THE AGE OF THE

TEXTS BY

EDITED BY DENYS HAY

London 1968

READERS UNION · THAMES AND HUDSON

RENAISSANCE

NICOLAI RUBINSTEIN

CECIL GRAYSON

PETER MURRAY

ROBERTO WEISS

DELIO CANTIMORI

I. D. McFARLANE

G. R. POTTER

A. A. PARKER

JOEL HURSTFIELD

L. D. ETTLINGER

JOHN HALE

600 illustrations

180 in colour

420 photographs, woodcuts,

drawings and maps

ACKNOWLEDGMENTS

The illustrations-sections have been the responsibility of the publishers, who would like to thank all the authors for their patient advice on the wording of the captions, and the following individuals and institutions for their generous help in providing the photographs:
Her Majesty the Queen; the Marquess of Bath; Dr A. Bettagno of the Cini Foundation, Venice; Dr Kurt Hannemann; Lt.-Col. Walter Luttrell, M.C.; the Marquess of Salisbury; Dr Fritz Schleifenbaum; Städtische Kunstsammlungen, Augsburg; Kunstmuseum and Öffentliche Bibliothek der Universität, Basel; Gemäldegalerie and Kupferstichkabinett der Staatlichen Museen, Berlin; Gemäldegalerie and Kupferstichkabinett der Staatlichen Museen, Berlin-Dahlem; Biblioteca Universitaria, Bologna; Museum of Fine Arts, Boston, Mass.; Herzog Anton Ulrich-Museum, Brunswick; Kunsthalle, Bremen; Fitzwilliam Museum and University Library, Cambridge; Musée Condé, Chantilly; Trustees of the Chatsworth Settlement; The Detroit Institute of Arts, Michigan; Staatliche Kunstsammlungen, Dresden; Scottish National Portrait Gallery, Edinburgh; Biblioteca Medicea-Laurenziana and Biblioteca Nazionale Centrale, Florence; Hessisches Landesmuseum, Kassel; British Museum (Departments of Coins and Medals, of Manuscripts, of Prints and Drawings and of Printed Books), Courtauld Institute of Art, National Gallery, National Portrait Gallery, London Topographical Society, Society of Antiquaries of London, Victoria and Albert Museum, University of London Library, Warburg Institute and Trustees of the Wellcome Foundation, London; Thyssen Bornemisza Collection, Lugano; Museo Naval, Madrid; Biblioteca Ambrosiana, Milan; Alte Pinakothek, Munich; Yale University Art Gallery, New Haven, Connecticut; Metropolitan Museum of Art, New York; Germanisches Nationalmuseum, Nuremberg; Ashmolean Museum (Department of Western Art), Balliol College, Bodleian Library (Departments of Western Manuscripts and of Printed Books) and Corpus Christi College, Oxford; Musée Jacquemart-André and Musée du Louvre, Paris; Národní Galerie, Prague; Musées de Rennes; Museum Boymans-van Beuningen, Rotterdam; Stadtbibliothek (Vadiana), St Gallen; The Huntington Library, San Marino, California; Siegerland-Bücherei, Hüttental-Weidenau; Opera della Metropolitana di Siena; Nationalmuseum Stockholm; Vatican Museums and Galleries, Vatican City; Biblioteca Nazionale di S. Marco, Venice; Kunsthistorisches Museum and Österreichische National-bibliothek, Vienna.

This copy is one of a small edition published by
READERS UNION LIMITED
and made available to its members only by arrangement
with the original publishers, Thames and Hudson Limited.
Full details of RU are available from
Readers Union Limited at Aldine House, 10-13 Bedford Street,
London, W.C. 2 and at Letchworth Garden City, Hertfordshire.

Designed and produced by THAMES AND HUDSON, London
MANAGING EDITOR: Ian Sutton BA
ART EDITOR: Ian Mackenzie-Kerr ARCA
EDITORIAL: Fiona Cowell MA
RESEARCH: Clarissa Cairns BA; Ronald Davidson-Houston BA, FRAI; Emily Lane BA
MAPS AND DRAWINGS: John Woodcock ARCA, MSIA; John Nowers
SPECIAL PHOTOGRAPHY: John Webb
BLOCKS: Klischeewerkstätten der Industriedienst, Wiesbaden, Germany
PRINTED in Western Germany by DuMont Presse, Cologne
PAPER: Woodfree White Art supplied by Gerald Judd Ltd., London
and Special Apex Smooth Grey supplied by Frank Grunfeld Ltd., London
BOUND by Van Rijmenam N.V., The Hague, Holland
© THAMES AND HUDSON 1967, LONDON

CONTENTS

CONTENTS

CONTENTS

INTRODUCTION

DENYS HAY

The significance of Renaissance Europe

EUROPEAN CULTURAL HISTORY has gone through a number of transfigurations since the time in the 4th and 5th centuries A.D. when the evolution of the continent became autonomous. These changes in public behaviour and in the assumptions about life and art shared by the dominant groups are often summarized by shorthand: Barbarian Europe, Gothic Europe, Renaissance Europe and so on. Such terms mislead of course if they suggest that historical periods are sharply distinguishable from one another. Contemporaries were usually oblivious of the breaks later ages have found it convenient to make in the past and, as we shall see, there was much that was 'Gothic' in the 'Renaissance'. This is a point worth insisting on at the outset. If by Renaissance we refer to a period of time, broadly speaking the 15th and 16th centuries, then everything that happens within the epoch is 'Renaissance', just as everything that happens in the 18th century is '18th-century'. But Renaissance or rebirth has for so long been applied to cultural history in a narrower sense, literature and learning, the fine arts, that the expression suggests not only a time span but problems arising within the time span. It is essential to bear this difficulty in mind. All men and all events belong to the Renaissance period; what we think of as characteristically Renaissance in style was far from being universal until towards the end of the age so described.

Italian Paradox

The great moments that have been artificially distinguished in European experience are associated with certain regions. The seminal rôle of northern France in the Middle Ages, of the Channel countries and then Germany in later times, was played in the Renaissance by Italy, the only occasion since antiquity when her experiences were avidly digested by neighbouring lands.

There is a paradoxical element in this. The Italy of the late 14th and 15th centuries was far less rich than it had been, for it suffered with the rest of Europe from an economic decline which lasted more or less throughout the 14th and 15th centuries; and its political life was full of wars within the small states and between them. The papacy, true to its ancient policy, continued to prevent the rise of any one predominating power, but this was achieved at the expense of the political power of the popes themselves. Out of Italy and in the city of Avignon for most of the 14th century, when the Curia returned to Rome it was to produce a Great Schism in 1378 which lasted until 1417 and was then followed by three decades during which the authority of the Vicar of Christ was challenged by the conciliar attempt to make him a constitutional monarch. Against this background Italian principalities evolved. The communes of the north came under local tyrants, the republics of Tuscany absorbed adjacent towns and in the south a chronically ill-governed Kingdom of Naples under a ruling house of French origin was distracted by ambitions in the east Mediterranean and by fear of the Aragonese established in Sicily. Some subsequent developments should be noted, for they were vitally to affect public life. From Milan the Visconti family had by the end of the 14th century come to dominate the entire plain of Lombardy; Giangaleazzo Visconti married a French princess, obtained the title of duke from the Emperor Wencelas for cash down in 1395, and he made no secret of his aim to extend his power southward, through the divided states of the church and into Tuscany. In this he was not successful, though it remained the ambition of Duke Filippo Maria Visconti (d. 1447). The Visconti did, however, establish a strong government, which was taken over by Franceso Sforza in 1450. In Tuscany the superiority of Florence was unquestioned and there, from 1434, the Medici family consolidated their effective mastery of the city while brilliantly preserving its republican form. Only one other great commercial centre challenged Florence. This was another republic, Venice, which had emerged successful from her long rivalry with Genoa for the fruits of Levantine commerce and which enjoyed, under a doge elected for life but shorn of real power, a constitution of enviable solidity, where the 'nobles' or patrician families governed the city and their overseas lands with a coherent and sophisticated administration. Early in the 15th century the wars of Italy compelled Venice to embark upon aggression on the mainland, and by the end of the century she had become a great territorial power, even though the Ottoman Turks were already rapidly stripping her of colonies in the Aegean. Finally it was to be of the utmost importance that from Sicily the Aragonese king Alfonso V moved to the mainland and conquered (1435–1442) the Kingdom of Naples. This was significant because on the death of Ferrante, the successor of Alfonso in Naples, the French king Charles VIII took up the claim to Naples and invaded Italy in 1494. Another French king, Louis XII, styled himself Duke of Milan from his accession in 1498, but by this time the King of Aragon wanted his share and from this point onwards Italy fell victim to foreign invaders. When the 'Italian wars' came to an end—effectively in 1538—the country was at the mercy of Charles V. This Hapsburg prince, reared in Burgundy, was ruler not merely of most of Italy, but of Aragon and Castile (with her growing American colonies), and the lands of Austria, as well as being titular head of the German principalities as Holy Roman Emperor. Under him Italy was managed by Spanish governors and viceroys and occupied by Spanish troops.

The European Scene: Politics

The political history of Italy in the 14th, 15th and early 16th centuries was violent. It would be mistaken to contrast this with peace elsewhere. France and England were involved in intermittent hostilities, the Hundred Years' War, from 1337 to 1453 and each country endured prolonged periods of internal strife. English kings were forcibly deposed by successful usurpers in 1327, 1399, 1471 and 1485 and the sordid troubles of the mid-15th century are given the deceptively pretty name of the Wars of the Roses. As for France, her king Charles VI was intermittently off his head from 1392 and this opened the way for the rivalries of the princes, who manipulated royal resources in their own interest: this inaugurated the period of 'Burgundian' and 'Armagnac' hostility which facilitated Henry V's invasion and which did not end until Charles the Bold, Duke of Burgundy, was killed in 1477. The internal histories of Germany, of the Scandinavian lands, of the kingdom of Spain were no less disturbed. There was little general peace in late medieval Europe.

Tempting as it is to pick out as explanations for the cultural innovations of Italy those aspects of the Italian scene in which that land differed from other countries, it is best to insist first on the features of public life found everywhere. And in doing this we can partly account for the rapidity with which Italian values were adopted elsewhere. Just as war and mercenary troops, as well as economic regression, were common to the whole continent, so were many other elements of society. England, France, Castile and Aragon were like many other parts of Europe, monarchies where royal power had been steadly growing from the 13th century. In Germany and Italy the control of princes was confined within smaller areas and did less to affect general unification just as it depended less on the centralizing consequences of patriotic sentiment and linguistic affinity. But an able Duke of Austria or Margrave of Brandenburg, a Duke of Milan or Marquis of Mantua behaved in their more restricted territories much as their contemporaries, the mightier Kings of France or Aragon or England. Likewise there were nobles, gentry, townsmen, clergy and lawyers everywhere and everywhere a growing value attached to literacy. New schools and universities multiplied in the later Middle Ages in all countries.

The European Scene: Culture and Learning

In the sphere of morality and culture the continent was also remarkably united. Doctrine was clear. Only by rejecting the world and its values could a man hope to attain salvation: 'to everyman according to his works'. An uneasy teaching this, for men whose works were battlements and entails, company contracts and ledger entries and the universal involvement in the marriage market. And the dilemma was all the more anguishing for the many who were moved by the gesture of Francis whose bride brought him no green fields, or rights of administration or houses with a counter on the High Street, whose bride was Poverty. It would be foolish to suppose that men and women necessarily involved in getting and spending, in raising families and managing the affairs of the neighbourhood or the greater business of government were always oppressed by the sense of living all their days under a moral cloud. But the moral cloud was there if and when they considered it. It was axiomatic that by cutting themselves off from the claims of everyday life the clergy and especially the regular clergy were fulfilling God's wishes more nearly than the laity.

As for the background of art and learning, it is important to remember how closely knit the continent was. Higher education, it is true, tended to be more regionalized. With their own universities available Scots went less frequently to Oxford; in 1300 there were five French universities, in 1500 there were seventeen and though some were small and not always effective, Paris naturally suffered. Nevertheless the ambitious German or Swiss lawyer in the 14th and 15th centuries still went to secure a qualification at Bologna, and the prestige of the Sorbonne for theology remained undimmed. Equally notable was the diffusion of literary manners: Chaucer owed much to French and Italian influences; the prose romances penetrated everywhere from their French homeland. Above all the artists reflected common preoccupations, as will be seen in Professor Ettlinger's essay in this volume.

Italy

Italy shared this broad background of European society and civilization. There were, however, significant differences which must now be noted. One was the high proportion of towns, which made members of the bourgeoisie much more significant there than they were elsewhere. Indeed in Italy even the nobility had one foot in the market place, and the princes and tyrants there were mostly of urban origin—the kingdom of Naples being the only major exception. Another difference in Italy was the large number of professional men, especially lawyers and clergymen, compared with the population as a whole. The lawyers (at this stage senior lawyers being often *doctores utriusque juris*, qualified in both Roman or civil and canon law) were often extremely well-read men, with an instinctive interest in ancient literature and antiquities. They were often employed in high office in the administration both of republics and principalities and they often canalized and expressed local loyalties. Even more impressive were the great merchants, especially in the larger commercial

centres, Venice, Genoa and the Tuscan towns, above all Florence.

The remarkable developments at Florence which constitute the early Renaissance are discussed below in the chapters by Professor Rubinstein and Dr Murray. By the middle of the century Florentine attitudes, shorn of their original republican attributes, and artistic manners and techniques had begun to penetrate the courts of Italy and this is the theme of the chapter by Professor Grayson. Later still the Renaissance came to the rest of Europe, a process examined here in chapters devoted to Germany (Professor Potter), France (Professor McFarlane), England (Professor Hurstfield) and Spain (Professor Parker). The diffusion of ideas and of artistic fashions was expedited by the invention of printing. This began at Mainz about 1450 and was quickly adopted in other areas, not least in Italy, where the two basic classes of typeface of the modern world were developed—the Roman and the Italic. One of the most impressive developments of the Renaissance is the steady assimilation not only of these Italian book styles but of the cursive handwriting associated with the papal chancery. Italic handwriting was practised by nearly all scholars in northern Europe by about 1550, at any rate wherever they wrote Latin in the new manner. For nearly all scholars were humanists.

The Humanists

Who were the humanists and what is humanism? The word humanist was used in late 15th-century Italy to describe a teacher of the humanities, that is those subjects which formed the curriculum in the educational programme formulated by Florentines like Leonardo Bruni and put into practice by Guarino da Verona and Vittorino da Feltre. The intention of this education was to prepare young men for an active life of service to the community by furnishing them with a solid stock of knowledge, a firm foundation of practical morality and the ability to communicate with fluency and grace in both speech and writing. The medium of instruction and the medium of communication were both Latin, a Latin recovered from antiquity and purified of medieval barbarism by constant contact with the classics, notably Cicero and Vergil. Both writers had, of course, been well-known in the Middle Ages. Now, along with other ancient writers of Rome and (for the teachers themselves and some of their pupils) the great writers of ancient Greece, they were studied as an essential training for a full life. Grammar, rhetoric and style, literature itself, moral philosophy and history (which taught by example), these were the 'humanities' and the humanist taught them. By extension the word came to be applied to all who were in sympathy with the aims of the humanist educators, for all who shared their conviction that Latin and Greek were the noblest vehicles for wisdom. In this way the scholars of the Renaissance are described as humanists, and notably those, whose work is described in later pages by Professor Weiss, who devoted their attention to the scientific examination of literary, historical and antiquarian issues. These men were far from being educators in a simple sense, for their voluminous works were directed at other scholars in much the same way as the theoretical physicist's research is communicable only to the other workers in the same field. In this way there was a genuine 'republic of letters'. Many of the scholars and writers who are important will be discussed by more than one of the contributors to this volume: an overlap which is essential and unavoidable. Among such scholars there were, of course, a few men who could claim to have advanced the frontiers of their subjects and at the same time to have participated to the full in the ethical or political issues of the day. Erasmus, for instance, was a considerable philologist and the bulk of his writing consists of editions of the Fathers, of classical authors and above all of the New Testament. Yet his pedagogical *Colloquies* grew into dialogues satirizing the corruptions in society and his *Adages* likewise developed into biting essays on current issues. In the *Praise of Folly* and the *Julius Exclusus* his criticism of the contemporary scene was direct.

Humanists were thus more than schoolmasters. Their very concern with moral problems led them into the public domain. Some of them, it will appear, espoused philosophical positions derived from neo-Platonic sources which led them to regard Man as the kernel of the Universe. Half earthly and half divine, his body and his soul formed a microcosm enabling him to understand and control Nature, to aspire to the comprehension of God. And for most humanists, on a lowlier level altogether, the tag from Terence was a self-evident proposition: *nil humani a me alienum puto*, 'I consider nothing human foreign to me'. In this way the humanists of the Renaissance may seem to be prefiguring if not anticipating the so-called humanists of our own day, who proclaim high ethical principles without the support of organized religion. Nothing could be further from the truth. Having profoundly modified the moral assumptions of an earlier day, the humanists almost without exception continued to believe in a Creator, in the divine mission of Christ, in the necessity of sacraments and in ecclesiastical organization. It is, indeed, the case that the accumulated criticisms of the Roman church burst into sustained revolt under the impulse of Luther's genius. But Professor Cantimori's chapter is a warning against too facile a connection being made between Renaissance and Reformation.

A plurality of Churches already existed in Christendom: the Greek Orthodox was separate (under Russian tutelage after 1453), while the Waldensians and later some Czechs had been driven into divorce from Rome. Luther issued his 95 Theses in 1517 and by 1522, in the face of papal condemnation, had moved to a more intransigent defiance. His doctrine of justification by faith was not new but the political division in Germany and long-standing German hatred of the Roman court secured for him lay support, while his own ability as a propagandist in both Latin and German gained him a wide popular following. In Germany it was the princes who determined the outcome, those who 'protested' in 1529 giving the movement its name. Elsewhere innovations in religious order were also instigated by monarchs, as in the royal break with Rome in England. But more radical changes occurred in some towns: the Anabaptists, with a programme of social revolution, were violently subdued, but the doctrines of Jean Calvin were adopted by Geneva and rooted themselves also in many other countries—parts of France, Scotland, the Low Countries. The extension of Protestantism forced the Roman Church to redefine its own positions on many central issues, and this was the main work of the Council of Trent (1545–63) which thus failed to reunite shattered Christendom. By the mid-years of the 16th century there were scores of Churches, though all of them still regarded unity as an ideal. But the humanist as such was found in all the confessional groups, just as earlier, before the hardening of attitudes involved in Luther's gesture and in comparable moves among Roman Catholics (Ignatius Loyola's Jesuit Order of 1534, for instance), humanists had been found of widely varying spiritual affinities.

Renaissance Achievements

It has often been too easily assumed that the origins of the astonishing advances in natural science during the 17th century should be explained by the 'Rebirth of Learning'. There were certainly men who were interested in what we would term scientific questions during the Middle Ages and in the Renaissance. And when we treat the Renaissance as a period then such men were indeed 'Renaissance scientists'. But they were, broadly speaking, not humanists. They were mostly men working in older academic traditions, and at centres like Padua and Paris where the humanities were not particularly flourishing. For this reason there is no discussion in this book of the progress of physics, mathematics, biology or anatomy. Progress in these fields was being made, but (apart from constructing better editions of some scientific or quasi-scientific books—though often the new texts were in fact very faulty) the humanist scholar had no hand in it.

We must be cautious, therefore, of treating the Renaissance as a mighty religious influence and as offering positive encouragement in the physical sciences. What of politics? Does the period see a characteristic shift in the possession of power, in the exercise of power, in the understanding of the nature of government? Here again our fathers would have said that it did. The Renaissance coincided with, if it did not provoke, the Nation State, the New Monarchy and, in a few particularly blessed areas, the Rise of the Middle Class. No one today would seriously argue that these muzzy concepts have any usefulness; they are monuments to 19th-century optimism. Countries, though harbouring populations with slowly maturing vernacular languages and—if one may put it this way—vernacular patriotisms, were for the most part governed by dynasts whose main preoccupation was the perpetuation of the princely line and the extension of the princely lands. Kings were not significantly more powerful, for example in England or France or Spain, in the 16th century than they had been in the 14th or 15th, though circumstances everywhere were driving the great landed nobles to court and political impotence. The gentry and the bourgeoisie were perhaps more obtrusive in northern lands than they had been, though their 'rise' is a long story and without doubt it had gone far before 1500. Only in two respects can one discern innovation. Educated laymen were staffing the administrative machinery; and there was a new sophistication in political thought. Humanists had occupied important positions in republican Florence and ducal Milan by the start of the 15th century. By the second half they were to be found everywhere in Italy as secretaries, councillors and diplomats. In the 16th century they were recruited by the sovereigns of large kingdoms and this fortified the conviction of the humanist that he had a crucial rôle to play in educating the 'governor'—the title of Sir Thomas Elyot's bulky treatise (1531), advocating the humanist schooling of the gentlemen and nobles. In this way the creaking apparatus of royal administration in France and England, mostly inherited from the Middle Ages, was made to work more efficiently, and in conciliar government, which spread everywhere but developed fastest in Spain, the new trained men could put to the service of their prince the expertise in mastering facts and the fluency in expressing advice which they had acquired at school. As for political thought, the early 16th century at long last witnessed the emergence of men who dared to analyze the practice of kings rather than preach sermons to them on their duties, and it also saw the emergence of unqualified support for the autocratic prince.

The Europe of the late 16th century was thus in many respects like the Europe of two hundred years before, though older trends towards stronger kingship had continued. Kings in many areas now had by Reformation or concordat made their *de facto* power over the Church *de jure*. Their wars were bloodier and the men they employed were mercenaries, whose discipline depended on regular pay—as was most dramatically shown by the sack of Rome by the ungovernable imperial army in 1527. And kings were now behind the advance of their subjects—curious, courageous, brutally acquisitive—to the Far East and the Americas, the subject of Professor Hale's final chapter. They also employed large numbers of 'humanists', though not as mariners or generals.

The change effected by the adoption of Renaissance concepts and practices was, in a sense, profounder than slowly evolving 'class' structure and government. It was producing—in Italy had by the 15th century produced—a conviction that civility was the most important social quality, that civility obliged one fully to serve one's community, and that it was to be obtained through education in the humanities. With this conviction went sympathy for an art which was at once realistic and ennobling and an architecture which exploited the serenity of Roman grandeur. The *lycée* and *gymnasium* (*anglice* grammar school) were the abiding products of the Renaissance. By the 17th century they had given the gentry and the bourgeoisie a culture common to the whole of Europe. It was perpetually refreshed by the Grand Tour which took the people who mattered to the home land of their civilization, Italy. That country, sunk in the peaceful slumber of the second rate, had still the power to inspire Poussin and Claude. When old St Paul's in London was burned in 1666, Wren built a Protestant temple which unashamedly recalled the new St Peter's in Rome.

On 13 September 1966 Delio Cantimori died as the result of a tragic accident. The editor and several of the contributors to this volume have lost an admired and generous colleague and a good friend, whose memory they will cherish. The proofs of Professor Cantimori's essay have been kindly read by Dr. John Tedeschi.

1 CRADLE OF THE RENAISSANCE

The beginnings of humanism in Florence

NICOLAI RUBINSTEIN

'Florence harbours the greatest minds:

whatever they undertake, they easily surpass all other men,

whether they apply themselves to military or

political affairs, to study or philosophy,

or to merchandize'.

LEONARDO BRUNI

'Our city of Florence,

daughter and creation of Rome, is rising and destined to achieve great things,' wrote the chronicler Giovanni Villani in the early years of the 14th century. Villani did not live to see the fulness of his prophecy. He died in 1348 when Florence was still enjoying commercial prosperity and with her constitution established on a broad civic basis. Curiously enough, it was when prosperity had begun to decrease, that there occurred an intellectual and artistic flowering which has no parallel in history. Part of the secret was that the Florentines believed in their own destiny and in their own right and power to control it. No city aroused fiercer devotion or prouder patriotism. The long panegyric on Florence that began with Villani was taken up by Boccaccio and then by Salutati, by Bruni, by Marsilio Ficino and Machiavelli, until it became the accepted judgment of European history. Every account of the Renaissance has to begin with Florence. But why?

Florence was lucky in her political background. She had no emperor or pope to squash every independent initiative and no family of tyrants to make government an exercise in murder. Power in Florence was in the hands of a cultivated bourgeois élite. This is not to say that life was especially peaceful: parties rose and fell, public men were exiled and ruined. But there was an openness to ideas that stimulated intellectual progress and made Florence the leader in the new *studia humanitatis*, the discussion of

moral values, of philosophy and religion, which were appearing in some form or other in many parts of Italy. Teachers of Greek from the Eastern Empire found a ready welcome there. From 1375 onwards the office of chancellor was held by a succession of brilliant men with wide cultural interests—Salutati, Bruni, Marsuppini and Poggio. Classical scholarship, neo-Platonic philosophy, the study of every aspect of ancient Roman life, could all be claimed with some justice to have begun in Florence. And parallel to this development in ideas went a development in art, closely related to it and clearly expressing the same ideals, which will be the subject of a later chapter.

The emblem of Florence is the *fleur-de-lis*, a medieval device whose origin has been lost. It may be connected with the old derivation of the name *Fiorenza*—the city built in a flowery meadow. In the first insignia the lily was white on a red ground; after the expulsion of the Ghibellines in 1251 it was changed to a red lily on a white ground. It appears on nearly every public building, perhaps most dramatically of all on the shield held by Donatello's *marzocco*, the heraldic lion which stood for Florentine power (the name seems to be a corruption of *Martocus*, 'little Mars', the Roman god held to be the first patron of Florence). Donatello's image of ferocity and pride was carved in about 1418, originally for the papal apartments of Sta Maria Novella. (1)

'**Within these walls** civilization began again', wrote Stendhal, with a touch of exaggeration. This woodcut of c. 1480 shows Florence at the peak of her greatness. In the centre rises Brunelleschi's lofty cathedral dome; in front of it the old Baptistery; Sta Maria Novella is nearer the foreground to the left, Orsanmichele and the Palazzo Vecchio on the right. Across the river is the Pitti Palace consisting as yet of only seven bays. (3)

The Cathedral, begun about 1300, still lacked the vault over its central crossing when Brunelleschi was appointed architect in 1420. He built over an octagonal drum a cupola, the model for all subsequent domes. (2)

The Baptistery (below) dates from the 11th century. Here every child born in Florence was baptized. Brunelleschi and Alberti believed it to be a Roman building and imitated many of its details. (4)

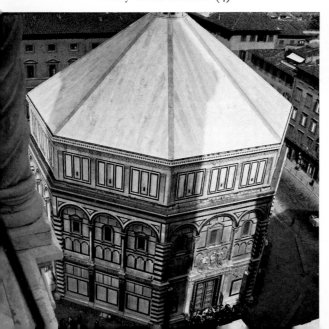

Santa Maria Novella is the Dominican church of Florence. The main structure is Gothic but between about 1456 and 1470 Alberti completed the façade using classical pilasters, pediment and scroll-buttresses (the first appearance of a motif that was to become universal). The lower row of arches belongs to the old building. (5)

The Strozzi Palace (right) testifies to the pride and wealth of other merchant families besides the Medici. Palla Strozzi, Cosimo's rival, was exiled from Florence in 1434 but Filippo Strozzi was recalled from exile in 1466 and in 1489 began a vast new palace that eclipsed even the Palazzo Medici. Designed by Giuliano da Sangallo and Benedetto da Maiano (the later cornice by Cronaca), it retains many of the features of the feudal town-fortress, though with a new regularity and elegance. (7)

Florence today is still a Renaissance city. This photograph, taken from the hill on the extreme right of the woodcut, shows the same dominant features—the Cathedral with its Campanile on the right, the tower of the Palazzo Vecchio in the centre, and the Ponte Vecchio, lined with goldsmiths' shops, on the far left. (8)

Orsanmichele (left) was originally simply a warehouse. The open ground floor served as market and exchange and had a small oratory. The city guilds were responsible for the decoration of the exterior piers, each one erecting a statue of its patron saint and striving to outdo its rivals. The building soon became an artistic showplace containing fourteen niches with statues by Ghiberti, Verrocchio, Donatello and others. (6)

Festive banners of the nobility, the *compagnie* (confraternities) and the guilds, carried in procession to the Baptistery on the Feast of St John, symbolize the strata of Florentine society. In its love of shows, pageantry and tournaments the city did not differ from the less democratic courts of the north. This *cassone* painting, of the late 14th century, is decorated with the Florentine lilies. (9)

The meeting-place of Renaissance Florence was the Loggia dei Lanzi, the high open arcade next to the Palazzo Vecchio. Built 1376–82, it appears in a fresco of Ghirlandaio of 1485 as a promenade for citizens and a playground for children. (10)

To be fashionable in dress as in everything else was a part of the Florentine character and one which is richly illustrated in art. These details (right) are from frescoes by Ghirlandaio and Masolino. First, ladies of the Sassetti family, 1485; second, anonymous gentlemen with a piazza in the background, c. 1425; third, members of leading Florentine families, against the closed doors of the Sassetti Palace. (11, 12, 13)

'**Equal liberty** exists for all—the hope of gaining high office and to rise is the same for all.' Bruni's boast of 1428 was in theory true. In practice the guilds, and the pressure groups within the guilds, could manipulate the political situation and rule indirectly. Florentine democracy turned into an oligarchy, though an oligarchy sensitive to public opinion. The highest magistracy was the Signory, of nine members, holding office for only two months but living all that time in the Palazzo Vecchio (below). The 'Old Palace' or 'Palazzo della Signoria' was built between 1299 and 1314; in front of it, in this detail of a painting of c. 1500, stands Donatello's *Judith and Holofernes*, symbol of tyranny crushed. (15)

The humanist Chancellor: in 1375 Coluccio Salutati (left), the leading humanist of his day, was appointed Chancellor of Florence. It was a significant event, linking the New Learning with the state. (14)

Appointment to high office was by a complex system of choice and chance. In periodic 'scrutinies', qualified citizens were elected and from among these appointments were made by drawing names by lot. The number of name–tickets which the citizens thus qualified had at their disposal depended on the number of tickets they had already used up. This detail is from the scrutiny of 1440 in the *Lion d'oro* district (L. Adaurum) for the 'three highest offices'. The meaning of each

'History is in mourning and eloquence is dumb, and it is said that the Muses, Greek and Latin alike, cannot restrain their tears'—the epitaph from the tomb (above) of the second great

Republican ideals lingered when the reality had faded. Brutus the tyrannicide had been a Florentine hero since the 14th century. Michelangelo, in making this bust of him for Cardinal Ridolfi, a leading opponent of the Medici after they had become Dukes of Tuscany, must have had a political purpose in mind. (18) ▶

column is as follows: (1) number of name-tickets available for the Gonfalonierate of Justice; (2) for the Signory; (3) name of qualified citizen; (4) number of name-tickets for the 'little purse' of the Priorate (there were eight Priors); (5) for the 'general purse' of the Priorate; (6) for the sixteen Gonfaloniers of Companies; (7) for the twelve *Bonuomini*. The last name shown here reads *Cosma Jo bicci demedici*—Cosimo de'Medici. (16)

humanist Chancellor, Leonardo Bruni. He wrote the first humanist history of Florence (in Latin) and lives of Dante and Petrarch (in the vernacular). He was also a Greek scholar. (17)

A council in session: an episode during the brief revival of the republic after the death of Lorenzo, when the Florentines decided upon war with Pisa (1494). Vasari, painting half a century later, included several portraits: the orator is Antonio Giacomini. Above their heads flies a Nemesis with flaming sword. (19)

One family came eventually to dominate both its rivals in commerce and finance and the city of Florence itself: the Medici. It was a despotism, but a constitutional despotism—as crucial in the history of civilization as that of Pericles or Augustus.

Cosimo de' Medici (1389–1464), named *Pater Patriae*, was painted in his old age by Gozzoli as one of the three Magi (left). He is dressed in blue, near the centre. His son Piero (1416–69) rides a white horse just ahead of him. Lorenzo, Piero's son (1449–92), seen (right) between two members of the Sassetti family, succeeded his father at the age of twenty and ruled Florence, in fact though not in name, for twenty-three years. (20, 22)

A plot to kill Lorenzo and his brother Giuliano was laid in 1478, the parties being the Pazzi family and Pope Sixtus IV's nephew Girolamo Riario. The place chosen was the Cathedral, the time the elevation of the Host at Easter Mass. Giuliano was killed but Lorenzo escaped and the whole conspiracy was ruthlessly crushed. In this medal the railed off space represents the choir. In the foreground Giuliano lies dead. (21)

In town and country the Medici and other patrician families owned palaces, villas and farms. Above right: the Pitti Palace, begun in the 15th century by Cosimo's friend Luca Pitti and acquired by the Medici in 1549. Below: the Medici villa of Trebbio, a medieval fortress surrounded by gardens and farm buildings. (23, 24)

Money was the foundation of Medici —as of Florentine—greatness. They were financiers in a city of finance. In 1422 there were seventy-two bankers or bill-brokers in or near the Mercato Vecchio, among them names famous all over Europe—the Strozzi, Pitti, Pazzi and many more. Others equally celebrated had not long before been exiled or made bankrupt—the Alberti, Acciauoli, Bardi and Peruzzi. Right: from a 14th-century painting, a Florentine money-changer with his scales, coins and account book.

The Medici, like the others, combined trade with purely financial business. They had extensive interests in the Flanders wool-trade, for instance. The drawing of a wool-merchant (far right) shows the woven cloth and bundles of wool, with the Medici arms on the pillar (they were enrolled in the Calimala Guild, which controlled trade in finished cloth). Under the founder of the family fortunes, Giovanni di Bicci de' Medici, banks had been established at Rome, Naples, Venice and Genoa. The great period of expansion was under Cosimo, when branches were opened in Bruges, Pisa, London, Avignon and Milan. (25, 26)

The bank at Milan was a superb palace (above), the gift of Francesco Sforza; since the entire staff was only eight, however, it could hardly have occupied the whole building. (27)

Lorenzo's villa at Poggio a Caiano (below) was bought from the Rucellai family in 1479. Giuliano da Sangallo remodelled it and the curving stairs were added in the 17th century. (28)

The gold coin of Florence, the *fiorino* or florin, was one of the foundations of her prosperity. First minted in 1252, weighing about 3½ grams, it remained unchanged for the next 300 years, even in face of the debasement of the silver coinage. The florin—the model for many other gold coins minted in Europe—was a small work of art, with the lilies of Florence on one side and St John the Baptist on the other. (29, 30)

As his head office combined with family mansion, Cosimo built the first of the great Renaissance palaces in Florence, designed by Michelozzo in 1444. The inner courtyard, carried on graceful arcades (below left), is somewhat belied by the heavy rusticated exterior (below), but the corner shown here was originally an open loggia. (31, 32)

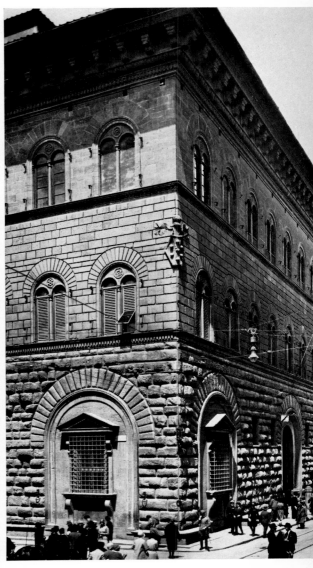

'He was so great a lover of antiquity that nothing enthused him more,' wrote Vespasiano of Lorenzo de' Medici. Medici patronage extended to every branch of the arts, though Lorenzo's natural bent was towards literature and history rather than painting. His collection of antiques was renowned. He had them inscribed with his name (LAVR MED) and often remounted in contemporary settings. Below: an agate cup, probably 9th or 10th century. Right: late antique ewer of oriental sardonyx and a covered cup of amethyst. (33, 34)

The priceless manuscripts and books collected by the Medici since the days of Cosimo were eventually (1571) made available to the public in a library designed by Michelangelo. The books were kept chained to the desks (left). Among other items, the collection contains a 5th-century manuscript of Vergil, Petrarch's copy of Horace and the only medieval transcript of the *Annals* of Tacitus. (35)

The Birth of Venus was painted by ▶ Botticelli for a cousin of Lorenzo, Lorenzo di Pierfrancesco de' Medici. His tutors were Politian and Ficino and the pictures that Botticelli painted for him (which include also the *Primavera*) are full of abstruse neo-Platonic meanings requiring considerable erudition to understand. The goddess, rising from the water, is wafted by the breath of Zephyrs (Politian's *zefiri amorosi* and *zefiri lascivi*) to the chaste Hour of Spring, who stands ready to clothe her in a flowered mantle—as all sacred mysteries should be veiled from the uninitiated. Venus herself symbolizes both aspects of love, the sensual and the pure. She is created from the sea (the formless element) by its union with the divine seed of Uranus (ideal form), represented by the white foam of the waves. (36)

The world of the humanists was a world in which the traditional concepts of Christianity were being flooded with an unfamiliar light from pagan philosophy. The result was not a rejection of Christian ideas, but an attempt to re-interpret them, to discover a basic harmony underlying all religions and all philosophies. The key to this new understanding was seen to be the mastery of Greek. A number of Greek scholars settled in the west, both before and after the fall of Constantinople to the Turks. John Argyropoulos (below), one of the most distinguished, became professor of Greek at Florence in 1456. Reuchlin and Politian were among his pupils. (37)

Leone Battista Alberti (1404–72) made himself the complete Renaissance man—famous as an athlete, musician, poet, scholar and architect. His emblem, the 'winged eye' signifies the union of supreme insight with supreme power. (39, 40)

Marsilio Ficino (1433–99), disciple, translator and 'Christianizer' of Plato, valued the word above the visual image. On the reverse of his medal is the single name of his master, *Platone*. (41, 42)

Politian—Angelo Poliziano (1454–94), scholar, translator and poet—was a pupil of Argyropoulos and the teacher of Lorenzo de' Medici's children. On his medal he places the allegorical figure of Study—*studia*. (43, 44)

Carlo Marsuppini (1399–1453), Bruni's successor as Chancellor (below), had been a teacher of Greek rhetoric and philosophy. (38)

Giovanni Pico della Mirandola (1463–94) evolved a mystical doctrine in which Christianity was proved through the Hermetic and Cabbalistic writings. The trinity of Beauty, Love and Pleasure stand for crucial ideas in Pico's thought. (45, 46)

The philosophy of love, destined to figure so largely in the imaginative literature of the next century, had its beginnings among the Florentine humanists. This diagram in Pulci's *Driadeo d'Amore* gives a naïve picture of Plato's theory of knowledge. The sun, top right, stands for the world of ideas; from it comes the 'idea' of a geometrical figure in the mind of the philosopher who then draws it physically in the world of appearances. (47)

The soul, according to Plato, was like a chariot being pulled down by one horse (the senses) and up to God by another (the love of the good). Trying to control them was the charioteer: Reason. But in neo-Platonism (derived from Plotinus and modified by theology), the charioteer has become Love. This detail (above) is from a bronze bust by Donatello. (48)

Humanists in daily life mixed on equal terms with the rich merchants who were their patrons. These portraits, from a fresco by Ghirlandaio, have been tentatively identified as Ficino, Landino, Politian and Demetrius Chalcondilas. Landino wrote quasi-Platonic dialogues in Latin, while Chalcondilas held the chair of Greek from 1475. (50)

The last of the great chancellors of Florence was Niccolò Machiavelli (1469–1527). A staunch defender of the republic, he expressed his ideals persuasively in the *Discourses on Livy* (1515–17). Earlier, in the disgrace which overtook him in 1512, he wrote his brief but famous work, *The Prince*, a ruthless analysis of the real sources of power unrestrained by ethical considerations. How far, in describing such a code, was he serious and how far ironical? The question is still unanswered. (49)

'The Sword of God over the land, swiftly and soon'. The last decade of the 15th century saw an extraordinary revulsion of feeling in Florence. Men turned away from the confident optimism of the earlier years. The international situation was threatening; Lorenzo had died in 1492 and there was no-one to take his place. And breaking across their anxiety came the harsh voice of Fra Girolamo Savonarola, prophesying doom. Humanist concern with paganism, he preached, was sin, beauty a snare. In a 'bonfire of vanities' women burned their jewellery and men their books. This medal records the vision seen and heard by Savonarola during an Advent sermon of 1492. (51, 52)

Florence besieged—a panorama by Vasari showing how the republic was finally crushed in 1530, nearly 40 years after Lorenzo's death. In 1494 Charles VIII of France had invaded Italy to make good his claims against Naples. Piero, Lorenzo's son, having opposed Charles, was driven out of Florence, and the republic was revived under the moral, and sometimes the political, leadership of Savonarola. He fell in 1498, executed for heresy. But the republic's survival depended on French support. Papal-Spanish victory in 1512 led to a restoration of the Medici on an autocratic basis. In 1527, after the Sack of Rome, they were again expelled, but three years later, abandoned by France, the city fell to the armies of Charles V, who re-established the Medici. The siege (in which Michelangelo took part as military engineer) lasted eight months—the last heroic act of the republican spirit. (53)

The beginnings of humanism in Florence

NICOLAI RUBINSTEIN

Savonarola's ideal of a good life, without luxury, vice or ostentation, is exemplified by the bareness of his cell, adorned only with holy books and crucifixes. (1)

WHETHER one defines the Italian Renaissance as a revival of art and letters, or in a more limited sense as a revival of antiquity, Florence occupies a leading, and in many ways decisive, place in it. The Florentines were fully aware of this, and their conviction of being pioneers of a new age forms an important aspect of Renaissance civilization. 'It is undoubtedly a golden age', writes Marsilio Ficino in 1492, 'which has restored to the light the liberal arts that had almost been destroyed: grammar, poetry, eloquence, painting, sculpture, architecture, music. And all that in Florence.' Poetry and painting, affirms Cristoforo Landino in 1481, which had been extinct since Roman times, were revived in Florence by Dante, Cimabue, and Giotto. This conviction of the special rôle assigned to Florence in the revival of art and letters pervades the 15th century; it had taken shape in the second half of the 14th. When the Florentine chronicler Giovanni Villani described the greatness of his city in 1338, he was still almost exclusively concerned with its material prosperity. Its population, he says, amounted to no less than 90,000, there were 200 shops of the wool guild with about 30,000 workers and an annual production of around 75,000 bolts of cloth. About forty years later, his nephew Filippo Villani, in his work on famous Florentines, traced the renaissance of poetry back to Dante, that of painting to Cimabue and Giotto. Giovanni Boccaccio (d.1375) had already praised Dante for having once more opened the road to the Muses, who before had been banished from Italy, and Petrarch for having restored the poetry of ancient Rome. The cult of the city's great poets and artists had begun. It reflects a broadening of Florentine patriotism, which had previously emphasized the Roman origins of the city and its political and economic achievements. Giovanni Villani's boast that 'our city of Florence, daughter and creation of Rome, was rising and achieving great things, whereas Rome was declining', was assuming a new significance.

In the panegyric on Florence which Leonardo Bruni wrote at the beginning of the 15th century in imitation of Aristides' description of Athens, he states that 'Florence harbours the greatest minds: whatever they undertake, they easily surpass all other men, whether they apply themselves to military or political affairs, to study or philosophy, or to merchandise'. The new classical studies, the *studia humanitatis*, founded by Petrarch, the son of a Florentine exile, flourish in Florence as nowhere else. 'These are', he writes in 1428, 'the best and most excellent of studies, and most appropriate to mankind'—and 'they took root in Italy after originating in our city'. But the dominant figure in the classical revival at Florence was not Petrarch but Coluccio Salutati.

In 1375, Salutati, the leading humanist of his day, was appointed Chancellor of Florence; and the influence which he exercised on the intellectual life of Florence was so profound that one may well date the beginning of a new period from that time. However varied the sources of the New Learning in Florence, however complex its manifestations, Salutati and his circle gave Florentine humanism the form which was to prevail throughout much of the 15th century, and made Florence the principal centre of Italian humanism.

In contrast to the princely states in which the humanist movement was focused on the court, in Florence it was shared by an intellectual élite of citizens, with the result that there arose a unique relationship between professional humanists and learned patricians. The New Learning in Florence has to be seen not only as an intellectual movement, but also in its social and political setting.

The Florentine Oligarchy

Freedom and law are the two cornerstones of our constitution, states Bruni in his panegyric on Florence. In his funeral oration on Nanni Strozzi of 1428 he elaborated the meaning of freedom: 'Equal liberty exists for all—the hope of gaining high office and to rise is the same for all'. In reality, the Florentine constitution did allow a large number of citizens to participate, on theoretically equal terms, in the highest offices, but it made it possible for small groups of leading citizens to get far more than an equal share of them. These oligarchical tendencies have considerable bearing on the development of the Florentine Renaissance. The two principal intellectual movements of 15th-century Florence, humanism and Platonism, affected only a small group of citizens, most of whom belonged to the upper classes; and the same is true of the private patronage of the arts. The Florentine 'patriciate' played a significant, and in some respects decisive, rôle in these manifestations of Renaissance civilization. At the same time, just as the Florentine structure of politics stood on a broadly democratic foundation, so did the people of Florence participate, though in a more passive manner, in some of the achievements of that civilization.

The prominent position enjoyed by the patriciate in Florentine politics was the more remarkable as the organization of the highest public offices in the city was designed to prevent not only despotism but also the seizure of effective power by the great families. Short terms of office and limited re-eligibility had the effect not only of admitting a large number of citizens to government and administration, but also of providing them with a great variety of public employment. Office-holding formed a normal part of a Florentine citizen's life. To be a member of the highest magistracies was a matter of honour and an indication of social status; but it could also be a matter of self-interest. Taxation was liable to become a political instrument, governmental authority could be used, in extreme cases, to deprive individuals or families of civic rights, and the high salaries of governorships in the city's territory could be an economic incentive. At the same time, public office could also mean sacrifices. The prosperity of Florence was based on trade and industry, and both business and family life were liable to suffer from public service. The nine members of the Signory, for instance, were confined, during the two months of their office, to the Palazzo Vecchio; other magistracies, as well as the two statutory councils, would normally meet at frequent intervals; the officials in charge of the territorial administration might have

p 18 (15)

to spend six months or one year in outlying districts; not to mention ambassadors who would often be absent from the city over long periods and with inadequate remuneration. The Florentine citizens paid heavily for the virtual absence of a permanent bureaucracy; they obviously did not consider the price too high.

p 18–19
(16)
After 1328, most Florentine magistrates were appointed by lot, to ensure a wider and more equitable distribution of political power than could be obtained by election. The 'purses' for the various offices were filled with the names of eligible citizens who theoretically stood an equal chance of having them drawn. In practice the way in which the purses for the government were arranged created substantial differences in the opportunities of being appointed by lot, and these differences reflect the limitations to which the principle of political equality was subject in fact.

Guilds, Families and Power

The most striking instance of such limitations was the different political status of the seven greater and the fourteen craft guilds.
f 2,3
p 22
(25, 26)
After 1282, participation in government depended upon guild membership, but the greater guilds scored heavily over the lesser craft guilds, for they included the wealthy cloth and wool merchants and the bankers on whom the prosperity of Florence largely depended, as well as the lawyers and notaries who were essential for the running of her administration; moreover, the citizens who lived from unearned income without exercising a trade had, by a legal fiction, the same political rights as the merchants of the greater guilds. The predominance of these guilds was challenged in the second half of the 14th century, but was fully restored after the collapse of the Ciompi revolt of 1378, with the result that the share of the craft guilds in the Signory and other magistracies was reduced to a quarter. The lesser guilds were never again to threaten the pre-eminent position of the greater guilds; but the Florentine merchants had not forgotten the past. 'Let this be a permanent warning to the leading men of the city,' writes Leonardo Bruni of the revolt, 'never to allow insurrections and weapons to be wielded by the arbitrary power of the masses; for once they have begun to seize the reins, they can no longer be kept back.'

If the distinction between greater and lesser guilds divided the Florentine citizens into two groups with different political opportunities, there were also ways by which the richer and more powerful members of the greater guilds could prevail over the less fortunate ones. As a result the great patrician families were heavily represented on the electoral rolls as well as in the highest magistracies. Moreover, once a family had achieved political prominence, only the victory of a hostile faction or economic decline could normally dislodge it from that position. Theoretically there was no bar to the rise of new men; in practice, social mobility was held in check by the oligarchical trend in Florentine politics. The Florentine patriciate was, however, not a homogeneous class. Side by side with the great merchants and manufacturers, it included rentiers as well as members of the old magnate nobility which had been excluded from government and subjected to legal discrimination at the end of the 13th century but which nevertheless continued throughout the 14th century to serve the republic in high positions as counsellors, diplomats, soldiers and fiscal experts. But while not homogeneous, nor politically exclusive like the Venetian nobility, the Florentine patriciate considered itself to be set apart from, and by right above, the rest of the population. Its members liked to describe themselves as 'noble commoners', thus combining, in one term, the two once contrasting attributes of nobility and people.

This was not only a matter of nomenclature. Just as the 13th-century magnates had included commoner as well as feudal elements, so the way of life of the feudal nobility had not lost its attraction for the patriciate of the 15th century. On the contrary, this attraction was probably increased by the close contacts with northern European courts. It was shown by the esteem in which knighthood continued to be held, although the legislation against the magnates had singled it out as a distinctive characteristic of that class; for this discrimination did not affect the

citizens who were knighted later, the more so as many of these received their knighthood from the republican government itself. Tournaments became, as we shall see, increasingly popular f 8 in the 15th century, and reflect the attractions of aristocratic customs. Finally, like the medieval civic nobility, the patricians of that century divided their life between town and country. Florence had owed much of its population growth to immigration from the countryside, and the desire to own landed property was common to all classes. For the patriciate, the country house was a status symbol as well as a source of pleasure and profit. It was traditional for merchants to invest in land for security of capital: the economic difficulties Florence had to face from the middle of the 14th century do not seem to have caused a significant shift to investment in landed property. However, such investment could at least serve as a hedge against inflation; and country estates, if prudently managed, could provide substantial returns. They were also a temptation to abandon city life for part of f 4 the year and enjoy the pleasures of the country. While in about p 21 1360, Paolo da Certaldo had warned merchants to stay in the (23,2. city and look after their business affairs, Alberti eloquently praised, around 1433, life in the country house. 'Who is the man who does not derive pleasure from the villa?' It alone is 'grateful, generous, and safe': in contrast to the turmoil of public affairs in the city, the villa is the source of the greatest happiness.

Wool and banking—two of the main items of Florentine economy. The quality and colour of Florentine cloth were world-famous, and even wool exporting countries like England were prepared to pay high prices for the finished cloth. Below: bankers from a 15th century tract, containing— among other useful tables—a list of exchange quotations in Lombard Street, London. (2, 3)

Yet there were limits to such affinities with the customs of the landed gentry. Florentine patricians might describe themselves as 'noble'; but Lapo da Castiglionchio's use of this term was significant: 'noble and honest merchandise' consisted in 'travelling to France and England and trading in cloth and wool, as do all the greater and better men of the city'. The utilitarian outlook of 14th-century merchants, with its caution and frugality, survived in the more pleasure-loving and sumptuous life of the 15th-century patriciate, and merged imperceptibly with aristocratic ideals and ambitions. There was a streak of austerity in Florentine life throughout the Renaissance, which helps to explain the success, at the end of the century, among all classes of the population, of Savonarola's sermons.

If there could be conflicts between aristocratic customs and commoner traditions, there could also be conflicts between office-holding and family interests. Treatises of practical wisdom, concerned with the management of the business and properties of the individual citizen, insist that these should take precedence over public office. The family remained the focal point of much of Florentine life, and the household could be considered an all but self-sufficient unit. Alberti's advice that the entire family should live under the same roof reflects the traditions of a city in which patrician families and their relatives would inhabit compact groups of houses. But the status of a family was raised or preserved by public office. If public office could be shunned for the sake of family interests, it could also be sought for the same reasons.

Humanism and the State

The country houses which surrounded Florence were only one aspect of her control of the territory. By the beginning of the 15th century, Florence ruled over extensive dominions which included a number of subject towns. Some of these, like Arezzo, had been acquired recently; in 1406 Florence added Pisa and in 1411 Cortona to her possessions. But Florentine aggrandizement clashed with the territorial ambitions of other Italian powers. From 1375 to 1378, the city was at war with the papacy, which was attempting to regain control of the papal territories neighbouring on Florence, and between 1390 and 1402 with Giangaleazzo Visconti of Milan, whose intervention in Tuscany, after his spectacular successes in Lombardy, threatened not only the pre-eminence of Florence in that region, but also her territorial integrity and political independence. The two conflicts were separated by the Ciompi rising of 1378. The city's success in resisting the lord of Milan, until his death in 1402 released her from mortal danger, was mainly the achievement of the patriciate which had, a few years earlier, triumphantly reasserted and strengthened its position. The struggle against Milan and its successful outcome no doubt gave this class fresh self-confidence and additional political influence, and helped to consolidate the new oligarchical regime which, since 1393, was headed by Maso degli Albizzi and a few prominent citizens such as Niccolò da Uzzano. Later generations looked back on the early 15th century as a golden age of unity and prosperity, in which Florence was ruled by a public-spirited patriciate. It was also the period during which Florence emerged as the leading centre of Renaissance humanism; the political and military events of the years of crisis, as well as the social structure of Florentine politics, form the background to this development.

Italian humanism was essentially a literary and scholarly movement, whose principal object was the study and imitation of classical literature. As such it had no immediate contacts with political life. 14th-century humanists, foremost among them Petrarch, would praise the solitary life as the only one conducive to true scholarship. But in so far as the *studia humanitatis* were concerned with ancient history, moral philosophy and rhetoric, they could also be used for political purposes.

Coluccio Salutati's long chancellorship not only made the city the intellectual centre of Italy, but also gave humanism an officially recognized position in Florentine public life which was to affect the writings and ideas of the Florentine humanists during the next decades. As students and teachers of rhetoric, the humanists were trained to defend opposing positions. As chancellors, they would

As well as being the rich man's retreat from city life, the villa was often an economic unit in itself. The house here—as the Medici villa at Trebbio (p. 21)—is surrounded by an outcrop of farm buildings. (4)

put this training to the service of their employer by writing official letters and speeches. Salutati was so successful in his post that Giangaleazzo Visconti was said to have considered his pen more dangerous than a detachment of Florentine horsemen. He died in 1406, and in 1427 the Florentines appointed his pupil Leonardo Bruni to the chancellorship which Bruni had already filled briefly in 1410–11. From that time onwards, it was Florentine policy to appoint only humanists to the highest post in the Chancery.

The Chancery brought humanists into close contact with the political problems and the ruling circle of Florence. In contrast to the short terms of office in Florentine government and administration, the personnel of the Chancery often held their posts over long periods and consequently acquired some of the attributes of a permanent civil service. They also could give Florentine propaganda a consistent and continuous character. During the war against the papacy in 1375–78, and especially during the wars with Giangaleazzo Visconti which followed it, Salutati formulated, in innumerable letters and manifestoes, a coherent and persuasive political image of Florence as the bulwark of freedom against despotic oppression. The idea itself was not new; but the use of classical rhetoric and ancient history gave it a fresh vigour, which was not lost on the Florentines nor on their enemies. Salutati's defence of Florentine republicanism was followed up, on a less polemical note, by his pupil Leonardo Bruni. By the early 15th century, the humanists had succeeded in providing the Florentine republicans with a coherent theory. In doing so, they were serving the republic in its relations with other states; but they also expressed the views and aspirations of the Florentine upper classes.

From the beginning, contacts between the professional humanists and patricians were close. Salutati became the teacher and guide of a generation of Florentines in the *studia humanitatis*, and the group of friends he gathered around him included young patricians such as Niccolò Niccoli, as well as professionals such as Leonardo Bruni and Poggio Bracciolini. The intellectual heir of Petrarch, he transmitted this heritage to the Florentine humanists; he assembled a large library of classical texts, and he was primarily responsible for inviting Manuel Chrysoloras from Constantinople to Florence to teach Greek, and thus in permanently establishing Greek studies in Florence.

p 122 (5)

p 122 (3)

Salutati received a State funeral during which he was crowned with the poetic laurel, a double ceremony which symbolized the two closely interrelated aspects of his life as a public servant and

p 18-19
(17)
p 26 (38)

Arts and crafts in Florence. In this engraving of the activities sacred to Mercury, the dome of the Cathedral is recognizable on the left and other actual buildings are suggested. At bottom right is a goldsmith's shop; opposite, a scribe and clockmaker; on the upper storeys are house decorators and a musician; and in the street a sculptor and philosopher with armillary sphere. (5)

man of letters. The same honours were rendered to Bruni (1444) and Marsuppini (1453). In these solemn ceremonies, Florence expressed her gratitude to her humanist chancellors. 'The Signory decreed', writes Vespasiano da Bisticci of Bruni's funeral, 'that his memory should be honoured in every possible way. It was decided that the ancient rule of delivering a funeral oration should be revived and Giannozzo (Manetti) was charged with this duty, and he was crowned with the laurel after the ancient custom.'

In Praise of Florence

At the time of Salutati's death, Bruni was apostolic secretary at the Curia; it was not until 1415 that he settled permanently in Florence. By the time of his master's death, he had written two works which contained some of the principal ideas of Florentine civic humanism, the *Dialogues* to Pier Paolo Vergerio, and the *Panegyric on Florence*. In the latter, he traces Florentine love of liberty to the Roman republic, for he believed, like Salutati, and contrary to medieval Florentine tradition, that the republican Sulla and not the dictator Caesar had been the founder of the city; in the second *Dialogue*, he vindicates the Italian works of the three great Florentine poets, Dante, Petrarch and Boccaccio, against those who upheld the absolute superiority of classical literature over the moderns. He had also begun his translations of *Lives* by Plutarch, which were to be followed by translations of Aristotle's *Ethics*, *Politics* and of the pseudo-Aristotelian *Economics*, all of which had a bearing on civic life.

On his return to Florence, he embarked on a vast *History of the Florentine People*, which he had not completed by the time of his death. Vespasiano da Bisticci later called it the first real history of Florence, thus denying that title to the great chronicle of the Villani: he meant that Bruni's work was the first history of Florence written in Latin, according to the rules of ancient Roman historiography. What was perhaps more important was that with Bruni the methods of textual criticism, which the humanists had been evolving in the study of literary works, began to make their impact on the use of historical sources. Bruni imitated Livy, but he also used archival documents. He had a high concept of history, and contrasted it with rhetorical eulogies like the one he had written on Florence: 'History should follow the truth, panegyric goes beyond truth in its praise.' Yet his *History* equally turns, in the end, into a praise of Florentine liberty. His account of the wars against the papacy and Giangaleazzo Visconti is pervaded by the praise of Florentine liberty, and echoes the letters in which Salutati had defended his city.

These were, however, not the only works in which Bruni gave expression to political values. Moral philosophy was considered to form part of the *studia humanitatis*—Salutati defines *humanitas* as moral learning—and in Florence it acquired civic overtones. This was natural enough: the humanists wrote for educated laymen as well as for other scholars, and the important rôle public office played in the life of the Florentine upper classes made them pay special attention to civic problems. The most important of these problems concerned the relative value of active and of contemplative life. Petrarch's preference for the latter was a legacy of medieval monastic ideals. These were still largely shared by Salutati, although he also affirmed the importance of civic life, and once justified his own commitment to it by saying that while monks served only themselves and a few brethren, he was trying to serve all the citizens. For Bruni, there was no longer any doubt about the need to merge active and contemplative life into a harmonious whole. While Petrarch had condemned Cicero for forsaking 'glorious solitude' and philosophy for 'the vain splendour of fame' as a statesman, and while Salutati was still hesitant in judging his political actions, Bruni regarded him as the ideal citizen-philosopher. While Boccaccio had blamed Dante for having aspired to 'the fleeting honours and the vain pomp of public office', Bruni praised him for having fulfilled his duties as citizen and soldier. 'Among the moral teachings through which man's life is formed', he says in the preface to his translation of Aristotle's *Politics*, 'those which concern the State and its government occupy, in a certain sense, the highest place, for they aim at achieving happiness for men.' Aristotle had qualified his statement that 'man is by nature a political animal' by observing that exceptional individuals may be able to exist without the state: Bruni was convinced that man 'achieves his perfection only in political society'. But if political life forms the external conditions for his perfection, the humane studies provide the intellectual and moral guidance for it: 'they are called *studia humanitatis*' he explains, 'because they perfect man'.

'The Worthy Citizens of the Time'

Bruni dedicated his translation of Plato's *Letters* to Cosimo de' Medici; and Cosimo, like other patrician students of the humanities, conformed to Bruni's ideal of the citizen who divided his time between active life and scholarship. A new generation of Florentine admirers of ancient learning and literature had succeeded the group of citizens around Salutati; older men like Niccolò Niccoli and Bruni himself preserved the link with the past. In the 1420s they would meet at the convent of Sta Maria degli Angeli, where the learned Ambrogio Traversari had come to occupy the same place as the guiding spirit of Florentine humanism which Salutati had occupied before in the Chancery. 'All the worthy citizens of that time', writes Vespasiano da Bisticci, 'would visit him almost daily .... Niccolò Niccoli, Cosimo de' Medici, his brother Lorenzo, Messer Carlo Marsuppini d'Arezzo, Messer Giannozzo Manetti ...' In its composition, this group exemplified the fusion of active and contemplative life preached by Bruni, although it included men like Roberto de' Rossi and Niccolò Niccoli (d. 1437) who preferred study to politics. But even Niccoli, who, Manetti says, did not strive after public offices and preferred to live unmarried and with his books, would accept such offices when he was appointed to them.

Not all the men who belonged to the first two generations of Florentine humanism were creative scholars, just as only a few of them were professional humanists who earned their living by their pen. At a time when manuscripts of ancient authors were rare, book-collecting formed an important aspect of humanist studies. Antonio Corbinelli (d.1425) built up one of the most important collections of Greek and Roman authors of his day; Niccolò Niccoli's famous library contained over 800 volumes (Petrarch and Boccaccio are thought to have owned not much more than 200 volumes; according to Poggio, Salutati's was about the same size as Niccoli's). Cosimo's library contained about 70 volumes in 1418, but was to grow rapidly under him an his heirs. Niccoli 'having spent on books a large part of his fortune', and being in financial difficulties, Cosimo and his brother Lorenzo 'ordered at the bank that whenever Niccolò might ask for money, it should be given to him'. Niccoli willed that on his death his collection should be made accessible to the public. Palla Strozzi (d. 1462), like Niccoli one of Chrysoloras' pupils, had procured for him Greek manuscripts required for his teaching and employed the best copyists to build up his own collection, which at one time he planned, in his turn, to make into a public library. He was, in Vespasiano's words, 'a fine scholar in Greek

and Latin'; but he was also, until his banishment in 1434, one of the city's leading statesmen. Another of Chrysoloras' pupils, Roberto de' Rossi, a member of a noble family, taught young patricians Latin and Greek: one of these was Cosimo de' Medici. A close friend of leading Florentine humanists, like Niccoli, Bruni, and Marsuppini, Cosimo helped their studies by patronage as well as book collecting. Vespasiano, who helped to build up his library, says of him that 'he had a knowledge of Latin letters which surpassed what one would expect from a great citizen who was engrossed in so many affairs'. But the combination of humanist studies with public life is perhaps most strikingly exemplified by Giannozzo Manetti (1396–1459). One of Florence's richest citizens, he was almost constantly employed in public office at home or abroad until his political enemies forced him to emigrate to Naples. A disciple of Traversari, 'he was most learned in Latin, Greek, and Hebrew', and was considered one of the best orators of his time; among his numerous writings and translations from the Greek, his treatise *On the Dignity and Excellence of Man* stands out as an eloquent glorification of human action and liberty, in answer to Pope Innocent III's *On the Contempt of the World*. Nor were public office and scholarship separate aspects of his life: in fulfilling his civic duties, he tried to live up to the moral ideals which his studies had inspired in him.

The interplay of professional and amateur interest in humanist studies, the close links between these studies and civic life, the eminence of her scholars and men of letters and the wealth of her libraries, all this had made Florence in the early Quattrocento a centre of unique importance for the development of Renaissance civilization. In 1428, Bruni likened her to Athens in a funeral oration modelled on that of Pericles in Thucydides' *History of the Peloponnesian War*. 'Even the knowledge of the Greek letters, which for more than 700 years had fallen into disuse in Italy, has been recalled and brought back by our commonwealth ... finally, the *studia humanitatis* themselves, surely the best and most excellent of studies ... took root in Italy after originating in our city ...' Poggio, in his funeral speech on Bruni, praised Florence for honouring and supporting these studies: 'There is no republic, and no prince, who rewards the men who are devoted to them more richly'. He was referring to the tax privilege which had been granted to Bruni as reward for his *Florentine History*. The award, like the less extensive one Poggio himself had received earlier, was characteristic of the difference between republican and princely patronage. In Florence, it was not the prince but the citizens who appointed prominent humanists as chancellors or university professors, and who were prepared to reward them for public service as well as for literary and scholarly merit. However, if the Florentine republic provided careers for humanists, the term patronage is inadequate to describe the support humanist studies received from private citizens like Palla Strozzi and Cosimo de' Medici, who were themselves committed to these studies and furthered them by building up great libraries. Only in the next generation, under the growing ascendancy of the Medici, does the patronage of men of letters by that family introduce into Florence some of the characteristic features of princely patronage.

Public Patronage

While the *studia humanitatis* were necessarily confined to a relatively small section of the population, the appeal of art and architecture was much wider, and consequently public patronage of the arts played a far greater rôle than that of letters. The construction and upkeep of the communal buildings, as well as of the cathedral and baptistery, were the responsibility of the Commune, which also contributed heavily to other ecclesiastical buildings, as for instance to the two friars' churches of Sta Croce and Sta Maria Novella. These extensive responsibilities were shared with the greater guilds; thus the Calimala guild was in charge of the supervision of the baptistery and of S. Miniato, and in the 15th century of that of Sta Croce, while in the early 15th century the wool guild was entrusted with that of the Cathedral, and the silk guild with the construction of Orsanmichele. Guild offices, like those of the Commune, were short-termed, and decisions of

p 14 (4)

p 14 (5)

p 14 (6)

artistic policy were therefore shared by a large number of citizens. This widening of public patronage must have helped to make art and architecture a popular concern. It no doubt also contributed to the many delays which beset the great building projects of the 14th and 15th centuries.

The continuity which was so marked in Florentine society and politics and which defies any clear cut division between 'medieval' and 'Renaissance' Florence, was also reflected in the public patronage of the arts. Nearly all the great enterprises of the early 15th century continue or complete work that had been undertaken in the preceding century or even earlier: the only major exception is the Spedale degli Innocenti (the Foundling Hospital), built between 1419 and 1444 from Brunelleschi's design under the supervision of the silk guild. The three greatest achievements of public patronage in the first decades of the century, Ghiberti's bronze doors of the baptistery, the façade statues of Orsanmichele, and Brunelleschi's cupola of the Duomo, all completed building projects whose beginnings went back into the distant past. Brunelleschi's cupola, which completed a structure which had been begun nearly one century and a half earlier, constitutes a dramatic and almost symbolical manifestation of this continuity, which also permeates the innumerable works by which during the 15th century private citizens adorned churches and chapels. The cupola of the cathedral, a revolutionary achievement of Quattrocento architecture, crowns the austere Gothic crossing.

Orsanmichele had been built after 1336 as a granary with an oratory on the ground floor—'a church in the form of a palace', as a contemporary document puts it. The Commune was to pay the expenses of the building, the guilds and the Guelf Party those of the sculptures of their patron saints that were to adorn its façades. But in 1406 most of these were still missing, and the Signory demanded that they be completed within ten years; it also decreed that they could be cast in bronze. Since the single guilds and the Guelf Party were responsible for one tabernacle each, the commissioning of the statues illustrates not only the collective commitment of public patronage but also its competitive aspects. Thus the decision of the Calimala guild to commission Ghiberti for a bronze statue of their patron saint, St John the Baptist, prompted the other greater guilds equally to set up such statues, which were far more expensive than stone ones. But more significant is the readiness of the guilds to accept the new artistic trends. Six of the statues that were executed between 1406 and 1428 were the work of the two greatest Florentine sculptors of their time, Ghiberti and Donatello.

The competitive spirit in Florentine artistic policy is shown even more strikingly by the history of the bronze doors of the baptistery. In 1401, the Calimala guild decided to commission a second bronze door (the first had been executed by Andrea Pisano in 1330—36), and held a competition in which Ghiberti triumphed over the other six final competitors, including Brunelleschi. His bronze door was set in place in 1424, and, in the following year, he was commissioned to model the third and last door. The 'Gates of Paradise' were completed in 1452. No other work of art of the Florentine Quattrocento was more admired in its time. 'Who would not be captured by beholding such wonders', writes Pietro Cennini in 1475; 'who would not stand transfixed almost out of mind?' Similarly, the most spectacular achievement of public patronage during this period, the cupola raised by Brunelleschi between 1420 and 1434, was the result of a competition held in 1418 which put an end to the long delays caused by the apparently insuperable problem of spanning the octagonal end of the nave with a dome.

While these great enterprises were under way, the interiors of Florentine churches were beginning to be transformed under the impact of the new art forms. Thus in 1432 and 1433 respectively, Luca della Robbia and Donatello were commissioned to provide the sculptures for the two singing galleries of the Duomo which Brunelleschi had designed in classical style, and which must have offered, when completed in about 1439, a sharp contrast to the severe Gothic nave.

Much of this transformation of church interiors was due to private patronage. As they had done in the past, the great Florentine families continued to build and embellish their private chapels and contribute also in other ways to the adornment of ecclesiastical buildings; and like the communal and guild commissions whose membership was often drawn from them, they were alive to the new creations of the artists. In patronizing the new Quattrocento art, Florentine patricians like Felice Brancacci showed much the same progressive attitude as others did in furthering humanist studies: the frescoes which he commissioned for his family chapel in Sta Maria del Carmine from Masolino and Masaccio mark a turning point in the development of Renaissance painting. And if artists like Ghiberti were deeply influenced by the classical revival, so were patrons of the arts: Niccolò da Uzzano, who, as one of the commissioners for the adornment of the baptistery, ordered the programme for Ghiberti's second bronze door from Leonardo Bruni, provides an early example of the contacts between artistic patronage and humanism which were to play so important a rôle in 15th-century Florentine art.

Felice Brancacci initiates the long line of patrician patrons of the arts whose judicious munificence did so much in creating Renaissance Florence. His political enemy Cosimo de' Medici was one of these great Florentine patrons; but Cosimo's patronage surpassed that of his peers, just as political and economic power gave him a dominant position among them.

The Rise of the Medici

One of the main achievements of the 'oligarchical' régime after 1382 was the unity of the ruling group. This unity was, despite occasional tensions and conflicts, preserved until the early 1430s, when it was finally disrupted. A new generation had taken over: in 1417, Maso degli Albizzi had been succeeded by his son Rinaldo; in 1421, Gino Capponi by his son Neri, and in 1429 Giovanni de' Medici by his son Cosimo; of the old guard, only Niccolò da Uzzano survived. After a long period of peace, war broke out in 1423 with Milan, whose Duke Filippo Maria was reviving the expansionist policy of his father. The war went badly for Florence until she succeeded in concluding an alliance with Venice (1426), and in the peace of 1428 she had to be satisfied with negligible gains. Nevertheless Florence embarked in 1429 on a war against Lucca, a city which she had already coveted in the preceding century, and as a result became embroiled with Siena, the other Tuscan city which had retained her independence from Florence. Milanese intervention followed, and the enterprise against Lucca collapsed in 1433. Rinaldo degli Albizzi, who had been one of its chief protagonists, had to face mounting criticism, and the death in the same year of Niccolò da Uzzano, who had advised against the war, further weakened his position. Cosimo de' Medici emerged as the potential leader of the opposition. In contrast to the Albizzi, his branch of the Medici family was of modest origin; however, his father Giovanni had a distant relative, Vieri di Cambio who was one of the city's leading bankers towards the end of the 14th century, and Giovanni laid the foundations of his fortune as manager of the Rome branch of Vieri's firm. By 1427, he was assessed for the second highest tax in Florence. After the débâcle of the war against Lucca, Cosimo appeared to many citizens as the principal rival of Rinaldo, and the city split into two factions. To forestall being ousted from the leadership of the régime, Rinaldo succeeded in having Cosimo banished in 1433; but, recalled to Florence by a pro-Medici Signory, he returned in October 1434, and now it was Rinaldo's turn to be banished. Many members of his party followed him into exile.

At first it may well have seemed that nothing had changed except the leadership and the composition of the ruling group, but it soon emerged that Cosimo and his followers were bent on creating institutional safeguards of their ascendancy that were far in excess of those possessed by the ruling patriciate before 1434. These safeguards were twofold: a preliminary selection of the candidates for the Signory who were then appointed by lot, and the substitution, for decisions of major importance, of special councils with wide powers (*Balìe*) for the ancient councils of the people and of the Commune. Contrary to a widely held view, neither of these institutional safeguards was established from the start on a permanent basis. It was not until 1458 that

p 86 (25)

p 14 (2)

p 14 (6)

p 82 (12)

p 82 (13)

p 82 (15, 16)

p 17 (12

p 80-81 (9,10)

the régime can be considered to be finally consolidated; for in that year the Mediceans, under the leadership of Cosimo and Luca Pitti, succeeded in having electoral controls, which had recently been abolished, restored for five years (they were shortly afterwards extended by another quinquennium), while a new permanent council was created to act as bulwark of the régime. Yet even now the régime was not entirely secure. After Cosimo's death in 1464, a rift developed among his followers, and the republican opposition gained the upper hand in 1465–66. As a result, not only were electoral controls once more abolished, but Piero de' Medici's ascendancy was threatened. This republican reaction remained, however, an interlude, for in September 1466 it was crushed by Piero and his friends; and now electoral controls were restored for no less than twenty years: they were to last until the fall of the régime in 1494. For this was the last constitutionalist challenge the Medici had to meet before 1494: the Pazzi conspiracy, which nearly cost Piero's son and successor Lorenzo his life, was due to family rivalry and intervention from abroad.

However much the establishment of the Medici régime changed the tenor of Florentine politics, it took some time to affect Florentine civilization. For one thing, the political changes were gradual and at first almost experimental; for another, they took place within the framework of long-established political traditions and institutions. It was not until the time of Lorenzo the Magnificent that they had become incisive enough to affect the cultural as well as the political life of Florence; and even then, there was no question of a complete break with the past.

Cosimo, 'Pater Patriae'

20 (20) The gradual nature of the changes wrought by the Medici régime may best be illustrated by the position of Cosimo himself. Cosimo insisted time and again that he was only a private citizen, and was careful to live up to this claim by avoiding the appearance of political privilege. He held three times the highest office in the state, the Gonfaloniership of Justice; and over long periods that of an official of the funded debt; but so did some other leading citizens. In his lifetime, Florentine eulogists would enlarge upon his public service, and compare him with Camillus and Cicero; and on his death the antique title of *Pater Patriae* was conferred on him for having served his country well. Before long this image of Cosimo as republican patriot was beginning to give way to that of Cosimo the ruler. This change was chiefly due to scholars and poets who were patronized by the Medici, and with it, the courtiers' adulation, which was a characteristic of princely courts, began to take root in Florence.

The eulogists who praised Cosimo as Augustus greatly exaggerated his real authority. The patronage that elicited their panegyrics was, on the other hand, a reality; and if they likened Cosimo to Augustus, they also compared him with Maecenas. If his patronage of the arts and letters surpassed that of his peers, and reflected in this way the leading position he had acquired among them he also took, like Palla Strozzi and other patricians, an active personal interest in the New Learning as well as in artistic production. Intellectual and aesthetic interests combined with religious sentiments and reasons of political prestige to make him the greatest Florentine patron of his generation.

According to Vespasiano da Bisticci, Cosimo felt that he had to expiate the unrighteous acquisition of some of his wealth if he wanted God to let him keep his worldly goods, and on the advice of Pope Eugenius IV resolved, after his return to Florence, to rebuild the convent of S. Marco, which the Pope had just transferred to the Dominican Observants. Cosimo spent over 40,000
p 126 florins on the convent, and provided it with the great library
(22) whose nucleus was formed by Niccolò Niccoli's collection. This was the first of his lavish gifts to churches and monasteries. In the forties, even before the building of S. Marco was completed, he erected the noviciate of Sta Croce and spent vast sums on the
86 (24) rebuilding of S. Lorenzo, thus continuing on a larger scale the work of his father, who had promised to contribute the sacristy (the *Sagrestia vecchia*) and the adjoining family chapel, and who appears to have been responsible for the acceptance of Brunelleschi's design for the new church. In 1456, Cosimo decided to rebuild the Badia of the Augustinian canons of Fiesole, and he

Quefto fie laffedio di Padoa

New weapons and a new ruthlessness were entering warfare. Orlando, in Ariosto's poem, throws to the bottom of the sea 'the murderous engine' which would destroy the virtues of chivalry. In this woodcut of 1521, cannon appear beside the bows, arrows, lances and heavy armour of the old order. (6)

1458804

provided it with a large library, which in this case was assembled anew: Vespasiano claims that it took him less than two years to produce 200 manuscripts. It was characteristic of Cosimo's patronage in favour of ecclesiastical foundations that it combined building enterprises with humanist book-collecting. Yet when it came to his private building activities, Cosimo showed remarkable restraint. It was not until 1444 that he decided to build a new family palace and he seems to have left its decoration and furnishing, as also the charge of his library, to his sons Giovanni and Piero. According to a later account, he rejected a design made for the new palace by Brunelleschi on the grounds that 'it appeared to him too great and sumptuous an enterprise', an explanation which would accord well with his attitude to his public image. He chose the more modest design by Michelozzi, who had been the architect of S. Marco. The palace, whose structure was completed by c.1460, served, with its rusticated façade which was p 23
based on medieval Florentine tradition, as a model for patrician (31, 32)
houses in the second half of the century. Overshadowing the houses of humbler citizens, they paraded the wealth and prestige of the great Florentine families. Yet none of them, including that of the Medici, could rival the palaces of despots. Strong enough to stand up to sudden attacks, they were, with their large windows and open loggias, turned towards the street, and formed an integral part of civic life. The private life of the patrician family revolved around the elegant courtyards, in which the layout of medieval cloisters was now adapted to the new classical design.

An author's income came not from the sale of his books but from the bounty of his patrons, whom it was his duty to flatter. It was a rule that applied to all, from the great humanists to the writers of romances like Masuccio da Salerno, here presenting his 'Novellino' to a noble lady. (7)

humanists began to collect antiques. Their collections of ancient statues, gems and coins were bound to mould their artistic tastes as well as those of their patrons, and thus, concurrently with the direct impact of classical art on creative artists, to influence the development of Renaissance art. Foremost among these early humanist collectors was Niccoli: admirers of his would go so far as to assert that he had revived not only classical literature but also painting and sculpture. Poggio went into raptures over antique works of art, and Niccoli combined the collecting of manuscripts with that of antiques. Patrician collectors, whose means gave them greater scope, followed suit. As in learning and literature, the humanists initiated new fashions which were then adopted by rich citizens. In the course of the century, the Medici were to assemble the greatest collection of antiques in Florence, but, once more, Cosimo was less susceptible to the new trend than some of his contemporaries: the real founder of that collection, after about 1450, was his son Piero. Nor was collectorship necessarily a corollary of patronage. As we shall see, Lorenzo de' Medici, while greatly expanding his collection of antique statues and *objets d'art*, did far less than his grandfather in patronizing artists and in thus furthering the development of Renaissance art.

The influence of antiquity on art and artistic patronage was not confined to the admiration and imitation of antique art. The humanists, in reviving the classical concept of fame, gave the individualism of the Florentine merchants and politicians a new dimension, which found its artistic expression in portraits and tombs. Portraits, which were largely inspired by antique models, became an integral part of Florentine sculpture and painting during the 15th century, and like the tombs provided individual citizens with an opportunity of perpetuating their memory; but while single portraits were designed for private houses, in the tombs individual fame could assume public significance. In Leonardo Bruni's tomb by Bernardo Rossellino in Sta Croce, which served as a model for later tombs such as that of Carlo Marsuppini, the traditional funeral monument of medieval Florence is given a new classical form. At the same time, with the religious imagery reduced to a minimum, with the Latin inscription celebrating Bruni's achievements, his tomb shows the impact of humanist studies and of classical art on the desire for individual fame.

p 18–1 (17) p 26 (3

The Two Cultures

Cosimo's ascendancy after 1434 did not materially change the oligarchical pattern of Florentine politics; it did not eliminate the republican ideas underlying it. Some families like the Brancacci and Peruzzi had been banished, and others deprived of political rights. New ones, like the Pucci and Martelli, had entered the ruling set. But this did not alter the fact that, as before, the Florentine upper class occupied a prominent position in the government of the city. The restraint with which aristocrats like Donato Acciaiuoli praised Cosimo as no more than a patriotic republican statesman reflected their conservative attitude to the republican framework of government. Indeed, Cosimo's ascendancy, as well as the institutional controls introduced by the new régime, could be considered by them, rightly or wrongly, as securing their own political and social status. As late as about 1440, the Chancellor of Florence, Leonardo Bruni, still described the city's republican constitution as if it was entirely intact. About the same time, Matteo Palmieri voiced the same brand of civic humanism which had been so popular at the beginning of the century. Patricians continued to consider public office as a right as well as a duty. A number of them combined it, as earlier generations had done, with humanist studies and creative scholarship. The Chancery continued to be headed by prominent humanists. When Bruni died in 1444, he was succeeded by Carlo Marsuppini, who had previously taught poetry at the University, and he in turn was succeeded on his death in 1453 by the most famous Italian humanist of his time, Poggio Bracciolini. Poggio, who returned to Florence after a lifetime in papal service, continued the tradition inaugurated by Bruni and wrote a Latin history of his city. But in it he no longer celebrated republican freedom: its main theme is the recurrent struggle with the Visconti whose final conclusion was the achievement of Cosimo de' Medici.

p 122 (

p 78 (4)

p 86–87 (28, 29)

While in 1418–23 Palla Strozzi had still built his family chapel in Sta Trinita in the late Gothic style, and had it adorned with the magnificent altarpiece by Gentile da Fabriano, Andrea de' Pazzi commissioned Brunelleschi, in about 1430, to erect his family chapel at Sta Croce—one of the purest examples of early Renaissance architecture. About ten years later Tommaso Spinelli commissioned a follower of Brunelleschi to build the second cloisters which surround the Pazzi chapel. If Brunelleschi, and later Alberti, were able to give Florentine architecture a new form, this was due to no small extent to private patrons; but while Felice Brancacci had ordered Masaccio, the pioneer of early Quattrocento art, to fresco his chapel in Sta Maria del Carmine, Cosimo commissioned Gozzoli to paint the *Adoration of the Magi* for his palace chapel in a style influenced by the International Gothic of Northern Europe. Perhaps the same caution which characterized Cosimo's political action also affected his attitude to art. Moreover, however much Florentine patrons supported the new artistic trends, there were strong traditionalist undercurrents, which were no doubt reinforced by the close contacts with the late Gothic art that was fashionable at the French and Burgundian courts. Florentine taste was sufficiently catholic to accept art forms which, while more conservative than the new classical style, were not necessarily *retardaire*, and which may have found an echo in the deeply rooted traditionalism of the Florentines. The greatest of these traditionalist artists was Fra Angelico.

p 80–81 (9, 10) p 20 (20)

The Humanist Position

The support which early Renaissance art received from public and private patronage forms part of a wider process. As men of letters the humanists were not necessarily susceptible to artistic experience, and their admiration for antique art was often motivated by antiquarian rather than aesthetic interests. Salutati's programme for a series of Famous Men in the Palazzo Vecchio and Bruni's for Ghiberti's Gates of Paradise were probably characteristic of the attitude of early 15th-century humanists to living artists: they were primarily concerned with the contents of artistic creation. Leone Battista Alberti marks the turning point in combining humanist learning with artistic theory and creation; but when he came to Florence from exile in 1434, the climate was already changing. Alberti was deeply impressed by the creations of the new art he saw in his city, and in his *On Painting* (1435) and *On Architecture* (around 1452) he provided it with a theoretical foundation derived from the teachings of the ancients and from antique models. Niccoli and Poggio achieved a fresh aesthetic sensibility by merging literary and artistic classicism in their love of Roman art. Whether for antiquarian or aesthetic reasons, the

p 26 (39, 40)

Donato Acciaiuoli (1429–78) and Alamanno Rinuccini (1426–99) are outstanding examples of the continuing commitment of Florentine patricians to the New Learning, as well as of their successful reconciliation of active and contemplative life. Of Donato Acciaiuoli, his 16th-century biographer says that 'while governing the republic, he applied himself to philosophy, and while philosophizing, he governed the republic'. Amidst his many offices at home and abroad, he found time to compose, among other works, a commentary on Aristotle's *Ethics*, and a life of Charlemagne. For the Florentine Signory, he translated Bruni's *History of Florence* into Italian, and for Federigo da Montefeltro, Aristotle's *Politics* into Latin. Rinuccini, who followed the customary civic career of Florentine patricians until he fell out with Lorenzo, was an accomplished Greek and Latin scholar; he translated several *Lives* of Plutarch, and composed many elegant Latin epistles and orations. In the fifties his house was the meeting place of a group of young humanists, among them Andrea Alamanni, Marco Parenti and Donato Acciaiuoli; they called their meetings an 'academy', and thus foreshadowed the Platonic Academy of Ficino. Rinuccini and Acciaiuoli were chiefly responsible for the appointment, in 1456, of the Byzantine scholar John Argyropoulos to the chair of Greek at the University. Argyropoulos' teaching (he held the chair until 1471) led to an Aristotelian revival and deeply influenced the Greek learning and philosophical outlook of his young disciples. In 1463 Donato Acciaiuoli affirmed, with some rhetorical exaggeration, that 'the liberal studies had never flourished more in this city' than after the arrival of Argyropolous, who 'educated the youth of Florence for many years not only in Greek letters, but also in those arts that are necessary to lead a good and happy life'. By his systematic programme of philosophical studies, which contrasted with that of the medieval schools, he gave his young disciples a wider and deeper knowledge of philosophy, which in its turn contrasted with the prevalently literary approach of the earlier Florentine humanists. By placing Aristotle into the context of Greek philosophy, he also gave them a new appreciation of Plato and thus prepared the ground for Ficino's Platonic Academy.

p 26 (37)

On the fringe of these groups of citizen scholars which are so characteristic of the Florentine Quattrocento, we find men who, while not actively participating in the New Learning, were attracted and influenced by it. One such citizen was Giovanni Rucellai (d. 1481), a wealthy patrician who after a long period in the political wilderness was accepted into the Medici fold, married, in 1466, his son Bernardo to a sister of Lorenzo, and became one of the leading personalities of the régime. His Roman guidebook combines the tradition of the medieval *Mirabilia* with humanist antiquarianism; a prominent patron of the arts, he had his family *loggia* and probably his palace built by Alberti, the pioneering theo-

rist of the classical revival in architecture, who also designed for him the façade of Sta Maria Novella. His *Zibaldone*, a kind of diary-cum-commonplace book, shows an interplay of civic traditions, religious sentiments, and learned interests which was no doubt more characteristic of the average culture of rich Florentine citizens than the erudition of the intellectual élite among them. However great the significance of Florentine humanism and however pervasive its influence, medieval vernacular traditions continued to prevail on a more popular level. This is shown, for instance, by the wide diffusion and proliferation of romances of chivalry, such as the *Reali di Francia* by Andrea da Barberino, and by the survival of the medieval legends of Florence's origins, despite their critical rejection by the humanists.

p 14 (5)

A meeting of the two cultures was promoted by the humanists themselves whose changed attitude to the value of the Tuscan language facilitated the spreading of their works and ideas. Bruni justified the writing of his *Life of Dante* in the vernacular by arguing that, like Greek and Latin, it 'has its own perfection'. Others were more on the defensive. Palmieri wrote his dialogue *On Civic Life* in his native language, although his friends warned him that in doing so he was liable to be misunderstood and derided by the uneducated populace. Leone Battista Alberti made it quite clear that he chose the same procedure in his *On the Family* because he wished to write in a language that was intelligible to all. Donato Acciaiuoli translated Bruni's, and Jacopo Bracciolini his father Poggio's, *History of Florence* from the Latin. Ficino himself translated his Latin Commentary on the *Symposium* into Tuscan (1475) so that Plato's message 'would be more readily accessible to a large number of people'. Yet the older prejudices survived. Giannozzo Manetti composed his *Life of Dante* in Latin on the grounds that learned men would not read Bruni's biography of him because it was written in the vernacular; and, as we have seen, Vespasiano da Bisticci, writing towards the end of the century, denied the status of true history to the city's 13th-century chroniclers because they were not written in Latin.

'Those Peaceful Days'

Art and architecture provided another channel by which the new humanist forms and values could reach a wider public and affect its tastes and interests. Girolomo Savonarola complained that people were often so delighted by a good painting that they would forget themselves. This warning was hardly addressed to patrons and collectors only. Most Florentine citizens would probably have agreed with Cristoforo Landino, who in his Dante *Commentary* (1481) praised the Florentine artists and architects of the 15th century as one of the glories of his city.

Public festivals and shows provided other points of contact. Festivals, processions and pageants formed a traditional element of Florentine, and indeed of Italian, civic life. Religious feasts, above all those in honour of the city's patron St John the Baptist, alternated with secular ones, such as celebrations of victories, and in their turn had often a partly secular character, and weddings and funerals could assume the form of public manifestations. In the 15th century, such feasts and pageants increased in number, sumptuousness and sophistication. The jousts, of which about thirty are recorded for that century, became increasingly occasions for the display of dress and armour, and religious and secular processions included dramatic elements in the form of allegorical floats and scenic representations. Among the many influences, local as well as foreign, which moulded form and contents of these public manifestations, humanism and antique art assumed an increased importance after the middle of the century. Historical or allegorical *trionfi* were modelled on Roman triumphal processions which could be observed in classical reliefs. Then there were the carnival masques, which might be based on classical mythology as well as on allegory or contemporary society. According to Machiavelli, Lorenzo de' Medici 'in those peaceful days always kept his city feasting, and there were often to be seen jousts and representations of ancient deeds and triumphs'. Whether he did so for political purposes is questionable. The Medici were not the only patrician family which presented the Florentines with spectacles of this kind. Bartolomeo Benci, for instance, organized a sumptuous joust in honour of his lady during the carnival of 1464.

p 16–17 (9)

f 8

Festivals, jousting and carnivals were not only sponsored by the patrician families to celebrate important events, but were also paid for by civic funds on regular occasions. No fewer than 30 jousts—to mention only one form of entertainment—were recorded in Florence for the 15th century. (8)

The fame of Cristoforo Landino (above), scholar, humanist and secretary to the Signory, rests largely on his 'Disputationes camaldolenses' a series of imaginary dialogues in which Lorenzo de' Medici discusses with Ficino and Alberti such topics as the good life, action versus contemplation, and the allegorical meanings in Vergil. (9)

When Lorenzo held a magnificent tournament in 1469, to celebrate his marriage to Clarice Orsini, he did so, according to his diary, 'in order to do as others', and adds that it cost him 10,000 ducats. The first prize he received was 'a silver helmet with Mars as its crest'.

Lorenzo the Magnificent

The Florentine, and indeed the Italian, Renaissance is often associated with the age of Lorenzo. In fact, Lorenzo's patronage lagged behind that of some of his Florentine contemporaries. Rather than create a new culture or political régime, he represented some of the major trends and problems of the intellectual civilization and the political system of Florence in the second half of the century. His literary gifts and learned interests, and his success in combining these with a life of constant political activity, corresponded to the ideal of Florentine Quattrocento humanism. Significantly, in Landino's *Camaldolensian Disputations* of c. 1475, Lorenzo appears as the defender of civic values and of a harmonious balance of active and contemplative life demanded by the early Florentine humanists. Yet by further depriving the Florentine republic of the spirit, if not the letter, of its constitution, he also robbed their ideas of much of their practical meaning.

Lorenzo succeeded his father in 1469 as head of the political régime which Piero had restored and consolidated three years earlier. He strengthened it by cautious constitutional reforms in 1471; but in 1478 the Pazzi conspiracy threatened to overthrow it by assassinating Lorenzo and his brother Giuliano. The conspiracy was hatched by the Pazzi, a wealthy Florentine family which had become increasingly hostile to Lorenzo, and Sixtus IV's nephew Girolamo Riario, whose projects of territorial aggrandizement Lorenzo had opposed. Lorenzo escaped with his life, while Giuliano was killed; but the war with the papacy and Naples which followed the failure of the conspiracy and the hanging of the Archbishop of Pisa, who had been implicated in it, went badly for Florence. Lorenzo succeeded in negotiating a relatively favourable peace in 1480, and on his triumphal return to Florence crowned his diplomatic success by a reform which gave the early Medici régime its final institutional form. Supreme power was vested in a council of Seventy recruited from the inner circle of the régime; and although the Seventy was established for a term of five years only, this was repeatedly extended until the fall of the régime. Lorenzo was a member of the new council and its leading figure; but, like his father and grandfather, he did not occupy an official post that could not have been held by other patricians, and he exercised his *de facto* ascendancy with the help of a group of loyal followers. Among these, 'new men' such as Bernardo del Nero played a somewhat greater rôle than they had done under Cosimo; however, the patriciate continued to be heavily represented in the highest councils and offices. And if Lorenzo collaborated, in every-day affairs, with a small number of friends, he had also to rely on the loyalty of a larger group of less influential supporters.

As a result of this progressive concentration of power, political patronage increased, and the older councils, commissions and magistracies, including the Signory itself, lost most of their earlier authority. The transfer of the real centre of government from the Palace of the Signory to the palace and villas of the Medici was all but completed. This change in public life was the climax of a development that had begun in 1434, and which was the more remarkable as it coincided, under Lorenzo, with a decline of the Medici bank which brought it, by 1494, to the verge of bankruptcy. The resulting transformation of the political climate had in its turn been prepared by earlier developments. While under Cosimo humanists could still extol republican equality, as if the republic were still intact, Alamanno Rinuccini accused Lorenzo of tyrannically suppressing the city's republican liberties. While Cosimo was still chiefly praised as a republican statesman and patriot, Lorenzo was eulogized as head of the State. Married to an Orsini and addressed by the King of France as cousin, his close relations with Italian princes, and especially with Pope Innocent VIII, probably contributed to this change of climate. It was not surprising that they should consider him the virtual ruler of Florence, and that this in its turn should react on his position at home, despite his protests that, like his grandfather, he was no more than a private citizen.

The Academy of the 'New Plato'

One aspect of this change in the political climate was a greater emphasis on contemplative as against active life, in contrast to the attitude taken by the humanists of Salutati's and Bruni's time. While such preference could be defended, as in Landino's *Camaldolensian Disputations*, with philosophical arguments, Alamanno Rinuccini, in his dialogue *On Liberty* of 1479, sees the withdrawal to a life of philosophical contemplation as an answer to the decline of republican institutions and civic values. The Platonic revival after the middle of the century helped to reinforce such attitudes. The leading spirit of that revival, Marsilio Ficino (1433–99), believed in contemplation as the means by which philosophical knowledge and moral perfection could be attained, and preached indifference to external goods. One of the maxims he had inscribed in his villa at Careggi read: 'Flee troubles, be happy in the present.'

Florentine Platonism may date back to the Council of Union in Florence (1439) when, according to Ficino, Cosimo was so impressed by the Byzantine scholar Gemistus Plethon that he decided to found a Platonic Academy. Whatever the truth of this story, it was Argyropoulos who prepared the ground for it. Cosimo commissioned Ficino to translate Plato's dialogues, and Ficino followed the completion of this work in c. 1468 with his *Commentary on the Symposium* (1469) and with his principal work, the *Platonic Theology* (1474). His small country house near the Medici villa at Careggi, which he had received from Cosimo, became the city's foremost philosophical centre. From there his influence was to spread throughout Europe, with the result that

p 22 (27)

p 26
(41, 42)

f 9

p 21 (22)

p 21 (21)

Florence played once more, and for the last time, a leading rôle in the intellectual history of the Renaissance. He called his villa Academy in memory of Plato, and he and his friends dreamt of the rebirth of the Platonic school, and celebrated Plato's birthday with a solemn banquet. In fact the Academy of the 'new Plato' was not a school and had little in common with the institutional academies of the 16th and 17th centuries. While it continued the tradition of humanist meetings, it had also some links with those of the religious companies of laymen which, like the Academy, provided a sense of spiritual community as well as a forum for the discussion of religious subjects. Like the confraternities and the humanist meetings of earlier days, the Academy included men of different philosophical views, and professional scholars as well as learned citizens. Among the former was Cristoforo Landino, since 1458 professor of rhetoric and poetry at the University, who in his Dante *Commentary* reinterpreted the Divine Comedy in Platonic terms, Ugolino Verino and Giorgio Vespucci Antonio; among the latter we find Lorenzo de' Medici, his brother-in-law Bernardo Rucellai, Giovanni Cavalcanti, Bernardo del Nero, and Piero Guicciardini. Ficino's rapidly growing reputation outside Florence, which is reflected by his vast correspondence, attracted

p 26
(45, 46)

visitors from abroad. The greatest of these was Pico della Mirandola, who joined Ficino's circle in 1484. But while influenced by Ficino, Pico developed his philosophical doctrine from a great variety of sources, including the Jewish Cabbala, and was closer to the medieval scholastic traditions of Paris and Padua than to Florentine humanism. It was characteristic of his attitude that he should defend the medieval schoolmen against humanist criticism of their 'barbarity', on the grounds that truth was more important than words, and philosophy superior to grammar and rhetoric.

But it was precisely with grammar and rhetoric that the humanists had been primarily concerned. Were Ficino and Pico still humanists in the traditional sense of that term? Some modern scholars, especially Garin, see in the Platonic Academy the unfolding of a philosophical humanism which complements and fulfils the highest aspirations of the literary humanism that preceded it; others, especially Kristeller, hold to the distinction between the two trends and would describe Pico as a humanist and philosopher and not as a philosophical humanist. This is not just a question of terminology. The philosophical doctrines of Ficino and Pico, preceded as they were by Argyropoulos' teachings, had not only widened the intellectual horizon of the Florentine élite; they had also given rise to ideas and speculations that had little in common with the prevalently literary, historical and political interests of the earlier humanists. Ficino's metaphysical doctrine of the immortality of the soul, his theory of love as a sustaining principle of the universe, and his attempt to reconcile Platonic and neo-Platonic philosophy with Christian theology, transcend the philosophical interests of men like Salutati and Bruni, which were chiefly confined to ethics. At the same time, the humanist belief in the dignity of man was given a new metaphysical significance by Ficino's concept of the soul as active centre of the universe. Moreover, the *studia humanitatis* not only remained the firm foundation of the new philosophical trends: Ficino's Platonism itself reflects their historical approach to antiquity. His doctrine of *pia philosophia* is based on his notion of a pre-Platonic philosophy and theology supposedly expounded by Hermes Trismegistus, Orpheus, Pythagoras and others, and in fundamental agreement with Plato. His belief in a basic harmony between pagan and biblical traditions could be taken to justify the study of ancient religions on theological, as well as on antiquarian, grounds.

Poet, Patron and Collector

Side by side with the complex and often esoteric discussions in the Academy, humanist studies continued according to traditional

p 26
(43, 44)

lines, and found their greatest exponent in Politian (1454–94). While in his youth he had come under the influence of Argyropoulos and Ficino, he described himself not as a philosopher, but as a critic, and considered Platonic dialectic 'too remote and difficult' for him. A Latin and Greek philologist of genius, he was also an accomplished poet in Latin and Italian, and thus personified the reconciliation between the exclusive admiration and imitation of classical literature by the earlier humanists, and the

'*Many are the Florentines who have made themselves memorable by the art of music*', wrote a 14th-century observer. Musical entertainments were encouraged by the Medici; this concert scene—with one listener asleep—is from Luigi Pulci's 'Morgante Maggiore' a semi-burlesque version of the epic of Charlemagne. (10)

growing appreciation of the Tuscan language as a medium of creative literature. Over many years a member of Lorenzo's household and tutor of his children, he was appointed to the chair of Greek and Latin rhetoric at the University in 1480. The University which at first had played only a minor rôle in the development of Florentine humanism, became one of its major centres from about the middle of the century onwards. The decision, taken in 1472, on Lorenzo's initiative, to restore the University of Pisa, and the consequent limitation of the Florentine University to classical and literary studies, while depriving the latter of other faculties, did not lessen its reputation, which was sustained not only by teachers of the calibre of Politian, but also by lesser men like Landino, and Demetrius Chalcondilas, who had succeeded Argyropoulos in the chair of Greek in 1475.

Humanism remained a pervasive influence in Florentine civilization. Alberti's designs may serve to illustrate that influence in architecture, Bertoldo's medals and reliefs in sculpture. Politian was said to have acted as his artistic adviser, and he may have composed the programme for the portico frieze of Poggio a Caiano. Politian also provided in his *Stanze* a theme for Botticelli's *Birth of Venus*. In the *Triumph of Aemilius Paullus*, which he had represented in 1491 during the feasts for St John the Baptist, Lorenzo de' Medici imitated Plutarch's account. But the Platonic school, too, left its mark on Florentine art, as in the *Primavera*, which Botticelli painted for Lorenzo the Magnificient's cousin, Lorenzo di Pierfrancesco de' Medici, and perhaps in the *Birth of Venus;* and Ficino's belief in the creative powers of music had a practical as well as a philosophical significance, and no doubt affected the enthusiasm for instrumental and vocal recitals in Lorenzo's circle. Examples of such contacts and interactions between different disciplines could be multiplied *ad infinitum:* they reflect the absence of narrow specialization which characterized Florentine civilization in the Laurentian age, and had its counterpart in the versatility of its major exponents.

p 25 (36)

p 77 (1)

f 10

No one showed that versatility more strikingly than Lorenzo. A friend and disciple of Ficino as well as his patron, his philosophical and poetic writings are inspired by the teachings of his master. Unlike Cosimo, Lorenzo was a creative man of letters. His Italian poetry—sonnets and carnival songs, eclogues and religious and philosophical poems—is influenced by classical literature and popular Tuscan traditions. A prominent member of Ficino's circle, he was surrounded by scholars and poets on terms of friendship and intellectual equality. His influence on the civilization of his age has been exaggerated: he was its representative rather than its inspirer.

f 11

Lorenzo's literary interests and activities may have been one of the reasons why he extended his patronage to men of letters rather than to artists and architects. Politian, like Ficino, owed his home and livelihood to Lorenzo, and had been educated at his expense.

The humanist Bartolomeo Scala, Chancellor of Florence since 1465, and the poet Luigi Pulci enjoyed his patronage. To these men and others like them Lorenzo was bound not only by common interests but also by friendship. No such bonds connected him with Florentine artists, although he seems to have encouraged young artists, including Michelangelo, to study his collection of antiques. It was his cousin Lorenzo di Pierfrancesco who was Botticelli's patron; the only artist continuously employed by Lorenzo was the sculptor Bertoldo di Giovanni. His small bronzes reflect Lorenzo's admiration of antiquity and his passion for *objets d'art*. These tastes are shown in Lorenzo's magnificent collection of antique and contemporary statuettes and plaquettes, medals and gems and precious tableware. He was a collector rather than a patron of the arts, and as such interested chiefly in antique works of art, as well as in manuscripts of Greek and Roman texts: he made Politian search for them in Italy, and John Lascaris in Greece. 'He was', says his 16th-century biographer, 'so great a lover of antiquity that nothing enthused him more.'

p 24 (33, 34)

If his architectural projects lagged far behind those of Cosimo and of other Florentine patricians like Filippo Strozzi, the chief reason was no doubt the financial straits of the Medici bank. Of his most important building project, the villa of Poggio a Caiano, Guicciardini says that although it was 'most sumptuous, he had not completed it when he died; and although in itself it was a great thing, nevertheless one may say that in comparison with the number and size of Cosimo's buildings, he did not build at all'. What remains of the original structure of Giuliano da Sangallo's building, with its classical portico, shows Lorenzo's plan to imitate an antique Roman villa.

p 22 (28)

Like other great patricians, Lorenzo succeeded in combining his manifold intellectual and artistic interests with a life of public activity; but there were significant differences. Unlike his grandfather, he neglected the central management of the bank, which had been the foundation of Medici power, with disastrous consequences for its fortunes; a neglect which was the more serious as his political position, and especially his personal diplomacy, involved him in vast expenses. Careful to avoid ostentation and to live like other great citizens, he was the virtual ruler of Florence; his son Giovanni was created cardinal in 1489; and his circle, despite its easygoing domesticity, had also, with its clients and eulogists, some of the characteristics of a princely court. In the fresco of the Sassetti chapel at Sta Trinita, Lorenzo is portrayed as standing between other citizens, in the simple dress of the Florentine patricians; but the gesture with which he welcomes Politian, who humbly approaches him accompanied by three Medici children, has a touch of seigneurial authority.

p 21 (22

Yet the fresco also reflects the continuity of patrician traditions. A less sophisticated painter than Botticelli, Domenico Ghirlandaio conveyed a faithful picture of the dignity and self-confidence of the Florentine upper class in the frescoes he painted for Francesco Sassetti in Sta Trinita, and for Giovanni Tornabuoni in Sta Maria Novella. The grave demeanour of the citizens in the Trinita fresco contrasts with the rich dresses of the Tornabuoni ladies; and the group of scholars in the foreground of the Sta Maria Novella fresco (possibly portraits of Ficino, Landino, Politian, and Chalcondilas) illustrates the traditionally close relationship between patricians and humanists. Francesco Sassetti (d.1490) was the general manager of the Medici bank; Giovanni Tornabuoni, Lorenzo's uncle and head of its Rome branch. Both belonged to families that had risen to prominence through the Medici. Filippo Strozzi, on the other hand, was a scion of an ancient family which had been exiled by the Medici for over thirty years. According to his son's biography, Filippo wished to erect a palace which would be a monument to him and his family all over Italy. The second half of the century was marked by the building of many Florentine palaces; of these, the Strozzi palace, begun in 1489, was destined to be the most magnificent. Its ambitious plan testifies to the survival of patrician pride of status at a time when the ascendancy of the Medici was at its highest.

p 17 (11, 13)

p 27 (5

p 15 (7)

Savonarola: Prophecy and Fulfilment

Ghirlandaio's frescoes also illustrate, by the way in which the wordly scene in the foreground overshadows their religious context, some of the secular aspects of Florentine Renaissance civilization. Certainly not 'pagan'—most Quattrocento paintings represent religious subjects—it had inherited the medieval merchant's attachment to worldly goods and values. Humanism had given these traditional attitudes a rational justification. On a more sophisticated intellectual plane, the study of ancient religions could lead to a reassessment of paganism; and the attempts to reconcile the latter with Christianity were, in their turn, symptomatic of such a reassessment. The ordinary Florentine citizens were no doubt little affected by such historical and philosophical trends, and were easily aroused by Girolamo Savonarola's relentless denunciations of worldliness and corruption in church and society, and by his prophecies of impending doom; but also members of the Platonic circle, including Ficino himself, and artists like Botticelli, came under his influence. Called from his native Ferrara to Florence in 1490 by Lorenzo probably on the recommendation of Pico della Mirandola, and appointed Prior of the convent of S. Marco, Savonarola soon became the city's most popular preacher. There had been other influential preachers before, and he himself had at first a serious rival in the Augustinian monk Fra Mariano da Gennazzano. Savonarola owed much of his sudden rise to spiritual leadership in Florence to the political events which took place after Lorenzo's death in 1492, and which to many Florentines appeared as a fulfilment of his prophecies.

p 28 (51, 52) f 1

These events changed the destinies not only of Florence, but also of Italy. Charles VIII of France, having inherited the Angevin claims to Naples, decided to conquer that kingdom. The Italian states had to take sides, and Florence, under Lorenzo's less capable and prudent son Piero, sided with Naples, thus abandoning its traditional pro-French policy. When the French army under Charles VIII entered Florentine territory in October 1494, Piero capitulated, but this did not save him from the mounting op-

An illustration from Lorenzo de' Medici's 'Canzoni a Ballo', lighthearted songs which were sung by the merrymakers at Florence's many festivals. Although Lorenzo's patronage of the arts fell short of Cosimo's, he was a talented and versatile poet in his own right. (11)

position in Florence, which was aggravated by dissatisfaction with his domestic policy. On 9th November he fled Florence in the midst of a popular rising.

The republican restoration which followed the fall of the Medici régime testified to the survival of republicanism during the sixty years of that régime. But the patricians who were hoping to put the clock back were faced by demands for a wider distribution of political power. These demands were supported by Savonarola, and it was no doubt due largely to him and his followers that in December 1494 a Great Council on the Venetian model was established. Composed of over 3,000 members, in charge of legislation and of elections to offices, the Great Council provided the most democratic form of government Florence had ever possessed. Savonarola, whom his followers regarded as its creator, exercised during the following years a powerful political influence in Florence, as well as a kind of moral dictatorship. His claim that the renewal of the Church was to begin in Florence gave his attacks on moral corruption an urgency which was not lost on the Florentines, and his denunciations of luxury and worldliness found a ready response in their traditional inclinations towards austerity and simplicity of manners. That he should also react against Renaissance values was not surprising. In his sermons, he violently attacked aesthetic attitudes to religious art; and in the 'burning of vanities' during the carnival of 1498, there perished, together with heretical books, mirrors, 'and many vain things of great value', 'nude figures'. Not only commoners like Landucci, but also many members of the upper classes were converted by his preaching of moral regeneration; and Francesco Guicciardini, who was not uncritical of him, records that 'there was never in Florence so much virtue and religion as in his time'. But Savonarola's chief support came from the masses of ordinary citizens who were enraptured by his sermons and distraught by the political crisis which had engulfed their city after long years of relative peace and prosperity. Florence had lost Pisa in 1494, and saw in the renewed French alliance her only hope of recovering it. The result was a war which dragged on until 1509, and the virtual isolation of Florence in Italy.

Savonarola's fall was as sudden as his rise to power. Political opposition to him had been growing, and his excommunication by Alexander VI, due partly to his reform sermons, and partly to his ardent support of the French alliance, had weakened his position. Arrested in 1498 after a refusal to go through with an ordeal by fire, he was tried and burnt at the stake in May of the same year. In his trial he was alleged to have confessed to having been a false prophet. His fall shattered the hopes of many an honest citizen who had believed that Florence was destined to become the new Jerusalem.

The End of Greatness

Savonarola's death did not have any substantial effect on the city's political development. Florence remained loyal to the French alliance and preserved its new constitution. A major problem was the technical one of making the Great Council a working proposition. Procedural reforms reinforced its democratic features, and estranged many patricians who had at first supported it. Patrician pressure led, in 1502, to the transformation of the two-monthly Gonfaloniership of Justice into one for life; but the democratic leanings of the new Gonfalonier Piero Soderini disappointed many aristocrats who had hoped that this would be the first step in an oligarchical reform of the constitution. Internal conflicts were sharpened by the war against Pisa and the financial sacrifices it necessitated. Florence had only the lukewarm help of France to rely on, and her exposed position was amply demonstrated by the threat to her independence from Cesare Borgia in 1501–2. Pisa was finally recovered in 1509; but the city's loyalty to the French alliance led to the restoration of the Medici by a Spanish army after the collapse of French power in Italy in 1512. This restoration had been prepared by the growth of the Medici faction in Florence: the Medici could appear as better guardians of patrician interests than the new democracy. Such sentiments found an intellectual centre in the meetings of humanists and citizens which took place in the gardens of Bernardo Rucellai, one of the patricians who had withdrawn from public life. After the Medici restoration, the Rucellai gardens were to become once more a centre of intellectual opposition; but this time against the Medici.

For the Medici had returned with a vengeance. Restored by force of arms, they could rely on the power of Rome after Lorenzo's son Giovanni had been elected Pope in 1513. Under Leo X Florence became, for all practical purposes, an annex of the papacy. It was first governed by Leo's brother Giuliano (d.1516), then by Piero's son Lorenzo, who in 1516 became Duke of Urbino. He died in 1519, and Florence remained under the government of Cardinal Giulio, son of Lorenzo the Magnificent's brother Giuliano. In 1521 Leo X died, and in 1523 Giulio became, as Clement VII, the second Medici Pope.

The new régime differed from that of the early Medici in that it depended far less on the co-operation and support of the Florentine patriciate. Under papal control, it constituted a step further in the direction of the principate. But the memories of the republic of 1494 remained alive, and inspired the members of the Rucellai circle, where Niccolò Machiavelli read his *Discourses on Livy* in which he celebrated the ancient Roman republic. Republican opposition led to an abortive conspiracy in 1522, and in 1527 to the last expulsion of the Medici. The immediate cause was the Sack of Rome: the prompt collapse of the Medici régime showed its dependency on the papacy. The republican constitution was restored in the form in which it had been abolished in 1512; there was a Savonarolan revival; but the city's last republican régime fell for much the same reasons as its predecessor in 1512. The republic's pro-French policy proved once more fatal. After a long and heroic siege, Florence capitulated in August 1530 to the Imperial Army; but this time, the restoration of the Medici was followed by the establishment of the principate. Alessandro, the illegitimate son of the younger Lorenzo, was created Lord of Florence by Charles V in 1531; in the following year, he assumed the title of Duke. The political transformation of the Florentine republic, which had begun almost exactly 100 years earlier, was completed.

We have tried to show how Florentine Renaissance civilization was rooted within the political and social framework of that republic. The republican revival of 1494, short-lived as it was, could appear not only as a return to the city's traditional way of life, but also as its most vigorous manifestation. Political power and responsibility were actively shared by more citizens than before 1434; political debate revived with freedom of speech; military challenges that would have daunted greater powers were met with a self-confidence reminiscent of the wars against Giangaleazzo Visconti. Public patronage assumed a political character. Michelangelo's *David*, a symbol of republican patriotism, was set up in front of the Palazzo Vecchio in 1504, where it joined Donatello's *Judith and Holofernes* which, having previously belonged to the Medici collection, had been placed outside the government palace in 1495, as an 'exemplar of public safety'. In that year, Simone Pollaiuolo was commissioned to build a new hall for the Great Council. Inaugurated in 1496, it was intended to be decorated with paintings celebrating Florentine victories by Michelangelo and Leonardo da Vinci.

That public patronage should have been extended to the two greatest Florentine artists of their time was in the tradition of the Florentine republic, and so was the competitive aspect of the commissions. Leonardo and Michelangelo personify some of its outstanding characteristics in the universality of their genius and in the harmonious fusion of art, learning, and literature. Their work shows, in its most powerful and mature form, the inspiring impact of antiquity: Leonardo's revolutionary scientific enquiries were inspired by classical sources as well as by empirical observation. In Michelangelo's Medici chapel at S. Lorenzo the creative interpretation of classical models reached a sublime individuality. The story of its execution, though belonging to the history of art, is not without political overtones. Commissioned in 1519 or 1520 by Leo X and Cardinal Giulio, work on it was interrupted when the republic was restored in 1527, and was never completed. Michelangelo's republican sentiments may have been largely responsible for his abandoning the tombs when he left Florence in 1534. Three years later, Duke Alessandro was assassinated by

p 47 (7)

p 28 (53)

f 1

19 (19)

his own cousin Lorenzino: a tyrannicide in the classical tradition which was meant to restore the republic, but failed to do so. Some time afterwards, one of the republican exiles, Donato Giannotti, may have persuaded Michelangelo to make a marble bust of Brutus for Cardinal Ridolfi, a leading opponent to the new Duke Cosimo. Whatever Michelangelo's personal views on Brutus, the republican inspiration of the unfinished work is evident. Michelangelo's bust of Caesar's murderer thus appears as the last artistic manifestation of Florentine republican ideals.

p 19 (18)

Machiavelli and Guicciardini

Brutus had been a symbol of Florentine republicanism since the 14th century. Before a young Florentine conspirator against the Medici was executed in 1513, he implored a friend who was trying to console him to get Brutus out of his head, so that he could die a good Christian. In his *Discourses*, which he completed in 1517, Machiavelli praised Brutus as an exemplar of republican patriotism. Machiavelli was the foremost intellectual representative of the republican revival after 1494. A prominent member of the Chancery between 1498 and 1512, an expert diplomatist and close collaborator of Soderini, he reminds us of the great humanist chancellors of the early Florentine Renaissance in his commitment to civic values and his admiration for the ancient Roman republic. But he was not a professional humanist, and his career was cut short by a revolution. His enforced leisure provided him with the opportunity, the contemporary political crises with an incentive, to reconsider problems and ideas of the past régime, and to investigate, in the context of a cyclical philosophy of history based on Polybius, the causes of the decline and fall of states and political societies. That in the *Prince*, which he dedicated to the young Lorenzo, he should have expounded the technique of autocratic power, not only shows his commitment to a new concept of objective political science, but also reflects the crisis of Florentine republicanism after 1512.

p 27 (49)

Machiavelli's political genius was rooted in the accumulated wisdom of the Florentine ruling class, to which he did not belong, and inspired by humanist admiration of antiquity. He was also faced by the problem of divided loyalties in an age of transition. Similarly Francesco Guicciardini, Florentine patrician and papal governor, could write, between 1521 and 1525, a blueprint for a new republican constitution, protesting at the same time that, a loyal servant of the Medici, he owed a superior loyalty to his city. The programme, cautiously couched in the form of a dialogue and never published by him, closely followed the example of the aristocratic Venetian constitution. Written at a time when the only real alternatives for Florence were democracy or absolutism, it was the fullest and most radical statement of the political ideals and aspirations of the Florentine patriciate of the Renaissance period.

Machiavelli and Guicciardini also inherited from the early Florentine humanists the concern with civic history and the belief in its political significance. 16th-century Florence witnessed a remarkable flourishing of municipal historiography, which was partly prompted by the political crises and revolutions of the first thirty years. Machiavelli and Guicciardini pioneered this development. But while Machiavelli confined himself to his *History of Florence* (1520–25), Guicciardini, after writing an unfinished history of his town in 1508–9 and beginning another in about 1528, composed between 1536 and his death in 1540 his greatest historical work, the *History of Italy*, which transcended the boundaries of his native city, and thus mirrors his own progress from Florentine patrician to Italian statesman. In doing so it also reflects a significant trend in Florentine civilization.

During much of the 15th century, Florence had been, despite its manifold contacts with the outside world, and despite its intellectual and artistic leadership, a relatively closed world, deeply rooted in its medieval traditions. Politically this continuity was expressed by the survival of a basically oligarchical structure of government, and, in foreign relations, of a system of equilibrium which secured Florence the status of an independent great power in Italy. The foreign invasions destroyed this equilibrium, created new and frequently changing alignments, and, while making it increasingly difficult for the republican régimes to

survive, widened the political perspective of the Florentines. The long dependency on the papacy contributed to this process. If Guicciardini wrote the history of the Italian wars, Machiavelli composed the *Prince* for an Italian ruler. The political stabilization of Italy under Spanish preponderance, which was finally accepted by France in 1559, counteracted this process by leaving the Tuscan duchy secure within its frontiers. These frontiers had been extended by the acquisition of Siena in 1557. At the same time, Florence lost her ruling position within the dominions of Duke Cosimo. Ever since the beginnings of communal independence, the Florentines had ruled the inhabitants of their expanding territory as their subjects. This distinction between rulers and ruled disappeared under the absolute prince, who treated Florentines and non-Florentines alike as his subjects.

To these political changes corresponded, though not necessarily in terms of cause and effect, changes in the position of Florence in art and learning. From the end of the 14th century onwards, Florentine humanists, artists and architects had secured for their city a dominant rôle in the development of the New Learning and in the revival of antique art; from Florence, their influence spread over Italy and beyond. After the middle of the 15th century, Florence gradually lost this position, although Ficino's Academy made her once more, for a brief period, the centre of an intellectual movement. Lorenzo, rather than patronizing Florentine artists, recommended them for employment abroad. In doing so he contributed to a general trend. The emigration, temporary or permanent, of Florentine artists and architects, while not a new phenomenon, is a significant trait of the history of Florentine art and architecture in the later Renaissance. While helping to spread Florentine artistic achievements abroad, it also deprived the city of much of their work. The career of Michelangelo presents the most striking example of this development. By the early 16th century, Papal Rome, not Florence, was the artistic centre of Italy.

To what extent was this development due to a decline in the public and private patronage which had contributed so much to the unfolding of Florentine Renaissance art? This question relates to the wider one of the effects of the political and social changes in the first half of the 16th century on Florentine civilization. It is often assumed that the end of the republic was decisive for the decline of that civilization. This is too facile an explanation. Art and learning have their own independent developments which are not necessarily affected by changing external circumstances. Yet Florentine Renaissance civilization, rooted as it had been in the social and political structure of the republic, was bound to be profoundly affected by its decline and fall. Moreover, these political changes coincided with economic ones. The wool industry, once the principal source of Florence's prosperity, had declined during the 15th century, but the rise of the silk industry had to some extent compensated for this, and trade with the Orient had opened up new markets. Despite many economic problems, Florence was a prosperous town at the end of the 15th century: the decline of the Medici bank was the exception to the rule, and largely due to personal causes. The wars after 1494 sapped the city's wealth; and the general European changes in trade routes and in the geographical distribution of industrial production further reduced her importance as a leading economic centre. The Florentine patricians, whose commercial ventures had once covered Europe, and whose accumulated wealth had furthered art and scholarship, became increasingly an aristocracy which derived their income from land. While they continued to participate in government and administration, the creation of the absolute monarchy deprived them for ever of the rights and responsibilities which had formed so much of the social background of Florentine civilization. While private patrons continued to commission artists, patronage was now, as in other Italian monarchies, centred in the court. The ancient Palace of the Signory became, in 1540, for a time the ducal residence, and the Hall of the Great Council was used for ceremonial receptions. At the centre of its ceiling, Vasari portrayed, in 1565, Cosimo crowned by a woman personifying Florence; in a neighbouring room, he represented him surrounded by artists and architects, as a princely patron of the arts.

II WIDENING CIRCLES

The Renaissance in Italy outside Florence

CECIL GRAYSON

*'Thus it may be seen how many noble works we possess
through the effort of these scholars and how much we are
indebted to them; and how greatly the students
of our own time have been enlightened
by their discoveries'.*

VESPASIANO DA BISTICCI

It was at Rome

that the intellectual revival and many of the innovations in art which had begun in Florence reached their fruition. From the end of the 15th century Rome was the cultural leader of Italy, although strangely enough few of the men who gave her that leadership were themselves Roman. They had come from all over Italy at the call of a series of outstanding popes—men, for the most part, of boundless ambition and consummate political talent, who were determined to make Rome culturally as well as spiritually supreme. The popes were princes in just the same way as were the other rulers of Italy, and they used their territories, the Papal States, both as a source of revenue and as a means to enriching their families. And at a time when rulers were competing for the prestige of employing the greatest scholars and artists, buildings and scholars in papal service symbolized papal grandeur.

The career of Aeneas Sylvius Piccolomini (his very name proclaims the advent of humanism) could only have been possible against such a background. Born in 1405 into an old Sienese family, he was educated at the University of Siena and at Florence, where he met Filelfo. From 1431 to 1445 he was involved in the troubled world of church politics: he supported the 'Conciliar' party which opposed the claims of Eugenius IV and aimed at the subordination of the pope's power to that of the Councils. As a secretary he slowly climbed the social ladder and explored Europe, visiting Scotland and Germany, and writing poetry, a comedy and a love-story (based on an affair of his own). Then in 1445, embittered by the disunion in his own party, he changed sides and became an ardent papal supporter. Thereafter his rise was rapid. He took orders in 1446, was made a bishop in 1450, cardinal in 1456 and, on the death of Callixtus III in 1458, Pope. All the time he was writing letters and books in fluent Latin.

The fresco by Pinturicchio (opposite) shows Aeneas Sylvius, who took the name of Pius II, entering the basilica of St John Lateran (the Cathedral of Rome, St Peter's being strictly in the Vatican). He is carried on a throne beneath a rich canopy. In front of him kneels a sacristan carrying a staff on which a tuft of cotton is burning, a reminder to the Pope that all human glory is fleeting.

Pius II reigned for six years. He did much to encourage scholarship and the arts, but his zeal in this direction was diminished by two other overriding concerns—the enrichment of his own family and the organization of a Crusade against the Turks. It was while trying to collect an army for this latter purpose at Ancona that he died in 1464. (1)

Sixtus IV (1471–84) built the Sistine Chapel in 1473 and a few years later had it decorated by the leading artists of all Italy—Botticelli, Signorelli, Ghirlandaio and Perugino. This fresco by Melozzo da Forlì (left) shows him receiving the humanist Platina. Platina was a member of the so-called 'Roman Academy', proscribed under Paul III for heresy and paganism. Characteristically, under Sixtus IV, he became Keeper of the Vatican Library, and was the author of an authoritative *Lives of the Popes*. (2)

Alexander VI (1492–1503), the Borgia Pope (below) employed Pinturicchio to decorate his apartments. A nephew of Callixtus III, he was made a cardinal at the age of 26 and became notorious, even at that time, for luxury and sensual indulgence. (3)

The heart of Christendom, the Vatican, was transformed by the Renaissance Popes into a truly imperial capital. Everything was conceived anew on a titanic scale. Sketches (below) made by Maerten van Heemskerck about 1534 show the old basilica of St Peter's, dating from the 4th century, partially demolished. In the first drawing (left) its nave arcade still occupies the foreground, with one of the old tombs on the right. Michelangelo's huge new crossing–piers tower over it. In the central picture, just in front of the new work, are the ancient round chapel of St Andrew, soon to be pulled down, and the Egyptian obelisk later re-erected as the centrepiece of Bernini's piazza; and in the background the Sistine Chapel. The engraving on the far right shows the same area from the east about thirty years later; work on the dome has now reached the drum stage. (4, 5, 8)

Julius II (1503–13), the warrior-pope, is perhaps the most dynamic figure of the age—a fitting patron for Michelangelo, whom he employed on a vast project for his own tomb and then (to the artist's annoyance) on the Sistine Ceiling. This portrait (left) is a detail from Raphael's *Stanze*, which he also commissioned. It was he too who initiated the rebuilding of St Peter's, originally to a design by Bramante. Julius was Sixtus IV's nephew, and can be seen as a cardinal, facing his uncle, in the fresco opposite. (6)

Leo X (1513–21) was a Medici, the son of Lorenzo the Magnificent. Cultured, worldly and generous, he made Rome a city of unequalled splendour. This portrait is a drawing made for one of the *Stanze* frescoes, and is probably by Raphael's pupil, Giulio Romano. (7)

Naples is the orphan of Italian history. Other states, despite their difficulties, were sustained by a sense of civic pride or at least civic identity. In Naples this was not so easy to feel. Throughout most of the Middle Ages it had been a prize or bargaining point to Spain, France, the Empire and the Pope, ruled over by foreigners who failed to win, or deserve, the good will of its people. In 1442, however, the Angevins were driven out, though their claims were taken up by the kings of France (this was the pretext for the invasion of Italy by France at the end of the century). The new king, Alfonso V, reunited 'the Two Sicilies' under his rule. It was the beginning of Naples' brief Golden Age. The panorama (above) shows the city in 1464. The fleet is entering harbour after the liberation of Ischia from Giovanni Torella, an Angevin supporter. The Castel Nuovo is prominent towards the left. On the hill in the background is the monastery of S. Martino. (9)

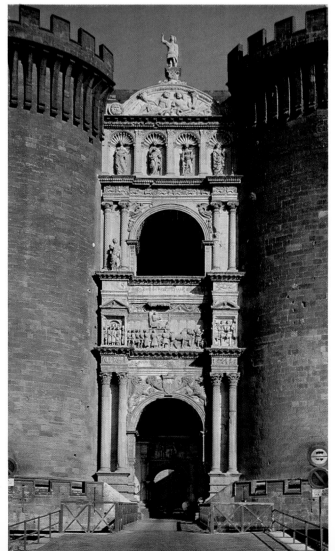

'**He entered Naples** like a conqueror of old', wrote Vespasiano. Alfonso, called 'the Magnanimous', is among the most sympathetic of Italian princes. His arrival in 1442 inaugurated the Renaissance in Naples and his death in 1458 brought to an end a brief but splendid era. During those sixteen years the city was the equal of any except Florence, attracting scholars as eminent as Filelfo and Valla. In architecture the best known monument of the period is probably the triumphal entrance (left) added by Alfonso V to the Castel Nuovo. The king's entry into Naples is depicted in the relief above the main arch (right). After Alfonso came the reign of his illegitimate son Ferrante, in whose time the poets Pontano and Sannazaro created Latin and Italian poetry and prose which was admired and influential throughout Europe. Then followed more civil war, the French invasion and the establishment of Spanish rule. The Neapolitan Renaissance was over. (10, 11)

ALFONSVS REGVM PRINCEPS HANC CON

ALFONSVS REX HISPANVSSICVLVS IT

Milan had ampler resources than the other city-states: rich land, prosperous cities, natural frontiers. Its handicap was disunity. The political system was only adapted to autocracy (as the 1447–50 republican experiment showed). Faction made stability precarious and the peace of the state was constantly being sacrificed to personal rivalries often leading to outside intervention.

In 1450 the old Visconti family, whose greatest member, Giangaleazzo, had carried Milan to its peak, was replaced by the *condottiere* Francesco Sforza. Under him and his son, Lodovico, Milan became a famous cultural centre. Left: Lodovico *'il Moro'* being presented by Bernardino of Treviso with his Commentary on the *Meteorologica* of Aristotle. (12)

Leonardo da Vinci came here about 1482, on Lodovico's invitation. His sketch for a bronze monument to Francesco Sforza (above) was unprecedented in boldness of technique and the statue was never cast. (13)

Antonio Filarete of Florence was Lodovico's architect and engineer. His heart, however, was in a vast imaginary city, to be called *Sforzinda*. He filled a large volume with plans and drawings (above) and notes on their symbolic meanings. (14)

Donato Bramante of Urbino, one of the leaders of the Roman Renaissance, worked in Milan as a young man, building the dome of Sta Maria delle Grazie (right). Bramante's version of the new style was to mould Lombard architecture for years to come. (15)

The fortress home of the Sforzas was the Castello (below left), built by Francesco Sforza from 1450 onwards. Several architects worked on it and Leonardo is thought to have designed these strange tree-knots painted on one of the ceilings. (16, 17)

Lodovico's wife was Beatrice d'Este, daughter of the Duke of Ferrara. Leonardo's portrait (above) brings out the intelligence and strength which we know her to have possessed. She died young, in child-birth. (18)

Wandering from court to court, scholars like Francesco Filelfo (above) were obliged to flatter a series of patrons in order to make a living. 'Duke Francesco granted him a salary', says Vespasiano, 'because he was writing an account in verse of his doings, called the *Sforziade*.' (19)

Venice, secure in her wealth and looking to the East rather than to Europe, was long unaffected by the new ideas stemming from Florence. But from the end of the 15th century she began to excel in almost every respect—in art (Bellini, Carpaccio, Giorgione, Titian, Tintoretto), in architecture (Sansovino), printing (Aldus Manutius), music (Willaert, Gabrieli) and literature. This bird's-eye view shows Venice in the mid-16th century. The Grand Canal, bridged by the Rialto, snakes its way through the city, lined with palaces. (20)

The Doge was theoretically the head of state, but his powers had been so diminished that he was little more than a figure-head. The real rulers of Venice were the Council of Ten, the committee of the Great Council—a body strictly confined to the 'nobility' of the city and closed to everyone else. Leonardo Loredan (left) was elected Doge in 1501 and reigned for twenty years. Giovanni Bellini's portrait has all the psychological insight and richness of colour that were to characterize Venetian painting for the next hundred years. (21)

Urbino between 1450 and 1508 was perhaps the most astonishing place in Europe; a poor mountainous duchy of 150,000 inhabitants, ruled by a mercenary soldier, which yet outshone practically every other city in art, scholarship and the cultural life of its court. Its position was due entirely to one man—Federigo da Montefeltro (right, with his wife Battista Sforza, in portraits by Piero della Francesca). His palace (below), was designed mainly by Luciano di Laurana. Built on a steep irregular site, it dominates the little city. (26, 27, 28)

Lecture in progress: Federigo and his young son Guidobaldo attend a discourse by a humanist scholar, probably Paul of Middelbourg. Federigo was devoted to the New Learning. His library contained practically every known classical text. Below: the courtyard and *studiolo* of the palace, the latter decorated with *trompe l'oeil* intarsia work. The books, musical instruments and pieces of armour symbolize the Duke's complex character. He was the complete Renaissance gentleman—well versed in all the accomplishments and arts, as well as being a successful general. 'Messer Federigo', wrote Vespasiano, 'had many praiseworthy qualities, and such another character, virtuous in every respect, the age could not produce.' (29, 30, 32)

Guidobaldo, Federigo's son (above), continued his father's policy and patronage, though he was a less astute politician. It was during his reign that Castiglione (below, in a portrait by Raphael) lived at Urbino and immortalized its ruling circle in his *Book of the Courtier*. Guidobaldo and his friends discuss the requirements of the ideal man—learning, honesty, courage in war, respect for women and talent in the arts. (31, 33)

At Ferrara the court shared many of the same ideals as Urbino, with perhaps even more emphasis on education. The Este family were established here as early as the 13th century. In 1441 Leonello d'Este became Duke. Educated by one of the most eminent humanist scholars, Guarino da Verona, he immediately set about remodelling his duchy according to the principles he had learnt. Pisanello's portrait of him (below) was painted probably in the year of his accession. (34)

The leisured life led by the Ferrarese court month by month is portrayed in a series of frescoes in the summer palace of the Estes, the Palazzo Schifanoia, by two leading artists of the school of Ferrara, Cosimo Tura and Francesco del Cossa. The scene on the right, by Cossa, shows Duke Borso, Leonello's brother, about to set off hunting with his courtiers, pages and falconers. Borso is the large man in the centre, facing left. In the left background is the 'occupation' for the month of March, pruning the vine, the agile movements of the boys contrasting with the deliberation of the older men. On the upper left, the hunt appears again, led by a hound hot on the scent. (35)

Ariosto (1474–1533), author of *Orlando Furioso*, a long romantic epic based on the story of Roland, lived most of his life under the patronage of the Este family. The poem instantly became popular and was widely imitated both in Italy and other countries. Besides receiving a salary from the Dukes of Ferrara, Ariosto was also employed on diplomatic missions and even acted as governor of a province for three years. This portrait, with the poet's laurel as background, is by Palma Vecchio. (36)

Tasso (1544–95) continued Ferrara's literary traditions later in the century. Born at Sorrento, he led a nomadic early life, visiting Rome, Urbino, Venice and Padua before settling in Ferrara in 1565. The Estes admired him, and he wrote his best work —the pastoral drama *Aminta* and the epic *Gerusalemme Liberata* (on the Crusades)—with their encouragement. His later years were clouded by quarrels and mental illness and he died, prematurely old, in Rome in 1595. (37)

Rimini lies only a few miles from Urbino, but there could scarcely be a greater contrast than that between their two rulers. Whereas Federigo of Urbino was extolled as the ideal prince, Sigismondo Malatesta of Rimini was a byword, even in that age, for ruthlessness and cruelty. In one respect, however, they were alike—in their patronage, and genuine appreciation, of the arts. Sigismondo's motives were no doubt mixed. Poets could transmit the name of Malatesta to posterity; painters could immortalize his features, suitably idealized; architects could make Rimini into an echo of ancient Rome. Yet, after all, the reality of his taste remains. Alberti and Piero della Francesca were only two of the famous men he attracted to his court.

Sigismondo inherited the lordship of Rimini in 1432. It was a small town with a medieval castle (right) and a large, rather bare church, S. Francesco. This latter Sigismondo transformed into a sort of pagan temple to his own glory, the *Tempio Malatestiano*. Alberti made the designs, basing the façade (below) on a Roman triumphal arch. It was originally to have had a superstructure with another arch, but was never finished. (38, 39)

Grim elephants—the Malatesta emblem—carry a classical plaque with Sigismondo's profile within a laurel wreath: one of the many heraldic ornaments and sculptured reliefs carved by Agostino di Duccio inside the *Tempio*. The iconography does, in fact, follow an orthodox scheme, but there are so many allusions to pagan Rome that Sigismondo's bitter enemy Pius II wrote: 'Sigismondo has built a noble temple, but he has so filled it with godless works that it seems to be a place not for Christians but for heathen devil-worshippers.' (40)

Mantua was the seat of another family made illustrious by its appreciation of the new intellectual currents, the Gonzagas. Alberti built here two of his most influential churches; Mantegna was court-painter; and later Giulio Romano made it one of the most fascinating centres of Mannerism. Among Mantegna's commissions was the decoration of a room in the palace with frescoes showing the family and leading members of the court. In the main scene (above) Lodovico Gonzaga is shown receiving a letter announcing that his son Francesco has been created cardinal. He leans back in his chair to speak to the messenger. Next to him sits his wife Barbara of Brandenburg with two other sons and (on the right) a court dwarf. In another scene (left) Lodovico greets the new cardinal. (41, 42)

Each of these small Italian courts, in spite of intermarriage, in spite of the fact that artists and writers were continually moving from one to another, displays a very clear personality of its own—of which, in most cases, one is still distinctly aware today. It is this sudden flowering of a dynamic new culture in a number of limited local centres that gives the Renaissance in Italy much of its peculiar diversity and its endless interest.

The Renaissance in Italy outside Florence

CECIL GRAYSON

Pre-Renaissance Rome: a German woodcut of 1493 showing the Vatican. The standard of accuracy is not very high, but old St Peter's and the Pope's palace are clearly indicated. The loggia in front of the atrium of the church stands out prominently. (1)

THE DIVISION of the Renaissance in Italy in this volume into Florence on the one hand and the rest of Italy on the other, already suggests an assessment of relative importance which would no doubt have appealed to the Florentines of that age as much as it has tended recently to dominate the direction of modern historical studies. There is a vitality and coherence about the traditions of Florence, about the relationship of thought and literature to social, political and economic evolution from Dante down to the end of the Republic, that have justifiably aroused admiration and attracted scholarly enquiry. In an overall view of the Renaissance Florence not only often appears to be the dynamo, the real force centre, but she seems at the same time unique in that the studies pursued and the energies released are somehow more rooted in the life of her people. At a superficial glance, by contrast, what appears as indigenous in Florence and to arise from or combine easily with her institutions, outside Florence, in different political-social contexts, more frequently looks like a superimposition or importation; not the pursuit of a society but the diversion of an élite or the adornment and prop of tyranny. There is some degree of idealogical interference in this picture, just as there is distortion of a different kind in an image of the Renaissance in which the major figures, most of them non-Florentines, are popes and princes, famous and nefarious, renowned for military valour, political cunning or moral laxity which they succeeded in combining with lavish patronage of the arts.

It is a question of angle of vision. But take out Florence, and the task of reviewing the Renaissance in the rest of Italy is made not easier but more difficult: for in a period of social and political disunity it will not too easily respond to unified consideration even on a cultural plane. Instead there would seem to be distinct advantages in maintaining the limitations imposed by geography and politics, if only to be made aware of what precise part the various principal centres played in the age we call the Renaissance. It was with such considerations in mind that the present chapter was written—that is, with a deliberate desire to outline the essential social and cultural developments that characterize the major states and cities: Rome, Naples, Milan, Venice and Padua, Ferrara and Mantua, Urbino and Rimini. This presentation aims to show particularly how and why these centres developed their own distinctive culture from indigenous and/or imported elements, and contributed to the social, intellectual and literary evolution of the 15th and 16th centuries. The aim is to demonstrate not only the similarities with, but more especially the differences from Florence, and to show how certain directions of thought and literature, many originating in Tuscany, come to full (and diverse) development in other centres.

Rome

The history of the Renaissance in Rome is closely bound up with the cultural interests and patronage of the popes; so much so that it appears to be personified by and identified with certain outstanding pontiffs, of whom there was a remarkable succession between Nicholas V (1447) and Paul III (1550). With the exception, however, of Pius II, who wrote a great deal, they were patrons not producers of the arts, and it is as such that they have stolen the limelight in the general picture of the age. This is certainly justified up to a point, since without their favour there would have been little or no cultural life in Rome. Before their time it is difficult to find much of an indigenous tradition. They created or continued the conditions which drew scholars and artists from the rest of Italy and from further afield as well. The result is that the Renaissance there is Roman only in as much as it is papal, and in fact hardly more Roman than the pontiffs themselves (which none of them were). In this sense it is more cosmopolitan than any other centre in Italy.

There were other factors in play besides the prospect of lucrative reward or employment. With the election at the Council of Constance of Martin V (1417) and the end of the Great Schism, the Church was restored to unity, and Rome began again fully to exert its natural and now undisputed attraction as the centre of the Christian world. Even before this time Rome had drawn men to contemplate or lament over her as the decayed museum of the ancient world, a storehouse of historical, archaeological, architectural and epigraphical material of vital interest to humanists like Poggio Bracciolini. The story of the Renaissance in Rome might be said to begin with the two Tuscan 'exiles', Poggio and Bruni, who were first employed during the brief but enlightened papacy of Innocent VII (1404–6). They initiated an important tradition of learned Latinists in the service of the Curia. From Bruni and Poggio down to Bembo and Sadoleto, the popes, with a brief interruption under Paul II, recognized and exploited the new humanism for their own glory as well as for the administrative, diplomatic and oratorical talents these men possessed. Almost all the great scholars of the 15th and early 16th centuries at some time found their way to Rome and a post in the Curia, and for all the political vicissitudes of the age and the unpredictable changes of popes, Rome provided a cultural focal point, an important instrument of patronage and a remarkably liberal refuge whose significance it would be difficult to overstress.

Leonardo Bruni is not, strictly speaking, a figure of the Roman Renaissance. He belongs primarily in the context of civic humanism at Florence where he spent most of his life. His ten years in Rome (1405–15) were not his most productive, but they were vital for his own reputation as a Latin and Greek scholar (without local limitations), and also for the establishment of the New Learning in Rome. The Florentine link is there too with Poggio both in his early studies and in his later chancellorship; yet his career is very largely Roman (and partly English), while a good measure of his fame as a discoverer of lost manuscripts depends on his being outside Rome and even outside Italy, albeit on ecclesiastical business. These difficulties of origin, education and movement are not untypical of 'Roman' scholars. With the exception of the years 1418–23, spent in England in the service of the Bishop of Winchester, Poggio was continuously with the Curia from 1403 to 1453. Abroad he made significant additions to the patrimony of antiquity by his discoveries in the libraries of Europe; in Rome his

p 18–19 (17)

p 122 (5)

classical interests extended to the study of ancient buildings and the collection of inscriptions and works of sculpture, and made him a central figure in the revival of Roman art and architecture particularly in the 1420s. A lively, polemical character, he was in contact or conflict with leading scholars of the day, using the Latin language as a racy, live idiom in his letters and *Dialogues* with an unrivalled fluency. Though these contain a serious vein, even at times pessimism, it is a comment on the times that his most popular work was his *Facetiae* (1438–52), a collection of humorous but often trivial and obscene Latin tales. Poggio forms a vital link between Rome and the Florentine humanist tradition of Salutati, though there is little in the 'Roman' Poggio of the Florentine civic inspiration. His humanism is also in a specific sense Roman by virtue of his interest in the antiquities of the capital, a 'local' interest which determined the cultural revival of Rome in the 15th century.

Physically the city was decayed and neglected when Martin V came there in 1420. Her political condition was hardly better, constantly threatened by noble factions and the remains of a republican spirit among the people. What Martin achieved in the way of basic repairs to streets and buildings was the modest beginning of a programme, pursued with more or less initiative by his successors, which in a century completely transformed Rome and especially the Vatican. Throughout this age, and with increasing momentum, Rome became, in a way that it never was before or since, both physically and intellectually, that unique centre and amalgam of ancient and modern, pagan and Christian that distinguishes it not only from the rest of Italy but from the whole of Europe.

Before this process got well under way, the papacy under Eugenius IV (1431–47) had to overcome important obstacles: within Rome, the rebellion of the Colonna family, and outside, the long-standing conflict with the Council of Basle. The former drove the pope from the city for nine years (1434–43); but at the end of that period he had won a victory over the Council, summoning instead the Council of Ferrara in 1438 (it moved to Florence, 1439–43) for the union of the Greek and Roman churches, and diverting attention toward the Turkish threat. If he had little time or opportunity to further culture in Rome, his pontificate saw the end of the struggle with the Council and led eventually to the disappearance of the last anti-pope. There were also two by-products of this period, both of no little cultural consequence: the physical presence of the exiled Curia in Ferrara and especially in Florence, and the contact there with the envoys of the Greek church. Among the latter was Bessarion, learned Archbishop of Nicaea, who became a cardinal and remained in Rome for the rest of his life. A revered and influential figure of a scholar and churchman, he stimulated Greek studies in Rome, and left to Venice during his lifetime the important collection of his manuscripts which formed the nucleus of the Biblioteca Marciana. More significant for Greek philosophical studies in Florence was the presence of Giorgio Gemisto Pletone, around whom there arose keen discussion of the merits of Plato and Aristotle, in which Bessarion took a part. Although Greek scholars had come to Italy before the Council and were to follow in greater numbers after the fall of Constantinople (1453), the Council of Ferrara-Florence was perhaps the most influential factor in the direction of Greek studies towards new philosophical enquiries.

Latin Renewal

In spite of this, and in some respects as a reaction against the claims of Greek, the emphasis remained and grew on Rome and Latin. This may be illustrated in the work of two leading scholars

The 'Urbis Romae Topographia' of Bartolomeo Marliano was first published in 1537. It is a painstaking study of the classical remains, with reconstruction maps of the city at various stages of its growth, beginning with Romulus (his Rome being a perfectly square wall round the Palatine). This detail (from the edition of 1544) is from the plan relating to imperial times. The shaded areas are the hills. Top left are the Baths of Diocletian; the Colosseum is near the middle; part of Trajan's Forum, to the left, is called the Baths of Constantine and wrongly drawn to fit the description. (2)

123 (8) of the day. Some degree of the reaction is present in Valla's *Elegantiae*, in defence of the power and purity of Latin, of its past, present and future as a *lingua universalis*: though the political greatness that was Rome has passed, this potentially perfect instrument still can and should represent her dominion. Valla was a Roman by origin, though he was in Naples when he wrote that work. He came to Rome in the later years of his life (1449–57), and there applied his philological talents to the biblical scholarship that aroused the admiration of Erasmus. Yet no contemporary expressed this spirit of Rome more strongly than Flavio Biondo, if in a different way from Valla. His work on the geography and history of Italy and of Rome is examined in Chapter IV.

Biondo's historical sense is also evident from his part in a debate concerning Latin which took place whilst the Curia was in Florence, Bruni (then Chancellor of the city) maintaining that Rome had possessed from the start two languages, Latin and vernacular, Biondo taking the view that Italian was the direct, if barbarously corrupted, descendant of Latin. This debate is equally important for the new historical perspective of Latin as for that of the vernacular, and it was appropriate, perhaps essential, that Florence, with its great part in the past if somewhat neglected Italian literary tradition, should be the place where it arose. But it is significant that the cue should be taken up immediately, not so much by the Florentines, but by a Florentine 'exile', Alberti, who, after a youth spent in northern Italy, became a 'Roman' of the Curia from 1430. The proem added later to the third book of his *Della famiglia* (composed earlier in Rome, before he was present at that debate) takes up and develops Biondo's view, and directs attention and practice to the modern language. By his theory and example, motivated by usefulness and a firm belief in the future of Italian, he opened the way for the ultimate transformation of Latin into vernacular humanism of the time of Bembo.

If this discussion was to have wide implications for Latin and Italian elsewhere, it had no repercussions in Rome. Although, following the same line of thought, Alberti composed the first Italian grammar about 1443, he himself wrote thereafter mainly in Latin, and his contribution to the Roman Renaissance was primarily architectural. His interest in architecture and art goes back to the circle of Poggio in the late 1420s and the revived study of Vitruvius, as well as to personal contacts in Rome with Florentine artists like Ghiberti and Donatello. This Florentine link is evident from his treatise on painting, the first of modern times, written in fact in Florence during those years when the Curia was in exile there. When his friend Tommaso Parentucelli became Pope Nicholas V (1447), these interests were given practical scope in the pontiff's grandiose plans for the reconstruction of the Borgo (unfortunately never executed) and a more modest restoration of churches and other buildings. From this experience and the study of Vitruvius and the architecture of Rome, Alberti wrote his ten books *On Architecture*, completed in 1452. This is not the place to elaborate on the content, importance and influence of this work, but merely to stress its origin and context, to place it, in spite of Florentine influences on Alberti's formation, in the Roman setting and experience from which it emerged. Some practical consequences which followed from and transcended this theory and experience, belong to the architectural history of Rimini, Mantua and Florence, to churches and palaces he designed or remade, that were no less, perhaps more, influential than his writings.

Nicholas V and Pius II: the first Humanist Popes

Nicholas V is often, rightly, referred to as the first Renaissance pope. His main object was peace, which he achieved in Rome, and (as far as it depended on him), in Italy; beyond this his prime concerns, as Vespasiano da Bisticci puts it, were 'books and buildings'. For the latter his ambitions far exceeded his achievement, which was considerable; for the former he was the real p 127 founder of the Vatican Library, whose holdings of manuscripts he (23) increased enormously by employing many copyists and illuminators and by commissioning original works or translations from Greek, sparing no expense. He also advised Cosimo de' Medici and Federigo of Urbino on their libraries, and was thus responsible for setting the pattern of great Renaissance collections in Rome

and elsewhere in Italy. The years of his pontificate (1447–55) were a golden age for culture in Rome. He has been called, for his character, piety and liberality, 'the most noble figure of a Pope in the whole of the Renaissance age'.

The reappearance of republican spirit in the unsuccessful plot of Stefano Porcari (1453) and the fall of Constantinople in the same year together cast a shadow over this picture. The early death of Nicholas and the election of the elderly Catalan Callixtus III deepened the gloom. But the latter's reign was even shorter, and the election of Aeneas Sylvius Piccolomini, Pius II (1458–64), p 45 (1) brought back light and hope. These high expectations, partly justified by his earlier career, were not altogether fulfilled. He had come late to holy orders (1446) after serving bishops, an anti-pope and an emperor outside Italy and as far afield as Scotland. Pursuing humanistic studies he had written things he later felt obliged to renounce: a Latin *novella*, a comedy and light verse f 3 that morally (in his later context) did him no credit. Changing careers, he rapidly advanced to the tiara; having gained which, he also changed course, renounced his levities, declared papal power absolute, and called a congress at Mantua for a crusade against the Turk. The latter overwhelming preoccupation led him to an early death at Ancona just as the expedition was due to set out. Nevertheless his pontificate was extremely favourable to arts and letters in Rome,—with some reserves. He gave time to his own studies, but his liberality to others fell far short of that of Nicholas V; he furthered reconstruction and building in Rome, yet he built his most magnificent palace at his native place, renamed Pienza; and favours went rather often to members of his own family. Though sincere in his aims to increase the power and prestige of the Church, there is something of the *bella figura* about Pius, a desire for personal glory that did not quite succeed. As a personality he appears in a sympathetic light

The early career of Aeneas Sylvius Piccolomini was that of a humanist and man of the world. In Germany, where he stayed for some years and was crowned poet by the Emperor at Frankfurt, he wrote a Latin 'novella' in the manner of Boccaccio. When he became Pope as Pius II—'Pius Aeneas'—he tried to suppress this memento of his frivolous youth but it had become popular and was translated into several languages. This woodcut is from the German edition of 1477. (3)

from his autobiographical *Commentarii*, a history of his own times full of digressions that tell us much of his love of letters, of nature and also of the pleasures of the world. His unfinished *Cosmographia*, in the geographical-historical vein of Biondo, rambles unevenly over Asia and Europe.

By the end of Pius' pontificate most of the figures so far mentioned, who had set the scene and tone of Roman culture, were already dead. A new generation of scholars, in the Curia or teaching in the university, continued the established traditions, less brilliantly and against some papal opposition. The Venetian Pope Paul II (1464–71) is a controversial figure. He had a passion for antiques, medals and coins, built the Palazzo Venezia at Rome, the loggia at St Peter's and a new bridge over the Tiber; loved magnificence and displays for which the city in his day was famous; supported the Vatican Library and the university. Yet he had a deep-seated suspicion of classical studies, and at one point forbade the teaching of pagan poets in the schools. He dissolved the college of abbreviators that under his predecessors had harboured many important scholars. When one of them, Bartolomeo Sacchi known as Platina, protested, he was imprisoned for four months. He was later imprisoned again in connection with an episode still shrouded in mystery. In 1468 an alleged conspiracy was discovered, with the support (it was rumoured) of Naples or France or the Malatesta of Rimini, to seize the pope and restore Roman liberties. Besides political charges, accusations were also made of heretical and pagan beliefs and practices. Those involved were members of the so-called *Accademia Romana*, a group of scholars who met in the house of Pomponio Leto, professor of rhetoric in the University, and who were united by a common interest in ancient history and literature, which they carried to the extremes of observing the Roman calendar with celebratory rites, assuming classical names, and exploring and making inscriptions in the catacombs. The trial dragged on for many months: the political charges were dropped, and the prisoners released. Although Paul II took the whole affair as a serious political and religious threat, it is generally agreed that it is an exaggeration to regard the Academicians as doing more than, perhaps foolishly, playing an imaginative intellectual charade without grave implications for their own faith, let alone for the security of the Church. More solid evidence than this would be required to substantiate the now exploded myth of the 'paganism' of the humanists. Yet such activities are an indication of the attraction and the assimilation of the past to the present, of the imitation of antiquity characteristic of the age. At the same time, this particular episode is peculiarly Roman, and an extension of that 'local' interest already evident in writers already mentioned.

Sixtus IV: the Leadership of Italy

f 4 Meantime an event of capital importance had occurred: the beginning of printing in Italy, first with Sweynheim and Pannartz in a convent at Subiaco (1465), then in Rome (1467), where in the same year Ulrich Hahn set up his press and produced the first book with woodcut illustrations. The initiative owed much to two humanists: Giovanni Andrea de' Bussi, and Giovanni Campano, friend of Pius II. Their publications were encouraged and increased by Pomponio Leto and the *Accademia Romana*, which, reopened under the new Pope Sixtus IV (1471–84), became a major centre of intellectual life. From this group and the university teachers came new editions and commentaries on the classics prepared with a more mature historical-philological sense. The old-style personal polemics of Poggio and Valla gave place to serious, if apparently pedantic, disputes over textual problems and interpretations among scholars who were the contemporaries if not the equals of Politian and Barbaro. Whatever criticism may be justified of the character, nepotism and politics of Sixtus, his pontificate was one of the most liberal and lavish for culture.

p 46 (2) Significantly, the disgraced Platina returned to favour as librarian of the Vatican Library, now re-housed in fine apartments decorated by Ghirlandaio and Melozzo da Forlì. Platina prepared the first catalogues and dedicated to Sixtus his *Vitae Christi ac omnium Pontificum* (1475) containing criticism of Paul II. The chapel bearing Sixtus' name (Sistine) was inaugurated; bridges, roads, squares were remade or constructed on a scale unprecedented even in the time of Nicholas V. Artists and artisans from all over Italy, but especially from Florence, poured into Rome, among them Signorelli, Botticelli, Perugino, Mantegna, Pinturicchio and Mino da Fiesole. Conditions and activities prevailed that were not to be surpassed until the age of Leo X, by which time the passion and the initiative for lavish building and artistic decoration had passed also to the higher ecclesiastics and private individuals.

Behind this magnificence the political, social and moral picture was far from reassuring, and was to grow worse. Sixtus' designs to establish his nephew, Girolamo Riario, in a state (that of Forlì) provides the model for similar papal ambitions to come: Alexander VI and his son Cesare Borgia; the Medici popes and their nephews in Florence and Urbino. These popes not only behaved like secular princes themselves, but wished to ensure the perpetuity of their families in that station elsewhere in Italy, and thereby they added further to the political confusion and internal weakness of the country. In Rome Sixtus' favours to the Riario and Della Rovere families exacerbated the factions; on his death riots

occurred and the old Colonna-Orsini feuds broke out again. Social and moral conditions deteriorated, especially among the higher clergy: ancient monuments (despite a bull of Pius II and the efforts of Leto and his colleagues of the Academy) were robbed for materials and cement. It is not surprising that Rome might give the impression at this time of preparing herself unconsciously to be the fine booty of the envious foreign invader. If such an arrival was deferred with the failure of the barons' revolt in Naples (1485) during the papacy of Innocent VIII, it came all too swiftly into the heart of Rome in 1494 in the first of a series of visitations that was to culminate in the sack of 1527. Before that disaster, which virtually closed the Renaissance in Rome, the city was to become not merely one of several centres but *the* cultural and political centre of Italy in the age of Leo X.

The Great Patrons: Alexander VI, Julius II, Leo X

Moral conditions were especially low during the pontificate of Alexander VI (Rodrigo Borgia, 1492–1503), years of French p 46 (3 invasions, the decline and fall of Naples, the meteoric rise and fall of Cesare Borgia. Though these were hard times for Rome, they were not without cultural activity. The city did not remain outside the contemporary developments in vernacular poetry; and even if what was written is not of high and lasting quality, there was no lack of activity in the 'courtly' lyric of a pseudo-Petrarchan character. Poets and men of letters found a welcome in the house of Paolo Cortese, a learned young Roman who engaged in correspondence with Politian on the current disputes over imitation in literature and language that were to be taken up and resolved for vernacular poetry by Pietro Bembo. A typical figure of this last decade of the century was the poet Serafino Aquilano, who had spent his youth in Naples and there, especially from Cariteo, had learned to compose, often improvizing, occasional and amorous verse. Employed then in Rome by Cardinal Ascanio Sforza and frequenting the house of Cortese, he rapidly acquired astonishing fame, and later toured the courts of Italy accompanying his lyrics on the lute, rather in the manner of a popular star of modern times. He was particularly successful in those cities where, unlike Rome, women had come to play a prominent part in society. It was to this superficial, often frivolous trend of poetry, characteristic of the period 1490–1510, that Bembo opposed a p 123 more serious imitation of Petrarch's language, style and content. (11) Without the flourishing of this kind of verse and its particular link with Rome, which under a Catalan pope and in years of international political agitation, attracted a more and more mixed and cosmopolitan clientele, it would be difficult to understand how and why there should then arise the theory of the *lingua cortigiana* (courtly language) appropriate to all Italy and centred on Rome. The problem of a 'national' language was discussed in the very same years in which an Italy, long divided among itself, achieved under political crisis some national consciousness. The focus on Rome rather than on Florence (despite her overwhelming linguistic-literary tradition, but because of her political decline after the fall of the Medici), is an indication that Rome was—at least for a time—politically and socially, if not culturally, in the ascendant.

Some measure of that national consciousness is present in the ambitions of the warlike Pope Julius II (1503–13) to rid Italy of p 47 (6 the foreigner; though France was expelled at the price of Spain's entrenchment on Italian soil. In Rome his greatest achievement was the foundation of the new basilica of St Peter's to the design of Bramante (1506), while at the Belvedere he assembled statues p 46–7 and antiquities unearthed during excavations. This was the great (4, 5, 8 period too of Raphael's activity in Rome (among other things, the p 150– Stanze della Segnatura), while Michelangelo was commissioned (7) to execute the tomb of Julius and decorate the ceiling of the p 154 Sistine chapel. Julius, indeed, was praised for having done more (12) to renovate Rome than Sixtus IV, by Francesco Albertini, whose p 99–1 *De mirabilibus urbis Romae* (dedicated to Julius in 1510) belongs to (57–8) that tradition of studies and descriptions of Rome begun with Poggio and Biondo. Julius was not so great a patron of men of letters as of artists; and even in this respect his reputation was overshadowed by the greater splendour of his successor Leo X, who in many ways simply continued, and got credit for the work begun under Julius.

p 47 (7) Under Leo X (1513–21) the Renaissance in Rome was at its most magnificent in every sense. The population increased rapidly with the influx especially of Florentines, who naturally expected much favour from their compatriot, and by and large they were not disappointed. Building, private perhaps even more than papal, proceeded on an unprecedented scale, and gave to Rome some of its finest palaces. Painting and architecture were then represented p 130 (30) by their most famous executants; besides Raphael and Bramante, Giuliano and Antonio da Sangallo, Jacopo Sansovino and Fra Giocondo. High living was the order of the day. Even contemporaries remarked on the wonderful transformation of Rome and its way of life. From the papal chancery issued elegant Latin epistles drafted by Bembo and Sadoleto, while the latter's villa on the Quirinale, together with those of the scholars Angelo Colocci and Giovanni Goritz, was the favoured rendezvous of great men of letters. The University too was at its best, counting (in 1514) some 90 teachers, among them Agostino Nifo and Paolo Giovio for philosophy, Inghirami, Beroaldo, Parrasio for rhetoric, Chalcondilas (in a special house for the purpose) and Lascaris for Greek. The Vatican Library grew and flourished under a succession of illustrious prefects. Theatrical representations of all kinds entertained prelates and laymen: classical Latin comedies and modern imitations, and Italian plays by contemporary authors, often with scenery painted by famous artists like Raphael and Peruzzi: Bibbiena's *Calandria*, Ariosto's *I Suppositi*, Machiavelli's *Mandragola*. Though little significant poetry was then written in Rome, it was a heyday for poets, buffoons and improvisers of verse. Latin poetry attained great perfection and novelty, being practised on a grand scale in all manner of compositions for the delight and reward of the pope. Leo X was very generous with artists and men of letters, and the Roman and Italian Renaissance owe much to his patronage.

In his age there came to fruition most of the trends in culture and material and social life begun under his predecessors since Nicholas V. At the same time there also came the reckoning with political and religious factors which had been badly handled, deferred or ignored: most important the reform of the Church. Leo made no effective reply to the Lutheran challenge, and it required a more resolute character than that of Clement VII (1523–34) to oppose or compromise with this and with the determination of the Emperor Charles V. The years from Clement's election to the Sack of Rome, though in some respects hardly less splendid than those of his cousin Leo X, were heavy with impending doom. When disaster came in 1527, not only were many of the fine things of Rome destroyed that had constituted the glory of her Renaissance, but many of the people who had adorned it or made it possible, were scattered over Italy.

After the Sack of Rome

It is possible to regard this event as signalling the end of the Renaissance in Rome; it is certainly the end of its most brilliant flourishing. Yet one might recognize in the pontificate of Paul III (Alessandro Farnese, 1534–50) the final phase of an epoch. Clement had the good sense to recall Michelangelo to Rome, and his *Last Judgment* was finished under Paul who employed him in many other works, especially the completion of St Peter's and the Vatican. Roman intellectual life in this period came to be centred more and more on private houses and on new academies. The pope enriched the Vatican Library with many manuscripts and printed books: fine private libraries were formed like those of the Ridolfi and Fulvio Orsini; and famous collections of antiquities in palaces and gardens. In these and other respects the age of Paul III, which is also that of the beginning of the Counter-Reformation with the Council of Trent (1545), may be regarded as p 153 (10) concluding the Roman Renaissance. After this, the liberties and licence, and the enlightened patronage that, with few interruptions, had characterized papal society for a century, gave place progressively to reaction, and to graver preoccupations with Councils and Turks. If we were to look for a definite signal of the end, we might find it in the actions of Pius V (1566–72), who excluded antiquities from the Belvedere, shut out the comedies, buffoons and feasts, and replaced them with the more sinister apparatus of the Inquisition.

Printing came to Italy from the north in 1465 when two Germans— Sweynheim and Pannartz—set up a printing press in the ancient monastery of Subiaco. Their first book (above) was an edition of the Church Father Lactantius; the type is a modified Gothic, not yet the 'Roman' or 'Italic' which became standard, but significantly it includes Greek. The writing going into the margin is manuscript. (4)

Neapolitan Golden Age

p 48–9 (9–11) The beginning of the Renaissance in Naples may be dated precisely from the triumphal entry of Alfonso V of Aragon into the city in 1442, bringing to an end the long and unhappy rule of the Angevin kings. The consequent reunion of the Kingdoms of Sicily and Naples did not, however, extinguish the Angevin claims to Naples. For a time Pope Eugenius IV, who supported René of Anjou, witheld the investiture from Alfonso until in 1443 he conceded it in exchange for military assistance against Francesco Sforza. Long afterwards these claims continued to provoke sporadic unrest until they finally formed the major pretext for the French descent into Italy at the end of the century. When this occurred, provoking Spanish intervention and subsequent domination, the conditions under Alfonso and his son Ferrante which had permitted the flourishing of Renaissance culture in Naples, virtually ceased to exist. It is, therefore, possible to set a term to the end of the Renaissance in Naples in the early 16th century with the advent of the first Spanish viceroys.

While it lasted, the cultural Renaissance of Naples was undoubtedly among the most significant in Italy, and owed its existence largely to the personality and patronage of Alfonso, surnamed *il magnanimo*. His rule (1442–58) came to be looked upon as a golden age in Neapolitan history both from the point of view of relative political stability and of enlightened protection of the arts. Alberto da Sarzana in a letter to Niccolò Niccoli of January 1443 states that he found in Naples 'no glimmer of letters, no learning'. Within a few years that picture had changed completely. Vespasiano da Bisticci, the Florentine bookseller who wrote the *Lives of Famous Men* (c. 1482), gives an ecstatic account of the character and actions of Alfonso, describing him as a deeply religious and pious sovereign who knew the Bible by heart, generous to an extraordinary degree with favours, and a paragon of justice. He compares him with Pope Nicholas V in his benefactions to letters, claiming that 'if princes had followed as these two began, men of letters would be far more numerous and be more respected than they are now'; and he especially commends both for commissioning original works and translations (from Greek and Latin). He has only one reserve about Alfonso, that he was very secretive in affairs and took counsel with no one. Otherwise he appears as the ideal of the enlightened prince.

Under Alfonso's rule Naples enjoyed a peace and reputation that impressed the rest of Italy. The feudal barons, independent overlords traditionally factious and open to provocation by Angevin instigation, gave little or no trouble. The kingdom entered a new period of economic prosperity due in part to the activities of foreign merchants, especially Florentines whose favourable treatment was continued under Alfonso in spite of the traditional Francophile (and consequently pro-Angevin) attitude of the Medici. The triumph of the Aragonese in Naples had not pleased Cosimo and, although economic relations were good, suspicions persisted as well as fears that the king's political ambitions extended not only to Lombardy but to Tuscany as well. Florence at first supported René of Anjou's attempts to regain Naples, and only much later, at the time of Lorenzo, entered into alliance with the Aragonese dynasty.

Cultural relations with Florence, on the other hand, were particularly close. Alfonso was always ready to receive, employ or reward scholars and especially from Florence. In 1441 Leonardo Bruni had dedicated to him a copy of his translation of Aristotle's *Politics;* Poggio sent him his *Ciropedia*. Many humanists were drawn for long or short periods to Naples by reports of Alfonso's generosity and learning, among them Filelfo, Gaza, Barzizza, George of Trebisond. Vespasiano recounts that in the year of his death Alfonso was spending 20,000 ducats on men of letters. His motives for such patronage were not merely to further his own reputation (though this undoubtedly determined the lavish scale on which he rewarded his biographers and historians) but also by a genuine interest in learning. Not only whilst at home in Naples, but even during campaigns abroad, he would have Livy's *Decades* read to him daily, and at other times the Bible and works of Seneca and other philosophers. So attentive was he to learned exercises, we are told, that he did not even move to brush a fly from his nose during an important speech by the Florentine ambassador Manetti.

The Humanists of Naples

In Alfonso's entourage the principal figure and mediator with humanists elsewhere was Antonio Beccadelli (1394–1471), called Panormita from his birthplace Palermo. He had studied in Siena and Bologna and had close relations with Cosimo de' Medici and Florentine scholars. Wealthy and of noble origins, Panormita entered Alfonso's service after five years in Pavia with the Visconti court, where he had been treated more as a professor than a gentleman. As a minister and member of Alfonso's council, he enjoyed considerable income and position, and received many gifts of land and property. In return Panormita celebrated the king in his Latin *De dictis et factis Alphonsi regis*, which was largely a collection of anecdotes illustrating aspects of his sovereign's character. Although he himself composed no works of great importance (his youthful *Hermaphroditus* enjoyed a *succès de scandale* in keeping with a characteristic gaiety he maintained all his life), Panormita was the real founder and focal point of learning in Naples. His villa was the scene of gatherings of scholars who discussed questions of textual interpretation, history, philosophy and natural science, and was the precursor of the later more famous *Accademia Pontaniana*.

The official historian of Alfonso was Bartolomeo Fazio of Spezia, a pupil of Guarino, formerly in the employ of Genoa. Entering the service of Alfonso during an embassy from Genoa in 1444, Fazio remained in Naples until his death in 1457, amply rewarded for his mediocre if stylistically competent history of Alfonso's reign. More than as a historian, Fazio deserves recognition as the author of one of the first works of contemporary biography, his *De viris illustribus*. As a scholar he came into violent conflict with

another protégé of Alfonso, the deservedly far more famous Lorenzo Valla (1407–57). A Roman by birth, much of whose career was spent in northern Italy and Rome, Valla served Alfonso for thirteen years (1435–48) and wrote some of his most influential works in Naples. His arrival in Naples was facilitated by his friend Panormita, to whom in his dialogue *De vero bono* (1431–33) Valla had assigned (not without justice) the rôle of expounding the philosophy of Epicurus. During his many years in Naples Valla wrote a history of the career of Alfonso's father Ferdinand (over whose accuracy he came into conflict with Fazio); his demolition of the Donation of Constantine; a work on free will; and his major contribution to Latin scholarship, his *Elegantiae* (see Chapter IV).

Another important figure of Alfonso's court, Giannozzo Manetti (1396–1457) belongs more to the story of the Florentine than to the Neapolitan Renaissance. He should, however, be mentioned, because one of his most important works *De dignitate hominis*, often quoted as a supreme expression of the Renaissance confidence in man's position and powers in the world, was written at Alfonso's invitation, issued while Manetti was on an embassy from Florence in 1451. Two years later Manetti settled permanently in Naples where he began or finished several translations from Greek into Latin of religious and philosophical texts, and enriched the cultural life of the city with his learning in classical and Oriental languages and his wide experience of political affairs.

Poetry of the South

Several of the important scholars protected and favoured by Alfonso, died before or soon after their patron. One, however, Giovanni Pontano (1426–1503), survived, along with Panormita, for many years to continue and further this tradition which reached its brilliant climax in the last two decades of the 15th century in vernacular literature as well as in classical works and scholarship. This was not due to a continuance of similar deliberate enlightened protection by Alfonso's son Ferdinand I (Ferrante), who was quite different in character and interests from his father. Brought up in Spain and educated later in Naples under the tutorship of Valla and the future Pope Callixtus III, he had more interest in (and justifiable preoccupations with) political affairs than learning, and during his long reign (1458–94) he favoured men of letters for their administrative uses, not for their scholarship. Harsh judgments have been passed on his severity and unscrupulousness as a sovereign especially in his treatment of the rebellious barons (1485), but there is no doubt of his political ability, and that his determined action against the Angevin attempt at the beginning of his reign (1459) deferred for many years the French threat and was vital for the peace of Italy in the second half of the 15th century. Throughout this time Ferrante played a leading part in the complex political and military scene, in the frequently changing pattern of alliances and counter-alliances between the Italian states and between the foreign powers, thus maintaining a precarious balance in Italy while containing the ever-present French and Turkish threats. It is impossible to summarize the vicissitudes of this period. Suffice it to mention here Ferrante's conflicts with the papacy in the 1460s and 1480s, his support of the Pazzi conspiracy and war against Florence (1478–80), his alliance with and plots against Venice (1470, 1476), his support of Ferrara against Venice (1483–85), his favouring Lodovico Sforza's claims in Milan (1480) that were subsequently to redound to the disadvantage of Naples.

Although lacking his father's disinterested concern for learning, Ferrante was not without taste for the adornments of life, and the climate of his court was favourable to the continued growth of the revival begun under Alfonso. In spite of often strained relations with Florence, even open hostility, the economic connections did not cease, and there was a continous flow into Naples of Florentine manuscripts, books, artists, singers and poets. Under Ferrante the Aragonese library begun by Alfonso grew into one of the most remarkable in Italy. In this context the collection of Tuscan poetry known as the *Raccolta Aragonese*, sent by Lorenzo de' Medici in 1476 with a famous preface by Politian, to Federigo of Aragon (Ferrante's second son), is an indication of, and was a stimulus to, the renewed interest in

p 21 (2

The chief Italian states in 1490; boundaries were constantly fluctuating. (5)

vernacular poetry in southern Italy that was to culminate in the lyrics of Sannazaro. Indeed, in the late 15th century, outside Florence, it would be difficult to compare any other Renaissance centre with Naples for brilliance and importance of production in both Latin and vernacular.

The principal figure was that Giovanni Pontano already mentioned. An Umbrian by birth, he came to Naples in 1447 and held various administrative and ambassadorial offices under Alfonso. He became of increasing importance under Ferrante, especially after the death of the unhappy Petrucci whom he succeeded as Secretary of State in 1485. As a man of learning he had few equals in the Renaissance. He was also a very able and successful political adviser and negotiator who was responsible for several treaties and alliances (e.g. the Peace of Bagnolo, 1484). A cloud hangs over his personal and public reputation in the later years of his life when, after many years of devoted service to the Aragonese, he did not follow Ferrante or his successors into brief exile, but remained to welcome and install the French invaders (1495); and when the Aragonese returned, he regained favour, surviving them to dedicate a work to Gonzalo of Cordova, the ouster of the young Federigo of Aragon (1503). None of this should be allowed, however, to dim the importance of Pontano as a humanist, scholar and poet, and as the focal point of the Neapolitan Renaissance at its height. The *Accademia Pontaniana* was famous throughout Italy (a learned academy bearing this name exists to this day in Naples); and its 'president' was recognized as the leading light of the revived Latin poetry. His production was vast. Particularly noteworthy, besides his amorous elegiac lyrics (many for his wife), are his elegant and realistic descriptions of Nature, his ability to assimilate the language, style and mythology of antiquity to the expression of sincere personal sentiments, and his astrological poetry inspired by Manilius. In prose Pontano also wrote much on moral philosophy, grammar and history, as well as several dialogues and allegorical tales involving or representing contemporaries and friends, and criticizing or satirizing himself as well as others.

In all these writings Pontano shows himself a master of Latin verse and prose, not in a pedantic sense, but in the capacity to use them as live media of art. His production represents, in consequence, a perfect adaptation of the antique to the modern.

As a Latin poet Pontano was surpassed in Naples, perhaps in Italy, only by Sannazaro (1456–1530). Born and brought up in the Abruzzi, he was in Naples from 1475 where he studied rhetoric and poetry under Giuniano Majo and became a member of the *Accademia Pontaniana*. Entering the household of Alfonso, Duke of Calabria, he rapidly acquired a reputation as a poet in Latin and Italian, and became closely associated with a group of literati nowadays less highly regarded but whose presence and influence at that time were highly significant: Gabriele Altilio, Tristano Carracciolo, Pietro Summonte (later editor of Sannazaro's *Arcadia*), Antonio de Ferrariis, and the vernacular poets Pier Jacopo de Gennaro, Francesco Galeotta, Giuliano Perleoni, Antonio Petrucci, and especially Benedetto Gareth *(Cariteo)*. From the late 1460s vernacular poetry, both local and popular and in the Petrarchan tradition, had been revived by these writers, who established a tradition second only in strength and importance to that of Florence. To this we may add the prose achievement of Masuccio da Salerno (*fl.* c.1460–69) whose *Novellino*, for all its defects, represents a notable attempt to imitate the narrative, language and style of Boccaccio. The Neapolitans tried to assimilate the Tuscan literary tradition and to rid their language of local dialectal elements. This fact, together with the vitality of neo-Latin poetry in Naples, goes some way to explain how and why Sannazaro's *Arcadia*, one of the most popular and influential works of the Italian Renaissance, should have been written here and not in Tuscany. A prose narrative interspersed with verses of different forms, this work is a remarkable amalgam of classical and Italian sources, of learned and popular traditions; yet it is the archetype of a new genre of pastoral literature that was to spread over Europe for nearly two centuries. Such a fusion may be compared, in a different genre, with the less substantial drama, *Orfeo*, of Politian. Both represent a characteristic tendency of vernacular

p 36 (7)

f 6, 7

EGLOGA QVARTA. 35

LOGISTO, ET ELPINO.

L.
I

Hi† vuol vdire i miei foſpiri
in time
Donne mie care , e l'angofciofo
pianto,
Et quanti paſſi era la notte e'l
giorno
Spargendo indarno vo per tanti campi,
Legga per queſte querce,& per li faſſi,
Che n'e già pien homai ciaſcuna valle.

E. Paſtori, vccel, ne fiera alberga in valle,
Che non conoſca il ſuon delle mie rime,

Ne

LA VERA EFFIGIE
DEL SANNAZARO

Tratta da vna Medaglia di bronzo,& rifcon-
trata col ritrátto colorito che è nella Sala
del gran Configlio in Venetia, fatto gia da
M. Titiano Pittore illuſtre.

MARCI ANTONII FLAMINII.

Quấtum Virgilio debebit ſylua Maroni,
Et paſtor, donec Muſa Maronis erit :
Tấtum penè tibi debent piſcator, & acta
Acti diuino proxime Virgilio.

*Jacopo Sannazaro (1456–1530) was the
most outstanding of the Renaissance poets
of Naples. His 'Arcadia', published in
1504, renewed the pastoral tradition in
Europe, idealizing the simple rural life
and influencing writers in Spain, France and
England. This portrait and illustration
are from an edition published in Venice
in 1578. (6, 7)*

literature in the late 15th century to adapt material and forms from antiquity and from modern times, using a type of imitation as yet free from any rigid historical or aesthetic criteria. Towards such linguistic criteria, we see Sannazaro move in his revision of the *Arcadia*, which he purged, after the first edition, of many dialectal terms and forms—moving, that is, in the direction later advocated in Bembo's literary and linguistic theories.

Sannazaro also excelled as a Latin poet, especially with his piscatory eclogues and his later religious work, *De partu virginis*. Although with the eclogue and the bucolic tradition generally, Tuscany has chronological precedence, there is no doubt that this genre was brought to perfection and a position of influence in both vernacular and in Latin by the Neapolitan poet. The European tradition takes its beginning from him.

Unlike his close friend Pontano, Sannazaro remained true to his masters and went into temporary exile in France with King Federigo (1501–04). With the final resolution of the succession to the kingdom in favour of the Spanish sovereigns (1502) and the death of Pontano (1503) the Renaissance in Naples may be said to come to an end. Sannazaro returned from France and lived on for many years, nostalgic for those better days. In the 16th century the culture of southern Italy was to produce or harbour men of a different kind—a few humanist scholars (Marcantonio Epicuro, Antonio Telesio), several important religious thinkers and reformers (Valdés, Bruno, Campanella), and a few but by no means insignificant lyric poets (Angelo di Costanzo, Luigi Tansillo, Galeazzo Tarsia).

Milan: Tyranny and the Arts

In the 'war' of pamphlets that accompanied the far more serious military threat of the Duke of Milan, Giangaleazzo Visconti, to Florence at the opening of the 15th century, the Florentines made much of the association of freedom with the liberal arts in contrast with the evils of tyranny. From the Milanese chancery the opposite view was expressed by a scholar in the duke's employ, Antonio Loschi, who praised the virtues of life under a prince. This debate, later repeated throughout the century, reflects a contemporary awareness of a distinction still valid for our own appreciation of the varied development of the Renaissance in Italy. Although Giangaleazzo is historically conspicuous for other things, and not

comparable as a patron with some of the great figures of the mature Renaissance, it is arguable that the first evidence of the Milanese Renaissance appears in his time; and not only in his appreciation and employment of men like Loschi (a pupil of Salutati), but in his magnificent building programme (the Duomo of Milan, the castle and Certosa of Pavia) and his development of the University of Pavia. Fortunately for Florence, his career was cut short in 1402 when his state extended from the Alps to Bologna, from Alessandria to Belluno. His eldest son Giovanni Maria (1402–12) was distinguished primarily for his cruelty, and was appropriately rewarded with assassination.

Many of the political ambitions of Giangaleazzo were renewed in his second son Filippo Maria (1412–47), who in spite of a notorious viciousness of character, gave some encouragement to Milanese culture. The leading humanists in his service were Pier p 122 Candido Decembrio (following his father Uberto in the Chancery), who enjoyed a reputation throughout Italy and abroad (he was in contact with Humphrey, Duke of Gloucester) as a Greek and Latin scholar, and subsequently wrote the lives of Filippo Maria and of Francesco Sforza; and later Francesco Filelfo p 51 (1398–1481), whom the duke especially favoured with a house and pension. Of all humanists, however, Filelfo is perhaps the most famous opportunist and time-server; a good example, often quoted, of the subservience of some men of letters to money and to the less noble ends and vanities of contemporary rulers. It would be true to say that in Filippo Maria's case there was a strong element of political and personal ambition in his employment of such scholars. He was nothing if not a realist; and this appears also in his insistence on the use of the vernacular rather than Latin in affairs. While elsewhere in Italy Latin was strongly supported and attaining ever greater purity, and while some disdain for Italian and its literary traditions still persisted among scholars, Filippo Maria frequently read the Italian poets and he had Filelfo write a commentary on Petrarch's *Rime* and Guiniforte Barzizza on Dante's *Inferno* (c. 1440) at a time when no comparable studies were to be found in other Italian centres.

But Filippo Maria's interests were far more predominantly political and military, and his long rule is remarkable rather for the extreme pressure he exerted in this way on Venice and Florence than for cultural brilliance. Nonetheless his political astuteness, especially in the employment of famous *condottieri*, Piccinino, Carmagnola and Sforza, paved the way in effect for a succession he did not intend. He had no male issue, and he married his only daughter to Francesco Sforza, whose career exemplifies the ascendance of a great soldier to political eminence. Although frequently betrayed or opposed by his suspicious and jealous father-in-law, Sforza not only survived but finally succeeded in realizing his claims to the duchy (1450) against those of Charles of Orléans (son of the duke who had married the daughter of Giangaleazzo Visconti) and of Alfonso of Naples. Indeed, after the precarious interlude of the Ambrosian Republic (1447–50) the city welcomed Sforza with open arms as a saviour of its freedom against outside pressure. His rapid rise to power is an object lesson in the political opportunism of the day, long before Machiavelli drew up the canon for the new prince. For this reason rather than for any other it is possible to date the beginning of the real Renaissance in Milan from 1450. Apart from the continued employment of certain humanists like Filelfo (who celebrated him in his *Sforziade*), his rule (1450–66) was culturally

p 50 (14)
p 51
(16, 17)

undistinguished. He employed the Florentine architect Filarete, but for practical works such as the reconstruction of the Castello Visconteo and the Ospedale Maggiore. More important was the consolidation and security of his large dominions, which included (besides Milan) Pavia, Como, Lodi, Cremona, Novara, Vigevano, Alessandria, Tortona, Bobbio, Piacenza, Parma and the over-lordship of Genoa. Some of these were later to be whittled away (Parma and Piacenza to the Church; Genoa became independent), but the state of Milan was to remain, despite the upheavals of the Italian wars, in and out of the hands of his descendants down to 1535.

f 10

Francesco Sforza saw to it, however, that his children received a good classical education from Barzizza and Lascaris; and brother and sister, Galeazzo Maria and Ippolita made Latin speeches that impressed contemporaries as prodigies of learning. While Ippolita went to Naples as wife of Alfonso of Calabria, her brother, after

f 8

a brief rule (1466–76) was murdered at the age of twenty-two. For a short and turbulent period the state was governed by his mother Bona of Savoy as regent and her late husband's minister Cicco Simonetta, acting on behalf of Galeazzo Maria's young son, Giangaleazzo, a boy of seven. This arrangement was brought to an end abruptly by the man whose name is identified most particularly with the Milanese Renaissance. Lodovico Sforza,

p 50 (12)

known as *il Moro*, younger son of Francesco, took over the guardianship of his nephew in 1479, dismissed Bona, and had Simonetta executed. When the young heir conveniently and mysteriously died in 1494, Lodovico obtained the investiture of the dukedom in spite of the renewed claims of France, Savoy and Naples (which had been strengthened by Giangaleazzo's marriage to Isabella of Aragon).

One of the founders of Italian music was Francesco Gaffurio of Milan (1451–1522) composer, teacher and musical director of the cathedral. His 'De harmonia musicorum' (1496) interprets harmony according to neo-Platonic theory. (9)

Lodovico 'the Moor'

Whatever political and moral charges may be made against Lodovico, there is no doubt that Milan under his rule enjoyed a reputation among the most brilliant of the age. Himself a man of some learning, and possessed with ambitions for cultural eminence, luxury and display, modelled in large part on contemporary example, he rapidly became one of the most liberal and enterprising patrons of the arts. In this he was encouraged and aided by the tastes of his wife, Beatrice d'Este, daughter of Ercole, Duke of Ferrara, and sister of Isabella, Duchess of Mantua. Artists and scholars were attracted, invited and commissioned from all over Italy: Leonardo da Vinci, Bramante and Giancristoforo Romano as engineers and architects; Demetrio Chalcondilas, drawn from Florence to set up Greek studies; copyists and illuminators, artisans of all kinds. Printing had begun in Milan in 1470. From the presses came new editions of classical texts; from the workshops fine bindings and illustrations. Music flourished with the practice and theory of Francesco Gaffurio. A brilliant picture of this court, rivalling all others in Italy for splendour, is given by Vincenzo Calmeta, secretary of the duchess from 1491–97:

p 50
(13, 15–18)
p 90–91
(36–41)

f 9

At that time Lodovico Sforza was invested with the Duchy of Milan, and to mark the occasion he ordered a great and memorable feast, at which all the princes of Lombardy were present including the Marquis of Mantua, who brought with him Serafino [Aquilano, the poet]. There were plays, banquets and various entertainments, recitations and displays ...

p 51 (18)

Lodovico's wife was the lady Beatrice d'Este, daughter of Duke Ercole of Ferrara, and though still quite young, she was of such lively intelligence, affability, grace, liberality and generosity, as to be comparable with any celebrated woman of ancient times; for she thought only of giving her time to worthy pursuits. The court was full of men of every skill and talent, especially musicians and poets; and no month passed but they were to present, besides other things, some eclogue or comedy or tragedy or other new production or play. Regular readings from Dante's *Comedy* were given at suitable times by a certain Antonio Grifo ... and Lodovico Sforza enjoyed no little relaxation from hearing these when he was free from the preoccupations of state ... The Duchess Beatrice was not content to praise and reward the outstanding men of her own court, but from any part of Italy from which she could obtain the compositions of elegant poets, she would keep and revere them in her own chambers as divine and sacred possessions ... So that vernacular poetry and prose, debased since Petrarch and Boccaccio, was first revived by Lorenzo de' Medici and his contemporaries and then restored to its original dignity by the encouragement of this and other remarkable ladies of our time ...

The murder of Galeazzo Maria Sforza in 1476. Galeazzo was the son of Francesco Sforza, the 'condottiere' who took over the Visconti Duchy of Milan. His reign of ten years was a chronicle of cruelty and oppression though he appreciated the arts of painting and music. He was murdered in a church, and his brother Ludovico 'il Moro' obtained power. (8)

The education of princes was by the mid 15th century in the hands of classical scholars, many of them from the Eastern Empire. Constantine Lascaris, who wrote the introduction to the Greek language shown here, was tutor to Francesco Sforza's children. Printed by Aldus Manutius in 1495, it gives the Greek text (with the letters of the alphabet) on one side, the Latin equivalent on the other. (10)

This brilliant period, coinciding with the first French invasions, was destined to be cut short by the early death of Beatrice (1497) and the eventual loss of Milan by Lodovico (1500). While it lasted, Milan was, among other things, a principal centre of Italian poetry, of that 'courtly' lyric which Calmeta virtually equated with Petrarch. Famous then among its poets were Niccolò da Correggio, Gaspare Visconti, Antonio Fregoso, Calmeta himself, with the temporary addition of the prestigious Serafino. Poetry then became fashionable among noble and elegant people; and like many fashionable things was to prove ephemeral. But for some two decades this style prevailed, especially in northern Italy and around the figures of the great ladies of the time. There is a striking contrast between this court poetry and the agitated political and military context in which much of it was written. In that last decade of the 15th century, Milan's most splendid, Lodovico overplayed his hand in the game of international politics, and he lost his state to the French whom he had welcomed into Italy under Charles VIII. After 1500 Milan was a victim of the rivalries between France and Spain. The sons of Lodovico enjoyed it for only short periods: Massimiliano for the years 1513–15; Francesco II from 1525 to 1535. In the intervals Milan was French; after 1535 it was Spanish. A bone of contention between François Ier and Charles V, Milan itself suffered much from military attack, internal uprisings, destruction of buildings and the plague, particularly during the siege of 1526.

Not all the cultural developments in the duchy depended, however, on patronage at the centre; though, unlike Rome, they lacked any very conspicuous private leaders. Little attention has been paid, except by specialists, to the cultivation of humanist studies outside Milan and outside institutions like the University of Pavia. Yet there is good evidence for the second half of the 15th century that there were local groups of scholars in many small towns and cities of northern Lombardy, who were in contact with humanists elsewhere. If they made no outstanding contribution to scholarship, their existence indicates a certain vigour of intellectual life independent of the court. But this quite rightly occupies the centre of the Renaissance picture of Milan; and without Lodovico and his wife Beatrice there would hardly be much to compare with the rest of Italy.

Venice: the delayed Renaissance

p 52 (20) Venice came late into the Renaissance field and stayed later than most other centres in Italy. The delay is somewhat surprising for various reasons. Since Petrarch's residence there (1362–67) the city had had no lack of contact with humanism, and in the early 15th century she was frequently visited by eminent scholars,

or provided the point of entry for Greek immigrants bringing new texts and knowledge. But none seem to have remained long, preferring to seek employment in cities where the reception was warmer. Secondly, throughout most of the 15th century Venice seems to disprove the Florentine contention that republican freedom and the cult of letters essentially go together. Only at a much later stage, in the 16th century, did Venice assume something of the rôle of Florence in the early 15th. Her Renaissance appears to begin when that in other areas is at its height or even drawing to a close. Yet from then on her place is consistently brilliant in art, architecture, music and printing, and in some respects decisive for the future of Italian literature. Thirdly, Venice remained for a long time unaffected by the fervour of Aristotelian studies centred on Padua, which provided also a focal point of new literary and linguistic ideas. The delay in the case of Venice can perhaps be partly explained in terms of political factors and orientation. Preoccupied after 1425 with extending her power on the mainland and ensuring her commercial prosperity on the sea against other Italian states and the Turk, she seemed to stand aloof from other than the political pressures of Italy. When compelled to defend her existence at the turn of the century, it was as though, under crisis, she changed from a power balanced between east and west, whose outlook was as mixed as her architecture, to a European and more precisely an Italian state.

Venice did not entirely lack humanists of her own in the first half of the 15th century, though they are isolated figures. Two of them had considerable reputation outside: Lionardo Giustinian (1388–1466), a pupil of Guarino (who taught briefly in Venice) and translator of Greek works, but more famous for his vernacular poetry; and Francesco Barbaro (1390–1454), also a pupil of Guarino, who had close relations with the Florentine humanists, but wrote only one work, *De re uxoria*, that alone could hardly account for his fame as a learned man. Both were employed in public office, but show none of the civic traits characteristic of their Florentine contemporaries. Relations with Florence were closer on the commercial level, and these, especially through the residence of many Florentines in Venice, assisted the diffusion of Tuscan language and literature there, and prepared the way for later Venetian initiative in these fields. Notable Florentine exiles also came to the Veneto: Cosimo de' Medici in 1434, and Palla Strozzi, 1434–62, in Padua. In spite of the anti-Venetian sentiments of the Medici, these contacts continued, and go a long way to explain some of the changes in interests and outlook of the Venetian patriciate in the second half of the 15th century. Bernardo Bembo, father of Pietro, is a good example of this generation of cultured ambassadors and officials of Venice. Friend of Lorenzo de' Medici and of the scholars of his circle, he had a deep interest in classical and vernacular studies, and made a collection of books and manuscripts, many of which are now in the library of Eton College. It would be difficult to overstress this Florentine connection for the education and development of Pietro Bembo.

To the same generation as Bernardo Bembo belongs the humanist who dominates the traditional picture of Venetian humanism in the late 15th century, Ermolao Barbaro (1453–93), p 52 (22) grandson of Francesco. His formation was, however, in good part Roman, and his major work, *Castigationes Plinianae*, was written in Rome. This philological revision of Pliny's *Natural History* was regarded by contemporaries and later historians as one of the outstanding achievements of humanist scholarship. One consequence of his initiative was the edition of the Greek text of Aristotle published by Aldus Manutius in Venice, 1495–98. Printing had begun there in 1467 and rapidly made Venice a leading centre of the book world. Aldus (1450–1515) made it *the* centre, especially for Greek texts. His publications were not f 10 confined to classical works, nor to the Italian 'classics'. One of his most remarkable books was the *Hypnerotomachia Poliphili* f 11 (1499) by Francesco Colonna, a curious romance in even more p 137 (7) curious Italian, with fine woodcuts by an unknown artist, now p 183 (3) prized as among the best of Renaissance illustrated books. The tradition of the humanist-publisher was carried on by Aldus' descendants throughout the 16th century. Together with other famous Venetian printers they constitute one of the outstanding and determining features of the Renaissance in Venice.

It will be evident from what has been said so far that this Renaissance did not arise from or depend upon the existence of patronage private or public, nor upon the attraction of foreign scholars from outside Venice. Slow to grow, in part from Florentine seed, it matured into a vigorous plant with its own roots and characteristics at a time when the Florentine Renaissance was beginning its decline. There the great humanist tradition of the 15th century ends with Politian (1492) when Pietro Bembo was only twenty-two. If it is possible to say that the real centre of humanist studies then moved to Venice and the Aldine circle, it is even more true that the focus of vernacular literature followed the same direction. The two are indeed inseparable for that significant transfer, which takes place in the first decades of the 16th century, from classical to vernacular humanism in which Bembo is the prime mover.

p 26
(43, 44)

The Venetian Achievement

This change took place at a moment when vernacular literature, especially poetry, had attained a new if chaotic and largely social vigour, as a pastime and courtly accomplishment rather than as a serious literary pursuit. Bembo's object was to give it dignity and gravity, to purify it linguistically and stylistically, to put it on the same level as classical poetry, not by injecting it with Latin, but by taking it back to its purest sources in the Tuscan writers. In his *Prose della volgar lingua* (begun c.1500 and first published in 1525) he accomplished several aims; he completed a process begun in the 15th century of placing Latin in historical perspective as a language of the past, established the validity of the modern language, and identified the true basis of literary Italian in the unique models of Petrarch and Boccaccio; it was a kind of takeover bid by a non-Tuscan, in the name of Italy, of the Tuscan literary-linguistic tradition. That this was practically possible, Bembo showed by his own *Gli Asolani* (1505). Others were soon to demonstrate how completely the assimilation by the rest of Italy of the Tuscan tradition was already an accomplished fact. Bembo's theory and practice in verse and prose decisively directed the course of much of Italian literature in the 16th century, and had a notable direct influence on major contemporary authors like Ariosto and Castiglione.

Bembo's influence was greatest in Petrarchan poetry, but hardly less in linguistic studies, and specifically in grammar. Alberti's much earlier grammar, based on modern Tuscan usage, had little diffusion, and nothing concrete remains of the teaching at Padua in this field of Giovanni Augurello, Bembo's tutor. Consideration

The handwriting of the Renaissance is one of its most enduring legacies, for upon it are based many of the Roman and italic typefaces still used today. Italic was the cursive script which was widely used by humanists. It was first made into a typeface by Aldus in 1501. This page is from Arrighi's 'Operina', a writing mannual published in 1539. (12)

of grammatical and orthographical questions was provoked in part by the invention of printing, but far more by the desire to regularize usage on some basis comparable to that of the classical languages. In the early 16th century much of the discussion and writing on these topics was centred on the Veneto, and owed its direction to Bembo and to contemporaries like Giangiorgio Trissino. In no other area of Italy was there at this time such a close association between humanistic and vernacular studies.

Bembo was also the historian of Venice in his later years, but his official Latin history, covering the period 1487–1513, is far less interesting, for all its humanistic elegance, than one of the contemporary sources he used, the *Diari* of Marin Sanudo. No work better than this record and compilation of political events, official documents and local *faits divers*, gives us such a clear and detailed picture of life in Venice between 1498 and 1535. In the arts in this period Venice could compare with any other centre. It is the great age of the Bellinis, Giorgione, Titian, Tintoretto, Paolo Veronese; and in architecture, a little later, of Sansovino and Palladio. The musical tradition, centred on the chapel of St Mark's, was to develop from the times of Adrian Willaert (1527) to its culmination in the following century with Monteverdi. The theatre too flourished from the early 16th century, and was distinguished by a vigorous popular tradition in local dialect written by actor-playwrights such as Antonio Molino, Angelo Beolco (*il Ruzzante*), and Andrea Calmo, precursors of the *commedia dell'arte*. The 16th century is indeed the golden age of the Venetian Renaissance, when to the rest of Italy and Europe, though shorn of her continental possessions, she seemed the model of free institutions and prosperity, the only major state to emerge politically unchanged from the Italian wars. After the Sack of Rome, and even more after the beginning of the Counter-Reformation, she became the delight and refuge of temporary or permanent exiles, protected from the long arm of the Inquisition or censorship. It was the ideal home for such as Pietro Aretino, 'scourge of princes', and later for apostates like Bruno.

p 106
(70, 71)
p 94–5
(47–50)
p 53 (25)

p 53 (23)

'Hypnerotomachia Poliphili' is a strange allegorical fantasy in a mixture of Latin and Italian (with a few passages in Greek and Hebrew). Conceived by Francesco Colonna in 1467, it was printed only in 1499, by Aldus Manutius of Venice. The woodcuts by an anonymous artist show extensive knowledge of classical remains. (11)

Two Humanist Courts: Ferrara and Mantua

These two states are distinguished among the governments of Italy by the remarkable continuity of their ruling houses throughout and beyond the age of the Renaissance. The Este (Ferrara) and the Gonzaga (Mantua) became established as lords of their cities in the 13th and 14th centuries and remained in possession until 1597 and 1701 respectively. In each the Renaissance may be said to begin about the same time with rulers who had received the benefits of a humanist education from the two most famous teachers of the century: Leonello d'Este (1441–50), pupil of Guarino da Verona, and Lodovico Gonzaga (1444–78), pupil of Vittorino da Feltre. Although humanist ideals of education were enunciated elsewhere in the 15th century (e.g. by Bruni, Vegio and Pius II), nowhere were they so clearly and effectively expressed and practised as in these two northern courts, and nowhere, except perhaps in Urbino, did they have such far-reaching consequences. Any consideration of the Renaissance in Ferrara and Mantua must, therefore, move from these two masters.

p 123 (9)
p 122 (6)

Guarino and Vittorino had both been pupils of Giovanni di Conversini da Ravenna in Padua in the late 14th century. The former learnt Greek from Chrysoloras, accompanying him to Constantinople, and then exercised considerable influence as a teacher in Florence, Venice and Verona, before establishing himself, on the invitation of Niccolò III d'Este, in Ferrara where he remained for thirty-one years (1429–60). Vittorino, after studying with Guarino in Venice, moved to Mantua, on the invitation of Gianfrancesco Gonzaga in 1423. There he maintained for more than twenty years the most famous school in Italy, the Casa Gioiosa. Although Guarino's teaching was more inclined to the production of good scholars, they both have in common as educators the ideal of an education designed to encourage, through a balance of sound learning in the classics and moral and physical instruction, the complete development of the individual. This ideal, represented perhaps most effectively in Vittorino's school, where rich and poor lived, worked and played together in an atmosphere of humanist studies and humane guidance, was the model for European education for centuries to come, and still continues to exert its influence in the modern world. By their fame they drew pupils from all over Italy and counted among them, besides the princes named, the young Federigo da Montefeltro, Duke of Urbino. We may rightly attribute to these teachers the deep cultural interests that, married to an aristocratic way of life, characterize the Renaissance courts of Ferrara and Mantua.

p 122 (7)
p 122 (3)

Leonello d'Este was the ideal of the educated prince, fond of reading the classical authors, collecting manuscripts, extending patronage and friendship to artists like Mantegna and Pisanello, and to men of letters like Alberti, whom he encouraged to write his work on architecture. Though his father, Niccolò, was not without letters, Leonello's short rule was by contrast like a spring of bright sunshine heralded by the brief but influential stay of the Papal Curia in Ferrara in 1438–9. The severe view of the vernacular expressed by one humanist at his court, Angelo Decembrio, does not, however, represent Leonello's attitude, and still less that of his successors under whom Ferrara was destined to achieve the greatest eminence as the home of Italian poetry. The University and the court continued to attract the most illustrious scholars in Italy; but under Borso, Leonello's brother (1450–71), Ferrara became more famous for its magnificence and spectacle, for the elegance epitomized in the Palazzo Schifanoia with its fine frescoes by Cosimo Tura and Francesco del Cossa. It was a society that gave new life to medieval ideals of courtesy and chivalry, inspiring and entertaining itself with the French and Italian romances in which the ducal library (Borso was given the title of duke in 1471) was especially rich. Nothing perhaps illustrates so well the difference of background and outlook between Florence and Ferrara at this time as the contrast between Luigi Pulci's *Morgante* (c. 1460–70), a somewhat chaotic, grotesquely comic reworking of Carolingian legends, and Matteo Maria Boiardo's *Orlando Innamorato* (c. 1476–94), in which the Carolingian heroes put on Arthurian garb and went on a quest for love with chivalric zeal. Written to entertain the court, Boiardo's poem faithfully represents, with some humour but largely seriously, the tastes and

p 56 (34)

p 56 (35)

p 147 (1)

ideals he shared with educated nobles and ladies of Ferrara. It is not only a marriage of Carolingian and Arthurian cycles (in which religious and political motivations have given place to those of love), but also one of a popular genre with episodes from classical sources. Boiardo thereby created the first of a series of great vernacular epics, all composed in Ferrara, that are among the most significant poetic achievements of Renaissance Europe. Boiardo, Ariosto, Tasso ensure the Ferrarese domination of a genre that was to be almost as influential abroad as the poetry of Petrarch.

What, therefore, begins and indeed continues in Ferrara as a Renaissance of humanistic learning, becomes overshadowed by a social splendour and an Italian literary flowering that draws increasing nourishment from classical studies. This is especially true of Ariosto and his poem, *Orlando Furioso* (1506–16, revised up to 1532). Yet, whereas it has much in common materially with Boiardo's epic, and celebrates the House of Este through its ancestors in the heroes of romance, Ariosto's poem is not similarly explicable in terms of the court society in which he served. His ideals were not those of Boiardo. For him the matter of the genre was a convenient but brilliant fantasy through which he could view the strength and weakness of human nature with tolerance and humour. Much has been made of the contrast between his world of unreality and the grim facts of contemporary Italy, as if it were an escape in some reprehensible sense. Inasmuch as it is the escape of a poet into his own imagination, and in particular this poet's escape from the oppressive employment of Ippolito d'Este, it is indeed an escape that permits Ariosto to express his own humanity. When this is magnificently done by skilful manipulation of complex material, and expressed in exquisitely beautiful verse, we have the most perfect poem of the Italian Renaissance.

p 57 (
f 3

Boiardo and Ariosto were also considerable lyric poets, untouched by the vogue of the 'courtly' lyric which had one of its most famous representatives in Ferrara in Antonio Tebaldeo (1463–1537). This kind of poetry found its ideal home in the northern courts presided over by educated ladies who shared the interests of Beatrice d'Este. Yet another form of entertainment, the drama, was to distinguish Ferrara among other centres almost as decisively as its cult of the chivalric epic. Duke Ercole (1471–1505) encouraged scholars in Ferrara (among them Boiardo) to translate many classical works into Italian; among these Latin comedies were produced in considerable numbers during his reign. In the same years plays in the original Latin were performed in Rome and Florence, but it was from Ferrara that there emerged the first important original vernacular comedies based on Roman models (the very first seems to have been written in Mantua, c.1506): Ariosto's *Cassaria* and *I Suppositi* (1508–9). Ferrara was to be no less influential in the development of tragedy and mixed dramatic forms. Although the first Italian tragedy (based on Greek models) was written in Rome by Trissino (c.1515), it was in Ferrara that Italian tragedy, tragi-comedy and pastoral drama ultimately developed a considerable tradition and related theory, with Giraldi (1504–73), Speroni (1500–88) and Tasso (1544–95). Giraldi in particular, with his plays and *novelle (Gli ecatommiti)* was to exert influence far outside Italy and provide source material for Shakespeare's dramas.

p 57 (.

A similar influence was exerted on drama by the *novelle* of Bandello (c.1480–c.1560), who spent some years in the northern courts including Mantua in the time of Isabella d'Este; yet their importance is greater in Italy for the light they throw on the social conditions and behaviour of these courts. Geographical proximity and family ties (Francesco Gonzaga married Isabella d'Este in 1490) partly account for the similar style of life in Renaissance Mantua. Though by long tradition first-class soldiers, the Gonzaga were also liberal patrons of the arts and built up a state as renowned for its prosperity as for its culture. Lodovico (1444–78) employed Alberti to design the remarkable Renaissance churches of S. Andrea and S. Sebastiano in Mantua, and the tribune of Santissima Annunziata in Florence; he also built or rebuilt the Casa del Mercato, the Torre dell'Orologio, and the Rocca di Cavriana, and employed Mantegna to decorate the Camera degli Sposi in Mantua with some of the most famous

p 87 (2

p 110

p 60
(41, 42

'Of ladies, knights, arms and love, of chivalry and courage I sing': so begins Ariosto's 'Orlando Furioso', at once striking the distinctive note of the romantic epic. Orlando is the ancient hero Roland, fighting under Charlemagne to defend Europe from the Moors. But the story wanders in a world of magic, enchantment and adventure. This woodcut is from the edition of 1542. (13)

92 (43) portraits of the Italian Renaissance. Lodovico also welcomed many scholars, among them Pico della Mirandola and Platina, and gave hospitality to Pius II's crusading congress. During the time of his successor Federigo (1478–84), Politian, temporarily estranged from Lorenzo de' Medici, composed in Mantua his drama *Orfeo*.

The city's most brilliant period, however, was that of Francesco II (1484–1519) and his wife Isabella, whose name is indissolubly associated with the refinement and grace of the aristocratic and cultured life of the north in the High Renaissance. While her husband distinguished himself on the battlefield (especially at p 130 Fornovo, 1495), Isabella was the courted queen of Italian *literati*, (28) receiving praise, letters, poems and other works from the most famous writers of the day, including Bembo and Castiglione, who for a period resided in Mantua. In character and accomplishments Isabella was the perfect counterpart to Castiglione's courtier. She was probably largely responsible for bringing to Mantua from Ferrara many social graces and entertainments, especially theatrical representations of Italian comedies based on Latin plays and on *novelle*, which were produced with increasingly elaborate scenic apparatus. Her correspondence is full of discussions of poetry and drama. In these activities she was much assisted by her secretaries Capilupi and Equicola. It is not surprising that she should have been called by contemporaries 'the first lady of the world', and that Isabella and her like should have inspired encomia of their persons and sex in a literature quite the reverse of the persistent anti-feminism of the preceding century. At the head of this literature might well stand the praise of Isabella, Elisabetta Gonzaga, Vittoria Colonna and others, in Canto xiii of Ariosto's *Orlando*. The rise of women to social and intellectual distinction is one of the remarkable features of the Renaissance in northern Italy.

Though militarily very much involved in the Italian wars and sometimes, paradoxically, on opposing sides, both Este and Gonzaga emerged from the final conflict between Church and Emperor (1530) secure and relatively unscathed. Throughout the 16th century Ferrara continued to be a favoured resort of poets and scholars and for a time also, under Ercole II (1534–59) who had married Renée of France, was a refuge for Calvinist sympathizers. The Gonzagas, created Dukes of Mantua in 1530, strengthened their estates and position by marriages, ensuring succession beyond the end of the century. From a cultural point of view, however, it is possible to say that the Renaissance in Mantua ends with the death of Isabella in 1539.

Federigo of Urbino, 'the Courtier'
Geographical proximity, unlike the case of Ferrara and Mantua, engendered rivalry and enmity between Urbino and Rimini in the days of the two famous soldiers whose names are associated with the Renaissance in this area: Federigo da Montefeltro and Sigismondo Malatesta. They are also contrasted in other respects.

Renaissance scholars often debated an old topic: the precedence of letters or arms. Federigo of Urbino (1444–82) appeared to p 54 (27) contemporaries as the embodiment of the perfect marriage of both: skilled and experienced in arts of war, which he exercised with distinction throughout his career, and learned in all branches of philosophy and the arts, which he cultivated in Urbino with a patronage unequalled even in Rome. He was a man of profound humanity and integrity of character, urbane and gentle, kind to his subjects, generous with all who served or needed him. It would be difficult to find any other man who combined such a universality of virtues. His early education in the school of Vittorino in Mantua had aroused in him a love of letters, and established a connection with that court which was to be cemented later by the marriage of his son to Elisabetta Gonzaga. To the north, and specifically to Ferrara, went his political sympathies when she was threatened by Venice, and in this cause, which he refused to abandon, he died from fever in 1482. These contacts point to a physical and spiritual affinity between Urbino and those courts which will have its most significant illustration in *The Courtier* of Castiglione, a Mantuan at Urbino. In his person Federigo seems to anticipate that ideal by half a century.

In Vespasiano's life of Federigo the buildings he constructed at Urbino fill two pages. But the most remarkable is the Ducal Palace designed by Luciano di Laurana, adorned within with Flemish tapestries, fine sculpture and marquetry, and portraits and scenes by Melozzo da Forlì and Joos van Gent. More famous still perhaps are the portraits of Federigo by Piero della Francesca p 54 (now in the Uffizi and the Brera). His employment and rewarding (26, 27) of artists and artisans is legendary. Vespasiano was an interested party in one of the largest and most expensive library collections of the century, for which Federigo (he writes) employed for some fourteen years some thirty or forty amanuenses making the finest manuscripts of classical and modern authors; and this went on in Florence and Urbino in spite of, indeed in defiance of, the invasion of the printed book. This collection, the finest for its beauty and size in Italy, ultimately found its way to enrich the Vatican Library. Where some other contemporary patrons of the arts may be suspected of giving favour for personal aggrandizement, Federigo impresses by his obviously sincere love of learning and the desire to create a harmonious and beautiful setting appropriate to a cultured life. It is remarkable that, during his very varied military career, he found time and leisure to enjoy the Urbino he created.

His life and times were celebrated by Giovanni Santi, Raphael's father, as well as by Francesco Filelfo, whose son Giammaria became tutor to Federigo's heir Guidobaldo. Apart from the p 55 (31) brief period during which he was expelled from his state by Cesare Borgia (1502–3), the latter ruled Urbino from 1482–1508. These were the years in which the fruits of Federigo's rule were gathered in what has been described as 'the most gracious of all the courts of the Italian Renaissance', presided over by the amiable but sickly duke and his cultured wife Elisabetta Gonzaga, sister-in-law of Isabella d'Este. Here Pietro Bembo resided p 123 (11) for a time (1506–11) and Baldassare Castiglione (1504–16), who p 55 (33) conferred literary and historical immortality on the company around the duke in the later years of his life, in his *Book of the Courtier*. This work, begun soon after 1508, completed in 1518, but not published until 1528, recreates the atmosphere and personalities of that period with a nostalgia for the cultivated society which was the natural context of the perfect courtier. It is unimportant whether the discussions that Castiglione represents did in fact take place in that form; it is more important that this kind of ideal could only emerge from this particular social and cultural background. Whereas humanist educational ideals and teaching in a democratic context like Florence developed the civic man and administrator, here the ultimate perfection of learning and the active life takes on the form of the urbane, cultured, universally equipped aristocrat, matched by a similarly cultured woman. Though an ideal, this image has actuality not only in the personality of the author and the society of Urbino, but in the topics of discussion current at the time affecting the accomplishments and behaviour of the courtier: language, poetry and love—neo-Platonic love which from the Florentine philosophers of the Laurentian circle passed elsewhere into vernacular literature and gave fresh impetus to the revived Petrarchan poetry.

The reality behind this ideal was broken at the death of Guidobaldo and never again recovered. While Castiglione perfected his picture (and his language) over the years, the old Urbino he represented became more remote, and the Italy it stood for was progressively engulfed, to his anguish and disillusionment, by the foreign invader. The duke had no children. He adopted as his heir his nephew Francesco Maria della Rovere, who ruled for thirty years, though almost always absent as captain of the Venetian armies. Urbino remained in the hands of this family down to the 17th century.

The Learned Tyrant of Rimini

As a political and military figure Sigismondo Malatesta, lord of Rimini (1432–68), was the opponent and opposite of Federigo of Urbino. Their disputes over Fano (which Federigo ultimately won in 1463) and other territories in Romagna, kept them in continual enmity: Sigismondo's frequent duplicity and violent actions contrast forcibly with the integrity and gentleness of the duke, whose quite different personality is illuminated by the fact that on the death of his enemy he supported his son Roberto Malatesta's claims to Rimini, and gave him his illegitimate daughter in marriage. Sigismondo's married life is sown with suspicions of murder: Ginevra d'Este who 'died' in 1440 after five years of marriage; Polissena Sforza who 'died' after seven years. Neither occasion endeared him to Ferrara and Milan. His military career begins and ends with a pope: as *condottiere* of Eugenius IV, and as the intending assassin of Paul II. In between he was excommunicated by Pius II and his effigy burned in Rome.

Yet this extraordinary figure was a genuinely learned man, who gathered around him a distinguished circle of scholars and writers, and promoted an artistic Renaissance in Rimini with quite remarkable features. Its greatest monument is the church
p 58
(39, 40)
of S. Francesco in Rimini, which in its reconstructed form (c.1450–58) has come to be known as the Tempio Malatestiano; and indeed it is a transformation of a medieval church into a kind of classical temple that is a mausoleum within of Sigismondo and his wife Isotta degli Atti, and without of the great men who served him. The architect of the new external marble shell, its
p 26
(39, 40)
form inspired by classical example, was Alberti, the executant Matteo de' Pasti, whose medallions of the Malatesta and of Alberti are among the finest of the 15th century. The interior, possibly designed by Pasti and executed in great part by Agostino di

Duccio, is rich with exquisite reliefs and sculpture of pagan divinities, allegorical figures, signs of the zodiac, Malatesta arms and monograms, and with the splendid tombs prepared for Sigismondo and Isotta. No other prince of the 15th century used (or abused) the resources of art in such profusion to celebrate himself and ensure his immortality. The Tempio is a monument to Sigismondo's pride. It is also the clearest symbol of the humanistic belief in the triumph of art over time.

Not only the plastic arts but letters too served this same end. The humanist Basinio Basini (like Filelfo with Francesco Sforza, Porcellio with Alfonso of Aragon) celebrated in a Latin poem *Hesperis*, Sigismondo's military exploits, and in elegies of Ovidian inspiration his love of Isotta. On his death Basinio was buried in the tombs on the north wall of the Tempio. With him, among others, is Sigismondo's military expert and general adviser, Roberto Valturio, author of a treatise on the art of war (*De re* f 14, 1 *militari*) that is remarkable also for its magnificent illustrations. Vernacular poetry too added its voice to the chorus of celebration, especially of Isotta, frequently using the fiction of the premature death of the lady to heighten the pathos of their love. Isotta in fact outlived Sigismondo by two years. This anticipation of death in poetry and in marble—which is in a sense the desire to triumph over death—is a unique feature of the personal cult of greatness practised at Rimini. It is uncertain whether the many poems attributed to Sigismondo were written by him or for him by others. The latter is the more probable, and it indicates yet another aspect of the deliberate myth of greatness he cultivated around him.

If Pius II disapproved of the Tempio Malatestiano on religious grounds, his and Paul II's major motives for disapproving of Sigismondo were political: to remove him from his support of the Angevin claims on Naples and from the Venetian alliance, and to oust him from the papal fee of Rimini. The succession of his son Roberto was in part ensured by his old enemy Federigo of Urbino. But Roberto (1469–82), though a good soldier, had no interest in art and letters. The unfinished Tempio remained and still remains incomplete, the symbol of a Renaissance begun and prematurely suspended. The history of Rimini in the late 15th-century was plagued by family rivalry and bloodshed. Overrun by Cesare Borgia (1500–03), sacked by Pandolfo Malatesta, sold to Venice, the city finally ejected Sigismondo's descendants in 1528. Continuously from Dante's time Rimini and the Malatesta had maintained a reputation for violence. For a brief period under Sigismondo the scene was brilliantly lit by a culture and an art among the most notable of the Italian Renaissance.

The art of war absorbed some of the best energies of many men of genius, including Leonardo and Michelangelo. Sigismondo Malatesta's military expert was Roberto Valturio, whose treatise on the subject published in 1472 gives a good idea of the practices and projects of the time. The illustrations—perhaps by Matteo de' Pasti—range from the severely functional (left, a scaling ladder with grappling hooks) to the uninhibitedly fantastic, as in this siege machine in the form of a dragon. (14, 15)

III A NEW VISION

Italian Art from Masaccio to Mannerism

PETER MURRAY

'The arts of painting, sculpture, modelling and architecture

had degenerated for so long and so greatly

that they almost died with letters themselves,

but in this age they have been aroused and come to life again.'

LORENZO VALLA

Between the world of ideas and the world of art

the threads are many, complex and—often—concealed. There are, in particular, three ways in which Renaissance art is a turning point. First comes a series of technical advances, beginning in the late 13th century with a new feeling for the solidity of bodies and the dramatic possibilities of design, and including the discovery of scientific perspective in the early 15th. Second, there is the rising interest in ancient Rome, leading to the imitation of classical architecture, sculpture and (as far as was possible) painting. Third, parallel with the New Learning, came a change in the *content* of works of art; ideas from philosophy and literature influence both the choice of subject and the way it is handled; iconography turns humanist.

Different artists were affected to different degrees by these three forces. Some, like Masaccio ('Giotto reborn' as Berenson calls him), enrich the Florentine tradition from their own resources, without special reference to classical models or humanist theory; others, like Mantegna, are almost obsessively absorbed by antiquarianism; others again paint in a style that retains many characteristics of earlier art, but use it to convey intellectual subtleties of which the Middle Ages never dreamed: and of this category the outstanding figure is Botticelli.

The esoteric meanings in Botticelli's *Birth of Venus* have already been briefly discussed (p. 24). Those of his other great allegory, *Primavera*, are even more complicated. It depicts the coming of spring. The shy earth-nymph Chloris is transformed by the touch of Zephyr into the calm, luxuriant figure of Flora (opposite), dressed in flowers. The story is taken from Ovid, and Botticelli achieves the extraordinary feat of actually painting one of the *Metamorphoses*—from Chloris to Flora. The allegory is expanded in the rest of the picture into a yet more elaborate symbol of neo-Platonic philosophy, with Venus, the Three Graces and Mercury. Yet the intellectual structure, organized to the point of pedantry, is suffused by Botticelli's art with tender lyrical beauty. (1)

The opening phase of Renaissance painting was one of exceptional variety. On the right are three panels of the *Madonna and Child*. The first belongs to the prevailing style of central Italy, deriving from the Trecento and ultimately from Giotto; it is by Masolino and dates from 1423. But simultaneously two new styles were emerging to challenge it. One of them was International Gothic and its leading exponent in Italy was Gentile da Fabriano; his Madonna (centre) sits elegantly but weightlessly in a flat setting of brocades and flower-patterns. The other was the art of Masaccio (far right)—monumental, firmly based, with the volumes built up in a space strictly defined by perspective. (2, 3, 5)

Richness to match the taste of the Florentine bankers was provided by Gentile da Fabriano and his followers. In his *Adoration of the Magi* (below) the delicate rendering of weapons, animals, clothes and jewelry shows the influence of the north. It was completed in 1423 for Palla Strozzi, Cosimo de' Medici's rival in finance and in patronage. (4)

'**Well did this holy friar** deserve the name by which he was always known, Fra Giovanni *Angelico*', says Vasari. Yet the religious devotion so evident in Angelico's painting has perhaps obscured his purely painterly qualities. His earliest dated work is a *Madonna and Child* (left) commissioned by the Cloth Guild in 1433. It has many features of International Gothic, but shows an understanding of Masaccio's innovations—an understanding that increased as he grew older. (6)

The impact of Gentile's *Adoration* on Florentine art can be judged by comparing it with Lorenzo Monaco's painting of the same subject of a year or two later (below). It has the same richness, the same love of naturalistic detail and the same lack of real depth. (7)

A young genius—Masaccio—revolutionized the art of Florence in the mid 1420s. He created a world clearly defined by perspective, lighting and modelling, and human beings who are embodiments of moral grandeur. Right: the *Tribute Money*; in the centre Christ directs Peter to take the coin from the fish's mouth; on the right Peter gives it to the tax-collector. Below: two cripples from another scene, *St Peter healing by his shadow*. Masaccio did not live to finish this series of frescoes. He died in 1428, aged twenty-seven. (9, 10)

The Deluge (left) by Uccello, of about 1445, has the charm of International Gothic combined with the new discipline of perspective. The latter is, indeed, prominent to the point of self-consciousness. All the defining lines and many of the bodies and the objects lie exactly at right-angles to the pictureplane and recede like a diagram to one vanishing point. Even the strange collar worn by the figure in the foreground is like one of Uccello's favourite exercises in foreshortening. God speaks to Noah on the right; the Ark is built on the left, and in the distance the dark storm breaks. (8)

When Masaccio was working in the Brancacci Chapel he probably took as a pupil one of the novices of the Carmelite monastery of whose church it forms part, Filippo Lippi. Although he entered the order Fra Filippo's real vocation lay elsewhere. The influence of Masaccio was soon modified by that of Donatello, but the prevailing character of his work is one of sweetness and sophistication. The dancing Salome (right) comes from his frescoes in Prato Cathedral completed after 1460. (11)

Sculpture followed a comparable development. Ghiberti's early *St John the Baptist* (above left) has the linear grace of a late Gothic figure. Donatello's *St Mark* (centre) is like a Masaccio apostle, sturdy and monumental. Donatello later evolved a highly expressionist style, as in his *Mary Magdalen* (above), carved in wood when he was nearly seventy. (12,13,14)

Ghiberti himself revolutionized his own art between his First and Second Doors. Far left: the *Annunciation* from the First Doors (1403–24)—even relief in a conventional setting. Left: the *Story of Joseph* from the Second (1425–52), utilizing every resource of modelling and perspective. (15, 16)

Donatello's study of antiquity enriched his art without leading him to imitation. The head of Gattamelata (right) derives from Roman portrait busts and the whole work—the first bronze equestrian statue to be cast since Roman times—looks back to the statue of Marcus Aurelius in Rome. 'Not only did it fill all the men of that day with amazement', says Vasari, 'but it astonishes everyone who sees it at the present time.' (18)

The clash of personalities is explored by Donatello in a brilliant series of low reliefs for the doors of the Old Sacristy of San Lorenzo (detail above). Their explicit subjects are saints, prophets and apostles; in fact they display human contact in all its variety— argument, agreement, expostulation, impatience, communion—expressed through fresh and vehement gestures which Donatello must have seen every day in the streets of Florence. (17)

Passionate grief: Donatello's *Entombment of Christ* (left), made for the Basilica of St Antony at Padua, unleashes a violence of emotion that had hitherto been characteristic of northern rather than of Italian art. Christ's body weighs with the heaviness of death; behind him the three Maries give way to a frenzy of sorrow. The figures are of grey sandstone, the background yellow and black mosaic, the sarcophagus inlaid marble. (19)

83

The drama of the Last Supper offered a challenge and an opportunity to painters. Andrea del Castagno (above) gives his figures the tense nervousness of Donatello, emphasizing the climax of the group Peter-Judas-Christ-John by the explosive patterns of the marble behind them. In Ghirlandaio's work (below) the scene is more relaxed and the pretty background of trees and birds adds charm rather than tragic power. (20, 21)

Bodies under stress were the special concern of the brothers Piero and Antonio Pollaiuolo. Their *Martyrdom of St Sebastian* (right) with its sense of violent muscular exertion and its careful anatomy looks forward to Michelangelo. The pairs of figures show the same pose viewed from opposite sides. Antonio probably painted the archers; his brother Piero, a less talented artist, the saint. (22)

EGO DISPONO VOBIS SICVT DISPOSVIT MIHI PATER MEVS REGNVM, VT EDATIS ET BIBATIS SVPER MENSAM MEAM IN REGNO MEO

'He was sent by Heaven to invest architecture with new forms, after it had wandered astray for many centuries.' Vasari's estimate of Brunelleschi's achievement is a useful simplification, though it exaggerates the revolutionary quality of his work. In Italy, and especially in Tuscany, the Gothic style was never firmly established and there is really no break in the tradition that links Brunelleschi with such buildings as S. Miniato al Monte and the Baptistery. But the work that made him famous, the dome of Florence Cathedral (see p. 14), would not have taken the form it has without his study of Roman techniques.

The loggia of the Foundling Hospital (above), begun in 1419, is a more deliberate attempt at revival. In his two churches of S. Lorenzo (c. 1419 below left) and Sto Spirito (1434 left) Brunelleschi again uses a severely classical style in the details, but for plans and elevations combines the traditional Christian basilica with his own system of proportion, all units being related to a simple module. (23, 24, 25)

Alberti's approach to architecture was that of a theorist. We have already seen him as a Florentine man of letters (p.26) and as the designer of Sigismondo Malatesta's *Tempio* (pp. 58,9). He wrote a very influential book based on Vitruvius, taking as his thesis the idea that architecture has immutable rules discoverable from a study of classical models. He was the first to formulate the doctrine of the five orders and, in the Palazzo Rucellai (below) of 1446, the first to apply them to a palace façade. In the church of S. Andrea at Mantua (right) he went to the Roman temple front, the triumphal arch and the *thermae*, and used the basic rhythm of bay-arch-bay for both the façade and the internal elevations. (26, 27)

The most perfect expression of Brunelleschi's ideals is probably the Chapter House of Sta Croce, known as the Pazzi Chapel. The façade (left centre) is a harmonious composition of straight entablature and round arch. The interior (left) consists of a square covered by a dome, a square chancel of exactly half the main dimensions (right, in the picture) and lateral extensions, or 'transepts', whose depth is one quarter. All these proportions are articulated in dark lines of *pietra serena* and also outlined on the floor. (28, 29)

Limpid colour, clear geometrical design and statuesque calm characterize Domenico Veneziano's *St Lucy Altarpiece* (above), an early example of the *sacra conversazione*, i. e. Madonna and saints shown together instead of in the separate panels of a polyptych. The form was carried further by Domenico's pupil, Piero della Francesca, in the altarpiece painted for Federigo of Urbino (below), where the space is a continuation of the church in which it was to hang. (30, 32)

Piero's first and last surviving works are the *Baptism* (above) and *Nativity* (detail below) dating from about 1440 and 1480. Sienese influence is evident in the *Baptism*, but there is a monumental quality that was to be personal to Piero. He must have seen Hugo van der Goes' *Portinari Altarpiece* (p. 287-9), for his own *Nativity* bears witness to the impression it made. The Child lying on the ground, the singing angels, the oil technique—all point to Flemish models.(31,33)

'**The best picture in the world** is painted in fresco on the wall of a room in the town-hall . . . Its clear, yet subtly sober colours shine out with scarcely impaired freshness.' The judgment is Aldous Huxley's and the picture is Piero's *Resurrection* at Borgo Sansepolcro (detail right). Christ, dynamic yet immoveable, plants his foot on the edge of the tomb, more like a Greek athlete than a suffering redeemer. 'The whole figure', writes Huxley, 'is expressive of physical and intellectual power . . . Piero achieves grandeur naturally with every gesture he makes.' (35)

The Dream of Constantine (above) is one small section of Piero's most sustained masterpiece, the *Story of the True Cross* at Arezzo. In spite of the virtuosity shown in the rendering of light and the angel plunging down from above, Piero's most salient quality is one of stillness. The figures, motionless and silent, seem engaged eternally in a scene of timeless significance. (34)

Leonardo's genius fits into no category. He excelled in painting, in mechanical invention, in scientific research, in the study of anatomy —yet somehow the man is always greater than his works and one has the feeling that he was capable of yet more. Each of his paintings (barely fifteen survive, and even fewer are finished) marks a significant step in the history of art and all had a tremendous influence. The *Adoration of the Magi* (above) was abandoned unfinished in 1481. Leonardo crowds his picture with figures but without sacrificing clarity; note especially the pyramidal composition and the two still figures (Age and Youth) at the sides. The background is filled with architecture and horsemen. (36)

'I can make' sound, indestructible armoured vehicles. If these reach the enemy with their cannon they can compel the largest forces to retreat' —so Leonardo, writing to recommend his services to Ludovico Sforza of Milan. The drawings shown here (right) were made during his Milanese period: at the top, a terrifying chariot with whirling scythes; underneath, an early form of tank. (37)

'One of you shall betray me'. Leonardo in the *Last Supper* at Milan chooses the psychological moment when the disciples draw back in dismay at Christ's announcement. (Compare this with the static treatment of the same scene by Castagno and Ghirlandaio). Judas leans back on his elbow so that his face is in shadow. Christ spreads His hands in a gesture of resignation. The painting, now almost ruined, shows Leonardo's new *sfumato* technique, by which the forms are modelled 'without lines or borders, in the manner of smoke', instead of being clearly defined as in previous Florentine art. (38)

In his drawings and notebooks Leonardo reveals a range of interests that is probably unique. His mind, too, was constantly looking for parallels in nature—between the spirals of a flower (above left: a Star of Bethlehem) and those of flowing water, of a woman's hair or (below left) the waves of a cosmic deluge. Right: two careful drawings of the human skull. Leonardo's example was decisive; to observe reality and to make detailed drawings became the normal practice of every artist. (39–41)

The antique world crumbling before the victory of the martyrs is the theme of Andrea Mantegna's *St Sebastian* (left). Mantegna formed his style on Florentine techniques, Roman sculpture and the art of Donatello. One of his early frescoes at Padua is shown later, p. 131, in the context of the growth of archaeological interest. 'Andrea always maintained', says Vasari, 'that the good antique statues were more perfect and beautiful than anything in nature. He considered that statues displayed the muscles, veins and nerves in a more accentuated manner than is found in nature, where they are covered by soft flesh . . . He clung tenaciously to this opinion, a fact which renders his style somewhat harsh, more closely resembling stone than living flesh.' (42)

The art of foreshortening has never been carried to more daring lengths than by Mantegna. Unusual viewpoints preoccupied him from the very beginning of his career, at Padua. In 1460 he moved to Mantua, where his greatest works are the frescoes of the Gonzaga family in the *Camera degli Sposi* (see p. 60). On the ceiling of this room he painted a round oculus opening on to the sky, with faces, birds, cherubs and even a tub of plants seen vertically from below —some of them outside the balustrade and in danger of toppling into the room! It is a piece of virtuosity that anticipates Baroque. (43)

Real space and picture space are merged by Mantegna in the altarpiece painted for the church of San Zeno at Verona, 1456–59. The frame is made part of the picture—four Corinthian columns with entablature standing against a square loggia which encloses the figures; swags of fruit and flowers hang between one world and the other. By unifying the whole space within the picture Mantegna achieves another variant of the *sacra conversazione*. Note too the very Roman details of the architecture. The predella panels underneath show the Agony in the Garden, the Crucifixion and the Resurrection. (44)

To Venice in 1475 came Antonello da Messina, an artist whose life is still something of a mystery. Vasari thought, wrongly, that he had learnt his technique of oil-painting from Van Eyck himself; it was certainly highly advanced and made a deep impression on the Venetians. Above: the fragmentary remains of his altarpiece for S. Cassiano, Venice. (45)

In its minute naturalism Antonello's *St Jerome* (detail above) is hardly distinguishable from an early Flemish painting. It is in fact almost certainly based on a lost work of Van Eyck. (46)

The Agony in the Garden (right) ▶ by Mantegna has all his personal characteristics—harsh metallic rocks, foreshortened bodies, classical allusions. Compare this with the Bellini opposite, painted at roughly the same time. (48)

The long career of Giovanni Bellini sums up the story of Venetian painting in the 15th century. When he was born about 1430 the Renaissance had hardly touched Venice. His father Jacopo Bellini had probably visited Florence as the pupil of Gentile da Fabriano, worked in a naturalistic International Gothic style and took a special interest in classical Rome. Of his children, Giovanni and Gentile became painters and his daughter Nicolosia married Mantegna.

Giovanni Bellini, versatile, inventive and ceaselessly open to new ideas, was practically the originator of the Venetian school as we know it. His *Madonna and Saints* painted for San Zaccaria in 1505 (left) is the culmination of a series of experiments in the *sacra conversazione* form. As in the Piero and Antonello altarpieces (and in two earlier works by Bellini himself) the space is continuous with the spectator's world. The group is placed inside a marble apse, behind which one can glimpse the open country. In these last works Bellini was influenced by a man nearly fifty years his junior—Giorgione—who was destined to explore the world of colour and light with even more sensuous mastery. (47)

'Nature had so richly endowed him that he succeeded wonderfully in both oils and fresco', writes Vasari of Giorgione, 'making certain things so soft and harmonious and his shadows so vaporous that many artists said that he was born... to counterfeit the freshness of living flesh better than any painter either in Venice or elsewhere.' Right: the *Castelfranco Madonna*, Giorgione's earliest known work (c. 1505). The Virgin sits on a high throne with St Liberale and St Francis below. All are wrapped in a dreamy calm, at one with the peaceful landscape behind them. In this 'atmospheric' quality Giorgione is the true successor of Leonardo. (49)

Two solutions to the same formal problem: *The Agony in the Garden* by Mantegna and by Bellini. Both show Christ kneeling on a rock, the sleeping Apostles in the foreground, Judas approaching with a group of soldiers further back and the walled city of Jerusalem in the distance. The Mantegna (far left) has perhaps a greater sense of urgency, with its striated rocks and sharp-edged drapery patterns. But Bellini (left) creates a drama of atmosphere—a landscape bathed in a softer light and Christ's head silhouetted against the sunrise. (50)

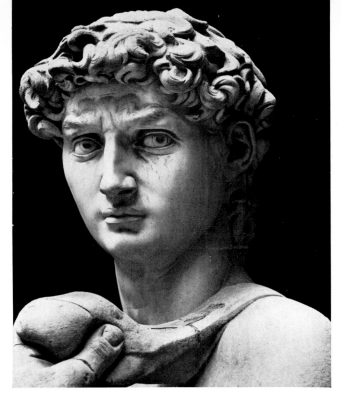

Pity and terror, for Aristotle the two components of tragedy, are more fully realized in Michelangelo than in any other artist in history. His genius was on the grand scale—unmistakable and unique. Yet he was the product of the Florentine tradition and is hardly to be understood outside it. *David* (detail right), completed in 1504, sums up the ideals of painters and sculptors from Masaccio and Donatello to Castagno and Pollaiuolo. The proud, fierce youth, confident of victory, became a symbol of Florence. In the *Pietà* (below) Michelangelo relates the figures of mother and son in a pose of great formal ingenuity, while at the same time revealing a tenderness that hardly appears in his later works. (51, 52)

Michelangelo's greatest patrons were the popes. For Leo X and Clement VII, both Medici, he carved the tombs of two minor members of the family—Giuliano, Duke of Nemours, and Lorenzo, Duke of Urbino, respectively brother and nephew of Leo X. This detail shows Lorenzo, symbol of the contemplative life, with allegorical figures of Dawn and Dusk reclining below. (53)

'**Unequalled** by any modern or ancient work' is Vasari's verdict on *Moses* (right). It was intended as one of over forty statues for the tomb of Julius II, an enormous project commissioned by the pope during his own lifetime. *Moses* is Michelangelo's image of the Old Dispensation—pitiless, omnipotent and terrible. (54)

The fate of two forerunners of the High Renaissance, Signorelli and Perugino, is an illuminating comment on the speed at which art was moving. Signorelli (above, the *Last Judgment* at Orvieto) was soon outmatched by Michelangelo in ferocity; Perugino (below, the *Charge to Peter*) by Raphael in elegance. (55, 56)

On the Sistine Chapel (right) three ambitious popes lavished their energies and patronage. Sixtus IV built it (1475) and commissioned the frescoes along the sides. Julius II commanded Michelangelo to paint the ceiling (1508–12), and for Paul III he returned to paint the *Last Judgment* in 1536–41. (58)

Fold out ▶

EZECHIEL

'Do as you please', Pope Julius told Michelangelo. It was unusual for a painter to be given such responsibility, especially when it concerned the most important commission in Christendom. But Michelangelo was accepted as no one's subordinate, and he did do as he pleased. 'Unless you have seen the Sistine Chapel', wrote Goethe, 'you can have no idea of what one man is capable of achieving.'

The section shown here is about a third of the whole ceiling, which is divided into compartments by means of painted pilasters and entablature. The Genesis series starts over the altar with *God Creating* and ends with the *Drunkenness of Noah*. Seen here are the *Creation of Adam* (far right), the *Creation of Eve*, the *Temptation and Expulsion*, the *Sacrifice of Noah* and the *Flood*. They were painted, however, in the reverse order, and Michelangelo increased the size of the figures as he went along, realizing better the effect of the vault's height. The ceiling was finished in four years (1508–12).

The *Flood* and *Sacrifice of Noah* are the least satisfactory—full of powerful and moving figures but crowded and not tightly integrated. With the *Temptation and Expulsion* he achieves his own heroic scale and superbly confident draughtmanship. The story is reduced to its essentials and expressed, as always with Michelangelo, entirely in terms of the gestures and attitudes of the human body. Next comes the *Creation of Eve* and then the *Creation of Adam*, one of the great masterpieces of the Renaissance: God, borne aloft by cherubim, touches the limp hand of the newly created Adam, and Adam, lying like a youthful river god, awakens into life.

At the sides are the huge figures of the *Prophets* and *Sybils*—a combination of Old Testament and pagan mythology that is typically humanist. The Sibyls were regarded as prophets of Christ, though not understood in their times. Michelangelo portrays them as superhuman beings, inspired by divine wisdom and strength. Those shown here are the Erythraean Sybil and Ezekiel (bottom) and Isaiah and the Cumaean Sybil (top). The *Ignudi*—naked youths at the corners of the smaller scenes—are at first puzzling in this context. But there is no doubt that for Michelangelo they represented perfect humanity, the highest ideal of beauty and the truest witness to God, as he says in one of his sonnets:

Nor hath God deigned to show himself elsewhere
More clearly than in human form sublime
Which, since they image Him, alone I love.

(57)

A radical break in the progress of Renaissance art can be detected in many of the important works of 1510–20. Raphael, always susceptible to outside influence, begins to emulate the *terribilità* of the Sistine Ceiling. Compare his earlier frescoes in the *Stanza della Segnatura* (p.150,154) with the later designs for tapestries to hang round the lower part of the Sistine Chapel, the so–called Cartoons which, taken to Brussels, had a strong influence on northern painting (below: *The Healing of the Lame Man*). Where the first is ordered, balanced and lucid the second is emotional and congested; where one shows only the noble and the beautiful, the other insists on pain. The same qualities appear again in Raphael's last painting left unfinished at his death, the *Transfiguration* (left). Here the nominal subject is placed at the back and the foreground is taken up by a disturbed and passionate scene whose significance is not immediately clear. The boy is in fact being cured of possession by demons; he screams aloud, the mother appeals for help, the Disciples gesticulate wildly. (59, 61)

Strident colours, distorted bodies, violence of composition and subject matter lead to the creation of a new style in the second quarter of the 16th century, a style which contradicts the old rules and introduces bizarre new effects to shock and surprise. Similar developments occur in architecture and sculpture, and are summarized in the useful but slightly oversimple term Mannerism. Left: one of its formative works, Pontormo's *Deposition*, painted about 1525, five years after Raphael's death. Gestures are exaggerated, figures elongated and intertwined in an unnatural way, and the general feeling, compared with the sanity and optimism of the Quattrocento, distinctly neurotic. History soon seemed to endorse the instinct of art. In 1527 came the Sack of Rome, a horrifying experience for artists and patrons alike, followed by the growing rigour of the Counter-Reformation. Of this new age Michelangelo's *Last Judgment* (previous page) was the grimmest symbol and a compulsive influence on painters of the next generation and beyond. (60)

Leadership in architecture after the death of Brunelleschi passed from Florence to Milan and then, decisively, to Rome. Bramante came to Rome in 1499, to be joined there in 1508 by his distant cousin, Raphael, whose interest in building was already evident in the circular temple of his *Sposalizio* (right) of 1504. The centrally planned church, symmetrical in all four directions, was a project dear to the humanists (Alberti held that the circle was the most fitting symbol of the divine), but was criticized because it gave no emphasis to the altar and was liturgically inconvenient. (63)

Raphael's own house in Rome, long since demolished, was designed by Bramante (above). It was impeccably Roman in its details, combining rusticated stone blocks on the ground floor with the classical orders above. (62)

The façades of palaces present a fascinating evolution. Sanmichele, in the Palazzo Bevilacqua, Verona (left), introduced rusticated pilasters, alternate wide and narrow bays and spiral fluting. Peruzzi (right: Palazzo Massimo, Rome) reversed the normal arrangement and gave the whole façade a curve. Palladio (right centre: Palazzo Porto, Vicenza) basically went back to the House of Raphael. Giulio Romano (extreme right: his own house at Mantua) almost abandoned the classical vocabulary, squeezing his windows into rusticated arches and pushing up the stringcourse over the door into a sort of mock-pediment. (64, 67, 68, 69)

Rome was a revelation to Bramante, although he was a middle-aged man when he arrived. Vasari tells us that he spent days exploring the ruins and it is clear from the change in his style that the size and grandeur of the ancient city impressed him deeply. His major task was the rebuilding of St Peter's, later transformed by Michelangelo. But a more perfect achievement is perhaps the *Tempietto* (right) of S. Pietro in Montorio, where Renaissance ideals and classical prototypes (in this case small circular temples like that of Vesta at Tivoli) meet in effortles harmony. (66)

Leonardo's teeming brain was probably the ultimate source of Bramante's new St Peter's. The two men knew each other in Milan and some of Leonardo's unrealized sketches (above) are uncannily prophetic. (65)

Italian Art
from Masaccio to Mannerism

PETER MURRAY

Vitruvius, the only surviving Roman writer on architecture, was read by Renaissance theorists with more respect than understanding. In 1511 the Veronese architect Fra Giocondo published the first illustrated edition. This is his idea of caryatids, based on Vitruvius' description. (1)

IN MANY FIELDS of historical enquiry there is nowadays a tendency to query whether the Renaissance, in the sense of a phenomenon distinguishable from the periods before and after it, ever actually took place. One of the strongest arguments in its favour is supplied by the history of the visual arts, since, unlike literature, there is a recognizable style of the 15th and early 16th centuries which cannot be confused with earlier or later periods and which is, basically, a realistic and classical style. This point can be established by direct comparison between contemporary works of art representing the same subjects.

The development of a specifically Renaissance style in painting, sculpture, and architecture began in Florence in a very short space of time—not more than about twenty years—and by 1430 the new style was established in Tuscany and already beginning to spread to other parts of central Italy. In the north, in such places as Padua, the presence of Florentine artists helped to spread the new ideas. By about 1460 it is possible to argue that the best work was being done outside Florence; the frescoes of Piero della Francesca or Mantegna, and Alberti's churches in Mantua are cases in point. Towards the end of the century the centre of gravity shifted back towards Florence again, although it must be admitted that Botticelli's work, important as it was, struck an old-fashioned note. The more progressive style was represented by Leonardo da Vinci, who worked for nearly twenty years in Milan (c. 1482–99), or by Perugino, an Umbrian, in some of his Florentine works.

From the early 1480s, when the Sistine Chapel was decorated by a number of artists, mostly Florentine, Rome resumed her rightful part as a centre of patronage; and it is perhaps the most important single fact in the creation of the High Renaissance style that it was the work of four men, none of them Roman, who came together in Rome in the years around 1500. These four were Pope Julius II, who came from Piedmont; Bramante, who came to

---

In the security of Venice High Renaissance confidence lingered longest. Titian preserves the noble ideals of Raphael, with a warmth of colour and richness of texture that were a legacy from Bellini and Giorgione. Titian was only slightly younger than Giorgione but outlived him by over sixty years. He was outstandingly successful, combining grandeur with sensuous lyricism in a way that was to influence painters as distant as Rubens and Renoir. In 1532 he met the Emperor Charles V and became his personal friend (a detail of his portrait is shown on p. 323). Titian worked slowly, leaving his pictures unfinished for months at a time and coming back to them again and again. The *Entombment* (above left) dates from his early period, when he was still under the influence of Giorgione.

Tintoretto, by contrast, was in many ways a Mannerist painter. In his version of the *Entombment* (below left) the whole group is turned at an angle to the picture plane, the darkness is more intense, the gestures more passionate. During the latter part of the 16th century Tintoretto was the leader of the Venetian School, painting enormous canvases for the Doge's Palace and the Scuola di S. Rocco, as well as numerous private portraits. He died in 1594 and Venetian painting dwindled into insignificance for over a hundred years. (70, 71)

Rome from his native Urbino by way of Milan; Raphael, also an Urbinate, but who received his most important education in Florence; and Michelangelo, a pure Florentine. Their great Florentine peer, Leonardo, spent some time in Rome in the early years of the 16th century, but he was of an older generation and his major contributions had been made much earlier in Florence and Milan.

There can be no doubt that the personality of Julius II was largely responsible for the creation of a climate of patronage which gave rise to the rebuilding of St Peter's, the enlargement of the Vatican Palace, the decoration of the *Stanze*, and the ceiling of the Sistine Chapel, as well as the gigantic project for the sculptural decoration of Julius' own tomb. All these were conceived in less than a decade, and although some were never completed in their original form, nevertheless their existence made Rome the undisputed centre of all the arts. This overwhelming concentration in one place and in one short span of time is a partial explanation of the fact that the High Renaissance lasted hardly more than twenty years, while the reaction against it dragged on for seventy or more before there was any sign of a new style establishing itself as an undisputed language.

p 47 (6)

p 46-7
(4, 5, 8)

This sudden change of style in the years around 1520 was to some extent determined by political and economic events, but it would be quite wrong to attribute everything to the Sack of Rome in 1527. The effect of the Sack was indeed devastating, but it did not do more than encourage artistic tendencies which already existed. In the same way, the effect of the Reformation movement in Germany was very slow in making itself felt, particularly in the arts, and it is not until the final sessions of the Council of Trent, in the 1560s, that we find a new formulation of the ideals of religious art which had been put into practice in some cases as much as forty years earlier. The artistic revolution is, therefore, only partly dependent upon non-artistic causes, but it would be as wrong to interpret the art of the Mannerist period solely in artistic terms as it is to interpret it in terms of Marxist economics.

The idea of an intermediate style between the High Renaissance and the Baroque is comparatively new, and Mannerism, as this interlude is called, is dangerously open to an interpretation based upon a partial selection of works produced in the period between 1520 and 1600. The paintings of Parmigianino, the architecture of Giulio Romano, and the last *Pietàs* by Michelangelo certainly have stylistic features in common, but the tendency to lump them all together as examples of 'Mannerism' leads either to an insensitive interpretation of the works themselves, or to a stretching of the definition of Mannerism to a point where it becomes almost meaningless. This blanket definition was, of course, the reason why the original concept of a single, homogeneous, Renaissance style beginning with Giotto and ending more than two and a half centuries later with the death of Michelangelo, collapsed under its own inability to serve as a sufficiently precise definition of the stylistic characteristics of any one work of art. At the present moment, Mannerism, which has taken over the 16th-century part of the earlier all-embracing concept, seems to be in some danger of a similar inflation and it is probably as important now to stress the differences between works produced in the mid-16th century as it once was to stress their similarities by comparison with works of the preceding century.

'Restored to Life'

What do we mean by Renaissance style? In some fields of history there are writers who think that the continuity of the web of history is such that we ought not to speak of 'the Middle Ages' or 'the Renaissance', and of course they are right if they mean that the world did not change much between 1399 and 1400 or any other such arbitrary dates. For the art historian the problem is simpler. We have the evidence of the works of art themselves, as well as the writings of contemporaries, and their answer is unequivocal. Alberti and Ghiberti, both practising artists, reject the works of their predecessors in an attempt to create a new style; Marsilio Ficino, writing in 1492, says: 'This century, like a Golden Age, has restored to life the nearly extinct Liberal Arts—Grammar, Poetry, Rhetoric, Painting, Sculpture, Architecture, Music...' and the story is taken up by Vasari in the mid-16th century.

It is clear that the new ideas were aesthetic in impulse, so that the situation is the opposite of that which obtained in the later Roman Empire, when Early Christian ideas were expressed in the forms of pagan late antique art: now there are new formal solutions to old iconographical problems. Aesthetic theory is rigidly classical and naturalistic, as in the treatises of Alberti, and theory itself assumes a new importance, as may be seen from the proliferation of treatises and the regrets expressed for the loss (or presumed loss) of so many of those written in ancient times. 'Thus it was', says Ghiberti, 'that Christianity gained the upper hand in the time of the Emperor Constantine and Pope Sylvester. Idolatry was so persecuted that statues and paintings, however ancient and perfect, were broken and disfigured and, at the same time, all the volumes and commentaries which contained rules and instructions for these noble arts were also consumed...' (Second *Commentary*, c. 1450). We have no reason to suppose that this was true, but Ghiberti took it for granted that such treatises must have existed once. Alberti, in *De re aedificatoria*, first drafted at about the same time, expresses similar ideas: 'It grieved me that so many great and noble instructions of ancient authors should be lost by the injury of Time, so that scarce any but Vitruvius has escaped this general wreck... He might also as well not have written at all... since we cannot understand him.'

Alberti's earlier *Della Pittura* (1435) is dedicated to Brunelleschi, Donatello, Ghiberti, Luca della Robbia and Masaccio; and he goes on to say: 'Our fame ought to be much greater if we discover new and unheard-of arts and sciences without teachers or models.' We are justified, then, in examining the works of these men for stylistic innovation: if we find common characteristics which are not shared by some of their contemporaries, then these must be the fundamentally new, Renaissance, characteristics. At the same time, we shall be warned not to read characteristics into Renaissance art which cannot be found implicit in the works themselves or explicitly stated in the theoretical treatises. We know, for example, from the theorists that the imitation of natural objects, and above all the illusion of relief, were regarded as self-evidently the main task of the painter, in the sense that all his technique was acquired for that end. To some extent this insistence on a literal naturalism was in itself a mark of the new art, since the workshop system which had obtained for centuries tended to produce painters who had mastered a series of formulae meant to produce visual images reasonably similar to those produced by their masters before them, and these technical tricks were not necessarily intended to give the illusion of nature. This can be seen by comparing the treatises on painting by Cennino Cennini and Alberti, both written at about the same time. (The date of Cennini is controversial, but it may be as late as the 1430s. The usual dating is 1390–1400.) Cennino gives an amusing series of recipes for painting landscapes—'If you want to acquire a good style for mountains, get some large stones, rugged, and not

cleaned up; and copy them from nature, applying the lights and the dark as your system requires'; while Alberti gives a complicated description of a method involving the use of a net. This allows the painter to construct a perspective system, so that the whole of his picture will appear to obey the laws of optics in the same way as actual objects in three-dimensional space.

The changes in artistic style in Florence can be dated with considerable precision in the middle 1420s, and the simplest way to do this is to compare three or four pictures painted at this time. To begin with, take the two versions of the *Adoration of the Magi*, produced in the first half of the 1420s by Lorenzo Monaco and Gentile da Fabriano. The Gentile is dated 1423 and it is likely that the picture by Lorenzo Monaco is a year or two later. Similarly, it is possible to compare three versions of the *Madonna and Child*; by Masolino, painted in 1423, by Gentile da Fabriano, painted in 1425, and by Masaccio, painted in 1426. Lorenzo was the oldest of this group of artists and the group of the Madonna and Child in the *Adoration* clearly shows his direct descent from the masters of the 14th century. This style is continued by Masolino in his *Madonna*, which may be taken as typical of the late 14th century in central Italy and typical of the style which prevailed in Florence until the eruption of the new ideas introduced first by Gentile da Fabriano (c. 1370–1427) and then, immediately afterwards, by Masaccio (1401–c. 1428). The International Gothic style, which took its rise in Burgundy rather than in Italy itself, created an immense impression in Florence when it arrived in the 1420s and triumphed in Gentile's *Adoration of the Magi*, painted for the wealthy Palla Strozzi in 1423.

This picture contains a vast amount of naturalistic detail in the animals and birds, in the costumes, and even in the facial expressions of some of the figures in the background. Nevertheless, the setting of the picture as a whole is highly artificial, with the stable of the Nativity represented as a sort of cardboard cave behind which there is a dark hedge effectively separating the narrow foreground stage from the far distance, where the cavalcade of the Magi can be seen approaching. The rather limited naturalism of the details and particularly the richness of the stuffs and the profusion of gold made an immediate impression, and Lorenzo Monaco's *Adoration* clearly reflects the excitement caused by Gentile's altarpiece. In fact, a closer examination of the individual figures in Lorenzo's picture shows that they have the elongated forms and the carefully contrived silhouettes which are characteristic of Trecento art, with figures in pale colours set against a plain gold background. Indeed, Lorenzo himself painted precisely this traditional kind of altarpiece on many occasions, examples being the two versions of the *Coronation of the Virgin* (one, of 1414, in the Uffizi, the other, of about the same date, in the National Gallery, London). This is the style which Masolino continued in his *Madonna* of 1423 in Bremen, but Gentile's *Madonna* of 1425 in the Royal Collection, and Masaccio's of 1426 in the National Gallery show two different styles, both new. The Gentile *Madonna* is a single panel from a larger altarpiece, now dismembered, consisting of several panels with figures of saints seen as separate entities. The Madonna and Child, however, are treated with the new realism of detail characteristic of the 1423 *Adoration*, so that the picture forms a strange mixture of naturalism—the smiling Child, with the teeth carefully shown—and the older, more symbolic, representation of the Madonna seated against a cloth of honour supported by half a dozen small angels, whose position in space is extremely uncertain.

It is here that the crucial difference between Gentile's International Gothic style and Masaccio's new realism is most clear, for the National Gallery *Madonna* is also part of a dismembered polyptych, with figures of saints in the other panels, but the realism of the Madonna and Child is different in kind, not degree, from that of Gentile's picture. In the Masaccio the spatial divisions are clearly established by an imposing stone throne and stone steps, so that the two angels seated in the foreground seem closer to the spectator than any of the other figures (the panel has been cut down and they have lost their feet, so the impression is less powerful than it must originally have been). On the next plane there is the throne, which is rendered in careful perspective so that it serves as a frame for the massive figures of Madonna and

p 78, 7
(4, 7)

p 78
(2, 3)
p 79 (5

0   75 F

0   25 M

Brunelleschi's unfinished church of Sta Maria degli Angeli in Florence was his most ambitious exercise in pure classical revival. Based directly on the Temple of Minerva Medica in Rome, it is the earliest centrally-planned church of the Renaissance. The elevation is one of several reconstructions. (2, 3)

Child. Behind the throne are two more attendant angels. The lighting of Masaccio's painting is also consistent; all the shadows are cast in such a way that the source of light must be at the upper left, whereas Gentile employs a generalized, diffused lighting. In short, Masaccio's aim is the re-creation of a three-dimensional world on a two-dimensional plane by means of the mathematical artifice of perspective—then being scientifically investigated by Brunelleschi—as well as by the use of controlled lighting and strongly modelled, realistic forms; whereas Gentile's style is conditioned by a desire to please, with enchanting naturalistic details grafted on to what is still fundamentally a non-naturalistic Trecento theme. As a rough generalization one might say that Masaccio sought truth, Gentile beauty.

p 82–83 (12–19) Precisely the same comparisons can be made between the sculpture of Ghiberti and that of Donatello, or even within the work of Ghiberti himself. Ghiberti's *St John Baptist* of 1414 represents a standing, bearded figure, with his right arm hanging at his side and his left bent, holding up the end of his robe. The same description is true of the *St Mark* carved by Donatello for the same church, Orsanmichele in Florence, two years earlier, but they differ markedly in the impression they make on the spectator. Donatello's figure is grave and massive, like a Masaccio apostle, because the weight of the body is carried on the right leg, which, with its drapery, looks like a fluted column; the huge left hand takes the weight of the book, and the tilt of the shoulders is expressed by the line of drapery crossing the chest. Ghiberti's figure is clad in beautifully arranged drapery—but the sweeping curves, and the placing of the weight on the left leg, combine to give an impression almost of fragility. Yet Ghiberti learned much from Donatello, not least the use of perspective combined with relief to give an overall pictorial quality to his panels for the Second

Baptistery Doors. Ghiberti's first great success came with the p 82 (15, 16) commission for the First Doors (1403–24). The *Annunciation* is a typical panel from these doors, while the *Story of Joseph* is equally typical of the panels from his Second Doors (1425–52). Here the difference in style is a development within the work of a single artist, so it is not surprising that the figures should have a family likeness: what is revolutionary here is the abandonment of the flat, neutral, background plane contained within an elaborate quatrefoil moulding, with figures in even half-relief set against patently unconvincing architecture. In the *Story of Joseph*, as in Masaccio's paintings and Donatello's reliefs, the stage is a single unified space, governed by perspective, with all the figures subject to the same optical laws. From Donatello Ghiberti has learned that gradations in relief give an additional feeling of recession, so that the foreground figures are not only taller but are also nearly free-standing. In his autobiography Ghiberti describes these Doors:

> I received the commission to make the other Door . . . and I was allowed to make it in any manner that seemed good to me, so that it should turn out perfect, rich, and ornate. I began the work in framed panels . . . with histories, containing many figures from the Old Testament, and in them I strove to observe every measure of proportion, seeking the closest possible imitation of nature . . . There were ten of these histories, each arranged in frames so that the eye could measure them, and, from a distance, they seemed truly in relief. The relief I employed was very low and against the backgrounds the figures seemed to be near if they were large, and smaller if they were at a distance, just as they would in reality. The whole work is founded on this principle.

In architecture obviously the naturalistic elements count for very little, but the new approach to formal problems made by Brunelleschi in the 1420s, as well as the deliberate attempt by Alberti, some years later, to revive classical forms, are both indicative of a profound change in the stylistic aims of architects, parallel to those of their contemporaries who were painters or sculptors.

Pioneers of the New Architecture

The new architectural ideas are clearly documented in the *Life of Brunelleschi* by Vasari, which is based on a much earlier *Life* by an anonymous writer of the late 15th century. These 15th- and 16th-century sources are definite about the innovations made by Brunelleschi. They say that he abandoned the prevailing style and rediscovered proportion and measurement, as well as the classical Orders, so that in their eyes he was the reviver of Roman architecture. These statements are undoubtedly exaggerated, and the amount of the exaggeration can be demonstrated by comparing Brunelleschi's Foundling Hospital, begun in 1419, with any sur- p 86 (24) viving Roman building. Comparison will show that the similarities are about equally balanced by dissimilarities, so that we are forced to conclude that Brunelleschi's ideas on architectural style certainly did not include a slavish emulation of ancient prototypes. Nevertheless, by comparing these early critical estimates of his work with the buildings themselves we can see that Brunelleschi had made a close study of Roman architecture. He had also learned a great deal about structural methods, and particularly the technique of building domes employed by Roman architects, which had gradually fallen out of use. Apart from these technical matters, he had learned something far more important, though perhaps more easily misinterpreted: this was the idea that proportion is the essence of architectural design, and proportion in turn is based upon simple mathematical elements. This is why his earliest biographers claim that he provided a norm of modern classical architecture. The unfinished Sta Maria degli Angeli thus became f 2, 3 the type of a centrally-planned church, while Sto Spirito, one of p 86 (23) his last and greatest works, became the model of a basilican type of parish church.

Outside Florence the course of Renaissance architecture was somewhat different. The principal figures were Leone Battista Alberti and the architect of the palace at Urbino. Alberti was an important architect, but he was probably still more important as a theorist and as a propagandist for the antique style. The palace at Urbino is almost certainly the work of Luciano di Laurana, whose career is otherwise somewhat obscure. Nevertheless, the palace is a major work in a style derived partly from Florence and partly from Rome, but which, in its fusion of various elements, attains to a classical harmony achieved even by Brunelleschi and Alberti only on rare occasions.

Alberti was born about 1404 and received a complete humanist education, so that when his family was allowed to return from exile to Florence and he met Brunelleschi and other leading artists of the day, he was well fitted to act as theorist and propagandist for their ideas. He was a fluent writer, both in Latin and in the vernacular, on most of the subjects which interested the humanists of his day; but his importance in the history of art rests on his three treatises on architecture, painting, and sculpture. By far the largest and most important of these was the treatise on architecture, *De re aedificatoria*, deliberately modelled on Vitruvius and, to a certain extent, intended both as a clarification and a continuation of the ideas set out by the only surviving writer on building to have come down from classical antiquity. Alberti earned his living in the Roman Curia, and quite early in his career he wrote a book on the monuments of Rome, the *Descriptio urbis Romae* of about 1432–34, which is very similar to the contemporary topographical treatises by Flavio Biondo and Poggio. All are based on the idea of the continuity of Roman civilization, though coupled with the idea of decay and rebirth. To some extent these treatises can be regarded as formal literary exercises, but they also prepared the ground for Alberti's much larger treatise on architecture. It seemed quite clear to him that the true form of a modern, classical architecture could be derived from a study of the ruins of ancient Rome checked against the theoretical principles laid down by Vitruvius; while at the same time the ruins and Vitruvius *f 1* could provide between them the basis of a system of mathematical proportions which would ensure the harmonious balance of the parts of a building. We know that Alberti made an intensive study of the ruins quite early in his career, and the most important thing about the *Descriptio* is his account of a surveying instrument, which, he claimed, made it possible to obtain accurate measurements of the ruins. The principal difference between Alberti's treatise and Vitruvius lies in the pragmatic approach to the antiquities and in the insistence on an underlying mathematical harmony. We know from a letter written to his assistant at Rimini in 1454 that Alberti attached the greatest importance to this—'if you alter anything you will spoil all that harmony'.

The treatise was certainly begun before 1450, and parts of it seem to have been known in the middle years of the century, although the final version was probably completed only shortly before he died in 1472. The first printed edition came out in 1485, so his ideas can have had only a limited circulation in the third quarter of the 15th century. Nevertheless, they seem to have been known in Florence, where he had many friends, and certainly in

Rome and Urbino. The Duke of Urbino, Federigo da Montefeltro, was the patron and friend of both Alberti and Piero della Francesca, and his palace, begun in a Florentine style about 1450, seems to have been transformed in the 1460s and 1470s into a building which followed Alberti's precepts and which resembles Piero's paintings to such an extent that attempts have been made to credit Piero with its authorship. In fact, we know from a brief of 1468 that Luciano di Laurana was the architect-in-charge and that Federigo had the fullest confidence in his abilities, so that the style of the building—unique in Italy—is almost certainly the work of Laurana under the joint influences of Alberti, Piero, and the duke himself. *p 54, 5 (28, 30 32)*

The principal innovations are in the main façade and, above all, in the extraordinarily beautiful court, which owes much to Brunelleschi's loggia at the Foundling Hospital. The loggia, of course, has no corners, but the court at Urbino neatly avoids the unfortunate visual effect which results from simply abutting two arcades, and this it does by the use of an L-shaped pier with attached half-columns. This was almost certainly Albertian in inspiration, and can be found in Rome, both in ancient buildings and, more appositely, in the court of the Palazzo Venezia. The *piano nobile* at Urbino has pilasters above the columns of the arcade, and the delicate adjustment of spaces between the columns in relation to the window openings, marks the designer as a man of the greatest sensibility. In a variation on the same theme the façade has rectangular window openings above rectangular doorways, but they are now arranged with four windows above three doors.

Like Brunelleschi, Alberti provided models for both the Greek and Latin cross forms of church, and his S. Sebastiano and Sant' Andrea, both in Mantua, were widely imitated in the 15th and 16th centuries. In Florence, his design for the Rucellai Palace provided a model for the disposition of the Orders on a palace façade which was partially followed at Urbino and more closely by the unknown architect of the Cancelleria at Rome. The remainder of the century saw the production of many fine buildings—for example, Giuliano da Sangallo's church in Prato, and several palaces in Florence—but the next great contribution to architectural design seems to have come from Leonardo da Vinci in the 1480s and '90s, when he was in Milan. *p 87 (26, 27 f 4, 5*

Masaccio's Legacy

Most of the great innovators of the early 15th century were personal friends, and, as we have seen, the preface to Alberti's *Della Pittura* (c. 1435) mentions Brunelleschi, Donatello—'our very dear friend'—Ghiberti, Luca della Robbia, and Masaccio as especially praiseworthy. The classically-based, severe style practised by Masaccio and Donatello, as well as by Brunelleschi, is therefore by far the most important stylistic phenomenon of the early 15th century; but it was a heroic style lacking in obvious attraction, whereas the International Gothic of Gentile da Fabriano, Pisa-

Alberti's S. Sebastiano at Mantua was the second important experiment in central planning. It embodied many of the principles laid down in his treatise on architecture—the flight of steps, the entrance portice, the symmetrical plan; but it was not completed according to his original designs. This reconstruction of the façade as it was probably intended is by Rudolf Wittkower. (4, 5)

nello, Masolino or Ghiberti, was more easily comprehensible and had a quality of delight which appealed to many more contemporaries than the harsher style of the real innovators. For this reason the first impetus of the heroic style died out in the 1430s, and some at least of the stylistic changes of the thirties and forties are due to the fact that Masaccio himself, having established the new style in painting with the Pisa altarpiece and the Brancacci Chapel frescoes, died in Rome when he was only twenty-seven. In effect, this left the painters without a leader and the figurative arts looked, therefore, to Donatello; but Donatello's own work, based on surviving examples of Roman portrait busts and Early Christian sarcophagi, developed more and more in the direction of a dramatic expressiveness which was admirably adapted to the rendering of miraculous themes, or themes of great pathos such as the Lamentation over the Dead Christ. Donatello soon discovered that expressiveness could best be obtained by the use of sharply silhouetted linear forms, often in very low relief, as well as by dramatic gestures and distorted facial expressions. The difference becomes evident in a comparison of Masaccio's apostles in the *Tribute Money* with those by Donatello on the Sacristy doors at S. Lorenzo; while his wooden statue of the Magdalen, of the 1450s, shows how far his style moved away from the calmer classicism of the 1420s. In architecture, Brunelleschi developed a much heavier, more Roman, style in his later works, probably as a result of a journey to Rome with Donatello in 1433/4; so that towards the middle of the century the deliberate imitation of Roman antiquities assumed a more important rôle than it had played in the classical and generalized style of the 1420s.

Almost the only painter to imitate Masaccio at all closely was Fra Filippo Lippi, who was very probably Masaccio's only pupil, and whose earliest works (of about 1432) are very close indeed to Masaccio's frescoes in the Carmelite convent where Fra Filippo lived. Nevertheless, Fra Filippo's style developed consistently away from Masaccio during the 1440s, towards something more lyrical and sweet, in an attempt to combine the naturalism of Masaccio with the sheer beauty and craftsmanship of the older style, in which gold and colours had been used for their own sake rather than to create an illusion of depth. Something similar occurred in the development of Fra Angelico, although he started from a much more conservative position and progressed steadily towards a more naturalistic style, showing that he had learned much from the example of Masaccio. In this he closely resembles Masolino, who, though much older than Masaccio, came under his spell for a few years while they were actually working together in the Brancacci Chapel. After his death Masolino reverted to the more decorative style he had practised earlier. In a similar way, Ghiberti can be compared with Donatello at Orsanmichele, where both men made standing figures of saints; the pictorial relief also, exploiting both linear perspective and varying depths of relief to give a three-dimensional stage-like effect, is something that had been invented by Donatello and taken over by Ghiberti. Uccello, who was a man of Masolino's generation, was away from Florence in the years when Masaccio was active. On his return he seems to have been so fascinated by the decorative possibilities of perspective, as set out in Alberti's treatise on painting and deduced from the practice of Brunelleschi and Masaccio, that he entirely overlooked the function of the mathematical system as a means of creating an illusion of reality. His famous *Battle Scenes*, painted for the Medici (and now divided between the Uffizi, London and Paris), show how his setting is no more realistic than Gentile da Fabriano's, in spite of the virtuoso foreshortening of the corpses and the splintered lances.

One of the most important painters of the next generation, Andrea del Castagno, who was probably born in the early 1420s, took as his starting point the linear style of Donatello rather than the paintings of Masaccio. In his work of the 1450s (he died young, in 1457) we can see how Donatello's use of expressive contour appealed to Castagno far more than the solidly built-up forms of Masaccio, largely because it permitted him to exploit dramatic gestures, and also because he was famous among his contemporaries for his skill in foreshortening. Castagno's use of contour rather than modelling was to become characteristic of Florentine painting for generations and so was his interest in

'Oh what a sweet thing perspective is', Uccello is supposed to have said when his wife was nagging him to come to bed. This analysis of a chalice is one of his many elaborate studies in foreshortening; in many of Uccello's paintings the objects are so obviously forced to conform to artificial schemes of perspective that the general effect is anything but natural. (6)

anatomy and perspective, the scientific pursuits which were taken up and developed by the Pollaiuoli and Leonardo da Vinci, to culminate in the most Florentine of all artists, Michelangelo. The second half of the 15th century in Florence saw, therefore, a consolidation of the conquest of line and of the exploitation of depth by means of perspective; but this way of looking at the world differs very sharply from that invented by Masaccio, and, in any case, the artists themselves ranged from the extreme naturalism, sometimes harsh and rebarbative, of a Castagno or a Pollaiuolo, to the lyricism of a Botticelli, whose aims can hardly be said to be realistic at all. The interest in naturalistic detail, which stemmed from Gentile da Fabriano rather than from Masaccio, persisted, not surprisingly, in the works of painters like Ghirlandaio, who, in the 1480s and '90s, produced admirable portraits and set-pieces masquerading as religious works. In fact, Ghirlandaio's frescoes in the Florentine churches can tell us an immense amount about the everyday life of well-to-do Florentines, although artistically they are little more than repetitions of the original ideas advanced by Masaccio more than sixty years earlier. So non-religious are they in their concentration on the status of the donors that they may well have been the target of Savonarola's denunciations of frivolous and irreligious art. In any case, Ghirlandaio's fundamentally prosaic mind was not capable of appreciating the gravity and stillness of Masaccio's figures, although he shows on occasion an interest in problems of movement and also in the adaptation of figures derived from antique sculpture, a subject which fascinated his contemporaries.

p 80–81
(10)
83 (17)
82 (14)

81 (11)

p 79 (6)

p 80–81
(8)
f 6

p 124
(12, 13)

p 16 (10)
p 17
(11, 13)
p 21 (22)
p 27 (50)

f 7   Botticelli, in his search for perfection of linear harmony, was
p 77 (1)   prepared to abandon naturalism altogether and his works of the
p 25 (36)   seventies and eighties, such as the *Allegory of Spring (Primavera)* or
the *Birth of Venus*, show what appears to be a stylistic regression
to something not far removed from Trecento ideals, although
expressed in different formal and iconographical language.
Something similar can be seen in the sculpture of Mino, or
Desiderio da Settignano, by comparison with Donatello, but the
case of Botticelli is more interesting. In effect, he returned to the
earlier notion of a two-dimensional surface which was an object
of beauty in itself and he took little interest in problems of
depth and recession, but, of course, the draughtsmanship of his
figures was both more naturalistic and more sophisticated than
that of any 14th-century artist. Above all, he had profited from
the experiments of Donatello, Castagno and Pollaiuolo in the
rendering of movement by means of a carefully adjusted contour,
the difference between him and them lying in the fact that they
sought movement for its own sake, where he sought it only as
part of a complicated linear rhythm covering the whole surface of
the picture. On top of this, the pictures are also made to carry
very involved allegorical meanings based (to some extent, at
any rate) on neo-Platonic interpretations of Christian ideas
expressed through pagan mythology, so that his work as a whole
is subtle and sophisticated and yet, in a curious way, also rather
mannered and old-fashioned. When he died in 1510 he left no
followers and his work had been neglected for a decade.

Leonardo and the High Renaissance

Botticelli was born about 1445, Leonardo da Vinci in 1452.
Vasari, a hundred years later, justly claimed that 'the good modern
manner' began with Leonardo, and it is certainly true that his
work was modern in a sense quite different from Botticelli's.
Unfortunately, he produced very little and most of his greatest
works were done outside Florence, so it is likely that the Florentines took some time to realize his importance. Nevertheless,
p 90 (36)   his unfinished *Adoration of the Magi*, worked on in 1481 and
abandoned when he went to Milan about 1482, was an epoch-
p 85 (22)   making work, like Pollaiuolo's *St Sebastian* of 1475, since it
attempted to find a solution to the problem of reconciling the
demands of the two-dimensional surface pattern—which had been
the strong point of the Trecento painters—with those of organized
spatial depth without too great discrepancies of scale between
the figures.

If one had to date the beginning of the High Renaissance at
any specific point in time there would be much to be said for the
p 91 (38)   year 1497. We know that Leonardo was then working on his *Last
Supper* in the Dominican convent of Sta Maria delle Grazie in Milan, and it is this painting, rather than any of the works of Michelangelo or Raphael which first makes a break with the practice of
p 84   the 15th century. Just before Leonardo left Florence Ghirlandaio
(20, 21)   had finished his *Last Supper* in Ognissanti (1480). This, like the
earlier version by Castagno, is simply a representation of a long
table, parallel to the picture plane, with Christ seated in the centre
and a group of Apostles on each side, with Judas very obviously
isolated on this side of the table. No action takes place and most
of the faces wear an expression of pious vacancy. Leonardo's *Last
Supper* attempts to recapture the moment of awful drama when
Christ announced that one of His own disciples would betray
Him. The disciples, appalled by the idea, give vent to their feelings
of horror and incredulity—with the exception of the one man
whose secret is thus exposed. We recognize Judas by his guilty
start and also—subconsciously—we recognize him by the fact
that, with characteristic subtlety, Leonardo arranged that his
should be the only face which is cast in shadow. In the earlier
pictures each disciple is rapt in his own thoughts and pays no
attention to any of the others. Leonardo arranges the groups in
threes or fours, so that each individual expression is heightened
by contrast with his neighbour. Ghirlandaio tends to group his
Apostles in pairs, but this emphasizes the rigidity of their poses
rather than giving interest to the composition as a whole. In the
same way, the light from the window is so arranged that it frames
and isolates the figure of Christ, where Ghirlandaio has a pretty
landscape with birds, which occupies nearly half the picture space

*Botticelli's poetic line finds its simplest expression in his drawings for
Dante's 'Divine Comedy'. Here Dante and Beatrice pass from the
summit of Purgatory to the outer sphere of Heaven at the beginning of
the Paradiso. (7)*

and effectively distracts the spectator's attention. In short, what
Leonardo is doing is to rethink in terms of drama the event which
he is representing, and he then employs his great technical skill
to make convincing visual equivalents. This is one of the distinguishing marks of High Renaissance art, and it can be appreciated more fully when one looks back from the early 16th
century—from the viewpoint of Michelangelo or Raphael—rather
than in the context of late 15th-century painting.

The development of painting, sculpture, and architecture in
the rest of Italy proceeded in a confusing number of directions.
For the greater part, sculptural activity was confined to Tuscany,
or to places like Padua which, under the influence of Donatello,
were virtually Florentine outposts. Very little sculpture of first-
rate importance was produced in the rest of Italy, with the single
exception of Venice, and even there the general level was much
below that of Florence or Siena until well into the 16th century,
when the Florentine Jacopo Sansovino had a powerful effect, both
in sculpture and in architecture, in the Venetian territories. Architecture also received its fullest development in the 15th century
in the hands of Florentines, but here the Tuscan dominance was
much less marked, since one of the noblest buildings, the palace
at Urbino, is certainly not a Tuscan work, while the greatest
architect of the age, Bramante, worked first in Milan and then
in Rome.

clear, colours, but in the background there are spectators in elaborate head-dresses which may derive from the exotic headgear worn by the Greek prelates in Florence for the Ecumenical Council of 1439. Fortunately, there is a document of that very year which tells us that Piero was working with Domenico Veneziano on a large fresco, now lost. For the rest, the National Gallery *Baptism* might almost be a Sienese picture; although the man in the background who is pulling his shirt over his head derives ultimately from Masolino, and the grave stillness of the angels may well reflect Piero's own version of the heroic mould of Masaccio's figures.

Certainly the frescoes at Arezzo, begun in 1452, which are Piero's masterpiece and one of the greatest of all Italian fresco cycles, cannot be imagined in their present form without the background of Sienese art as well as the Brancacci Chapel. The Arezzo cycle contains references to antique battle sarcophagi and to other, later, forms of art combined with a complex and condensed narrative derived from two separate accounts of the story of the True Cross given in the 'Golden Legend'. These frescoes were probably finished by 1460 and form the strongest possible contrast to the cycle in the choir of Prato Cathedral, by Fra Filippo Lippi, painted at exactly the same time. The Lippi frescoes, in their search for movement and drama and their attempt to pack in as many narrative details as possible, end by giving an impression of confused richness which is characteristic of Florentine art in the middle of the century. Nothing could be more truly classical, or further from this narrative abundance, than Piero's fresco of the *Resurrection* in the town-hall of Sansepolcro, painted about 1460. It has often been observed that the calm grandeur of the figure of the risen Christ makes it akin to Greek sculpture of the 5th century BC, which Piero could not possibly have known. Nevertheless, his imagination must have revived Greek sculpture, or the Roman copies of Greek originals (which he must have known), perhaps seen in his journey to Rome in 1459.

The same dependence on the ancient world occurs in the work of Mantegna, although he was more consciously an archaeologist. Piero, however, developed in a slightly different way, for he seems to have become interested in the technique of oil-painting, with all its possibilities of elaborate detail. This is clearly visible in the *Nativity*, probably painted about 1475–80. Here the open mouths of the singing angels derive directly from the literal realism of the *Ghent Altarpiece* by Jan van Eyck, while the unusual pose of the Child, laid flat on the ground, may derive from the huge altarpiece by Hugo van der Goes, painted for the Portinari family of Florence, which arrived in the city about 1475. It is one of the largest of 15th-century Flemish pictures and displays a dazzling mastery of the possibilities of oil-painting in the rendering of minute detail and in depth and richness of colour. For this reason it was an object lesson to Florentine painters, whose experiments with the new technique were still very uncertain.

Piero must certainly have known the Flemish painter Joos van Gent, who was working in Urbino in 1473–74, but it seems quite possible that he may also have paid another visit to Florence and seen the Hugo altarpiece. Even more important than the *Nativity* is the large altarpiece (Milan, Brera) representing the Madonna and Child with angels and saints and with Federigo da Montefeltro, Duke of Urbino, as donor. This, which must have been painted about 1475, is one of three large altarpieces of the type known as the *sacra conversazione*, which represent the scene as taking place in a continuation of the real space. The *sacra conversazione* shows the Madonna and Child seated in a room or garden with saints, angels, and donors so that all the figures are in the same space and may, as the name implies, be represented as conversing. This marks a great change from the earlier type of altarpiece in which the Madonna and Child were set against a gold background in a compartment by themselves, while the figures of the attendant saints each occupied their own niches. Even Masaccio's Pisa polyptych, or the dismembered polyptych by Piero himself, still show this type; but the *sacra conversazione* can be found in Florence in the work of Fra Angelico and Fra Filippo in the late 1430s, or in the work of Domenico Veneziano a few years later.

The Spreading Wave: Piero della Francesca

In painting, the second half of the 15th century saw the development of several regional schools and a number of major artists. Most of the greatest masters of the second half of the century had some connexion with Florentine painters or painting, but the use they made of their models varies interestingly. Six of these painters—Piero della Francesca, Mantegna, Antonello da Messina, Giovanni Bellini, Perugino, and Signorelli—demonstrate the different ways in which the great Florentine advances of the first half of the century were assimilated into Italian art generally.

Piero della Francesca was born in Sansepolcro, near Arezzo, about 1416, and his working life extended from about 1440 to 1480 at the latest. Two pictures in the National Gallery, London, the *Baptism of Christ* and the *Nativity*, are probably his earliest and latest surviving works. Both are intensely personal, although there is a marked stylistic difference between them and both seem to indicate contacts with wider artistic horizons than he could have known in Arezzo. To begin with, Piero seems to have studied in Florence under the mysterious Domenico Veneziano, who may well have been a Venetian living in Florence. Certainly Domenico was the least Florentine of all the painters working in the period 1440–60, and his obsession with colour and light, which may be seen in his masterpiece, the *St Lucy Altarpiece*, places him apart from the general trend of Florentine art towards the expression of movement and energy. Piero's first experience of modern art must have come from Sienese painters such as Sassetta, whose *St Francis Altarpiece* was painted for Piero's native town. The *Baptism* shows this Sienese delight in pretty, pale,

p 89 (34)

p 81 (11)

p 89 (35)

p 88 (32)

p 88 (31, 33)

88 (30)

Piero could thus have seen one or more examples of the type when he was in Florence in 1439, but his Brera altarpiece makes a step forward by the introduction of an elaborate architectural setting and the use of perspective, so that when it was placed above an altar it would give the impression of the chancel of a domed church, with the light from the dome coming down from the top of the picture. The architectural forms at the sides continue towards the spectator, so that we feel ourselves to be in the actual building. It is one of the unsolved mysteries of Italian painting that no fewer than three large altarpieces of this type seem to have been painted at almost the same moment, the other two both in Venice. One was the altarpiece for S. Cassiano, which Antonello da Messina is known to have painted in 1475–6, but which now exists only as fragments. The third—but possibly the earliest—was by Giovanni Bellini and was burnt in the 19th century, although copies exist. It is possible, therefore, that in his very last works Piero was continuing to make innovations and was moving towards a greater naturalism, made possible by Flemish technique. Piero lived on until 1492, but no surviving work seems to be later than 1475–80, and the story that he died blind may well be the explanation.

Antonello:
the Lessons of the North

The presence of Antonello da Messina in Venice at this critical moment has never been adequately explained, but there is no doubt that the S. Cassiano altarpiece of 1475–6 was a work of the same importance as Piero's *sacra conversazione*, and, unlike it, this can be dated with great precision. We know that it was commissioned by the noble, Pietro Bon, and a letter of 16th March, 1476, from him to the Duke of Milan says that the picture is just being completed and will be one of the best in Italy or anywhere else. Unfortunately, we now know it only from three fragments in Vienna, of the Madonna and Child and two cut-down figures of saints, but a 17th-century copy allows us to reconstruct it. Like Piero's, the figures are comparatively small in scale—the full-length figures in the foreground occupy less than half the total height of the picture, so that the greater part of the imaginary space is taken up by the architecture which defines it. Much the same could be said of the third of these altarpieces, that by Giovanni Bellini, which is also known only from two poor copies. It was painted for another church in Venice, and the style has led most critics to date it at about the same time as the other two, although some think that it was the earliest and that Antonello was imitating it when he painted his *pala* for S. Cassiano, rather than the other way round. There can be no doubt at all, however, that Giovanni Bellini learned much from Antonello during his stay in Venice.

Antonello was born, and spent most of his life, in southern Italy, mostly in Sicily. In the whole of the 15th century he was the only major painter active there, so that he was entirely cut off from the stream of experiment which started in Florence and fertilized all the rest of central and northern Italy. Antonello, in effect, was closer to French or Flemish 15th-century painters than he was to other Italians, and many works of his could easily be mistaken for pictures painted in Flanders in the earlier part of the century: the *St Jerome* in the National Gallery, for example, is almost certainly based on a picture by Jan van Eyck and, as early as 1529, a Venetian writer said of it: 'The little picture representing St Jerome reading in his study, robed as a cardinal, is ascribed by some to Antonello da Messina, but the great majority, with more probability, ascribe it to Jan van Eyck or Memlinc.' His portraits are also closer to Flemish prototypes than to other Italian portraits and here there is a point of resemblance between him and Piero della Francesca. Vasari, writing in the 1540s, says quite definitely that Antonello was trained by Jan van Eyck and introduced the technique of oil painting into Italy. The first of these statements is almost certainly untrue, and the second is improbable; but nevertheless Vasari had some grounds for them since Antonello's pictures are really quite like those painted by Jan van Eyck at the time of Antonello's birth, and Antonello's mastery of the Flemish technique was much greater than that possessed by any other Italian of his generation.

He died in February 1479, according to Vasari at the age of forty-nine. It seems likely that he really was about this age at the time of his death, so that he must have been born around 1430—which means that he was eleven when Jan van Eyck died in 1441. More probably, then, Antonello learned the Eyckian technique in Naples, where we know that it was practised by Neapolitan, French, and perhaps even Flemish, artists. There is no real reason to believe that Antonello ever went to Flanders, and he seems to be fairly well documented in Sicily and south Italy until 1475, when he went to Venice for eighteen months. We do not know whether he went there on his own initiative or whether he was sent for to paint the S. Cassiano altarpiece; but while he was in Venice he had, and refused, an offer of the post of Court Painter in Milan. The previous holder, a very minor artist called Bugatti, was trained in Flanders, so that Antonello's skill in the Flemish technique was responsible for the regard in which he was held by his contemporaries. Antonello, however, returned to Messina, where he died some three years later. There can be little doubt that the effect he had upon his compatriots was due to the detail which the Flemish technique allowed him to pack into his pictures. This can be seen in the *St Jerome* or the *Crucifixion* (Antwerp) which is dated 1475 and carries a mysterious inscription that seems to claim that it is painted in oil, thus advertising to the Venetians his mastery of a difficult technique. This concern for finesse and minute detail hardly seems consistent with the style of his *sacra conversazione* (which we can estimate to have been something like 12 feet high) and it has been held that this exceptionally large picture was therefore derived from the types established by Piero and Giovanni Bellini. This is not necessarily true, since other pictures by Antonello (e.g. the damaged *Madonna* of 1473 in Messina) show that his style had a monumental quality before he went to Venice. On the other hand there can be no doubt that Giovanni Bellini certainly learned something about the use of oil paint from Antonello, both in his altarpieces and in his portraits. Antonello's effect on Venetian art was not inconsiderable, since the evolution of Venetian painting in the second half of the 15th century can be summed up in the career of Giovanni Bellini.

Mantegna, Bellini and the Venetian School

Before attempting this, however, it is necessary to go back in time to consider the importance of the link between the early Florentine Renaissance of the 1420s and Venetian work of the 1470s. The gap is largely bridged by painting and sculpture in Padua from the 1430s onwards. Padua was one of the great university cities of the Middle Ages and stood in somewhat the same relationship to Venice as Oxford to London. Politically, Padua was an important part of the Venetian State: artistically, the Paduans responded far more readily to the intellectual art of Florence than did the Venetians, whose taste remained essentially Byzantine until well into the 15th century. This was largely due to the trade links between Venice and the Eastern Mediterranean, but it is probably also true that the splendour of gold and rich colour of a Byzantine church like St Mark's appealed more to the average Venetian than did the austere and geometrical art, with its Roman classical overtones, of a painter like Mantegna or a sculptor like Donatello. In effect, Donatello virtually created the Paduan School, although we know that Florentine painters such as Uccello and Fra Filippo Lippi were active in the city in the 1430s. Nevertheless, the sculpture for the high altar of the Santo in Padua, as well as the equestrian monument of Gattamelata outside it, were Donatello's masterpieces of the 1440s.

The influence of sculpture is predominant in Mantegna's paintings; indeed, Vasari criticized his work as being more like bronze or stone than flesh and blood. Mantegna, however, married Giovanni Bellini's sister and through this marriage something of Donatello and of Mantegna's austerity came as a sort of intellectual stiffening into the art of Giovanni Bellini and, through him, into Venetian painting of the 16th century. This was not entirely Mantegna's doing since his father-in-law, Jacopo Bellini, had almost certainly worked in Florence as a young man. He seems to have been trained under Gentile da Fabriano (he gave the name Gentile to the elder of his two painter sons) and he was probably the Venetian painter who got into trouble in Florence

P 94 (45)
f 8

P 94 (46)

for an assault upon two boys who were throwing stones at a picture by Gentile da Fabriano which had been put in the sun to dry. Certainly Jacopo's own art, with its insistence on the importance of draughtsmanship, reflects the International Gothic style of Gentile and, more distantly, Florentine painting of the 1420s. Two large collections of drawings by him have come down to us, showing that he was fascinated by Florentine experiments in perspective, and also by the study of classical antiquity, although his knowledge of both was rather limited. Nevertheless, his drawings were used by both his sons as well as by his son-in-law, and Mantegna must have found his father-in-law's ideas congenial, although there was no comparison between the two men in technical skill.

Andrea Mantegna and Giovanni Bellini were both born about 1430–31, but Mantegna was much more precocious than his future brother-in-law. He died in 1506 and Giovanni Bellini outlived him by ten years. Most of Mantegna's important work was done quite early in his career, while Giovanni Bellini matured more slowly and made some of his greatest innovations after 1500. Mantegna's career falls naturally into two parts: the first being the early years in Padua, when his style was modelled directly on Donatello, and on a close study of classical antiquity. In 1460, before he was thirty, he went to Mantua as Court Painter and spent the rest of his life there. Much of his time was devoted to the study of archaeology, and, although he produced many masterpieces, his work shows a straightforward development from his Paduan style. That style was shown in frescoes of SS. James and Christopher, and in an altarpiece for S. Zeno in Verona.

p 131 (34)

The fresco cycle was almost entirely destroyed in 1944 but is, of course, known from photographs. He was recorded as working on these frescoes in 1448, when only about seventeen, so that the two principal influences on his style seem to have been evident before he was out of his teens. All the frescoes by him showed that he had already mastered the most difficult effects of perspective, since all of them set the figures in their surroundings in such a way that the spectator, looking upwards, saw the figures high above eye-level and in an architectural setting that was archaeologically completely Roman. All the details of architecture, weapons, and armour were treated with a scholarship far beyond even the most classically-minded of his Florentine contemporaries. The use of Roman armour or triumphal arches he obviously learned from Donatello, but the effect is quite different. What is more, the details have an esoteric significance over and above their importance as ancient objects. Thus, in the fresco of St James led to martyrdom, the saint is shown passing through a triumphal arch, which is itself a symbol of his victory; but the panels of the arch also bear hieroglyphic symbols which have been interpreted as a vase, a rudder, a circle and a palm tree, together meaning a well-guided life leading to eternal victory. Most of Mantegna's religious works contain symbolism of this sort: one of the most famous is the *St Sebastian* (Vienna) which also represents a Christian victory through martyrdom over the crumbling pagan world, represented by a defaced statue.

92 (42)

The S. Zeno altarpiece in Verona is iconographically straightforward and less obtrusively classical, but in some ways it is even more important, since the perspective, which in the Padua frescoes was rather insistent, is used here to create a completely convincing spatial enclosure. This altarpiece, painted between 1456 and 1459, can well claim to be one of the early examples of the *sacra conversazione*, developed in the seventies by Piero, Antonello, and Bellini. Fortunately, it is still in the church for which it was painted (although some of the predella panels stolen by Napoleon are still in France and have been replaced by copies). The frame divides the *pala* into three equal panels by means of four richly carved Corinthian columns. Behind these wooden columns there are painted piers, so that it is very difficult to decide where the three-dimensional world represented by the columns merges into the painted two-dimensional scene. The shape of the frame is probably taken from Donatello's sculptured altarpiece in Padua, but Mantegna, by means of perspective, has created an imaginary space where Donatello's figures actually exist in three dimensions. The S. Zeno altarpiece anticipates the spatial continuity of the

93 (44)

All that remains of the S. Cassiano altarpiece by Antonello da Messina has been illustrated on p. 94. The whole work is reconstructed here by Johannes Wilde from a later copy, so that its affinities with the Piero and Bellini altarpieces (p. 88 and 94) can more readily be appreciated. (8)

later *sacre conversazioni* and there can be no doubt that Giovanni Bellini learned as much from this treatment of the theme as from any other single source.

Mantegna had thus already made his principal innovations before he was thirty, and the depth of his influence on Giovanni Bellini can be judged by comparing the *Agony in the Garden* as painted by both men. Mantegna's picture must have been painted about 1459, when they were both in their late twenties. The landscape is harsh and rocky, with a sort of promontory in the centre, on which Christ kneels. In front of Him, on a flat piece of rock, there are the sleeping figures of three disciples, foreshortened and awkward. Behind Him, in the middle distance, there is a pink walled town, like any Italian hill town, and emerging from it is the long procession led by Judas. The figure of Christ is thus in the centre of the depth of the picture, and nearly in the centre of the picture-plane. His attention is entirely concentrated on the small angels appearing in the sky.

p 94 (48)
p 95 (50)

The same description would almost serve for Bellini's version, where the figure of Christ, facing in the opposite direction, occupies the middle of the picture in depth and is slightly to the right of centre on the picture-plane. Again, the sleeping disciples are awkwardly foreshortened in the foreground, and in the background there is an approaching file of soldiers. Christ kneels on an outcrop of rock, but the picture as a whole is far less stony in feeling and the great difference between the two really consists of the effects of light. In Bellini's picture the head of Christ is silhouetted against the bright sky, which is pink at the horizon, with little flecks of sunlight here and there on the clouds. This understanding of the emotional possibilities of light and of the elements of landscape Bellini was to carry much further in his *Transfiguration* or *St Francis receiving the Stigmata*, and it was this feeling of unity between man and the world around him which was his most important legacy to Giorgione and Titian, and, through them, to the 16th and 17th centuries. Nevertheless, it was Mantegna's painting which was his starting point and in a similar way some other works by Mantegna were to be carried further by later artists.

Mantegna's most important works in Mantua were the frescoes in a room in the Ducal Palace, known as the Camera degli Sposi, completed in 1474. These frescoes occupy two walls and the

p 60 (41, 42)

whole ceiling of a fairly small room, and they represent episodes in the life of Lodovico Gonzaga and his family. Even more than in the Paduan frescoes or the S. Zeno altarpiece, the structure of the room is worked into the illusionistic design so that painted pilasters support real capitals and the mantelshelf becomes a support for painted figures. In the centre of the ceiling there is what seems to be a round opening, through which one looks up towards the sky—and sees with horror small boys balanced precariously on the wrong side of the balustrade, as though at any moment they might fall down into the room. This extreme illusionism looks forward to the great Baroque ceiling decorations, but it was a piece of virtuosity which attracted no immediate followers. In the same way the extraordinary picture of the dead Christ (Milan) seen in extreme foreshortening was probably not well known in Mantegna's own day, since it was in his studio at his death. Nevertheless, it is another example of the way in which, like Donatello, Mantegna employed distortion and foreshortening as a means of heightening tragic effect.

p 92
(43)

Such effects were not sought by Giovanni Bellini, who soon began to go his own way and to develop a much gentler style, better suited to Venetian taste. Many examples of this can be found in the small devotional Madonna pictures produced by Bellini himself, or under his supervision in his very large studio, or by Venetian imitators of this popular type of picture. Giovanni's own innovations can be seen in large altarpieces, such as that painted in 1505 for S. Zaccaria, in Venice, where the *sacra conversazione* type is developed about as far as it will go. In his portraits, such as the *Doge Loredano* (National Gallery), Bellini adapted the type which he knew both from Flemish originals and from Antonello's version of them, but he treated this bust-length type of portrait with much greater breadth of handling and with a concentration on the face, rather than on enchanting but irrelevant background details, to produce a portrait type which could be taken up by Titian and developed far beyond the rather stiff image-making of the Flemings. Bellini continued to be an important innovator into extreme old age, and the two major painters of the early 16th century in Venice, Giorgione and Titian, were both his pupils. Giorgione, indeed, died young in 1510 and some of Bellini's last works show that he had learned from his own pupil.

p 94 (47)

p 52
(21)

Ferocity and Sentiment

Two of the most important non-Florentine painters active in the last quarter of the 15th century and the early years of the 16th were Perugino and Signorelli. Although the general impression made by their work is so entirely different, Perugino being gentle and rather sentimental, and Signorelli dramatic to the point of ferocity, yet the two men were friends and had more in common than might appear at first sight. Both were born in the years immediately before 1450 and both died at an advanced age in 1523. Although they lived to be well over seventy, their major works were painted before 1505; that is, when both were in their late fifties. In the last years of their lives both retired to their birth-places and produced large numbers of old-fashioned, hack altarpieces, in which the participation of inferior assistants is all too evident. Perugino retired to his native Perugia in 1506 when it became clear that the Florentines were no longer content with the type of painting which had suited them well enough ten years earlier. Signorelli also retired at about the same time to his native Cortona, although he visited Rome about 1508 and again about 1513. He received no commissions and was even reduced to borrowing money from Michelangelo. This is the key to the sudden eclipse of both Perugino and Signorelli: their importance in the years just before 1500, as forerunners of the High Renaissance can hardly be over-estimated, but as soon as Raphael and Michelangelo began to produce their first masterpieces it was evident to everyone that Perugino and Signorelli had had their day.

p 98
(55, 56)

Both men were probably pupils of Piero della Francesca in the 1460s, at about the time he was working on the Sansepolcro *Resurrection*. We know very little about their own style at this stage of their careers, but it does seem clear that they both went to Florence as soon as they could, to learn the latest artistic

fashions. Perugino seems to have been influenced by Verrocchio at this time, although his early works still contain many elements taken from Piero. Signorelli, on the other hand, in his *Flagellation* (Milan) combines a Piero type of composition with obvious borrowings from the anatomical studies of Antonio Pollaiuolo.

Perugino went to Rome in 1479, and in 1481 he received a considerable share of the commission given by Sixtus IV for the series of Old and New Testament frescoes on the walls of the Sistine Chapel in the Vatican. Signorelli seems also to have come to Rome about this time and to have received a share in the commission, perhaps through the influence of Perugino, although Signorelli's name does not occur in either of the only two documents known to us.

Perugino's frescoes include the *Charge to Peter*, which is the most important statement of his artistic principles. It is also the key picture in the cycle, which is based on the idea of the papal primacy. What is so important about Perugino's fresco is its restraint, its balance and symmetry. There is a large centrally-planned temple in the centre, with a long band of figures arranged symmetrically in the foreground on either side of the group of Christ giving the keys to St Peter. The action is lucid, and there are no (or very few) unnecessary and distracting figures. This was the essential antidote to the uproar, the violent action and the irrelevant posturings which Pollaiuolo and others had introduced in an attempt to gain greater expressiveness and to demonstrate their mastery of anatomy and foreshortening. This calm, ordered, composition is, of course, particularly desirable in a wall-painting and no doubt it was Perugino's principal inheritance from Piero della Francesca. Certainly, this Early Classicism, as it is sometimes called, was historically necessary, but it can very easily degenerate into insipidity. Two other works by Perugino, the large fresco of 1496 in the convent of Sta Maria Maddalena de' Pazzi in Florence, and an altarpiece painted at about the same time (National Gallery, London), demonstrate both the success and failure of Perugino's style just before 1500. The Pazzi fresco is painted on the wall opposite the entrance in a rather small room opening off the cloister. The room is not very well lit and as one comes in from the arched openings of the cloister one sees three more arched openings with a landscape beyond. In the central arch there is a representation of the Crucifixion and on either side there are groups of meditative saints. The illusionistic effect is quite strong, but it soon wears off. The gentle piety of the figures, on the other hand, becomes the more impressive the longer one contemplates the scene. In this case the sentimental religiosity which ruins so many of Perugino's works has been avoided and we see a gentle, harmonious, style which must have come as a great relief in Florence in the 1490s. The National Gallery altarpiece, on the other hand, though similar in type and composition, seems to consist of vapid insubstantial figures posed in all-too-evidently stock positions in an improbable Arcadian landscape. About 1500, when Perugino was painting the frescoes in the Sala del Cambio in Perugia, Raphael, aged sixteen or seventeen, became his pupil. In the next four years Raphael learnt everything that Perugino had to teach him and, by 1504, when he painted the *Marriage of the Virgin (Lo Sposalizio)*, now in Milan, Raphael had already surpassed his master. From that date Perugino ceased to have any importance in the history of art.

p 98
(56)

p 104
(63)

Something rather similar happened in the case of Signorelli, whose masterpiece is the series of frescoes in Orvieto Cathedral, painted between 1499 and 1504. This fresco cycle represents the signs and portents of the End of the World, together with the Last Judgment, but the iconography is rather unusual. The cycle was begun in 1447 by Fra Angelico who painted some figures on the ceiling, including a representation of Christ as Judge in the space immediately above the altar. The cycle was left unfinished, although its iconography was determined, and it was not until 1499 that the patrons finally employed Signorelli to complete it. The long delay from Fra Angelico's death in 1455 is partly explained by the fact that both Gozzoli and Perugino failed to secure the commission, but a new urgency was imported in the 1490s by the troubles of Italy. During the French invasion Orvieto had been bypassed by the armies of Charles VIII on their

p 98
(55)

'*Whoever departs from Bramante departs from the truth*', said Michelangelo, when in his design for the new St Peter's he returned to Bramante's original idea for a centrally-planned church surmounted by a huge dome. Bramante's plan (left) had ingenuity and elegance, though it may be doubted whether the central piers would have supported the superstructure. The façade (right, from the Foundation Medal, 1506) would have been completely novel for the early 16th century, and the dome (unlike Michelangelo's but like the Pantheon) was to have been hemispherical, not pointed. (9, 10)

way to Rome, although the danger to the town at one time seemed very great. This was the moment when Savonarola, in Florence, had been preaching sermons which echoed round the whole of Italy threatening the tribulations to come. He had predicted a French invasion as an instrument of the wrath of God and there seemed therefore cogent reasons in 1499, when the danger to the city had been removed, for completing the cycle. Signorelli was evidently the right man to employ, for the violence and the harshness of colour which are characteristic of his style were eminently suited to the scenes of the last days of the Earth, the coming of Anti-Christ, the Resurrection of the Dead, and the representation of the Blessed and the Damned. Characteristically, it is the Damned who call out Signorelli's powers to their fullest extent, while the Blessed seemed to have interested him rather less. The dependence on outline, the use of the human figure as the sole vehicle of emotion, the subordination of incidental background, even the disdain for beauty of colour, all combine in a synthesis of the principal aims of Florentine artists over a period of more than half a century. Nothing could be further from the classic art of Piero, but nothing makes a better preparation for the art of Michelangelo. Michelangelo may actually have known these frescoes, but by the time they were finished he could hardly have learned much from them, since he had already carved p 96 his *Pietà* for St Peter's, and, indeed, had completed the *David*, 51, 52) which established his fame as the greatest living artist. Signorelli was thus already superseded, and, like Perugino, the rest of his life was passed in provincial obscurity.

The Roman Consummation

Rome in the years around 1500 was, therefore, the centre of all those developments which we call the High Renaissance. Michelangelo, Raphael and Bramante all emerge from the traditions which had formed them, and, largely under the inspiration of 47 (6) Julius II, the years of his pontificate (1503–13), saw the creation of Michelangelo's Sistine ceiling, the greater part of Raphael's *Stanze* and the idea of the rebuilding of St Peter's.

In a sense it is extremely difficult to discuss the style practised in Rome in the first decades of the 16th century. One reason for this is evident if we refer to it as 'Roman art'. The unfamiliarity of the phrase in connection with the 16th century is justified by the fact that it was the art of Rome but it was produced by people who, without exception, had been born and trained elsewhere. p 105 Even Julius II came from the north of Italy, and Giulio Romano, (69) the first important native-born Roman artist for centuries, was a child in 1500, and his whole career is connected with the rise of Mannerism and not with Renaissance art at all. The characteristics of the High Renaissance style in so far as they are common to the work of Michelangelo, Raphael and Bramante are really the characteristics of Julius' patronage. How far he actually inspired and directed these great artists is impossible to guess; but certainly both Raphael and Bramante changed their styles

—and Bramante was then nearly sixty—and the changes were in every case for the better, towards a greater simplicity of composition and a more heroic conception of the figure. Probably no man, not even Julius II, could have made Michelangelo produce anything that was not deeply personal, but it is worth remembering that the Sistine ceiling was a commission he never wanted, that he did his best to evade, but that once started he enlarged it far beyond its original rather restricted scope. It became one of his most important works and was to some extent a substitute for the enormous tomb that Julius had planned for himself. Michelangelo must have realised by about 1508 or 1509 that this titanic mausoleum, with forty-odd lifesize figures, was not going to be realized, but, nevertheless, the enormous scale of the undertaking, worthy of the pope and of himself, haunted him all his life. He referred to it as a tragedy when it was finally completed, in a much reduced form and by inferior hands, poked away, not in St Peter's for which it had originally been planned, p 97 (54) but in S. Pietro in Vincoli.

The phrase 'High Renaissance art' covers Michelangelo's Sistine ceiling and the Moses from the Julius tomb; it also covers some of Raphael's *Stanze*, particularly such frescoes as the *School* p 150–151 *of Athens*, the *Disputà*, the *Miracle at Bolsena*, and *Heliodorus in the* (7) *Temple*. Bramante's works would have been even more awe- p 154 inspiring, and would certainly have been more readily visible to (12) the public, but almost nothing remains of the gigantic project for *f* 9, 10 St Peter's. His other most important building-types are represen- p 104 (62) ted by the house he built for himself, and the little temple com- p 105 (66) memorating the crucifixion of St Peter. Both were certainly known to every architect of the 16th century, but the palace, later known as the House of Raphael, was destroyed in the early 17th century and is known to us only from an engraving and a drawing by Palladio. The Tempietto survives, but its dome has been altered and it stands rather forlornly in the courtyard of S. Pietro in Montorio instead of inside the circular colonnade which Bramante intended as a setting. In practice, therefore, the High Renaissance style really means those stylistic characteristics which we can actually see, in the Sistine ceiling, the Vatican frescoes and a few other works by Michelangelo or Raphael (such as the tapestry cartoons now in the Victoria and Albert Museum). p 103 (61) All these works do possess characteristics in common, and those characteristics differentiate them on the one hand from the works of painters like Perugino and Signorelli, and, on the other, from the works of younger men such as Giulio Romano or Parmigianino. Familiar as they are, these works are nevertheless of permanent importance because of the way in which they combine a carefully thought out intellectual content with a complete mastery of difficult techniques.

This achievement in two fields is what really distinguishes p 99–101 them from their predecessors, so that if we compare the Sistine (57, 58) ceiling, or the *School of Athens* with Giotto's frescoes in Padua, p 150–151 Masaccio's in Florence, or Piero della Francesca's in Arezzo, we (7)

p 80 (9, 10)
p 89 (34)

can see that all speak the same language, but Michelangelo and Raphael were fortunate in possessing a language which had been given a range and refinement certainly lacking in Giotto's time, and perhaps even still in Piero's. This is why Vasari, much as he praised a Giotto or a Masaccio, was always careful to add that they were good by the standards of their day and perfection had only been attained in the good modern manner, in Michelangelo and Raphael, and in Leonardo, whom he regarded as the forerunner. Leonardo's approach to the *Last Supper* was to become characteristic also of Raphael and Michelangelo, and we can see that Raphael learned his artistic lessons in Florence in the series of Madonna groups, all of which are variations on a composition formed by two or more adult figures and one or two children. By 1508, however, when he began to paint in the Vatican, he had obviously learned more than the technical disposition of groups of figures. His *School of Athens*, completed by 1511, marks an enormous advance upon Perugino's *Charge to Peter* of 1481, even though, in its day, the Perugino fresco had been of primary importance in the subordination of purely technical achievements to an overriding religious theme. Raphael himself said that he worked from 'a certain idea' in his mind, and his tapestry cartoons such as *Feed my Sheep* not only show an advance upon Perugino in pure technique, but also demonstrate Raphael's power of creating visual types for the Apostles themselves, which became accepted almost immediately as valid characterizations.

p 96 (52)

The marrying of a Greco-Roman figure type with the ideas of the Old and New Testament can be seen differently expressed in Michelangelo's early *Pietà*, completed by about 1500. Like Leonardo's *Last Supper*, it takes a Christian theme charged with emotional possibilities and expresses these emotions in terms of Hellenistic beauty and restraint. The original idea of the representation of the dead body of Christ in His mother's lap was not Italian but German, and medieval northern piety had tended to exaggerate the physical suffering at the expense of deeper theological implications as well as of artistic naturalism. Michelangelo faced the problem of representing a full-grown man in a more or less horizontal position across the lap of a seated woman, which, if treated realistically, could easily present a most unpleasing outline. He solved the purely artistic problem by very careful adjustments of scale, by the use of a mass of drapery as a sort of base, and, above all, by the beautiful gesture of the Virgin's left hand which breaks up the sharpness of the silhouette and, at the same time, expresses complete resignation. All the Germanic emphasis on suffering is minimized, and his effect is made by means of a Greco-Roman beauty of form which, in the hands of its inventors, had never been made to carry so great an emotional charge. In this respect Michelangelo departed abruptly from the line of development laid down by Donatello and he was to persist in this reconciliation of antique beauty and Christian sentiment throughout the whole enormous undertaking of the Sistine ceiling.

p 99–100 (57)

This consists of nine rectangles separated by painted architectural ribs, which serve also to divide the ceiling at the sides into spaces filled with figures of the Prophets and Sibyls who foretold the coming of the Messiah to the Jews and the Gentiles respectively. Below these, partly on the side walls and partly on the lower part of the cove of the ceiling, are four scenes of Divine intervention on behalf of the Chosen People, as well as a series of the human ancestors of Christ. Since this elaborate arrangement of scenes was painted for the private chapel of the Vatican it is evident that the theological complexities are deliberate, and an analysis of the subjects shows that the ceiling was intended to complete the 1481 fresco cycle on the walls, largely by representing scenes of life on earth before the coming of the Law.

The primal act of Creation is symbolized immediately above the altar, and from there, running back towards the door, there are scenes of the Acts of Creation, the Fall and the Deluge and, finally, the Drunkenness of Noah, which symbolizes Man in a state of degradation. This gigantic work was completed virtually single-handed by 1512, and thirty years later Michelangelo finished another enormous painting in the Sistine Chapel, the *Last Judgment*, which occupies the entire altar wall. Work was begun in 1534, and the difference between it and the ceiling is extremely striking. The subject itself is necessarily rather pessimistic, but the whole atmosphere could hardly be more different from that of the ceiling with its pale, bright, colours, its perfectly proportioned forms, and its general air of the perfectibility of Man. The *Last Judgment* is dark, even gloomy, in colour and tone, and the atmosphere is charged with violence. The Martyrs are crying out for vengeance, and it has often been observed that Christ is more like Jupiter Tonans than an impartial judge. The forms themselves are heavy, almost muscle-bound, and seem roughly carved out of huge blocks of stone. These basic differences are to be explained in terms of the great change that came over Europe, and Rome in particular, between 1520 and 1540. The spread of Lutheranism, and later Calvinism, had produced a new defensive mentality, far removed from the neo-Platonism current in Michelangelo's youth. More than this, the Sack of Rome by Imperial troops in 1527 had caused a shock of surprise and horror throughout Europe which made men look back to the Sack of Rome by the Visigoths under Alaric in 410. Michelangelo expresses the new mood in a number of poems as well as in his later frescoes and the two versions of the *Pietà*, one of which was originally destined for his own tomb.

p 101 (58)

From these religious, political, and economic circumstances and perhaps most of all from Michelangelo's own stylistic evolution there grew the restless, dynamic style known as Mannerism, in which expression, invention, and imagination seemed more important than the precision and harmony which the arts had attained in the Golden Age of Julius II. The only important exception to this rule, at any rate in the first half of the 16th century, was Venice. Giorgione and Titian, Sansovino, Veronese and Palladio carried on a rich and decorative tradition, much of it firmly based on Roman antiquity as interpreted by Bramante, Raphael and the young Michelangelo. Tintoretto was the only Venetian with a real sympathy for the later works of Michelangelo, and, perhaps for that reason, he was the mostly deeply emotional and religious artist of his time. Tintoretto was born in 1518, some 30 years later than Titian (whose actual birth-date is a matter of controversy). Titian was the artistic heir of Giorgione and Giovanni Bellini, and, in his early years, continued the voluptuous and colouristic tradition established by them. The splendid *poesie* painted in his old age for Philip II of Spain are erotic mythologies which are the logical successors of Giorgione's *Venus* or Bellini's *Lady at her Toilet*: they are, however, contemporary both with Titian's own late religious pictures, such as the *Entombment* or the *Martyrdom of St Laurence*, and Tintoretto's first works for the Scuola di S. Rocco. Tintoretto was almost exclusively a religious painter—some magnificent portraits and a few mythological and allegorical subjects are the exceptions—but the real difference between the two men is simply that of generations: Tintoretto was a boy of nine at the Sack of Rome, and his earliest surviving works date from about 1545, the year the Council of Trent opened. He belongs in spirit to the world of the Counter-Reformation. That world grew out of the Renaissance, but was impatient with many of the aims and ideals, artistic or intellectual, which had been the rule of life to men like Raphael or Leonardo.

p 95 (4
p 106 (70, 71
p 296 (42)

SCIENTIÆ
IMMVTA
BILIS

IV THE NEW LEARNING

Scholarship from Petrarch to Erasmus

ROBERTO WEISS

'After the darkness has been dispelled,
our grandsons will be able to
walk back into the pure radiance of the past'.

PETRARCH

The hidden source

of what is most splendid and significant in the Renaissance lies in the labours of a relatively small number of dedicated men who rediscovered the heritage of Greece and Rome and made it available to the world—Latinists, Greek scholars, collectors of antiquities and manuscripts: in short, the humanists. Humanism is a vague concept; it implied no particular body of belief, as the word does today. There were humanists among Catholics and Protestants, despots and republicans, rationalists and mystics. What held them together was a common passion for the ancient world and a common conviction that it held the key to civilization. The New Learning meant first the 'Rebirth' of the old.

The Renaissance in its beginnings, therefore, was entirely a matter of books: the correction and interpretation of those already known (which included most of the Latin classics, but often in corrupt and incomplete texts) and the search for others that might survive in obscure places. This latter was an enterprise of which one can still catch the feeling of excitement. The *Annals* of Tacitus, the complete poems of Catullus, Tibullus, Propertius and Lucretius, the *Satyricon* of Petronius—these and many more were read for the first time by their delighted discoverers in monastic or cathedral libraries where they had lain forgotten for centuries. When Poggio found the unique complete copy of Quintilian's *Institutiones* at S. Gall in 'a sort of dungeon, foul and dark, at the bottom of a tower', he says it seemed to be stretching out its hands to him, begging to be rescued.

After Latin came Greek—practically unknown in the west before 1400. During the next century a few teachers made the journey from Constantinople, and when the city fell to the Turks in 1453 their numbers increased. But Greek was still a relatively rare attainment, not to be acquired without difficulty and effort. The task of collecting the texts and translating them into Latin became the second great mission of humanism. Gradually the riches of Greek literature were unveiled to a marvelling world—most of Plato, Homer, Thucydides, Herodotus: mere names to the Middle Ages, now living realities.

Something of the urgency and fervour of the humanist adventure is caught in Botticelli's painting of St Augustine for the church of Ognissanti in Florence. The saint is shown as the inspired scholar, the heir of the classical world, transmitting its wisdom to future ages. Behind him on a shelf are an armillary sphere (based on Ptolemy) and a book of geometrical diagrams (Euclid); the other object is a clock with twenty-four hour dial. It is important to remember that the humanists (as distinct from their reactionary opponents) saw no conflict between the New Learning and the authority of the Church. On the contrary, the new critical and linguistic techniques were in their eyes tools for the elucidation of true Christian doctrine, while Platonic philosophy could only illuminate, never undermine, theology. For, says Augustine, 'the true and highest good, according to Plato, is God, and therefore would he call him a philosopher who loves God; for philosophy is directed to the obtaining of the blessed life, and he who loves God is blessed in the enjoyment of God.' (1)

SIC AVGVSTINVS SACRIS SE TRADIDIT VT NON
MVTATVM SIBI ADHVC SENSERIT ESSE LOCVM

A scholar's books were necessarily few, and much of his life would be spent travelling from city to city simply to read the basic texts. Printing relieved the situation during the second half of the 15th century; before then, the cheapest way to acquire a book was to copy it out oneself, and many humanists did. Above: a book cupboard, from a medal of Galeotto Marzio da Narni, teacher of the humanities at Bologna. The Lucretian motto reads: 'Being born we die, and the end depends on the beginning.' (2)

'Knowledge of Greek', wrote Leonardo Bruni, 'after an interval of seven centuries, was revived by Chrysoloras of Byzantium... My dreams at night were filled with what I had learned from him by day.' Chrysoloras (above) taught Greek in Florence from 1397 to 1400 and later elsewhere in Italy. (3)

Pier Candido Decembrio, who died in 1477 at the age of nearly 80, typifies the way in which the services of humanists were sought after. He was secretary to the Visconti in Milan until 1449, and was retained in the same capacity by the Ambrosian Republic. From 1450 to 56 he was Papal Secretary in Rome, later serving at the courts of Naples and Ferrara. He wrote elegant Latin and translated Greek according to the tastes of his patrons—including Plato's *Republic*, Appian, much of Plutarch and five books of the *Iliad*. (4)

Poggio Bracciolini, one of Bruni's fellow-students, also held an appointment at the Papal Chancery. He was among the luckiest of literary explorers. Besides the Quintilian already mentioned, he discovered Lucretius' *De rerum natura*, several of Cicero's *Orations* and many other lost works in Italy, Switzerland and France. (5)

Vittorino da Feltre tried to integrate the New Learning into a broader social education. In his school at Mantua, 1425–46, he combined Latin and Greek (including poetry, oratory and philosophy) with mathematics, natural history, music, athletics and guidance in manners and morals. (6)

Giovanni Conversini da Ravenna, teacher of rhetoric at Padua from 1392 to about 1405, was one of those who passed on the heritage of Petrarch to the generation of Vittorino da Feltre and Guarino da Verona, both of whom were his pupils. His favourite author was Cicero. (7)

With **Lorenzo Valla** (1409-57) humanist scholarship came of age. His first notable work, the *Elegantiae*, was an examination of classical Latin usage which cleared up points of grammar, meaning and style with a finality that was accepted for a century. The critical mastery displayed here was put to its most famous use when Valla exposed the Donation of Constantine as a forgery. In support of Alfonso of Naples' quarrel with Eugenius IV, he showed that this document, the legal basis for the popes' claim to temporal sovereignty, contained expressions not current until after Constantine's time, and mentioned towns that had not then been founded. He went on to apply the same acumen to other writings hitherto accepted and revered, such as the correspondence between Seneca and St Paul and Christ's letter to Abgar of Edessa. Even St Jerome's Vulgate, officially an inspired work, came in for criticism on philological grounds. Nicholas V, by a piece of enlightened self-interest, made Valla an official of the Curia. He was buried in St John Lateran and his tomb (above) has the form of an antique sarcophagus. (8)

Guarino da Verona actually went to Constantinople to learn Greek, bringing back with him a considerable number of new texts. From 1429 to 1460 he taught Latin and Greek at Ferrara and translated, among other authors, Strabo and Plutarch. Among his pupils were the first English humanists, Gray, Free, Flemmyng, Gunthorpe and Tiptoft. (9)

Pietro Bembo (above) learnt Greek at Messina, helped to popularize 'Platonic' love in his *Asolani* (1505), reformed Italian lyric poetry, became secretary to Leo X, then official historian of Venice, and died—a cardinal—in 1547. (11)

Nicolas of Cues (left), one of the first humanists north of the Alps, absorbed Plato into his own speculative system of theology. He was a zealous seeker after ancient manuscripts and visited Constantinople as papal representative before the Council of Florence. (10)

123

The most illustrious of Greek humanists to visit Italy was Archbishop Bessarion, who came in 1438 for the Council of Ferrara-Florence and remained to become a cardinal. His magnificent collection of Greek and Latin manuscripts formed the nucleus of the library of St Mark's in Venice. This painting (right) by ▶ Gentile Bellini shows him presenting another precious gift—a Byzantine reliquary still in Venice—to the brethren of the Scuola della Carità. (15)

Precursors of humanism were Petrarch and Boccaccio—seen here in Castagno's idealized representations of about 1450. Petrarch (1304–74) assembled the best private Latin library in Europe and originated modern textual criticism, while Boccaccio (1313–75) began the study of Greek as early as 1360. (12, 13)

An angel dictating to St Matthew before a kneeling donor seems to belong to the Middle Ages. But the date is 1509, the donor John Colet, and the manuscript a double Latin version of the Gospels, one the Vulgate, the other the translation of Erasmus. Renaissance scholarship in England was challenging old ideas long before this was reflected in the arts. (14)

124

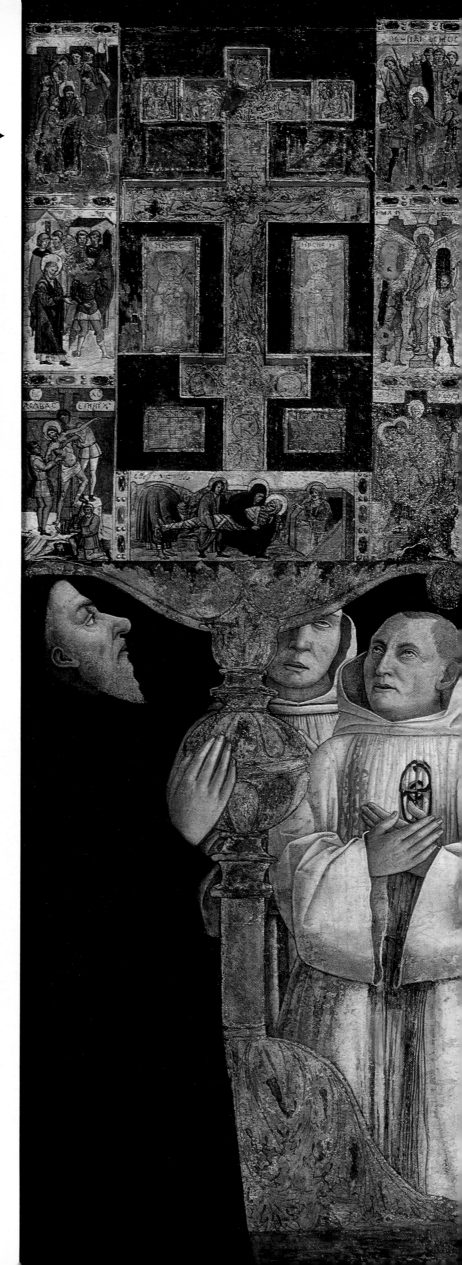

Three astronomers: Giorgione's strange allegory of human thought at the cross-roads. The old man perhaps stands for Aristotle, the eastern figure for Ptolemy, and the young man for a modern astronomer (possibly Regiomontanus). (17)

In the north, humanism was engulfed by the conflicts of the Reformation, though Erasmus (see p. 197) and his followers struggled to avoid the extremes of either side. Erasmus' heir, in a literal as well as figurative sense, was Boniface Amerbach (above: portrait by Holbein). Amerbach taught civil law at Basle, read Hebrew and could write accomplished Greek —for instance a treatise, characteristically, on moderation. (16)

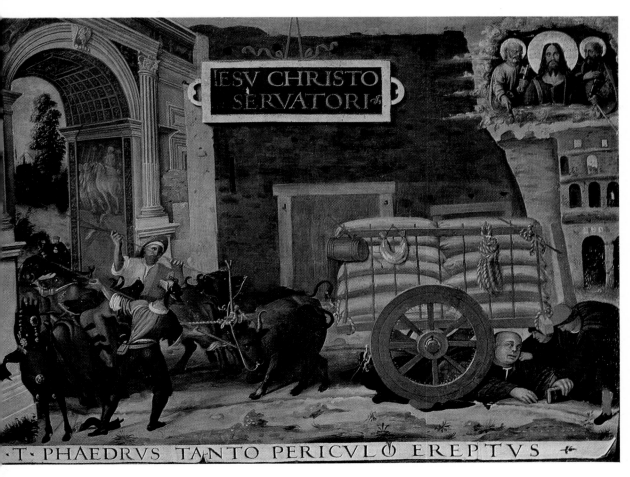

'Saved from so great a danger'—a vivid little vignette that illustrates one of the less remembered hazards of the scholar's life in the 15th century. Tommaso Inghirami, born at Volterra in 1470, came to Rome at the age of 23 and rose rapidly in the papal service, becoming Vatican librarian under Julius II. (His performance in the title-rôle of Seneca's *Phaedra* earned him the nickname which appears beneath the *ex voto*.) Inghirami's Latin orations were famous; Erasmus called him 'the Cicero of his age'; Raphael painted his portrait. The accident here commemorated happened near the Roman Forum, between the Arch of Titus and the Colosseum, and the concern for archaeological accuracy in such circumstances must reflect the scholarly personality of the donor. (18)

To the larger public the New Learning came in three ways—through lectures, through libraries and, eventually, through the printing press. The first public library was that given in 1440 to the monastery of S. Marco in Florence by Cosimo de' Medici (right). Designed by Michelozzo, it contained some 400 volumes, mostly from the collection bequeathed by Niccolò Niccoli. It was well-lit, the books being placed on desks between the windows, and was soon imitated in other Italian courts. (22)

Petrarch built up his library by buying books, by having them copied by scribes, receiving them as presents or, when all else failed, by copying them out laboriously himself. When he did this he would compare all the available texts, choose the best of variant readings, make emendations and add explanatory notes. Above left: a page from Livy, copied and annotated by Petrarch. The marginal note gives the reading of another manuscript. (19)

Lecture notes (left) survive from a student of one of the first teachers of Greek in England, William Sellyng, Prior of Christ Church, Canterbury. Sellyng had studied at Bologna and knew Politian; he returned to England in 1470. The notes, in Latin with examples in Greek, show his lectures to have been at a fairly elementary level. (20)

How many attended the lectures given by famous teachers is difficult to assess. Jacopo Bellini, in this sketch for the tomb of an imaginary professor (below), shows a crowded hall with 115 students, 21 of them standing. (21)

The 'Apostolic Library' of the Vatican had been in existence throughout the Middle Ages, but it was Pope Nicholas V (who, as Tommaso Parentucelli, had helped to organize the Library of S. Marco) who first gave it a humanist direction. At his death in 1455 it contained 824 books in Latin. The next twenty years saw the addition of numerous Greek manuscripts. In 1475 Sixtus IV appointed Platina as librarian (see p. 46). This fresco (right) shows Sixtus visiting the library; the books lie flat on the desks rather than upright on shelves—a medieval fashion which still persisted. (23)

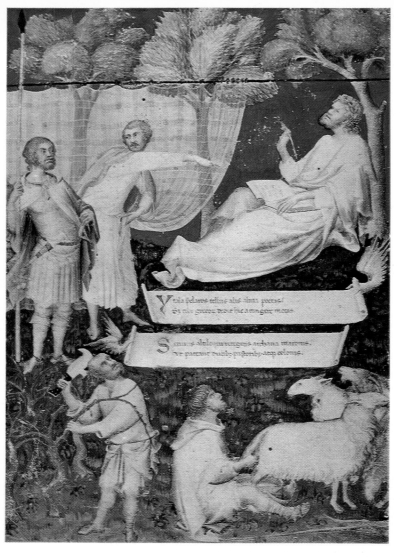

Renaissance manuscripts enjoyed a brief period of glory before being eclipsed by printing. Petrarch's copy of Vergil, illustrated by Simone Martini (left), may fairly claim to be the first. The two men met at Avignon about 1341. Simone's frontispiece shows Vergil sitting pen in hand, seeking inspiration. On the left is Aeneas, symbolizing the *Aeneid* and between them is the commentator Servius, who symbolically lifts the veil obscuring the poet. Below are a peasant *(Georgics)* and a shepherd *(Eclogues)*. (24)

An intellectual art, often of baffling subtlety, grew up within the neo-Platonist schools of philosophy. This page from Aristotle's *Nichomachaean Ethics* (c.1495) by Piramo da Monopoli ▶ (opposite) is supposed to illustrate a passage from Book VII on the nature of moderation. In the centre stand Heracles and Hermes, types of heroic and intellectual virtue. At the top are sacrificial scenes, at the bottom examples of bestial cruelty— Phalaris of Agrigentum roasting his children (the only subject actually mentioned in Aristotle's text) and Diomedes of Thrace feeding his horses with human flesh. The elaborate ornamental borders introduce Renaissance candelabra, putti, *bucrania*, Pegasus, cornucopia, trophies and medallions with the heads of Roman emperors. (27)

Ptolemy in his study (above), from a copy of the *Geography* made for Cardinal Bessarion about 1450, has a touch the exotic appropriate, in Renaissance eyes, to its Alexandrian theme. Note the astronomical instruments and books. (26)

The scroll title-page (left) held up by cherubs puts a classical motif to a new use. It was produced in Italy for an English patron, John Tiptoft, Earl of Worcester, who studied under Guarino at Ferrara in 1459–60. The work is by Basinio of Parma *(Basinius Parmensis)*, a humanist employed by the Este and later by the Malatesta. His *Astronomicon*, evidently valued by Tiptoft, is a Latin poem based on Manilius, but of little merit as either astronomy or poetry. (25)

BASINII
PARMEN
SIS·ASTR
ONOMI
CON·LI
BER·I·

λέγεται ἀγαθός· οὐ κεν δέχεται· ἅμα γὰρ τῇ φρονήσει μιᾷ οὔσῃ πᾶ
σαι ὑπάρξουσι· δῆλον δέ, καὶ εἰ μὴ πρακτικὴ ἦν, ὅτι ἔδει ἂν αὐτῆς
διὰ τὸ τοῦ μορίου ἀρετὴν εἶναι· καὶ ὅτι οὐ κέσται ἡ προαίρεσις
ὀρθὴ ἄνευ φρονήσεως, οὐ δ᾽ ἄνευ ἀρετῆς· ἡ μὲν γὰρ τὸ τέλος, ἡ δὲ
τὰ πρὸς τὸ τέλος ποιεῖ πράττειν· ἀλλὰ μὴν οὐ δὲ κυρία γε ἐστὶ τῆς
σοφίας, οὐ δὲ τοῦ βελτίονος μορίου· ὥσπερ οὐ δὲ τῆς ὑγιείας ἡ ἰατρι
κή· οὐ γὰρ χρῆται αὐτῇ, ἀλλ᾽ ὁρᾷ ὅπως γένηται· ἐκείνης οὖν ἕνε
κα ἐπιτάττει, ἀλλ᾽ οὐκ ἐκείνῃ· ἔτι ὅμοιως κἂν εἴ τις τὴν πολιτικ
φαίην ἄρχειν τῶν θεῶν, ὅτι ἐπιτάττει περὶ πάντα τὰ ἐν τῇ πόλει.

ἐπὶ ταῦτα λεκτέον ἀρχὴν ποιησαμένους ἄρχην, ὅτι τῶν περὶ τὸ
ἦθος φευκτῶν, τρία ἐστὶν εἴδη· κακία, ἀκρασία, θηριότης· τὰ

The 'sacred ruins' (in Du Bellay's phrase) of Rome had been seriously examined and studied since the early 15th century—the beginning of modern archaeology. Greece, on the other hand, was known only from the sketches of one traveller, Ciriaco d'Ancona, who visited Athens in 1436 and again in 1448. His drawing of the Parthenon (right, copied from the destroyed original by Giuliano da Sangallo) shows the sculpture fairly correctly but the capitals are wrong and the metopes arranged in a non-existent attic storey. Below it is a detail of the frieze. At the bottom, a fallen arcade from Hadrian's Aqueduct, the inscriptions carefully copied. (29)

In honour of Vergil, poet of Mantua and of Italy, the Marchioness Isabella d'Este Gonzaga proposed to erect a statue. She consulted the Neapolitan humanist Pontano, and Mantegna made a design (above) evoking Vergil's own age. (28)

'I have given much study to these ancient edifices', wrote Baldassare Castiglione (who was the actual author of Raphael's Report on Ancient Rome for Pope Leo X); 'I have taken no small effort to look them over with care and to measure them with diligence.' Raphael's drawing of the Pantheon survives (right)—then as now the best preserved of all ancient Roman buildings. (30)

Triumphal arches begin to appear frequently in art—symbols of glory either worldly or spiritual. Above: the imaginary Arch of Niccolò Tron, Doge of Venice from 1471 to 73. Right: the Arch of Constantine, painted for the first time with something like archaeological accuracy by Benedetto Bonfigli about 1470; S. Ercolano's body is being carried to St Peter's in Perugia. (31, 32)

The past baptized: the Renaissance architect who rebuilt Santi Apostoli in Rome for Cardinal Giuliano della Rovere (the future Julius II) had no scruple in placing in the vestibule an imperial eagle from Trajan's Forum. Roman power, no longer a symbol of paganism, is part of civilization. (33)

To rebuild Rome in the imagination was part of Mantegna's vision. A tireless scholar of inscriptions, sculpture and architectural remains, he yet used his knowledge with great freedom. In his *Trial of St James before Herod* (right) he succeeds in uniting motifs from various sources into a scene of convincing classicism. The arch is a free rendering of the Arco dei Gavi at Verona. (34)

The hill of knowledge was as steep as ever, and the way up it still usually followed the well trodden path of the Middle Ages. Humanism had revealed new fields for study and had transformed most branches of learning; exceptional men like Vittorino da Feltre had tried to put teaching on an entirely new basis. But it took time for these ideas to become accepted at university level, and still longer for them to percolate down to ordinary school education. For most of Europe the *trivium* and the *quadrivium* remained all-powerful.

This Florentine miniature of the late 15th century shows the old *schema* of the Seven Liberal Arts painted, it is true, in the style of Botticelli and embodying a beautiful Renaissance doorway, but otherwise reflecting only traditional concepts. Each Liberal Art is represented allegorically with her most famous exponent sitting at her feet. At the bottom Grammar—'of all the other Arts, the way and the gate'—welcomes the youug aspirant. The grammarian who sits writing is the Roman Donatus. Next comes Arithmetic gathering reeds, with Pythagoras; then Logic holding a scorpion, with Zeno. Music plays an organ, with Tubal Cain hammering on an anvil. Astronomy holds a sphere, with Ptolemy beneath her. Next comes Geometry with compass, and Euclid; and Rhetoric, with Cicero. Just below the summit sits St Augustine, who had first given the whole allegory a Christian meaning; he had made Theology rather than Philosophy the highest branch of knowledge to which all the others lead. Here she holds a triangle (the Trinity) in one hand, and with the other points upward to God. He sits enthroned above the heavenly spheres, which meticulously include the sun, the moon, the planets and the fixed stars. (35)

Scholarship
from Petrarch to Erasmus

ROBERTO WEISS

THE MIDDLE AGES forgot Greek and debased Latin: the Renaissance brought back Greek and restored Latin. Admittedly there were pockets in the medieval west where Greek was not unknown, just as there were medieval scholars who wrote what was good Latin by classical standards. Moreover, the great writers of ancient Rome had not been forgotten and Vergil, Ovid, and Horace continued to be sedulously flogged into schoolboys, while late antique writers like Orosius, Boethius and Isidore came to mean history, philosophy and encyclopaedic learning, in fact were the sources of much knowledge for nearly a thousand years. When all is considered, the Middle Ages offered a Christian civilization tempered by the classics. What then is the revival of classical learning and what did this revival really consist of?

The history of Europe between 600 and 1300 reveals several classical Renaissances, one in Ireland about 700, one at the court of Charlemagne, a revival of Roman law in the 12th, and one of Aristotle in the 13th century—and these were by no means the only ones. Some of them left only a faint legacy. Others proved more robust. But none of them dominated so entirely every aspect of life as that which 19th-century historians labelled *the* Renaissance.

Needless to say, the Renaissance was more than a revival of classical learning. But it did include such a revival. Standards in scholarship were completely overhauled, while the approach to the classics was changed beyond recognition. Renaissance humanism meant a total revaluation of the ancient classics, an investigation into what they stood for and what they had to say, and this is what the humanists set out to do between the time of Petrarch, who died in 1374, and that of Erasmus, who died in 1536.

'Humanism' was one of the words which were introduced into historical currency by 19th-century historians. The Latin word *humanista* was used first in the late 15th century and frequently in the 16th, but its meaning was rather narrow; it merely

indicated a teacher of one or both classical languages, in short of what constituted then the *studia humanitatis*. To us it means something more—a teacher who was no longer the medieval *doctor puerorum* (though he retained the old partiality for flogging) but a man of broader horizons, to whom the classics, instead of serving as quarries for stray facts and fine sentences, represented the accumulated wisdom of a civilization which it was imperative to rescue before it was too late.

p 196 (2)

f 4

Humanism did not start abruptly—its beginnings were already perceptible in north Italy during the second half of the 13th century—nor were its causes simple. The widespread interest in Latin rhetoric, which already in the later Middle Ages was considered to have practical value; the revival of Roman law in the 12th century and of Aristotelian philosophy in the 13th, which directed the attention of theologians, lawyers and doctors to certain aspects of classical antiquity; a small group of scholars in Padua gaining access to the library of the Abbey of Pomposa; another in Verona suddenly discovering the treasures of their own cathedral library . . . all these and many more seemingly insignificant straws in the wind showed the way in which the intellectual climate was changing.

Another important contributing factor was the beginning of private book-collecting. Individuals began to acquire and to read books for their own sake, not as part of their profession. Groups of these 'pre-humanists' were already flourishing in some

This vivid sketch of a Renaissance school comes from the manuscript of Antonio Filarete (see p. 50): students dine on the left, masters at the high table. At this date (about 1460) the word 'humanista', was just coming into use, in the narrow sense of a teacher of Latin or Greek. The critical study of texts, however was still confined to an enlightened few. (2)

Francesco Petrarca (Petrarch) is most famous as a poet: for his 'Canzoniere' that had such a decisive effect on Renaissance literature. He was, however, equally eminent and original as a scholar. He collected and collated texts of the Latin classics and his library was from that point of view the best in Europe. This sketch was made by a friend in a copy of one of his works. (3)

towns of north Italy between 1270 and 1320. Not only did they effect a decided improvement in the standard of written Latin, both prose and poetry, but they also achieved considerable successes in the realm of scholarship proper—such as the resurrection of Latin classics (e.g. Catullus) that had been forgotten for centuries; the unravelling of the metres of Seneca's tragedies, incomprehensible until Lovato Lovati (1241–1309) succeeded in explaining them; and the differentiating between the elder and the younger Pliny, regarded as one person, until Giovanni Mansionario proved during the early years of the 14th century that the Pliny who wrote the *Natural History* could not have been the one who wrote the Letters. This same Giovanni also revealed himself as a student of Imperial Roman coinage through the drawings he made on the margins of the autograph of his *Historia imperialis*. Ancient Roman inscriptions also began to be studied. The Middle Ages had been the heyday of abridgments of classical writers, when Livy meant Florus and Trogus meant Justin. Now they were no longer enough. Petrarch's father's volume of Vergil and Landolfo Colonna's rescue of the third Decade of Livy were typical of the change. In short, by 1320 it was already clear that a new study of classical antiquity was on the move.

f 1

Petrarch the Scholar

f 3
p 124
(12)

As a scholar Petrarch (1304–74) had not been exactly a slow developer. But although he received a traditional education at Carpentras and wasted three years at Bologna, it was at Avignon that he really found his vocation. His meetings here with the Provençal 'clerk' Raymond Soubeyran and the Roman noble Landolfo Colonna opened his eyes to the new classics and especially Livy. He succeeded in assembling the first, third and fourth Decades into one volume, displaying exceptional acumen as a textual critic. Soon he was doing the same for other authors. He discovered Cicero's forgotten *Pro archia* at Liège in 1333 and the letters *Ad Atticum* at Verona in 1345, corrected both texts and freed them from scribal interpolations and corruptions. The works of some Christian authors like his beloved St Augustine received similar attention. Modern textual criticism in fact begins with Petrarch—not because he was consciously preparing what we call today a critical edition, but because he felt the necessity that the volumes in his own library should contain texts as accurate as possible.

p 126
(19)

Petrarch's own literary achievement was very great—the whole lyric poetry of Renaissance Europe, for instance, would have had a different complexion without him. Yet the creation of his library was a feat of at least comparable importance. It was unique in its time for the number of its classical Latin texts, and it contained two items of even greater significance for the future—Plato and Homer in Greek.

Petrarch himself never learned Greek, though it seems to have been the energy rather than the opportunity that was lacking. His first teacher, a Calabrian monk called Barlaam, broke off the lessons, but in cosmopolitan Avignon it would have been easy to find another master, had he really wanted to. When, some twenty years later, he met another Calabrian Greek he preferred to hand him over to Boccaccio. Yet there is no doubt that Petrarch's interest in and encouragement of the study of Greek exercised a powerful and pervasive influence. He stands behind Leon Pilatus' translation of Homer into Latin.

It would be a mistake to assume that Petrarch's pursuit of the classics sprang only from a disinterested love of learning. He himself aspired to be one of them: a new Vergil in the *Africa* and a new Livy in the *De viris illustribus*. His Italian as well as his Latin works were coloured by his classical scholarship, and he addressed the Latin writers of antiquity as equals in the *Antiquis illustrioribus*.

Inevitably he had to remain very distant from the models that he admired—not so much because of the number of centuries that separated him from them as because those centuries were Christian. Christian outlook and Christian prejudices could not be disregarded at will. Yet his writings do mark a decisive break with previous literature both in their style (the abandonment of medieval conventions in order to conform to classical practice) and in their values. He looked at classical antiquity not only as a Golden Age and a lost Paradise, but also as the teacher of a way of life which could be regained. It was therefore, so he felt, his duty to restore the true letter of the ancient writers and emphasize the exceptional significance of their message, by gathering all the available evidence which would make these texts intelligible. This also meant turning to the tangible remains of the ancient world. He examined inscriptions and ancient coins to throw new light on obscure passages in a writer, and set one text against another to solve a problem of history or scholarship. Of course Petrarch was not infallible and there are cases when he misunderstood a passage or accepted an unreliable legend; it could hardly have been otherwise with the means at his disposal. Perhaps his most serious limitation was his underestimate of Greek. For all his interest in Homer he never doubted that Rome was the classical civilization *par excellence*.

Boccaccio, Scholar and Story-teller

This was a field where Boccaccio not only felt differently but, by bringing Leon Pilatus to Florence, did something positive. Before Pilatus Greek had been virtually unknown outside eastern Europe and some parts of south Italy and Sicily, and those who translated Aristotle and some of the Fathers during the 12th and 13th century and Galen during the first half of the 14th established no tradition of Greek scholarship. The Boccaccio-Pilatus partnership, on the other hand, led to the public teaching of Greek in Florence, to the translation of Homer as well as of a little Euripides, not to mention a pseudo-Aristotelian tract. These versions as well as his own notes on Homer reveal Pilatus to have been a far better scholar than has hitherto been suspected. As for Boccaccio, Pilatus proved a godsend to him, and during their three years together he succeeded in learning enough Greek for his needs. The fact that after Pilatus' departure from Florence Greek dried up there for some thirty years was due not so much to lack of the essential texts, as to his teaching being so much above the heads of most of his hearers.

As a scholar Boccaccio (1313–75) differed greatly from Petrarch, whom he always regarded as his master. As slovenly as Petrarch was accurate, Boccaccio was the most unreliable of scribes. Their outlooks also differed, for to Boccaccio the encyclopaedia was clearly the best way for gathering together the results of scholarship. Both were bibliophiles and Boccaccio too was anxious to assemble as many classical texts as possible; yet the remains of his library do not betray that work of revision and emendation which appears on so many volumes from Petrarch's. Some writers (Tacitus in particular) whose works came into Boccaccio's hands had been unknown to Petrarch. Boccaccio's passion for classical mythology, which he saw as an essential key to the understanding of ancient poetry, never abandoned him

p 124
(13)

and made him spend many years on a huge compilation, the *Genealogiae deorum*, which remained the standard work on the subject for nearly two hundred years. He was also supposed to have unearthed some long forgotten texts of Varro, Tacitus, and Apuleius in the library of the Abbey of Monte Cassino, but the real discoverer was another friend of Petrarch, Zanobi da Strada, who, by bringing the famous Laurentian archetypes of Tacitus and Apuleius to Florence, made them available to Boccaccio.

Petrarch never taught, but his interests and way of thinking spread far and wide. Barbato da Sulmona wrote a commentary on one of Petrarch's letters as if it had been an ancient classic. On the other hand, Giovanni Dondi, the Paduan physician who was a very close friend of Petrarch in his old age, did valuable work in his own right. He was a very keen antiquary who went deeper than Petrarch in this field. For when visiting Rome as a pilgrim in 1375, he not only recorded the principal monuments of the city but measured some of them and copied inscriptions. Thus when Petrarch died in 1374 there was no danger that his influence would fade away.

The Heirs of Petrarch

Apart from a host of lesser names, the principal continuators of his lifework were three: Lombardo della Seta, who saw to the spreading of Petrarch's literary inheritance, Giovanni Conversini da Ravenna, whose teaching as well as his activity as chancellor was instrumental in popularizing the new humanist doctrines, and, above all, Coluccio Salutati.

Like Petrarch, Salutati (1331–1406) sedulously collected classical texts and annotated and emended the volumes he owned. He was particularly interested in Latin orthography, consulting manuscripts and inscriptions in order to establish correct spellings. He compared all the available sources in order to settle a doubtful point and he intervened in defence of poetry against the theologians. Salutati never held a university chair, though his influence was paramount on the Florentine humanists who came after him, Poggio and Bruni included. His greatest achievement, however, was the re-awakening of Greek studies in Florence, which had been slumbering since the departure of Leon Pilatus. The coming of the Byzantine Manuel Chrysoloras to Florence in 1397 to occupy a chair of Greek was the direct outcome of Salutati's efforts. Chrysoloras' lectures began in March 1397 and proved popular at once, pupils flocking to his classroom also from other parts of Italy. An initial difficulty encountered in his teaching was the scarcity of suitable books. Thanks to Palla Strozzi, then the wealthiest citizen of Florence, this was however only a temporary setback.

Chrysoloras emphasized the importance, when translating, of rendering the spirit rather than the bare letter of the original. His lectures covered most of the major Greek writers, with Thucydides and Ptolemy along with Plato and Homer. And although his Florentine teaching lasted only three years, it was sufficient to establish the study of Greek on a permanent basis.

From Florence it spread to Rome, where many of Salutati's most promising young friends, Poggio and Bruni among them, went to seek employment in the Papal Chancery. Leonardo Bruni (1374–1444), the most brilliant of all, expressed his Hellenism mainly in translating, though he was also the author of a tract in Greek on the Florentine constitution. As a translator he had started by assisting Salutati in his controversy against Dominici in defence of classical writers through making a Latin rendering of a tract by St Basil in defence of classical letters. But his main fame as a translator rests on his versions from Aristotle, which enjoyed a European popularity long after his death.

In his *De interpretatione recta* Bruni had put forward his views on translating, though he only followed them to a limited extent. His versions are marred by a preoccupation with stylistic elegance, and whenever another translation was available (and this was so with Aristotle), Bruni's own production was little more than a decorated rendering of the earlier text.

If Bruni was the leading translator of his time, the leading teacher of Greek was Guarino da Verona who, after mastering the language at Constantinople, eventually settled at Ferrara, where he taught from 1429 until his death in 1460. As a translator

Marginal references (left column):
122 (7)
18 (14)
122 (3)
19 (17)
123 (9)

Guarino da Verona's 'Grammar' of which the title-page is shown here, was a school textbook in the new style. The humanists saw one of their main tasks as that of purifying Latin from medieval 'barbarism'. But in the small scenes at the bottom it is evident that they did not relinquish the idea of beating knowledge into their pupils. (4)

Guarino directed his attention to Plutarch and Strabo. As a teacher his secret lay in both the appeal of his engaging personality and his painstaking method. There is no doubt that he and Vittorino da Feltre (1373–1446) were the greatest educators of Renaissance Italy. But whereas Vittorino's teaching was meant for schoolboys, that of Guarino was mainly at a university level. If he had a rival, it was Francesco Filelfo (1398–1481), his superior in actual knowledge of Greek, but a man handicapped by a difficult temperament. He had a troubled career, wandering from city to city in quest of employment. His translations, however, were sensitive and accurate, which was more than could be said for Poggio or Valla, whose versions were far from reliable.

Marginal references (right column):
f 4
p 122 (6)
p 51 (19)

The Classics Restored

Even before the fall of Constantinople in 1453 Greek scholars had been coming to Italy in increasing numbers, though they were generally handicapped by their indifferent knowledge of Latin. There were, however, exceptions, and Theodore Gaza, George of Trebizond and John Argyropoulos had no linguistic difficulties and proved outstanding teachers. Yet even with them and Italian teachers like Guarino and Filelfo, to mention only the most distinguished, knowledge of Greek did not spread as widely as one might have thought. The fact that instruction in Greek was available at a particular place, was no guarantee of continuity, for when a teacher left or died, many years often elapsed before teaching was resumed. Thus, for example, Alessandro Farnese,

Marginal references (right column):
p 26 (37)

the future Pope Paul III, had to move in 1487 from Rome to Florence in order to learn Greek. The great popularity enjoyed by the humanists' Latin versions of Greek authors are in themselves indicative of ignorance of that language.

f 5 The texts chosen for translation were very seldom purely literary works. Like the medieval translators, their Renaissance successors generally chose those writings which might further some definite branch of knowledge. Except for Homer, poetry was left alone, the versions of Theocritus by Filetico and of Hesiod by Niccolò della Valle being exceptional cases, while it was not until the very end of the Quattrocento that the first humanist translation of Aristotle's *Poetics* appeared, a work which was overlooked until the 16th century although it had been available in Latin since the 13th.

With the resurrection of Greek went that of many Latin classical writings, which had been gathering dust unread in the cupboards of monastic or cathedral libraries since the Carolingian age. Or practically so, for there were occasional instances during the 11th, 12th and 13th centuries of the use of texts (Varro's *De lingua Latina* and Tacitus' *Germania* are typical examples) otherwise unknown until the rise of humanism. The first half of the 15th century was the period when most of the forgotten texts were discovered. The letters of Cicero and the younger Pliny, the histories of Tacitus, and the poems of Propertius and Tibullus had already come to light during the 14th century. But during the

p 122 next century Poggio Bracciolini (1380–1459) alone discovered
(5) between 1415 and 1417 a very considerable number of Cicero's orations, the epic of Valerius Flaccus, the poem of Lucretius, the *Silvae* of Statius, and Asconius on Cicero's orations, as well as a complete Quintilian, while later he found Petronius' *Coena Trimalchionis* in England and Frontinus' book on the aqueducts of Rome at Monte Cassino.

Needless to say, all these discoveries were greeted with jubilation by the humanist world of Italy. Other discoveries which also aroused much enthusiasm were those of the hitherto unknown *Brutus* of Cicero and of complete copies of the *Orator* and *De oratore* by the same author, made by Gherardo Landriani, Bishop of Lodi, in his own cathedral in 1421, and of Pliny's *Panegyric* and the *Panegyrici veteres* made at Mainz in 1433 by Giovanni Aurispa. In importance they were, however, surpassed by the discovery of the minor works of Tacitus and the *De grammaticis et rhetoribus* of Suetonius made at Fulda, not at Hersfeld as was believed until not so long ago, by Enoch of Ascoli about 1455. With those made at Fulda the age of great discoveries seemed to be over. But in 1494 Giorgio Merula or, more exactly, his secretary Giorgio Galbiate, carried out a successful exploration of one of the forgotten treasure houses of north Italy, and in the library of the ancient Irish monastery at Bobbio, was able to lay hands on a host of unknown writings by late Roman authors, mainly grammatical manuals, but including also the poems of Dracontius and the *De reditu suo* of Rutilius Namatianus. Some important discoveries were also made during the 16th century, the most outstanding ones being those of Books I–VI of the *Annals* of Tacitus, the correspondence between Pliny and Trajan, the history of Velleius Paterculus, and part of Livy's fifth Decade.

The discovery of new classical writings brought with it a desire to have correct copies of them. Here Petrarch and Salutati had been pioneers and, as the 15th century went on, such efforts became increasingly numerous. Of course in many cases what were intended as corrections were actually corruptions, a criticism voiced at the time by Niccolò Niccoli (1364–1437). A very common source of corruption was that even learned scribes often substituted their own spelling for that of the original they were transcribing, so that archaic forms disappeared. Even so accomplished a humanist as Poggio was guilty of such a practice; indeed Niccoli was one of the very few scholars of the first half of the 15th century who was not. As for emendations, these were only too often the result of guesswork. It was according to such a method that Poggio emended, or rather corrupted, Cicero's *Philippics*. On the other hand, Lorenzo Valla's corrections to Livy were backed by such acumen and command of classical usage that several of his suggestions have been accepted by modern editors.

At times even great humanists would be rather naïve. Guarino da Verona, for instance, having found that quotations from Herodotus in his Gellius appeared to stop abruptly, did not hesitate to take his own Herodotus and complete the passages in question. Even further went Tommaso Seneca who, when preparing a copy of Tibullus for a friend, did not scruple to fill in the lacunae with lines of his own. Again when sections of a text were missing in their copy, it was usual for humanists to supply what was not there from another manuscript, thus contaminating the tradition represented by their own. These humanist copies were the immediate predecessors of the printed editions. On the whole they have proved somewhat of a curse to modern editors. All the same it was all this work on the text of the Latin classics which led directly to the new philology.

The New Philology

The key figure is Lorenzo Valla (1407–57). Until him classical p 123
scholarship had mainly expressed itself in the commentary and (8)
emendation of texts. But for Valla, feeling as he did that written Latin had not achieved classical purity and that the way to achieve it was a thorough reform of grammar, this was not enough. The result was the *Elegantiae*, a work which ruled over humanist Europe for over a century. A comparative examination of classical and modern Latin usage, the *Elegantiae* emphasized that the latter should be based on the ancient writers of Rome, though the coining of new words could sometimes be permissible. At the same time, he did not advocate a blind imitation of Cicero, in fact he occasionally even disagreed with him. The *Elegantiae* stressed the real value and meaning of words, though wider issues were also discussed in it.

The comparative method, which was so evident in the *Elegantiae*, was also followed in the *Orthographia* of Giovani Tortelli (c. 1400–66), which meant to do for Latin spelling what Valla's work had done for usage, but included also discussions on other subjects connected with antiquity. For instance the section dedicated to *R* (each letter of the alphabet was assigned a section in Tortelli's treatise) included a long and extremely interesting description of the topography of ancient Rome, as an extension of the discussion on the correct spelling of the name of the city. Another work in which the new philology inaugurated by Valla was very much present was the *Cornucopia* of Niccolò Perotti (1429–80) which, started originally as a commentary on Martial, grew eventually into a philological and grammatical repertory of the Latin language. But Perotti did not limit himself to philological works. Like other humanists, he also felt the urge to revise and overhaul the teaching of elementary grammar in the light of the new humanist knowledge. This led to his *Rudimenta* which, together with the Latin grammar by Gaspare da Verona, ended the grip exerted by the old medieval grammars over education, at any rate in Italy. On the other hand, except at Rome, where Antonio Mancinelli and Sulpizio Verulano compiled some very successful elementary Latin grammars, the age when humanists were preoccupied with works of this kind was over by 1470.

The new philology carried in its wake a new criticism. Here also Valla was in the forefront. What prompted him to attack the so-called Donation of Constantine, the document which gave a legal basis to the temporal power of the papacy, was the conflict between Pope Eugenius IV and Valla's own protector, King Alfonso of Naples. Yet politics did not figure in this treatise, where the authenticity of the Donation was denied solely on historical, philological and legal grounds. There was the fact that no mention of it occurred in the early biographies of Constantine and Pope Sylvester; there were the legal contradictions; there were the numerous anachronisms and other howlers; and finally there were the phraseology and vocabulary, which had been complexioned by the Vulgate and did not conform at all with the usage of the Constantinian age. Valla's treatise showed fully the powers of the new philological criticism when backed by a mind of exceptional acumen. Even bolder were Valla's annotations on the Latin New Testament, which were so much admired by Erasmus, for what was questioned here was the accuracy of part of Holy Writ itself. The annotations were a philological comparison between the text of the Vulgate and the Greek original, supported

HERODOTI HISTORICI INCIPIT.
Laurentii Vallen. conuerfio de Græco in Latinum.

ERODOTI Halicarnafei hiftoriæ explica
tio hæc eft: ut neqꝫ ea quæ gefta funt: ex rebus
humanis obliterentur ex æuo: neqꝫ ingentia &
admiranda opera: uel a Græcis edita: uel a Bar
baris golria fraudétur: cum alia: tum uero: qua
de re ifti inter fe belligerauerũt. Perfarũ eximii
memorat diffenfionũ auctores extitiffe Phœ
nices qui a mari quod Rubrum uocatur: in hoc noftrum profcif
centes: & hanc incolentes regionem: quam nunc quoqꝫ incolunt:
longinquis continuo nauigationibus incubuerunt: faciendifqꝫ
Aegyptiarum & Affyriarum merciũ uecturis in alias plagas: præ
cipuèqꝫ Argos traiecerunt: Argos &enim ea tempeftate omni

One of the revelations of Renaissance scholarship was Herodotus, un-
known in the west until the first half of the 15th century. The text was
translated into Latin by the great Lorenzo Valla, pioneer of the new
philology. The opening page, shown here (from a Venetian edition of 1494)
belongs to an early stage in the history of printing, space being left for an
ornamental initial to be added by hand. (5)

by evidence drawn from the early Fathers. And here his verdict
was that St Jerome's version was not faultless, owing to an imperfect knowledge of Greek and his use of corrupt manuscripts.

Valla's annotations were a philological work which inaugurated modern Biblical criticism, and the immediate predecessor of
the work of Erasmus and Nebrija in the same field. Nor should
one forget that Valla's achievement as a critic also included the
proof that the correspondence between Seneca and St Paul was
spurious and that the writings ascribed to Denys the Areopagite
could not possibly have been written by a contemporary of St
Paul. He showed the spuriousness of the Letter of Jesus to Abgar
of Edessa and laughed away the belief that each of the Apostles
in turn had composed one of the lines of the Creed.

The Past Rediscovered

19 (17)
The first half of the 15th century witnessed a complete change in
the writing of history. Leonardo Bruni initiated humanist, and
Flavio Biondo modern, historiography. Before them history writing had remained traditional, and even Petrarch had been medieval enough to see history as either a series of biographies of great
men or a collection of anecdotes. But Bruni, during the long
struggle between Florence and Milan, came to see Florence's rôle
in it as a championship of freedom against tyranny, which in
turn aroused an urge in him to glorify what his town had done
for democratic liberty. He saw Florence as the new Rome, while

the rival Pisa was presented as the new Carthage. To this was
added a conviction that a history such as his would also prove
valuable in the interpretation of what was taking place in the
present.

Historiography advanced one step further with Flavio Biondo
(1392–1463), mainly because his vision of history was wider than
Bruni's in both time and space. For he was the first to conceive a
history of medieval Italy, indeed of medieval Europe, during the
thousand years stretching from 410 to 1441. Also striking was his
approach to authority. In the *Decades* he was obviously not over-
awed by the prestige of famous historians, even when they were
called Procopius or Paul the Deacon, neither of whom escaped
his criticism, so that we find him, for instance, producing the
evidence of a mosaic seen in a church at Ravenna in order to re-
fute a statement in Procopius.

The sources of Biondo's *Decades* were many and various, ranging from Strabo and Ptolemy to ancient monuments and inscriptions as well as medieval chronicles, and when evaluating the
authority of a writer he assumed that the closer he was to the
events he described, the greater would be his reliability. As a
humanist, Biondo possessed a good knowledge of Roman history. But in the *Decades* he disagreed with his fellow humanists,
who had traced the beginnings of the decay of Rome to the
abandoning of republican institutions in Caesar's time, believing
instead that it had started during the later Empire. Biondo was
naturally not infallible; moreover, his style lacked distinction
when it was not decidedly flat, and occasionally his chronology
was at fault and some of his facts confused. Yet after his presentation of the Middle Ages as a distinct period, any serious writing
of history could no longer be the same.

The originality of Biondo's *Decades* is beyond doubt. Still the
work where he showed himself at his most original was the *Italia
illustrata*, which surveyed the peninsula province by province and
inaugurated historical geography. It showed a merging of history
and geography backed up by a deep knowledge of antiquity and
a cunning use of personal observation and information received
from friends and correspondents. In the *Italia illustrata* one feels
that Biondo was more at ease than in the *Decades*, and what emerges is an Italy united geographically and historically. The effect
is achieved through its descriptions of regions and towns, which
include not only historical details and geographic features, but
also accounts of their most famous men and their more prominent monuments, both ancient and modern.

Biondo's lavish references to ancient remains in his historical
works is not surprising, for he and Poggio were the real founders
of modern archaeology. It is true that the monuments of Rome
had been examined before them and ancient inscriptions copied
and collected. But Poggio's account of ancient Rome in the first
book of his *De varietate fortunae* inaugurated new archaeological
standards. For Poggio, not content with describing what he saw,
set about finding what the ruins could reveal through an examination of their structure and materials and even their nomenclature. Along with classical writers he also consulted early
Christian and medieval texts and, of course, considered the evidence supplied by inscriptions.

It was left to Biondo's *Roma instaurata*, however, to give the
first methodical description of the ancient city. In this he was not
moved solely by archaeological passion. He saw in these ruins a
deeper meaning, and felt that to neglect them was tantamount to
forsaking, indeed losing for ever, what had been ancient Roman
civilization. Besides studying what was still left of the old city and
the ancient writers, he consulted the old catalogues of the urban
regions and the medieval descriptions of the town. Nor were inscriptions and coins, Christian and medieval texts, and even documents in the archives of churches overlooked. In his reconstruction of what the city had looked like, he followed a logical
plan based on the catalogue of the city regions traditionally
ascribed to Sextus Rufus. Thanks to the *Roma instaurata* it was now
possible to have a reasonable idea of the old town from the topographical angle and, furthermore, an account of its growth and
the functions of its main buildings. p 130-131
(30-34)

Greek archaeology, on the other hand, started and ended with
Ciriaco d'Ancona (1391–c.1455), since after him the Turkish con- p 130
(29)

quest of the Greek world stopped any archaeological activity until the middle of the 16th century. As a traveller in Greek lands, Ciriaco had been preceeded by the Florentine priest Cristoforo Buondelmonti, who spent about sixteen years (1414–30) exploring the islands of the Aegean. But he was more of a geographer than an archaeologist. Not so Ciriaco, whose travels included Asia Minor and Egypt as well as Greece. During his many journeys he was tireless in his archaeological activity, which mainly consisted in his copying countless Greek and Latin inscriptions and drawing a large number of buildings, statuary, carvings, stelae, etc. The details which he gathered about the great temple of Hadrian at Cyzicus, now lost for ever, testify to his scientific accuracy. For in order to record its dimensions, he not only measured its remains carefully, but even employed an astrolabe in order to record accurately the height of the pillars. Nor did Ciriaco devote himself exclusively to Greek antiquities; he worked also in Italy and made two visits to Egypt, examining and measuring monuments there with equal enthusiasm. Unfortunately he failed to record his findings at all systematically and much of the immense amount of information gathered in a lifetime of travel remained undigested.

Renaissance Libraries

Thanks to the humanist effort the number of classical writings available had increased very considerably since the time of Petrarch. Such an increase was of three kinds. There were the newly discovered Latin works. There were the numerous Greek manuscripts which had been flowing into Italy or transcribed there since the beginning of the 15th century. And there were the ever increasing Latin translations of Greek classical authors. Now, in medieval libraries, volumes of classical authors had generally been an exception, but in the new libraries being created by the humanists the classics had pride of place, though theology, civil and canon law, and medicine continued of course to figure in them.

p 129
(27)

'The Wonders of Rome': cheap guides to Rome for pilgrims and visitors included religious pictures as well as secular ones like this woodcut of about 1500. It shows Romulus and Remus suckled by the wolf and their mother Rhea Sylvia praying before a statue of their father Mars. (6)

The first library with a large collection of classical and humanist volumes was that of the rulers of Milan, which was kept in the Castle of Pavia, until Louis XII removed it to France in 1500. What made this library so exceptional was that it included a substantial part of Petrarch's library, brought to Pavia after the conquest of Padua by Giangaleazzo Visconti in 1388. But the library of the Visconti, like those of the Este at Ferrara and the Gonzaga at Mantua, was a private library, to which only a few privileged persons could have access and even fewer were able to borrow books. It was left to Cosimo de' Medici to inaugurate in Florence what was in every sense the first Renaissance public library.

Medieval libraries consisted as a rule of a rectangular room with cupboards against the walls or, alternatively, two rows of desks with the volumes resting on them and securely chained, so that they could be read without being removed. The one built at S. Marco in Florence for Cosimo de' Medici was quite different. Designed by Michelozzo Michelozzi in 1440, its hall was basilican in form, with a high barrel-vaulted ceiling supported on two rows of pillars and two side 'aisles' containing the rows of desks with the chained volumes. It was an immediate success, not only on account of its elegance but also because it allowed a window between every two rows of desks. Of its contents the nucleus was the outstanding collection of Greek and Latin manuscripts assembled by Niccolò Niccoli, and new books were continually being added by its founder. For the first time, too, the growth of a library was planned according to a rational principle. For at Cosimo's request a list of essential works, sacred and secular, was drawn up by the humanist Tommaso Parentucelli, later Pope Nicholas V. (The same list was used again later for libraries at Fiesole, Pesaro and other places). The other great novelty was that it was open to the public. In this, and in its design, it was quickly imitated at Cesena by the lord of the town, Malatesta Novello, whose library is still open and functioning today.

p 126
(22)
p 24
(35)

Parentucelli's list was also used for the library established at Urbino by its ruler Federigo da Montefeltro, who mostly relied for the supply of volumes on the Florentine book-seller Vespasiano da Bisticci. It is true that Politian looked down on these recently executed books. Yet by the time of its founder's death Urbino had become the most important repository of classical and humanist manuscripts in Italy next to the Medici and the Vatican libraries. What then of the Vatican? Of course a papal library had been in existence for several centuries and even at Avignon it had included classical and even a few humanist works. Yet decay had set in with the Great Schism. It was Pope Nicholas V (1447–55) who founded the new Vatican Library. What he created was certainly the greatest library of his time. Further developed under Sixtus IV (1471–84), when Platina, one of the leading members of the Roman Academy, became its head, it was supervised for a very long time by a series of distinguished humanists.

p 127
(23)
p 46 (2)

Humanists were also in charge of the library at Naples, which King Alfonso V of Aragon had founded and his son Ferdinand I increased. But important as it was, it mostly consisted of manuscripts either made expressly for the Aragonese Kings or presented to them by their authors, so that it had less appeal to humanists than other libraries. A library which would, on the other hand, have greatly attracted them was that of St Mark's at Venice. But the magnificent collection of books presented to it by Cardinal Bessarion in 1468 was still unpacked as late as 1494, so that it was only in the time of Aldus Manutius that it began to exert a vigorous influence on Venetian scholarship. In fact it was almost entirely Bessarion's books that made possible the achievements of Aldus and his colleagues in the field of Greek editing.

p 124
(15)
p 126
(26)

Books in Print

The first printing press in Italy began to function at Subiaco in 1465; two years later there was one in Rome. Other Italian towns quickly followed and it was not long before the potentialities of the new invention were appreciated by the humanists. Inevitably many of the first printed books shared the drawbacks of manuscripts. Apart from the fact that compositors were no more accurate than scribes, some of the traditions of the medieval *peciae* were preserved in the printing of some university texts, where

p 65 (4)

every page was likely to consist of two columns, each with sixty lines and at least thirty letters in every line. Moreover a blank space was generally left at the beginning of a paragraph, to be filled in by a rubricator, who often supplied the chapter headings as well. Nor was it uncommon to have the first page decorated with illuminated borders and initials and have special copies printed on vellum instead of paper. It took some time before the scribes were completely ousted. Throughout the last quarter of the 15th century they were still as active as ever, and even in the late 16th century the *scriptores* of the Vatican Library were still engaged on the activities denoted by their title. Even manuscripts which were actually copies of printed books were not uncommon, most of them being made for patrons who preferred to have texts not produced by mechanical means. Yet even the most famous libraries of Italy eventually came to admit printed books; before the 15th century was over they were already appearing on the desks of the libraries of Naples, Mantua, Ferrara and the Vatican.

Until the invention of printing what we understand by a 'critical edition' hardly existed, the texts 'edited' by humanists being as a rule merely copies made for personal use and circulating, if at all, within a very small circle. But scholars now had the task of producing correct texts of classical authors for issue by the printers. Thus between 1469 and 1472 Giovanni Andrea de' Bussi, Bishop of Aleria, edited a considerable number of Latin classics for the Roman press of Sweynheim and Pannartz, the two German typographers who had introduced printing into Italy. The rate at which these editions poured out meant that the standard of editing was rather superficial. The venture on the whole did not succeed—perhaps because the texts were not accompanied by a commentary. Later on, the Latin classics, especially the poets, were printed framed by a copious running commentary, as was usual with the *Pandects* and the works of Aristotle. These commentaries or collections of short dissertations on the text of an author were often printed on their own, as for instance the annotations on Catullus by Girolamo Avanzo (1495) or those on Pliny by Ermolao Barbaro (1491–93), these consisting of discussions of difficult passages or words as well as textual corrections.

A return to the plain text without commentary was inaugurated by Aldus (1450–1515) whose editions of the classics in a pocket format led to a new era in book production. Furthermore with Aldus the printing of Greek ceased to be very exceptional and editions of the classics in several volumes also started to appear. They were the result of considerable editorial effort. To Aldus the edition of a classic no longer meant a manuscript just being handed over to the printer with the more obvious errors corrected and the abbreviations expanded. Instead each text was assigned to a particular editor, often Aldus himself, and the manuscripts were very carefully revised and emended and the proofs carefully corrected. Of course at the rate at which the Aldine classics appeared, it is obvious that editorial revision must have been somewhat hurried. But his press did establish a standard in editing that made it very difficult for anyone to return to the old slipshod ways.

Politian and Barbaro

As we have seen, during the first half of the 15th century, there were ample opportunities to learn Greek, and several of the early humanists had done so. But with Politian (1454–94) we find for the first time an Italian scholar with a grasp of classical Greek not inferior to that of the best Byzantine masters. As a philologist he certainly depended largely on the pioneering work done by Valla but he proved to be much the more thorough and imaginative of the two. When lecturing on a text he skipped no problem, and if a passage was not clear he sought every possible help in order to throw light upon it. Instead of publishing running commentaries on authors, as was the fashion in his time, he preferred to subject them to a searching textual criticism, with full exegesis and illustration. If he was examining the work of a particular writer he consulted all the manuscripts he could find, and here he was fortunate in having both the public and private libraries of his Medici patrons available to him. Not only did he make a point of searching for the oldest manuscripts but he also made use of the scholiasts and considered the evidence offered by similar usages in

A colossal elephant of black stone, bearing on its back an obelisk of 'verde antico'—from Aldus Manutius' famous edition (1499) of the 'Hypnerotomachia Poliphili'. This is one of the ancient monuments seen by Poliphilus in the early part of his dream, a section full of strange archaeology. The author and illustrator had no doubt seen something like it. Egyptian obelisks were known, having been brought to Italy in classical times. The fact that their hieroglyphics could not be deciphered gave them the added fascination of the occult. (7)

other writers, the testimony of archaeology and numismatics and the theories of the ancient grammarians. In the *Miscellanea* (1489), for instance, he adduces a coin of Brutus to explain a passage in Dio Cassius. Politian's learning was accompanied by an exquisite taste and a sensitive feeling for poetry. As his versified inaugural lectures show, he was often able to turn erudition into elegant Latin verse of real merit. His Greek and Italian verse was also outstanding. No wonder then that he was universally recognized as the greatest humanist scholar of his time.

The only scholar who could stand up to Politan during his lifetime was the Venetian patrician Ermolao Barbaro (1453–93). His original overriding interest in Aristotle gave way to Pliny when he moved to Rome, possibly because he now had Politian's *Miscellanea* and the Vatican Library available to him. Yet his choice of Pliny also shows the same concern for what was then called natural philosophy; for Pliny, though infinitely inferior, was in many ways the Latin Aristotle.

In the *Castigationes Plinianae* (1491–93), Barbaro proved himself almost the equal of Politian. His emendations of corrupt passages and explanations of difficult words display exceptional learning and acumen, particularly in those places where he demonstrated that some alleged corruptions were actually correct. Neither Politian nor Barbaro left any real successors in Italy. Despite his great industry, Pietro Crinito never rose above the second rate, while Giano Parrasio for a variety of reasons did not fulfil the exceptional promise shown in his commentary on Claudian (1505).

New Tools for Philosophy

Alongside the achievement of the translators and the speculations of Platonists and Aristotelians, a new element soon began to be noticeable in Renaissance philosophy—the impact of grammar and philology. As in other fields, so here the pioneer was Valla, whose *Disputationes dialecticae* of 1439 were a fierce onslaught upon traditional dialectics. He condemned the vocabulary of the dialecticians, which he thought obscured instead of illuminating philosophy. In his view one of the chief aims of philology was to make Aristotle intelligible. Accordingly he advocated that his interpreters should be fully aware of the precise meaning of every word they used, verbal accuracy being in his opinion of paramount importance. By urging a return to the original terminology, he was trying to do for philosophy what he did in his *Elegantiae* for rhetoric.

Valla's novel approach was continued more than a generation later by Politian. In between had come John Argyropoulos, one of Politian's teachers who had lectured on Aristotle in Florence from 1457 to 1471. Argyropoulos went back to the original Greek text, explaining Aristotle's ideas within the framework of the whole history of Greek thought. The only scholar who could stand up to him was another Greek, Cardinal Bessarion (1403–72), a Platonist equally at home with Aristotle and his Greek interpreters, and who also appreciated Averroes. Compared to them Marsilio Ficino (1433–99), despite his immense achievement as a Platonist, was ultimately but a translator and speculative philo-

f 5
p 168 (10)
p 169 (12)
f 8

p 26 (43, 44)

p 53 (22)

p 26 (37)
p 124 (15)
p 26 (41, 42)

sopher, whose only real purpose was the resurrection of Plato, and who was not prepared to stoop down to the level of the grammarian. Pico della Mirandola (1463–94), on the other hand, for all his esoteric mysticism, was far too intelligent not to see that philology could contribute to philosophy. Most of Pico's knowledge of Plato and the Platonists came from Ficino, but he preferred to read them in the original and it was a desire to have direct access to the original text of the Old Testament that led him about 1486 to learn Hebrew and Aramaic. Pico had been humanist trained, besides going through the conventional university schools. It is true that when it came to defending the schoolmen against Barbaro, he maintained the supremacy of philosophy over rhetoric and grammar, which looked like a condemnation of humanist exegesis. Yet, when in Florence he had a dispute with Ficino about dialectics, it was to Politian's philology that he turned in order to test the validity of his opponent's objections.

p 26
(45, 46)

Politian's return to philosophical studies, which he had practically abandoned since his youth (though they were not altogether absent from the *Miscellanea*) was due to a belief that the texts of the ancient philosophers needed revising and that only a 'grammarian' like him could do it. Hence his courses on Aristotle's writings on logic were above all attempts to give them a grammatical and linguistic interpretation. He had to bring in the Greek commentators, the neo-Platonists, and even some of the medieval interpreters, with the result that his lectures on the *Organon* were also accompanied by courses on Porphyry and Gilbert de la Porrée. In the introductions to these lectures and particularly in the *Lamia*, he strenuously defended his methods, stressing the vital rôle played by the grammarian in the interpretation of classical philosophy.

Ermolao Barbaro followed much the same policy, challenging the orthodox Aristotelianism of such centres as Padua, firstly by demonstrating the ignorance of the modern schoolmen and Averroists, and then by showing that Averroes himself had depended largely on the early Greek commentators. Barbaro scrutinized Aristotle's logic with constant reference to the Greek text, proving how it had hitherto been corrupted and misunderstood. His own translations were attempts to present Aristotle anew in the language of humanism.

More than anyone else Barbaro made the philosophers of his time Greek-conscious. For many leading Aristotelians now began to learn Greek in order to defend their positions, while those who, like Nicoletto Vernia and Pietro Pomponazzi, had no Greek, found it necessary to employ tame humanists to read and explain the original texts to them. The appointment of Leonico Tomeo in 1497 to lecture at Padua on the Greek Aristotle was a recognition of the new needs, another one being the complete edition of Aristotle in Greek issued by Aldus in 1495–97. It was just at this time that the Latin translation by Girolamo Donato of Alexander of Aphrodisia's *Paraphrases de anima* (1496) was adding new fuel to the disputes on the immortality of the soul, then the most debated philosophical issue in Italy.

Humanism and the Law

Another field which felt the impact of the new philology was that of legal studies. Humanist distaste for the barbarous Latin of the lawyers and their unhistorical approach to the *Digest* found an expression in Valla's attack (1433) on the 14th-century jurist Bartolus, which marked also the opening of jurisprudence to humanist influence. Valla's explanation in his *Elegantiae* of many hitherto misunderstood terms in the *Digest* showed what humanism could contribute to legal science. Politian envisaged a new edition of the *Digest* but died before he could carry it out. Yet his collations of the famous Florentine *Pandects* were sufficient to show the corruption of the texts in circulation.

The work of both Valla and Politian lay behind later legal scholarship: Budé's annotations on the *Pandects*, and the achievement of Andrea Alciato (1492–1550). Both a humanist and jurist by training, Alciato did not hesitate to apply humanist methods to the interpretation of Roman law. He appealed to the classics for the explanation of legal terms, expounding the *Pandects* in elegant humanist Latin and drawing from them a picture of the administrative practice of Imperial Rome. His

principal achievement as far as the text was concerned, was the re-introduction into them of the Greek words and quotations which had been left out in the medieval manuscripts. At the same time, he followed Bartolus in considering them as a living system of common law. Indeed he defended the medieval jurists and particularly Bartolus, who had been Valla's favourite target, against the grammarians of his own time.

Humanist philology also affected other fields. One example was medicine, where Politian was likewise a pioneer, though it was left to his English pupil Thomas Linacre and to Niccolò Leoniceno to bring the impact of Greek learning upon it. Still there were also cases when the influence of humanist studies was not entirely beneficial. For instance insistence upon correct Latin brought with it a worship of Cicero as the sole model worth following, which proved as much of a curse as the slavish imitation of Petrarch in lyric poetry. A reaction against it had been inaugurated by Valla, who launched an attack on the sacred cow, though by his advocacy of pure Latin he really encouraged the Ciceronians. Not so Politian who, besides practising a wide eclecticism, defended this against Paolo Cortese, who had maintained the necessity of imitation and held up Cicero as the best model available. The dispute flared up again in 1512, when eclecticism was defended by Gianfrancesco Pico and Ciceronianism by Pietro Bembo. But despite the efforts of Bembo and Sadoleto and the idolatry for Cicero of Christophe de Longueil (Longolius), the days of Ciceronianism were nearly over, though the imitation of Cicero continued on the school level for centuries. For the *Ciceronianus* (1528) of Erasmus, a most devastating satire of Cicero's devotees, was really the mocking epitaph of Ciceronianism and all it stood for.

p 260
(22)

p 123
(11)

The New Learning in France

The deaths in rapid succession of Barbaro, Pico and Politian left an irreplaceable void in the humanist scholarship of Italy. During the early 16th century the classical scholars who really mattered were Linacre, Nebrija, Budé, and above all Erasmus, none of whom was Italian, though each of them was heavily indebted to at least one of the three scholars who had been the teachers of humanist Europe, Valla, Barbaro, and Politian.

That Guillaume Budé became the greatest classical philologist of his generation, greater even than Erasmus, may be surprising. For French humanism, which had suddenly bloomed in the late 14th century with Jean de Montreuil and Nicolas de Clemanges, soon died out, to begin again only with Gregorio Tifernate's teaching of Greek and rhetoric in Paris from 1456–59. After Gregorio intellectual life in Paris was never quite the same again; for a small but influential group of Paris masters were completely conquered by the new rhetoric of the humanists. It was typical that when the first printing press was set up in Paris in 1470, its first book was the Latin epistles of Barzizza, one of the most popular formularies of humanism.

The outlook of the early admirers of the Italians was exemplified by Robert Gaguin (1425–1502) whose Latin letters and orations tried to conform with the new Italian rhetoric. Yet personally he preferred the early Christian poets and Battista Mantovano to Vergil and Ovid, and did not approve of the study of pagan philosophers. As for the Italian humanists who came to teach in Paris, first Beroaldo and then Balbi, Vitelli and Andrelini, there is no doubt that they found a receptive public.

Despite the humanists, the University of Paris went on being scholastic and Aristotelian, though even Parisian Aristotelianism gradually came to assume a new look. The new Latin versions of Aristotle began to be printed in Paris, though the same printers who published them were issuing at the same time Duns Scotus and medieval manuals like the *Doctrinale*. But humanism implies Greek, and after the departure of Gregorio Tifernate, the instruction in this language by his pupils was neglible. Furthermore the Greek George Hermonymos, who came to Paris to teach the language about 1476 and settled there, proved extremely incompetent; those of his pupils who became Greek scholars—and they included Reuchlin and Budé, Erasmus and Lefèvre d'Etaples—did so in spite of him. To find some competent instruction of Greek in Paris we have to wait for François Tissard.

The art of calligraphy was revolutionised by the Renaissance. The humanists revived scripts based on the most ancient manuscripts they knew (thought by them to be classical but in fact usually Carolingian), and it is from these that modern type-faces derive. Before being finally superseded by the printing press, however, a great deal of fine writing was produced. Even in the late 16th century a large library would have its staff of 'scriptores'. This woodcut from a writing manual of 1524 shows pen, penknife, scissors, dividers, inkwell and rules. (8)

Tissard, who had learnt Greek in Italy, began his Paris courses in 1507, when he also had some short Greek texts printed for the use of his students. Competition from the much superior teaching of Gerolamo Aleandro, who had turned up in Paris in 1508 surrounded by the aura of the Aldine Academy and an introduction from Erasmus, soon drove Tissard to Hebrew studies. By then the two principal French humanists of their generation, Lefèvre d'Etaples and Budé, were already scholars with a European reputation. Jacques Lefèvre d'Etaples (c. 1456–1536) had no real interest in rhetoric and his Greek remained very indifferent. But his meetings in Italy with Pico and Barbaro and, almost certainly, Politian, aroused in him a strong enthusiasm for the new philology and its approach to Aristotle, so that once back in Paris he began to lecture on Aristotle in the way Barbaro had indicated to him. Visits to Padua and Venice in 1500 led to an interest in Aristotle's logic and in 1503 to his edition of the *Organon*, based partly on the Greek original. His knowledge of Hebrew, limited as it was, made possible his edition of the Psalms, where he gave the four Latin Psalters and tried to reconcile their discrepancies by reference to several manuscripts as well as the Hebrew text. Equally ambitious was his edition of the letters of St Paul, which included both the Vulgate and a new Latin text of his own, unfortunately not devoid of errors, as Erasmus was quick to note. (Lefèvre, incidentally, agreed with Budé's judgement that the Vulgate could not be by St Jerome.) All the same, he was not endowed with exceptional critical powers—he accepted as authentic the spurious correspondence between Seneca and St Paul and other notorious forgeries, and believed that the pseudo-Dionysian writings had really been written in the Apostolic age.

Such powers were, however, outstandingly displayed by Guillaume Budé (1468–1540), whose education had not included a period of instruction in Italy. After some utterly useless teaching of Greek by Hermonymos and a few lessons by Lascaris, his penetrating intelligence had enabled him to master the language by himself, his Latin translations of some tracts of Plutarch published in 1503–5 showing that by the time Tissard and Aleandro had started to lecture, he was too advanced to profit from their teaching. Fra Giocondo's course on Vitruvius, held in

p 178 (41)

p 179 (44)

107 (1)

Paris in 1500, on the other hand, had impressed him and perhaps brought him face to face for the first time with the new philology. But Budé was really a lawyer turned humanist. It was Valla's praise of the *Pandects* in the *Elegantiae* that moved him to undertake his first serious work—an examination of their text from a humanist angle. Needless to say he found it very corrupt and decided to correct it, his decision being strengthened by a visit to Florence where, it is true, he was only allowed a short glimpse of the celebrated copy of the *Pandects* but, as a compensation, he was given access to Politian's collations of it. The eventual result was the *Annotationes*, which were published in 1508, and in which he displayed his formidable acumen and humanist learning in restoring the original readings of the *Pandects* and explaining those words which had been left unexplained by the glossators or had been misunderstood by them.

The *Annotationes* displayed a scholarly quality not seen since the death of Politian. But the philological masterpiece of Budé was the *De asse*, which saw the light in 1515, the outcome of nine years' labour. The aim of the *De asse* was the study of ancient metrology, that is to say a subject which had baffled even Barbaro and Politian. What Budé proposed to find out were two things: the exact value of the coins and measures of the ancients, and their modern equivalents. This meant scrutinizing every ancient writer—an extraordinary feat in itself. But the *De asse*, like the *Annotationes*, went well beyond its avowed aim through its countless digressions. It was undoubtedly the most brilliant achievement of early 16th-century philology. Compared with it his *Commentarii linguae Graecae* of 1529, for all their value, are certainly less important. By then the end of Budé's career was not so very distant, and the treatise in which he held that knowledge of the eternal truths was the final aim of philology, was the swan song of the greatest Renaissance humanist of France.

The First English Humanists

Scholarship in England pursued a course different from that in France. At first humanism here had meant the new rhetoric of the Italians and an interest in the new translations from the Greek. Humphrey of Gloucester's employment of Italian humanists as secretaries may have been mostly vanity, plus a subtle estimate of the value of elegant Latin in politics, but his lavish donations of books to Oxford University in 1439 and again in 1444 were genuine attempts to arouse his fellow-countrymen to emulate the Italians. A similar intention was expressed in 1460 by John Tiptoft, Earl of Worcester (?1427–70), in a letter written from Padua to Oxford University, in which he announced a forthcoming present of books, which did not in fact materialize. But Tiptoft, like most of the Englishmen who had gone to Ferrara to sit at the feet of Guarino da Verona, never developed more than a taste for the classics and the new rhetoric and of course book collecting. Another of Guarino's English pupils, Robert Flemmyng, who became Dean of Lincoln in 1452, also took up Greek. But the only one who reached the exacting standards of humanist Italy was John Free, who died still young in 1465 and never returned home. By then the starting of Greek studies in England itself was only a matter of time. In 1470 William Sellyng, who became Prior of Christ Church, Canterbury in 1472, and had learnt the language at Bologna, was teaching it in his monastery. It was also studied in the household of George Neville, Archbishop of York (?1433–76), until 1472, when his exile to Calais dispersed his household. His protégé Manuel of Constantinople went on, however, practising as a copyist of Greek manuscripts, and together with another Greek, John Serbopoulos, appears to have eked out a living by copying texts for an academic clientèle. But humanist philology proper had to wait until the return from Italy of the two English pupils of Politian, Grocyn and Linacre.

William Grocyn (?1446–1519) was one of those scholars who preferred reading to writing. A Latin letter he sent to Aldus in 1499 was, however, deemed worth printing by that fastidious scholar and discloses a predilection for Aristotle as well as enthusiasm for Aldus' plan, which never materialized, to publish a polyglot Bible. Politian's stringent standards and critical integrity left their mark on his English pupil: while delivering a course of lectures on the Dionysian writings in St Paul's, London,

f 9

p 128 (25)

p 126 (20)

about the turn of the century, Grocyn found himself compelled, despite his intention to uphold the authenticity of the writings, to prove just the opposite to his audience.

Thomas Linacre (?1460–1524) too had sat at the feet of Politian, as well as meeting Ermolao Barbaro in Rome and securing a doctorate of medicine in Padua in 1496. His mastery of Greek was such that Aldus gladly included his Latin translation of Proclus on the sphere in the *Scriptores astronomici veteres*. Some of the Greek commentators of Aristotle and especially Simplicius and Alexander of Aphrodisia are also known to have aroused Linacre's interest. But what gave him a European reputation were his Latin translations of Galen, which provided a text translated by a humanist who was also a physician and therefore knew what Galen was talking about. His Latin syntax proved hardly less famous and it was used for a long time in school teaching, both in England and abroad.

p 260
(22)

In the England of his time Linacre was one of the very few (Croke and Pace and perhaps Grocyn being the others) who had really assimilated the new philology. John Colet (?1467–1519), the man who exerted so great an influence on Erasmus, was really a theologian with a leaning towards humanism. But the humanism he found irresistible was not the critical type of Barbaro and Politian, but the esoteric kind of Ficino and Pico, who may be considered his real masters. In Italy Colet learnt no Greek, but developed a taste for Plato and the Platonism of Ficino; and although he thought that the Bible and the Fathers were the only things that really mattered, he also felt a profound distaste for scholasticism and the allegorical mode of interpreting the Bible, which was still being followed in England. He believed that the classics could be useful in helping us to understand Holy Scripture. Thus, when lecturing on the Epistles of St Paul he refused to follow the conventional allegorical interpretation, preferring to approach the Pauline text as a whole and from a grammatical and historical standpoint, taking into account also the circumstances in which the letters had been written. As for their meaning, he saw them in the light of what he had learnt from St Augustine and the pseudo-Dionysius, Pico and Ficino.

p 260
(23)

p 124
(14)

Colet's contribution to scholarship in England mainly consisted in applying to theology what Pico and Ficino had taught him. Nor was he alone in England in feeling the impact of Pico. Thomas More (1478–1535) felt it, though what attracted him to Pico was rather the new religious feeling emerging from his writings than his esoteric doctrines. More never went to Italy; as a student he had attended Linacre's course on Aristotle's *Metheor*, and both Linacre and Grocyn had taught him Greek. Among the writers of antiquity, his special admiration went to Plato, and when Greek studies at Oxford seemed to be in danger at the hands of the more conservative theologians, it was his intervention with Henry VIII that silenced the opponents of the New Learning. More's work on Plato and his translations of Lucian show his complete mastery of the language (as his epigrams do of Latin prosody); yet the author of *Utopia*, the greatest of English humanists, was not a philologist in any narrow sense. He belonged with Colet and Erasmus, among those for whom the

p 261
(26, 27)

New Learning, controlled by Christian revelation, was both the supreme civilization and the way to truth—ultimately to God.

The teaching of Greek at the universities began in 1511 when Erasmus arrived in Cambridge, and after his departure his pupil Henry Bullock had kept the study alive and eventually published a translation of Lucian in 1521. Yet what really consolidated Greek at Cambridge was the appointment of Richard Croke to a readership in 1518. A pupil of Grocyn who had also been taught by Erasmus in Cambridge and Aleandro in Paris, Croke was a philologist who had previously lectured at Cologne, Louvain, and Leipzig before being appointed at Cambridge. His *Introductiones ad rudimenta Graeca*, first published while at Leipzig, was, though successful, an elementary manual. His edition of Ausonius, however, was a remarkable achievement, as well as being the first humanist edition of a Latin poet by an Englishman. At Oxford the beginning of Greek studies dates from 1516 when the trilingual college (Latin, Greek and Hebrew) of Corpus Christi was founded.

This account of English humanism shows how the Italian impact on it was not primarily philological. Thomas More even proves that it was possible to become a great humanist without ever setting foot in Italy. Admittedly England did not produce a Budé, though Richard Pace (1482–1536) might have become one. His enthusiasm for Greek, in praise of which he delivered a Latin oration in Venice in 1505, had been followed by Latin renderings of Plutarch and the *De fructu*. But his great promise was lost for good in the labyrinths of politics and diplomacy.

Spain and the Polyglot Bible

The impact of Italian humanism in Spain became first noticeable about the middle of the 15th century. But until Nebrija its influence did not go beyond grammar and rhetoric and it was only at the end of the century that humanism could be said to be well established. As usual, Greek followed quickly in its wake. At Salamanca it was first taught during the very last years of the century by the Portuguese Arias Barbosa (died 1540) who had been a pupil of Politian; he was succeeded by Hernán Núñez (?1475–1553) who eventually became the most distinguished Hellenist in Spain, though his philology appeared at its best in his edition of Seneca published in 1536 and in his emendations to Pliny, which appeared six years later. But the greatest Spanish humanist was Elio Antonio de Nebrija (1444–1522), whom ten years in Italy had acquainted with Greek and acclimatized to the new philology.

p 232
(22)

Nebrija's enormous output ranged from grammar to history, from archaeology to lexicography, from geography and law to the Bible. Perhaps the most lasting achievement was his setting down rules for the pronunciation of Greek (forestalling Aleandro and Erasmus). But his heart was really in sacred studies, in the study of the Bible, and in fact as early as 1495 he had declared to Queen Isabella his intention of devoting his life to it. As a biblical scholar he did not avoid feeling the overwhelming impact of Valla. Nebrija's first two series of philological dissertations on the text of the Bible were impounded by the Grand Inquisitor; but a third series succeeded in appearing in 1508 and consisted of a philological revision of the text of the Vulgate. Nebrija insisted on a comparison with the original Hebrew and Greek texts. Little wonder then, that Cardinal Jiménez was glad to secure his editorial services for the Polyglot Bible.

It was the opinion of Cardinal Jiménez (Ximenes) de Cisneros (1436–1517) that no one without Greek could be a good theologian, and his newly founded university at Alcalá quickly became the leading centre of Greek studies in Spain. The Cretan Demetrius Dukas, who had edited texts for Aldus in Venice, held a chair from 1512–18 and published while at Alcalá a collection of grammatical tracts and the poem of Musaeus. But his presence at Alcalá, and also that of Nebrija, Hernán Núñez, and Diego de Zuñiga, was not really prompted by purely humanist interests. The real reason for their presence was the edition of the Polyglot Bible, that is to say the Bible in Latin and its original languages, which was to be printed by a special press installed by Cisneros and at his expense, and in which the original Old Testament was to be edited by some Jewish converts.

p 232
(26, 29)

'Cest livre est a moy homfrey duc de gloucestre le quel Jay fait translater de grec en latyn par Antoyne de Becaria Veroneys mon serviteur': This book is mine, Humphrey Duke of Gloucester, which I have had translated from Greek into Latin by my servant Antonio Beccaria of Verona. Duke Humphrey, Henry V's, brother, was one of the great book collectors of his age and a generous benefactor of Oxford University, founding the Library which still bears his name. This ownership note is inscribed in a copy of six theological treatises by St. Athanasius. (9)

From the philological point of view the Polyglot Bible was not faultless. Its editors proved on the whole too conservative. The Greek New Testament was corrected on the Vulgate and not vice-versa, while the so called *Comma Johanneum* which did not figure either in the Greek or the earliest manuscripts of the Vulgate, was inserted into the Greek text. Besides, following the Cardinal's instructions, no readings commonly attested by ancient manuscripts were corrected. Yet even with such shortcomings as well as many others, the Polyglot Bible was a tremendous step forward and certainly revolutionized biblical scholarship. The first volume, containing the New Testament, was ready from the press in 1514. A lexicon of the languages of the Bible, i.e. Greek, Hebrew and Aramaic, followed in 1515, while the Old Testament came out in 1517. But it was only in 1520, after Cisneros was dead, that its publication was finally licensed by Pope Leo X. Another ambitious scheme of the Cardinal, a new and complete Graeco-Latin edition of Aristotle, petered out after only three of his works had been re-translated by his secretary Juan de Vergara.

Schools and Scholars in the Netherlands

Humanism only started to exert some influence in the Netherlands during the second half of the 15th century. Grammar and rhetoric were given most attention, which is not surprising since it was the schools of the Brethren of the Common Life, with their concern for efficiency and up-to-date teaching methods, which contributed most to the rise of humanism.

One of the first humanists educated at these schools was Johann Wessel of Gansfort (c. 1420–1489). His education predisposed him towards grammar and rhetoric, and he never entirely renounced his early allegiance to scholasticism. But his stay in Greek lands led to a mastery of Greek, the reading of Aristotle in the original, and a weakness for Plato, which found encouragement later in the Florence of Marsilio Ficino. Rudolf Agricola (1443–85) was a more complete humanist, staying eleven years in Italy, first at Pavia and then at Ferrara. His translations of Isocrates, Lucian and the pseudo-Platonic Axiochus, testify to his proficiency in Greek, which he also taught after leaving Italy. His greatest achievements, however, were the *De inventione dialectica*, an introduction to logic full of new and stimulating ideas and including a fierce attack on the schoolmen, and the *De formando studio*, where he advocated the exclusion from education of what we now call medieval learning. In the next generation Christophe de Longueil (Longolius, 1488–1522) when in Italy fell under the spell of the Ciceronianism of Bembo and Sadoleto, and thereafter he never ceased to worship at Cicero's shrine.

Humanist rhetoric was being taught at the University of Louvain during the last quarter of the 15th century. The introduction of the printing of Greek in Louvain about 1515 and the founding of a trilingual college (that is to say one providing instruction in Hebrew, Greek and Latin) in 1517 thanks to the munificence of Jerome Busleiden, speak for themselves. Greek and other innovations were, however, strenuously opposed there by more conservative schoolmen such as Johannes Latomus and Martin van Dorp (Dorpius).

German Enlightenment

Petrarch's exchanges with the Imperial Chancellor Johann von Neumarkt furnish the earliest evidence for a penetration of Italian humanism into the Empire. But it was not until the 15th century that humanism really established itself in Germany. In its earlier stages it did not go beyond grammar, rhetoric, and Latin versification; Nicholas of Cues (Cusanus, 1401–64), who learnt Greek and competed with the Italians in the discovery of classical manuscripts was by no means typical of contemporary German scholarship. But by the second half of the century a few Latin classics were being edited by German scholars. The humanist-astronomer Johann Müller of Königsberg (Regiomontanus, 1436–76) was responsible for the first edition of Manilius' *Astronomicon* (c. 1472), while Conrad Celtis (1459–1508) edited two tragedies of Seneca in 1489 and Tacitus' *Germania* in 1500. These early attempts at editing classical texts (they were by no means the only ones) went little beyond the handing of a manuscript of a classical author to the printers. In fact we must reach the editions

p 123
(10)

213 (5)

Hrotswitha, a 10th century nun of Gandersheim, wrote a number of Latin farces based on Plautus and Terence. These were recovered and published in 1501 by the German humanist Conrad Celtis, a patriotic enterprise designed to enhance the reputation of medieval Germany. Dürer, or one of his assistants, made this woodcut for the frontispiece showing Hrotswitha presenting her works to the Emperor Otto I. (10)

of Velleius Paterculus (1520) by Beatus Rhenanus (1485–1547), of Jordanes by Conrad Peutinger (1465–1547) and those of Florus and Avianus by Johann Spiessheimer (Cuspinianus, 1473–1529), to find texts edited according to the standards prevailing in Italy.

Celtis' edition of Tacitus is interesting for another reason. It is among the first examples of that preoccupation with national history that became typical of German humanists immediately before the Reformation. There was keen interest in both ancient and medieval Germany. Peutinger, for instance, edited Jordanes, wrote his *Sermones conviviales* (1505), modelled on Macrobius and discussing topics connected with German antiquity, and made a collection of Roman inscriptions found there. Beatus Rhenanus, in the same spirit, composed a commentary on Tacitus' *Germania*. Interest in the Middle Ages is shown by Celtis' editions of the plays of the 10th-century nun Hrotswitha (1501) and the *Ligurinus* of Gunther the Cistercian (1507); and among his projects there was a *Germania illustrata* intended to be on the same lines as Biondo's *Italia illustrata*, which was never completed. Jacob Wimpheling in 1501 produced a *Germania* in which he sought to prove that Alsace was German, and an *Epitome rerum Germanicarum*, a history of Germany from the earliest times. Some years later, in 1518, Franz Friedlieb (Irenicus, 1473–1529) provided a survey of medieval German history. The best effort was probably the *Annales ducum Boaiorum* of Johann Thurmair (Aventinus, 1477–1534), which really constituted a landmark in German historiography. But it was left to Ulrich von Hutten (1488–1523) to voice the contrast between Rome and 'Germania' in his *Arminius* (written in 1520 but not published until 1528), where the conqueror of Varus was set up as the national hero and a symbol of resistance to Rome.

p 211 (2)

f 10

p 217 (9)

Erasmus, aged 64, in a room of Freiburg University, dictates to his secretary Gilbert Cousin (Gilbertus Cognatus). Cousin, a Protestant and later an active Reformer, was a young man from Burgundy whom Erasmus brought with him to Freiburg in 1531. He took his duties extremely seriously. In his book 'On the Duties of Secretaries' he maintained that choosing a secretary was as important as choosing a wife. (11)

Many towns in Germany could boast humanist circles; one of Celtis' favourite activities was the founding of academies—his *Sodalitas danubiana* was followed by the *Sodalitas rhenana* and the *Collegium poetarum et mathematicorum* at Vienna. Celtis himself had very little Greek, which is not very surprising, as no Greek was taught in Germany before the second half of the 15th century, when Agricola taught it at Heidelberg and Andronicus Cantoblacas at Basle. Some German scholars, Reuchlin and Beatus Rhenanus for instance, learned it abroad, but by the second decade of the 16th century there were chairs of Greek at Leipzig and elsewhere and Greek grammars were published by Croke and Melanchthon.

p 196 (4) In his inaugural lecture at Wittenberg (1518), Melanchthon, whose main interest at the time was the Greek text of Aristotle, stressed the great importance of Greek in humane studies.

Latin translations from the Greek were, at any rate at first, mainly confined to short texts. Thus Reuchlin translated a homily by Proclus. Two sermons of Gregory of Nazianzum were turned

p 196 (3) into Latin by Beatus Rhenanus, while Willibald Pirckheimer turned his attention to Lucian. What was, however, particularly appreciated was the usefulness of Greek in theological studies, this being a field in which Hebrew also aroused considerable interest. Several German humanists, Trithemius, Celtis and Peutinger among them, did definitely study Hebrew so that they could read the Old Testament in the original.

p 197 (8) Hebrew was the particular province of Johann Reuchlin (1455–1522), who studied it partly for the Old Testament and partly because, like Pico della Mirandola, he was anxious to penetrate the mysteries of the Cabbalistic writings. The result was the *De arte cabbalistica* (1517), in which he gave an explanation of the Cabbala and its cosmology. But Reuchlin's principal title to glory, even greater than his being the initiator of modern Hebrew studies, was his spirited stand for Hebrew books against the Dominicans of Cologne, which led to a long-drawn struggle and

p 212 (3) the *Epistolae obscurorum virorum*—a collection of satires against the 'obscurantist' theologians who maintained that the study of Jewish books was heretical. After him Hebrew studies were pursued by Conrad Pellican and Johann Husschin (Oecolampadius), but in their hands they were above all an instrument for the furthering of their reforming ideals.

The Last of the Humanists

Renaissance scholarship ended with Erasmus (?1466–1536). p 197 (Although born and brought up in Holland, it would be impossible to claim him as 'belonging' to any country. He was educated *f 11* by the Brethren of the Common Life, and it was at their schools that he mastered the rhetoric of the Italians and felt at the same time the impact of the *devotio moderna*. From Colet he learnt the importance of the new approach to the Bible and the Fathers, while Aldus' house in Venice brought him into contact with what was best in humanist Italy. At an early stage he had gauged the importance of Greek for his studies; as Hermonymos had proved utterly useless as a teacher, he went on learning it by himself, with the result that he never acquired more than a working knowledge of it and always found Homer difficult. His Cambridge teaching of Greek never went beyond the grammar. Yet his views on the pronunciation of Greek found wide acceptance and are still followed to this day. The man who perhaps influenced him more than anyone was Valla, whose *Elegantiae* pointed to him the way to better Latin, just as his annotations on the New Testament showed what could be done in biblical studies.

Of all Erasmus' numerous writings, the *Moriae encomium* was p 197 the most popular; the *Adagia* was the most important, and its (5, 6) second edition in 1508 made Erasmus famous at once. The *Adagia* p 215 had implied a thorough exploration of the whole of Greek and Latin literature for, although it was meant to be a repertory of proverbs and sayings out of the classics, it also included countless discussions and digressions, the phrases commented on being often an excuse for the airing of opinions or the display of learning tempered by wit. For sustained effort, however, Erasmus' main scholarly achievement were his labours on the New Testament and the Fathers, which to him were his real life work. One of the first after Valla to approach the New Testament as a philologist, he had started by turning it into Latin, this being in itself a challenge to the Vulgate, and then by editing the Greek text. As a textual critic he remained a long way behind Politian and Budé, his conjectures being the result of guesswork and his use of manuscripts unmethodical. Having found, for instance, that the last lines of the Apocalypse were missing in his manuscript, he translated into Greek the corresponding passage in the Vulgate and inserted it into his edition.

The Greek New Testament was prepared in a hurry, but Erasmus tried to improve on it later and actually re-edited it four times. His many volumes of the Fathers betray a similar haste, but it was mainly due to him that many of the Fathers became available in standard editions at all. Though neither a deep nor an original thinker, he certainly captured the imagination of his contempories by his intellectual honesty, the charm and flexibility of his Latin, his repugnance for any kind of extremism and his belief in toleration. He embodied all that was best in the European culture of his time. A Catholic to the end, he unhesitatingly exposed the abuses in his Church, of which he certainly represented the conscience.

After Erasmus a new scholarship dawned upon Europe. The study and interpretation of antiquity became deeper and more methodical. Manuscripts were considered more critically and with the younger Scaliger the reconstruction of the archetype was considered for the first time. The tangible monuments of antiquity, whether large or small, became the auxiliaries of philology, which was no longer quite the same as before.

Needless to say, what occurred in scholarship, between the death of Erasmus and the end of the 16th century, would not have been possible without the foundations laid down in the two centuries before, beginning with the work of Petrarch. After Erasmus humanism no longer covered both rhetoric and philology, but each went its own way. The philologists who came after Erasmus may have been his heirs, but they were at the same time the heirs of Petrarch and Valla, of Politian and Budé. Humanist scholarship, one might claim, lies behind all the great upheavals and innovations of the Renaissance.

PIETAS AD OMNIA
VTILIS EST 1.Timoth.4.
SACRIFICIVM DEO
COR HVMILIATVM. Psal.50.

V REASON, UNREASON AND FAITH

Challenges to traditional Christianity

DELIO CANTIMORI

'The divine ray cannot reach us unless it is covered by poetic veils'.

EGIDIO DA VITERBO

'It will be intelligible only to a few'

writes Pico della Mirandola about one of his own essays, 'for it is filled with many mysteries from the secret philosophy of the ancients.' What secret philosophy? asks the modern reader, having heard of no such thing. The answer takes us to an aspect of the Renaissance which is little dwelt on today but which was of the profoundest moment to the men involved. We have to remember that in the rich legacy which the humanists inherited from the world of late antiquity were many items whose value they wildly overrated. With equal awe and equal fascination they read not only Plato but Plotinus, not only the Hebrew Scriptures but the Cabbala, not only the Church Fathers but Hermes Trismegistus. The spirit of these writings was esoteric. They sprang from a background of Gnosticism, of 'mystery' salvation religions whose deep truths could be communicated only to the initiated. Plotinus, the 3rd century philosopher of Alexandria, had made of Plato's 'Form of the Good' a transcendent power which seemed to be a prevision of the Christian God. The Cabbala was a body of Jewish mystical writing supposedly handed down from the time of Moses and incorporating secrets not fully explained by the Patriarch in Genesis. Hermes Trismegistus was believed (by Augustine and Lactantius, not just by Renaissance humanists) to have been a priest of the time of Moses whose works hinted, in veiled terms, at doctrines such as the Trinity and the Incarnation, though in fact they date from the 2nd and 3rd centuries AD. Cosimo de' Medici ordered Ficino to translate Hermes (first brought to Florence in 1460) before starting on Plato.

The obscurities and ambiguities of these writings were accepted and even welcomed by the humanists. It meant that the wisest thinkers of the ancient world could be seen, given sufficient latitude of interpretation, as essentially in communion with Christianity; indeed they confirmed the central tenet of Christian mysticism that God's nature was inexpressible, or expressible only darkly. And no doubt there was also the special appeal of knowledge confined to a small circle of the élite.

The task of 'Christianizing' the mysteries thus became one of the missions of humanism. In 1486 Pico della Mirandola arrived in Rome with 900 theses drawn from every conceivable text which he offered to prove were consistent with one another. Reconciliation of apparent opposites is henceforward a *leitmotif* of the Renaissance, and one which (as we have seen in the case of Botticelli) is frequently conveyed in the visual language of art.

About 1460 Duke Borso d'Este of Ferrara commissioned a series of frescoes in his Palazzo Schifanoia. The theme was to be the Months of the Year, set out in a complex allegorical scheme probably devised by the court astrologer, Pelegrino Prisciani, and executed by painters of the school of Ferrara, notably Cosimo Tura and Francesco del Cossa. Prisciani's sources were many and included several of the works we have been discussing. The frescoes are in three sections or levels: first the god or goddess presiding over the month; then the three *decans*, or 10-day periods; and beneath them the occupations and court life at Ferrara. (A detail from this third level has already been shown on pp. 56–7.)

This detail (opposite) is from the first and second levels of April. Venus sits on a throne drawn by swans, holding in her hands a flower and an apple (her prize from Paris). Before her kneels Mars, chained to her by the fetters of love—opposites reconciled. 'It is well-known', says Pico, 'that in the fables of the Greeks, Harmony was born from the union of Venus and Mars, of whom the latter is fierce and contentious, the former generous and pleasing.' On the river banks rabbits play (a fertility symbol) and groups of young lovers wander.

In the section below are the *decans*—an astrological element from Egypt absorbed into Hermetic philosophy. Prisciani probably relied for his information on the *Picatrix*, an Arabic work going back to the same Alexandrian background. Pico had a copy in his library. In it the 36 *decans* are described in detail. The one seen here is a naked man holding a key which opens *(apre)* the new season. (1)

▶

In riddling images, Correggio decorated the Camera di S. Paolo in Parma for the Abbess Giovanna da Piacenza, who had lately won a dispute with the Curia in Rome over claustration. Above: the Three Graces, here Friendship, Concord and Peace, who face the goddes of war, representing her adversaries. Below: Juno symbolizing the Air—the golden chain round her wrists is Fire or the Stars, the two anvils tied to her feet the heavy elements Water and Earth. Bottom: Pan blowing a conch, a rare attribute mentioned only by another Hellenistic writer. As the source of panic ('Pan'-ic) terror he symbolizes Giovanna's papal opponents. (2, 3, 4)

'Hermes Trismegistus, contemporary of Moses': in this pavement design of 1488 the mythical Hermes penetrates into the very Cathedral of Siena. To an oriental figure (possibly Moses) he hands a book saying *Suscipite o licteras et leges Egiptii*—'Take up letters and laws, O Egyptians.' (5)

The four 'humours' or temperaments (melancholic, choleric, sanguine and phlegmatic) had been a popular theme during the Middle Ages and Dürer had, in fact, based his Four Apostles (p. 299) upon it. Until the Renaissance, the 'melancholic man' had been depicted as one diseased by excess of black bile or as a bad character, grasping and slothful. Dürer, under the influence of Ficino, now draws Melancholy herself (right), a winged figure with many of her medieval attributes but given a new meaning: the clenched fist of avarice now denoting frustrated purpose; the 'black' face now cast into the deep shade of depression; the symbols of her riches, keys and purse, now hanging neglected at her side. For to the humanist, melancholy was the particular affliction of genius. The signs of intellectual prowess (geometry, pure and applied)—polyhedron and sphere, compass, plane, set-square and hammer—are nullified by total inability to act. Her wreath of waterplants is an ineffectual remedy (wet against dryness), as is the square of numbers behind her—a talisman to attract Jupiter (hot against cold). The putto next to her enhances her anguish: happy activity unconscious of the suffering of thought. (6)

149

The essential unity of man's varied efforts towards understanding is given its clearest and most powerful expression in the four frescoes of Raphael's *Stanza della Segnatura* in the Vatican. Together they sum up the all-embracing confident world-view of the Renaissance before that became darkened by religious conflict. The reconciliation of opposites here finds its apotheosis.

Each fresco stands for one of the paths by which mankind approaches Truth—the spiritual (Theology), intellectual (Philosophy), imaginative (Poetry) and social (Law). 'Theology' is represented by the *Disputà* (see p. 154); 'Poetry' by the *Parnassus*, showing the great poets of the past gathered round Apollo; 'Law' by scenes of the great lawgivers Gregory IX, Moses, Justinian and Solon.

'Philosophy' is the subject of the fresco shown here, known as *The School of Athens*—the attainment of wisdom through purely human reason. At the centre stand Plato and Aristotle, types of the two chief schools of philosophy. Plato, venerable and bearded, holds the *Timaeus* in one hand and points upward with the other (an allusion to the Platonic theory of Ideas, as interpreted by the neo-Platonists). Aristotle, holding his *Ethics*, gestures towards the earth, indicating his belief in the study of the real world. The two systems of thought are brought into aesthetic harmony by the calm attitudes of the figures and by the soaring Roman architecture in which they stand—inspired by Bramante's new St Peter's, which was just being started. Around them are grouped the philosophers of the ancient world, many of them portraits of Raphael's own contemporaries. The man seen in profile to Plato's left, bearded and snub-nosed, is Socrates. Others include Euclid (bending down, right foreground, demonstrating a geometrical theorem); Ptolemy (to his right, crowned and holding a globe); Diogenes (reclining alone on the steps); and Pythagoras (left foreground, writing; in front of him a youth holds a tablet inscribed with a diagram of musical harmonies and the Pythagorean decad).

It is ironic to remember that within seven years of Raphael's painting these frescos, and while the great new cathedral that he saw in his imagination was rising nearby, Luther would nail his Theses to the door at Wittenberg and found a Church which would repudiate Rome and the type of 'Christian humanism' that she had evolved—opposites indeed, and in a sense which the humanists did not foresee: opposites which could not be reconciled. (7)

Luther's protest forms part of a long tradition of reforming movements going back to the Middle Ages (Wycliffe, died 1384; Huss, died 1415) and therefore need not be seen as having any necessary connexion with the Renaissance. Nevertheless, the fact that most of the protagonists were also eminent scholars gives the whole controversy a distinctly humanist bias. This group (left) by Cranach the Younger shows Luther in the foreground with some of his early supporters, including Erasmus (fourth from the right) and Melanchthon (extreme right).

Below: the reading of the Confession of Augsburg to Charles V in 1530. Drawn up in moderate terms by Melanchthon, it was signed by the German princes who 'protested' against papal jurisdiction. When this was rejected the two sides were in open conflict. (8, 9)

The Catholic answer came with the Council of Trent (1545–63). Until then, and even during its early sessions, there had been some hopes of reconciliation. Protestant representatives, in particular Melanchthon, were expected and a few Protestant observers, including the historian Johann Sleidan, did actually attend. The Emperor Charles V worked for a settlement, but the Pope and Curia were too entrenched in their position. This painting shows the final session (1563) in the Cathedral of Trent (Trento, in northern Italy). The era of 'Christian humanism' was over. Catholic doctrine had been defined with a new strictness that made acceptance by the Protestants impossible. (10)

Paul III, Pope from 1534–1549, illustrates the tragic *impasse* of humanism almost as strikingly as Melanchthon, Erasmus or More, though from the opposite point of view. Cultured and intelligent (he commissioned Michelangelo to paint the Last Judgment), he had in youth moved in the circles of Lorenzo de' Medici and Pomponio Leto. But as the Council of Trent dragged on and both sides became more intransigent and extreme, the old humanism of the papal court gave way to distrust and intolerance. Titian's cruelly realistic portrait (left) shows Paul in old age. (11)

In the Eucharist, the central mystery of the Christian faith, earthly wisdom and divine revelation meet: part of Raphael's 'Theology' or *Disputà* which stands opposite the *School of Athens*. The stages by which grace is bestowed on mankind are displayed in the simplest possible way. In one vertical line are God the Father, Christ, the Holy Ghost and, in a crystal monstrance on the altar, the Holy Sacrament. With Christ in Heaven sit saints, martyrs and patriarchs. On earth are the great theologians who have illuminated the doctrine of the Eucharist—on the right St Ambrose, St Augustine (whose book *De civitate Dei* lies at his feet) and St Thomas Aquinas; on the left, St Jerome, with the Bible and his Letters, and Gregory the Great with the *Moralia*. (12)

Challenges to traditional Christianity

DELIO CANTIMORI

Giuliano de' Medici worships Venus, from Politian's unfinished poem 'La Giostra' (1475–78) describing Giuliano's love for Simonetta Vespucci. The way in which classical mythology and Christianity are interwoven in these stanzas characterized much of the new literature. Humanist philosophy found a hidden Christianity in paganism and a hidden divinity in earthly love. (1)

DURING THE 19TH CENTURY, it was widely held that the Renaissance and the Reformation were two quite distinct phenomena, and both (depending on the taste and prejudices of individual historians) were credited with marking the beginning of modern Europe. Burckhardt, for instance, saw 'the modern age' as starting with the Renaissance, which he characterized as humanist, individualistic (producing a new era in art and architecture), man-centred, outward-looking, innovatory in techniques (political systems, printing, etc.) and in thought. The source of all these new ideas was Italy, and everything was interpreted from this premise. Thus, the work of Erasmus was placed in the context of Florentine neo-Platonism; the most important events in Dürer's life were his visits to Italy . . . and so on.

The other point of view may be represented by Leopold von Ranke, the historian of the papacy and of Reformation Germany. For him, modern Europe and the states that make it up stem from the Protestant Reformers—Lutherans, Calvinists, Anglicans. The Reformation, on this theory, was also individualistic, but theocentric rather than humanist. It re-established the rôle of conscience, using the methods of humanist philology and criticism not for the analysis of the world of the imagination but for the study of divine revelation as set down in the Bible. It encouraged philosophical speculation and science more than the arts, although it did incidentally stimulate painting (it had its Rembrandt to set beside Raphael) and especially music. Above all, it led to a new morality and a new social system better suited to the fundamental conditions of the age (in spite of the unhappy experiences of the German people in the 16th and 17th centuries) than was the Italian system. In Europe great military states, calling for vast administrative organization, were created, bringing with them a new political ethic by which men were the state's servants. Elsewhere new communities were founded on new principles. Humanism and the Italian Renaissance, it was conceded, had perhaps discovered new continents, but it was the Reformation which sent out the men who settled them.

Whether one was a disciple of Burckhardt or of Ranke, it was assumed that there was nothing wrong in thus treating Renaissance and Reformation as separable events capable of separate evaluation. The assumption was still very much in evidence at an international congress of historians held as recently as 1955, and indeed it has been kept alive largely by romantic notions of a gulf between the Mediterranean temperament (neo-Latin, Catholic, artistic, immoral, poetic, idle) and the Nordic (Protestant, devout, industrious, moral and prosperous). The whole quarrel may perhaps seem somewhat remote from the traditions of Anglo-American scholarship, which has never been so deeply and bitterly involved in it as that of France, Germany and Italy. In fact the history of English institutions and culture during this period shows how unworkable such an oversimplification is, though it has encouraged the growth of another: for in England all the various attitudes, beliefs and disciplines could be seen to co-exist and to merge—especially in the peculiar constitution of the Anglican Church, over which (or so it appeared to the liberal historians of Europe) the tolerant spirit of Erasmus still seemed to reign: an interpretation impossible to maintain seriously, and as misleading as either of the two positions already described.

Renaissance and Reformation are concepts which belong together and which cannot usefully be discussed in isolation. There were not two Europes, but one; and it is the framework of cultural relationships that held it together rather than the conflicts that seemed to be tearing it apart which will be emphasized in this chapter.

After his father's funeral, Hamlet wishes to return to his old university of Wittenberg. Claudius forbids it:

> For your intent
> In going back to school in Wittenberg,
> It is most retrograde to our desire.

And the Queen:

> I pray thee, stay with us; go not to Wittenberg.

This was at a time when the Renaissance was over in some countries and on the point of ending in others. But Wittenberg was reaching its peak. It was the most famous university of northern Europe. Giordano Bruno praised its seriousness and scientific freedom. Martin Luther and Philip Melanchthon had lectured there. It was fitting that a prince of Denmark should go there for his education. What would he have learnt? p 196 (4)
p 152 (8)

The Secrets of Humanism

If Hamlet and Horatio had been at Wittenberg in the time of Philip Melanchthon, that great and wise man would certainly have been able to teach them (besides his own subjects, Latin, Greek, philosophy and theology) many unsuspected secrets of the occult. He would indeed have confirmed that there were more things in Heaven and Earth than were dreamt of in philosophy—things even stranger than dreams but to which dreams might be the key. For Melanchthon had developed an inquiring interest in dream interpretation, astrology, divination and other systems of foretelling the future and had convinced himself that such things were possible. And in this he was by no means an exception among European humanists of the Renaissance. On the contrary, it was an integral part of the scholarly tradition.

It derived largely from a body of writings ascribed to an Egyptian priest, Hermes Trismegistus ('thrice-great'), who was thought to be a contemporary of Moses. In fact they are a collection of prophetic and philosophical pieces written during the 3rd and 4th centuries by various neo-Platonists of Alexandria. Translated into Latin by Marsilio Ficino in 1471 and subsequently into Italian, these 'Hermetic' writings, edited, retranslated and republished many times, became revered texts for meditation throughout Europe. Although couched in mysterious language, they were regarded as containing predictions of Christian doctrine (the Incarnation and the Trinity), profound truths about human p 26
(41, 42)

nature handed down from the Egyptians to the Jews and then to the Greeks and Romans, and finally justifications and recipes for magical practices which had a special appeal to Renaissance intellectuals since they came from a source so apparently in accord with the Old and New Testaments. Orthodox theologians might express disapproval, but the extent of Hermes' acceptance can be judged by the mosaic portrayal of him made in 1488 by Giovanni di Stefano for the floor of Siena Cathedral and inscribed 'Hermes Mercurius Trismegistus, Contemporaneus Moisi'.

p 148 (5)

We need not, therefore, be surprised to find Melanchthon studying the occult, especially as he was a great-nephew of the most famous Hebraist and Cabbalist of all, Johann Reuchlin. The 'Reuchlin affair', which had taken place only a few years before Luther made his great protest, reflected in miniature some of the coming conflicts of the Reformation. The question was whether, in view of the 'inspired' translation of St Jerome's Vulgate, it was permissible to go back to the Hebrew text of the Old Testament. (There was an analogous argument about the Greek text). The humanists, or 'New Men' as they called themselves, maintained that the original texts should be consulted on matters of such vital importance to the spiritual life. Erasmus in 1505 restated Lorenzo Valla's arguments in support of this view.

p 197 (8)

The quarrel, though fierce, was at first confined to the small circle of the learned. When ordinary uneducated people began to take an interest in it, and it was conducted not in the Latin of schools and academies but in the low Saxon of the streets and shops—then the scholars withdrew, surrounded by their books, and settled for compromises and half-measures. Not all of them, however: Melanchthon, the progressive, mild, highly distinguished teacher, went to Wittenberg. Here he re-introduced the traditional Aristotelian teaching, purified of scholastic sophisms, and brought back the rigorous discipline of good all-round education, earning the title of *praeceptor Germaniae*. But he did not leave his Hermetic and astrological trappings behind, and these were not without effect on his fanatical colleague, Martin Luther.

Dividing Lines

Melanchthon was one of the first thinkers of the north to attempt a systematic historical account of his own epoch and to see it in terms which we can still largely accept today. Within a large general framework of the development of human life on earth (which was itself part of an even vaster cosmic picture), he set out a clear definition of the 'Renaissance'. The rebirth of literature and scholarship, he decided, began in Italy, though it was at first a rather limited and uncritical imitation of the ancients. However, after the fall of Constantinople to the Turks, the learned men of Byzantium, custodians of the store-house and precious essence of antiquity (which was Greek, incorporating ancient Egyptian discoveries), were forced to flee from their own country and find refuge elsewhere. Melanchthon exalted the Florentines, because unlike the rest of their contemporaries, they were not satisfied with merely offering hospitality and alms to these exiles. With their love of knowledge, they realized that the Byzantines' learning had great importance and they treated them with respect, asking them to teach and providing them (as Melanchthon puts it with professional realism) with adequate and suitable means to support themselves and continue their studies. Melanchthon dwells on this point at such length that it deserves to be repeated: the Florentines had understood the importance of the Byzantines' studies (he implied that members of the University of Wittenberg were trying to follow their example and should not therefore be regarded as inferior; they too should pursue such philological, humanist and philosophical studies); the Florentines had also understood (and the University of Wittenberg was trying to do likewise) that the Greek and Hebrew knowledge and learning brought to Italy by the guardians of the ancient, true and primeval learning and doctrine, of fundamental importance and divinely inspired, formed the basis not only of a good literary education, but also, and principally, of the good and true theology of Wittenberg.

The historical division proposed by Melanchthon—making the year 1453 or thereabouts the beginning of humanism and the Renaissance of art, scholarship and neo-Platonist philosophy—was regarded as valid up to the first decades of our own century.

But while accepting the theory, almost all scholars overlooked at least two fundamental points: first that these Greek sages brought with them (according to Melanchthon, if not in fact) the Hermetic prophecies which gave rise to so much unease in 16th-century European culture; second (again in Melanchthon's view, if not in fact) Wittenberg followed Florence in the study of occult wisdom as well as in the pursuit of good education.

It is tempting to adopt Melanchthon's system of dating and division into historical periods, and to begin our exposition with the Councils of Florence and Ferrara, in the time of Pope Eugenius IV. Reuchlin and Melanchthon in effect made that period the beginning of a new era, and made their fathers' and grandfathers' time the 'prehistory' of their philology and culture. This must be specially emphasized in the case of Melanchthon, a competent and well-informed theologian, strict and intransigent in his own sphere, and a loyal supporter of the fundamental Protestant concept of faith as the unique source of salvation. Despite his reputation for mildness and gentleness, due to the fact that his work contains none of Martin Luther's vehemence, he was always a firm and decided supporter of the new religious ideas, even when he could have seemed inclined to compromise. He suffered from none of Erasmus' uncertainties over theological matters. Erasmus, at first sympathetic to the Reformation as a movement of both moral and cultural rebirth, detached himself from it at an early stage and turned back to the traditional Church: revolted by the violence the Reformation had caused, he again upheld traditional attitudes and the doctrine of 'free will'.

p 197 (5, 6, 7

The Catholic attitude to Erasmus was nevertheless one of extreme suspicion. His work was officially condemned in 1559 by Pope Paul IV, and even at the fifth Lateran Council many voices had been raised in protest against his *Colloquies* on the grounds that their anti-clerical satire was unseemly. But despite his humanist culture and impatience with scholasticism, Erasmus belonged to the old, the pre-Reformation, generation. So did Tommaso di Vio, Thomas More, Cardinal Sadoleto and Cardinal Contarini, not to mention Pope Hadrian VI and Girolamo Aleandro. None of them could or would accept a complete break with religious and ecclesiastical tradition, though they criticized it in every possible way (Anabaptists and even Antitrinitarians were able to find arguments in Erasmus and some Anabaptists used to read More's *Utopia*), and hoped for thorough-going reforms of the Roman Catholic Church, *in capite et in membris*, ('in head and members').

The 'modern generation', by contrast, was ready for a fundamental break with tradition, and with various degrees of enthusiasm accepted the doctrine of justification by faith, a concept which involved a reorganization of dogma, the liturgy, the hierarchy and ecclesiastical administration. This is true of all radicals, from the more moderate, such as Luther and Melanchthon and most Anglicans, to those with the most extreme views on dogma and organization, such as various Anabaptist groups, who appeared on the scene between 1520 and 1525. In any case, they can all be given a common identity, though they lived at different times, because they were all to take the final step of making a break with tradition, and starting on a new road, whose direction they did not and could not know.

Naturally there were many retreats, regrets and reconversions to the old doctrines and discipline; opinions diverged radically, bringing bitter persecutions (extreme examples are the suppression of the Anabaptists at Munster in 1535 and Servetus' condemnation to death by the Geneva Calvinists) and there were polemical disputes, as between Luther and Zwingli. 'Reformation' too meant something different from country to country, from the Anglican Reformation in England and the Lutheran in Germany, both under the supremacy of the sovereign, to the Presbyterian-Calvinist Reformation in the Swiss and Rhenish towns (Zürich, Berne, Geneva and Strasbourg) and the Palatinate. But all these internal conflicts have clouded and obscured the one basic antithesis between the old and the new. Everyone, great and small alike, was keenly aware of a decisive break in their lives. For some (Ulrich von Hutten in Germany, for example), it was a revelation; for Catholics it was either an unprecedented outrage or a source of inner torment. But the overall experience was that

f 2

p 252 (
p 200–
(13–17)

The wolf-monk devouring an innocent sheep—a satire on the covetousness of monks which is typical of the crudity and violence of Reformation controversy. (2)

an important, crucial event had taken place in western Christian society. People were prepared to kill or be killed for issues which had suddenly come into their lives.

These considerations (to return for a moment to the distinction outlined at the beginning of this chapter) tend to make us agree with the 'Ranke' view of history whereby the 'modern age' would start, not with the Renaissance and humanism, but with the Protestant Reformation. After all, except for some exceptional cases, very few people died in the cause of Hermes Trismegistus and the philosopher's stone. But a great many died, and a great many were ready to kill, over questions of justification by faith, the invocation of saints and the real presence in the Eucharist. The tragedy permeates the whole 16th century. Without bearing this in mind we cannot fully understand the value of the slow, persistent growth of humanist attitudes, largely religious in content, *within* the sectarian disputes—even if in the end it only leads us to understand the ensuing weaknesses and renunciations, oppressions and injustices, deceits and subterfuges.

The Language of Protest

p 148
(2, 3, 4) One protest against the 'oppression' of Rome was made in symbolic imagery as skilfully arranged as the pieces in a complicated game of chess. It came from a pious, devout and aristocratic abbess in charge of a small community of nuns in a city which was certainly important for strategic reasons, though it did not have the independence or fame of Florence or Venice: Giovanna da Piacenza, abbess of the Benedictine convent of San Paolo at Parma. She took issue with the Curia over the question of claustration, from which her convent had been for some time exempt. Aware of the accusations and humiliating suspicions which the vulgar-minded secular clergy would level at a community of nuns to which courtiers and cultured men had access, she wished to answer them not only in terms of canon law and of her own personal authority, but also in terms of a larger symbolic language which would express her contemptuous indifference for Roman oppression, for the vulgarity of the clergy and for those who were not of her own world. She won; she established her independence of the Curia in administrative, social, intellectual and spiritual matters. And to leave a record of her triumph she chose a painter of genius, Correggio. His frescoes

in the Camera di San Paolo were enigmatic then and are doubly so today—unusual, mysterious and 'Hermetic' in more than one sense. But they typify a certain stage of humanism as it relates to the conflict against Rome.

Giovanna da Piacenza became abbess of San Paolo in 1507 and died in 1524. The world changed in those seventeen years. By its end, the revolt was no longer the affair of aristocrats, the cultured few and the intellectually superior, grouping themselves together in academies and closed circles of the initiated, who could indulge in criticism of a private kind while remaining faithful in principle to Rome. It had now begun to move to peasants, artisans, townsmen and lawyers, and some powerful princes. A great monarch might soon join the movement, and other great monarchs would then have to keep an eye on it. The genteel system of symbols and devices (see p 159) was, of course, *f* 3, 4 to continue in European culture, but it would no longer be the only way of expressing protest, or marking the stages of a conflict, though it had been the only way open to the abbess Giovanna, with her aristocratic upbringing and refined cultural background. Even Philip Melanchthon, in spite of his liking for and interest in devices and other kinds of hieroglyphs and emblems, always expressed himself in clear straightforward terms when it came to teaching and disputation.

Good Latin, wide learning, and the vast fund of information of men such as Melanchthon, Zwingli, Calvin, Peter Martyr Vermigli, and later Matthias Flacius, Pierre de la Ramée and John Knox, commanded the respect of the humanist sections of the cultural world. Martin Luther is an exception. Admired and p 200
(13) respected by theologians, even those whose views were most far-removed and hostile to his own, he was always a source of some embarrassment to the humanists. Even Melanchthon, his most devoted friend, makes this apparent in his memorial to him. Who, after, all, was Luther's favourite poet? Battista Mantuanus, a didactic and tedious Carmelite monk, whom Luther liked for some of his attacks on the clergy, or more precisely, the Roman Curia.

The greatest and most respected humanists in general European culture or the *respublica literarum* in the 16th century are those we have just mentioned. It is significant of this urgent attitude to scholarship that when St Philip Neri, for example, had to give a general outline for future work to one of his followers, Cesare Baronio, he set him the task of compiling an answer to the survey of church history known as the *Centuries*, organized by Matthias Flacius Illyricus, one of the most rabid Lutherans, who was hated even in Lutheran universities for some of his theological attitudes. In spite of his undoubted merits as a historian (he started a kind of Institute of Historical Research, and was accused of making his researchers dress up as friars and go into Catholic convents to seek out ancient texts), Flacius' book is of no interest to us at the moment. The point to be stressed is that Baronio's *Annales ecclesiastici*, a history of the Church to the 12th century, is still on the reference shelves of great libraries, unlike the pioneering work of Flacius.

Hermetic and philosophic humanism had by now been inaugurated and was proving seminal. Italian and especially Florentine in origin, it raised problems and stimulated curiosity, following an indirect and illusive path. The Protestant humanism of Melanchthon (using him as a prototype or symbol of a much broader movement, which was often not directly connected to any definite sectarian attitude; Erasmus might be considered an equally good representative) and Calvin and their immediate successors set the movement under way. It defined issues, and problems, and asked questions and found new answers. Erudite Italian humanism kept up a continual flow of answers in an aggressive counterblast. It made a brilliant defence of its position from the doctrinal academic point of view, but it suffered, on the whole, from a certain ambivalence. The position of the supporters of the Catholic point of view was that they were defending a cause—that of the Roman Catholic Church—in which they believed whole-heartedly from a personal subjective stand-point, while being aware that their argument was invalidated by humanist methods and criteria of philological criticism in which they also believed.

The Split Widens

People were very much aware of individual events, sensing that they were, or could be, turning points in their lives. The dates stressed in history books stood at the time for radiant hopes, violent upheavals, fearful memories. Let us look at some of them. 1513: the election of Leo X, which raised great expectations among the faithful. 1515: the Fifth Lateran Council, called some years earlier (1512) by Julius II to provide an opposition to the pro-French party, but now seeming to be a harbinger of peace among Christian leaders. 1519: Charles of Burgundy became Emperor Charles V—a step towards European unity, but would Europe be unified? 1518–21: Luther's revolt; his agitation and propaganda now made themselves felt, though their political effects were not immediately apparent. First came purely religious controversies, then social disturbances (1525, the Peasants' Revolt; 1535, the Anabaptist rising in Münster); only later did Luther's ideas emerge as a factor determining the balance of power between great nations. There was a spontaneous proliferation of manifestoes of doctrine, opinions and views covering a whole range of topics from the mystical insights and visions of individual people and small groups to the re-emergence of the ideas and doctrines of John Huss, the launching of the Swiss Reformation by the humanist priest Ulrich Zwingli in 1522–1525, and the formulation of doctrinal systems and canon law, particularly after the English Reformation and the establishment of the Anglican Church.

The Sack of Rome of 1527 was an epoch-making event in the lives of Italian humanists and men of letters. Poets have described the misery they felt on seeing the end of the happy age they had known under the aegis of the papacy. In many other European cultural circles—literary, philosophic and theological, both Catholic and Protestant—it seemed a just punishment approved by God. In 1530 the last Florentine republic fell after fierce resistance. Clement VII's successor, Paul III, began a new and obviously necessary policy, by which the patrimony of St Peter, or the Papal State, would no longer play an expansionist part in Italian politics (as it had done under Alexander VI, Julius II, and even under Leo X and Clement VII). Instead it was to be the seat of the Roman Catholic and Apostolic Church and had to prepare itself for a General Council on the reformation and the reorganization of Christian society, setting itself up in competition with and in opposition to the various different shades of Protestant opinion.

Paul III was Pope from 1534 to 1549. Many well-educated men of letters were still in the Curia under him. Among the cardinals who produced the plan of reform for him in 1536–37 were Gasparo Contarini, Pietro Carafa, Jacopo Sadoleto, Reginald Pole, Giovan Matteo Giberti, Girolamo Morone, Gregorio Cortese . . . philosophers, humanists, theologians, political theorists and lawyers. Their sympathies, indeed, were sometimes too wide. The most theologically-minded of them all, Pietro Carafa, later Pope Paul IV (1555–59), had Cardinal Girolamo Morone imprisoned in the Castel Sant' Angelo on the grounds that he favoured the dissemination of Protestant ideas in Italy. An able philosopher and a good diplomat, Morone, it appeared, had failed to understand the Protestantism of the *Beneficio di Cristo*, the most famous devotional work of the Italian Protestant movement. Other good theologians, however, had at once discovered that under its ascetic mysticism, under its wonderful expressions of love for Christ, and exhortations to moral and religious endeavour, it was a heretical work.

A report was drawn up which proposed the reform of many abuses, but repeated that Erasmus' *Colloquies* and various other philosophic doctrines such as those of Pomponazzi should be condemned because they were considered dangerous. A copy came into the hands of Jacob Sturm, the humanist Protestant of Strasbourg, who published it with a letter of criticism addressed to Contarini before the text had been printed in Italy. In the first twenty or thirty years of the 16th century, open letters between Protestant and Catholic humanists were not unusual, as is shown by the exchange between Sadoleto and Calvin. The scandal, on this occasion, lay in the fact that a document of this kind, secret at Rome, could come so quickly into the possession of a 'Lutheran'. Sturm made it the pretext for a concise critique of the Church of Rome, but expressed his delight that a pope was at last prepared to listen to the voice of truth. In 1559, Sturm's letter and the *Consilium delectorum cardinalium* were placed on the Index, and this put an end to free communication between humanists and their exchange of exhortatory and polemical letters. Sadoleto made an attempt to start a discussion on theological and humanist ideas with Melanchthon, but Melanchthon did not respond.

Words and Deeds

One of the cardinals at the Council of Trent, defending a humanist colleague from the charge that he showed insufficient respect for papal supremacy, said contemptuously that there was no need to give any weight to the speeches 'those humanists' made, because they merely juggled with words. It was not, of course, an allusion to the 'words but not deeds' that Martin Luther had said of Erasmus, but the idea was the same—the notion that humane letters were a matter of indifference in the battle of rival doctrines. It was a sign of the times. With Paul III the reaction was beginning. Humanists on the Catholic side were going back to theology and devotion. Cardinal Gabriele Paleotti, Archbishop of Bologna and a friend of St Charles Borromeo, turned at the end of his life to write *De bono senectutis*, an 'art of living in old age' (1595); while between the controversies in which he was engaged Bellarmine worked on the medieval theme of 'the art of holy dying' (1621).

This peculiarly Italian situation (it was also to be found in other predominantly Catholic countries, due to the immediate link with the papacy) had various consequences. The most lively, 'advanced' or 'progressive' cultural circles (usually aristocratic) were humanist in inspiration—humanist in the most general sense. They wrote Petrarchan poetry; they were interested in Greek and Latin culture, philological criticism and antiquarianism. Their paramount interest was in the philosophy of love and the reassessment of rhetoric and the emotions, or (to put it more philosophically) in the theory of the pre-eminence of the will over the intellect. Many of them applied the philosophy of love to divine love—that of human beings for Jesus Christ, and that of God and Jesus for humanity; they derived their views sometimes from traditional, orthodox mysticism, and sometimes from the new ideas on dogma, the Church and morality coming from beyond the Alps. But a situation was developing to which the Protestant humanists and their friends found it increasingly difficult to adjust. Even the reading of St Paul's Epistles came to be regarded as suspect. In such an atmosphere, when Catholics might be urging greater understanding and Protestants concealing their true allegiance, it was difficult to judge between them dispassionately. The preaching of Bernardino Ochino, general of the new Franciscan order of the Capuchins, and a very famous and popular speaker, came (about 1540) to be suspected, although he did not attack Rome, but developed themes of ascetic mysticism of a Franciscan kind, the sort associated above all with Bonaventura. The little tract *Beneficio di Cristo*, apparently the result of collaboration between a Benedictine monk and Marc' Antonio Flaminio, a classical traditional humanist and Latinist, appeared to be controversial, although it can now be safely regarded as Protestant. The ideas and insights of Juan de Valdés (who died in 1541) were very popular in aristocratic and cultured circles. His theories were clearly Protestant in background and outlook, but vague and cautious in their actual content, as is seen in his writings, and particularly in the *Christian Alphabet* (the fundamentals of Christian doctrine), which was dedicated to Giulia Gonzaga. Among other things he advised regular attendance at mass and other ceremonies that Protestants regarded as superstitious (in fact considered a serious offence, almost amounting to blasphemy, by Lutherans and Calvinists) but he interpreted them in a 'spiritual' sense.

Naturally, with the passage of time, such attitudes could be used to justify either complete submission or complete concealment, particularly perhaps among the aristocracy, but also in popular circles (among humble 'humanists', village school-masters, merchants, etc.). Recent research has shown that the Protestant movement was more widespread in all classes in Italy than used to be thought twenty or thirty years ago. There were parti-

p 28 (53)

p 153 (11)

p 147 (1

f 1

cular groups who made no secret of their beliefs (e.g. the Calvinists of Lucca, and the surviving Waldensians in the valleys between Piedmont and France, who were now Calvinists) and a
few brave or eccentric individuals. But apart from these, the vast
majority of the followers and 'pastors' of the new religion preferred to take Juan de Valdés's advice and as far as possible stay
underground in their own country. Some, like Ludovico Castel-
vetro, a man of letters, literary critic and commentator on Petrarch, had to flee, after being publicly denounced. Some were put
to death, after a long series of abjurations and hair-splitting decisions, as were Pietro Carnesecchi, one of the most prominent
and respected members of the Roman Curia in Clement VII's
time, and the poet, Aonio Paleario. The case of Fausto Sozzini may
be taken as a typical example. He came from a famous and noble
family of Sienese lawyers, and he spent about ten years at the
Medici court, and a further twenty or thirty in Poland, all the
time without having to make any declaration of faith. He wrote
tracts under various pseudonyms, and managed to make a living,
even in Poland, for about thirty years, demanding and getting his
income as an Italian *rentier*, until members of the Italian Inquisition
caught up with him, and his authorship became known.

Calvin and his friends in Geneva urged their supporters to
open action, to face martyrdom, or at least to make every sacrifice
short of life, but to little effect. The Italian Protestant movement
preferred allusions, readings and secret studies. Renée of France,
Duchess of Ferrara, left the court at a fairly late stage in her life;
she may possibly have received Calvin there, certainly did receive
Clement Marot; but not even in France, where she was freer
than in Italy, since she belonged to the royal family, did she ever
want to go further than the Italian Protestants, in spite of Calvin's
exhortations. French and German Protestants were always far
more outspoken than Italian; at an early stage, crude German
books printed in Alsace (Karsthans for example) have engraved
frontispieces showing Martin Luther and Erasmus of Rotterdam
beside a peasant who is making a priest vomit out all his ill-
gotten money; but there are no similar Italian works. They made
no direct polemic or satirical attacks on the Catholic religion—any
attacks they made were anticlerical—either in painting or literature.

A characteristic example of the Italians' allusive roundabout
modes of expression is to be found in the use of 'emblems', intelligible only to the initiated. Those of the Camera di San Paolo
are an example: they are not too obscure for an audience that
knows the secret but they are incomprehensible to the layman, or
even to an Inquisition spy. The Bolognese humanist Achille
Bocchi dedicated some emblems to Renée of France. They were
published at Bologna in 1555, under the title '*Symbolicarum
quaestionum libri quinque*', with engravings attributed to one of
the Carracci. They include a picture of Proteus, bound and tied
into the form of a human being, after having cast off various
monstrous and diabolical forms. This seems to be a warning to
Renée of France to stay faithful to the true religion (Catholicism):
as truth can assume a vast number of forms, it is sufficient to
remain constant to any one of them. The legend runs *unam viden-
dam veritatem in omnibus*, and the accompanying lines encourage
the reader to pursue the 'true faith'. Another emblem, almost a
copy of the upper part of Raphael's *Transfiguration*, showing people fainting at the apparition of Christ is a sort of repetition o
Dante's theme 'Mankind, content yourselves with the fact' (from
the Divine Comedy). It is here expressed as *archana quaerens curio-
sius, perit*. The Christian (Catholic) faith is *intimus amor in Deum*.
The same motif, symbolized by the image of Ganymede snatched
up to heaven by Jupiter's eagle, is dedicated to Reginald Pole:
pacati emblema hoc corporis atque animi est; disputes should not be
polemical or bitter, but peaceful: *ex disputatione veritas patet, con-
tentione evertitur;* those who seek truth in open conflict will never
achieve it, but rather those who work alone, each lighting his own
lamp with a flame he has himself kindled:

> *Sic disceptando studiosi in luminis oras
> verum ipsum e latebris excutiunt facile.*

In the second half of the 16th century, Theodore de Bèze and
others published clearer and more explicit metaphorical pictures
and allegories of the European religious conflicts.

f 3, 4

*Emblems intelligible only to the initiated were especially useful in the
dangerous labyrinth of religious dispute. These two engravings are from
Bocchi's 'Symbolicae quaestiones'. Top: Proteus, bound in the form of a
man, having thrown off various shapes. Symbolically it exhorts the
French-born Duchess of Ferrara, who favoured Protestantism, to adhere
to the Catholic Church, truth in its only real form. Bottom: Ganymede
being snatched up to heaven by Jupiter. The Greek inscription, 'to enjoy
intelligence', reflects the neo-Platonic interpretation of Ganymede's name,
and the emblem represents the Mind, beloved of the Supreme Being, rising
above the lower faculties of the soul to the ecstasy of contemplation. (3, 4)*

Sleidan took twelve years to complete his monumental history of the Reformation (published 1555), collecting documents even in England. The printer's colophon in the 1559 Basle edition, 'Time drawing forth Truth', is particularly apt for a history so impartial that even Melanchthon was dissatisfied. (5)

The First Protestant Historian

Let us return to the chronological sequence of events. Juan de Valdés had a brother Alfonso de Valdés. Alfonso spent some time in the chancery of Charles V in the early years of the reign, when Mercurino da Gattinara and the followers of Erasmus were still in the ascendancy. They favoured a general 'Italian', 'imperial' policy, with the restoration of imperial authority on a par with papal authority. (They went back to the theory of the *duo soles*, two suns, and also proposed an edition of Dante's *De monarchia*.) Such was the climate of opinion in which, in 1526, Alfonso de Valdés wrote a famous Latin admonition for Charles V, inviting Clement VII to the Council, and loading him with eloquent abuse: *Tu non pastor, sed invasor*. Some people even advised Clement VII to oppose Luther not by a war against the Turks, but by receiving the separated Christians of the great and powerful Muscovite empire into the Church.

The Society of Jesus had been founded in Italy and Spain in 1534, and was given official approval in 1540. Charles V turned his attention from Italy and the Universal Empire to Spain and the Low Countries. He implemented his policy by war with François Ier. The French were defeated at Pavia in 1525 but war went on in Italy until 1538, and even then the Hapsburg-Valois struggle troubled the peninsula until the settlement of Cateau-Cambrésis in 1559 by which time Italy was dominated by Spain. At Charles V's abdication (1556), the kingdom of Spain, Naples, Sicily and Milan (of course under separate administration), the American colonies and the traditional feudal possessions in Franche Comté and the Low Countries all passed to Philip II. The Imperial title and the traditional Hapsburg possessions in Germany went to Ferdinand.

p 152 (9) Meanwhile, in Germany, at the Diet of Augsburg (1530), Melanchthon's *Confessio fidei Augustana* was presented to Charles V in person, and he provisionally agreed to accept it. This sanctioned a first consolidation of the movement and a first, inconclusive, informal, if not yet official recognition. Lutheran princes and cities (the Zwinglians were excluded) united in the Schmalkaldic League (1531) to maintain the position they had now achieved. For some time—until 1549—they managed to assert themselves, taking advantage of the difficult position the Empire and the Hapsburgs had been put into by the war against the Turkish invasion of eastern Europe. The Schmalkaldic League had aroused high hopes among declared and secret Protestants even outside Germany, because it seemed a sufficiently strong political and military force to be able to play a diplomatic and military part in the machinations of the great powers.

f 5 The princes of the League entrusted Johann Sleidan, an able and learned humanist from Strasbourg, with the task of writing a history of the Reformation which would give the 'republic of letters' an account and explanation of the work of Martin Luther, and the motives of the German princes who helped and protected him. Strasbourg had been deeply involved in the humanist and religious upheavals and Sleidan had remained faithful to the original Protestant, mainly Lutheran, attitudes of the Reformation. His opinions were confirmed when the city sent him to the Council of Trent in the capacity of observer but with the hope that he might act as representative. This came to nothing, partly because Melanchthon, expected at Trent from day to day, never came.

The Council of Trent took place between 1545 and 1563. It was interrupted many times, the main sessions being held 1545–47, p 153 1551–52 and 1562–63. Owing its existence largely to the initiative (10) of Charles V, its aims were ostensibly threefold: to resolve the religious dispute by doctrinal decision, to reform ecclesiastical abuses, and to discuss a Crusade against the Turks. The Emperor, the humanists and men of moderation everywhere had long pinned their hopes on a General Council (it was held in the extreme north of Italy in order to tempt the Protestants to attend) but the Pope and the Curia closed the door on compromise. It soon became evident—to Sleidan and to everyone else—that the Council was only ready to accept total submission, though this they would accept benevolently enough. It was impossible to have a serious discussion or to make peace with the 'Romans'. This was a very influential experience in the life of the Protestant historian.

When Sleidan's work was published in 1555 the Schmalkaldic League had been disbanded, and the political and cultural atmosphere had changed so much that even his family and friends were puzzled by the book. Old disputes had been over the rôle of critical reason, the problems of faith and works, and the right of the individual on humanist grounds to be protected against authority. Now, with compromise about, no one in power wanted trouble from humanists—who were indeed often tiresome pedants. But Sleidan's work is far from being pedantic in the frivolous sense. He insisted that he must have precise documentation provided by those who played important parts in the events described, and he obtained many authentic records from Luther and others. (Calvin never answered; the matter he was being asked about was an unpleasant one, Servetus' trial.)

Sleidan's narrative is in the humanist tradition; although he was an ardent and convinced Protestant, he saw religious life principally as a matter of church institutions in relation with secular authority—the emperor and his councillors, kings, princes and town councils. After the point when Luther brought the true faith to the world, doctrinal differences interested Sleidan less than political and moral judgments on secular and ecclesiastical authority. His work deals more with legal issues than religious or theological ones. With his access to the documents in the princes' chanceries, especially that of the Elector of Saxony, he was able to improve on the methods previously used in humanist historiography. His constant endeavour to write good Latin in the style of Livy, with various *excursus* of antiquarian interest, in the *Commentaries* is directly connected with his endeavour to maintain the typical traditional humanist ideal of an impartial narrative, written in eloquent, but restrained language; he did not use imaginary speeches, as even Guicciardini did.

Such a synthesis of humanist concepts and religious faith was very original and new, even if it reduced religious life to the history of the different Churches and their leaders; for the first time, religious events were discussed in the same context as political events. Sleidan and Luther had the same views on history. Luther, (in spite of his theological and mystic conception of universal history and the history of the Church) when making a collection of his own writings, added many of those of his first companions in the struggle, because he felt they would be useful and important for historians.

Fact, Faith and History

Other historians understood Sleidan's lesson—for instance William Camden in England and Thuanus (Jacques-Auguste de p 260 Thou) in France. Camden in his *Annales rerum Anglicarum et* (25) *Hibernicarum regnante Elizabetha* (1615) used a restrained style and tried hard to be impartial. He included religious questions in his concept of history, believing that 'there can be no divorce between religion and the state'. Thuanus (1553–1617) was a humanist with a precious and somewhat pedantic style. But in his *Historia sui temporis* he expounds his theories with great lucidity. In order to save France from the terrible evils of religious civil war, he says, force should not be used, but rather tolerance and persuasion by teaching, discussion and good example. Unlike Sleidan and Camden, Thuanus was a Catholic and he deplored the 'division in the Church'. But the fact that he called it 'division' (*scissura*) instead of rebellion or heresy shows his tendency towards conciliation.

This was history written by humanists. History written by professional theologians presents a different picture. Even the most learned allowed their convictions to get the better of their objectivity. When Melanchthon, for instance, recast the *Chronicon*, the universal history originally written from a Lutheran standpoint by the astrologer and diplomat Carion, he tried to show not only that Lutheranism was the true form of Christianity which had existed ever since Adam and Eve, but also that divine intervention was apparent in every decisive moment of history. He made a collection of edifying examples and cases to show the truth of Luther's theology. A less simple, and much more important work is Flacius Illyricus' *Ecclesiastica historia . . . secundum singulas centurias*, which has already been mentioned. In spite of his humanist education in Venice, Flacius approached his work, not as a humanist or historian, but as a theologian, and thus he separates Church history from the general aggregate of historical facts, ignoring the humanists' methods. While Sleidan was introducing a new concept of history, treating not only political and military issues, but also religious and cultural ones, Flacius and his collaborators were evolving a theory which saw the Church as the pivot and determining factor of history as a whole. They not only went back to the old idea that theology is the queen of all branches of learning, but they also completely rejected the fundamental humanist ideal that all knowledge forms a consistent and harmonious unity.

Unity, in fact, is the key to the humanist view of history, as of all other aspects of human life and culture. Language and literature, scholarship, the arts, religion (or religions, in the plural)—all were seen as wholes, as universals, whose values remained the same for all times and places. It is a view which comes through in many different ways: in Melanchthon himself, speaking of the heritage of the Greeks; in Giovanni Pico della Mirandola and his neo-Platonic Christianity; in Raphael's *School of Athens;* in Dürer's studies of figures and proportions; in the work of Leonardo da Vinci. Sleidan, therefore, may be included in the humanist sphere, though only in a limited sense, while Flacius and the Centuriators (as his team of collaborators are known) put themselves outside it, in spite of their consideration of non-Christian religions, their study of doctrine and their improved methods of research. Their successors were to be the compilers of 'books of martyrs'—edifying material and good sectarian propaganda, but not history.

Humanism in the Wilderness

Erasmus—hesitant and uncertain as he seemed to many—was always the epitome of the religious humanist, and his reputation rose and fell with that of the philosophy he represented. Towards the end of the 16th century many people felt a new sympathy for his position. His literary works, such as the *Praise of Folly*, had never ceased to be read, and the *Colloquies* were used in schools in Protestant countries, particularly Holland and England. But now, after so many bitter controversies and violent persecutions, he began to seem an almost legendary figure: a scholar, a deeply religious man, a friend to Protestant and Catholic alike, a symbol of the longing for peace and agreement. Officially he was still condemned; Lutherans and Calvinists despised him, the Inquisition banned or expurgated his works (the *Adages*, of which Catholic preachers very frequently made use, were censored and printed under the name of Paulus Manutius, a descendent of Aldus, instead of Erasmus).

Rightly or wrongly, people began to see in his work a synthesis of the kind of humanism and sincere religious feeling which no longer existed as a cultural reality—humanism was exhausted. There was of course no lack of learned men—philologists, excellent Latin, Greek and Hebrew scholars, antiquarians and historians. But the philosophic and encyclopaedic humanism of the Renaissance was now dead. We can certainly find something of it in Francis Bacon (1561–1626), but a definition of Renaissance thought would not provide an adequate description of his ideas, or bring out any of his salient characteristics. At this time, religious humanism and humanist religion, in the Renaissance meaning of the words, only survived in a relatively concealed position in European culture, where it fostered a useful and

A satirical world-map of Papalism, published in 1556, is attributed to the French humanist Theodore de Bèze. This small section (the complete map is over a yard wide) attacks the worship of saints. Mountains of images and relics (including a pair of dice) lie beside a coffer of asses' and horses' bones. (6)

fertile heritage which was to emerge at a later date. However, for the time being it remained in the background.

The proud intellectual tradition of Petrarch, Valla and More was now reduced to the ability to write good Latin and Greek, a useful aid to communication between scholars and theologians of different nationalities. Interest in the life and history of men, in their customs, in philosophical ideas and in historical and philological criticism either dwindled into affected conceits and artificial exercises, or became divided and subdivided into specialized studies. Theodore de Bèze (1519–1605) and his friend George Buchanan (1506–82) may serve as examples. They had the virtuoso style of Latin and Greek epigrammists and elegiacists, and the Scottish writer was also an excellent imitator of Livy. But as a historian, Bèze used the popular theme of the 'Book of Martyrs', and Buchanan completely ignored the religious conflicts of his time, although he did in fact take a direct part in them. Interest in Renaissance humanism became separated from interest in religion, the former becoming a literary exercise, often a very accomplished and successful one, the latter a matter of sectarian disputes.

Humanism, properly so called (that is, scholarship combined with a lively interest in religion), seemed to survive only among a certain class of heretic, the 'radical reformers' as we should call them today. They were often close to Anabaptists of various different shades, but can be distinguished from them by their greater and more conscious humanist background, (a sound knowledge of philosophy, good Latin and Greek, and often good Hebrew), and by a certain taste for concrete rationality, which sometimes recalls the clear-cut terminology of lawyers. In their customs, in their practical and moral fervour as well as in their ideas, some of them are comparable to the first generations of Quakers. When faced with exile, persecution and poverty, they showed great simplicity and resignation; freedom of conscience and the Sermon on the Mount were the mainstays of their thought. For them, the spontaneity of true religious feeling (in the evangelical Christian sense which is generally accepted among Protestants) lay principally in religious freedom. Without this freedom there could be no genuine voluntary belief.

By 'religious freedom' or 'freedom of conscience' they meant the right of each individual, provided he lived his life according to the precepts of Christian morality, to profess only those doctrines, or dogmas, of which he was fully convinced, and to reject those of which his powers of thought (his reason) and his culture (humanism) made him in any way doubtful, of which he could not be wholly sure, and could not therefore accept as the word of God. This is the essence of Sebastian Castellion's *De arte credendi et dubitandi:* true religious faith lies in absolute conviction and belief in free salvation; therefore no one should

p 26
45, 46)
p 150–
151 (7)

p 197
5, 6, 7)

f 6
p 179
(46)

say he has faith in a specific doctrine unless he has examined its validity in the light of sacred texts, and analyzed it from a critical and philological standpoint. It follows that no one (among those who call themselves Christians and practise Christianity) should prevent others from doubting, discussing and criticizing this or that particular doctrine or dogma.

The Pressures of Intolerance

The essence of humanist religion, therefore, was tolerance. Only faith can bring salvation, but faith is mystical and spiritual. A learned man may not *force* another learned man to accept his own doctrines, but should convince him by the use of persuasion and reason. It was a philosophy that found a ready home in the Protestant countries, where private conscience was acknowledged a surer guide than the appeal to authority.

All the greater, therefore, was the scandal which arose in enlightened circles when in 1553 these principles were contradicted; when a humanist, a theologian and a poet—Calvin—positively desired, or at any rate did not hinder, and certainly did not disapprove of, the execution at Geneva of another humanist, a mystic, Hebraist, doctor and geographer—Michael Servetus. The political and ecclesiastical reasons for the condemnation are understandable enough, given the time at which it took place. The Protestants were going through a difficult, critical period, and could not let themselves be accused of tolerating doctrines which were held to be dangerous by the vast majority of Christians. Servetus' criticisms of the dogma of the Trinity would certainly be considered dangerous not only by Catholic princes, but also by Protestant princes and cities. The acute disquiet felt by the humanist world was formally expressed by Castellion, Curione, Camillo Renato, Lelio Sozzini and others, and there is a certain unease in the argumentative arrogance of Calvin's and Bèze's answers. They had abandoned the humanist use of argument and proof, and turned to authority and the power of law; they had abandoned the principle of Christian freedom. From a theological and legal point of view, they could prove that their action was politically and ecclesiastically necessary; but Sebastian Castellion and his friends answered that what is necessary politically and ecclesiastically may not be necessary morally.

It was an age when the old attitude was becoming increasingly difficult to maintain. Anabaptists, even able scholars of Latin and Greek, often ended by rejecting humanist Renaissance culture as worldly knowledge, leading to un-Christian pride and arrogance. But other groups tried to continue the work of purifying the Christian religion which this culture had begun. Their general view was analogous to that of Melanchthon: Latin scholarship, followed by Greek and Hebrew scholarship and, to some extent, the revival of Platonic philosophy were the means of freeing the Divine Word and true doctrine (theology) from scholastic 'barbarisms'. By barbarisms they meant clumsy expressions, sophistry, linguistic ignorance and gross oversimplifications. It was the old programme of the previous century, of men like Pico della Mirandola and Barbaro, but now carried to greater lengths—to a basic re-examination of traditional practices like baptism and traditional dogmas like the Trinity and the Incarnation. The process took many different forms, leading eventually to the multiplicity of sects which characterizes the 17th century. The Unitarians, for example, acknowledged the 16th-century humanists as their distant forerunners.

The main practical issue, however, was still that of toleration. How much freedom of conscience could a Christian state allow? According to Sebastian Castellion, those who are considered heretical should not be persecuted or put to death because, first, it is difficult to reach a perfect understanding of truth on religious matters, even for those who are convinced that they are the bearers of the one true faith, and second, because it is always possible that the heretic may be converted before he dies. According to Jacopo Aconcio, doctrinal differences and theological interpretations are the snares set by Satan to make discord between Christians; the only way to avoid them is to reduce to a minimum dogmatic and theological definitions (which remain necessary in order that the true followers of Christ on earth

should be able to make themselves known and recognize their brothers), so that they will even allow an eventual union with the Catholics. Mino Celsi, on the other hand, laid emphasis on legal and political points (secular authorities are not empowered to judge heresy or to punish those who have been condemned by religious authorities). All the same, those who expounded theories such as these felt they were doing so because they had to defend their own way of following Christianity and the inspiration which had led them to their opinions. In a work of 1526, Hans Denck started from a meditation on the inner and disinterested nature of perfect love, which he expressed in quietist, mystical terms, forming the conclusion that the true Christian was one who suffered in quietness and love for Christ on the Cross, while his persecutors were the personification of Satan on earth. Castellion started from the *Theologia Deutsch* and the *Verba idiotae*, a strange medieval mystical text which had attracted the attention of Giovanni Pico della Mirandola. Others took the desire for peace between Christians as their starting point; yet others, the right of the scholar to inquire into, confront and criticize the errors of the ignorant. Present in many of them, (those whom Calvin later called 'libertines', and in Fausto Sozzini for example), was a complete indifference to every form and method of ecclesiastical organization and 'ritual'; sometimes particular ideas emerged on the after-life, re-echoing Hermetic motifs—that is, motifs which take up some central themes of Renaissance humanism. In the *Institutio* of 1559–60, Calvin discusses the Platonists and the critics of the dogma of the Trinity. This suggests that there were connections between the Florentines and the new heretics, between the old humanist attitudes and the humanist religion of Calvin's contemporaries. This implication must not be overlooked, even if it needs reservations.

Christ's Kingdom

What, finally, was the relationship between the humanist Renaissance and the rebirth of 'radical' religion? The Protestant tradition (that darkness reigned before Martin Luther; with him the light of religious truth once more dawned on Europe) is easily seen to be too crude. Writers at the time had no simple answer. Fausto Sozzini (an Italian Protestant of very independent views whom we have already met) in an early work (1570) tried to define the essence of Christian belief by referring to a few well-known passages from Dante's *Divine Comedy*. Sozzini's vision of Christian history is not out of keeping with the 'spiritual' religion propounded, for instance, by Celio Secondo Curione. He believed that the Kingdom of Christ and the Kingdom of Satan are not separated by geographical boundaries (between Catholic countries and Protestant countries, and Christian and non-Christian countries), but they both exist inside all men; the conflict is in men's minds; therefore it is universal in space and time. Thus it is useless, indeed the work of the devil, for one Christian to fight another (Catholic or Protestant); it is useless to leave a Catholic country for a Protestant one, since Antichrist, Satan, exists everywhere in the guise of persecution and the spirit of oppression. Almost the same conclusion is reached, not in good Latin but in vernacular German, by Sebastian Franck (1499–1542), the author of various works and compilations among which the most famous has the title *Chronica, Zeitbuch und Geschichtsbibel vom Anbeginn bis 1531*. Franck, a deeply religious man of letters (though certainly not a humanist), recognised the merits of some popes, and criticized the overbearing attitudes of various emperors, who had been hostile to the clergy but unfriendly to true religion and the poor. In his severe judgments on the Renaissance popes, in which he reproduces Erasmus' themes in the *Julius exclusus* (a dialogue in which the Pope is barred from heaven for his violent and overbearing character), Franck allied himself with the condemnations made by the first reformers. However he is not concerned with polemics or historical reconstructions; like Sozzini, his main concerns are outside the realms of history. The example of such men was to be followed in the next century, when attempts were to be made to write 'impartial' histories of religious life and doctrines. But this takes us far beyond the religious humanism of the Renaissance.

VI FRANCE IN TRANSITION

Cultural values in a troubled age

I. D. McFARLANE

'I see highwaymen, hangmen, soldiers of fortune and stable-boys nowadays more learned than the scholars and preachers of my time.'

RABELAIS

The crown of France,

during the years when the Renaissance was leading to a radical break with the old traditions, was worn by François Ier – one of a trio of princes, born within eight years of each other, whose subjects looked upon them as harbingers of a new Europe. Each, as he ascended his youthful throne – Henry VIII in 1509, François in 1515, Charles V in 1516 – was tempted to see himself in that light also. Each offered himself as a candidate for the Holy Roman crown in 1519. Each was proud of his humanist education and conscious of his responsibilities to scholarship and the arts. Each strove, by means that he could ill afford, to outshine the others in pomp, luxury and prestige.

The fourth power in Europe was the Pope, but neither he nor Henry of England could seriously claim to be one of the protagonists. These rôles belonged to François and Charles, between whom a bitter struggle for supremacy was inevitable and indeed ancestral (Charles was descended from Duke Charles the Bold and therefore claimed Burgundy as part of his patrimony). It was a struggle which worked itself out mainly in Italy. Popes, intimately involved, gave their support to one or the other as the situation fluctuated, before deciding finally in favour of Charles. Henry, from a safer distance, tried to do the same, concluding treaties of alliance with François (1519) and Charles (1522) and breaking both.

Of the two great problems of François' reign one was external –

the war against Charles; the other internal – the religious schism. In France, as in England, the country was divided. François held firmly to the Catholic cause, though he did not pursue it wholeheartedly: the Protestants within his own dominion were powerful enough to deserve conciliation, and those in Germany dangerous enough to his rival to repay discreet encouragement. By temperament François was not a fanatic; nor indeed was he markedly endowed as a statesman. In his early years he could act with spirit and boldness, but his policies were indecisive, his judgment of men poor and his industry unsustained.

His reign is remembered, not for political success, but for the flowering of French culture which it saw and which François to some extent made possible. While he occupied the throne (from 1515 to 1547) France emerged fully into the Renaissance. He founded royal readerships which developed into the *Collège de France*, supported and protected Budé, appreciated Marot and employed Cellini. Handsome, accomplished and avid for amusement, he gave the French court a charm which it might not otherwise have possessed. Power indeed was often in irresponsible hands; revenue was spent on ostentatious displays and offices were distributed according to the whims of pretty women rather than by merit. This was excused at the time and has been excused since. The King, as a historian of the next century observed, 'had a noble passion for everything beautiful.' (1)

French ambitions in Italy went back to the 13th century, when the House of Anjou ruled Naples. François' two predecessors, Charles VIII and Louis XII (above), had tried to assert this claim and both, aided by hostility between the Italian states, had partially succeeded. In 1515 François Ier conquered Milan and ruled it for six years. But Pope and Emperor united against him and in 1525, at the Battle of Pavia, he was ignominiously defeated and taken prisoner. Pavia, in the background (below) was being besieged by the French, when their camp was attacked by the Imperial army. In the foreground the king is shown on a kneeling white horse surrendering his sword. Fifteen years later François met his old enemy again. In a painting commemorating the occasion (above), he is prominently in the centre, the sombre figure of Charles next to him on the right. (2, 3, 4)

The religious conflict, which had smouldered all through the reign of François, burst into flame during that of his son Henri II (above left). Married in 1533 to Catherine de Médicis of Florence (centre), he was killed in a tournament accident in 1559. During the minority of their son Charles IX (right) the French Protestants, or Huguenots, seemed to be gaining political power and on St Bartholomew's Day 1572, in a plot organized by the Queen Mother and the Duke of Guise, nearly all the Huguenots in Paris, about 2000, were suddenly attacked and murdered. In a contemporary picture of the massacre (below) several incidents of that day are combined. In the centre the young king inspects the decapitated body of Admiral Coligny, the Huguenot leader, and further back, Catherine gloats over a pile of corpses. Charles IX died soon afterwards, reputedly filled with remorse. (5–8)

The supreme patron relaxes among a circle of cultured friends—the picture of himself which François Ier hoped to transmit to posterity (right). Here the king listens to a reading by Antoine Macault from his translation of the Greek historian Diodorus Siculus. The date is about 1532. To the left of the king are his three young sons, to the right Cardinal Duprat, Chancellor of France. Macault, the friend of Marot, made several classical writers available in French, including much of Cicero. (9)

The king's sister, Marguerite of Navarre, not only provides evidence of the emancipated position of women at this time but is a fascinating personality in her own right. Twice-married, witty, cultured and talented, she gathered round her a group of men of letters which tended to outshine that of her brother. The most famous of her own works, the *Heptameron*, modelled on Boccaccio, evokes the atmosphere of Renaissance France as vividly as do the painters of the School of Fontainebleau. In religion she inclined to Reform, and it was her daughter Jeanne who became the mother of Henri IV. (10)

Anctiffimo patri/Sixto Quarto po tifici maximo/ Guillermuf fichetuf nunntiuf theologozum Parifienfium doctozum deuota pedum ofculu ag

Growing awareness of humanist ideas made France the first country outside Italy to feel the new intellectual currents. As early as the 1460s Robert Gaguin was pressing for a reform of university education and a deeper study of the classics. It was his friends Guillaume Fichet and Jean de la Pierre who first brought printers from Germany to France. Fichet's *Rhetorica* (1471) is among the earliest books printed in Paris. This presentation page (left), on vellum, is from the copy sent to Pope Sixtus IV. The picture and decoration have been added by hand. (11)

Le premier chappitre parle cõ
ment les francois descendirct
des tropens.

Patre cens et qua
tre ans auant que
Romme fust fõde
regna priant en
trope la grant. il
enuoia paris laisne
de ses fil3 en grece
pour rauoir la royne helaine la femme
au roy Menelaus pour soy benger du

ne honte que les grec3 lui auoiēt faitte.
les greiois qui moult furent courouciez
de ceste chose sesmeurent et bindrent
assieger trope. a ce siege qui. p. ans du
ra furent occiz tous les fil3 au roy pri
ant. mais que bng appelle elenus il et
la royne ecuba sa femme. la cite fut ar
se et destruicte le peuple et les barons
occis. mais aucuns eschapperent de ceste
pestilence et plusieurs des princes sespā
sirent en plusieurs et diuerses parteis
du mõde pour querre nouuelles habita
cions cõme elenus eneas anthenoret

The first book in French to be printed in Paris was the *Chroniques de France* (1477), of which the first page is shown here. The arms are those of Jean de Malestroit, its original owner. Like the volume of Fichet shown opposite, this belongs to a transitional stage of printing, when the ideal was to imitate a hand-written book as closely as possible. The type-face is based on manuscript forms and a space was left blank for the illumination. The *Chroniques* are also of interest in showing the rising nationalism that often accompanied the New Learning. At the beginning of the text is the heading: 'The first chapter tells how the French are descended from the Trojans.' (12)

The personal voice of Renaissance man speaks in the *Essays* of Michel de Montaigne (above), for whom ordinary private life, daily experience and meditation, were of absorbing interest and value. Fully aware of what was happening in the world, alive to the new races, societies and moral codes which exploration was bringing to light, Montaigne pleaded for tolerance and understanding. Peace of mind, the discovery of one's true self—these are the highest goods. In quiet prose studded with classical allusions he reveals his own character, his prejudices, passions, fears and deepest thoughts: 'I desire therein to be delineated in mine owne genuine, simple and ordinarie fashion, without contention, art or study; for it is my selfe I pourtray.' (13)

The face of Paris was changing at a pace that had no precedent in history. The stages of growth can be traced, like the rings of a tree, on this map of the late 16th century. The circles, originally lines of fortifications, are today occupied by the *boulevards* (literally 'bulwarks')—the wide streets laid out when they were demolished. (14)

Few of the architects who were creating the new Paris had a real insight into the Renaissance style, which indeed came far less naturally to them than to their Italian counterparts. French Gothic was deeply engrained, and for the new style they had to depend on brief visits to Italy and books of engravings. In Philibert de l'Orme's screen for St-Etienne-du-Mont (right) he combines Milanese motifs like the foliated pilasters and baluster columns with an airy elegance that was to become typically French. (15)

The mythical founder of the city—Paris, son of Priam—appears as a contemporary Frenchman in this tapestry. (16)

Gothic translated into Renaissance idiom but with structure and proportion unchanged: the strange transitional church of St Eustache, begun in 1532. (17)

A wave of new building began with François' return from captivity in Spain. Below: Château de Madrid, begun in 1528. (18)

The focus of François Ier's cultural ambitions became the Château of Fontainebleau, which grew by gradual accretions from a hunting lodge to a vast palace. Here he collected his choicest treasures and employed his most valued artists. Rosso Fiorentino, Francesco Primaticcio and Benvenuto Cellini were all lured from Italy to work on the decoration. The style they created, based on Italian Mannerism, was new to France and new to Europe. Taken up by native French painters, the 'School of Fontainebleau' characterized a whole generation. Left: Diana the Huntress, a mythological portrait of Diane de Poitiers, the mistress of Henri II, painted about 1550. (19)

'The King cried aloud' in astonishment and could not look at it long enough', says Cellini describing the salt-cellar that he made for François Ier (below). The male figure, with trident, represents Sea, the female Land: 'Both figures were seated with their legs interlaced, just as the arms of the sea run into the land.' (20)

Arts overflow into one another in Rosso and Primaticcio's *Galerie François Ier* at Fontainebleau. In a design of immense vitality and inventiveness, the lithe elongated figures of the paintings seem to climb out into three dimensions, mingling with the sphinxes, putti and swags of fruit that surround them. The strap-work, echoed in the wooden panelling below, became a favourite motif in Flanders and England. The picture in the foreground is the *Shipwreck of Ajax* by Rosso; note, above it, the heraldic salamander of François Ier. The gallery was originally open, with windows on both sides, but has been considerably altered since. (21)

The promise of French sculpture at the turn of the 14th century was not immediately fulfilled. Claus Sluter's *Well of Moses* (detail right), carved soon after 1395, has no parallel in Italy until the work of Jacopo della Quercia some twenty years later. From there the development led on to Donatello and Michelangelo, but in France it lapsed, to revive again only after the High Renaissance had passed, and in a style almost wholly dependent on Italian models. (23)

The Risen Christ of Germain Pilon, part of a never completed *Resurrection*, seems inspired by Michelangelo. Primaticcio had brought with him to Fontainebleau plaster casts of several famous statues both antique and modern, including one of Michelangelo's *Risen Christ* in Rome. (22)

Italy and France interpenetrate at every stage of the story. Above: Michel Colombe's *St George and the Dragon* (1509), a late Gothic work in a Renaissance frame supplied by an Italian sculptor. Right: the tomb of Louis XII, commissioned by François Iᵉʳ from two other Italians, Antonio and Giovanni Giusti. (24, 25)

Question: whether the famous *Diana of Anet* (right) was made by a French or an Italian artist. The most brilliant of the French sculptors, Jean Goujon, was long the favourite candidate, but this is now doubted and the name of Cellini has been suggested. The Diana, with her slim long body and small head, is indeed a characteristic product of the School of Fontainebleau, where both traditions met. It was originally part of a fountain which stood in the courtyard of Anet. (26)

The clinging draperies and sinuous forms of Goujon's most famous work, the Nymphs for the *Fontaine des Innocents* (below) show a delicacy surpassing even Cellini's. The strained poses derive from Mannerism but the drapery patterns are, typically, more classical. Goujon also worked on the decorative reliefs of the Louvre; see p. 295. (27–30)

A new exuberance bursts into life in French architecture during the first years of François Ier's reign. The nearest parallel is the flamboyant Gothic of a century earlier, and indeed much of the feeling behind these buildings is medieval. Chambord (right), begun in 1519 and not finished at the king's death, is grouped round a square *donjon* with corner towers. Its most striking exterior feature is the roof—an extravaganza of chimneys, turrets and dormers which would be unthinkable in Italy yet which is Renaissance in all its details. (33)

In a magical transformation of the medieval moated castle, French architects produced a series of *châteaux* in the valley of the Loire which have never been surpassed for picturesqueness and charm. Water, no longer a defence, now adds a cool dimension of its own. Above: Azay-le-Rideau, 1518–27. The flat pilasters and horizontal string-courses show Italian influence, but the steep roof and dormer-windows are traditionally French. Below: Chenonceaux, begun in 1515. The earliest part is the square block to the right of the long gallery over the water; the gallery itself was added in 1576. Both these houses were built for rich bourgeois patrons independently of royal example. (31, 32)

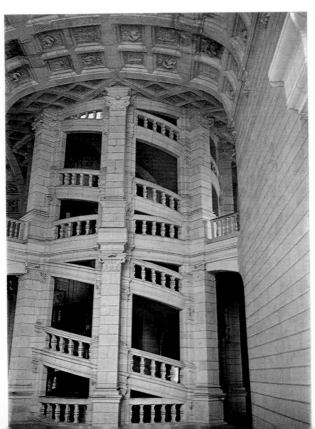

The spiral staircase was French, not Italian, and it was some time before the French could bring themselves to forego it. In the original plan for Chambord, by an Italian architect, the staircase was to be two straight flights of steps (as had already been used, in fact, at Chenonceaux). But in the event this was replaced by the fascinating double-spiral now to be seen in the centre of the main block (left). The external staircase at Blois (right), one of the earliest works of the new reign, is still Gothic in structure and in such details as the gargoyles and statues under canopies. Everything else is Renaissance, and the king's salamander proudly climbs its way up the balustrades. (34, 35)

'**François in war** is Mars, in peace Minerva, Diana in the chase, ▶
Mercury in eloquence and Cupid in love.' The somewhat grotesque
allegorical portrait (right) shows the king in all five rôles combined. It is attributed to Nicolo da Modena, another Italian artist
working at Fontainebleau. (37)

Teachers at the *Collège des Lecteurs Royaux:* **Oronce Finé,** reader
in mathematics (top: frontispiece of his *De mundi sphaera,* 1542,
showing Finé with the muse of Astronomy, Urania; **François
Vatable** (above left), reader in Hebrew; and **Jacques Toussaint**
(above right) in Greek; 'he spoke', says one of his students, 'in
choice Ciceronian Latin, but always clear and always within the
grasp of those who were listening'. (36, 38, 39)

Michel de L'Hôpital (above left), himself a scholar of distinction,
was able by his position at court (he became Chancellor of France
in 1560) to encourage both patronage of the arts and toleration in
religion. **Lefèvre d'Etaples** (above right) combined scholarship
with practical religious concern. He edited both Aristotle and the
Church Fathers, studied mysticism and translated the Scriptures
into French. (40, 41)

The greatest name in French humanism is that of Guillaume Budé, one of the few scholars who can stand beside Valla and Erasmus. Born in Paris in 1468, he was sent as ambassador to the Pope by Louis XII and attained a position of influence over François Ier. To him are due most of the king's progressive measures, including the founding of the royal readerships. His first notable work was the *Annotationes*, a commentary on Roman law published in 1508. In 1515 came his masterpiece, *De asse*, a treatise on classical coins and measures. Both these works go far beyond their nominal subjects, containing discussions and digressions on almost every aspect of ancient life and culture. In this portrait by Clouet he holds an open book with a quotation from the Stoics. (44)

Scholar-printers, such as the Estiennes and Simon de Colines, played a vital part in the spread of humanist ideas. Below left: the Hebrew Psalter printed by Robert Estienne in 1540, with his device of the olive tree. Right: a plate from the *Anatomy* of Robert's brother Charles (1546), printed by de Colines, their stepfather. (42, 43)

Jean Dorat came to Paris from Limoges in about 1530 and established himself as a poet, teacher and scholar of antiquity. Ronsard was first his pupil and later his rival when they were both made *poeta regius*, Dorat championing Latin and Ronsard French. (45)

George Buchanan was a Scot but spent much of his working life in France and had the distinction of teaching both Montaigne and Mary Queen of Scots. Besides poetry and religious satire, he wrote on history, political theory and astronomy. (46)

Nicolas Bourbon (below) illustrates the dilemma of the humanist poet—the vernacular or Latin? Bourbon chose the Latin of the classics and of humanism. His work is impressive in its range but the future belonged to French. (47)

179

The passion plays of the Middle Ages continued to be acted during the 16th century, while a revival of classical drama was beginning among the intelligentsia. This drawing of the stage at Valenciennes, where the whole Passion story could be performed, shows that by 1547 the sets were wholly Renaissance in style. The various parts are labelled—Paradise, Nazareth, the Temple, Jerusalem, the Palace, the Priests' House, the Golden Gate, Limbo and Hell. (48)

Renaissance pageantry blended with medieval habits of thought in a way that is reminiscent of architecture. This curious painting by Antoine Caron (below) shows a fête such as was popular in the second half of the 16th century. Caron himself might have contributed décor. It is based on an old play, *Octavien et les Sibylles*, dealing with the meeting of Augustus with the Tiburtian Sibyl. In the foreground the Sibyl points to the Virgin and Child as the object of true worship. On the right her servant approaches a fountain which it was prophesied would run with oil when Christ was born. Four more sibyls and three imperial officials stand on the left. The scene is set in the Tuileries Gardens: from left to right are a tourney held in the *Grandes Ecuries*; Catherine de Médicis, centre, in red; the two-gabled pavilion built 1570–72 by Jean Bullant; and the river Seine. (49)

Cultural values in a troubled age

I. D. McFARLANE

The press of Josse Bade (Jodocus Badius Ascensianus), one of the first scholar-printers to settle in Paris. During his travels in Italy he learned not only the new art of printing, but also Greek, which he taught at Lyons for some ten years. (1)

WE ARE no longer prepared to accept the view which conveniently but too simply, linked the advent of the Renaissance in France with the Italian wars of Charles VIII and Louis XII; many currents had penetrated long before. On the other hand, we are still meagrely informed about the so-called fallow decades of the 15th century in its cultural aspects. This is a period when the political unity of the country is still far from assured and the Royal domain is only a fraction of what it will become later in territory and authority; moreover, the vernacular has not reached the stage when it can be considered the normal vehicle for cultural communication. We are, however, on the threshold of the days when these two elements will become realities, and in so far as the French Renaissance includes a growing national awareness and seeks to break with what is thought to be a static past, the middle third of the 15th century may serve as a useful starting point.

'Intellectual Reform'

The full influence of the Renaissance did not make itself felt for some decades, but both internal deficiencies and external pressures made men of good will aware that France had lost something of its former cultural momentum. The court of the dukes of Burgundy, and even Lyons, proved more attractive to some men of letters than did the capital; and the prestige of Paris, as the centre of theology, was at a very low ebb: the dreary disputations and the wrangling between Ockhamists, Scotists and others had taken the vitality out of religious discussion, and it seemed to many that the gap between learning and life was widening rapidly. Contemporaries also deplored the decay of Paris as a centre of Latinity; and there were persistent complaints, not only about the *mores* of the ecclesiastics and the various religious orders, but about the decline in teaching standards and the ignorance of the average clerk. Small wonder that the first generation of humanists called out for what Renan was later to describe as the 'moral and intellectual reform of France'. Sporadic attempts had been made earlier to put the house in order: Cardinal d'Estouteville had vainly urged university reform in 1453, and renewed exhortations some years later had been scarcely more effective. It is only after the 1460s that reforming zeal began to assert itself vigorously, and here the rôle of Robert Gaguin and his wide circle of friends becomes apparent.

Gaguin (1433–1501), head of the Trinitarian Order, more than once Rector of Paris University and a diplomatic envoy, was not himself a true scholar: he had scarcely the time to become one and his life was essentially one of administrative and pedagogic crusades. Like his friends, he saw the great need for the restoration of the Sorbonne to its pristine glory—though he was inclined to lay less stress on certain theological pre-occupations; above all, he sought the introduction of educational reforms which would give the student the proper moral and cultural foundation on which to base his life. In practice, this meant a return to the classics, the proper approach to which should inculcate virtues likely to develop the Christian attitude to life. Gaguin did much, it is true, to reform his own Order; he exercised useful influence in the University, he also strengthened the links between scholarship in Italy and France. He rapidly grasped the importance of the recent advances in printing for educational ends. One of the first books to be published in France was his friend Guillaume Fichet's

Rhetorica (1471); he himself, laying much stress on the value of Latin verse composition, composed an *Ars versificatoria* (c.1478) which ran through innumerable editions before his death; and various friends had their Latin compositions published: Pierre de Bur, canon of Arras, whose poems appeared posthumously; Nicolas Horry, the author of sacred verse printed in Lyons and Paris; Simon Nanquier, whose curious elegy *De miseria hominis* enjoyed an unprecedented success throughout the 16th century; Guillaume de la Mare, the enlightened Rector of Caen University, one of the most engaging figures in this first wave of humanists. p 168 (11)

In this campaign, the early humanists were helped, not only by enlightened ecclesiastics and teachers, but by the appearance of the scholar-printers, the outstanding example being Josse Bade (Jodocus Badius Ascensianus, 1468–1535). This scholar from the Low Countries, after an apprenticeship in Lyons with Trechsel, moved to Paris, where he was responsible for an immense number of classical texts and school manuals on which the younger generation was to feed. His editions of Horace, Vergil and of moderns such as Battista Spagnuoli ('good old Mantuan') or his imitator, Pierre Rosset, as well as of various reference books, stretched over nearly thirty years; the most significant period of his activity ran from 1505 to 1515. A glance at his classical editions shows what he was about: first, a genuine attempt to provide a more reliable text, second a grammatical exegesis (including metrical observations where this proved necessary), and finally a 'moral' commentary which often claimed more space than the linguistic. The stress was indeed on the moral elements: aesthetic matters and questions of Golden Latinity were left aside, so that no distinction was made between Vergil and the other 'swan of Mantua' (Spagnuoli) whose eclogues were used in schools down to the 17th century. A further factor in this educational drive was the presence of a number of conscientious pedagogues from the Low Countries in Paris colleges: Petrus de Ponte, the blind poet of Bruges, who settled in the capital and eked out a precarious existence for over thirty years, teaching, composing vigorous but incorrect Latin verse and publishing manuals; Gilles de Delft, one of the early editors of Aristotle; Michel l'Anglois and others of more modest achievements. The importance of this element in Paris cannot be neglected: but, for all its pedagogic fervour, it may be that it delayed the full action of Renaissance currents flowing directly from Italy. f 1

Finally, mention should be made of the serious attempts made by certain colleges to put themselves in order, in particular the Collège de Montaigu, whose Principal, Standonck, also came from the Low Countries and was closely connected with the Brothers of the Common Life at Windesheim.

Patriotism and Culture

In all this, there may also be detected a rising sense of patriotism. Gaguin himself had written a chronicle of France; and many of the early humanists were concerned to make France recover the lead it had lost to Italy in cultural matters. During the reigns of Charles VIII and Louis XII, one notes the infiltration into court circles by humanist poets, where they developed a curious form of Vergilian propaganda, and by their celebration of French victories produced a type of committed poetry intended to act as publicity and often, for that reason, translated into the vernacular. Indeed, during these years a real symbiosis between Latin and vernacular poetry came into being. Germain de Brie (c.1490–1538), later to achieve fame as a Greek scholar, wrote a poem on a naval encounter between French and British vessels (*Herveis*, 1513); another composition on the same episode came from the pen of Valeran de Varanne, who later wrote an extensive epic about Joan of Arc (1516). And the Benedictine monk, Humbert de Montmoret, wrote abundantly on various military events towards the end of Louis XII's reign. The importance of the humanist, in ceremonial, propagandist or wider cultural respects, was reflected in the increasing patronage shown not only by royalty, notably Anne of Brittany, but also by ecclesiastics and members of the nobility.

This stage in humanism marked a conscious effort to remove the degenerate elements in recent theology and education, and to

p 166 (2)

f 2

Anne of Brittany as Juno in the dedication of a book by Jean Lemaire de Belges, of stories linking the history of Troy with that of Gaul. The queen is given the attributes of Juno on the basis of a laboured pun between 'Juno' and 'Juvans omnes' (helping all). (2)

return to a healthier and more illustrious state in which France and particularly Paris could enjoy the fame they once knew. These early humanists were instrumental in clearing the ground; one should not, however, think of them as being in any sense 'modern'. Though stirrings may be found among younger spirits as, for instance, Jean de Vitrier, who incurred the displeasure of the Sorbonne, and though Gaguin himself was more interested in behaviour than in theology, the outlook of these men was still essentially medieval. When Gaguin did enter the theological fray, as in the dispute on the Immaculate Conception, he was on the side of the conservatives. When, in a later generation, the Scot George Buchanan showed his contempt for his compatriot, John Major, he was referring to a man who had done his best to reinvigorate traditional theology in the Sorbonne; and the Collège de Montaigu at which Erasmus and Rabelais laughed was the college already reformed by Standonck. This impression is confirmed by a glance at the books printed in Paris during the last thirty years of the century: they are nearly all in Latin, and the prominent categories are books of established devotion, pedagogic manuals, Church Fathers or classical texts from a restricted number of authors: no Catullus, no Tibullus, Horace only as a moralist, the satirists suitably bowdlerized, the historians, Vergil or Ovid acclimatized to the medieval tradition. Even the manuals are not as advanced as one might think: the most successful manuals tend to be adaptations of earlier works, and Despauterius' various grammatical textbooks owe much to Alexandre de Villedieu. The foreign humanists who made an impact are either the Netherlanders already mentioned or, among the Italians, Beroaldo, Faustus Andrelinus and Spagnuoli who, at best, represented only one facet of the Italian Renaissance. The gap which showed between these early humanists and the younger generation of the 1530s is revealed by the oblivion into which most of these forerunners fell after François Iᵉʳ came to the throne. These pioneers had shown the need for educational reform and had supported the view that moral formation lay through the classics, but the classical world they knew was that of their predecessors; important aspects of the ancient world remained a closed book to them, and few showed sensitivity to the aesthetic aspects of the Italian Renaissance. In a sense they were sorcerer's apprentices: they unleashed forces they had hardly suspected.

p 179 (46)

In some provincial centres, encouraging progress was being made. At Caen printing went ahead fast and Guillaume de la Mare's impressive figure gave an important lead. At Orléans, the home of civil law, an important group of humanists was to be found. Not only was Orléans to be associated with the renewed study of Roman law, but much was to be done there for the development of Greek studies, stimulated by the presence for a short while of Girolamo Aleandro. Troyes also was an important cradle of humanism. Above all, Lyons, closer to Italy, relatively free from supervision owing to its lack of university and Parlement, and one of the major centres of European trade, was entering a phase of high economic and cultural activity. Standing at an international cross-roads and inhabited by a largely Italianate population, it was more receptive to currents from abroad. Symphorien Champier, the eminent polymath and disciple of Ficino, lived in Lyons; and it was not long before many printers established themselves there. It was in Lyons that many of the pseudo-Aldine editions were printed after 1505. It is significant that, among the vernacular writers of distinction, Jean Lemaire de Belges (1473–?1525) remained for a long period outside the influence of Paris. Connected with the court of Margaret of Austria and with Lyons, he certainly shows in his writings some adherence to the *Rhétoriqueur* traditions, but in his balanced view of national sentiment in literary development, his creative use of the French language, his wider range of sensibility which moves from a delicate *badinage* to an imaginative sympathy with the pagan elements of the ancient world—the description of the temple of Venus, condemned at conscious level in his *Concorde des deux langages*, triumphs by its artistic fervour over the temple of Minerva—in all these ways, Lemaire is the herald of a new age.

f 2

To equate humanism with the Renaissance would be quite misleading, but at this stage, there is no doubt that French humanists played an essential part in preparing the way for a wider awareness of the Renaissance. Not only did they by their philological approach, as well as by their fresh look at religion, make it easier for the next generation to develop new intellectual attitudes, but by their strengthening of links with Italy they facilitated the penetration of other aspects of the Italian Renaissance.

The Age of François Ier

165 (1)
p 178
(37)
In many minds, the reign of François Ier is connected with the flowering of the French Renaissance, and in a sense this is true: the numerous contemporary homages paid to him were not all lip-service; there is no doubt that court life with its refinement of
f 3, 4
social and aesthetic considerations acclimatized certain aspects of the Italian Renaissance; moreover, during this period the population of the country was increasing, a considerable economic prosperity was developing, and in certain strata of society a more luxurious and refined way of living was becoming apparent. Changes in taste were reflected more especially in architecture. Nevertheless, this blossoming covered only part of François' reign: the early years showed a reduction of patronage, humanists
166 (4)
suffered during his captivity after the Battle of Pavia (1525), and it was not until the return of the Royal children, held as hostages, that things really got under way. On the other hand, the last decade of his life, clouded by foreign policy troubles, religious dissension, economic perils and his own illness, is reflected in a literary *rallentando* and the waning of the cultural optimism, so marked a feature of better days. Nevertheless, we see the seeds of new things between the final years of Louis XII's reign and Pavia.

First of all, the development of serious scholarship. Gaguin and his friends, for all their humanist enthusiasms, were not learned. And among those who made their mark before the advent of
p 178
(41)
p 179
(44)
François Ier, only Lefèvre d'Etaples (1450–1536) and Guillaume Budé (1468–1540) stand out, and of these two Budé is the one who had the true scholarly urge. One of the features of the French Renaissance is that it produced scholars of greater depth and distinction than Italy, less *belles lettristes*, no doubt, but wider-ranging and methodologically sounder—Budé, Toussaint, Vatable,
p 178
(38, 39)
Turnèbe, Postel, Lambyn, Muret, Estienne, Vinet, Passerat. Budé's early works were more obviously limited to erudite ends—*Annotationes in pandectas* (1508) and the *De asse* (1514)—works which go far beyond the limits of their professed domains, law and numismatics, and which show a quite unusual gift for the proper interpretation of sources and a most comprehensive knowledge of the ancient world. Nevertheless, Budé was no ivory-tower *savant*, and he is typical of the Renaissance in the sense that his learning was not divorced from a keen awareness of the *vita activa;* his later writings shown his eager concern with problems of government, his appreciation even of economic issues, a horror of war, and though his religious outlook still retained many medieval elements, one can see in him too the shift of emphasis from doctrine to inner religion.

Lefèvre d'Etaples' scholarship was certainly less impressive than Budé's, nor would he have claimed to rival him; in his eyes, scholarship was the handmaiden of a revitalized religion, and this is seen in the choice of texts he edited. First, he sought to produce an edition of Aristotle which was shorn of the accretions of medieval commentary and which allowed the philosopher to appear as he truly was. Second, he interested himself in the Church Fathers; thirdly, he turned to the study of Nicolas of Cues and writers of the mystical tradition; finally, he concerned himself with the sacred texts and their translation into the vernacular. From the religious point of view, his activities revealed the conviction that religion must touch the inner man and not confine itself to arid discussion of dogma or outward observance of precept—with the further implication that since the scriptures held the key to religion, their diffusion must logically follow in the vernacular. It is in these respects that Lefèvre can be seen as a link-figure between the older humanists and the generation of Guillaume Briçonnet and Marguerite de Navarre. From the scholarly point of view, Lefèvre did much to promote Greek studies: before him, there had been some interest shown as a result of isolated teachers sojourning in France, and men such as Jan Lascaris were also important agents. Among those who exerted some influence on the Greek studies of the younger generation

The translation of Italian culture to France: the French version of the 'Hypnerotomachia Poliphili' is based closely on the Venetian edition of 47 years earlier, but whereas the first (above) was simple, linear and clear, the French artist gives the scene an atmosphere of slightly menacing gloom. (3, 4)

were Germain de Brie, editor of St John Chrysostom, and Jacques Toussaint, who encouraged his pupils to translate the *Greek Anthology* into Latin verse. Nevertheless, though the penetration of Greek culture was undoubtedly important, the number of competent Greek scholars in France in the 16th century was rather smaller than is generally supposed. It is curious how many Greek authors were rendered into Latin throughout the century, and one is struck by the extent to which the traditional views in scientific matters, originally so coloured by the Greek attitudes, remain unchanged by the New Learning.

Printers, Books and Readers

Nevertheless, scholarship did make noteworthy progress during the 1520s and 1530s, and in more ways than one. The multiplication of more reliable texts, edited both locally and abroad, proceeded on a very great scale, and here the rapid development of printing contributed handsomely. We note the presence of several major printing-houses interrelated often by marriage—a genealogical tree shows connections between Hygman, Josse and Conrad Bade, Regnault Chauldière, Pierre Roffet, Simon de
f 5, 6
Colines, the Estiennes, Michel Vascosan and Frédéric Morel. The Estienne family is the best-known, and more especially Robert
p 179
(42, 43)
Estienne I and Simon de Colines stand out for their enterprise,

François Ier as one of the three Magi, from a book of hours printed by Simon de Colines in 1543. (5)

Colines introducing the italic type and publishing very many manuals, Estienne developing Greek editions and bringing out the contemporary equivalent of the Penguin. Certain foreign printers of distinction came to swell the ranks, notably Christian Wechel in Paris and Sebastian Gryphius at Lyons. Nor should one forget the pioneer work of Attaignant whose musical publications were not only milestones of technical skill but an indication of the rôle of music in the cultural atmosphere of the time. These men, often scholars in their own right, could draw on the services of distinguished humanists for the correction of their proofs. They were often associated with the newer religious currents, and men like Henri Estienne II later found their way to Geneva. Not only were some very useful editions printed in the 1530s, but serious attempts were made to overhaul the manuals and reference works. The grumbles about the old primers persisted—Nicolas Bourbon and Sussannée had harsh words to say about Despauterius—and many Frenchmen tried to compose adequate substitutes; but the fact remains that French originals did not succeed in establishing themselves: either we find the older works revamped (and even later the Jesuits give Despauterius a new look) or foreign volumes became popular—Niccolò Perrotto on Horatian metres, Mancinelli, Ulrich von Hutten, and Buchanan's Latin version of Linacre's *Rudimenta* which went through nineteen editions in quarter of a century. Where French initiative made greater headway is undoubtedly in lexicography; here the pioneer work of Robert Estienne established precedents which were respected for many decades.

Further impetus to scholarship was given by the creation of the royal readerships, from which later developed the Collège de France. Nevertheless, there was delay in the establishment of these posts, because of the religious implications of the project. Lefèvre's interest in Greek studies had contributed in some measure, not only to the furthering of Greek scholarship, but also to an interest in Hebrew; and humanists, anxious to return to the original sources, found themselves suspected by the orthodox, and the introduction of a comparative element on the philological side of religious studies was thought by many to threaten rather than to consolidate tradition. The matter came to a head first in Germany over the Reuchlin affair (1516, see Chapter VII), which was closely watched by French scholars; then shortly afterwards the emergence of Luther meant that the religious question became central for many people associated with the cultural revival. The story of these upheavals is told elsewhere, but the impact on the humanist cannot be ignored, as is shown by the

episode of Guillaume Briçonnet and the Groupe de Meaux in the early 1520s, whose reforming activities were inspired in great measure by Lefèvre d'Etaples. By the intrusion of this religious problem, and also, at a cultural level, the wider penetration of Italian humanism and Renaissance literature, the gap between the first and second waves of humanists became wide indeed. The names of many earlier humanists disappeared overnight, and even a printer like Bade was quickly eclipsed. The humanists who made the transition from the one period to the other were few in number; and they achieved this, either because they were associated with the development of Greek studies with all that this implied—hence the survival of Lefèvre, Germain de Brie, even the curious figure of Pierre Rosset (died 1532), and perhaps Nicolas Barthélemy de Loches (c. 1478–c. 1540)—or because they had shed their old skin: a striking example of this is Salmon Macrin (1490–1557), the neo-Latin poet, who before 1515 had produced orthodox or ceremonial verse, but who after 1528 emerged as a major lyric poet, deeply imbued with the spirit of the Italian Renaissance and more than somewhat sympathetic to the evangelical currents.

How Much Freedom?

The average humanist certainly found himself under pressure from various quarters; for him, no doubt, the Reformation in its early stages was seen as a force for intellectual liberalism, and in any case the distinction between orthodoxy and beyond was not always crystal-clear in the years before the Council of Trent. On the other hand, in so far as the new humanism was deeply patriotic, there was a reluctance on the part of many to carry things to the point of schism and therefore to the rupture of a traditional unity. In practice, it would seem that many professed a fairly advanced inward religion, without breaking formally with the Church— though their children often turned to Geneva (Salmon Macrin, Guillaume Budé, Nicole Bérault). Nevertheless, one does notice during these years a tendency for the Establishment to part company with humanism. Those who saw in reform the need for a return to stricter standards and unshakable authority, such as Calvin, might leave France in search of new pastures; but Calvin remained medieval in his stress on theology, in his abhorrence of classical literature, so corrosive in its influence, in his totally theocentric attitude. Others, who saw reform as the need to improve morality, to remove abuses and move towards a more personal religion, but were as yet reluctant to cross the Rubicon, might leave Paris and try their luck in the provinces. It is noteworthy how many pedagogic ventures were carried out beyond the confines of Paris—one thinks of the Collège de Guyenne at Bordeaux, staffed by many former teachers at Sainte-Barbe, the establishments at Nîmes, the Collège de la Trinité at Lyons. At the same time, the humanist was subjected to new literary and philosophical influences, from Italy more particularly, but also from classical authors whom a previous generation had neglected or denounced. Through the activities of publishers like Gryphius, Colines, Wechel, the spectrum of literature was greatly widened: among the classical writers, the moralist strain no doubt persisted at school level, but Catullus, Propertius, Tibullus and Horace the lyrical poet were now read with enjoyment, as was the *Greek Anthology*. Neo-Latin writers, known before the death of Louis XII, but ineffectively, now acquired great popularity: Marullus, the Strozzi, Pontano, Politian, Angeriano, in addition to Vida, Sannazaro and Navagero who followed perhaps more beaten paths. Then there was the steady influx of neo-Petrarchan currents, which often blended uncritically with the philosophically important neo-Platonic tradition represented not only by Ficino's edition of Plato, but also by later followers such as Ebreo or Speroni. These authors in their Platonic dialogues as well as more austere sources brought new elements to the discussion of questions like the immortality of the soul. Many scholars too had made the journey to Italy; some had studied at Padua and had absorbed the rudiments of a rationalist approach to philosophical problems. Moreover, certain classical authors—and one thinks more particularly of Seneca, Cicero and Lucian, and possibly Lucretius—were exercising subtle pressures on the humanist mind: the aversion from theology, initiated by the errors of the theologians themselves, was fanned by the study of these authors, the very great stress which the Stoics in particular laid on ethics in this world helped to strengthen the shift from the contemplative to the active life and the sudden exposure to varied philosophical currents was bound to encourage sympathy for some form of syncretism and, later, relativism; all this, added to the shift from intellectual definition to personal sentiment in the field of religion, began a process destined in the long run to affect the structures of the mind.

When we look at the world picture of the average Renaissance Frenchman, it does not, in certain respects, differ greatly from that of his medieval forebears. It is, for instance, curious how long it took for a recognizable scientific spirit to take shape; the return to the classics in this respect was in fact an impediment to a rational, empiric attitude, and the dependence on authority in this domain stifled the spirit of enquiry. There were, it is true, a number of humanists, more especially on the medical and biological sides, who made valuable contributions—Charles Estienne in the study of anatomy (1545), Jean Fernel (1497–1550), Rondelet (1507–66) and Belon (1517–c.1564) in the field of zoology; but, though Copernicus' view of the universe was published in 1543, Buchanan's conservative *De sphaera* (1585) was completed in the last quarter of the century and used as a text-book in French schools at the beginning of the next century. The disturbing *Cymbalum mundi* was published anonymously in 1538 and Robert Breton came under suspicion for irreligious views, but it is clear that in the first half of the century there were very few genuine atheists or sceptics, though these terms were bandied about freely in moments of irritation and choler. Rare was the humanist prepared to go to the logical conclusion of his beliefs; the theocentric view of the universe was accepted well nigh universally; and the conception of man (one can hardly call it a psychology yet) owed much to earlier times. Ronsard's view of man is not very different from Gaguin's, even though he may have hesitated on certain doctrinal points, such as that of the creation *ex nihilo*.

p 179
(43)

The Discovery of Man

f 7
Nevertheless, a change had come over the view of man in society, of his *condition humaine*. There were certainly old-guard attempts to restore theology and the Church to its former authority; but one notices that for many there was, however unconsciously, some gap between overtly accepted doctrine and one's personal world view and the attitude to behaviour that goes with it. Significant in this connection is the attitude adopted by certain humanists to monasticism. Rabelais (?1494–1553) no doubt followed a well-established tradition of satirizing monks for not obeying their rule, for accumulating capital, for immorality and so forth, but the core of his attack was new, in that it stemmed from his conviction that monasticism is against nature. Nature, no doubt as part of the divine cosmos, was not held in abhorrence, and man was not asked to turn his face to the wall and shun human society; the stress was moving away from an obsession with salvation to an awareness of life fully lived upon this globe. Man had therefore his part to play in the conduct of a society which had something positive to offer. Of course, the relations between man and his God formed part of the debate in theological circles—the extent to which man can consider himself a free agent and under what circumstances, the precise point at which grace may operate, the degree to which man can collaborate in his own salvation—matters which are raised also in the work of Rabelais; the problems themselves were not new, but they were seen in a changing context, the context of a man aware of the society in which he must evolve. The claims of the active life became gradually stronger than those of the contemplative. In this, the classics brought grist to a mill already functioning, and it is no coincidence that in a mind steeped in the classics like Dolet's there should emerge something that looks very much like an impersonal Deism, an attitude which reminds us of Herbert Spencer's division into the Visible and the Invisible, with the stress on the Visible.

It is thus not surprising that from the first days of the Renaissance earnest thought was given to the problem of the nature of wisdom, human and divine, and recent scrutiny of the terms *scientia, sapientia* and *prudentia* has underlined this shift to the active

A fine example of the printer's art allied to a work of scholarship: the titlepage of Oronce Finé's 'Euclid' printed by Simon de Colines. Finé made his life's work the recovery, translation and explanation of ancient works on mathematics, a science which was then being revived in French universities. (6)

Pantagruel at table—a scene from Rabelais' long burlesque epic in which the characters and humour are as overwhelming as the meals. Rabelais' mockery touched everything, from the old pedantry of the schools to the new pedantry of the humanists. This woodcut is from the Lyons edition of 1547. (7)

life, for knowledge was seen to have important connections with behaviour. It is equally significant that interest in education should have increased so sharply and enthusiastically. A belief in education implies a belief in the possibility of progress, in man's ability to help himself and shape his destiny, here and now. Every attempt was made to sweep away the cobwebs of the older methods, and the contrast between Thubal Holoferne, Gargantua's first schoolmaster in Rabelais, and his more humane teacher, Ponocrates, is representative of the times. Not only was a new attitude encouraged towards the classics, with their stress on ethical matters (Seneca, Cicero, Plutarch), but a wider field of knowledge was embraced; all paths did not lead by implication to theology, and moreover a concern was shown for the whole man. In Rabelais' ideal upbringing, the physical well-being of the man is not neglected. Many of the leading humanists were more than scholars, they were educationalists as we would call them today—Vives, Erasmus, Sturm, Cordier, Buchanan, Gouvea, Baduel. Readers today may find the daily programme of the new approach hopelessly loaded and overdependent on authority, but the principles underlying its planning introduced at least a breath of fresh air. Later in the century Montaigne was also to see the importance of man developing according to the potential within him, without his having to be forced into the procrustean bed of preconceived notions. Equally important was the recognition that man was being prepared for a career in this world; it is significant that the inmates of Rabelais' imaginary community, the Abbaye de Thélème, did not take vows of asceticism or seek permanent withdrawal from the world: sojourn in that Renaissance establishment was for a time only, and the door is always open for man to walk into the outer world. It is true that Rabelais' ideal education is aimed at a limited section of the population (the leisured classes), but it is nonetheless an important move in the same direction.

Humanism in Society

This gradual secularization of mind is apparent too in the various treatises on wider education and on behaviour which were so popular at this time. Sadoleto (1476–1547), an illustrious pillar of the Church, and Bishop of Carpentras, praised philosophy almost more than theology; Castiglione, though he made orthodox remarks about religion in his *Courtier* paid less attention to religious instruction than to ethical matters, and his hymn to love, his attention to social comportment and personal relations are further illustrations of the same trend. The inhabitants of the Abbaye de Thélème were not merely humanists, they were men and women of the Renaissance, spiritual relatives of Castiglione's ideal figure. Marguerite de Navarre (1492–1549), a disciple of Briçonnet but also of the Italian neo-Platonists, was concerned with an inward form of religion in which moral purification seems more important than the search for eternal life: though she conformed in her outward practice, her religious position was one which, taken to its logical extreme, diminished the rôle of the Church. And in her *Heptameron*, we not only see the reflection of her religious attitudes more thoroughly expressed in her poems, but also the Renaissance awareness of the need for proper comportment in society. If there is little at this time in France to correspond to the various Italian academies, it is not surprising that we should see in the second half of the century the gradual emergence of *salons*: the Morel group, the *cénacle* of the Duchesse de Retz, and indeed many others, sometimes imitated in the provinces (the Dames des Roches at Poitiers). In this context too, the traditional attitude towards women was changing—an attitude reflected in literary works such as the *Heptameron*, Scève's *Délie*, Héroët's *La Parfaicte Amye*. Here and there we witness the gradual organization and indeed civilization of social life. The question of communication was taken seriously; this is a period in which the epistle and the literary dialogue in a sense reflect a trend in society itself. No doubt, in due course, the development of social intercourse was to wield some influence in shaping French as the language of civilization, though certainly not to the extent we associate with the *grand siècle*. The poetry of

p 55 (33)

p 168 (10) f 8

'Tell me the grief and the pain you suffer' … Marguerite of Navarre, who in the 'Heptameron' had treated love as a serious passion, shows a vein of sentiment in 'La Coche', the lament of three ladies crossed in love. (8)

Clément Marot (c.1496–1544) reflects a higher degree of urbanity than can be found in previous generations of French poets, where any attempts in this direction appeared over-sophisticated, hyperconscious. Marot in many ways is an *écho sonore* of the times. He reflects the courtly currents, the humanist enthusiasms (witness his eager adoption of classical genres) and also a more popular vein. To imprison him in the formula *élégant badinage* is unfair, for there is also a serious poet in Marot, the one who wrote the *Deploration de Florimond Robertet*, the epistles from Ferrara and the translation of the Psalms. What he did above all was to reintroduce vitality into poetry, and also a personal dimension. There was something of the court clown in Marot, with his detachment, his ability to watch himself as part of the action he was describing, his awareness of the reactions of his audience, his mixture of serious and comic, and above all, the tempo of his verse. No doubt his thematic range was considerably wider than his poetic sensibility, but in his own way he reflected the emerging Renaissance man, living in this world, but also aware of the need for religious liberalization, possessed of strong convictions about human behaviour, by no means insensitive to the message of the classical world. What Marot often lacks is a certain body, and he sometimes appears as a man of reaction rather than of action; his very ability to respond to the moment and the circumstance has perhaps masked his more permanent features.

The Ideal King

One way in which the humanist concern with the relations between the proper education of man and his subsequent career upon earth was manifested was the interest taken in the 'institution of the Christian King'. From one angle Rabelais' work is a blue-print for the ideal philosopher-king; and other writers such as Budé, and later Michel de l'Hôpital and Ronsard, orchestrated this theme eloquently struck by Erasmus, whose attitudes and ideas dominated the humanist generation of the 1530s. Indeed, the problem of the formation of the sovereign recurs frequently in political theory. More and Erasmus gave their views in classic texts; and later animated, but not always well-informed, reactions greeted the appearance of Machiavelli's *Prince*. No doubt, the gradual emergence of royal authority as a centralizing force counted for much, and a good deal was written in theoretical support of the king's expanding power, partly from the pens of scholars trained in the new school of Roman law under the stimulus of Alciati and later Cujas, but also by writers such as Claude de Seyssel whose *Grant Monarchie* appeared in 1518: this latter work is a good example of the way in which attemps were made to find the theoretical bases for the *de facto* monarchy. Seyssel preferred a pragmatic approach to a theory based on abstract principles, and his chief concern was to give a rational account of guarantees for stability. Much was written on problems such as the nature and origin of royal authority, the practical and traditional limits which might curb the uninhibited exercise of royal prerogative (Christian principles, Salic law, non-alienation of rights or domain, the rights of the individual within his private domain). But much was also written on the qualities which should be possessed by any ruler of Christian persuasion, and also on the relations between Church and state. Later in the century, when religious dissensions complicate the problem, other humanist currents came to the surface. Roman law did not give such unambiguous support to the principle of monarchy as some enthusiasts thought, and authors like Nicolas de Grouchy (died 1572) saw in Roman institutions the germs of democratic principles which were not unwelcome to Protestant writers such as Hotman or Buchanan.

p 178 (40)

In short, active political theory was widespread; and it was a sign, not only of the desire to rethink basic principles in the dawning of a new era, but also of the need to provide the theoretical correlative of the emerging political situation. But it also went hand in hand with a rise in the prestige and power of the magistrature; during the 16th century, an extensive legal machine was coming into being: the Parlements were growing in power, and the Parlement of Paris, owing to its close relationship with the monarchy, increased rapidly in stature, both jealous of its

One of the accusations levelled against Henri III by his opponents, the Catholic League, was that he practised sorcery. When the Leaguer troops took Vincennes in 1586 they found two silver-gilt statuettes of satyrs holding bowls. 'In these vases were unknown drugs . . . used as an oblation; and what is more detestable, they were in front of a gold cross in the middle of which was set a piece of the True Cross'. This anti-royalist propaganda was published in a pamphlet in 1589. (9)

f 9

special rôle and also eager to be the spokesman of informed opinion and perhaps something more. In this period too, the local customary laws of the various provinces were scrutinized and properly codified, and we shall see that towards the end of the century, though certain elements in the magistracy identified themselves with the interests of the *Ligue* (the Catholic opponents of Henri III and of centralized rule), most lawyers, humanist at heart, supported a policy of moderation and national unity. In the present context, one further point should be mentioned: it is the considerable development of interest in history. In this there was no doubt impetus from Italy, but the growing concern with man's situation, and also the patriotic urge, induced humanists to examine the historical perspective. We saw that this tendency was present in Gaguin, but it was very much stronger by the middle of the century, and one notices a publisher like Vascosan devoting a major part of his activity to the publishing of historiographical works. In some cases, the past acted as a guide to, or perhaps a justification of, present policy: this aspect is very much to the fore in Buchanan's *Rerum Scoticarum historia*, on which he seems to have been engaged as early as the 1540s when still in France.

French versus Latin

This new spirit was also abroad at a wider literary level, where the patriotic urge to overhaul the Italians was very strong. The attitude to Italian literature was understandably ambivalent: on the one hand there was the admiration for the new wine which was splitting old bottles, but on the other, there was national resentment at having to be so beholden to foreign currents and a sense of shame at the vanishing of earlier prestige. One of the curious features of this reaction is the way in which many writers hoped to achieve victory in the field of Latin, and it is only during these years that the claims of French became a burning issue. The idea that the vernacular was less serious died hard, and all the more so at this time when many believed that the French language was in poor fettle. But other arguments also carried weight: Latin had stood the test of centuries, and purified by new scholarship, could last for a very long time yet. A number of contemporaries had also noted the speed at which French was evolving, and had wondered whether under these conditions they could hope to be understood by their successors. The aristocratic view of culture gave further impetus to the Latinist attitude, and the fact that for many humanists the Italians had succeeded in Latin (or, like Petrarch, thought they had) was not negligible. Finally, the attitude of the Church and the ambitions of those who wished to achieve fame abroad coincided in that they both supported the tradition of a common language transcending national boundaries as well as the ravages of time.

In the long run, of course, other forces were to move in favour of the vernacular: a shift in the patriotic attitude itself, the penetration of culture to wider sections of society (as the Protestants realized in their propaganda), the growing inadequacy

of Latin to cope with scientific advances and perhaps, in time, the impact of the Ciceronian attitude which was essentially a static one and accentuated the gap between Latin and the culture and society it sought to manifest linguistically. Furthermore, if Latin had to evolve in order to maintain its position, why could the vernacular not follow suit?

In the 1530s, however, the issues were not so clear-cut, and many men of letters were in two minds, trying to make the best of both worlds. Nicolas Bourbon and Macrin are both said to have written in the vernacular, Boyssonné certainly did, and writers like Dolet and Scève seem to have changed camps; and this indecision persisted right through the century, even among members of the Pléiade of whom only Ronsard remained faithful to his decision to abandon Latin as a poetic medium.

p 179 (47)

Neo-Latin Poetry

It is therefore not surprising that many writers made serious attempts to win their laurels in the classical tongue. The first important date here is Salmon Macrin's *Carminum libellus* (1528): after a period of twelve years' silence, he brought out this collection of lyric verse inspired by his love for and marriage to Guillonne Boursault: the poems rejoin the traditions of Horace, Catullus, Marullus and Italian love-poetry, as well as being an interesting document about humanist circles in those years. Love poetry in lyric metres appears here for the first time, and Macrin shows a happy mastery of his medium. The religious element, so evident in his earlier writings, moves into the penumbra, but soon to return, sometimes in sacred poetry purely and simply, at others as a vital aspect of his amatory verse. Macrin's lyrical poetry, published from 1528 to 1531, established him as the leader of humanist poetry in France, and the formula of epigram collections, so popular in Italy, spread rapidly during the 1530s, associated in great measure with the Lyons *sodalitium* which flourished chiefly during the years 1536–38. The emergence of this group was due in part to the tendency for younger humanists out of sympathy with the Establishment to find a more congenial milieu, and many of these who had previously worked and taught in Paris, and perhaps Bordeaux or Toulouse, foregathered for a time at Lyons. At the same time Dolet, the printer-scholar, had tried to bring cohesion into the group, taking the opportunity of the Dauphin's unexpected death (1536) to organize an anthology of poems in his honour, in which the majority of the tributes were in Latin and may be seen as an attempt to substantiate the claims of the humanist poets. During the next few years a stream of verse, variable in quality but wide-ranging in inspiration, vigorous and open to new ideas, came from the pens of men such as Bourbon, Visagier, Boyssonné (unpublished but circulated), Dolet, Macrin and Ducher. It is partly through their efforts that Petrarchan poetry became acclimatized; and the developments of new genres under classical influence started long before the Pléiade. For instance, it is probable that Marot was much influenced by these writers with whom he was in close touch, and that he owes something to them, especially in the field of the epigram in the style of Martial, greatly favoured by Ducher and Visagier. Love poetry, of an *élégant badinage*, no doubt, also throve in these years, with dilute neo-Petrarchism, neo-Catullan elements and native ingredients; and indeed the lineaments of the love-cycle first appear in the Latin verse of this period. What emerges from these neo-Latin centres more particularly is, in spite of some orthodox currents existing as it were by contradiction, a greater liberalism in things religious—and some of the Latin religious poetry written in this decade is impressive—a missionary love of letters, an unquenchable patriotism, a serious concern with matters of form and language. There is a good deal of gossipy verse, and the perpetual squabbles of these 'College Apollos' (as Lucien Febvre calls them) can become tedious; moreover, their effort was short-lived for a variety of reasons, but the fact remains that their activity was far from insignificant. Macrin's claims to be a poet of some stature are real enough; and these poets acted as a filter for the flow of new literary currents and genres; moreover, their thematic range is probably wider than what may be found then in French poetry, and they helped, by their cultural cohesion, to give more sense and purpose to the literary impulses which were soon to make themselves felt also in the vernacular. Most of these poets, as we have seen, were out of sympathy with the Establishment, with the exception of Macrin, whose position was perhaps at times ambiguous, but who functioned for nearly twenty years as a court poet. The other writers tended to be peripatetic, with only rarely a fixed post, but they did have some support in high quarters: thus the Bohiers patronized Jean Visagier, who died in the odour of sanctity in 1542, and others were protected by Guillaume du Bellay (the patron also of Rabelais) a diplomat of outstanding ability and with a generous sympathy to many men of letters whose reputations in the purlieus of the Sorbonne were not reassuring.

The Pace slackens

What has been said of these neo-Latin writers in the 1530s and early 1540s is no doubt true of humanism and the Renaissance as a whole. We have before us a complex state of mind—an undoubted optimism in the humanities and an eager desire to experiment in the field of education, a welcome note of liberalism, particularly in the field of religious belief, a gap between Establishment and humanism in certain important respects, the comparative eclipse of Paris therefore as the cultural centre of France (though this point must not be overstressed), the continuing closeness of contacts between France and Italy on the cultural front, a certain secularization of the attitude to life. One should perhaps not exaggerate the intellectual advances of these years. Though aesthetic considerations are particularly evident in the fields of the visual arts and especially architecture, I am not sure that the same awareness had yet penetrated significantly into letters. Scholarship was still massively predominant, the reliance on authority was as strong as ever, the preoccupation with man as a moral being was profound, and some of the results of a new view of the classical world were not to show themselves in all their significance for some time to come. France could indeed boast a Marot and a Rabelais by the end of the 1530s, but the rest of the literary scene was less rich in achievement. Rabelais, of course, is magnificent in his dynamic expression of contemporary currents: through his books runs an awareness of the intellectual issues of the epoch, and his work carries the signs of vigorous committed writing, both in the way in which his characters refer to current events and in the development of satirical gifts, which may be found, though in lesser degree, in a number of his friends and fellow humanists. Above all, the vitality of his world view is seen in the handling of language; but his awareness of the classical world is far distant from that of Ronsard, and in him the moral preoccupation is a long way ahead of the aesthetic.

The last years of François Iᵉʳ's reign are depressing: court life, with the King's illnesses, had lost something of its former brilliance, and the sharpening of the religious conflict, together with the hardening of the King's heart, had helped to damp the optimism of the previous decade. Many humanists of distinction or promise had left the scene: in the older generation, Budé, Lefèvre d'Etaples and, of course, Erasmus had passed on, and among the younger ones, some, like Farel and Calvin, had moved to Geneva or abroad, and others had died prematurely. Dolet's enthusiasm was soon snuffed out in martyrdom; he was finally condemned for an allegedly heretical treatment of a classical text. The economic prosperity of the country, after the wars, was less than brilliant; and indeed in many ways the 1540s marked a regression. Nor did the reign of Henri II (1547–59) show much improvement: the King, strongly resentful of his father's treatment, discarded old humanist links and did not patronize the arts in the way that his father and his aunt, Marguerite de Navarre, had faithfully done. Marguerite herself died just over two years after her brother, and it was not greatly to the credit of her *protégés* that the first anthology of poems in her memory (1550) should have been so slim a volume, and that the more distinguished writers of the time should need to be hectored into action by the faithful Charles de Sainte-Marthe. At all events, François Iᵉʳ's reign went out with a cultural whimper, and it is only after a little while that the tide began to flow again in strength.

p 167 (5)

Harmony amid Discord

The stage of the Renaissance which we associate more especially with the Pléiade spans the reigns of Henri II and of his sons by Catherine de Médicis. Before we turn our attention to the literary manifestations of this epoch, a few remarks on other aspects are apposite here. Broadly speaking, we may say that this is the period in which the Renaissance, after a stage of experiment, ebullience and even dispersal of effort, becomes organized and more fully integrated into the life of the country. We noted that in the 1530s and 1540s there was an unmistakable gap between the humanist Renaissance and the Establishment. The religious wars of course continued some of this fragmentation, and came moreover to threaten the unity of the country, but on the whole, the gap narrowed and indeed disappeared altogether at certain points. As the Council of Trent settled down to business, many humanists of Protestant sympathy quite simply left the country (Bèze had already packed his bags in the autumn of 1548)—though it should be noted that religious differences did not always interfere with cultural affinities: Henri de Navarre's librarian, Florent Chrétien (1541–96), who remained stoutly Protestant, was a curious kind of humanist translating into and out of French, Latin and Greek, striking out in the field of parody, and ending up as one of the authors of the *Satire Ménippée* (1593). Nevertheless, in spite of political and religious troubles, Renaissance culture drew closer to the Establishment, and Paris once again became the clearly recognizable centre of activity.

p 167 (6, 7)

A welcome change in cultural fortunes occurred when Michel de l'Hôpital (1505–75) was appointed first Chancellor to Marguerite de France and then Chancellor of France (1560); his own humanist and literary distinction, as well as his powerful position at court, were of inestimable value to the rising Pléiade. It was in this period, particularly after 1558, that the poets and artists played a conspicuous part in the ceremonial of the time, and the amount of court and encomiastic verse rose steeply, both in Latin and in French. During these years, indeed, pageantry and court ceremony assumed large proportions, and all the arts, visual, musical and literary, played their part. Ronsard (1524–85) was appointed court poet, but so was his counterpart in Latin verse, Jean Dorat (1508–85), who signed himself *poeta regius* from 1567 onwards. As the clouds darkened over Charles IX's reign, the humanist poets not merely celebrated the hatches, matches and despatches of court society, but they became, as they had been half a century earlier, the spokesmen of government policy. Ronsard's poems in the early 1560s were dominated by these considerations, and so were Dorat's. Generally speaking, these propagandists adopted the middle-of-the-road attitude which was that of Michel de l'Hôpital himself, the attitude of a man deeply versed in classical humanism, who avoided extremes, was imbued with a sense of national integrity, eschewed schism and violence, and no doubt, with his neo-Stoic leanings, attached greater importance to behaviour than to doctrine. There were occasional lapses from grace: Ronsard, Léger Duchesne (died 1588) and Jean Dorat went to unlovely lengths, either in the dispute with Pierre de la Ramée or in connection with the Massacre of St Bartholomew.

p 178 (40)

p 180 (48, 49) f 10

p 179 (45)
p 167 (8

Humanism Established

This closer collaboration is to be seen also in the field of scholarship. Whereas earlier the royal readerships had been viewed to some extent with suspicion, in that philological research could be seen to threaten theology, now the Collège de France, as it was to become, formed a central part of the Establishment. Turnèbe, Léger Duchesne, Toussaint, Vatable, Lambyn and others were solid pillars of academic orthodoxy; sometimes too strict perhaps, for anyone who threatened to disrupt the paths of scholarship in original fashion was liable to get short shrift, such as Pierre de la Ramée (1515–72), whose views on the reform of teaching were not unreasonable in their substance. Newcomers were viewed as interlopers, as the Jesuits found when they sought to enter the teaching lists of the University, and became the butt of a splendid satire by Turnèbe (*Ad Sotericum gratis docentem*). Original scholars like Guillaume Postel (1510–81) could hardly have found the climate of the period entirely to

Despite the troubled political atmosphere, court entertainments under Catherine de Médicis were frequent and lavish. The festivities to celebrate the wedding of the Duc de Joyeuse in 1581 included a 'ballet comique', a musical drama with dancing. The Salle de Bourbon is seen here arranged for the performance, with Henri III and Catherine in the foreground, and the mass of billowing cloud on the left concealing singers and musicians. (10)

their taste. It was a time in which scholarship became powerfully organized, a time when works of impressive erudition were produced. Lambyn's Horace (1577), not to speak of other works of his, was the envy of Europe; Muret's Catullus (1554) is another example, though he himself moved early to Italian pastures, thus breaking a fruitful link with the Pléiade; Duchesne lectured with authority on Martial, and in the provinces Elie Vinet was hard at work on his Ausonius. Such was the prestige of Paris in the world of scholarship in these middle years of the century that men came from all over the Continent to hear these humanists, especially men from the Low Countries and Germany, without regard to religious opinions. More has yet to be written on these humanist contacts during the reign of Charles IX in the history of European culture. The increasing severity of classical erudition in its fidelity to the Golden Age—and of this Scaliger's posthumous *Poetice* (1564) is in some measure a symbol—was doubtless destined to spell ruin in the long run to neo-Latin poetry, whose elated freedom in the thirties was gradually curbed by the increasing Ciceronianism of the scholars. In this respect, neo-Latin literature, though much more closely linked with court ceremony

and the like, underwent a further restriction through another phenomenon which was emerging. As we have already suggested, this was the period in which the magistrature and the Parlements established themselves as a central feature of the cultural scene, not to mention their increasing rôle in public life. When one surveys the various literary centres in Paris and the provinces, one is struck by the proportionately high number of lawyers taking part. The leading examples of this trend were Scévole de Sainte-Marthe (1536–1623), a figure of some stature in both literary and governmental spheres, and Etienne Pasquier, the author of the *Recherches de la France*. When the meetings of the *Grands Tours* (assizes) took place here and there, literary activity might be intensified (at Poitiers in the house of the Dames des Roches, or at Troyes, where Pasquier's *Hand* became the subject of much occasional verse). One may also note the remarkable increase in collective composition, more especially, but not exclusively, in the field of the *tombeau* (a poetic memorial), now a very popular genre; these collective tributes to literary figures (Ronsard), lawyers of distinction (Christofle de Thou) or ecclesiastics (Viole) served not only to consolidate the fame of the deceased, but also to express a certain political (or religious) attitude, as well as the solidarity of some humanist group. This literary activity of the lawyer for various reasons restricted the range of neo-Latin poetry in some degree. Apart from this, the emergence of the lawyer at this time is a sign of two things from our point of view. On the one hand, he took precedence more and more over the ecclesiastic and pointed thus to the gradual secularization of the state (though he might be strictly, even fanatically, orthodox in his religious opinions); and on the other, he revealed how the humanist, now solidly entrenched in the fabric of society, had become fully committed to the service of his country.

It is in this period that the literary life of the country became more closely organized, and that various trends earlier adumbrated came to fruition. We have seen how humanism had begun to nourish the roots of French literature; and we know that Petrarchism also helped to rejuvenate poetry, affording, as it were, a trellis on which the French poetic imagination could grow and flourish; but before the middle of the century, these trends had not acquired a distinctive personality in the poetic field, with the exception of the remarkable work of Scève in his *Délie* (1544). Here Scève, whose humanism had strong Lyonnais roots, acclimatized and developed many poetic themes which were 'in the air', but he gave to love-poetry a dignity which the compositions of previous decades had not possessed, and he showed how a powerful imagination of marked intellectual fibre could use a foreign poetic convention to express itself in original and indeed unforgettable fashion. Moreover, Scève's pioneer effort revealed itself in the way in which he tackled the problem of language, for many of the features of the *Délie*, which is the first Petrarchan love-sequence in France, anticipate the pro-

Ordōnā cede le A, faict de trois I. sus la fleur du Lisslābe.

Notez bien icy, & entendez.

An illustration from 'Champfleury' (1529) by the humanist printer Geoffroy Tory—a treatise on the alphabet containing not only directions for the construction of 'Roman' letters, but also anecdotes on their history and little moralising stories. The letters I and A were reputedly 'fantasticated' from a purple iris (lisflambe). (11)

gramme of the *Deffense et illustration* which the Pléiade were to publish five years later. Nevertheless, his venture had only a limited success; published at Lyons without the fanfares which were to announce the Pléiade's entry on the literary scene, it was appreciated only by the happy few; to many it seemed difficult, for Sebillet complained of its numerous newly-coined words. It certainly did not elicit the response to which it was richly entitled, and it is indeed only during the last fifty years, in the critical climate of the post-symbolist period, that Scève has established his claims as a poet of singular beauty and startling originality, both at linguistic and at imaginative levels.

The Rising Pléiade

Nevertheless, kindred spirits were about to explore similar veins, and in 1549 Du Bellay published the notorious *Deffense*. No doubt the tone of the pamphlet was sharpened by the fact that Sebillet had got in first with his *Art poétique* in the previous year, and what was worse, had associated some of his good ideas with the 'reactionary' school of Marot; but it was with the Pléiade that the poetic fruits of the Renaissance were gathered in. To begin with, we have here the collective endeavour of a group of talented poets, closely linked with the humanism of their times, to establish by precept and practice the claims of French in the field of serious poetry. The seven members, taking their name from the constellation of seven stars, embarked on a conscious programme of reforming French poetry by basing it on classical and Italian models. Ronsard was the leading poet of the movement; Du Bellay (whose *Deffense* is in many ways its manifesto) its critical spokesman. Later there was backsliding, of course—most of them took out a belated insurance policy in Latin verse—but with the hindsight of posterity we can see that it is with the Pléiade that the victory of the vernacular was finally won. It was necessary that this should come about through the enthusiasm, talent and disciplined taste of a group. The language was developing very rapidly, and dialects were still vigorous, so that it needed a measure of authority for a happy balance to be struck between the enrichment of the language and its proper control, and for due attention to be paid to questions of clarity and order. This trend was already apparent in the *Deffense*: if Du Bellay put forward various suggestions for increasing the range of poetic language, he also introduced remarks to underline the importance of precision and controls. And Ronsard's own evolution, as it is revealed in his variants throughout a long career, shows equally the movement towards a more highly organized poetic vehicle. With the arrival of the Pléiade, many of the trends we have already noted were brought together. Its members harmonized the vital elements of the French tradition and enriched them with the experience filtered through classical literature and Italian writings. The range of poetic endeavour was greatly broadened, and here support was given by foreign models and, as I mentioned before, poetry was closely related to the leading scholarship of the time: Dorat, Turnèbe, Muret, Lambyn, Léger Duchesne, Daniel d'Auge, Hélie André, Henri Estienne and later Jean Passerat, were all on friendly terms with the Pléiade. Impressive in the members of the Pléiade was the desire to build on solid foundations; and what strikes one in their verse is the structured quality of their language as well as of their poetic form. A more modern awareness of the formal qualities of poetry came into being, very different from that of the *Rhétoriqueurs*, for the stress was not on form in itself, but on the proper balance between content and vehicle. By drawing on Italian poetry, the French achievement returned to a wider European tradition; this Italian phase was not necessarily long-lived, and indeed some anti-Italian attitudes soon began to assert themselves, but the Petrarchan experience accelerated a process which was only slowly getting under way. It is indeed important not to overstress the Petrarchan element, in so far as one may tend in addition to give too much weight to purely aesthetic considerations; the Petrarchan experience was essentially a springboard for the French poet. The Pléiade is remarkable for the way in which its members tried to integrate poetry into all the most vital currents of contemporary culture. The links with scholarship are one indication; the ambition to extend the range of poetry into philosophical territory, very evident in Ronsard and Pontus de Tyard, is another; so is the eagerness with which these poets sought to be associated with the political and social manifestations of their day; and there is their desire to be in close contact with the other arts—were not Ronsard's *Amours* accompanied by musical settings, and did not the Pléiade's awareness of the neo-Platonic tradition and its Italian developments lead to the foundation of the Academies? In all this the main burden was carried by Ronsard; the work of Du Bellay (1522–60) is impressive in more ways than one, and he is the true elegist of the Pléiade, but much of his best work was written in Rome, and when he returned, he was on the threshold of death. Jean-Antoine de Baïf (1532–89) never rose much above the level of a competent versifier, though he asserted himself in other cultural ways; Pontus de Tyard (1521–1605), though a distinguished mind and the Pléiade member most endowed with an inclination and talent for philosophy, did not have the personality that would make an immediate impact upon his times, so that his influence worked chiefly indirectly; and Belleau (1528–77) and Guillaume des Autels (1529–81) were minor figures.

The World of Pierre de Ronsard

It was Ronsard who, thanks to his poetic stature and also to his continuous activity throughout three and a half decades, carried the venture to its successful conclusion. To reduce him, as some have done, to the status of an 'Epicurean' writer is to do him a great injustice. He has a wider range of inspiration than any other French poet; lyric, philosophical, ceremonial, national in turn, he makes the French language the undisputed vehicle of national sensibility. His poetry is characterized at once by an exceptional gift for apprehending his material in pattern and movement—even when he is developing some theme of Petrarchan origin—and by a highly developed awareness of the resources of the French tongue for poetic ends. In consequence, his poetry gives a greater sense of controlled vitality and 'body' than does that of any other poet of the century. And at political level too, the ideas which informed his poetry in the early years of Charles IX's reign found their echo in the *Satire Ménippée* of 1593 with its humanist ideals of moderation, its stress on national unity, its dislikes of faction and partisan interest, and with its conviction that principle carried to extremes will disrupt the proper business of living. It was in these years therefore that the cultural Renaissance reforged its links with the Establishment, and that the movement which was to culminate, at literary level, in the *grand siècle*, began to take shape.

It is nevertheless evident that Ronsard, in his philosophical attitude the spokesman of order and stability, possessed an imagination only too aware of the fluidity of human life, its transience and its standing under the shadow of death. Ronsard was also the poet of the moment. He was not the only writer in those troubled times to reveal this sensibility; and indeed the end of the French Renaissance coincides with the *monde cassé* of the last years of the Valois; the contrast between the optimism of the early years and the uncertainty of the end of the 16th century was very marked. In Ronsard and others, we detect frequently the awareness of this strife and insecurity, and a corresponding yearning for peace and permanence; and in Ronsard more especially, this response was no doubt also fed by certain aspects of his classical culture. These uncertainties were beginning to show in the field of thought as well; the full impact of rationalism and relativism was not to declare itself awhile, but the weakening of authority in various domains, notably political and theological, the beckonings of classical philosophies, empiricism and neo-Stoicism (though sometimes absorbed into the Christian tradition) were there for the observant to see. The widening of the known world—this was a time when travellers and geographers were rife and eager—led Montaigne (1533–92) to ask where was the 'norm' in human existence and encouraged Bodin to see human societies in terms of the local conditions in which they could prosper; and the outbreak of barbarity in the religious wars and the devastation of region after region of *la doulce France* made man increasingly aware of his isolation, as one can see in the poems of Sponde (1557–95) or of Chassignet (c.1570–1635). Reactions were many and various; some yielded to doubt and scepticism; others managed to keep

The Architect: a Mannerist fantasy by Philibert de l'Orme. He needs four hands and winged feet to accomplish so many things in a short time; the vases hold his secrets, which he must share with others: the buildings show several new features (such as the so-called French Order, with rusticated columns) that appear in Philibert's own work. (12)

their faith and their scepticism in some curious watertight system which allowed fideism and rationalism to co-exist. Montaigne seems, on occasion, to offer solutions by seeing himself in different contexts: the Mayor of Bordeaux, the sceptic, the supporter of the Establishment. Others yet sought to provide an orthodox answer in the purification of a shop-soiled and discredited system —the Council of Trent, the development of the Society of Jesus, the Counter-Reformation. And those who thirsted after an orthodoxy, but could not reconcile themselves with the Catholic tradition, often found themselves on the road to Geneva. p 169 (13)

France in a Changing Image

Nevertheless, in this period we see the gradual emergence of a more practical, empiric attitude, though it rarely manifested itself in its pure state. We saw that scientific progress was in many respects hampered by the return to the classics, but there are examples of scientific observation trying to free itself from bookish authority. Bodin in his *La République* (1576) attempted a description of states as they exist, according to the logic of their principles and their circumstances, but his attempt was not totally disinterested, since his scholarship was subordinated to the desire to show the claims of the *status quo* in France; on the other hand, his excursions into philosophical speculations were more adventurous, and were not without good cause viewed with suspicion by the orthodox. The claims of Roman law were adapted often to interested ends, monarchist or democratic, according to the dictates of the moment; nevertheless, the attempt to see things for what they were and not to impose upon events the dogma of authority and tradition was gaining ground. At all events, the past was being used to elucidate and guide the present, and whatever the despair and the discouragement, the Renaissance man saw in knowledge and its widening horizons the means of coming to terms with the human condition (the message given by Montaigne in his final essay). The secularization of the mind, of which so much has been written, was certainly gathering speed in the second half of the century. Much too has been written about the devotion of these years—the obsessive interest in the Passion, the suffering of the world and its nothingness, but these preoccupations were not incompatible with the active life. The sense of social obligation was growing stronger with the gradual development of the realm and the waning of feudal institutions. Through the fog of civil troubles during the last thirty years we can see that the mercantile class with its energy and its massive contribution to the cadres of the civil service was strengthening its positions; and by the end of the century one may think that the symbol of the times is not a chevalier Bayard, but a Sully. Knowledge was seen, not as the temptation of the devil, but as an instrument and a guide. As the religious wars subsided, attempts were made not only to restore the political unity of the realm, but also to bring into shape and pattern the various currents developed during the high tide of the Renaissance. The prestige of the national Church was changing in emphasis; theology was no longer the queen of the sciences, and the religious life contained a strong vein of inward devotion; Gallicanism was developing more strength and preparing to play a vigorous part in the secular world. The Jesuits quickly learned one lesson of the Renaissance, the importance for the Church to put its pedagogic house in order, and there is no need to insist on the importance of Jesuit schools in the decades to come.

No clear dates can be given for the end of any movement, and the Renaissance is as elastic a term as any. Nevertheless, the end of the Valois dynasty is not an unsuitable point at which to break off. With the disappearance of Henri III, peace and central authority began to assert themselves in more lasting fashion; and Henri IV's acceptance of Catholicism was the public recognition of the Church as the Church of France, a proper element of the temporal order. By the end of the Valois, the great majority of humanists still resident in France had become reconciled with the Establishment. Whereas in the first half of the century the new forces came to the surface in excitement, ferment and disruption, by the end of the century the search for unity and order was apparent not only at political, but at cultural level. We think of the literature first and foremost, but we shall be unwise to forget parallel developments in the realms of painting and architecture. Of course, there was no close synchronization, the various currents were to remain turbulent awhile; and the growing classicism could not absorb all the tendencies which recent study of the Baroque spirit has thrown into sharper relief. It was during this period, too, that Paris entered a new phase of its existence. Though an important amount of building had been undertaken in the first half of the century, a further enlargement of the precincts occurred by the end of the Valois, and its architectural image reflects a new era.

In the world of the universities, theology was now less prominent, and the Sorbonne of the nominalists and the realists had become a memory. Instead, philological scholarship, jurisprudence, medicine were assuming greater importance, and the links between government and education were developing strongly. Political theory began to take on, for various reasons, an urgency which it lacked half a century earlier, in France at least. And then too, one notes the increasing number of books in which problems of behaviour and knowledge were discussed. One may stress Montaigne's interest in the nature of the self, on the *passage* rather than the *être*, but a substantial portion of the essays is devoted to the problems of man in society—education of children, *exempla*, how to organize oneself—so that problems of self and the outside world are mainly prolegomena to the question of how to live a better life.

p 170–
177
f 12

p 170
(14)

What was the French Renaissance?

In France, then, one may see the Renaissance as a composition in three movements. At the outset we saw the first generation of humanists seeking to return to a purer medieval tradition in the best Christian sense; themselves ecclesiastics, they sought no innovation of principle, but a return to proper authority, with the help of a reformed classical tradition and support from countries like Italy where stimulus was already forthcoming. There might be some questioners of principle, and the claims of the *vita activa* were perhaps already asserting themselves here and there, but, by and large, Gaguin and his friends were thinking of a spring-cleaning of a house which, though in need of repair, was still structurally sound. The artistic and more worldly elements of the Italian Renaissance were not perceived by the great majority of educated Frenchmen before the Italian wars.

In the second stage, we saw the development of trends going far beyond what the precursors could have imagined: an even greater stress on education, a questioning of certain aspects of tradition, a wider awareness of what was going on abroad in the cultural sphere, important shifts in the pattern of social life, but above all, a growing divorce between humanism and Establishment. In the third stage, which took place in a heavily troubled world politically and socially, we witnessed the gradual reunification of those trends and their maturation at artistic level under the aegis of the Establishment, however threatened that Establishment might have seemed to be in the first uneasy decades. In this period of synthesis the new trends were being absorbed and harmonized with the French tradition.

In all this, what so often dominated was a desire for proper authority; the view which used to equate the Renaissance with individualism will not find much support, in this period at least. What one notices at the end of our epoch is precisely relief at finding authority more in harmony with the times and trying to come to terms with the forces in ferment in the previous decades. These trends are reflected in some measure in the rapid development and organizing of the French language which was recognizable as such and capable of being the proper vehicle for French culture. At the same time, this period of synthesis had absorbed elements which carried in themselves the germs of future transformation. We observed that a new reading of certain classical authors, a tendency to separate faith and reason (as may be seen in certain humanists associated with Padua), the move towards a more empiric attitude in things scientific were certainly present in this period; one can see that the tendency to syncretism and sometimes euhemerism would ultimately lead to a more relativistic view of religion; the widening of geographical horizons would also strengthen the comparative attitude; and finally, certain shifts in social conditions, in which a mercantile, positive layer of society was gradually pushing aside the remnants of a feudal order, can be clearly discerned. Nevertheless, the minds in whom a rationalist and anthropocentric view is taken to an extreme were rare indeed, and, though secularization pointed the way to the idea of a man-centred universe, the process had barely started at this stage. At most, one may note something of a gap between the intuition of the world as apprehended by some humanists and the more or less easy way in which they allowed the traditional formulation of faith to correspond to that intuition. This explains in some measure the divergence of views that appeared about the religious attitude of certain humanists on their death-beds (Budé, Turnèbe, Montaigne); it also accounts for the fact that Ronsard's pantheistic intuition of the universe did not seem, in his eyes, to conflict with a genuine profession of orthodox faith. It is only later that free-thinking *(libertinage)* crystallized into recognizable patterns, that the logical consequences of rationalist and empirical attitudes became apparent, and that the time-honoured foundations of religion came under more intense fire. Into the structure of this third stage were absorbed elements which, in the fullness of time, were to take the enquiring spirit of man a step further.

VII 'THE EGG THAT LUTHER HATCHED'

Renaissance and Reformation in Germany

G. R. POTTER

*'I laid a hen's egg; Luther hatched a bird
of quite a different species.'*

ERASMUS

Germany did not exist

as a political entity in the Renaissance. Instead of a nation there
was an idea, and to symbolize the idea there was one man: the
Emperor. Otherwise it was a collection of separate states, large
and small, ruled in any number of ways—by kings, dukes, arch-
bishops, margraves, landgraves and town councils—but all sovereign, each ready to do battle for its own cause, none willing to
make concessions in the interests of unity. It was a land where the
Church had more temporal power than anywhere outside the
Papal States, but also where variety of opinion could flourish and
where, alone in Europe, heresy and revolution could gather head
without any single authority being able to stop it.

The idea of German nationhood was nevertheless dominant in
the minds of most citizens of the Empire. Why should not
Germany go the way that England had gone, and France and
Spain were going? The machinery seemed to be ready, but, as so
often before and since, moral authority without sanctions found
itself powerless. The Diet was theoretically a meeting of all the
leaders of state presided over by the Emperor, though it was not
until 1489 that the free towns had won the legal right to be represented. In practice it proved to be almost unworkably cumbersome
and for long the real decisions were taken by the 'Electoral
College'—the seven rulers who elected the Emperor: the Arch-
bishops of Mainz, Cologne and Trier, the Count Palatine (ruler of
a Rhineland state), the Duke of Saxony, the Margrave of Branden-
berg and the King of Bohemia.

But if a German state did not exist, a German culture emphatically did, and by 1500 it was a distinctly humanist culture. Humanism, indeed, had made German intellectuals look beyond their own
city or province, where local patriotism had always been intense,
to the idea of *Germania*. At first, naturally, they had been dependent
on Italians (Aeneas Sylvius Piccolomini's stay had a pronounced
effect) but before long there were German scholars able to stand
besides those of any other country. To Melanchthon, appointed
professor of Greek at Wittenberg in 1518, it seemed that at a time
when the fire was dying down in Italy, it was just coming to full
blaze in the universities of the north.

Maximilian inherited the Empire in 1493 (it was not, of course,
hereditary; but the Hapsburg lands, his chief claim to be chosen,
were). He was intelligent, well-educated, far-sighted—and inevitably national and cultural ambitions fused in his mind into one rosy
ideal: to revive on German soil the Empire of which his own was
the heir, that of Rome. *Caesar Maximilianus*, says the inscription
on his portrait. Intellectually he was a true Renaissance prince,
a personal friend of nearly every outstanding artist and scholar of
his time—Trithemius, Pirckheimer, Celtis, Peutinger, Dürer,
Burgkmair. He was active in reorganizing the universities of
Vienna and Freiburg, giving more emphasis to the New Learning.
Dürer's portrait (opposite) brings to life the description given by
a Venetian ambassador: 'He is not very fair of face, but well
proportioned, exceedingly robust, of sanguine and choleric complexion and very healthy for his age'. Dürer met Maximilian at
Augsburg in 1518 and did some charcoal sketches from which the
oil painting was made. The Emperor died a few months later,
before it was finished. (1)

POTENTISSIMVS MAXIMVS ET INVICTISSIMVS CÆSAR MAXIMILIANVS
QVI CVNCTOS SVI TEMPORIS REGES ET PRINCIPES IVSTICIA PRVDENCIA
MAGNANIMITATE LIBERALITATE PRÆCIPVE VERO BELLICA LAVDE ET
ANIMI FORTIDVDINE SVPERAVIT NATVS EST ANNO SALVTIS HVMANÆ
M·CCCC·LIX· DIE MARCII IX VIXIT ANNOS LIX MENSES IX DIES XXV
DECESSIT VERO ANNO M·D·XIX MENSIS IANVARII DIE XII QVEM DEVS
OPT·MAX·IN NVMERVM VIVENCIVM REFERRE VELIT·

Learning began in infancy, and the methods in the early 16th century had not changed appreciably since the Middle Ages. Schoolmasters were often men debarred from a clerical career by marriage. This realistic little scene shows a schoolmaster beating the alphabet into one small pupil, while his wife instructs a little girl. It was painted in 1516 as an advertisement probably for Oswald Myconius by his friend Hans Holbein. Although at this time he claimed to teach no more than elementary reading and writing, Myconius later attained eminence as a Reformer. He became a Professor at Basle and wrote the first biography of Zwingli. (2)

'The schoolmaster of Germany', Philip Melanchthon, stood for all that was best in German humanism when the time came to choose between Luther and the Pope. By nature and education a teacher (he was Professor of Greek and Hebrew at Wittenberg for many years), he worked consistently for moderation but his intellectual gifts and mastery of theological exposition made him a key figure in the conflict. He was a great-nephew of Johann Reuchlin (right) who had first won the right to study Hebrew in Germany against the narrow-minded opposition of the Dominicans of Cologne, for whom Jewish books were heretical and therefore dangerous. (4)

'I read with pleasure what you write, as witty as it is wise', wrote Erasmus to Willibald Pirckheimer (seen left, standing next to Dürer in the latter's *Martyrdom of Ten Thousand Christians*). Pirckheimer was a celebrated patrician patron in Nuremberg: he patronized artists, learned Greek, translated Lucian into Latin and collected books and antiques. (3)

The life of Erasmus spans almost every important aspect of both the Renaissance and the Reformation. He was a brilliant scholar, editing texts in both Greek and Latin, including the first edition of the Greek New Testament. But underlying all these achievements was a deep concern for the troubles of Christendom, expressed with wit as well as compassion in his *Colloquies* and his great satire *The Praise of Folly*. Above left: two drawings by Holbein in the margins of *The Praise of Folly*. At the top, Erasmus writing, with this note: 'When Erasmus saw this he said, "Oh ho, if Erasmus still looked like that he would quickly find himself a wife."' Below, Folly descending from the pulpit. Above right: Erasmus aged 57 by Holbein. (5, 6, 7)

The Triumph of Reuchlin: at the gate of his native town of Pforzheim Reuchlin is received with music and laurel wreaths. A crowd of defeated monks in chains go before him and his arch-enemy Pfefferkorn, his tongue torn out, is dragged along by a scythe. Reuchlin's victory, when Leo X stopped his trial, came in 1516, after seven years of bitter persecution. (8)

Between rich and poor, between the nobility who held nearly all the constitutional power and the peasantry without rights or opportunities, a new class was growing up, destined eventually to become dominant: the burghers (literally 'townsmen').

Right: Maximilian and his court enjoy a day's hunting and fishing. Note the substantial picnic being prepared at one side. (9)

The imperial free city of Augsburg, about 1530 (below), was among the commercial leaders of Germany. Here Charles V called the Diet (1555) that was to settle the religious question—a fitting choice in many ways, for it was the Augsburg banking house of Fugger which had played a large part in the scandal over the sale of indulgences in 1517. It had then acted as agent for Albert of Brandenburg, half the proceeds going to Rome for the building of St Peter's, the other half being divided between Albert and the Fuggers. It was Fugger loans, too, which buttressed the shaky imperial exchequer. Augsburg was in all respects highly progressive and was among the first German cities to welcome the Renaissance style in sculpture and architecture. (10)

An itinerant pedlar leaving a dilapidated farm-house, one of Bosch's realistic portrayals of life among the very poor. Travellers in Germany were struck by the apalling poverty of the countryside. Economic changes were working to the detriment of the peasants, who were not allowed even to fish or fell timber, while their meagre crops could easily be destroyed by the upper classes hunting across their land. Their natural sense of grievance, coupled with Luther's unintentional encouragement to defy the authority of the Church, led to the hideous Peasants' War of 1525. (11)

Jacob Fugger the Rich in his office with his secretary Matthäus Schwarz, a miniature of 1519. In the cupboard behind are files dealing with cities all over Europe from Cracow to Lisbon. A complete district of Augsburg with six streets and a church, known as the *Fuggerei*, was being laid out at this time, as a semi-business, semi-charitable project. Dürer assisted with the designs. (12)

199

'The difference between the true religion of Christ and the false idolatrous teaching of Antichrist': a woodcut published as Lutheran propaganda about 1545. This left half shows the Protestant communion and baptism. Luther expounds the doctrine of salvation by the sacrifice of Christ: 'Neither is there salvation in any other, for there is none other name under Heaven given among men, whereby we must be saved'. In his audience, piously bearing the cross, is the Elector John Frederick. (13)

God in Heaven with St Francis looks down in horror as the modern friars collect money for the Church of Rome. The one in the pulpit preaches that there are many easy ways to be saved, all available to the Catholic Church, while the devil at his ear puffs him up with bellows. On the right the Pope hawks indulgences, holding a text which reads 'As soon as the money falls, the soul flies up to Heaven'. In the background various Catholic ceremonies are satirized. (17)

When Maximilian died in 1519 the prospects for German unity, even on the level of scholarship and culture, were dark. Perhaps the last symbol of the unfulfilled promise of Celtis' and Rudolf Agricola's Germany is Maximilian's own tomb (right) erected some time after his death in the Hofkirche at Innsbruck. It was not completed until 1583 and makes a curiously muted impression in spite of the splendour of its parts. Round the sarcophagus and facing it kneel a line of life-size bronze figures of Hapsburg ancestors and legendary heroes, 'silent witnesses', as they have been called, 'of the vanished grandeur of the Holy Roman Empire'. (19)

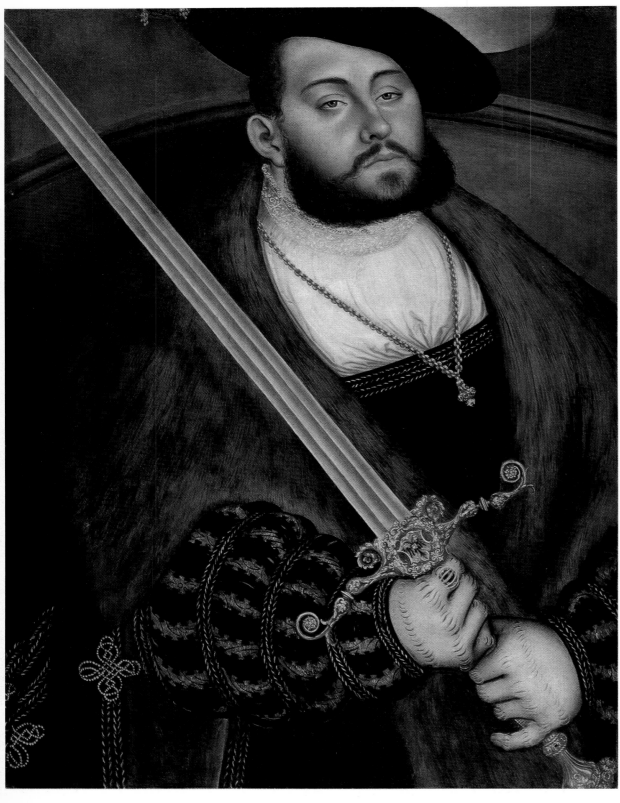

The Protestant princes were led first by John of Saxony, the son of Luther's protector, and then by his son John Frederick the Magnanimous (above). Full scale war came in 1546. John Frederick was defeated by Charles V at Mühlberg (1547). It is said that Lucas Cranach, his court painter, interceded for him, but John Frederick was deprived of his electoral dignity. This portrait by Cranach was painted several years earlier, in 1531. (18)

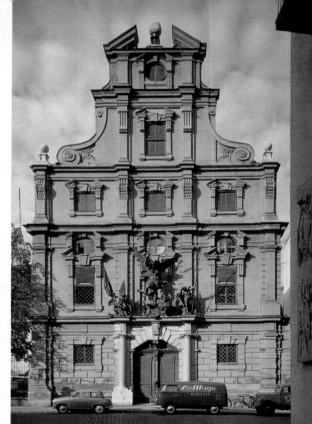

Architects looked south but translated what they saw into their own idiom. Elias Holl visited Venice in 1600–1 and on his return became city architect at Augsburg. His Arsenal (above), a reaction against the richness of the Ottheinrichsbau, adapts Mannerist features, like the volute and broken pediment, to the traditional gable-roof of Germany. (20)

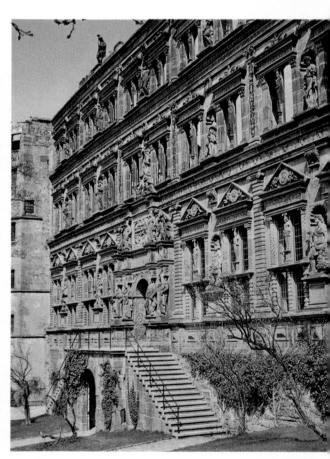

An Italian façade to a German elector's palace—the Ottheinrichsbau at Heidelberg, built by the Count Palatine in 1556. Renaissance motifs, however, are crowded upon it with a profusion that an Italian would have avoided. It is now an empty shell. (21)

Paracelsus (1493–1541) began his career in the mining business of the Fuggers, learning chemistry and later medicine. Nature, not authority, was his professed teacher, but the result was less science than a new form of alchemy. (22)

Vadian (1484–1551), also a doctor of medicine, wrote voluminous works on many subjects. After lecturing at Vienna he became burgomaster of St Gallen and an active friend of the Reformer Zwingli. (23)

Nicholas Kratzer (1487–c.1550), mathematican and astronomer, illustrates how small the circle of humanism still was. Born in Bavaria, he came to England as a young man, lectured at Oxford and became official astrologer to Henry VIII. His portrait by Holbein (above), painted in 1528, shows an interesting array of scientific instruments. (24)

Andreas Vesalius (1514–64), greatest of Renaissance anatomists, was born in Brussels, studied at Louvain and Paris, and at the age of 23 became Professor at Padua. His *De humani corporis fabrica*, published at Basle in 1543, is the foundation of modern anatomy. This detail from the title-page shows him performing a dissection. The artist who engraved the plates was another Fleming, Jan Stephan van Calcar, a pupil of Titian. (25)

Genuine science did not begin with the humanists, who were in general uninterested in observing the physical world. It was Germany that took the lead. The first globe of the earth ever made (below) was the work of Martin Behaim of Nuremberg. It was commissioned by the Nuremberg city council and utilized all available geographical knowledge. But the date is 1492; Columbus had not returned; there is no New World. (26)

A year later Johann Stöffler of Constance produced the first globe of the heavens (below). This too embodied the most up-to-date information. Stöffler wrote a book on the use of astrolabes and built the clock of Constance Cathedral. (28)

The astrolabe, a navigational instrument for co-ordinating the time of day with the angle of the stars and so calculating position, employed the talents of mathematicians. This one (above) is by Regiomontanus of Königsberg—humanist, Arabic scholar, and friend of Bessarion. (27)

Science and superstition were still inextricably blended in the 16th century. This intriguing painted table, dating from 1533 shows in schematic form the cosmic harmonies thought to hold good between the planets (in the centre), the days of the week, the Liberal Arts (seated women), the virtues (their attributes), the colours (their dresses) and the metals (the vessels standing next to them). It begins top left with a scholar, perhaps the owner of the table, drawing up the whole scheme. Then, in anti-clockwise order, come the Sun (Sunday, Grammar, Hope, yellow, gold); the Moon (Monday, Rhetoric, Faith, white, silver); Mars (Tuesday, Arithmetic, Strength, red, copper); Mercury (Wednesday, Logic, Love, grey, quicksilver); Jupiter (Thursday, Geometry, Justice, blue, tin); Venus (Friday, Music, Holiness, green, lead), Saturn (Saturday, Astronomy, Prudence, black, iron). The artist was Martin Schaffner of Ulm, painter, wood-engraver and medallist, who died about 1549. (29)

Renaissance and Reformation in Germany

G.R. POTTER

A students' drinking bout, from the two exhortations delivered to the Heidelberg students in 1489 condemning the drunkenness and prodigality of students. They were soon afterwards printed in Strasbourg with a treatise on the morals of the lower clergy, also a frequent target for criticism. (1)

IF WE THINK of Germany in the age of the Renaissance as including those areas in which one of the innumerable German dialects was spoken and in which the emperor had some nominal authority, we shall not be far wrong. North of the Alps the Holy Roman Empire comprised a good deal more than 19th-century Germany, embracing the Low Countries, Bohemia, the Hapsburg possessions (of which Vienna and Innsbruck were the administrative centres), modern Switzerland, Franche Comté and Luxembourg.

195 (1) Neither Frederick III (1440–93) nor Maximilian I (1493–1519) was in any effective sense ruler of Germany, although Maximilian's influence in the Netherlands, where he entered into his wife's inheritance, was considerable. In general, however, Germany was a land of warring princes and flourishing, independent cities—the Seven Electorates were well defined, but, before 1450 at any rate, not one Archbishop of Cologne, Mainz, or Trier, no Elector Palatine, King of Bohemia, Margrave of Brandenburg or ruler of Saxony was concerned to promote any 'new' learning. The common people secured a bare livelihood from the soil only with difficulty: travellers who came from, or

p 199 who had visited, Italy, were mainly impressed by the poverty,
(11) dirt and ignorance of the countryside over which they rode.

The Old Learning

Before 1450 there was little sign that the ideas of the Italian Renaissance would cross the Alps. None the less, some factors favoured the humanities: those rulers, and their officials, who were in touch with the princes and councillors of France and Italy, and, most obviously of all, with the Papal Curia, were aware that a certain degree of correct, and even elegant, Latinity was expected from their chancelleries; residence at a university was becoming fashionable, while the richest inhabitants of the cities, secure behind their as yet impregnable walls, had some leisure and capital which might be made available for scholarship. Some were university centres; some, such as Nuremberg, first and foremost, Ulm, Strasbourg, Augsburg, Rothenburg and Zürich, were not.

In addition to the cities there were the universities. After the foundation of Prague (1349), Vienna (1365), Erfurt (1379), Heidelberg (1386), Cologne (1388), Leipzig (1409) and Louvain (1426), there was a pause, followed by the appearance, almost in a bunch, of Freiburg (1455), Basle (1459), Ingolstadt (1472), Trier (1473), Mainz (1476), and Tübingen (1477), and then Wittenberg (1502) and Frankfurt am Oder (1506), demonstrating that there was a public with a taste for, and conscious of the need of, higher education. None of them was directly a humanist foundation—the first overt public sign of this is the foundation of the *collegium trilingue* at Louvain in 1517—but they brought together men accustomed to subtle arguments, nice distinctions and a certain acquaintance with Latin style. The students usually knew their Vergil, almost alone of the great classical authors, and some attempted Latin verse. Philosophically the not entirely barren controversies of the two 'ways', ancient and modern, Thomist and Ockhamist, encouraged independence of thought and logical reasoning; success in the university disputations might lead to employment in the service of a prince or to rapid promotion in the Church. There were, as yet, no theological colleges or seminaries; the higher clergy, at any rate, were for the most part trained in, or had been exposed to the influence of, the university cities. The teaching was traditional and conservative and there were many vested interests to keep it so.

Behind the universities lay the schools. Every aspirant to holy orders (and there were many), every civil servant, doctor, lawyer or accountant needed Latin—to be literate was to have been to school, and Germany was well provided with grammar schools, many of good quality. It was taken for granted that the acquisition of Latin syntax and grammar from the church liturgy, Donatus, Alexander of Villa Dei and the traditional grammarians, was a painful business; underpaid schoolmasters, often men barred from a clerical career by marriage, beat the essentials into reluc- p 196 (2) tant boys in quite appreciable numbers. Much of this was learning by rote: books were rare, parchment expensive, paper difficult to come by. The medieval scholar had this in common with the blind today—he learnt to listen carefully and to remember what he heard. There were a few teachers who reflected upon the purpose of education, especially those in the more prosperous and settled north-east where Gerard Groote (1340–84) and Hegius (1433–98), with their centres at Deventer and Zwolle, gave conscious thought to the moral welfare, as well as to the intellectual advancement, of their pupils. The schools of the Brethren of the Common Life, or their imitators, spread along the Rhine into Germany. At Strasbourg, Schlettstadt and Colmar in particular, there were to arise excellent schools which attracted a good deal of attention.

The adoption in the mid-15th century of the art of printing with movable type, inseparably associated with Gutenberg's press at Mainz, unquestionably reflects the rising literacy of the Rhineland but had, at first, little direct connection with the Renaissance, as the predominantly theological output of the early presses makes clear. None the less, cheaper duplication on paper made texts more readily available and ensured that the same text was in many hands. This was true even of the Bible, and with the study of the Bible went much else. The rapidity with which printers and their presses expanded, and the popularity of their wares, is striking; when new ideas and new information became available they could be disseminated rapidly. No printer was redundant, and river transport, especially along the Rhine, facilitated traffic in books and ideas still further.

Light from Italy

Geography and tradition alike ensured constant intercourse between Germany and Italy; at all levels, from the emperors whose nominal empire reached to Rome and beyond, to the clerics, merchants and students who visited the shrines, markets and universities of the peninsula, there was constant coming and going. The renewed attention to antiquity, the consciousness of new ways of considering man and the universe in which Italians were taking the lead in the late 14th century, the attraction to Greek studies, the passionate hunt for manuscripts—none of these things had gone entirely disregarded. Petrarch and Charles IV exchanged letters, while Sigismund, present in person at the Council of Constance, came into direct contact with Vergerio and his circle.

p 45 (1) Both Constance and Basle, meeting places of councils, were German cities. It was from Basle that Aeneas Sylvius Piccolomini came to put his gifts for rapid drafting in elegant Latin at the service of the Imperial Chancery, writing *Historia Frederici Imperatoris* between 1452 and 1458, and demonstrating in *Germania* that there was a German nation which could claim Caesar, Strabo and Tacitus as classical witnesses. Aeneas Sylvius, in fact, spent a good deal of his earlier years north of the Alps. After his coronation as 'poet' he was actively employed in the chancery at Vienna from 1442 onwards. For the best part of a decade he helped to compose official documents and was sent on a number of diplomatic missions. That the emperor and Caspar Schlick, the chancellor, were willing to use the services of an exponent of Italian humanism is significant, and Aeneas used his leisure for writing. Neither his masters nor the German universities were yet interested in anything outside routine and practical affairs, but something was moving none the less. This is apparent in the way in which Aeneas' work was in fact supported by his rival and opponent, Gregory of Heimburg (1400–72). A solid German and a sound lawyer, as practical as Aeneas was flighty, he illustrated by his p 51 (19) writings, his eloquence, and his acquaintance with Valla, Filelfo p 123 (8) and Poggio, that another step in the Renaissance direction had p 122 (5) been taken.

From much further north one of the best known and most controversial of the products of the schools of the Brethren of the p 123 (10) Common Life at Deventer was Nicholas of Cues (1401–64), student in Italy, brought by the existence of the Council to Basle, political thinker, philosopher, reformer, hardly at all a Renaissance figure yet tinged with much that belonged to it, and adding German seriousness and profundity. He knew some Greek, he collected ancient manuscripts, he corresponded with Aeneas Sylvius. The more his works are studied the more he seems to be a compact of later scholasticism, compromise, open-mindedness and understanding, the embodiment of a changing northern Europe.

The New Schools

When Gerhard Groote initiated at Deventer one of the many semi-monastic reforms, advocating a life in community of men devoted to learning, prayer, and welfare through education, he could not have foreseen how widespread would be the influence of *devotio moderna* and the schools of the Brethren of the Common Life. Quietly, but decisively, their influence spread all through the Rhineland; one German humanist after another derived inspiration from that source. The schoolroom became a different place under the influence of the Brethren; pupils were to be persuaded rather than bullied, and the purpose of education became moral rather than merely academic. While there was no organic connection between the northern schools of Hegius and the southern educa- p 122 (6) tional revolution connected with Vittorino da Feltre, in a measure the two met in Alsace, with Wimpheling and Dringenberg, and from Alsace fertilized much of south Germany.

The perfect product of the schools of Deventer and Zwolle, (although probably he actually attended neither but was powerfully influenced by them) was Rudolf Agricola (1442–85). When only twelve years old he had enough Latin to be able to attend lectures and take part in disputations at Erfurt, and he anticipated Wolsey as the 'boy Bachelor' at Louvain, where, at the age of sixteen, he was admitted as a Master of Arts, presumably having obtained exemption from the statutes. Having considerable talent for metaphysical speculation, as well as for mathematics, he natu-

rally moved to Cologne, but found the arid exposition of scholastic theology there little to his taste. He learnt French, visited Paris, and then secured tutorships which allowed him to visit north Italy. At Pavia there were opportunities, of which he took some advantage, for studying Roman law, but he soon went on to Ferrara where Theodore Gaza and Guarino da Verona taught p 123 (9) him Greek very successfully. He managed somehow to stay in north Italy for a decade, an Aristotelian scholar of parts, and a personality whom many sought to know as a translator and writer.

Thence, in 1478, he returned to the Netherlands to a sinecure which left him time for study, visits to friends and an extensive correspondence, moving in 1484 to Heidelberg where professors and students persuaded him to lecture and dispute although he was without any university appointment. He was in Heidelberg for less than a year, returned to Italy on a mission for the Elector Palatine in 1485 and died on his return to Heidelberg in the autumn. He had expounded his views on the art of logical public speech in *De inventione dialectica* and had cast an educational treatise in the form of an open letter calling for character-training through moral philosophy, and independence of thought secured by wide reading of, and reflections upon, the best ancient authors. Agricola impressed his age, and in a short life demonstrated that a German could have something to teach, as well as to learn from, Italians.

Education at the Cross-roads

Strasbourg, where Agricola's work was early known and appreciated, was favourably situated. It was on the line of communications between north and south, closely involved politically with Zürich, Basle and Berne, an island of security amid the uncertainties of the Hapsburg lands in Alsace, with leisured ecclesiastics and wealthy business men stimulated to mental activity by the consciousness of living in a German outpost in the west. Like Cracow in the east, also a humanist centre, it was almost a border town, a kind of advanced German position never indifferent to what was going on in France. In the age of the Renaissance it was regarded, and rightly, as a peculiarly free, German-speaking imperial city, and a notable ornament of the Empire. Alsace was a singularly independent region, with some parts in the south under Hapsburg rule and with many enclaves under the control of nobles or ecclesiastics. There was thus scope for independent development, while at the same time the Rhine provided communications with the Netherlands in the north and, through Basle, with the Swiss in the south. In the seventies of the 15th century, Burgundian influence and pressure had been increased; if events had gone only slightly differently, Alsace might have become the fourteenth state of the Swiss Confederation or the capital of a Greater Burgundy.

It was in such surroundings that the schools of Strasbourg and Ensisheim became renowned. Jacob Wimpheling (1450–1528) typifies the Renaissance in this area, just as Bucer does the Reformation, and in each case local conditions made for moderation and compromise. Wimpheling came from Schlettstadt. Greek, apparently, he never learnt, and his Latinity did not quite match the easy grace of Agricola or Erasmus. Yet in two ways he illustrates his age. Thoroughly orthodox, he was yet as critical as Valla: for example, being himself a secular priest, he demonstrated that the claim of the Augustinian Order to follow a Rule drawn up by their nominal founder was untenable. He could be described as an educationist and a patriot: he exalted his homeland in *Germania* and insisted that the whole Rhine valley appertained to it and not to France. John Geiler of Kaysersberg had already aroused enthusiasm in Strasbourg by his sermons, and when Wimpheling urged the City Council there to set up a grammar school (*Gymnasium*) in which Latin literature was to be the chief subject of instruction, with morality, strategy, architecture and agriculture all studied from Roman writers, he met with a good deal of support. It is interesting to find Wimpheling taking this viewpoint because, although his own training in Heidelberg where he was Dean and later Rector, had been along traditional lines, he nevertheless valued university education much more highly than did some other Renaissance figures. He admired the school set up by Louis Dringenberg in Schlettstadt and he would have been delighted with the elaborate and logical advanced classical studies arranged later by Sturm.

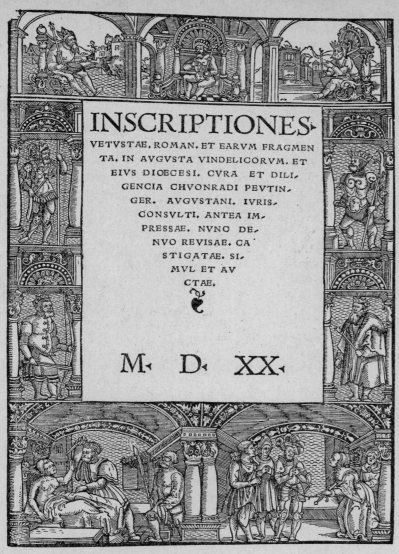

'Ancient Roman Inscriptions,' published by Peutinger in 1520. The inscriptions came from the environs of Augsburg, some supplied by such eminent burghers as the Fuggers and the Paumgartners. The titlepage shows the rape and suicide of Lucretia, and seven Roman emperors. (2)

Reluctant Universities

Humanism north of the Alps depended much more upon institutions, schools and universities than was the case in Italy, and herein lies part of its enduring success. None the less humanism was in no way the product of the German universities but was, in a sense, imposed upon them, just as the teaching of Greek at Oxford was reluctantly undertaken only at the orders of the government. Heidelberg, Erfurt and Vienna were more willing than the others to accept the modifications of the traditional courses, to allow the study of letters together with logic, to encourage the writing of Vergilian hexameters and Ciceronian prose side by side with the nice distinctions and often sterile arguments of current scholasticism. The transition was, indeed, gradual, if it was ever fully accomplished, and the 'poet' long remained something of an exotic rarity. The Renaissance in Germany was part of a wider European movement. Locally it became an affair of personalities, of institutions and of communications. The universities could not fail to be affected in some measure by the currents of European thought. At Cologne, for example, later regarded by the humanists as the citadel of theological obscurantism, Greek and Hebrew were being taught before the end of the 15th century and there was a printing press there in 1467. All the German universities knew something of the New Learning. What is true of Erfurt, Vienna and Tübingen is fully paralleled elsewhere.

The University of Vienna, founded in 1365 by Rudolf of Hapsburg, at first without a theological faculty, flourished from the outset. Both Gerson and Aeneas Sylvius praised its scholarship and the advocacy of proper Latinity there was quite remarkable.

Although Zwingli left after only a short stay, Vienna helped to make him the humanist theologian that he became. Scholastic and medieval its earlier traditions necessarily were, but an undercurrent of restlessness becomes apparent before the end of the 15th century. In 1492 there were lectures on Vergil, Cicero, Horace and Sallust from Bernhard Perger; in 1494 Jerome Balbi, the jurist from Venice, was asking that his lectures on poetry might be compulsory as well as remunerated, and by 1501 there were two professors, one of oratory, one of poetry, who, with the professors of mathematics and physics, might bestow the laureate on behalf of the emperor upon approved applicants. There was a tinge of humanism about Viennese university studies at the opening of the 16th century, and this was significant.

Erfurt was a quasi-university town even in the 13th century; Clement VI in 1379 merely regularized what had long been going on. Well and centrally situated, equi-distant from Heidelberg, Cologne and Prague, the institution moved with singular independence. It was, in a sense, purely German, for there were no 'nations' as there were elsewhere, and it received substantial support from the city. Law and theology were stressed, there was a rich library, especially of bible-commentaries, and John of Wesel and Nicholas of Lyra were influential names. Directly, perhaps, there was little that could be called humanism, but indirectly there was much. There was a good deal of exposition of the best Latin authors, free discussion and argument were encouraged, and the spirit of critical enquiry there did something to shape the thoughts of Luther, its best known *alumnus*. There was an early interest in mathematics and astronomy and care was taken to introduce new methods of teaching style and rhetoric rather earlier than elsewhere. Visiting lecturers from Italy were encouraged and Locher, Mutianus Rufus, Wolf, Zell, Spalatin, Crotus Rubianus, Jodocus Trutfetter, were all there at different times.

The foundation of Tübingen in 1477 required confidence and courage, with Heidelberg and Freiburg so close at hand. Perhaps because of this, the university authorities deliberately set out to attract some distinguished scholars as teachers—the realist Johann Heynlin von Stein, the nominalist Gabriel Biel whose commentary on Ockham was appreciated by Luther, and Heinrich Bebel who lectured on oratory. Greek and Hebrew were taught, mathematics and astronomy were popular, and lecturers were instructed to expound their texts briefly and clearly and to avoid 'inane and frivolous questions'. *Via moderna* and *via antiqua* were both catered for, and special care was taken to secure the best possible texts of Aristotle and a wide range of commentaries on them as well.

There was no university in Augsburg, Ulm, Strasbourg or Nuremberg, yet each of these cities, together with others, was in a measure a focus of new tendencies. Their buildings, and the ornamentation of their great churches, were expressive of a characteristic approach to the age; the Rathaus was the centre of civic life, and, at a time when ecclesiastical and domestic architecture were still undifferentiated, the Town Hall of Nuremberg was different both from a French late Gothic cathedral and an Italian palazzo. Guarded by their walls the citizens had security; they had a tradition of personal freedom and some had both money and leisure. The merchants who were painted by Cranach and Holbein had taste and encouraged it in others; they were ready to support the literary societies, the Rhine and Danubian *Gesellschaften* which were the parallels to the renowned academies of Florence and Rome. Augsburg, for example, employed Conrad Peutinger, the scholarly editor of Roman inscriptions, as its Town Clerk; other towns directly and indirectly encouraged the production of their own chronicles or histories.

p 198–9 (10)

f 2

Wandering Scholars

Among the penniless wandering students who moved from city to city, publicizing and exaggerating their poverty and their attainments, was Peter Luder (1415–74) of Heidelberg, where Frederick, Elector Palatine, set an example of encouragement to letters. Luder left the university without a degree, and as soldier, mendicant and clerk made his way to Italy, to the eastern shore of the Adriatic and to Asia Minor, picking up what he could of the attainments of his tutors and acquaintances. By 1456 he had

The titlepage of the second instalment in 1517 of the 'Epistolae obscurorum
virorum' represents the obscurantists (scholastic theologians) so bitingly
satirized by Crotus Rubianus and Ulrich von Hutten, and exhorts the
reader to exercise his lungs with laughter. It brought Reuchlin's opponents
into such ridicule that the victory of humanist studies was secured. (3)

returned to the Neckar and offered to lecture in his former university on rhetoric and poetry. This was not acceptable to the
Establishment and it required a special grant from the Elector and
an order to 'his' university before recognition and a lecture room
were provided. The lectures on the Epistles of Horace, on Ovid
and on Valerius Maximus attracted no very considerable following
and Luder made ends meet by taking private pupils in Augsburg
and Ulm during vacations and by delivering a course on Terence
and Ovid at Erfurt in 1461. From thence he moved to Leipzig,
where he taught Hartmann Schedel (1440–1514), obtained a
temporary success and then, after further wandering, entered the
service of the Duke of Saxony. All this he expounded freely in his
autobiographical verse and letters. Luder was scarcely more than
a sign of the times: his scholarship was superficial and his influence
slight, he had no serious pupils or disciples, but he led the way.

Polished Latinity and a great deal of versifying combined with
relentless self-advertisement to magnify, in his own age and later,
f 5 the achievement of Conrad Celtis (1459–1508). In time, and also in
aims and method, Celtis is Luder's successor and, for a variety of
reasons, was able to achieve more than his predecessor. Luder
was ignored by Frederick III, Celtis was patronized by Maximilian I, but then Frederick III was neither humanist nor Renaissance prince while Maximilian would have wished to be remembered as both. A peasant's son, after an adventurous career as a
poor student at Cologne and Heidelberg, Celtis managed to move
north, south and east, to Rostock, Erfurt and Leipzig, and was
accepted as a mathematician and astronomer. He learnt some
Greek in Rome and Florence and with almost modern publicity
received the laurel crown from the emperor at Nuremberg in
April 1487. How it all happened and how it was paid for is a
matter for speculation, but it showed what was possible. The

vainest of men, he was disappointed with Rome, Florence and
Ferrara alike, partly because they had less that was new to offer
than a generation earlier, partly because there he was among
equals, if not superiors, whereas in northern Germany he was a
prodigy.

Indefatigable in the formation of learned societies, some of
which existed on paper only, he moved east to Cracow for two
years, then via Nuremberg to Ingolstadt for a further two (1494–
96) and finally became an ornament of the University of Vienna,
president of its Poetry Society. He was enormously popular with
the young men, and wrote extensively both the elegiacs on the
theme of love for which he was best known, and treatises on the
potential greatness of Germany, presenting everything with the
gloss of the Golden Age of the Roman Republic. Within the little
world of books he was a minor Erasmus, knowing much, inspiring confidence, praising rather than criticizing his fellow humanists, and possessing in no small measure the instinct for original
research, constant questioning rather than simple exposition.

Exposition, however, was indeed very necessary in Germany;
in scientific knowledge, information about the physical universe,
in politics, philosophy and law, the ancient world was still ahead
of the modern. Celtis helped it to catch up. Never long in one
place, accepting Church money without performing clerical
duties, refraining from open criticism of accepted beliefs, he
showed his fellow-countrymen how to use language as a weapon
of power and effect. Small in stature, often in ill health, always
on the move, he was interested in painting, music, drama, geography, printing (which he highly commended), natural history,
astronomy; sceptical about astrology and magic, a conventional
churchman who defended the Immaculate Conception, he lived
to see some of his teaching brought to fruition after Maximilian
had opened in 1502 the *Collegium Poetarum et Mathematicorum* at
Vienna. It was as a poet that he wished to be remembered, but his
encouragement of science was valuable for Germany.

John Tritheim, Trithemius (1462–1516), was Celtis' contemporary and his equal as an exponent of German humanism. He
made his profession as a monk at the age of twenty and was
satisfied with the life of cloistered scholarship which the age
allowed and expected. He was orthodox yet critical, he followed
St Augustine in rejecting the superstitions of the astrologers, yet
he studied the stars with intense care; perhaps something of a
conjurer, he gained the reputation of a magician. Immensely
industrious, an experimental chemist on occasion, he turned his
attention to the history of German monasticism so that he could
demonstrate the superiority of clergy to laity and of Germans to
other nations. For the greater glory of Hirschau he resorted to
forgery and deliberate misinterpretation of documents, and history

The virulence of the Reuchlin-Pfefferkorn controversy increased with every
pamphlet. This woodcut is from Pfefferkorn's 'Mitleydliche Claeg' ('Pitiful
Plaint') against Reuchlin's advice to the emperor in 1510 that Jewish
books should not be suppressed; it shows the author pointing to Reuchlin
who is bewailing the loss of his case, wearing sackcloth and eyeglasses (a
pun on his 'Augenspiegel' condemned by Imperial mandate in 1512). (4)

in his hands became an instrument of propaganda. He disliked and defamed the Jews of his day, he neither wrote, nor persuaded others to appreciate, Latin verse, yet in his enormous breadth of knowledge, his wide classical reading, his consistent friendship with humanist circles, he illustrates the seriousness, the political-mindedness, the patriotism and even the piety that marks much of the northern Renaissance.

The Study of Hebrew

The cult of polished Latin prose, the new-found recognition of what the literature and language of ancient Greece had to offer, was one aspect of the German Renaissance. It was paralleled by another—a revived interest in Hebrew. There had been little concern with this language in the Middle Ages; St Jerome had translated the Old Testament from the original tongue with which he was so well acquainted into Latin and there was little desire to go beyond this. Only rather exiguous Oriental contacts and efforts at conversion of Jews were factors favouring the study of the language; some university teaching in the subject, following the decree of the Council of Vienne (1311), was intermittently available.

There were, however, special reasons why Renaissance Germany should show an interest in Hebrew. In so far as the New Learning bred a critical outlook which was applied to religion, interest in Bible study and the difficulty of adequate New Testament exegesis without Hebrew, which Christ quoted and used, turned attention to this. The humanists, following St Jerome, regarded Hebrew as the first original language and, since the Old Testament is quoted in the New, each word of the original had special value. To isolate the whole Bible, including the Apocrypha, from any Renaissance study is to misunderstand the age.

Further, there was a considerable Jewish population in some German cities, the result, partly, of the expulsion of Jews from the more highly centralized states, France and England. A succession of learned rabbis meant that Hebrew scholarship had been maintained and it was to this source that interested parties could turn. Humanist Hebrew, if the phrase is admissible, was the result of the work of the gifted linguist Johann Reuchlin (1455–1522), lawyer, Latinist with some knowledge of Greek, who was induced by intellectual curiosity and by acquaintance with Pico della Mirandola to learn Hebrew and to examine with interest the Cabbala. In *De verbo mirifico* (1494) and *De arte cabbalistica* (1517) he directed attention to the special Jewish contribution to theological speculation and he wrote for German students an elementary grammar *De rudimentis hebraicis* (1506), and a more advanced commentary *De accentibus et orthographia linguae hebraicae* (1518). Thus, even if some of it was plagiarized without acknowledgment, there was now a working text-book available and printed.

The result was publicity of an undesirable kind, but still publicity. The Dominicans of Cologne made use of the enthusiasm of a Jewish convert to Christianity, John Pfefferkorn (1469–1522), to attempt to suppress Jewish books, and an imperial mandate was obtained in 1509 ordering their confiscation. Reuchlin's works were soon included. This led to investigation, consultation of various universities, information volunteered by interested parties which aroused public interest and which led to a kind of pogrom. Any learned controversy in the 16th century, as the writings of Sir Thomas More illustrate, easily became a slanging match: Reuchlin answered his opponents in 1511 in *Augenspiegel*. This was promptly condemned by the University of Cologne, as heresy was suspected. The issue moved up to papal level, the stormy petrel Franz von Sickingen got himself involved, and the case went against Reuchlin, who was ordered to be silent and pay costs. All this aroused ever-widening interest. Testimonials to Reuchlin's scholarship came in from many quarters and were printed as *Clarorum virorum epistolae* (1514) and *Epistolae illustrium virorum* (1519). A kind of party organization developed. The Reuchlinists were those who cared both for the arts in the wider sense (*studium humanitatis*) and for people, while their opponents were men of darkness and obscurity. Then came the famous satire, anonymous and by several writers, but bearing unmistakably the hands of Crotus Rubianus and Ulrich von Hutten, *Epistolae obscurorum virorum*. The satire has lost much of

p 26
(45, 46)

f 4

f 3

In 1507, Conrad Celtis, feeling the approach of death, commissioned a memorial of himself from Hans Burgkmair in the style of a Roman funerary monument. He survived until February 1508, however, and an extra stroke had to be added to the VII. The laurel wreath around his hat, he complacently rests his hands upon his works: odes, epigrams, love lyrics and 'Germania Illustrata', and his coat of arms lies broken before him. (5)

its sting across the ages now that the allusions have to be laboriously interpreted, but Ortuin Gratius of Cologne is set up as the incredibly learned, pious, skilled master of all the arts, and the stories of sexual irregularities are as crude as the bad grammar or names like Dollenkopfius, Mammotrectus, Bunstemantellius, Langschneiderius. The fact that some, like one Dominican prior in Brabant, failed to realize that it was satire at all, says much for the need for the New Learning. Erasmus characteristically urged peace and tried to escape being drawn in. It may be noted that Reuchlin's chief supporters came from Erfurt, that no question of heterodoxy was involved (for Reuchlin, who was teaching Hebrew at Ingolstadt in 1520 and at Tübingen in 1521–22, remained steadfastly Catholic), and that in the end the cause of Hebrew won. After this controversy the three languages, Latin, Greek and Hebrew became part of the necessary equipment of the educated scholar.

p 197 (8)

Some Humanist Careers

The German humanists lacked the spacious inspiration and encouragement of Florence, Rome or Venice, and the incipient signs of what later seems to be a universal tendency have to be traced in the works and careers of somewhat minor and not individually very significant figures.

Selection of these is inevitable and thus the narrative is likely to become, in part, a series of biographies. Erasmus tends to dominate the scene and to overshadow his fellow workers, but

Sebastian Brant's vernacular 'Das Nar-renschiff' tells of a shipload of fools who embark for Narragonia, a fools' paradise. In jaunty verse it satirizes contemporary failings, both clerical and lay, and its wide popularity led to a whole 'fool' literature. This woodcut from the fully illustrated first edition shows the foolish boatman who comes to grief by failing to take the necessary precautions against misfortune. (6)

he was eager enough to correspond with them, to compliment them, and to make use of their brains. The centres of German population were further apart than were the Italian cities and local life was active and intense. Hence some of the exponents of the New Learning, men like Locher, Pirckheimer and Murner were influential chiefly in their own immediate neighbourhood: much depended on the spoken word which has escaped record and the personality of its exponent. Men like these prepared the way for successors who could address a wider public.

Jacob Locher (1471–1528) was a kind of minor Celtis. There is the same background of the wandering scholar, the Basle boy who studied at Freiburg, Ingolstadt, Tübingen, Padua and Bologna, lectured on rhetoric and poetry at Freiburg in 1495, was *poeta laureatus* in 1497 after which he delighted in the epithet or nickname of Philomusus and succeeded Celtis as *lector in poesi* at Ingolstadt in 1498. Anti-clerical, bitter in his attacks on the scholastic theologians, he had a following and was an invaluable subordinate in the humanist ranks. Thomas Murner (1455–1537) abandoned the study of antiquities for violent controversy against Brandt, Luther, Wimpheling and any enemies of the faith to whom his attention could be drawn. There is something of the foil about him: more of permanent worth could have come but that his attention was diverted elsewhere. Willibald Pirckheimer (1470–1530) was Locher's almost exact contemporary, better known, chiefly because he was painted by Dürer and because he was rich enough to be extravagantly complimented by Erasmus. The taste of that age, P. S. Allen once remarked, liked the butter spread thick and Erasmus' was the best butter. A wealthy Nuremberg patrician, joining the select throng of those who, like Reginald Pole, learnt Greek in leisurely fashion at Padua and Pavia, he was a Platonist who translated the works of Lucian and St Gregory Nazianzen into Latin, and he was justly proud of the intellectual achievements of his sisters, Charity and Clara. The furniture and pictures of his house showed his own good taste, he inherited and added to a considerable library, he collected and used mathematical instruments, studied maps and was a kind of minor Lorenzo de' Medici in his renowned city. Because of his wealth his scholarship may well have been overrated; he was a soldier and man of affairs as well as a student.

Such were some of the 'poets', and not one of them cared for the vernacular. A partial exception is to be found in Sebastian Brant (1457–1521), one of those marginal figures, no true humanist, and yet powerfully influencing humanism. The *Ship of Fools* (*Das Narrenschiff*) was first printed in 1494 at Basle and soon translated into several languages, Locher (Philomusus) being responsible for a Latin version in 1497. The ship-load of fools was a satire touched by the Renaissance spirit, the 'fool' being an almost indispensable accompaniment of the thought of the age. The *Praise of Folly, Moriae encomium* (1509) connects directly with it, as do the Pasquinades of Rome and the crude street-plays which brought the Reformation to Berne.

p 196 (3)

f 6

p 197
(5, 6)

214

The Making of Erasmus

The notion that there was an Italian Renaissance which was pagan, and a northern Renaissance which was Christian, has long since been abandoned as untenable. The fact that Lorenzo Valla demonstrated that the Donation of Constantine was of a much later date than it asserted, or that the Apostles' Creed could not be assigned to the Apostles, no more made his circle unbelievers than the elimination of the 'three witnesses' text involved the rejection of the inspiration of the Bible. It is true that most of the books that came from the early printing presses were 'religious' in their titles and contents, but this is because they reflected the general interests of their age. However inevitable it may be to consider the Renaissance as characterized by a revival of interest in classical antiquities and in the study of Greek and Latin, contemporaries need not have seen anything unchristian in this, nor did they. There was in northern Europe from the beginning of the 15th century a fusion of the study of antiquity and of the Bible which was so complete as to make them inseparable. Indeed, many of the early Reformers were so conscious of the difference between the Christian community of the time of the Acts of the Apostles and that of their own age that part of their case was based upon a desire to return to the primitive practices. It was much the same as the conviction that ancient Rome should be copied in its laws, institutions and terminology, which powerfully affected a good deal of 16th-century political and even military thinking.

There had long been criticism of the Church in Germany, some of it bitter enough, as for example that of Conrad Mutianus Rufus (1471–1526), Canon of Gotha, whose orthodoxy was tinged with scepticism but who refused to leave the Catholic Church. Agricola and Reuchlin were the most notable early exponents of critical thought, linguistic attainments and deep acquaintance with the past, and their names were widely known in the 15th century. They were transcended by Erasmus in whom the p 197 (northern Renaissance reached its highest point. Every aspect of his life has been studied with care by devoted admirers and also by critics who disparage his Latinity, demonstrate the manifest imperfections in his knowledge of Greek and dislike him for his refusal to abandon the Catholic Church while at the same time equating him with Luther as a solvent of established beliefs.

The natural son of a priest, a monk by unwilling profession, forced to earn a living by his pen and therefore to flatter wealthy patrons with almost sickening adulation, he secured for himself, a little late in life, the comfort and security without which penetrating scholarship and continuous writing were impossible. *Roterodamus*, he was Dutch by birth, brought up in a wealthy corner of a poor continent, where Burgundian achievements were apparent in buildings, pictures and books, and with relations who were well enough off to send him to school at Gouda, and thence to the best school in Europe, St Lebuin's, kept by Brethren of the Common Life at Deventer. He was in the atmosphere of the *Imitation of Christ*, of the mysticism of Gerson and the *devotio moderna*, and at the same time he was taught by men who were scholars, transcribers and accurate grammarians. He had already learnt to sing, and a choir-boy's trained voice brought him into the Cathedral of Utrecht and the organization of a great collegiate church.

In later life he criticized his own early upbringing; he hated the harsh methods of learning medieval Latin grammar in hexameters and he hardly realized that Hegius, his headmaster, was an up-to-date scholar who made his school representative of the best that the age had to offer. Hegius himself knew and studied with Agricola and thus learnt a little Greek and also was acquainted with what Italy had to offer. Erasmus met Agricola once and remembered the meeting long after. He also came into touch with John Wessel (Gansfort) who had also been to Italy and was trilingual, knowing Latin, Greek and Hebrew, but concerned with doctrine and pastoral work rather than style and the niceties of scholarship. At Deventer there was a simple printing press, actively issuing many of the Latin classical texts just as Erasmus was leaving and thus bringing him early into touch with the new medium for reaching a widening reading public. In 1484, having learnt by heart most of the comedies of Terence (whose plays were popular in the 16th century both for their style and their

The image on the title page with portraits, framed text in Latin:

IO. FROBENIVS PO/
litioris literaturæ cultoribus, s.

Adnifi fumus æditione proxima, ut hoc
opus cum primis frugiferu, quàm emen/
datiffimu prodiret in lucem, nec arbitror
quenq̃ inficiaturu, id nos infeliciter fuiffe
conatos: nunc quicquid in arte mea pof/
funt promittere curæ, id totu expromptu
eft. Acceffit & autoris opera, qui multa uel
auxit, uel reddidit meliora. Atq̃ utinã hoc
diu illi liceat, in ftudiorum lucrum potius
quàm meu. Sed ucreor ne hãc recognitio
nem ab illo fimus habituri poftrema. Qui
literario gaudēt lucro, habent hic lucru nõ
afpernandu: quibus res eft anguftior do/
mi, quàm ut identidē idem opus mercenẽ,
habēt poftremã, ni fallor, autoris recogni
tionē, fimul & locupletationē. Bene ualete,
& noftræ induftriæ, fi promereor, faucte.
BASILEAE, AN. M. D. XXIII.
Ex autoris recognitione poftrema.

Portrait labels: HOMERVS POETA · SALOMON REX · HESIODVS · ARISTIDES · DEMOSTH · PLATO · ARISTOT · EVRIPID · ARISTOPHAN · PLVTARC? · LVCANVS · THEOCRIT · PINDARVS · CICERO · QVINTIL · VERGIL · HORATIVS · PLINIVS · A. GELLIVS · LIVIVS · SALVSTIVS

The '*Adagia*' of Erasmus was among the most popular works of the age. It began as a small collection of Greek and Latin proverbs with which readers could embellish their prose and increase their reputation. But Erasmus went on adding to them all his life and his original brief commentaries grew into lengthy disquisitions on manners, morals and religion, so that by the end the book was a fascinating record of his opinions on a host of subjects. This titlepage from Froben's *1523* edition has fanciful portraits of the authors from whose works the '*Adagia*' was compiled. (7)

content), Erasmus left Deventer and was ready for a university course. Why he did not beg his way to Louvain, Cologne or Paris, as others like Butzbach had done before him, is uncertain. For local and family reasons perhaps, the young man, for so, at fifteen, he would regard himself, moved on to the house of the Brethren of the Common Life at Bois-le-duc, 'sHertogenbosch. There he fretted and found little scope for his abilities and inclinations. Pressed by relations, anxious for some settled stability, in 1487 he was admitted as a novice, and in 1488 became a full professed monk, an Augustinian Canon Regular, at the monastery of Steyn. It was a critical decision and it influenced much of his life through his later attempts to evade or wriggle out of his vows. The books were few, the services long, monastic routine was boring, the food was not properly cooked, there was no one of his own intellectual calibre in the society. He had no real vocation. If he had remained at Steyn the northern Renaissance would have been both delayed and different. It did mean, however, that when at long last he managed to study at the University of Paris he was an older monastic student, cynical and disappointed. He had also learnt that the Regulars were the avowed opponents of 'good letters' and it was to the production of aids to classical Latin style that he was to devote his early attention.

The 'Adagia' and World Renown

This he did the moment he was able to exchange the cloister for the study. In 1493 he had become secretary to the Bishop of Cambrai, was drafting letters which would go out in the Bishop's name, and engaged upon an abstract defence of the monastic life and an attack on the obscurantists, *Liber antibarbarorum*, which he circulated among friends in manuscript. It is a kind of dialogue in which the defence of classical learning against its narrow-minded and ignorant opponents is left to James Batt with a good deal of success. At about the same time the young Canon produced a summary or paraphrase of the *Elegantiae* of Lorenzo Valla which, again, was not published in book form until many years later when any printer was only too glad to produce a volume with Erasmus' name attached to it.

Such was, in a manner, the emergence of German humanism. With this, and with some Latin poems of youthful mediocrity also circulating among a few friends, Erasmus arrived at the Sorbonne in 1495. He was at once admitted to the society of the Masters of the University of Paris and proceeded to the degree of B.D. in 1498. This first sojourn beside the Seine gave Erasmus the fullest possible insight into the thought and expression of the theologians of the principal centre of learning in the civilized world. The 'Scotists' of the Collège de Montaigu ignored the ardent, argumentative pupil who retaliated by noting for future uncomplimentary use their methods, language, expressions and habits of thought.

He met Faustus Andrelinus and the historian Robert Gaguin, he attended the statutory lectures and disputations and he started to learn Greek. It was late in life if he was to become a Greek scholar of renown and to this he hardly attained. He was doing, however, what he could not have done east of the Rhine which is in itself a measure of the cultural insignificance of Germany at the end of the 15th century. Money was obtained by securing a tutorship to young William Blount, Lord Mountjoy, and by gifts wheedled by flattery out of the wealthy Anne of Veere. If he was to go further and synthesize for northern readers what had been achieved further south, if something could be distilled from the early editions of the Latin classical writers now available new from various presses, he might make his name more widely known.

f 7   This he did, partly by a visit to England where he received mild encouragement from More and Colet, but essentially by writing *Adagia*. This compilation which was to be enlarged again and again in the course of the hundred and more editions and issues through which it went, brought European renown almost immediately upon publication. It consisted of a kind of set of classical gems, a Dictionary of Proverbs and Quotations with a commentary, and was published by a German printer at Paris in 1500. Although Polydore Vergil had preceded him with the idea, Erasmus' collection was much larger and more useful. Recent years had indeed made texts more accessible, but few could collect, or even obtain access to, a large library. With a combination of immense industry, acute sensibility and an eye to utility and popularity, Erasmus enabled those who knew only school-boy Latin to quote from the best authors, to have model sentences which could be copied and adapted, and also to understand the allusions with which they were accompanied.

As in his later biblical annotations, Erasmus used the opportunity to bring gentle satire to bear on those who despised good classical prose, on those too for whom the traditional verbal disputations of the schools were the end of advanced study, and on the reactionary theologians, monks, mendicants and prelates. At the same time the compiler advocated sweetness and light; his pacificism was in the medieval tradition of St Bernard, deploring armed conflicts between Christians, urging a return to the simple precepts of the Gospels. But it was as a guide to good classical Latin prose that men bought it and it showed that the ideals of Locher, Celtis and Agricola had now reached a wider northern public.

England, Rome and Venice

p 261   In England he had made contact with the rising young lawyer,
(26)   Thomas More; with the wealthy and earnest exponent of preaching based on the text of the New Testament, John Colet; and
p 260   with Grocyn and Linacre, full of universal knowledge, including
(22, 23)   Greek acquired in Italy. Adroitly obtaining a glimpse of life at the English court, pleasing his hosts and patrons, on his return to Paris he plunged into intensive study of Greek. This was indispensable both for the proper knowledge of the New Testament, to which his thoughts were constantly returning, and for any adequate understanding of the Latin authors whom he would edit and expound.

Writers were not paid by royalties in the 16th century, and there was no law of copyright. To write a best seller did not bring any money of itself; reputation and the good-will of patrons might follow, but this was all. Money had to be begged if Greek texts were to be procured; Erasmus was the self-taught home student in Greek, but he soon realized that a visit to Italy was indispensable. The times were propitious for him. There could not be an effective expansion of Greek scholarship north of the Alps until books were available, and the mass production of these was beginning in 1500. A money-collecting and book-buying tour through the Netherlands in 1501 was accompanied by concentration upon Greek whenever opportunity allowed, followed by a longer stay in Louvain where he ignored suggestions that he should lecture regularly in the university there. In this way the northern Renaissance, beginning with humanism in Vienna, Erfurt and Heidelberg, had shifted its sights somewhat. As in England, it was the independent thinkers and writers rather than the university professors who carried forward the new fashion.

After little more than a year of Greek study, Erasmus was translating Greek authors, including some remarkably obscure ones, into Latin. Lucian suited his quiet mordant wit admirably, and he was to interest More, and many others, in the content, rather than the style, of the author. He and his disciples were, in fact, conscious that their Latin should be that of the Golden Age but there was no such conviction about Greek, no differentiation

Two doodles from a manuscript in Erasmus' hand—one an ironical self-portrait (right)—show a lighter side of the great humanist's character. (8)

between the style of Thucydides and the Hellenistic Greek of the New Testament. It was sufficient to have grasped the elements of the language. When the most suitable gift to the Archbishop of Canterbury seemed to be a translation of the *Hecuba* of Euripides into Latin verse, the donor was as much anxious to demonstrate his facile Latin style as to expound a difficult play.

One sign of the times came in 1504 with the appearance of *Enchiridion militis christiani*. Enchiridion was a Greek word for handbook or for dagger—very few can have known the meaning of this when the book came to the Dutch or Frankfurt bookfairs, but there was subtle flattery in the assumption that they did—the introduction of the knight suggested the fashionable bastard chivalry of the age of Louis XII. 'Christian' indicated that the contents were edifying. No one was disappointed. You learnt how to fight the spiritual battles of the Christian soldier, how to differentiate between faith and works, and why one should rely less upon the mechanical performance of fasts, ritual prayers or the intervention of the fashionable saints. Physical warfare must be eliminated, the true Christian fights for the welfare of the soul, rising above the temptations of the flesh. There is little that is humanist about it except the title, yet the same ideas would have been put very differently half a century earlier.

With popular books to his name, with some money and much commendation from England, Erasmus reached Italy in 1506. He was now forty, or nearly forty, years old. A generation previously, Agricola had found that in Italy alone were the men and the materials available for the humane studies: now, there was, in fact, little new that Erasmus was able to gain intellectually from his ultramontane expedition. A doctor's degree from the University of Turin, a useful dispensation, a visit to Rome and exploration of the libraries of Bologna, continuous reading, trips to Padua, Ferrara, Siena, Naples, some work at Venice for the supreme Renaissance printer, Aldus Manutius, filled nearly three years. While there was much in Rome to criticize or to satirize, and papal patronage was not forthcoming, Erasmus respected the city's reputation.

> Had I not torn myself from Rome, I could never have resolved to leave. There one enjoys sweet liberty, rich libraries, the charming friendship of writers and scholars, and the sight of antique monuments. I was honoured by the society of eminent prelates, so that I cannot conceive of a greater pleasure than to return to the city.

But he never did.

'The Philosophy of Christ'

By 1514, when Erasmus was back in Germany after a second, more lucrative, stay in England, with more steady work done in the rural retreat at Queens' College, Cambridge, than almost any- p 260 where else so far, he was now a world celebrity. Travelling up the (21) Rhine to Basle he was no longer a missionary of culture, he was the honoured embodiment of an incipient intellectual revolution. By now, too, he was an indefatigable correspondent with everyone who mattered, and with many who mattered only because they were rich or influential and could thus help the cause of letters, on both sides of the Alps. Many of his epistles were, after the habit of the age, carefully composed with a view to publication, but, partly because they have been so admirably edited, and are so informative, there is danger lest they overshadow other important aspects of Erasmus' work. He himself probably gave pre-eminence to his great folio editions of the Fathers, Jerome first of all, then Cyprian, Ambrose, Augustine, Origen and Chrysostom which were with him to the end of his life. They have long been superseded, and the study of patristics has ceased to be fashionable, but they illustrate the uses to which Erasmus put his knowledge of Greek, his time and energy.

Best known is *Novum instrumentum* (February 1516), the edition of the New Testament in Greek, extravagantly praised in its day and depreciated since. It had all the weaknesses of pioneer work and Erasmus was no minute Greek scholar: it was hurriedly printed and it contained many mistakes, yet it enormously influenced its age—neither Luther nor Zwingli would have taught as they did without it. It was based upon a comparison of such manuscripts as were available and it opened the way for modern exegesis. Erasmus himself perhaps rather spoilt matters by his explanations and paraphrases, for many knew his commentaries better than the text and opponents made much of their uncertain orthodoxy. In his preface Erasmus returns to the 'philosophy of Christ' as the supreme objective of scholarship. He defended the

p 264 (34)

vernacular versions of the Bible, and maintained that the Gospels should be accessible to all, men and women alike, so that 'the peasant might sing them at his plough, the weaver repeat them at the loom and the traveller find solace in them on his journeys'.

Without Froben's printing press at Basle the history of European scholarship would have been different. The Greek New Testament might have come from Aldus at Venice if Froben had not been available, and in any case the *Spanish Complutensian Polyglot Bible* was already in print although not on sale. Froben did

237 (3)

much for the humanists. The Renaissance printer had to be

181 (1)

scholar, manager and capitalist at the same time. Author and publisher were often present in person at the printing works and corrected the proofs as they came from the matrices, passing to an assistant, such as Pellican, in the background, the Hebrew in which he specialized. There was money to be made by successful publishing, editions were small and reprints were many, while printing, and even publishing, being regarded primarily as duplication, meant that anyone could print anything in any language. It says a good deal for German scholarship that Froben, and still more that Amerbach, could sell, and even make a profit on, the

p 125 (16)

ponderous learning of their great folios. Men gladly spent large sums to buy books for themselves. The minority who were literate could hardly resist the cultivation of style which was fashionable and the promise of salvation through knowledge of the Divine Word which none doubted. Private libraries were small, but they represented, as with Zwingli, real sacrifices by their owners.

'The Egg that Luther hatched'

f 9

On his way to Basle in 1514 Erasmus met Ulrich von Hutten, one of the impoverished nobles who had attached themselves to Albert of Brandenburg, Archbishop of Mainz. The two men felt at first the attraction of opposites—cleric and layman, bourgeois and aristocrat, delicate finicky scholar and rough adventurer, the best-seller who died in prosperity in his bed and the young knight-errant who perished in exile of disease and poverty before he was forty. Hutten was a celebrity almost *malgré lui*. Entirely German, as ready to live by rapine and violence as any robber noble of the Rhineland, he had shown a youthful devotion to 'poetry' which brought him the laurel crown in 1517, he admired Erasmus' early writings and he had supported Reuchlin with characteristic impetuosity, helping forward and contributing to *Epistolae obscuro-*

f 3

rum virorum.

This performance was ill taken by Erasmus who preferred the rapier to the bludgeon, but in 1520 he was still prepared to think of Hutten as a co-worker. By the end of this year, however, they had drifted apart. Hutten was the avowed friend and admirer of Luther whose writings were already the target of the theologians, especially of Louvain, and whose later excommunication was, for Erasmus, a serious matter. Besides, Hutten was also associated with Franz von Sickingen whom many regarded as a dangerous revolutionary. The gap between Hutten and Erasmus steadily widened: by 1522 they were not on speaking terms when Hutten

In contrast to Erasmus, Ulrich von Hutten, poet laureate, deeply committed himself to the issues of the day. Son of a knight, he supported von Sickingen's attempts to restore the power of the knightly order, and the anti-Roman, anticlerical prejudices of his class helped to make him a supporter of Luther. (9)

visited Basle. A controversy was soon in print, Hutten issuing an *Expostulation* and Erasmus answering with *Spongia, adversus aspergines Hutteni*, published by Froben in 1523. It was an effective counterblast, but by then the enemy, broken by disease, miscalculation and misfortune, had crept away to die, unobtrusively harboured by Zürich, on the little island of Ufenau.

Without the German Renaissance there would have been no Luther. The latter may have been, in Acton's phrase, a rude, angry and not very learned monk, but this was by Acton's standard of learning. Luther had been a good Latinist at Erfurt and he was not alien to the humane studies of his time. He never failed, for example, to uphold the cause of the expansion of education and the need for better schoolmasters. But he had been through an unforgettable religious experience and he had broken with the pope.

p 152 (8)
p 200 (13)
p 201 (16)

It would also be quite unhistorical to treat Erasmus as a humanist for whom religious issues were not to be pushed beyond academic differences of opinion in contrast to Luther, the fundamentalist who could interpret infallibly the revealed faith of the Gospels. In spite of differences they were at first much nearer than this. Both men had somewhat similar backgrounds of early study and Erasmus had shown his distaste for scholastic theology very clearly. The *Handbook of the Christian Knight*, the *Praise of Folly* and the anonymous *Julius Exclusus* had demonstrated the

p 197 (5, 6)

concern of the humanist for Church affairs while the *Colloquies* provided a mine of satire for those who would attack relics, indulgences, sporting monks, and idle, self-indulgent priests.

Erasmus had suffered at the hands of the schoolmen and pointed the way to an entirely different approach to Bible study and exposition. Luther welcomed Erasmus' edition of the New Testament and found support for his attitude to justification by faith and to free will. Yet all too soon Erasmus was to repudiate the doctrines of Wittenberg, re-assert his acceptance of transubstantiation and papal supremacy and, in the end, leave Basle when the Mass was abolished there.

Luther in his turn made it clear that he had the Gospel to preach and a new view of the Church to put forward and he soon lost patience with the aloof sage of Rotterdam who constantly preached moderation and would not break with Rome. It had been possible, if difficult, for the humanists and the traditionalists to live side by side, but when pope and emperor had decided against Luther, Erasmus, repudiating the suggestion that he 'had laid the egg that Luther hatched', set out his position in *De libero arbitrio* (1524) and *Hyperaspistes* (1526) and then returned to his beloved Fathers.

Having stated his religious position, Erasmus directed his attention to a characteristically Renaissance topic. This was how Latin should be spoken. There are still those alive who remember Latin being taught with the 'English' pronunciation and the difficulty with which a satisfactory compromise on this complicated matter was reached. Latin quantities were known to the Middle Ages and were explained by the grammarians: there was an ecclesiastical 'Italian' Latin which meant that clerics could understand its speech across the frontiers. But that something more was required was obvious and in 1528 *Dialogus de recte latini graecique sermonis pronuntiatione* started a flood of pamphlet-arguments which went on until well into the next century. The content is unimportant: what is notable is that the issue had now advanced a stage forward and that what before Erasmus' day would have interested a few

The legend on the map reads:

1 Archbishopric of Mainz
2 Palatinate of the Rhine
3 Archbishopric of Trier

- - - - Boundary of The Holy Roman Empire
⌐⌐ Imperial Cities
▨ Hapsburg possessions
▤ Lands of the 7 Electors of The Empire

The Empire in 1519 was a loose confederation of many states. On this map only the most important territories and the chief of the Imperial free cities (subject only to the emperor) have been shown. Since 1485 Saxony had been divided into Electoral and Ducal Saxony (the former is shaded).

The signatories of the Confession of Augsburg 1530 (see p. 201), were the princes of Saxony, Brandenburg, Hesse, Brunswick-Lüneberg, Anhalt, and the representatives of Nuremberg, Reutlingen, Windsheim, Kempten, Weissenburg and Heilbronn. (10)

Italians only was now a topic for discussion among the scholars of Europe. Therein lies some part of the achievement of the northern Renaissance.

Similarly, while abused on all sides, and in poor health, still busy with the Fathers, in 1528 Erasmus produced *Ciceronianus* wherein he demonstrated that his gifts for satire were undiminished. The issue was not entirely simple: Erasmian Latin could easily degenerate into a sub-language, but the exclusive imitation of Cicero only, which Scaliger defended, markedly limited the study of a language which had been a living and developing one.

Zwingli and Protestant Humanism

Among the students at the University of Basle who admired Erasmus and, in his earlier phase, all that Erasmus stood for, was Ulrich Zwingli (1484–1531). If Zwingli had died at the age of thirty he would have been known only as a minor figure in the history of German scholarship. At Vienna he had sympathized with the young men to whom Celtis appealed: at Basle he had been impatient with both 'ways' of scholastic philosophy and had shown a nice capacity for Latin prose. A musician and a linguist, he was ordained and became a kind of papal chaplain in order to obtain money for books, corresponding eagerly with Crotus Rubianus, Hedio, Beatus Rhenanus, Pellican, Glarean and Myconius, and being accepted as a prominent exponent of the new ideas in south Germany.

With his belligerent parishioners from Glarus he visited Italy, where he had friends at the Papal Curia: as soon as he was free to resume his studies he was making himself as good a Greek scholar as Erasmus and a better Hebraist. That this could be done at all from a small Swiss town is an eloquent tribute to the reality of a German Renaissance. In the mid-15th century this would have been impossible, for the vocabularies, grammars and texts did not then exist in print, whereas by 1510 Zwingli could apply his papal pension to the purchase of books and his training at Basle University to understanding them. The range of his classical reading is wide—Vergil, Cicero, Ovid, Livy, Juvenal, Pliny, Valerius Maximus as well as Homer, Euripides, Demosthenes, Aristotle, Plato and Lucian. Perhaps the most remarkable tribute to his humanist attainment was the preface that he wrote to a selection from the poems of Pindar, commending them because they helped towards an understanding of the Psalms, but demonstrating thereby his close knowledge of one of the more difficult of the Greek authors. Even more than with Luther his early humanist training was to be of value for biblical studies and for rapid controversy in fluent Latin. He was anxious for wider facilities for learning Greek, not so much out of special respect for the unique contribution of the ancient Greeks to civilization, as because without it the full meaning of the New Testament could not be apparent. In one particular he went further than, for good reasons, most of his contemporaries dared to go—he maintained the possibility, at any rate, that some pagans living before the Christian revelation might hope for salvation because, by the goodness of their lives, they might hope to benefit retrospectively by the merits of Christ.

From Zürich he was able to do something for humane studies in his own land, especially in Berne where Wöllflin had been his early teacher; in Lucerne where he constantly encouraged Myconius whom he later brought back to Zürich to teach Greek; in St Gallen where the polymath Vadian was his peer as a scholar, and, by a kind of cross-fertilization, in Basle, which he knew to be a constant and valued source of inspiration to him. Had his political schemes for a great Swiss-South-German Protestant Confederation come to pass, it is manifest, from the reforms that he introduced into the school set up in connection with the Grossmünster, that education would have received marked encouragement there.

Italian Models in Architecture

The Germany of Maximilian, Charles V and Ferdinand I was, in the main, a poverty-stricken country knowing a great deal of civil war, in constant danger from the Ottoman Turks, split in two by the Lutheran Reformation. Imaginative experiment in the fine arts, such as Italy had long conducted, was not likely to flourish in such conditions; so far as buildings were concerned, there was little scope for the architects, patrons were few and not much attracted to the great domed churches and palaces of Italy. Slowly, and a little reluctantly, French Gothic had come to be accepted as the conventional style if a new church was required and such little major building as went on was often for churches. Occasionally, as at Heilbronn, a distinctly Italian innovation might be introduced, but this was rare. The new influences are apparent either in the decoration of the interiors or in the enlarged Rathaus or in the town houses of wealthy merchants. Not until the very end of the 16th century, as at Salzburg, were great princes able or interested to make their castles into residential palaces, many of which suffered during the Thirty Years' War.

It was at Nuremberg and Augsburg, where there was safety and capital, that something was tried, but neither the Tucherhaus nor the Fuggerhaus was striking for plan or design. It was only at Prague in Bohemia, where there was space and encouragement, that an Italian architect was able to find employment on the Imperial Palace (and later on the Wallenstein palace) and these late buildings had little influence elsewhere.

On the Rhine, almost in the shadow of the unfinished Cathedral, the City Council of Cologne rebuilt its headquarters in almost the Venetian manner in 1570, complete with loggia and colonnades. What is, however, commonly thought of as Renaissance building in Germany is the gabled hall proceeding by rectangular steps to a centre point, the high, steep-pitched roof being broken by a series of dormer windows. Apart from the considerable number of these, as at Brunswick and Rothenburg, it is in gateways, porches and decoration that Italian models were sometimes deliberately and consciously copied. The Fürstenhof palace at Weimar, Schloss Schobber (Hameln), Schloss Leitzau, Schloss Ambras are (or were) examples of buildings that would not have been out of place in Rome or Florence, but this sparseness, compared, for example, with the great outburst of Renaissance château-building in the France of François Ier is revealing.

French influence is apparent in Heidelberg where the Elector Palatine Otto Henry (father of the 'Winter King' of Bohemia) was responsible for the older parts of the castle with staircase, caryatids, pilasters, statues and window-frames which are as agreeable examples of their type as can be found anywhere north of the Alps. The continuation of his work by Frederick (1601–7) shows what more might have come but for the wars. It all, however, merged strangely rapidly and easily into the Baroque of which Munich was a leading example, but so soon as a building can be confidently labelled 'Baroque', Renaissance, used adjectivally, ceases to be applicable.

Even in the Netherlands, more exposed to French influence, much the same story is true. It was still Gothic that inspired, and Bruges remained a Gothic city in the 16th century. At most, generally speaking, it was in ornamentation, the use of the column at Liège, or a classical gateway at Breda and some other buildings like Granvella's palace at Brussels (known only by descriptions and imperfect engravings), that distinctively Renaissance tendencies were apparent. Sometimes buildings, like the

196 (2)
p 206
(23)

p 301
(64)

f 11

176–7
p 205
(21)

In 1570 a new porch was added to the old town-hall of Cologne. It is typical of German 16th-century architecture in combining a somewhat florid Renaissance style with such traditional features as a steep-pitched roof with dormer-windows and (on the upper story) pointed arches. (11)

Cloth Hall at Ypres, have been reconstructed, but it was not until the 17th century that much was done and then not in any characteristically Renaissance way.

The achievements of the major German painters and sculptors of this period—Dürer, Riemenschneider, Vischer, Viet Stoss, Cranach and Grünewald—are discussed at length in Chapter X. Their significance is far greater than that of the architects, and the style which evolved was a unique combination of Italian influence and Gothic tradition, a true union of north and south, although the emphasis varies in each individual case.

Scientific Advance

There is now no danger that the German contribution to scientific knowledge may be overlooked. None the less, to have produced great mathematicians and geographers in a somewhat hostile climate was something of an achievement. The age, fortunately, did not think of the arts and sciences as separate departments of knowledge or as comprehensible only to the specialist. On the contrary, in Germany even more than in Italy, the whole range of human knowledge was thought to lie within the compass of the individual. The seven liberal arts included arithmetic, geometry and astronomy and these, conventionally, were studied by all. In every country physicians (for surgery, like carpentry, was a matter of manual dexterity only) were also often humanists, good Latin scholars, cultivating words and style, corresponding on equal terms with Erasmus and Budé. Linacre, whose medical knowledge was admirable, had his counterparts on the Continent, particularly in Vadian, city doctor of his native St Gallen, yet more devoted to the New Learning than most academics.

For the most part, in the realms of physics and the mathematical sciences men were content to expound, but with ever-growing qualifications, the Aristotelian teaching: Jodocus Trutfetter (1460–1519) of Erfurt and Wittenberg, wrote at length on physics, but there is not the slightest evidence that he ever conducted an experiment. The neo-Platonists were fascinated by the study of numbers and joined forces with the astrologers whose studies were to lead to a revolution in thought, little though most of them, casting horoscopes and expounding the nature, paths and supposed influence of the planets, realized it or contributed to it.

Copernicus (1473–1543) was no German (he was born at Thorn in Poland), but some part of the way that he was to open up was explored by Peuerbach and Regiomontanus. All of these worked by direct observation within the currently accepted theories and not one was quite happy with his result. From Königsberg (in Franconia, not the better-known Baltic birthplace

p 196 (3)
p 204
(18)

p 207
(26-28)

p 132
(35)

p 179
(44)

p 208
(29)

p 207
(27)

of Kant) came the penetrating thinker, Johann Müller (1436–76), Regiomontanus, philologist as well as experimental scientist, mathematician, astronomer and instrument-maker. He advocated the need for accurate chronology and thus contributed to the movement towards the 'New Style' of dating. His work was linked with the new calendars, *Ephemerides*, such as the examples edited by Johann Stoffler which in turn encouraged the map-makers, geographers and explorers. Georg von Peuerbach of Vienna (1523–61), who taught Regiomontanus, has been called, extravagantly, the father of modern trigonometry: his *Theorice nove planetarum* was reprinted many times and his tables of eclipses were much consulted. Regiomontanus accompanied Bessarion to Italy and Hungary and settled finally in Nuremberg. There he

p 207
(26)

was in contact with the wealthy and well-born Martin Behaim (1459–1507) whose maps and globes, well known in Portugal, not only advanced geography but may have influenced, indirectly, Columbus and Magellan. The German Renaissance was not specially, still less specifically, 'scientific', a concept then unknown, but its contribution to the advancement of the study of the natural sciences was far from entirely negative.

p 206
(23)
p 206
(22)

Two Swiss-Germans illustrate all this admirably. Joachim von Watt of St Gallen (1484–1551), known as Vadian, was doctor of medicine like his friends Cuspinian and Collimitius and the incomparable Theophrastus Paracelsus von Hohenheim (called, with, reason, Bombastus, 1493–1541). His voluminous writings were, however, mainly on poetry, history and geography, that widely-embracing subject. Nature, he thought, should be studied in all its works and expounded in elegant Latin by those whose studies included the meaning of words and the elements, at least, of philology. After studying and lecturing at Vienna, the young humanist, knowing little Greek but with a number of hastily published Latin works to his name, returned to St Gallen in 1517 to act as city medical officer and advise about the plague, to become actively involved in politics as Bürgermeister and thus in religious controversy. He was the friend and supporter of Zwingli and carried through the Reform of his native city. It is in the combination of stylist, *poeta laureatus*, medical practitioner, active politician and serious religious thinker that Vadian exemplifies the transition from Renaissance to Reformation in Germany through which he lived, hardly conscious of its implications.

P 339 (7)
p 331
(31)

Conrad Gesner (1516–65) is in the same tradition. Succeeding with difficulty in reaching a university, he graduated at Basle in medicine, practised, and helped to make gynaecology scientific and respectable. He compiled a renowned *Bibliotheca universalis*, a critical bibliography which has earned him the title of 'father' of that subject, and he became known as the 'Pliny of his age' on account of his *Historia animalium* and, more valuable, the first modern scientific treatise on botany, *Historia plantarum*, which helped to inspire Linnaeus.

The name of Agricola is inseparably and rightly associated with the German Renaissance. But there were two men who adopted this name, Rudolf Agricola (1442–85) whom Erasmus knew, and the much younger and unrelated George Agricola (1494–1555) who moved from the study of Latin letters, philology and Roman history to natural science, particularly to acute observations in geology and mineralogy. He was the first to issue a systematic descriptive catalogue of the various rocks and minerals grouped by their qualities and he is also acclaimed as the first scientific metallurgist. His *De re metallica* (1530) is best known, together with *De ortu et causis subterraneorum* (1546) and *De natura fossilium* (1546). The most profitable strata that he wished to study lay in the Protestant states but he himself was a Catholic and thus found many impediments to research in the field. With him and his associates the Renaissance ideal of universal knowledge merges into the specialized achievements of the 17th century.

Renaissance and Reformation

The impact of the Renaissance on the study of law in Germany was of considerable importance. The generation of Maximilian was also that of the 'Reception' of the Roman law—the imperial Court of Appeal (Reichskammergericht) accepted the Code of

Justinian and Roman procedure as applying to the Empire with consequences that were of far-reaching significance. The progress of absolutism among the German Princes was greatly enhanced. In general, the German humanist tended to regard the civil lawyers as stupid, backward, prejudiced and ignorant; the Glossators and Post-Glossators had often written execrable Latin. Law, however, could not be shrugged off. Cicero had been at home in the courts and the 16th century could not overlook jurisprudence. Law was actively studied at those universities into which the humane letters were infiltrating. Reuchlin himself was no mean lawyer. At least one professor was able to meet the humanists on their own ground. Ulrich Zasius (1461–1535) demonstrated that the Roman law could be expounded in gracious and eloquent Latin and that its principles and abstractions were worthy of close study. He argued convincingly that it made for moderation and equity. Further, he investigated, and thus seriously corrected and improved, the accepted text of the *Corpus juris civilis* and his lectures at the University of Freiburg attracted large numbers. A convinced Catholic, he had none the less many Protestant friends in the Upper Rhineland and it was largely owing to his influence that, on the Continent, law and the New Learning became reconciled in the mid-16th century.

The German Reformers, Luther, Melanchthon, Zwingli and Bucer, were concerned with the state of the Church and the path to eternal salvation, with the Sacraments, clerical marriage, the use of images, the claims of the pope and the interpretation of the Word. Of them Zwingli approached nearest to Erasmus in training, interests and early outlook: indeed in 1515 Erasmus, More and Zwingli could have conferred together on common ground. The fluent Latinity of the Reformation controversialists made for active exchange of views, if not for conviction, and was linked in the popular mind with the New Learning. It is easy to show how the Reformation diverted the course of the Renaissance in Germany, how men turned back to theology and even to a 'Protestant scholasticism' because of the overwhelming force of the conflicts between the churches. There was, in fact, no looking back and no wish to revert to any pre-Erasmian world of thought and scholarship. Religion and politics were notoriously intertwined and so, equally, were religion and letters. Men thought in theological terms and the Reformers constantly preached that faith and belief mattered more than knowledge—and they had the New Testament on their side. When the Latin classical authors had become more widely known there were naturally those who perceived that some were solvents of simple faith and others merely hedonist and ill-suited to young minds. The cult of Lactantius as 'the Christian Cicero' is significant but the Rubicon had, in fact, been crossed. The German and Dutch Reformed divines of the later 16th century wrote far purer Latin than had Thomas à Kempis or Gabriel Biel. Controversy continued as violently as ever, but more and more the words and sentences used would have been intelligible to Livy or Tacitus.

The schoolmasters of Geneva were required first to be properly grounded in the Calvinist creed, but they had also to teach their pupils good Latin. Moreover, the attachment of the Reformers to the Bible-text helped to save the study of Greek. More and more it was apparent that every clergyman—and there were many of them in an age when every one went to church—should be able to read the Greek Testament in the original, and the implications of this are obvious.

For central Europe the age of the Renaissance merged into that of the Reformation. It did not 'begin' with imitation of the Italians and it certainly did not 'end' with Wittenberg. Side by side with Luther was the scholarly Melanchthon, and the German presses continued to print classical texts and treatises on the history, government, coinage, monuments and natural science of the ancient world.

With the advance of the Ottoman Turk central Europe had to be at one and the same time the bulwark of Christianity and of the culture of the age. 'Renaissance' and 'Reformation' are labels applied for convenience to the years when the West re-shaped itself into the community of sovereign independent states which owes much to both.

VIII AN AGE OF GOLD

Expansion and scholarship in Spain

A. A. PARKER

'Now there has returned to Spain the glory that in times past
has lain asleep; those who have written in praise of Spain say that
when other nations sent tribute to Rome, Spain sent
emperors . . . and now the empire has come for its Emperor to
Spain, and our King of Spain, by the grace of God, has
become . . . Emperor of the World'.

PRESIDENT OF THE CORTES OF SANTIAGO, 1520

The long crusade

that had been Spain's history during the whole of the Middle
Ages ended in 1492 when the 'Catholic Kings', Ferdinand and
Isabella, rode into conquered Granada. The Moors had ruled in
the southern part of the peninsula since the 8th century. Their
culture and ways of thought had taken deep root, and as the
Christian rulers of Aragon and Castile had gradually pushed the
frontier further and further south they found themselves governing subjects who were more mixed in race, religion and social
customs than any others in western Europe. Spain was a country
where the forces of disunity were stronger even than in Germany;
yet she became a united and powerful state and for the next
century dominated not only Europe but the whole world. How
did she do it?

First by political union, through the marriage of Ferdinand of
Aragon with Isabella of Castile. Although constituting in reality
several distinct states governed by a cumbersome system of diverse
administrations, the nation could be treated as a single unit.
Second by the ruthless imposition of a state-controlled religion,
the suffering involved by this being the counterpart in a politically peaceful country of the ravages caused elsewhere, for much
longer, by the Wars of Religion. Third by the gold of America.

The greatness of 16th-century Spain is thus causally independent of the Renaissance, but the civilization which it produced was
to be a Renaissance civilization. The Aragonese royal house ruled
in Sardinia and Sicily and after 1443 in Naples. The Spanish
College of San Clemente, in the University of Bologna, founded in
1365, gave Spaniards another contact with Italian humanism. And

throughout the 16th century there was scarcely a Spaniard of
renown in scholarship and letters who did not visit Italy. Spain
welcomed the humanist innovations, translated the classics, transformed her art and expanded her education earlier than France,
England or Germany.

Scholarship, however, like everything else in Spain, had to be
subservient to the church. There was no room for dissent or for
the liberal semi-paganism of the Italian courts. University patronage was for the most part ecclesiastical, and although the results
achieved were often spectacular (for instance the Polyglot Bible of
Alcalá), it is impossible to separate them from the demands of
religious orthodoxy. The Inquisition, an institution peculiar to
Spain in the form given to it by Ferdinand and Isabella, that of a
Council of State, was founded to make that orthodoxy universal
and permanent. And the weapon, forged at home, was transferred
to Spain's new empire in the New World.

This coloured relief by Felipe Bigarny de Borgoña (i. e. of
Burgundy) is part of the predella of the altar in the Chapel Royal
of Granada (about 1521). Beside King Ferdinand and Queen
Isabella as they enter the Moorish city rides, fittingly, the great
Archbishop of Toledo and Primate of Spain, Cardinal Francisco
Jiménez de Cisneros. Cisneros was not actually present on this
occasion (though his predecessor Cardinal Mendoza was); the
portrait here is a compliment to him as the man who had commissioned the altar and had presided over the destinies of Spain
between the death of Ferdinand in January 1516 and Charles'
arrival in Spain in the autumn of the following year. (1)

The moral dilemma facing Spain as the great imperialist power of the Renaissance was an agonizing one. It has been customary to think of the Conquistadors as ruthless exploiters of the native population and of the government at home as the official instigators of this policy, but the truth is much less crude. The government never instigated or approved such actions. In Spain the whole question of the rights of the Indians was passionately debated, while in America the Church (though implacably hostile to the indigenous pagan religions) tried hard to exercise a paternal guardianship over its new converts. The first group of Dominicans arrived in Hispaniola in 1510. Above left: Fray Domingo de Santa María, Vicar of Tepozcolula in Mexico, a famous teacher who gave most of his life to the cause of the natives. He is seen here (in a surprisingly realistic portrait) with two of his flock. The place-name is given in Aztec hieroglyphs at the bottom, the names of the two Indians above their heads. They wear an adaptation of European dress. (2)

'The deeds of the Castilians' in the discovery of the New World, related by Antonio de Herrera in 1601 (right). The roundel portraits of the title-page show Ferdinand, Isabella, Christopher Columbus and his brother Bartholomew, and the pictures tell the story of Columbus' voyages. At the top he leaves the port of Palos and arrives at Hispaniola; on the left he builds the fort of Navidad, on his return finding it burnt and the inhabitants murdered; on the right, a battle against the natives who seek to pull down the Cross; at the bottom, he discovers Trinidad and the mainland of South America. (5)

The catechism in Aztec: part of a manual (above left) used by the friars in teaching their Indian parishioners. The signs represent the fundamental doctrines of the faith in hieroglyphic form.

Left: Don Juan López de Zárate Bishop of Oaxaca, here instructing Indians in Christian doctrine. The well-dressed man facing him is Don Domingo, Señor of Yanhuitlán, an Indian put in a position of authority by the Spaniards. Bishop López is known to have visited Yanhuitlán in 1541 to baptize and confirm Domingo and this scene may well refer to the event. He is explaining the meaning of the rosary, which he holds in his hand; behind him stands an interpreter, and from the way they are all holding up one finger the subject seems to be the 'one' God of Christianity. (3, 4)

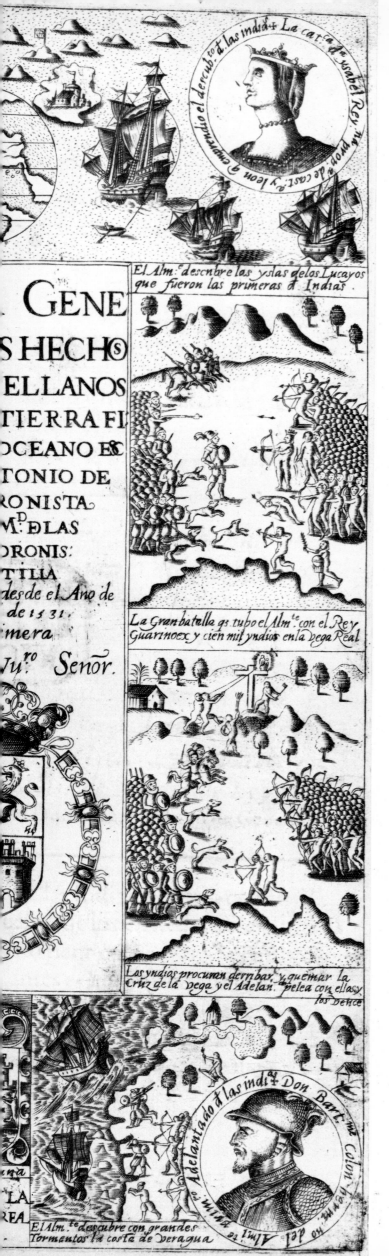

El Alm.ᵉ descubre las yslas delos Lucayos que fueron las primeras d'Indias.

GENE s HECHo ELLANOS TIERRA FI OCEANO ES TONIO DE RONISTA M: DLAS DRONIS: TILIA des el Año de de 1531. mera ᵗᵒ Señor.

La Gran batalla q's tubo el Alm.ᵗᵉ con el Rey Guarinoex y cien mil yndios enla vega Real.

Las yndias procuran derribar y quemar la Cruz de la vega y el Adelan. pelea con ellas y los peñe.

El Alm.ᵗᵉ descubre con grandes Tormentos la costa de Veragua

The case for imperialism was put by Juan Ginés de Sepúlveda (right). In a treatise circulated in 1547 with the encouragement of some members of the Council of the Indies, he argued that some races were by nature inferior and destined to be the slaves of others. Sepúlveda was a classical scholar; one of the authorities whom he quoted was Aristotle. For him it was lawful to subdue uncivilized nations and subject them to the rule of the more civilized.

The opposite principle, that 'Spanish rule should be exercised in the interests of the Indians and not merely for the profit of the Spaniards' was held by Queen Isabella and officially by the Catholic Church (Pope Paul III condemned the enslavement of the Indians in 1537). Its two greatest spokesmen were Francisco de Vitoria, a Dominican professor of theology at Salamanca, and another Dominican, Bartolomé de las Casas, who became Bishop of Chiapas in Guatemala. Las Casas laboured for fifty years, crossing the Atlantic many times, writing, preaching, rousing public opinion and pleading with the governors to enforce the humane laws that had been passed at home. The controversy between Las Casas and Sepúlveda reached the stage of a full debate before a special council of theologians and state officials, held at Valladolid during 1550 and 1551. The ultimate decision has not been recorded, but Sepúlveda's book was not allowed to be published and Las Casas continued his propagandist activity. It is interesting to note that in this quarrel the side of intolerance was taken by the humanist and that of enlightenment by the friar. (6)

Gold was the lure that drew colonists to Mexico and Peru, and whatever the missionaries and their sympathizers could do, the native peoples were forcibly organized to provide labour. Slaves were allocated to the colonists by a system called *encomienda*. When they died, more were provided. The Government at home sided with the missionaries and made several attempts to abolish or modify the *encomienda* system, but it was always up against an insoluble problem: the incapacity of the primitive Indian to live, in freedom, a civilized life.

Right: two drawings, from the same source as those shown opposite, the Codex Yanhuitlán, showing an Indian panning for gold and giving the result to his Spanish master. (7, 8)

Three races

and three religions made up Spanish society and culture at the end of the 15th century: Christians, Muslims and Jews. The government of Ferdinand and Isabella determined upon religious conformity as a means of uniting all three, and the Inquisition founded in 1478 was their instrument. Though administered by churchmen, its primary purpose was political. Jews were forbidden to practice their religion as early as 1492. Those who refused baptism were expelled. Large numbers were nominally converted, while trying to preserve their own faith in secret. But, being 'Christians' they were now subject to prosecution for heresy.

The Moors had been promised freedom of religion before the surrender of Granada, a promise broken within ten years. In 1502 they were compelled to renounce their faith or be exiled in poverty to North Africa. This relief (right), also from the altar of the Chapel Royal of Granada, shows the baptism of Moorish women. (9)

The Christians enjoyed hardly more freedom. Any questioning of the Church's doctrine or authority might be an offence. Offences ranged from the slight to the serious and serious heresy, if not abjured, was punishable by death. Trials were in secret, but executions and the imposition of lesser penalties were public. This painting by Pedro Berruguete (far right) represents a medieval scene— the Inquisition, with St Dominic presiding, persecuting the Albigensian heretics in France—but it belongs to the period of the Renaissance and depicts the customs and procedures of that time. (10)

227

The many faces of Spain are nowhere more apparent than in her architecture. In this chapter we shall concentrate on the assimilation of Renaissance ideas from Italy, but these had to contend with other living traditions. Gothic was by no means exhausted. The Cathedral of Segovia was not begun until 1525 and only finished in 1616. Late Spanish Gothic, probably as a result of Moorish contacts, was characterised by a frantic profusion of ornament, and exactly the same trait is the keynote of the early Spanish Renaissance—the Plateresque style, which leads into the Baroque. The sober classical Renaissance on the Italian model, however, also continued well into the 17th century.

One of the earliest examples is the Palace of Charles V at Granada. Its architect, Pedro Machuca, was also a painter and possibly a pupil of Raphael. Begun in 1527 and never finished, its circular courtyard (above left) of Doric and Ionic columns is as pure as anything in Italy.

Above right: the Plateresque style —the west front of Sta Maria la Grande at Pontevedra (1541). The façade of Salamanca University (pl. 29) is another instance in which Gothic analogues are even more evident. (11, 12)

First of the non-Gothic cathedrals was that of Granada by Diego de Siloé. He adapted an earlier design by transforming the piers into Corinthian columns and turning the choir into a huge centralized space covered by a dome. This photograph (above left) shows the view from the ambulatory through the massive supports of the dome into the choir.

Above right: Jaén, the finest of Spanish Renaissance cathedrals. The plans were drawn up in 1534 by Andrés de Vandaelvira, though it took nearly 200 years to carry them out. Jaén is a hall-church with central dome carried on remarkably slender piers. (14, 15)

'Do not forget what I have told you', wrote Philip II to his architect Juan de Herrera: 'simplicity of form, severity in the whole, nobility without arrogance, majesty without ostentation'. The recipe is splendidly fulfilled in the Escorial (left), begun in 1563 by Juan Bautista de Toledo but completed by Herrera between 1567 and 1584. Combining palace, college, monastery and cathedral, it was praised by a contemporary for 'the manner in which it follows the rules and orders of Vitruvius, abandoning as vanities the pretty projections, reversed pyramids, brackets and other foolish things'. (13)

229

The response to Italy came with equal sureness in the arts of painting and sculpture, though the influence of the Netherlands and Burgundy was still strong. Right: St Matthew, by Felipe Bigarny, from the same altar as that illustrated in pl. 1 and 9. It shows that Bigarny had taken careful note of Michelangelo's prophets in the Sistine Chapel. St Matthew, resting his book on his right knee, turns to dip his pen in an inkwell held by an angel. Far right: the tomb of Bishop Alfonso Madrigal, 'el Tostado' (1518) by Vasco de la Zarza. Zarza worked in both Gothic and Renaissance idioms, this work being his purest essay in the latter; his training had been in Lombardy. The overcrowded decoration, typical of the Plateresque style, includes representations of the journey and adoration of the Magi, as well as many north Italian ornamental motifs. 'El Tostado' himself, who sits reading in the centre, had died more than sixty years earlier in 1455. He was Grand Chancellor of Castile, Bishop of Avila and one of the most learned theologians of his time, who also, incidentally, adapted into Castilian the *Medea* of Seneca. (16, 18)

The humanist Crusader: Martín Vázquez de Arce had died in 1486 in the war against the Moors of Granada. On his tomb in Sigüenza Cathedral (below) he is shown as a young warrior, but sitting up reading—an attitude which was to become typical of Renaissance tomb sculpture. (17)

The change to Mannerism appears in the work of Pedro Berruguete's son Alonso, who studied in Florence and Rome in the early part of the 16th century. *Elijah* at Toledo (above) has a new sense of dynamic movement. Berruguete's younger contemporary, Juan de Juní, went further in the direction of drama and pathos. His *Entombment* (detail below) at Segovia (1571) points forward to the extravagant emotionalism and passion of Spanish Baroque. (19, 20)

'The uprooting of barbarity from Spain' meant—for the great classical scholar Elio Antonio de Nebrija—raising the standard of Latin to Augustan purity. This miniature (left) from his *Institutiones Latinae* shows him in the centre delivering a lecture in the house of his patron Don Juan de Zúñiga, who sits on the left. Nebrija, who held posts at Salamanca and Alcalá universities, was also the author of the first Spanish grammar, thus giving Spanish something of the status of a classical language. (21)

Socrates drinks the hemlock, from the first Spanish translation of Plato's *Phaedo*, made in the mid 15th century for the Marquis of Santillana. The translation, by his chaplain Pedro Díaz, was made from Leonardo Bruni's Latin version, not the original Greek. Santillana, one of the earliest patrons of the New Learning in Spain, classified literature into 'sublime', 'mediocre' and 'low'; he confined the first category to Greek and Latin works. (22)

New universities sprang up under the patronage of the Church, usually with the specific purpose of training an educated and reformed clergy. The first of them was the College of Santa Cruz at Valladolid, founded by Cardinal Mendoza (left), the son of the Marquis of Santillana. The building (1468–93) is an early instance of the Renaissance style—the express choice of Mendoza. His successor, Cardinal Cisneros (right), though not himself a scholar, was intensely conscious of the need for better education. His foundation of the University of Alcalá in 1486 was the most ambitious step so far taken in this direction. He tried to tempt Erasmus to lecture there, without success. The façade (far right) by Rodrigo Gil de Hontañón, dates from the 1540s and already shows many Mannerist features. (23, 24, 25, 28)

Luis de León (1527–91) an Augustinian friar who lectured in Scripture and theology at Salamanca, was the finest exponent of the Christian Platonism of the age. One of Spain's greatest poets, he was a humanist scholar of distinction who wrote in Spanish and not in Latin in order to make the fruits of his biblical scholarship accessible to the layman. (26)

Benito Arias Montano (1527–98) edited the work which made Cisneros' Polyglot Bible out of date within fifty years of its publication—the great Antwerp Polyglot of 1569–72. (27)

The ancient foundation of Salamanca (it began as a cathedral school in the 13th century) retained eminence and prestige despite the new foundation of Alcalá. It was the academic home of Nebrija, Arias Barbosa, Hernán Núñez, El Brocense, Vitoria, Luis de León and many other famous scholars. The principal façade (above), completed in 1529, displays at the bottom portraits of Ferdinand and Isabella; in the centre the arms and imperial eagles of Charles V; at the top the pope giving out privileges. (29)

Luis Vives (1492–1540), the greatest Spanish humanist, preferred to live out of Spain, possibly because he was of Jewish descent. He taught at Louvain, Oxford and Paris and wrote widely on philosophical, ethical and religions subjects. (30)

'**Such is the reward** of him who has served God and His saints' —words said to have been spoken by St Stephen and St Augustine when they assisted at the burial of Count Orgaz, here immortalized by El Greco. Gonzalo Ruiz de Toledo, Count of Orgaz and Chancellor of Castile, endowed several religious houses in or near his native city, including one dedicated to St Stephen and occupied by canons of the Order of St Augustine. He died in 1323 and was buried in the church of Sto Tomé, which he had rebuilt. During the ceremony, says the Chronicler, after the Office of the Dead had been sung, those present saw 'visibly and clearly, the glorious saints Stephen and Augustine descend from the heavens, their features and dress easily recognisable by everyone; going to where the body lay, they took it up and placed it in the tomb'. El Greco's painting, commissioned by the church of Sto Tomé in 1586, turns the scene into a mystical vision of earth and heaven, united in a Baroque composition of supreme eloquence. The heads are nearly all portraits of his contemporaries, the little boy in the foreground being the artist's son Jorge Manuel. (31)

Expansion and scholarship in Spain

A. A. PARKER

The arms of Isabella and Ferdinand, from a woodcut of 1498. The castle and lion are of Castile; the vertical strokes and the eagle, of Aragon; while the pomegranate stands for recently-won Granada. At the bottom the yoke and sheaf of arrows signify strength through unity. The motto 'Tanto Monta' means 'of equal importance' and is the beginning of a couplet affirming Isabella's equality with Ferdinand. (1)

IT WAS CUSTOMARY, not so long ago, to deny that the Renaissance bore fruit in Spain. This was in large part due to the simplification that opposed humanism to both the Middle Ages and the Counter-Reformation; but it was also due to the awareness that Spain was different from the rest of western Europe. Historically, the difference lies in the fact of the Moorish conquest, which meant that from 711 to 1492 parts of the Iberian Peninsula belonged to Islam and not to Christendom. Although from the middle of the 13th century Arab rule had been confined to the small Kingdom of Granada between Gibraltar and Cartagena, the presence of Islam was still strongly felt at the time of the Renaissance. There is indeed a tendency nowadays to explain all the differences between Spain and western Europe, in the present as well as the past, by the enduring effects of the Semitic element in her civilization. But while this influence certainly went deep, it is an exaggeration to imply that Spanish culture is basically non-European. Spain indeed had her own type of Renaissance, but its roots were still deep in Italy, not in Islam. The differences between Italy and Spain were, none the less, very great, though cultural and political contacts between them were close throughout the 15th and the 16th centuries. The Renaissance is the period in which Spain emerged as a united (though not a centralized) nation, in which her imperial expansion overseas began and in which imperial duties of another kind fell to her lot when her king was elected Holy Roman Emperor in 1519 as Charles V. Renaissance Spain was a 'world power'—the first of modern times—in a sense in which no other country then was.

The differences between Spain and western Europe are also geographical. One crosses the Pyrenees into the steppes of Aragon, or ascends the Cantabrian Mountains to the plateau of Castile, and one is virtually in another continent, in a land that is very unlike France and practically indistinguishable from Morocco. It is mostly an arid, hard, austere land. In such surroundings the art of the Renaissance is less elegant, less refined and sensuous than in Italy, but not on that account does it lack beauty.

The Bonds of Unity

The joint reign of Isabella I in Castile from 1474 and of her husband Ferdinand II (V of Castile) in Aragon from 1479 is a clear dividing line between medieval and modern Spain. Isabella died in 1504 and was succeeded nominally in Castile by her eldest daughter Joan the Mad, whose husband reigned as Philip I until his death in 1506. Ferdinand then became Regent of Castile and ruled both kingdoms until his own death in 1516. These forty-two years constitute really one reign, that of *los Reyes Católicos* (for which the mistranslation 'Catholic Kings' instead of 'Sovereigns' has become established in English). This reign saw the unification of Spain, first by the union of Castile and the realms of the Crown of Aragon through the marriage of the two sovereigns, then by the conquest in 1492 of the last Moorish kingdom of Granada, and finally by the conquest of Navarre in 1512. It saw also the discovery of America in 1492. Politically, socially, culturally this was a period of vitality and renewal. As anarchy gave way to discipline and as rebellious barons were brought to heel, the return of order was felt to be the fruit of the new national unity, and Spaniards were conscious of the dawn of a new age.

But unity was not just a question of bringing under a single rule different states with different traditions. Spain was more deeply disunited than that, for alone of European countries it was a land of three races and three religions. The Jews had prospered under the enlightened tolerance of the Spanish Arabs. As the Reconquest pushed the frontier southward and Jews and Muslims came under Christian rule, toleration and official protection became the policy of the Christian governments, for the conquered lands could not have been peacefully held under a policy of repression. Throughout the Middle Ages toleration between the three religions was thus traditional when they lived side by side. None the less, religion had been the only bond of unity that had ever existed between the different Christian kingdoms; they had been united in spirit only when fighting for the Cross against the Crescent. Religion was thus a logical basis for the new national spirit that was to keep Castile and Aragon united. To achieve religious unity the Catholic Kings decided to proscribe the two alien religions. In 1492 all Jews, and in 1502 all Muslims, who would not accept Christianity were banished from the Spanish kingdoms. Prior to this, in 1478, the Inquisition had been established to ensure that conversions from Judaism, of which there had already been many as a refuge from a growing anti-semitism, should not be merely nominal. The Spanish Inquisition was not an extension of the Holy Office (which had never existed in Castile) but a tribunal of a new type, an organ of the State, not of the Church. Established to prevent or extirpate heretical deviation from Catholic orthodoxy among professed Christians, the Inquisition became the instrument of a policy of enforced conformity through persecution that had never characterized Spain before her unification. The change of policy was dictated more by political than by religious motives. Religious uniformity seems to have been considered essential for cementing national unity by creating a homogeneous nation. In this respect it is significant that the Inquisition was the only instrument of government that broke down the regionalist barriers; the Council of State that ran it was the only one that functioned with uniformity in all the states that made up 'the Spains'; despite their diversity of parliaments and administrative systems, there was only one Inquisition.

Religious intolerance and persecution meant that an element of reaction offset the elements of enlightenment that were entering with the Renaissance. The deep roots of Mohammedanism and Judaism in Christian Spain created an extraordinarily complex social situation, precisely because the Renaissance gave energy and vitality to the creation and consolidation of a new nationality. No justice is done to Spain unless it is realized that the Inquisition represented, in effect, until towards the end of Charles V's reign, a policy of 'Europeanization'. By its very nature the Spanish Inquisition worked against humanity (and Spaniards were to be slow to see it), but it did not work against humanism.

p 226–7 (9, 10)

f 1

223 (1)

Classics in Castilian

Humanism, in the narrow sense of a revival of classical studies, is the main innovating feature in Spanish education during the reign of the Catholic Kings. But the influence of the classics does not begin then: there is a long period of preparation which makes it impossible, as far as Spanish literature is concerned, either in Castilian or Catalan, to separate a 'Renaissance' 16th century from a 'medieval' 15th. A marked and sudden change comes, if anything, a hundred years earlier. During the Middle Ages the outside influences that had helped to mould and guide the native traditions of Spanish culture had come from France and Arab Andalusia, the two cultures bordering on Spain to the north and south. With the coming of the 15th century these influences gave way to two others, that of Italy and, through Italy, that of the classics. Dante and Petrarch became the favourite reading of educated Spaniards, the latter especially among the Catalans. Dante's influence was felt as early as 1405 in Castile. His Christian philosophy and spirituality did not interest the poets of this century; what they took from him was an allegorical structure, that of a dream or vision whereby life past, present and even future could be surveyed as a whole. This they used as a device that enabled them to return to the world of classical antiquity and to visit the shades of Clytemnestra, Hero, Leander, Dido and others Classical literature opened its doors; that of Greece for the first time, though mostly at second hand through Latin versions. Translations were made of Thucydides, Homer, Livy, Seneca, and fragments of Plato. The first complete translation of the *Aeneid* into a modern language is the Castilian version (1427–28) of Enrique de Villena. Literature was classified by the Marquis of Santillana (1398–1458) into 'sublime', 'mediocre' and 'low': into the first category went only Latin and Greek. The result of these new

p 232
(22)

Antonio de Nebrija (1442–1522) was the first humanist scholar of international stature produced by Spain. His Latin Grammar became the standard text-book; the title-page shown here is from the edition of 1510. (2)

influences was that literature moved away from reality, in the sense of direct experience, into a world of abstractions or an idealized world of fancy. It also became secularized by very largely ignoring religion. These are tendencies that are to characterize the Renaissance period proper. Acquaintance with classical literature also meant the discovery of the power and majesty of language. Writers attempted to raise Castilian to a level of expressiveness as near to Latin as possible by latinizing Spanish in vocabulary and even in grammatical constructions, syntax and word order, thus beginning the process of enriching the language by learned borrowings which continued until well into the 17th century.

Though one ecclesiastic, Alfonso de Cartagena (1384–1456), Bishop of Burgos, deserves a place among these precursors of humanism as a translator and annotator of Seneca and Cicero, the movement was essentially lay. It marked the changes in the structure of society whereby the cultural predominance of the clergy declined. Feudal aristocrats were transformed from warriors into gentlemen of leisure, many of them collecting manuscripts, forming private libraries, and cultivating literature. The Marquis of Santillana, a poet of considerable distinction, is a striking example of this patronage of literary learning. The secularization of culture, which went hand in hand with the growth of interest in the classics, more as cause than effect, is the natural outcome of these changes.

'Language accompanies Empire'

This classical interest, though very real, cannot be called scholarly till the reign of the Catholic Kings. Queen Isabella's reputation as a patroness of learning attracted Italian humanists to Spain and one of them, Pietro Martire, to the court itself. The first great name in classical scholarship is that of Antonio de Nebrija (1442–1522), who held various chairs at Salamanca from 1476 to 1513, when he transferred to the Chair of Rhetoric at the new University of Alcalá. He envisaged his life's work as the 'uprooting of barbarity from Spain', by which he meant raising the knowledge and use of Latin to the level of classical purity. His Latin Grammar and Latin Dictionary became the standard tools. He was also the author of a Spanish Grammar—the first grammar of any European vernacular—which was presented to the Queen with the statement that 'language accompanies empire': Spanish was entitled to the dignity of a grammar since it was now to be carried overseas to people still barbarous and so attain, like Latin, to an imperial status. Arias Barbosa (d.1540), from his chair at Salamanca, did for Greek in Spain what Nebrija had done for Latin. The first Greek Grammar was published in 1538, seven others by different scholars were published at intervals up to 1600: contrary to what used to be believed there was no decline in the study of Greek during Philip II's reign. The greatest successors of Nebrija and Barbosa were Hernán Núñez de Guzmán (1475–1553) and Francisco Sánchez *el Brocense* (1523–1601). Both held chairs of Greek at Salamanca; both edited many Latin and Greek texts; the latter, in addition, was a literary theorist and critic, and also published many scholarly treatises such as *Minerva, sive de causis linguae latinae* (1587) which remained a standard work in Europe for two centuries, being constantly reprinted with new commentaries.

p 232
(21)
f 2

The great Maecenas of humanism during the reign of the Catholic Kings was the Archbishop of Toledo and Primate of Spain, Cardinal Francisco Jiménez (Ximenes) de Cisneros (1436–1517). He presents a striking contrast to the great prelates of the Italian Renaissance in that he was an observant Franciscan friar of humble origin until the Queen selected him for preferment, a man of saintly and austere character, and a practical reformer of ecclesiastical life. His first task on appointment to the primacy was to reform the indiscipline and laxity that was as rife in this sphere in Spain, especially among the religious orders, as it was elsewhere. Isabella had employed vigorous methods in stamping out social anarchy; Cisneros paralleled these in exercising his own jurisdiction. He conducted visitations of many of the great monasteries, expelling those inmates whose lives were a cause of scandal, imprisoning some and also punishing in other ways any laxity in observing the rules of religious life. It is recorded that some four hundred friars left for Morocco and embraced Mohammedanism rather than submit to this unwelcome discipline.

p 223 (1
p 232
(25)

Ἀποκάλψις.　　　　　Cαp.ϰϰιι.

ψῶμ'ἐρχέσθω∙ο'θέλω∙λαβέτω∙ὕδωρ'ζωῆς
'δωρεάν. μαρτυρῶ'ἐγὼ' παντὶ'ἀκούοντι
ι'Τους'λόγους'Τῆς'προφητείας'Τοῦ'Βιβλί
ου'Τούτου'ἐάν'Τις'ἐπιθῇ'ἐπ'αὐτὰ'ἐπιθήσαι'ἐπ
'αὐτὸν'ο'θεὸς'τὰς'ἐπτὰ'πληγὰς'τὰς'γεγραμ
μέρας'ἐμ'Τῳ'Βιβλίῳ'Τούτῳ∙καὶ'ἐὰμ'Τις'ἀφέ
λη'ἀπὸ'τῶμ'λόγωμ'τοῦ'Βιβλίου'τῆς'προ=
φητείας'ταύτης∙ἀφελοῖ'ο'θεὸς'το'μέρος'αυ
τοῦ'ἀπὸ'τοῦ'ξύλου'τῆς'ζωῆς∙καὶ'ἐκ'τῆς'πο
λεως'τῆς'ἁγίας'τωμ'γεγραμμένωμ'ἐμ'τω'Βι
βλίω'τούτω∙λέγει∙ο' μαρτυρῶμ'ταῦτα'ναι
'ἔρχομαι'ταχύ∙ἀμήμ∙ναι∙ἔρχου'κύριε'Ιη
σοῦ∙Η'χάρις'τοῦ'κυρίου'ιησοῦ'χριστοῦ'με
τα'πάντωμ'τωμ'ἁγίωμ∙ἀμήν.

Τέλος'Τῆς'ἀποκαλύψεως.

Θεογρατίας.

veniatɪτ'ꝗ'vult'accipiat'aquam'vite ∞
'gratis.'Contestoꝛ'enim'omni'audienti
'verba'prophetie' libri ∞∞∞∞∞∞∞∞∞
buiꝰ.'Si'ꝗs'appoſuerit'ad'bec'apponet
'deus'ſuper'illuꝰ'plagas'ſcriptas ∞∞∞∞
'in'libro'iſto.'Et'ſi' quis'diminuerit ∞∞
'de'verbis'libri'prophetie ∞∞∞∞∞∞∞∞
'buius:'auferet'deus'partes'eius ∞ ∞∞
'de'libro'vite' τ'de'ciuitate ∞∞∞∞∞∞∞∞
'ſcta et de bis'que'ſcripta' ſu'in'libro ∞∞
'iſto.'Dicit'ꝗ'teſtimoniū'pbibet'iſtoꝛ.'E
nā'venio' cito:'amē.'Veni'dñe'ieſu.
'Gratia'dñi'noſtri'ieſu'chꝛiſti'cuʒ ∞∞∞
'omnibus'vobis.' Amen.

Explicit liber' Apocalypſis.

Among the greatest monuments of humanist learning was the 'Compluten-sian Polyglot Bible' of Alcalá. Commissioned by Cardinal Cisneros it gave the text of the Pentateuch in Hebrew, Aramaic, Greek and Latin; the rest of the Old Testament in Hebrew, Greek and Latin; and the New Testament in Greek and Latin. This last page of the New Testament was printed in 1514. There followed another volume of vocabularies. (3)

Cisneros realized that such measures did not strike at the root of the trouble and that reform of religion had ultimately to flow from the reform of education. Thus, though not a scholar himself, he became the greatest single patron of the New Learning. In this respect he followed in the footsteps of his predecessor at Toledo, Cardinal Mendoza, who had founded in 1479 the College of Santa Cruz at Valladolid. This College is one of the earliest Renaissance buildings (1486–93) in Spain, the style in this case being imported from Italy by the architect Lorenzo Vázquez de Segovia. It was originally of Gothic design but when Mendoza visited the site he was so distressed at the building's lack of grandeur that it was re-designed and reconstructed. In recent years it has been restored to its original use as a residential college of the University. Cisneros, for his part, founded the University of Alcalá de Henares in 1498, which immediately surpassed in prestige and influence all the older universities except Salamanca, whose principal rival it became. Transferred to Madrid in 1836 it is now the *Universidad Central.*

p 233 (29)

The curriculum of Alcalá was directed towards philosophy and theology, but with a special emphasis on the classical languages and literatures. As regards professors, Cisneros aimed at the very best. He offered chairs to Erasmus and Luis Vives, but neither accepted. He did succeed, however, in persuading Nebrija to transfer from Salamanca.

The new University, while still in its infancy, was associated with one of the monuments of Renaissance scholarship, the *Complutensian Polyglot Bible,* so-called from the Roman name,

f 3

Complutum, of the town that the Moors renamed Alcalá. The humanist orientation of the reforming mentality of Cisneros was evident in his conviction that the basis of theology was scripture, and that scripture could not be properly studied without the restoration of the authentic texts. He therefore commissioned a group of scholars to prepare texts of the Old Testament in Hebrew, Greek (Septuagint), Latin (Vulgate) and, for the Pentateuch, also Aramaic (Targum), and for the New Testament, texts in Greek and Latin. Printing began in 1502 and was completed in 1517 in six folio volumes, the last containing the vocabularies. Cisneros lived to see the completion of this great enterprise, which he hailed as 'a powerful means for the resurrection of theology'. Half a century later Philip II was to sponsor and Spanish scholarship to produce a similar enterprise, the great *Antwerp Polyglot Bible* of 1569–72 under the direction of the biblical scholar and orien-talist, Benito Arias Montano (1527–98); as was to be expected, this surpassed the Complutensian Bible in its much more extensive *apparatus criticus.*

p 233 (27)

'All Authority is to be Condemned'

The direction given by Cisneros to the New Learning coincided with the type of religious reform advocated by Erasmus. But it is convenient, before embarking on this subject, to look at some individual examples of the Renaissance spirit, selected to indicate the range of the movement in Spain. Learning was not confined to academics in the universities. It was typical of the age, for instance, that a man engaged professionally in the municipal administration of a large city could be at the same time a scholar of a wide, encyclopaedic learning. Such was Pedro Mexía (c.1499–1551) author of the *Silva de varia leccion* (1540), a work that was well-known abroad, especially in France. It is a miscellany of scientific, philosophical and historical information of a 'curious' kind, drawn from ancient authors and from the Italian 15th-century humanists. Mexía's interests are humanistic in that he extols the dignity of man and the nobility of reason although, like his age in general, he is not yet able to distinguish in scientific matters between fact and fancy. Another type of humanist was Juan de Mal Lara (1524–71), who founded in 1548 a grammar school in Seville at which he him-self taught. He also presided over a literary academy which was the centre of the city's intellectual life. He was not by any means the only Spaniard to follow Erasmus in collecting proverbs, which he did in *La filosofía vulgar* (1568); but he was the only one to use them as expositions of a 'natural philosophy', expounding their views on the world and men and arranging them systematically; in fact, he saw in proverbs nothing less than the origins of thought. This is an example of the Renaissance tendency to idealization: the belief, in this case, that wisdom can be extracted from the common people, whose untutored tradition has preserved it because they are and always have been close to nature.

In philosophy Spain has never at any time been noted for much original speculation: her thinkers have mostly belonged to already existing schools of thought whose tenets they have expounded and developed. In the Renaissance period they tended to follow either the newly revived Platonism or the tradition of Aristotelian scholasticism, which underwent a revival within the Roman Catholic Church that was centred chiefly in 16th-century Spain. This revival was itself due to a revitalization by the critical spirit of humanism. Francisco de Vitoria (?1483–1546), for instance, one of the great minds of the time, was a Dominican theologian, professor at Salamanca, who rejected dialectical subtlety and all argumentation based on fine metaphysical points, in favour of the study of real problems which were to be found in contemporary political and social life, to the discussion of which he applied the principles of philosophy and theology. He was a scholastic, but at the same time one of the founders of modern international law. Even a theologian like Melchior Cano (1509–60), who showed himself a clerical conservative in public life, insisted on a return to original sources in theology and assessed the value of tradition and the authority of the Church with a free and liberal mind. Among laymen, two thinkers can be cited as examples of this wider mental horizon and (within limits) independence of tra-dition. Gómez Pereira (1500–60) declared: 'In matters not concerning religion I will not subject myself to the opinion or authority of any philosopher unless it be grounded on reason. In questions of speculation, not of faith, all authority is to be condemned.' This is a quotation from his philosophical treatise *Antoniana Margarita* (1554), whose odd title is composed of his parents' names. True to this principle, he broke new ground by attempting to derive ideas solely from sensation and by making the individual mind's analysis of its own process of cognition the starting-point of speculation. Much more influential was Juan Huarte de San Juan (1529–?88), who was, in a sense, the first proponent of specialization in education. Having noted at school that one of his fellow-pupils was better at Latin than anybody else, another at astronomy and another at philosophy, he later wondered why. His *Examen de ingenios* (1575) studies the different types of intellectual talent in order to determine the special aptitude that points toward excellence in each discipline and thus to facilitate at an early age the choice of the right profession. He also speculated on the possibility of parents' producing a genius by devising an education in conformity with their child's 'type'. This interesting work had considerable influence abroad, notably on Bacon; it was, nearly two centuries later, the subject of Lessing's doctoral thesis.

Humanism versus Conquest

p 224–225

f 4

In the world of ideas the optimism, idealism and humanity of the Renaissance are most strikingly exemplified in the controversies concerning Spain's colonial activity in the New World. The leading promotor of the anti-imperialist cause was the Dominican friar, Bartolomé de las Casas (1474–1566), who laboured tirelessly for over fifty years, backwards and forwards across the Atlantic, against the slavery and oppression of the American Indian. An indefatigable writer as well as preacher, he propagated his basic principles in a number of books and tracts, namely that war is irrational and a travesty of civilization; that no force must be used against the natives, even forcible conversion to Christianity being iniquitous; that the rationality and freedom of man demand that he be taught religion and everything else only by gentle and loving persuasion.

Vitoria, from his Chair of Theology at Salamanca, put these humanitarian principles into the context of a law of nations in his famous lectures *De Indis*, delivered in 1539, which have come down to us in the form of notes taken by his students. To those who asserted that the King of Spain was, as Holy Roman Emperor, civil lord of the whole world since the Pope had delegated to the Emperor the universal temporal jurisdiction that belonged to him by divine right as spiritual ruler, and that America thus belonged by law to Charles V, there being in consequence no question of unjust conquest, Vitoria replied that the Pope had no universal temporal jurisdiction, and that even if he had he could not delegate it to the Emperor or any other ruler; that Charles V therefore had no claim on these grounds to his American possessions and that right of conquest did not constitute any such claim; that the Indians were fully rational beings, like all men free by nature, and therefore that they alone were the lawful owners of the New World. None the less, he continued, there were titles by which Spaniards could lawfully claim to enter these lands, and in expounding these, Vitoria was the first to affirm the basic concepts of modern international law. The whole human race, he taught, constitutes a single family, and friendship and freedom of intercourse among men, as brothers, is a rule of the Natural Law. It is right that men of different nations and races should trade peaceably among themselves provided they do each other no hurt. Vitoria thus affirmed the basic freedoms of international relations: freedom of speech, of communication, of trade and of the seas. Because these freedoms are intrinsic in human society Spaniards had a right to go to America and open up intercourse and trade with the Indians, provided they did them no physical or political harm; but they had no right, he affirmed, to make war on them, except in defence of humanity's right to free intercourse and trade. On this plane of international relations war is justified only if it is for the good of the international community as a whole. But, of course, the fact that the Indians were undeveloped communities, with no political organization or means of trading, meant that they and Spaniards were not fully able to exercise their natural freedom of intercourse; as a result, Vitoria adumbrated the system

of mandates, laying down the right and duty of a state, on its own initiative or under mandate from the international community, to prepare backward peoples for sovereignty on a footing of equality with other states. On these grounds alone could Spain claim a colonizing mission in America: 'Spanish rule should be exercised in the interests of the Indians and not merely for the profit of the Spaniards.'

p 225

The opposite, or imperialist cause, was defended by Juan Ginés de Sepúlveda (?1490–1573), a distinguished classical scholar and historian, in his treatise entitled *Democrates alter, sive de justis belli causis apud Indos*. On returning to Spain in 1547 after a voyage to Mexico and Guatemala, Las Casas found this work circulating in manuscript and he immediately attacked it as pernicious in order to prevent its obtaining a licence for printing. To Sepúlveda's indignation the universities of Alcalá and Salamanca did in fact pronounce against its publication. As a result of the furious controversy that followed, Charles V took the astonishing step of ordering all overseas conquests to cease until a special council, formed of theologians and members of the Councils of State, should decide the issue, which Sepúlveda and Las Casas were summoned to debate before it. The sessions took place in Valladolid during 1550 and 1551. Sepúlveda's case followed from the denial of what Vitoria had postulated, a universal international law binding on all peoples. For him, instead, only civilized nations could have a conception of law and morality; uncivilized peoples, who were unable to apprehend these concepts, could have no moral rights. Inferior races must be governed by superior ones, and this doctrine of national aristocracy implied a doctrine of natural servitude. Basing himself on the authority of the ancient Greeks, particularly Aristotle, Sepúlveda argued that inferior peoples like the American Indians were slaves by nature, and it was in their own interests to be conquered and governed by superior races. Civilized nations had a natural mandate to subdue uncivilized nations; if the latter refused to submit voluntarily, warfare against them was morally lawful. Sepúlveda therefore defended the right of conquest and slavery. Against this theory of

Here se cõtienē vnos auisos y reglas para los confessores q oyeren confessiones delos Españoles que son/o han sido en cargo a los Indios delas Indias del mar Oceano: colegidas por el obispo de Chiapa don fray Bartholome dlas casas/o casa vela orden de Sancto Domingo.

'*Advice and rules for confessors who hear confession from Spaniards in charge of Indians*'—one of the many works of Las Casas aimed at obtaining justice and humane treatment for the native peoples of America. (4)

imperialism Las Casas reiterated at great length a doctrine that can be summed up in this one sentence of his: 'No nation exists today or could exist, no matter how barbarous, fierce, or depraved its customs may be, which may not be attracted and converted to all political virtues and to all the humanity of domestic, political, and rational man.' This impressive statement is an example of the idealism and faith in humanity that are marks of the Renaissance. It should be noted that the reactionary in this controversy was the classical humanist who was tied to the concepts of the past, while the apostle of enlightenment was a member of one of the religious orders which had all been stigmatized not so long before by Erasmus as being bigoted and obscurantist. The decision of the Council of Valladolid has not been preserved; historians have deduced from this that it was probably inconclusive. The fact, however, is that *Democrates alter* was never allowed to be published, while Las Casas continued his propagandist activity without hindrance.

Erasmus, Erasmians and Reform

The controversies over America are a sign of the liberal forward-looking minds of many Spanish churchmen in the first half of the 16th century. The revival of classical studies, never in Spain an end in itself, was only one aspect of the general movement of revitalization and reform directed to education, social life, morality and above all religion. Here the greatest single influence, coming after the ecclesiastical reforms of Cisneros, was that of Erasmus. His aspiration to reform theology through classical learning and literary study, and to combine this with the reform of spiritual life by a return to a more evangelical and personal piety, was shared by the humanists of Alcalá. During the 1520s the writings of Erasmus became so widespread and popular that Erasmus himself was almost worshipped. The greatest Spanish humanist, Luis Vives (1492–1540), was closely associated with him. Vives himself exercised little direct influence in Spain; he preferred to live abroad, probably because of his Jewish origins. Erasmus was the main influence behind the ecclesiastical policy of Charles V, who was his patron. The movement of reform thus became characteristically Erasmist, fostering on the positive side a movement towards a 'religion of the spirit' freed of observances and devotions that had become superstitious, and on the negative side a widespread anti-clericalism, especially anti-monasticism. Typical of the movement among laymen are the writings of Alfonso de Valdés (d.1532), a secretary of the Emperor's. One is a Dialogue discussing the Sack of Rome in 1527 by imperial troops. Valdés maintained that the pope had brought this misfortune on the Church by having turned himself from a spiritual ruler into a political potentate. Rome had departed from the spirit of Christ and had become corrupted by wealth. Not only the sack of the city but even Luther himself were hailed by Valdés as instruments of divine providence to call the Church's attention to abuses. A second work, *Dialogo de Mercurio y Carón* (?1528), is closer to imaginative literature, consisting of conversations that Charon and Mercury hold with the souls who come to be ferried over the river Styx on their way to Hell. These are representative of the various professions and stations in life. All are cynically unashamed in recounting their immoral lives while demanding entry into Heaven, which they claim to have purchased by bequeathing money to monasteries and other such pious practices. One of them is especially indignant to find himself damned despite his having expressly guarded himself against that eventuality by wearing a religious habit on his deathbed and holding a specially blessed candle. Saintly souls on their way to Heaven come next, each one of whom is an example of a pure mind and a charitable heart. Four of these six saintly types are churchmen, but this does not really mitigate the anti-clericalism. One of them, a Cardinal, reveals that he had to escape from the Curia after only three weeks in order to save his soul. After hearing the life story of another, a Bishop, Charon asks Mercury how many such prelates are to be found among Christians, and the latter replies that he had searched all Christendom and had not been able to find even that one. There is more satirical literature in this vein, some of it more virulently anti-clerical; but the greater part of this Erasmian literature is theological and devotional.

A defaced portrait of Erasmus, from a copy of Sebastian Münster's 'Cosmographia' (1550) imported into Spain. Erasmus' criticism of the Church had won much early support but by the middle of the century many of his opinions were being condemned as heretical, both inside and outside Spain. Hostility was particularly intense among the friars, whom he had uncompromisingly attacked. (5)

Erasmus had followers among the leaders of the Church as well as of the State. Both the Archbishop of Toledo, Alonso de Fonseca (d. 1534), and the Inquisitor General and the Archbishop of Seville, Alonso Manrique (d.1538), were included among them. The latter had prohibited any public attack on Erasmian doctrine, but when presented by the religious orders with a list of alleged heretical statements culled from the works of Erasmus, Manrique had to summon a conference to adjudicate on their orthodoxy. This met at Valladolid in 1527, the same year in which the University of Paris condemned certain propositions of Erasmus. After two months of discussion Manrique suspended the conference because of the danger of pestilence in the city. The fact that no adverse judgement had been passed on Erasmus was hailed by his followers as victory. But this triumph was short-lived: trials for heresy of some individual Erasmians began in 1529, who 'abjured their errors'. For the next thirty years the growing breach between Luther and Rome made Erasmus suspect because of the closeness of much of his teaching to the reformed doctrine.

The hostility to Erasmus was everywhere fed by the natural antagonism of the religious orders, whose manner of life and the very principle of whose existence he had strongly condemned. One of his leading Spanish disciples, the secular priest Juan Maldonado, wrote to Erasmus in 1526, pointing out that there were monks and monks: many were wholly on his side in condemning their unworthy and uneducated colleagues, and would publicly support him but for their consciousness that Erasmus had wronged the associations to which they belonged by his wholesale condemnation; such men, said Maldonado, could easily be won over completely if only Erasmus would show himself disposed to distinguish the good monks and friars from the bad ones. But all through the turbulent religious controversies of the age tact, fairness, and moderation are hard to find on any side.

239

Erasmus Rejected

p 153
(10) The condemnation of Erasmus came with the end of the second phase (1552) of the Council of Trent. No reconciliation or compromise between Protestants and Catholics had been effected and it was obvious that none would be possible. The need to choose between Luther and Rome crushed the Erasmian movement. For Spain there could be no doubt where the choice lay. There thus followed the persecution of the small Protestant communities that had formed on her soil, and her path was set once more, this time within Christianity itself, in the direction of religious unity and enforced conformity to which Ferdinand and Isabella had first guided her sixty years before. Since it was a reformed Catholicism (though not in the Protestant sense) that emerged out of Trent, it is not correct to call the period of Spanish history that now followed one of 'reaction' in the modern sense of the term; but it was definitely one of conservatism. The Counter-Reformation now began and, in this sphere, the Renaissance had come to an end. Spain was, however, on the threshold of the greatest vitality and creativity that she had ever shown in religion—theological speculation, spiritual literature, mysticism, art—but it was a creativity within narrower limits than the ones the Renaissance had originally pointed to. What died with Erasmus was the spirit of tolerance in Spain, and this was an enormous loss. But as regards depth of religious experience nothing was lost: Erasmian piety is subdued, cold and unimaginative compared with the flame-like ardour of St John of the Cross, the human warmth of St Teresa or the poetic vision of Luis de León's Christian Platonism. The literature of the Spanish Erasmians is superficial in comparison with the great literature that follows. The most influential factor in this religious transformation was the new order of the Society of Jesus, founded by St Ignatius of Loyola (1491–1556), one of the greatest religious figures in Spanish history. The Jesuits prolonged much of the humanist movement into and beyond the Counter-Reformation, not only by giving Spain a long line of scholars in nearly every field, but by incorporating, in their schools, classical studies into a Catholic religious education.

Poetry and the Religion of Love

It is generally considered that the Renaissance emerges in Spanish literature when Italian metres and rhythms are adopted into Castilian lyrical poetry, a transformation of the craft of poetry that is paralleled about the same time in France and later in England. At a chance meeting in 1526 the Venetian ambassador, Andrea Navagero, suggested to the Catalan poet Juan Boscán (1474–1542) that he should try to imitate the Italian poetic style in Castilian. This aroused the interest of his friend Garcilaso de la Vega (1501–36), a much greater poet, and together the two men revolutionized their manner of writing and, after the publication of their poems in 1543, greatly enriched the whole tradition of Spanish prosody. Garcilaso was resident in Naples from 1533 to 1536, the most formative and fruitful period of his short life, during which he devoted himself with enthusiasm to the study of Latin and Italian literatures, writing poems in Latin as well as Spanish, and immersing himself in Renaissance culture. He sent Boscán from Italy a copy of Castiglione's *Courtier* with the request that he should translate it. Boscán complied, and his admirable translation was published in 1534. The fact that Boscán wrote in Castilian though a Catalan is a further mark of the Spanish Renaissance—the disappearance, for the time being, of Catalan as a literary language.

At this same time neo-Platonism, the characteristic philosophy of the Renaissance, enters Spain to colour her literature. All this should be taken as marking the height of the Spanish literary Renaissance, not its beginning. The poetry of Garcilaso and the acceptance of the doctrine of human love in neo-Platonism are one phase in what is essentially a continuous development from the mid-15th century. This is obscured if a dividing line between medieval and Renaissance literature is placed here. The criterion is not Italian metrics but the emergence of 'humanism' in the wider sense of the word—not just the revival of classical studies and the liberal tolerant mentality that this new education fostered, but a concern with purely human values as distinct from divine or

The '*Cárcel de Amor*' by Diego de San Pedro, an allegory of the Religion of Love, became a European best-seller. In this woodcut (from the 1493 edition) a hairy savage representing Desire entices men into captivity by carrying a statuette of the naked Venus. (6)

religious ones. In Spanish literature this kind of humanism is first apparent in the lyrical poetry of the 15th century. There is a change of fashion in Castile about 1450. The first big collection of Castilian lyrical poetry is the *Cancionero de Baena* compiled about 1445. The great majority of the poems it contains are moral and didactic, dealing with religion, death, the uncertainty of worldly fortune, and so on; very little prominence is given to the theme of love. The poetry of the second half of the 15th century, which is covered by two other *cancioneros*, shows a sudden change. Nearly all of it is love poetry and of a type new to Castile. There are hundreds of these poems and every one assumes or expounds the same conception of human love. This is not based on the physical and the sensuous, but on love as the faithful service of a lady who never rewards her servant, a love from which there is no escape and which therefore produces a suffering akin to death, but this suffering is not only accepted, it is actually desired and found pleasurable. The lover is condemned by fate to love faithfully, without hope of happiness, a cruel and indifferent lady; yet better this living death than not to love at all.

This conception of love is purely medieval in origin: it derives ultimately from the courtly love of Provençal poetry and is much influenced by the poetry of Petrarch. Both these influences had previously met in the Catalan poet Ausias March (1397–1459), who is the greatest exponent of this erotic humanism in the peninsular poetry of this century. In Castile it becomes an all-pervading literary fashion. It is often expressed in specifically religious terms—for instance, the liturgical prayers of the Church or the psalms of the Old Testament are used as prayers to Cupid, the god of love, and the suffering and passion of the lover are even equated with the passion of Christ and the lover is often presented as a martyr for his faith. This religion of love is not peculiar to Spain; it comes belatedly from France, but in Spain it is carried rather further in extravagance.

The structure of these poems follows a fairly uniform pattern. The expression is always abstract, the imagery is never sensuous or concrete. For this reason, and because the same ideas are constantly repeated in hundreds of poems by dozens of poets, we are justified in concluding that this is not a genuine expression of personal experience but a fashion or convention, and accordingly this poetry has never been taken very seriously. The conventionality of the literary form alone suggests that this conception of love is an artificial attitude to life, which is certainly borne out by what we know of actual life in the 15th century. This was therefore a poetic convention divorced from reality. But that in itself is significant. All literary conventions have some purpose; by the mere fact that if they constitute a prevalent fashion they give pleasure, they must satisfy some need. A poetic convention divorced from reality points to some sort of aspiration or ideal. If 15th-century poets found satisfaction in posing as suffering martyrs of love, we may conclude that they would have liked to be such; in other words that this convention was a kind of wish-fulfilment. The aspiration it embodied was that of a perfect love, one that transcended the carnal and spiritualized the lover, endowing him with moral perfection through the virtues of fidelity, fortitude and complete selflessness. In other words, human love enshrined in theory the highest values of life, and spiritual values were thus circumscribed within a purely human activity. Since this is an idealized conception of love, the literature that promulgated it was not a literature of experience. A divorce is thus effected between literature and reality such as had not occurred to any appreciable extent in the literature of the 12th, 13th and 14th centuries. This is also connected with the first influence of Italian and classical literatures in this century.

Divorce from Reality

If this had been a passing fashion one would not be justified in attempting to explain it in this way. It started, however, a literary movement that lasted for a century or more. The most famous of the 'sentimental novels' of the period was the first Spanish work
f 6 to become a European best-seller, *Cárcel de amor* (1492) by Diego de San Pedro. Here the expression of love in directly religious terms finds its extreme form. Love, being without hope of fulfilment, is presented as faith—a faith and a consequent suffering which, fully accepted, ennoble the lover. Woman, aloof and unattainable, is the source of grace, infusing into the lover not only the cardinal virtues but also the theological virtues of faith, hope and charity. Since woman is the object of the lover's faith, the supreme value in which he believes, human love is unequivocally associated with the mystical union of the soul and God. And finally, since 'greater love hath no man than this, that a man lay down his life for his friends', the lover in this novel, in order to prove his love by the supreme sacrifice, chooses death in suicide in order to die a martyr for his faith, attaining a sacramental communion with his beloved by tearing up her letters and drinking them from a goblet.

This equation of love and religion is so extravagant that it has never been taken particularly seriously. But the vogue it enjoyed points to the widespread popularity of a spiritualized mystical conception of human love, of an attempt to centre the highest values of life in the love of man for woman. Because this was remote from actual experience, the plot of this novel is unfolded in an unrealistic setting, in a largely allegorical form.

The basic divorce from reality lies of course in the separation of love from the physical. This particular idealization of love in religious, mystical terms could find no room for sensuality; it was in fact something that aspired not to refine the sensual but to transcend it. The suffering of these literary lovers is the flesh seeking to assert itself against the ideal of a spiritualized and therefore chaste love. In San Pedro's novel the lover is led into the allegorical 'prison of love' by a hairy savage who represents Desire, and who entices men into imprisonment by carrying the statuette of a beautiful woman, who in a woodcut in the first edition is represented as the naked Venus.

In medieval art, from the 14th century onwards, lust had frequently been represented by a wild man, a hairy savage with a cudgel, a traditional folk figure that had come to represent the bestial side of human nature. The chivalrous or courtly love of woman was represented by a knight who fought the savage. These savages became supporters of heraldic shields, indicating that their strength was ready to defend them. In Spain, in the 14th and 15th centuries, these heraldic savages are chained, i.e. defeated, and heralds on horseback, blowing trumpets, announce the outcome of the battle. The savage, with or without the accompanying knight, is a recurring symbol in Spanish Renaissance literature. In Gil Vicente's play *Don Duardos*, written between 1521 and 1525, a 'savage knight', who has defeated all the knights at court, must be vanquished in his turn by the hero before the latter can win his lady's hand. In pastoral novels savages invade Arcadia, threatening to abduct the shepherdesses; they can only be rescued by those whose love is chaste. This symbol of the wild man or savage is the connecting link between the medieval ideal of courtly love in its 15th-century form and the Renaissance ideal of Platonic love; what they have in common is the aspiration for a perfect love to be achieved by the permanent chaining of the wild man. This is the principal way in which the idealistic tendencies of the Renaissance find expression in literature; the foundation is, however, fully medieval.

'*The Tragedy of Calisto and Melibea*' is one of the most fascinating works of the Spanish Renaissance. Written by Fernando de Rojas in the form of a dialogue, it tells a realistic story of intrigue and seduction, dominated by the bawd Celestina. Above left Calisto meets Melibea for the first time, and on the right Celestina pays a call on her still-innocent victim; below, Melibea throws herself from a tower after the affair has ended in ruin and disgrace. (7, 8)

Realism and Romance

The most famous work of this period stands apart as an exception to the main literary trend, in that it is a pessimistic refusal to admit that an ideal or idealized love of this kind is possible. This is the *Tragedia de Calisto y Melibea* (1499), better known as *La* *f 7, 8* *Celestina*, by Fernando de Rojas (d.1541). Like *Cárcel de amor* it enjoyed an international vogue. It is one of the masterpieces of world literature. The hero Calisto is a worshipper at the altar of love, and the heroine Melibea is his deity. To the question whether he is not a Christian, Calisto replies, 'I am a Melibean, I adore Melibea, I believe in Melibea, and I love Melibea.' But the mediator between him and his human divinity is Celestina—the professional bawd—in other words it is lust. And lust does not ennoble the lovers, on the contrary it plunges them into social degradation and death. The religion of love is thus brought down to earth, is directly associated with lust and the exploitation of vice for mercenary ends, and is thereby shattered as an ideal of salvation. The promise of happiness that love holds out is only a bait, and men are so bewitched by the promise of joy that they cannot escape from the hook on which the bait is set. Rojas here condemns erotic passion for being what it is, precisely for not being divine; yet in this humanistic work there is nothing else to take its place, and love is the only human value that is given any kind of fulfilment. Because of this uncompromising confrontation of the ideal with the reality of human nature, the *Celestina* departs from the literary tradition of its times in that its technique is starkly realistic. In contrast to the unreal allegorical world of the *Cárcel de amor* it presents real people who move through the world of human society as it actually exists. These two works thus point a contrast between the two different literary techniques of idealism and realism: the one based on the idealization of human values, the other based on the affirmation of moral evil. The former is the one that characterizes the Renaissance, and for this very reason the *Celestina* remained outside the main stream of the literature of its age. Though it had one or two successors that tried to imitate it, these were insignificant and uninfluential. The *Celestina* could not divert the continued flow of Spanish literature from the channel of idealism.

f 9 The next prose work of historical importance is *Amadís de Gaula*, the third Spanish work of this period to become known and influential abroad. Though not the first Spanish novel of chivalry, it initiates the great vogue of this *genre* in the 16th century. The form in which we know it dates from 1508, and is the recasting by Garcí Ordóñez de Montalvo of an earlier 15th-century work, of which only some fragments have survived. The world of chivalry in *Amadís de Gaula* is one that never existed nor ever could have existed in space and time. None the less, despite the complete unreality of its setting, *Amadís de Gaula* does present a certain ideal of human personality. There is a nostalgic idealization of the virtues of bravery, magnanimity, loyalty and abnegation, but these chivalrous virtues are presented almost exclusively in relation to love. Amadís, the perfect knight, is devoted, loyal, faithful and self-sacrificing in relation to his lady. She, Oriana, implicitly usurps the place of the divine: it is she who calls forth adoration and devotion in the knight, it is for her sake and to prove his faith that he lives ascetically and even undergoes penance. Love and the adoration of woman are the centre and circumference of life, and true love is imbued with an aspiration to chastity and purity, which makes Oriana, in effect, equivalent to a goddess placed high on a pedestal. Because *Amadís de Gaula* created a whole novelistic *genre* it contributed greatly to perpetuating the divorce between literature and experience.

Neo-Platonic Relationships

This whole idealization of human love, in implicit or explicit religious terms, became crystallized in the philosophy of neo-Platonism, the characteristic philosophy of the Renaissance which came to Spain from Italy. Two of the works exemplifying it had a great influence on Spanish literature. They are *Dialoghi d'amore* by the Sephardic Jew exiled from Spain, Leone Ebreo (Judah Leo Abravanel), published posthumously in 1535, and *The Courtier* (1528) by Castiglione, which in its closing section contains an exposition of the neo-Platonist doctrine of love. Plato's philosophy of love is based on the ascent from the material to the immaterial, an ascent in which the mind is drawn upwards by the love of beauty. From the beauty of material things the mind is led to the beauty of human bodies, from there to the beauty of goodness, then to the beauty of ideas and from there to the knowledge and love of Absolute Beauty, which is God. On this basis Renaissance neo-Platonists expounded a conception of ideal

human love that gave it more importance and a more central place than Plato himself did; for them it is in and through human love that man progresses from the physical plane, through the intellectual, to the spiritual. Castiglione and Bembo developed the conception of so-called Platonic love (which is not found in Plato at all), whereby a man overcomes sensuality when his reason makes him realize that beauty is all the more perfect the more it is removed from corruptible matter. Through this realization love is transformed into a chaste and Platonic attachment, which is the union only of the minds and wills of the two lovers. This mutual attachment will lead in both of them to the contemplation of universal beauty and so on to the contemplation of God, which Castiglione expresses in terms of Christian mysticism. For Ebreo, too, beauty does not reside in matter, which by itself is ugly: the beauty of material things consists in the ideas which fashion matter. So that though physical beauty stirs the mind to love it, such love is only fitting if it leads the mind on to love of the beauty of the spirit. The physical beauty of a body is not itself corporeal, it is the image or reflection of spiritual beauty, and it is this essential beauty that the human soul should aspire to know and love. Love for physical beauty is therefore a stepping-stone to the ultimate goal of union with the final and only real Beauty, which is God. So the physical union of lovers can be transcended and surpassed in the union of their souls through the communication of their minds and the fusion of their wills; and this spiritual union between man and woman leads to union with God. For Ebreo, therefore, the ultimate nature and purpose of human love is religious. There is no gulf between the human and the divine, but a natural ascent.

It is difficult to take Platonic love, as expounded by Castiglione, or even Bembo, seriously as a practical moral ideal. Behind the cultured and elegant way of life portrayed in *The Courtier* there is the smugness of a self-satisfied aristocracy able to sanction the frivolity of Platonic attachments with other men's wives by surrounding it with an aura of religious mysticism. This is not so, however, with Ebreo, whose deep earnestness is unquestionable. This is apparent above all in the note of suffering that runs through his presentation of human love, which is imbued with an underlying sense of anguish, a real existential hurt that it can never, in this life, fully be what the human mind and heart are compelled to yearn that it should be: even the body is hurt at the imperfection of the only love it can achieve. This is a genuine and deep religious note, far removed from any complacent optimism, and it is because of this that Ebreo came to exercise a deeper and more enduring influence in Spain than Castiglione. This underlying note of suffering makes his philosophy of love the link between neo-Platonism and the 15th-century form of courtly love.

The philosophy of neo-Platonism thus places human love in the setting of divine love and gives it a spiritual value, which is what the love poetry of the 15th century and *Cárcel de amor* had in a confused way been trying to do. Love of woman is a stage towards and a part of the love of God; it is a stage that is not left behind but carried up. This is a philosophy that, in effect, idealizes and glorifies human love to the highest possible degree within a religious or theistic view of life. As such, by giving a philosophical sanction to the conception of ideal love, it offered a justification for centering the values of life exclusively in human love to the disregard of all other human values. In this respect it could consolidate and continue the literary movement that has so far been sketched. But at the same time this return to Plato could also appeal (as Platonism had always done) to a different type of mind, one whose interests and aspirations were purely religious; this it could do by its emphasis that in the last resort ideal love was divine love, that the response to the attraction of beauty found its complete fulfilment in the apprehension and contemplation of God. Neo-Platonism could thus point in two different directions: ideal love can continue to be the main preoccupation of literature, but now, so to speak, on two different levels instead of only one.

The modification of the courtly love tradition by the influence of neo-Platonism is seen in the two major humanistic poets of this century, Garcilaso de la Vega and Fernando de Herrera

Spain gave a new lease of life in Renaissance Europe to tales of chivalry. 'Amadís de Gaula', an older story retold as a prose romance by Garcí Ordóñez de Montalvo in 1508, was the first of a long line of popular novels which were to be the object of Cervantes' satire in 'Don Quixote' almost a century later. (9)

(1534–97). The former, as has already been stated, is the most characteristic poet of this phase of the Renaissance in Spain through having assimilated the Italian style to perfection. He also adds a new element into Spanish poetry by adopting the pastoral convention from Vergil and Sannazaro. Garcilaso's poetic experience passes from the suffering caused by the conflict between reason and sensuality to the achievement of a resigned serenity, not in the self-assurance of being in contact with the Divine through love of woman, but in acceptance of the sadness inherent in life through the fact that love and beauty are perishable. The note of suffering and melancholy links Garcilaso with the 15th century; its gentle, more restrained expression within a pastoral setting and the perfection of his craftsmanship is what he owes to the Italian Renaissance. From Garcilaso to Herrera this idealized and suffering love within a humanistic 'spirituality' becomes conventional. Herrera is the type of humanist for whom the scholarly and critical study of poetry becomes a life's devotion; he exemplifies the fulfilment of Platonic love in a reciprocated attachment to a married woman, but he remains greatly inferior to Garcilaso, despite the more classical elaboration of his style, in not rising above a subjective conventionality.

The Deceit of Love

The new pastoral convention was adopted also by the novel as the background setting for idealized love in its neo-Platonist form. This began in Spain in 1559 with the *Diana* of Jorge de Montemayor (?1520–61), another of the works of Spanish literature that was influential abroad. The unrealism of the *genre* is something that it is difficult for us nowadays to stomach, but there was never, of course, any intention on the part of these novelists to reproduce reality; on the contrary, they had every intention of rising above it into the realm of ideal love. Most of them, from the *Diana* of 1559 to the *Galatea* of Cervantes in 1585, illustrate various aspects of the doctrine of love of Leone Ebreo, whom they directly quote. What must be judged is not the verisimilitude of the pastoral setting but the adequacy of this philosophy of love as material for a novel. What is obvious in the first place is that this ideal love, faithful and chaste, in which all trace of passion is absent, cannot produce any sort of conflict. The only possibility of having anything approaching a narrative plot is to make the love of each shepherd and shepherdess unrequited. And this is what Montemayor does: thus A is in love with B, but B with C, and C with D and so on. The characters are thus

f 10

unhappy, and the purpose of the novelistic plot is to bring about a happy ending by making B transfer his affections from C to A, and so on with the other characters. But this is not easy to do, because since the majority of the charctaers exemplify ideal love, they must be constant and faithful in their affections and it is therefore not in their power to cease to love. Some *deus ex machina* is therefore required, and this takes the form of magic. The characters who are in love with the wrong people are given a potion by the high priestess of the temple of Diana, the effect of which is to make them cease to love the persons they are in love with and fall in love with those who are already in love with them. Thus all are rewarded with happiness, but only at the cost of violating all plausibility. Attempts at a more realistic psychology in later novels only makes the artificiality of the pastoral convention all the more incongruous.

These few examples out of many must suffice to indicate that the type of humanism that came into Spanish literature in 1450—a humanism based on the idealization, even divinization, of love—was a very narrow and limited view of human nature and life. It disregarded extensive and vital spheres of experience: in the first place, the whole setting of human life, namely the environment of society with its complex of political and social relationships, its laws and customs; in the second place, the fact of evil—whether physical evil like disease and death, or social evil like oppression and poverty, or moral evil, namely the power and freedom that individual men have to debase their human nature. This idealistic literary humanism did not just fail to face up to these aspects of life, it turned its back on them and ignored them. Neo-Platonism was upholding a dream vision when it placed no obstacle in the ascent from the human to the divine, when it made human love the continuous chain linking the two. This is not what humanity has ever at any time experienced. It has always known in practice that somewhere between man and God (or, if one prefers, between man and the ideal) there lies the obstacle of evil—an obstacle to be overcome, an enemy to be conquered. In so far as neo-Platonism considered this at all, it was only as concupiscence, which it tended to present as a potential aberration that an intelligent and rational man would either never fall into or would quickly surmount. The problem of evil in human life is not quite as simple as that. This is ultimately the great weakness of the humanist idealism with which the Renaissance imbued Spanish literature.

The Love of Deceit

A few years before the publication of *Diana*, the first of the pastoral novels, there had appeared *La vida de Lazarillo de Tormes* (1554), generally but inaccurately called the first of the picaresque novels. This anonymous and internationally popular work has an importance in the history of European literature out of all proportion to its length, for it is a precursor of the modern novel. After the lapse of half a century we return to the real world of *La Celestina*. There is no vestige of any courtly or Platonic love; instead, this little novel deals, ironically, with a more practical human value—a social one. For life to have a minimum of dignity it is necessary for the individual to have a social position that gives him a decent standard of living. Lázaro, the hero of this tale, enters the world lacking every single social advantage, but manages by the end to win a respectable position: he has a wife, an honourable job and sufficient economic well-being. He is, as he says himself, 'at the summit of all good fortune' and is thus in appearance an example of humanist fulfilment. But his wife is an archpriest's mistress; by marrying her he has made the continuance of this liaison possible, and by accepting it he has received certain economic advantages in exchange. In order to achieve one value in life, Lázaro has trampled another underfoot. He has thereby only been putting into practice the lessons he has learned from his fellow-men in the art of living. All the characters of *Lazarillo*, without exception, lead double lives—an outer life in which they pay respect to social decorum, honour and religion, and an inner life in which these values are non-existent. In addition to a realistic narrative with life-like characterization, we have here a witty, ironical vision of men in society, in which religious satire is prominent—there is,

'Diana' by Jorge de Monte-mayor (first published in 1559) began a new fashion for love stories in bucolic settings, influenced by neo-Platonism. It proved influential far beyond the borders of Spain. (10)

for instance, a cynical seller of indulgences who advertises his wares by false miracles. These qualities align it with the Erasmist literature of religious reform.

Erasmus himself had no interest in contemporary vernacular literature, but at least two of his Spanish disciples, Vives and Juan de Valdés (d.1541), a brother of Alfonso, were concerned with the effects of secular literature on the minds and morals of its readers. Modern theologians can argue whether the religious works of Valdés are Protestant or Catholic, but Valdés himself took no chances and moved to Italy. Here he wrote *Diálogo de la lengua*, a most interesting treatise on the Spanish language, which also contains some literary criticism. Both he and Vives, long before Cervantes, attacked the contemporary novels of chivalry for their improbabilities and impossibilities, for being untrue to human nature and experience. The literary ideal of Valdés, in particular, was coherence within a framework of events and characters that could happen and exist in reality. This is an ideal of realism that was not then, in the 1530s, being exemplified in fiction; but it was exemplified twenty years later in *Lazarillo de Tormes*. This pointed the way to a literature of social realism, but for nearly fifty years it remained without a successor and without influence, impotent to stem in isolation the tide of idealistic literature. The literature of social realism did eventually emerge, and it did so as a result of the continuing movement of religious reform, for the churchmen of the Counter-Reformation developed more effectively the same criticism of contemporary literature which the Erasmian humanists had been the first to make.

'A New Gladness'

Part of the policy of reform that followed from the Council of Trent was the endeavour to turn literature into religious channels. The churchmen who tried to carry out in Spain this policy of Christianizing humanistic literature began by launching an attack on the whole tradition of idealistic love literature—explicitly on Garcilaso, on the novels of chivalry and the pastoral novels. The whole of this literature was condemned not only for not being religious, but also for being irresponsible in its unreality, since, by failing to show its readers what the real problems of life were, it encouraged them to take refuge in what we now call escapism. They therefore advocated replacing the 'untruthful' romances by a literature that would be 'truthful', by which they meant one that would promulgate a Christian view of life and a sense of moral responsibility by presenting human nature as it actually is instead of idealizing it.

The period 1560–1600 saw the flowering of Spanish religious and mystical literature, which is one of the most remarkable features of this culture. It is worth noting that this literature also had a considerable vogue abroad, and not only in Catholic countries, for writers like Luis de Granada and Diego de Estella were translated and widely read in Anglican England.

p 233 (26) The first thing that strikes one about this literature is its contact with the real world. Two descriptions of the dawn from a pastoral novel and from the pen of Luis de León, an Augustinian friar, will illustrate the point. In the *Diana enamorada* (1564) of Gil Polo we read: 'The hour came when ruddy dawn with her golden gesture swept away the nocturnal stars, and the birds with their sweet song announced the approaching day.' The description is perfunctory and the expression stilted. There is no indication at all that Gil Polo had ever actually seen the sun rise or heard the birds welcome the dawn—he need only have read about it, for this kind of conventional description occurs time and time again in the pastoral and chivalry novels. By contrast Luis de León, in *La perfecta casada* (1583), remarking how mistaken it is through a sluggish desire to sleep to miss the most delightful experience that life can offer, which is the coming of the day, writes:

Because at that hour the light, since it comes after the darkness and is as if finding itself after having been lost, seems quite different from what it is at other hours and strikes the heart of man with a new gladness. The sight of the sky, with the clouds slowly reddening and the appearance of the beauty of the sun, is something most lovely. As for the song of the birds, who can doubt that they sing then more sweetly than at other times?... The flowers and the grass give out a gracious scent; the animals, the earth, the air and all the elements rejoice at the coming of the sun and in order the better to welcome him they beautify and clothe themselves with their finest raiment.

There is a world of difference: here the writer is describing what he has actually seen and is telling his readers not to miss this experience, while Gil Polo is not in the least bit interested whether his readers ever see the dawn or not.

Similarly with the descriptions of nature. Although the pastoral novels are ostensibly nature literature, we can look in vain in them for any indication that the writers have ever directly observed any scenery, for the descriptions are always a succession of conventional stock phrases like 'thick wood', 'green and spacious meadow', 'rushing stream' and so on. If, on the other hand, we turn to *Símbolo de la Fe* (1582), an exposition of Christian doctrine by the Dominican Luis de Granada (1504–88), we find page after page of detailed descriptions of the beauty of nature drawn from direct and loving observation, all of which are imbued with a sense of joy. Granada's attitude to reality is always positive and welcoming: the sea, he says, not only separates nations it also unites them, 'leading them to friendship and harmony' by the intercourse it facilitates, for the sea is like 'a great fair and market, in which are found great numbers of buyers and sellers with all the merchandise needed to sustain our lives'. The note of joy stems from a belief in the essential goodness of the world, of human relations and even of commerce. Although this religious literature is dogmatic and ascetic, and as such would not normally be considered humanist, it would not have had this tone and this human quality without the Renaissance; in this particular respect, in fact, it exemplifies the Renaissance more positively and fruitfully than secular literature, for if one wants to find a real love of nature in the literature of 16th-century Spain it is not to the pastoral novelists or even the poets that one goes. These religious writers of the Counter-Reformation loved nature because they were true Platonists, seeing in nature the visible reflection of the beauty of God and the tangible evidence of his existence. But their contact with reality was not limited to nature: it embraced the practical and material facts of everyday life. A work that in this respect points an illuminating contrast with the preceding literature is *La perfecta casada* by Luis de León (1527–91), an Augustinian who held Chairs of Theology

and Scripture at Salamanca. It is a work in praise of women, which had been a favourite topic in the literary tradition of courtly love. In the numerous works treating of this subject woman had, of course, been idealized as a sort of goddess, and was not a creature of flesh and blood with a real life to live in the material world. In *La perfecta casada*, however, she is, as the title indicates, a married woman, and at once the idealized feminist literature is brought down to the plane of social duties and moral obligations. Luis de León takes us through the practical tasks of daily routine—the stocking of the larder, the making and mending of clothes, the looking after the servants and so on, insisting all the time that it is in a busy domestic life and not in idle luxury that women find their fulfilment. Yet this does not mean that he considers women to be inferior drudges. A good woman, he says, is something finer than a good man because ultimately it is upon her that human society depends. The goodness of a woman is creative, and communicated to others: it is not in her nature to attain to a self-centred perfection, but to give. For this reason, the love she inspires in man is, or should be, the love of reverence, based upon the realization of her unique worth in the task and art of living. In this way the ideal of woman and the ideal of human love are brought down from the clouds to reality and are, in fact, ennobled in the process, for this is a work that retains all that is best in Renaissance idealism—a belief in and an emphasis on what is good and noble in human nature.

This Augustinian friar has, indeed, been called the finest and most typical representative of the Spanish Renaissance in its complete, fully developed form. And this is certainly true, for Luis de León was a humanist, a Latin and Greek scholar, a translator of Vergil and Horace, among whose verse translations are also to be found an ode of Pindar and some fragments of Euripides; he studied also the Italian poets, and wrote sonnets modelled on Petrarch; he was a devout Christian with a liberal and enlightened outlook, and a theologian whose doctrine was scripturally based from first to last; a Hebrew scholar, a translator of the *Book of Job*, of the *Song of Songs* and of many of the *Psalms*, all his writings are pervaded by a deep love of the Bible; he was also a Platonist, whose whole work is imbued with a sensitiveness to the beauty of nature, the beauty of human living and the beauty of ideas, and who brought a Platonist mind to biblical exegesis in *Los nombres de Cristo* (1583 and 1585), an exposition of the significance of the names given to the Messiah in the Old Testament and to Christ in the New. Lastly, to crown all this activity, he is one of the greatest of Spanish poets in his own right; since he conceives poetry as a search for beauty that leads the mind to God, his most characteristic poems exemplify the Platonic process of contemplation in the ascent from material to divine beauty. So that nothing should be wanting to complete in Luis de León the complexity of the Spanish Renaissance, it must be added that he spent nearly five years confined by the Inquisition (1572–76). Proclaiming the necessity of revising the traditional Latin version of the Bible direct from the Hebrew text rather than from the Septuagint, he was accused by the conservative theologians of Salamanca of, among other things, belittling the authority of the Vulgate as a reliable medium of revelation. He was finally declared innocent of heresy and returned to a triumphal reception in Salamanca.

Christian Platonism

León is only one of a number of Counter-Reformation theologians who are Platonists. Although they directly attack humanistic secular literature, they at the same time continue and bring to fruition the philosophy on which its conception of ideal love was based. In them Platonic doctrine finds its proper fulfilment in divine love without being led astray by the unreal illusion of a spiritualized human love. A representative example is *La conversión de la Magdalena* (1588) by the Augustinian friar, Pedro Malón de Chaide (d.1589). This is a treatise on love; Part I is in fact the clearest and simplest exposition in Spanish literature of the Platonic doctrine of love, which Malón presents as a cosmic circular movement from God down to creatures and back to God, this unbroken circle being the ideal of love. In this First Part of his work Malón is the pure Platonist, and as such a man of the Renaissance; he becomes the Christian Platonist and a man of the Counter-Reformation by his insistence, after this First Part, that this ideal is not just lying at one's feet, ready to be picked up and absorbed without difficulty. The tragedy of man lies in the fact that, since in his nature spirit is compounded with matter, he is strongly impelled to break the cosmic circle of love by remaining bogged down in an imperfect and inferior love. In his preface Malón attacks Garcilaso, *Amadis de Gaula*, and *Diana* for being unaware that they are representing a broken circle. By contrast the figure of the lover that he puts forward is the historical Mary Magdalen. A repentant prostitute becomes a heroine of love to replace Oriana and the shepherdesses of the *Diana*. In that she was a sinner she represents, unlike the heroines of fiction, the reality of human experience; yet in her answer, through repentance, to the call of a higher love, she also represents the ideal. In Malón's presentation of the Platonic doctrine of love the emphasis therefore shifts away from the confident pursuit of divine beauty through the beauty of woman, away from the confident reliance on the spiritual nature of human love, to the recognition of the essential weakness of human nature, a weakness which is such that men can have no natural confidence in their ability to attain to the divine, but can only seek to love God through the plea for his forgiveness and mercy.

It was in this way that the religious literature of the Counter-Reformation brought the ideal of perfect love down from the clouds, while at the same time retaining the vision of the ideal—the union of the soul with God. It counteracted the prevailing idealistic humanism by placing the ideal where it properly belonged, in the realm of the spiritual, and by laying stress on the real world, on the reality of human nature, and on social obligations and moral duties. In this latter respect the Counter-Reformation is influential in transforming secular Spanish literature from a literature of idealism to one of realism: and this is what produces its greatest period. The retention of the ideal of love, spiritualized, is seen in the mystical movement within the Counter-Reformation, whose outstanding figures are St Teresa of Jesus (1515–82) and St John of the Cross (1542–91), both of whom are major classics of Spanish literature, the latter often being called the greatest of all Spanish poets, a title to which he has indeed a strong claim.

The Mystical Path

Looked at as a cultural phenomenon this mystical literature must be considered the culmination of the doctrine of love in Renaissance neo-Platonism in its truly religious form, as in Leone Ebreo. Mysticism cannot properly be included under humanism, whether this term be used broadly or narrowly; none the less it is something that can be explained historically only by the Renaissance. This Spanish mystical movement is confined to the second half of the 16th century and is unique in Spanish history: there was no similar movement before, there has been none since. This restriction in time means that it was produced by cultural and historical causes that have operated only then. It can be argued that these are three: a widespread aspiration for an ideal, perfect love; a philosophy that could both give it form and satisfy the minds of ordinary educated people; and a revival of religious life within Spain as part of the renewal of the Church. The conjunction of these three pressures occurred during the Spanish Renaissance.

The mystics claimed to achieve the spiritual ideal of love, not as the humanist neo-Platonists had thought they could, by reaching God through attachment to creatures, but by rising above this attachment and following the path of purgation which leads to what St John of the Cross calls 'the dark night of the soul'. In the suffering of this dark night the soul must be stripped bare of all attachment to things and images of sense before the light of the divine can flood the darkness. There must be a direct link, somewhere deep in human nature itself, between the suffering love of Spanish 15th- and 16th-century poetry and St John's dark night. One is a confused intuition, the other a real and agonizing threshold to a deep spiritual experience. Midway between the two there is Ebreo's realization that the body itself, in the midst of the ecstasy of its own kind of love, feels anguish at being a barrier to the much higher love that the mind can apprehend. The link is also a literary one. The secular poets had one and all referred to their suffering as 'a living death'. St John of the Cross repeats this commonplace image, but no secular poet came anywhere near giving it the tremendous significance that St John does as he applies it to his own experience. The suffering of emptiness that produces the darkness, when there is nothing in creation left that the soul can love while searching for God, is expressed as dark, deep caverns of meaninglessness: the flame of love is burning and wounding as the senses die, but the flame heals as it kills and suddenly the caverns, in which the soul without God is empty and blind, are flooded with the burning radiance and heat of meaning as God communicates his presence.

These mystical writings are a literature not of aspiration but of experience. Secular literature, for its part, exemplifying the truthfulness and responsibility which the Counter-Reformation had desiderated, begins by the end of the century to return, through realism, to the analysis of human experience by presenting moral issues within a social setting. Human love, which in an idealized and artificial form had been for 150 years the dominant theme of Spanish literature, ceases to be its almost exclusive preoccupation. One theme out of many, it is now placed in the context of social duties—it is related to family life, to parental authority, to marriage and to social honour. Don Quixote and his Dulcinea are a satirical parody of the idealized love of the 16th century, the *reductio ad absurdum* of Platonic love. There is one great, if excessively diffuse, work in which the Spanish 17th century can be said to pass a judgement on the 16th: *La Dorotea* (1632) by Lope de Vega. It contrasts the idealization of love with reality. The lovers in it live in the beautiful but illusory world of 16th-century love poetry, having this poetry and the language of neo-Platonism on their lips. But they are the victims of this idealization of love, in that they are tied to their own feelings: they cannot escape but must go round and round themselves in an aimless futility. Faced with the problems of reality they prove spineless and irresolute, incapable of facing up to social obligations, incapable of preventing their ideal of altruistic love from debasing itself in financial self-interest, jealousy and vengeance.

Disenchantment

This note of disenchantment is not only, in this particular case, the disillusionment of a poet in his old age, it is one of the marks of the new literature in Spain as elsewhere. Although the idealization of nature is found in the sumptuous and sensuous baroque poetry of Góngora, optimistic idealism and a belief in the perfectibility of human nature did not otherwise survive the Counter-Reformation. Platonism gave way to Stoicism as the dominant philosophy behind literature, and disenchantment deepened at times into pessimism. But because disenchantment can be a profounder experience than optimism, there is in 17th-century Spanish literature a deeper probing into the problems of human character and the complexity of life than anything that the Renaissance achieved. For this reason the Baroque—the age of Cervantes, Góngora, Lope de Vega, Quevedo and Calderón—is the great age of Spanish secular literature. It is also the age in which this literature had the greatest impact abroad, exercising a decisive influence in the development of the European novel. Although the Latinization of the language of poetry reached its height with Góngora, neo-classicism took no root in Spain. The national drama that Lope de Vega created was deliberately anti-classical in order to appeal to the people as a whole and not to a select minority. Attacked at the beginning as a 'barbarous' art because it rebelled against the authority of the ancients, it was defended and established as the imitation of nature—not of a dead culture but of life as the audience knew it, and thus as in keeping not only with the spirit of the age but also with the national temperament, to which Lope de Vega explicitly appealed in justifying his departure from the classical rules. In so far as classicism meant any degree of remoteness from real life it was rejected in Spain; but in so far as it meant a training in language and literature, in style, technique and critical appreciation, and thus an enrichment of the intellectual and aesthetic experience on which writers could draw, it remained the basis of education and the foundation of culture.

Interest in ancient Roman architecture followed the introduction of Renaissance motifs from Italy. From Diego de Sagredo's book on the measurements of Roman buildings comes this illustration of a cornice related (on the right) to the proportions of the human face. (11)

Architecture Transformed

At the beginning of the reign of the Catholic Kings the architectural style in vogue was the flamboyant Gothic known as the Isabelline style. The College of S. Gregorio in Valladolid (1488–96) is perhaps the best example of this astonishingly ornate style, which is much more 'Baroque' in feeling than Gothic. The influence of Italy made itself felt in the latter half of the reign, and this marks the Renaissance period in architecture. A fusion of Gothic with the decorative features of the Italian style, producing a distinctively Spanish Renaissance style in Plateresque, preceded the classicizing movement proper, or adaptation of the canon of Roman architecture. Gothic and Plateresque overlap, and nothing is more remarkable than the versatility with which architects could turn from one style to the other. Rodrigo Gil de Hontañón (d.1577), perhaps the outstanding architect of his day, not only designed some of the finest Plateresque buildings, but completed the Gothic Cathedral of Salamanca (1513–60) designed by his father, and modified and developed his father's Gothic design for the Cathedral of Segovia (1525–1616). Renaissance influence brought Gothic back in these fine buildings to a massive simplicity, almost a bareness, which gives an air of solemnity and gravity. Segovia is the last cathedral of first rank to be built as a whole in Gothic style, not only in Spain but in the world—a striking example of the strength of tradition in the Spanish Renaissance.

The first imitation of Italian models is seen in the College of Santa Cruz at Valladolid, already referred to, and in the Castle of Calahorra (1509-12) in the province of Granada, which marks the transition from the medieval castle to the Renaissance palace, a grim exterior giving way to an elegant courtyard. A slightly later example of pure Italian classicism is the Palace of Charles V adjoining the Alhambra in Granada, a striking juxtaposition of the Oriental and the European that only Spain can offer. This grandiose building was designed by the painter Pedro Machuca (d.1550), who is thought to have been a pupil of Raphael's. This is his only architectural work; it was begun in 1527 and never finished, the construction being abandoned in 1633. The exterior is square but the courtyard is circular; all the Italian examples of buildings with this pattern are later in date.

p 228 (11)

The term *plateresco* means 'like silversmiths' work'. The style retains the structural forms of the Isabelline Gothic but superimposes upon it the new Italian ornamentation. This decoration is used exuberantly in the florid Gothic manner rather than in a classical one. The Gothic effect is exemplified in the Dominican Priory of S. Esteban in Salamanca, begun in 1524 to the design of Juan de Alava (d.1537), although the sculptures and carvings of the west front were not completed till the 17th century. The west front of Sta María la Grande in Pontevedra (1541) is an even more sumptuous example of Renaissance decoration on a basically Gothic structure. The florid use of Renaissance ornamentation is best seen in the façade of the main University building in Salamanca, attributed to Enrique de Egas and completed in 1529. The same architect is thought to have designed the beautiful Hospital of Santa Cruz in Toledo which, built in 1504–14, is the first large Plateresque building. There is no uniformity about these buildings: theirs was an open style that

p 228 (12)

permitted any number of original variations. Its range can be exemplified by two of the buildings of Rodrigo Gil de Hontañón: the Palace of Monterrey in Salamanca (1539), and the façade of the University of Alcalá (1543) where the style finds perhaps its most harmonious and refined expression. Large Plateresque buildings in which the effect is one of horizontality, closer to the Italian style, rather than of Gothic verticality, are the Town Hall of Seville (1527) by Diego de Riaño (d.1534) and the Priory of S. Marcos in León (1539) by Martín de Villarreal; only half the façade of this latter building was completed at the time, the other half being copied in 1711–16, when the section above the centre doorway was designed.

The first of the non-Gothic cathedrals of the 16th century is the gigantic one of Granada. The first design was Gothic, by Egas, who began the construction in 1523. Five years later he was replaced by Diego de Siloé, who altered the Gothic design into a classical one. The pillars were turned into Corinthian columns and a dome was constructed on 'stilts': technically this is said to be a brilliant solution to the problem of placing a dome above the plan of a Gothic apse, but opinions are divided on its aesthetic merits. The cathedral was not finished till 1703 and its façade is Baroque. The slightly smaller Cathedral of Málaga (1528–1783) is similar in design. The finest of these Renaissance cathedrals is Jaén. Although not completed till 1726, the design, apart from some modifications in the west front, is essentially the one drawn in 1534 by Andrés de Vandaelvira (1509–75). It has been said that the only other church in Renaissance style that can equal Jaén Cathedral in artistic quality is Wren's St Paul's. The movement towards a pure classical style reaches its culmination with the great architect Juan de Herrera (1530–97). His masterpiece, the enormous granite monastery-palace of El Escorial, commissioned by Philip II, was built between 1563 and 1584, and was hailed by contemporaries as the eighth wonder of the world. This is classicism in naked purity, devoid of any Plateresque ornamentation. Especially austere in its mountain setting, it is dignified and impressive, and in some parts, particularly the church, elegant. Another major example of Herrera's work is the unfinished cathedral of Valladolid, which he designed in 1580. Herrera's restrained classicism was in vogue for some twenty years after his death. One of his disciples, Juan Gómez de Mora, was responsible for the magnificent Plaza Mayor of Madrid (1617–19). The church of S. Isidro el Real in Madrid (1626–51) marks the transition to the Baroque, which by the end of the century came to rival the floridity of the Isabelline Gothic of two hundred years before.

p 229 (14)

p 229 (15)

p 228-9 (13)

The Sculptor's Contribution

The sculpture of the period is nearly all on or in churches—stone figures on façades and on tombs, stone or marble screens beside or behind the high altars or, especially characteristic of Spain, the polychrome wood-carvings on the great retables above the altars. As in architecture, the Renaissance meant first a turning away from Flemish to Italian influences and later the emergence of a native style. Italian influence penetrated the Gothic style with a realistic presentation of draperies, attitudes and facial expression instead of stylization and conscious piety. This transition is evident in the *trasaltar* (screen behind the high altar) in Burgos Cathedral in 1499 by the Frenchman Felipe Bigarny. The general influence of humanism is seen in a tendency to represent on tombs and sepulchral slabs not the dead but the living figure. A noteworthy example is the tomb of Martín Vázquez de Arce in Sigüenza Cathedral. Killed in 1486 in the war of Granada, this young man is represented as a crusader with his legs crossed, but only half reclining, and in the very unmilitary but very Renaissance attitude of reading a book. The most distinguished sculptor of this early Renaissance is Damián Forment who completed the splendid retable (1509–15) of the basilica of El Pilar in Saragossa with Renaissance figures within a Gothic framework. His alabaster retable in the monastery of Poblet, designed in 1527, is more Italian in style. Many Spanish sculptors received their training in Italy. One of these was Vasco de la Zarza whose art is pure Renaissance, notably the beautiful *trasaltar* in Avila Cathedral with the tomb of El Tostado in the

p 230, 231 (16, 20)

p 230 (17)

p 231 (18)

The female nude is extremely rare in Spanish art, probably because almost all patronage was ecclesiastical. This panel of Eve from the choir-stalls of Toledo Cathedral is by Alonso Berruguete (see pl 19). Though clearly in the classical tradition she lacks some of the sensuousness which an Italian sculptor would have given her. (12)

centre. The classical movement was strong at Granada, not only in Siloé's cathedral but in the tombs of the earlier Chapel Royal. That of Ferdinand and Isabella (1514–17) is the work of an Italian, Domenico Fancelli; that of their daughter Queen Joan and her husband Philip I (1526) is by Bartolomé Ordóñez, who might have been apprenticed to Fancelli before he went to Italy. Siloé himself left a great of sculptured work, mostly purely decorative, in Burgos as well as in Granada. The Madonna and Child on the choir-stalls of S. Jerónimo in the latter city is characteristic of his adoption of Italian idealization. This classical movement in sculpture, which had a secular side in the provision of civic statuary for Granada and Seville, culminated in the work for the Escorial. The chief sculptor was an Italian, Pompeo Leoni, but he was preceded by a Spaniard, Juan Bautista de Monegro, whose work is less naturalistic, more sober and austere than Leoni's.

Departure from idealization characterizes the more distinctively Spanish style which emerged with Alonso Berruguete (c.1490–1561), the greatest of all these sculptors, who studied in Italy, copying Michelangelo in Florence and the Laocoön in Rome. The pioneer of Mannerism in Spain, he disowned grace, elegance and anatomical accuracy, exaggerating muscles and dynamic expression; instead of serenity and classical composure there is a sense of fervour, passion and drama. Berruguete must have influenced El Greco, whose distortions represent a transformation in his style after his arrival in Spain. In a panel of Eve in his choir-stalls for Toledo Cathedral Berruguete has given us one of the rare representations of the female nude in Spanish art. The absence of something so characteristic of the Italian Renaissance is to be explained both by a strain of puritanism in Spanish life and by the fact that nearly all this art was commissioned by ecclesiastical patrons. Berruguete's Eve, not being Venus, is not sensuous but austere. Mannerism was continued by Juan de Juní (c.1507–77), a Frenchman who came to Spain about the age of twenty-five and underwent the influence of Berruguete. He was a sensualist who could express human happiness and grace, as in his Madonna in the church of Sta María at Medina de Ríoseco, but more typical of his art is the sense of anguish and desolation. Within the Counter-Reformation this Mannerist sculpture developed into Baroque, represented by such artists as Pedro de Mena and Alonso Cano: there is greater restraint in posture and draperies, expressiveness being concentrated in the faces in which the artists try to convey the idea of sanctity by a mystical rapture.

Mysticism in Paint

The strength of religious feeling in Spain throughout the Renaissance period is also evident in her paintings, nearly all of which are either religious subjects or portraits. The greatest painter in the reign of the Catholic Kings is Pedro Berruguete (c.1450–1504), father of Alonso. His work at first sight seems Flemish, even primitive, yet until 1483 he worked in Italy, collaborating with Piero della Francesca and painting some of the portraits of philosophers for the Duke of Urbino. In his religious pictures, behind the Flemish atmosphere of his style, one can detect the art of perspective and a power of endowing each figure with a human personality. A charming instance of the fusion in art of the old world and the new is the *Virgin of the Navigators* by Alejo Fernández (1508–43), in which the Virgin spreads her cloak, medieval-wise, over a fleet of ships like those that sailed to America; one of the kneeling figures, seen in profile on the left, may be Columbus. All trace of medievalism disappeared with the full influence of the Italian Renaissance, more particularly of Leonardo, in Hernando Yañez and Hernando Llanos, who both spent a long period in Italy. This Italian influence, rather sentimentalized, was transmitted at second hand to Juan de Juanes (c.1523–79). A Spanish style, with a dignified and unemotional naturalism, emerged with Francisco Ribalta (c.1551–1628), who foreshadows Zurbarán.

The period of the Counter-Reformation is dominated in Spain by the Cretan El Greco (Dominikos Theotokopuli, 1541–1614) who settled in Toledo in the 1570s. Though his strange and novel art did not always meet with the approval of his royal and ecclesiastical patrons, he was never short of commissions. It is difficult to conceive any other country's stimulating and accepting his art, which is the nearest that paint has come to expressing a mystical *élan*. One of his great canvases, the *Burial of Count Orgaz*, painted in 1586 for the little church of Sto. Tomé in Toledo where it still is, sums up better than anything else the spirit of 16th-century Spain. The lower and upper halves represent the human and the supernatural worlds respectively. The former is presented with great dignity; the faces of the living are calm and serene, thus being a human society consicous of its worth; in the foreground the theme of death is treated with tenderness and is dominated by the Church which is the threshold to the afterlife, for the two parts are linked by the priest who is looking upwards to Heaven; this is presented as full of light and movement, the static and dignified human world explodes upwards into vitality.

The great age of Spain's painting, like that of her literature, is the 17th century. The revaluation of the human, which the Renaissance had brought about, is apparent, for instance, in Zurbarán's paintings of female saints, who are ordinary women, unidealized and unexalted, but gracious with an unaffected candour. It is seen also in the dignity and composure with which Velázquez portrays his sitters, even the beggars and the dwarfs. Like the literature, this is an art that neither worships an idealized antiquity nor feels any festive sensuousness: when Velázquez paints Bacchanalia in *The Topers*, his god Bacchus is a good-looking but perfectly ordinary youth and his companions are ordinary men from the streets, good-humouredly tipsy but treated with sympathy and respect.

p 231 (19)
f 12
p 231 (20)
p 322 (13)
p 234 (31)

IX TRADITION AND CHANGE

English Society under the Tudors

JOEL HURSTFIELD

'We will unite the white rose and the red.

Smile heaven upon this fair conjunction,

That long have frowned upon their enmity.'

SHAKESPEARE, 'RICHARD III'

After a generation of bloodshed

a new dynasty, the Tudors, brought lasting stability to England. Henry Tudor united the claims of Lancaster and York, being descended through his mother from John of Gaunt and marrying Elizabeth of York the eldest daughter of Edward IV. It would be misleading to interpret the Tudor Age that followed as a direct result of this settlement. Many of the developments that took place might well have occurred whoever sat on the throne; and in fact some of the administrative 'innovations' of Henry VII can be traced back to the reigns of Edward IV and Richard III. Nevertheless it is a significant moment. The wound that was sapping the best energies of the country was healed. Henry's government was that of a businessman; abjuring glamour and glory he consistently pursued the more solid virtues of commercial success and financial solvency, and was accordingly accused of meanness.

In the realm of ideas the change was not immediately felt. England lagged behind the rest of Europe in the new scholarship, in humanist culture and the revival of classical art. Henry created the conditions by which this backwardness could be made good, but was himself little inclined to intellectual and artistic pursuits. His son Henry VIII, however, had the opposite temperament, and it was with his reign that the Renaissance became a living force in England.

In reading English history against the background of the Italian Renaissance it is difficult to believe that they belong to the same world. When the Battle of Agincourt was fought Ghiberti was at work on his first doors, Brunelleschi was thirty-eight and Alberti eleven; when Richard III was killed at Bosworth Botticelli, Perugino and Ghirlandaio were at the height of their careers; in 1509, when Henry VII died and when, in England, the last glories of the Perpendicular style were rising at King's College Chapel and Bath Abbey, Michelangelo was painting the Sistine Ceiling, Raphael the *Stanze* and Bramante's new St Peter's had just been started. The chapel begun by Henry VII to be his chantry in Westminster Abbey is perhaps the masterpiece of Perpendicular, with pendant vaults, delicate tracery and expressive sculptured figures subordinated to the architectural scheme. But in the centre, within a screen still in the old style (by an English artist, Laurence Imber) stands the bronze monument of Henry VII and his queen by Pietro Torrigiani of Florence—and at one step we move from the English Middle Ages to the Italian High Renaissance. The tomb had not been commissioned in Henry VII's lifetime and the choice of Torrigiani was, it seems, Henry VIII's. It was begun in 1512 and completed by 1518. Effigies of the king and queen, swathed in ample drapery, lie on a classical sarcophagus, decorated with candelabra shapes. Other motifs include medallions surrounded by wreaths, winged putti and at the corners child-like angels of a pure Italianate beauty.

The tomb of Henry VII was no more than an augury for the future. Native artists were slow to follow its example, and when the Renaissance style did become general at the end of the 16th century it was a typical compromise of traditional elements and Italianate features adapted via France and Flanders. (1)

Church and State were knotted together in all European countries, but perhaps nowhere more so than in England, where the solution of the Reformation conflict was to make the king the head of the Church. Here Henry VIII lies on his deathbed passing the succession to his son Edward VI. Beside him stand the Protector Somerset, and the Council of the Protectorate, including Cranmer. In the foreground is the Pope, mortally sick, whom two monks are hurriedly forsaking. In the view through the window soldiers hurl down an image of the Virgin. (2)

Resistance to the religious changes came at every level, though most churchmen settled down fairly comfortably to the new order. This drawing (right) shows a judge riding out of Colchester after the trial of Abbot Beche (1539). The Abbot had been accused of high treason and, as Cromwell expressed it, 'sent down to be tried and executed' in his own diocese. In the tiny scene top right the sentence is being carried out. (3)

Propaganda was carried out extensively during this period by means of pamphlets and above all by sermons. The most influential pulpit of them all was that at Paul's Cross, in London (right). It stood to the south of old St Paul's Cathedral and was sometimes used by the government to disseminate its policies, but it was, on occasion, an organ of dissent. (5)

'The Bussop of Rome, the Four Evangelists casting stones at him'— the Protestant position expressed crudely but forcibly in visual terms. This is an Italian work, owned by Henry VIII. (4)

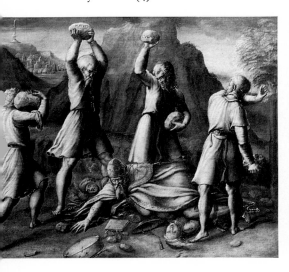

Thomas Cromwell, the king's chief adviser for eight years, presided over the dissolution of the monasteries, to his own considerable profit. In 1540 he lost Henry's favour and was executed for heresy and high treason. (6)

Thomas Cranmer, appointed Archbishop of Canterbury by Henry VIII in 1533, was chief architect of the English Reformation. He was executed, like Latimer and Ridley, in the reign of Mary Tudor. (7)

Reginald Pole stood for the English Catholics' opposition to Henry. Forced to live abroad, he returned as cardinal on the accession of Mary and worked to restore Catholicism, dying on the same day as the queen. (8)

ANNO DÑI   1544

LADI MARI   DOVGHTER TO
THE MOST   VERTVOVS PRINCE
KINGE HENRI   THE EIGHT

THE AGE OF   XXVIII YERES

Henry VIII's personal character is of perennial interest and looms large on the pages of history. In his early years he was a generous patron and a man of considerable literary and musical talent. When he came to the throne Erasmus and others looked forward to a Golden Age in England which would eclipse every other country in Europe. Their hopes were disappointed, though the fault was not entirely Henry's. England was caught up in the larger conflicts of the Reformation. Henry attempted a compromise—roughly, to retain Catholic doctrine but to renounce allegiance to the Pope. His difficulties were aggravated by his grandiose foreign policy (which gave him an added motive for despoiling the Church) and by his domestic troubles. The end of his reign contradicted its hopeful beginning. Intellectual freedom was severely curtailed, and to think differently from the king became heresy and treason. (9)

Mary I, Henry's daughter by Catherine of Aragon, was all her life a staunch Catholic. On her accession in 1553 (her brother Edward VI only lived to be sixteen) she set about reversing the Reformation. She married Philip of Spain in 1554, but failed to produce an heir and died four years later. The foreign marriage was unpopular and the next swing of the pendulum back to Protestantism under Elizabeth had overwhelming public support. (10)

Elizabeth, aged twenty-five on her accession, succeeded in uniting the nation as her father, brother and sister had never done. Religious passion was damped down and her Catholic subjects were for the most part loyal (the alternative seemed to be Spanish domination). Practical affairs were in the hands of a statesman of immense skill and patience, William Cecil, Lord Burghley. She was sometimes at loggerheads with her Puritans and Parliamentarians who wanted more freedom of speech. But she possessed sufficient charm and political sense to retain the affection and loyalty of her people.

Elizabeth reigned for nearly 45 years and became a familiar figure to her subjects. Every year she would go on a 'progress', visiting the country houses of the gentry (though never too far away from London), entertaining, being entertained, flattering and receiving flattery. She was extremely intelligent, spoke several European languages fluently, had a good knowledge of Latin and Greek, and was among the most learned women of her time. This picture, painted towards the end of her reign, shows her on a progress or on some ceremonial procession. (11)

'The ancient and famous city of London', as one proud contemporary described it, was growing fast throughout the Tudor period. Most of these details are taken from drawings by a Dutchman, Antony van der Wyngaerde, made about 1550. Above: Westminster, with St Stephen's Chapel on the left, then Westminster Hall and behind it the squat shape of the Abbey without its towers. Right: old London Bridge, for many centuries the only bridge across the Thames at London. It was constructed in the late 12th century and many times repaired. Houses began to be built on it as early as the 13th century. It was the custom to nail the heads of executed criminals above the main gateway. (12,15)

Old St Paul's (above) stood until the Great Fire of London. It was one of the largest churches in Europe; the nave dated from the 12th century, the choir from the 13th and the spire from 1315 (this was destroyed by fire in 1561). (13)

St Mary Overie (left), on the south bank of the river ('Over-ie' means 'over the water') still survives as Southwark Cathedral. This view is from Norden's engraving of 1616. (14)

The Renaissance came to London in two buildings now destroyed—the Protector's Somerset House (1547) and Gresham's Royal Exchange (above), begun in 1566 in a style that was more Flemish than Italian. (16)

The Tower looks in Wyngaerde's drawing much as it does today. London in the 16th century was outwardly still a medieval city. (17)

Greenwich Palace (below) was Henry VIII's favourite residence. Here Elizabeth was born and Edward VI died. (18)

The life-story of an Elizabethan gentleman is depicted in the curious memorial-painting of Sir Henry Unton (above). Born into a prosperous county family of Berkshire in about 1557, he fought in the Low Countries with Sir Philip Sidney and was knighted in 1586. In 1591 he was sent as ambassador to France and died there in 1596. The painted narrative begins in the bottom right-hand corner with his birth (to the left are scenes from his private life at Wadley, including a gay banquet with musicians and masquers). Next, on the extreme right, we see his career at Oriel College, his travels in Italy (Venice and Padua), his war-service in the Low Countries, his embassy to France and his death in the camp before La Fère. His body is brought back across the Channel and the rest of the bottom of the picture (going from right to left) shows the funeral and burial in Faringdon Church. (19)

Fashions for the middle-classes: Joris Hofnägel's panorama of English society about 1569 is set at Bermondsey, then a pleasant district for relaxation, but does not seem to represent any particular occasion. The clothes range from expensive dresses that would not have been out of place at court to ordinary working-clothes and military uniforms. (20)

The seats of learning, the ancient and well-endowed universities of Oxford and Cambridge, put up at first some conservative opposition to the innovations of humanism. Greek studies began at Oxford when William Grocyn returned from Italy in 1491. At Cambridge, seen (below) in an engraving of 1574, only the arrival of Erasmus, who taught Greek at Queens' College from 1511 to 1514, brought it firmly within the sphere of the New Learning. Some years later it was the home of an early group of Protestants. (21)

Galeni de sanitate tuenda Libri sex Thoma Linacro Anglo Interprete.

The English humanists formed a close group mostly of personal friends. Thomas Linacre, like Grocyn, studied in Italy. His translation of Galen was made for Cardinal Wolsey, and the frontispiece (left) shows Galen on one side, Linacre on the other, and the Cardinal's hat above the shield. (22)

John Colet (c. 1467–1519), after travelling in France and Italy, lectured on the Epistles, challenging the orthodox view on philological grounds and arousing strong opposition, though he remained a loyal Catholic. (23)

Richard Fox (c. 1448–1528), Bishop of Winchester and Lord Privy Seal, founded Corpus Christi College, Oxford, in 1516, making provision for a lectureship in Greek. (24)

William Camden (1551–1623) belonged to a later generation. His *Britannia* (1586), an antiquarian survey following the pioneer work of Leland, did for Britain what Biondo had done for Italy. (25)

'The house at Chelsea', wrote Erasmus of his friend Sir Thomas More, 'is a veritable school of the Christian religion. In it is none, man or woman, but readeth and studieth the liberal arts.' This drawing by Holbein shows More himself, in the centre, his father next to him in judge's robes, his three daughters, his son John and daughter-in-law Anne. Left: the Island of Utopia, a woodcut from an early edition of More's greatest work. (26,27)

The anatomy lesson: John Banister (1540–1610), one of the best known of Elizabethan surgeons, demonstrates a dissection. Banister was the author of several medical works, mostly based on foreign writers—'sucked from the sap of the most approved anatomists,' as he put it. (28)

Portraiture 'in little' was an art in which England excelled the world. Nicholas Hilliard, the greatest of the miniaturists, expresses with unique vividness the freshness and romantic fervour of Renaissance England. His pictures often conceal an allegorical message. About the youth dressed in Italian fashions (above), standing with his hand on his heart among thorny roses, many theories have been proposed. It has even been suggested that he is Shakespeare's 'Mr. W. H.' (31)

Artistic inspiration came overwhelmingly from abroad. Hans Eworth (see Chapter x) migrated from Antwerp to London in 1547. His curious allegorical portrait showing Sir John Luttrell (above) is typical of the new taste. The theme seems to be the triumph of Peace after storms. Peace herself, holding Sir John's raised right arm, is probably an addition by a French artist of the Fontainebleau School. (29)

Henry VIII's answer to Chambord was the huge palace of Nonesuch (right). Although boasting an unparalleled wealth of ornament by 'the most excellent artificers, architects, sculptors and statuaries of different nations' it clearly had little of true Renaissance discipline. (30)

The mystery of Longleat (above) is how a house of such consistent classicism could have been designed in England in 1568 (possibly even earlier). Nothing so accomplished was seen until Inigo Jones in the 1620s. The builder was Sir John Thynne, 'an ingenious man and a travalier', but who was the architect? Possibly Robert Smythson, possibly an Italian, possibly Thynne himself. The use of the orders comes from Italy or France, but the crestings above the bays are Flemish. (32)

The native tradition continued in the humbler arts almost untouched by the Renaissance. This embroidered table-carpet dates from the late 16th century. The hunting scenes form the border of a floral patterned tapestry. (33)

George Gascoigne (c. 1525–77), seen here presenting his poems to Queen Elizabeth, was among the early 'popularizers' of the Renaissance. He adapted plays by Euripides (in blank verse) and by Ariosto—the first English comedy in prose. (35)

Sir Philip Sidney (below) embodied the ideal Renaissance 'courtier' perhaps more completely than any other man. His poems are full of Italianate ideas; his *Arcadia* introduced the pastoral to England; while his *Apologie for Poetrie* combines humanist theory with genuine personal feeling. (36)

'The Byble in Englyshe'—Henry VIII's official version of the Old and New Testaments issued in 1539—was a decisive step not only in the Anglican religion but in English culture as a whole. Whether the Scriptures should be available to the non-learned had long been a subject of controversy. English translations had been made, and banned, since Wycliffe; but with Henry's 'Great Bible' they began to be part of the thought and language of everyone. The text was based on that of the great translators of the previous thirty years. The titlepage (above) shows Henry presenting the new work (*Verbum Dei*) to Cromwell and Cranmer, who distribute it to the clergy who expound it to the laity, all uttering sentiments of gratifying loyalty. (34)

It was in drama that the English Renaissance found its clearest and deepest expression. The medieval theatre, with its Mystery Cycles, and allegorical Miracle Plays, finally died out in the early 16th century. The new impetus came from abroad. Plautus' comedies were translated, tragedies composed in imitation of Seneca and blank verse adopted as their fitting medium. In the country houses of the nobility private companies of actors were formed, and these went on to build theatres of their own. The first public playhouse in London opened in 1577. Soon there were half a dozen, each under the nominal patronage of a nobleman. This was the situation when Shakespeare came to London about 1587. Shakespeare was a genius of a peculiarly self-sufficient kind, but his dependence upon European Renaissance sources is undeniable, ranging from Sir Thomas North's translation of Plutarch to sentimental Italian romances. (37)

Ben Jonson's debt was more direct and was frankly acknowledged. Proud of his classical learning, Jonson attempted in his tragedies to revive the forms and even the words of ancient Rome—much of *Cataline* is a free translation of Cicero and Sallust. (38)

Shakespeare's theatre: the exterior of the Globe Theatre in 1616; the interior of the Swan c. 1596; and the only known contemporary illustration of a Shakespeare play—*Titus Andronicus*, a sketch of 1594. (39, 40, 41)

Entertaining the Queen could be the occasion of almost limitless expense. Scenery, costumes, music, poetry and every kind of spectacle were brought in. Such performances had an important effect on the professional theatre, as the free use of stage machinery, pageantry and music in Elizabethan drama shows. This woodcut illustrates the masque arranged for the Queen at Elvetham by the Earl of Hertford in 1591. A crescent-shaped pond was dug, leaving three islands, one of them with a fort on it. The Queen was received by Nereus and his tritons blowing conches. A mock attack was staged on the fort; a pinnace with singers and musicians sailed past; and dinner was accompanied by volleys of cannon from another island. (42)

English patriotism reached its peak in 1588 with the defeat of the Spanish Armada. The immense fleet of 129 vessels assembled by Philip II was to sail to the Netherlands, join with the Spanish army and invade the south coast. When it reached the Channel it was opposed by a powerful force of English ships under Lord Howard of Effingham. The engraving (above) is from a series of ten published in 1590 to illustrate the course of the battle. The left hand side shows an incident of July 24th when the Triumph and four other ships were cut off from the rest until rescued by the main fleet. On the right the Lord Admiral divides his ships into four squadrons, 'by means of which division the enemy might be greatly and more continually troubled.' When the Spaniards reached Calais, ships blazing with pitch were sent into the harbour; the Armada panicked, sailed north, abandoned the invasion and returned home by way of the Orkneys and Ireland. Only 54 ships managed to reach Spain. (43)

Robert Dudley, Earl of Leicester, commanded the land forces at the time of the Armada. He was Elizabeth's first and dearest favourite. They had perhaps known each other since youth. When Elizabeth came to the throne he rose rapidly at court. For a time she thought seriously of marrying him, but had to give way to the opposition of the country. His unpopularity increased when his wife died mysteriously but Elisabeth continued to favour him. In 1585 he was given the command of the army in the Netherlands (Sir Philip Sidney, who died on this campaign, was his nephew). When the Armada was already dispersing towards Scotland she visited his headquarters at Tilbury and made the most famous of her speeches: 'I know I have the body of a weak and feeble woman, but I have the heart and stomach of a king, and of a King of England too.' Leicester died a few weeks later, without (perhaps fortunately) having to prove his military talents against the invaders. (44)

English Society under the Tudors

JOEL HURSTFIELD

'*The Groundworke of Conny-Catching*' by Robert Greene (*1592*) was 'a warning to all men to shun the crafty cozening sleights of these both men and women that have termed themselves Conny catchers', that is, cheats, vagabonds and crooks of all sorts. The book contains a vocabulary of their slang and full descriptions of their tricks, some of which are illustrated on the titlepage—for instance card sharping and the Curbing Law, or hooking at windows. At the top the judge, scourge and gallows point to the conny-catcher's end. Greene himself had first-hand knowledge of the Elizabethan underworld, spending most of his short life on the fringes of 'cozening'. (1)

IN ITS CULTURE, as in its geography, England in the early 16th century lay on the edge of Renaissance Europe. Separated from the continental land mass by a narrow channel of water, at one point not much more than twenty miles across, it somehow escaped, as it did for centuries, the impact of major European developments, or received them late and changed by their sea journey. The structure of English society, too, although it formally resembled the kingdoms of north-western Europe with monarchy, aristocracy, clergy and commonalty, displayed also a marked difference from them in the gap between the form and reality of its class distinctions. To more than one foreign observer, the subtle inflections of its social order, and its traditions and attitudes, seemed insular and self-contradictory.

A Venetian diplomat, *en poste* in London at the beginning of the new century, saw England as a prosperous country with fertile soil, beautiful landscape, and a martial people, yet one inclined to set great store by their physical comforts, especially food and drink. He said that they were a proud people too, who thought well of themselves and rather less of foreigners. They were quick and intelligent rather than educated, regular in church attendance but in many cases sympathetic to novel opinions. (The diplomat here confirms what historians have only recently rediscovered, namely that the Lollards had made greater inroads among Church and people than was at one time believed.) This independence of mood, he believed, extended even to their relations with their monarch, for they were not as devoted to their Crown as were the Scots. The English by nature, apparently, 'hate their present sovereign and extol their dead ones'. The Wars of the Roses had ended only half a generation before but the threat of dynastic war was by no means banished. Henry VII he respected, describing him indeed as the most secure monarch since the days of William the Conqueror. It is interesting and significant to notice, in passing, that while the ambassador refers to the king as 'His Majesty', contemporary Englishmen usually did not: he was known as 'His Highness'; but the style was coming in. Majesty belonged much more to the next reign and a new generation. It belonged also to an outlook more in keeping with the political and cultural trends in Renaissance Europe.

With such a degree of physical and intellectual isolation, it is hardly surprising that the effects of the Renaissance came slowly and late to England. In the middle of the 15th century, large-scale intellectual intercourse through print did not exist. Communication, whether by land or sea, with the great Italian cities was still primitive; and to these inhibitions were added the hair-raising travellers' tales of the hazards—physical and moral—which lost nothing of their terror to successive generations. Long afterwards, late in Queen Elizabeth's reign, Lord Treasurer Burghley was to warn his son against crossing the Alps where a man would learn nothing but atheism, blasphemy and vice. In Thomas Nashe's *The Unfortunate Traveller*, published in 1594, we have these monitory tales in their most extravagant form. It is not a one-sided story, however. Our Venetian diplomat unwittingly reciprocates the compliment. The English law-courts, he observes, are extremely harsh; but severe measures are apparently ineffectual. '. . . There is no country in the world', he writes, 'where there are so many thieves and robbers as in England, in so much that few

f 6

f 1

venture to go alone in the country, excepting in the middle of the day, and fewer still in the towns at night, and least of all in London.'

A Portrait of England

England in the 15th century was, and long remained, a place of small towns. London was the only significant exception and even here the population did not exceed 50,000. There were also ancient cathedral towns like Winchester, Canterbury and York; industrial centres like Norwich; ports like Southampton and Bristol. But in most places no traditions of urban culture had ever existed or could even be remotely conceived. On the other hand, aristocratic patronage was equally rare. The heads of the great baronial families looked to war and to internal territorial expansion as their most attractive and rewarding enterprises, not the unlikely prospects of some enduring fame as patrons of art or literature. The English baronage was rural in wealth, influence and outlook. To turn from them, for example to the cultured patriciate of Florence, is to move from the darkness into the light. Humphrey, Duke of Gloucester, was the exception not the rule. The poets were not members of a cultured group gathered round some provincial court but monks, baronial officials, civil servants. The town chroniclers could on occasion provide fascinating narratives but, for the most part, they were content to record the repetitive trivia of municipal officialdom.

f 2

Such other prospects as may have existed of widening the range of patronage were drowned in the intermittent wars with France, lasting until the middle of the 15th century, followed by an internal struggle for power between those magnates, or their heirs, who had at last been driven from French territory. This internal poverty, war and instability were, of course, reflected in the Court itself where no 15th-century monarch (other than Edward IV) had more than a decade of settled power. Even Henry VII, the first of a new and powerful dynasty, had no really secure hold on his throne until the opening years of the 16th century. Hence, until the time of the Tudors, any significant Court patronage was out of the question.

When we turn from the monarch and the baronage to the other source of power, the Church, the story is comparable. For a large part of the Middle Ages, government had been administered by churchmen and paid for by the Church. The servants of the Crown held bishoprics, deaneries and other ecclesiastical offices, usually *in absentia*. Their stipends as churchmen enabled them to take on the secular duties of administration. Where they had

267

Bristol in 1611 is described as 'one of the greatest and famous Citties in England' but is still comparatively very small. One of its unusual features is that 'ther is no dunghill in all the Cittie nor any sinke that cometh from any house into the streets but all is conveyed under ground'. (2)

'Scholars like Ingenious Bees'

Yet, in spite of the built-in resistance to alien influences, England in the late 15th and early 16th centuries was by no means immune to the prevailing winds. Certainly, from the middle of the 15th century, churchmen like William Grey (the future Bishop of Ely) and baronial leaders like John Tiptoft, Earl of Worcester, had come back from Italy with new attitudes to culture and perhaps also to society itself. But the central event was the return to England in 1491 of William Grocyn after his period of study in Florence and Rome. It was now that Oxford had its first experience of Greek scholarship where Grocyn's disciples included Erasmus and More, whose fame would shortly outdistance his own. His fellow-Englishman in Italy, Thomas Linacre, took the whole Italian world within his sphere of interest. Bologna, Florence, Rome, Venice, Padua, Vicenza gave Linacre access to classical sources in the arts and sciences, as well as enabling him to study medicine under the leading teachers of his day. On his return he too taught at Oxford, and then in the royal household, becoming in the new reign physician to Henry VIII. Yet Linacre, the founder of the Royal College of Physicians was, like Grocyn, a priest. For them there was no conflict between ecclesiastical doctrine and classical learning. Erasmus says of his patron, Grocyn, that he was 'exceedingly observant of ecclesiastical rules, almost to the point of superstition, and to the highest degree learned in scholastic theology; while he was, at the same time, a man gifted by nature with the most acute judgment and exactly versed in every description of educational knowledge.' If their influence began in Oxford, it did not end there. It was Linacre's Latin Grammar which John Colet adopted for his new school, St Paul's, founded in 1510.

p 128 (25)

p 260 (22)

p 260 (23)

No less influential was the work of Richard Fox, administrator, diplomat, scholar, architect, bishop, founder in 1517 of Corpus Christi College, Oxford, and himself a great sponsor of humanist studies in the university. But it is clearly a humanism planted firmly in a Christian context. Nowhere is his mood better revealed—and with it the climate of his whole generation—than in the founding statutes of Corpus Christi, of which the preamble runs:

p 260 (24) f 3

> In honour of the most precious body of Our Lord Jesus Christ, and of His most Holy Mother, and of all the other saints, patrons of the cathedral churches of Winchester, Durham, Bath and Wells, as also of Exeter, We Richard Fox, by Divine Vocation, Bishop of Winchester, founder, builder, and endower of the College of Corpus Christi in the University of Oxford, first invoking the most dread name of the most holy and undivided Trinity, have framed our Statutes for the same college, and have written them in this original book, for their constant and everlasting remembrance and establishment: and We, the aforesaid, have set our seal thereto in manner following:

It is followed by a clear exposition of the role of learning in society:

> We have no abiding city here, as saith the Apostle, but we seek one to come in heaven at which we hope to arrive with the greater ease and dispatch if while we travel in this life, wretched and death-doomed as it is, we rear a ladder whereby we may gain a readier ascent. We give the name of virtue to the right side of the ladder, and that of knowledge, to the left, and between these two sides lie steps; for either side hath rungs of its own by which we may either soar on high, or sink into the lowest depths. We, therefore, Richard Fox, by Divine Providence, Bishop of Winchester, being both desirous ourselves of ascending by this ladder to heaven and of entering therein and being anxious to aid and assist others in a similar ascent and entrance, have founded, reared, and constructed in the University of Oxford, out of the means which God of his bounty hath bestowed on us, a certain bee garden which we have named the College of Corpus Christi, wherein scholars, like ingenious bees are by day and night to make wax to the honour of God, and honey, dropping sweetness, to the profit of themselves and of all Christians.

And then, having made provision as to the curriculum of the

---

intellectual interests as well, these tended to be part of the thought and culture of the Church and the schoolmen.

All this is not to say that English culture passed through bleak decades of sterility, unease and social disorder. English ecclesiastical architecture, for example, magnificently displayed its vigour and initiative. Merchants, gentry, nobility sometimes raised impressive buildings full of vitality, dignity and enduring beauty. Local guilds produced miracle and morality plays, civil pageants and other lively expressions of a traditional art form. But, over a large field, inspiration came from domestic sources and the impact of Italian culture was at first minimal. What was true of culture in general was equally true of education, whether at school or university. So, when humanism began to make its impact on English life it was both cause and effect. It caused a fundamental re-direction in education and produced a profound change in all branches of culture. But, on the other hand, its acceptance and dissemination were the effect of political and social changes and needs, calling for an outlook and training which medieval institutions and doctrines were quite unable to provide.

But although the Church had always known of the advantages to be gained from recruiting educated men to its service, the English nobility and the upper classes in general were much slower to grasp the point. The Venetian ambassador, whom we have already cited, expressed astonishment at the speed with which Englishmen—however wealthy they were—sent their children, aged nine or less, to be boarded out in other men's houses, while they took in strangers' children themselves. When he asked them why they did this, he was told it was so that the children 'might learn better manners'. In his report home, however, the diplomat rejected this explanation and suggested that the real reason was their wish 'to enjoy all their comforts themselves'. They believed themselves to be 'better served by strangers than they would be by their own children'. In any case, they could then 'indulge in the most delicate fare themselves and give their household the coarsest bread and beer, and cold meat baked on Sunday for the week'. If they had their children at home with them 'they would be obliged to give them the same food they made use of for themselves'. Englishmen had, too, great advantages for study with two such well-founded and well-endowed universities at Oxford and Cambridge. Yet, although they were quick at learning, few of them, except the clergy, were 'addicted to the study of letters'. The invasion of the universities by the sons of gentlemen had yet to come. Before the end of the 16th century it would be familiar enough.

p 260 (21)

College, resting on the three pillars of Latin, Greek and Divinity, and for the qualifications of the staff, Fox tried to ensure that his foundation should have access to foreign scholars rather than succumb to a perpetuated insularity in which only Oxford graduates could be appointed to Oxford posts:

> And if no person in our College shall be found competent in the judgment of the President and the electors for the office of any lecturer vacating, or if any person in our College be found competent, and yet a stranger shall be found much more learned . . . then we will that he shall be preferred to that office and as public lecturer before all the fellows and scholars of our College . . . provided only he is born in England, Greece, or Italy, beyond the Po.

Meanwhile, Italian influence of a lesser kind began to make itself felt in England. The papal collectors, Giovanni Gigli and Polydore Vergil, found patronage at the English court. Vergil's career was, for a time, blasted by the enmity of Cardinal Wolsey; but he lived long enough to see the publication, after the fall of the Cardinal, of his *Historia Anglica*, begun many years ago at the end of Henry VII's reign. Another of their countrymen, Pietro Carmeliano, was the first holder of the office of Latin Secretary, established by Henry VII; while some of his lesser contemporaries sought access to the royal bounty with undistinguished Latin compositions in verse and prose.

If, in the intellectual field, English priest, physician, bishop, as well as Italian poet and historian, made characteristic contributions to the Renaissance in this country, it was a cardinal who gave it its greatest impetus in the world of affairs. Wolsey's recruitment of lay scholars and churchmen alike to his service—of the calibre of Richard Pace, Richard Morrison, John Clement, Richard Sampson and Cuthbert Tunstall—ensured for men of the New Learning advancement and reward in the state. At the same time, Cardinal's College, Oxford—not long after his death to become King's College and, in due course, Christ Church—was an impressive monument to the state's hopes of the next generation. Here, too, liberal humanism flourished and, in spite of conservative resistance, Oxford found room also for the beginnings of religious dissent, a process already at work at Cambridge. Thus in this brief interval of moderation, it was possible for some diversity of opinion to be sheltered by the Cardinal of England himself, against the accustomed rigours of the Church. And if the New Learning flourished in Oxford under the high patronage of Wolsey, far away in Padua, in the household of Reginald Pole, kinsman and future critic of Henry VIII, there gathered alumni of Cardinal's College like Richard Morrison and Thomas Starkey to continue their apprenticeship in scholarship or statecraft, or both.

f 4, 5

An edition of Polydore Vergil's 'Historia Anglica', printed in Basle in 1534, was much enlivened by drawings scribbled in the margins in about 1550. The illustrations here are of Augustine preaching to King Ethelbert, and Canute forbidding the sea to rise. (4 and 5)

Intellectuals and Utopians

Yet, in summoning scholars to positions of influence, the state took serious risks. The Tudor intellectuals, for all their high distinction in a distinguished age, were hardly a success in the upper ranges of government. At the end of the 16th century, and in the early 17th, we have examples of the all too familiar experience of what happens when an intellectual takes up politics as a career. Sir Walter Ralegh was a failure; so was Sir Francis Bacon. Edmund Spenser got nowhere. All three wrote bitterly about the high cost of the climb to political power: the price to be paid, the sham rewards, the false standards, the disillusionment. In the earlier years of the 16th century, we have the most famous case-history of all in the rise and fall of Sir Thomas More.

p 261
(26, 27)
p 197
(5, 6, 7)

Like his friend Erasmus, More represented the finest expression of the early Renaissance. They brought to bear the full weight of classical scholarship and modern critical techniques upon the literature and tradition of the Church. They were remorseless in their onslaught upon inherited and hallowed superstitions, incisive in style, formidable in the range of their thought and culture. More's *Utopia*, probably completed in 1516, is a brilliant critique of the practice and the fundamental thinking of his own society. But it is much more than a *livre de circonstance*. It reaches beyond Tudor concepts and even Christian doctrine itself to ask what are the basic principles upon which a good society is organized. Here in *Utopia* was the vision of a nation at peace with itself and with its neighbours. Here was a land where men worked freely for all men's welfare and all men had easy access to the wealth they had created. There was no slavery, no oppression of the weak by the strong, no ruthless power based on an intolerable concentration of wealth in few hands. Here was the Christian life, lost to Europe, but re-discovered by the Utopians who were themselves not Christian. *Utopia* was early humanism at its best. But the greatness of its concepts carried the gravest threat to its fulfilment, and indeed to the life, and, more important, the whole way of life of its author. For early Tudor humanism was a compromise: an unworkable one in face of the new political situation which was developing. For the future did not lie with Erasmus and More but with Richard Rich (who betrayed More) and with Thomas Cromwell.

In his recent study of *Utopia*, Professor J. H. Hexter has shown how the driving force behind More had been the belief, in which he followed Erasmus, that true Christian ideals and practice had been perverted by the Aristotelianism of the schoolmen and the social rigidity and inequality of Roman law. The original Christian ideals of poverty, love and spiritual well-being had given place, at least in practice, to private property, material well-being, social hierarchy, usury and all the other abuses which had corrupted

Although Oxford suffered numerous confiscations at the Dissolution, the century also saw a fresh series of academic foundations. Corpus Christi, founded in 1516, was first envisaged as a monastic establishment, but was finally founded on a wider basis 'for such as by their learning shall do good in church and commonwealth'. (3)

the purity of Christian doctrine. So the spirit had been drained out of Christianity and all that remained were the formalities, ritual, a worship of saints amounting almost to idolatry, and all the trappings and rigidities of a narrow creed. Could one bring back to the Church, and at the same time to government, the lost principles of the Christian faith?

The short answer to this question was that one could not. But before we consider the series of events which destroyed all prospects of a society governed by the beliefs of Christian humanism, it is worth examining the inherent strains which were tearing asunder More's compromise. Men like More thought that they had found a way of assimilating the secular approaches of the Renaissance with the teachings of the New Testament. He thought that the humanistic beliefs in the supremacy of intellect and the high classical ideals of the perfectability of man in a man-centred world could somehow be merged with Christian humility, biblical doctrine, and a world centred on God, in whom sinful man found his only perfection in the true life of the spirit. Perhaps More's own life represented such a compromise which succeeded. Perhaps even in his own life the compromise was throughout under heavy strain, which might offer some explanation why so many of us find it difficult to see him whole, to account for his cynicism mingled with saintliness, his compassion with his persecution, his pagan republic which he invented and which was superior to the Christian world he lived in. If, within More's own personality the compromise was difficult to fulfil, in early Tudor England it assumed the character of a contradiction in terms and an anachronism. Edmund Spenser tried, half a century later, to rediscover this compromise in his Christian Platonism; but his very greatness as a poet sets him in a world of his own.

It may be that Henry VIII himself was something of a humanist. Certainly he loved the trappings of a Renaissance court, with its elaborate ceremonial, its high patronage of scholarship: a learned prince presiding over a cultured court. He may too have felt genuinely sympathetic to Erasmian aims to rediscover the foundation of Christian doctrine in terms of the original texts. Perhaps, indeed, this amateur theologian saw in himself some remote resemblance to the Platonic philosopher-king. But such humanism as he adopted stopped far short of that Christian poverty and humility which More continued to believe might be attainable amidst the worldly considerations of Tudor society. Decades before, Machiavelli had pointed out how inappropriate Christian ideals were in the practice of politics. 'The religion of the ancients', he wrote, 'beatified none but men crowned with worldly glory, such as leaders of armies and founders of republics, whereas our religion has glorified meek and contemplative men rather than men of action.' The times were changing. If *Utopia* was indeed nowhere, *The Prince* stood with both feet firmly on English soil.

p 254 (9)

'This Opulent and Ample Realm'

The generation which saw *The Prince* come to power in England and His Highness transformed into His Majesty saw the end of More's world. But, if England was changing intellectually, it was changing physically as well. We are fortunate, therefore, in this period of change, to have the work of one of the greatest of English antiquaries, John Leland, who put on paper in the 1530s his impressive, detailed, scholarly account of the rich diversity of the land, as he saw it with his own eyes. If the discovery of the world is a characteristic of the Renaissance outlook, then Leland set about his discovery of England in the true Renaissance spirit. He was, he told the king,

> Totally inflamed with a love to see thoroughly all those parts of this your opulent and ample realm that . . . I have so travelled in your dominions, both by the sea-coasts and the middle parts, sparing neither labour nor costs, by the space of these six years past, that there is almost neither cape nor bay, haven, creek or pier, river or confluence of rivers, breaches, washes, lakes, meres, fenny waters, mountains, valleys, moors, heaths, forests woods, cities, boroughs, castles, principal manor places, monasteries and colleges, but I have seen them; and noted in so doing a whole world of things very memorable.

It is sad after all this to record that Leland died bankrupt, broken-hearted and insane, his work unfinished. But he left voluminous notes of his itineraries; and we can therefore follow him some of the way. We know that the way was difficult, the roads bad, the population sparse. He found many of the old chartered boroughs in decline but he noted also that some insignificant towns, like Liverpool, were showing signs of growth. He found many of the medieval castles decaying shells except for those like Warwick which had undergone a process of internal reconstruction to meet the needs of comfort rather than civil war. Before he was much older he would know that the monasteries and abbeys had been submitted to faster destructive processes, save those converted into Protestant churches or into the country seats of the new nobility or the gentry, like Woburn in Bedfordshire which went to the rising family of the Russells, future Earls of Bedford.

But Leland's England was not a static society. There was plenty of evidence of movement and change. There was movement along the coast bringing coal from Newcastle and carrying wool textiles from the outports overseas; movement down the Thames estuary to France, Flanders and beyond; movement down the navigable rivers of food, timber, industrial products; movement across country as cattle was brought on the hoof, to be fattened in the home counties for the London food market. And there is plenty of evidence too of the drift to London, already reaching impressive dimensions, that ceaseless process which has lasted on into the present century.

Yet, when all is said, England remained a lightly populated country, and Wales and Scotland even more so. By the middle of the 16th century the population of London was approaching 100,000 but that of the rest of the country stood at no higher than about three million. (The population of France was perhaps four times as high.) It was still a country occupied by scattered communities, with some concentrations of people in the cities and ports, but even these were intimately linked with the patterns and rhythms of the countryside. It was a country with a backward economy, a primitive transport system, wasteful agricultural practice and rudimentary industries.

The major force which destroyed the established pattern of English society and culture, as it does in most communities, was the growth of population. How and why this came about is only imperfectly known and the same is true of its extent. But it is clear from the evidence already available that the fall in population which had been going on throughout a good part of the 14th and 15th centuries was somehow arrested in the course of the 15th and then it began to rise; that this rise was followed by a sharper rise for roughly a century from the 1530s and that the process thereafter slackened greatly. We know too that the effects of this rise were exactly those we encounter today in any under-developed economy which experiences the same pressures of population growth. There was a manifest inability of technically backward industries and agriculture to absorb the increased supply of labour available, so there was unemployment, poverty and the continuous threat of social disorder. No less important, though industry could with an effort meet a good deal of the increased demand for its products, agriculture could not: the result was an inflation of prices which made itself felt throughout the whole economy and was made worse by the heavy debasement of the currency late in Henry VIII's reign. Inflation is always a great social solvent. It always leads to a redistribution of power and influence. Hardship it undoubtedly brings: to the wage earner, to the agricultural day labourer and, at the other end of the social scale, to the landlord-rentier and the monarchy itself, if they draw a large part of their income from rents where these are held fast by legal and tenurial restraints. But inflation brings benefits too. In moderation it stimulates production and trade, though its bounty is unevenly given. It favours the producer and the merchant; it favours the landlord if he finds some means of breaking through the existing restraints on rents; it favours the lawyers whose professional services are greatly demanded in such times of boom.

Prosperity extends beyond the material world and a new pattern of culture emerges. Mid-Tudor England displayed all the features of a shift in the economic, social and cultural balance of the time.

The titlepage to Coryat's 'Crudities', a lighthearted warning to travellers, is crammed with incidents which befell him abroad. At A we see him on a rough crossing to France; in the bottom right-hand corner (E,F) he is having trouble with a Venetian courtesan because 'he did but kisse her and so let her go'; at G a Rabbi, who objected to his attempts at converting the Jews, is chasing him with a knife; and I shows

> *'Old Hat here, torne Hose, with Shoes full of gravell, And Louse-dropping Case, are the Armes of his travell'.*

Beside his engraved portrait are the figures of France and Italy, while above him Germany 'spews on him out of her Tunne'. (6)

Even though a clumsy attempt was made to arrest inflation in 1551, and a more successful one a decade later, the process could not be fully arrested and its effects lasted on throughout the century and beyond. Painting, architecture, literature, the drama were called into the service of the newly prosperous classes, at a time when these classes were in any case adopting the postures of the social leaders of the past. If the College of Heralds was busy manufacturing pedigrees for new aristocrats and new gentry, time and judicious marriages would inject a large measure of truth into the romances of the antiquary. By the end of the century the sources of patronage were much wider than ever before, ranging from the Elizabethan court through the great landed aristocracy on to the greater bourgeoisie of the capital and to the volatile mob who crowded into the Globe theatre to see the latest play by Shakespeare.

p 265 (39–41)

Reformation by Stages

But before these processes were fully at work there occurred a major upheaval which left its own impress upon the rapidly changing social and cultural scene. The Reformation, which took more than a generation to establish itself, roughly spanning the middle decades of the 16th century, exercised an ambiguous influence on the Renaissance in England. It severed old connexions with the Continent but established new ones; it released speculative, rational thinking and at the same time tried to suppress it; it greatly reduced ecclesiastical patronage yet gave the Church for a time a more powerful hold on the intellectual movements of the age.

The Venetian ambassador had, at the beginning of the century, seen England as virtually independent of the Holy See. Norman historians, he said, recorded that William the Conqueror did homage to the pope but 'the English histories make no mention of this; and it is a forgotten thing'. Equally forgotten was the tribute arising from King John's submission to the pope. All that was now paid, he said, was Peter's Pence. He cannot have discussed ecclesiastical grievances with many Englishmen. But with these we are not here concerned for they did not cause the breach with Rome. The breach itself derived from a crisis in the monarchy, a crisis shortly to be reflected in another form in the monarchy of France. For if, as Michelet believed, the kings of Renaissance

Material riches are held by the devil in a net, towards which ride 'men wordly minded'. Bateman, a 16th-century moralist, deplored the state of society in which 'persons of gentilitie... are not contented with sufficiencie' and 'the yeomandry... seeketh... promotion from the dunghill to a gentleman'. (7)

Europe emerged as the new Messiahs they were none the less as vulnerable as the humblest of mortals. France in the second half of the century was convulsed in an exhausting dynastic war as the Valois kingship sank into oblivion for want of an heir. The Tudor dynasty, much more recently established, faced the same threat when, after nearly thirty years of marriage, Henry had no one to succeed him but his daughter Mary. To understand what followed, and indeed much that happened for decades to come, one must be aware that the Wars of the Roses had ended within living memory and that Elizabethans had the vicarious experience of living through them again as they watched the collapse of government in war-divided France. To reinforce their folk-memory they had the history plays of Shakespeare with the lamentation put into the mouth of Henry VI:

p 254
(10)

> *O piteous spectacle! O bloody times!*
> *Whilst lions war and battle for their dens . . .*

It was to guard against these things that Henry VIII broke his allegiance to Rome when he found that there was no other means of ending one marriage and starting another. Here was no planned campaign of advance to a new ecclesiastical order. Rather, an opportunist king felt his way towards this simple objective of a new legitimate marriage hoping that each threat, each blackmail, each cautious advance would be the last that was needed. But having failed to gain his end with a papal blessing, he found that he gained it more easily against a papal excommunication. In the process the monarchy itself was transformed.

For our immediate purpose we are concerned only with two of the great Reformation statutes, the Act in Restraint of Appeals of 1533 and the Act of Supremacy of 1534. They are worth citing because they seem almost a landmark in the history of English literature as they certainly are in the history of the government, religion and society of England. By now Thomas Cromwell was the closest adviser of Henry VIII, and gathered round Cromwell was that group of writers and publicists who had absorbed many of the new secular ideas abroad in Europe. Moreover they were writing when the English language was approaching its best period of sensitive, lucid vigour which was soon to make it a wonderful instrument for politician and poet alike. For power of language, rich cadence, and inexorable advance to a grand climax, few contemporary prose passages could have equalled these opening words from the statute of 1533:

p 253
(6)

Where by divers sundry old authentic histories and chronicles it is manifestly declared and expressed that this realm of England is an empire, and so hath been accepted in the world, governed by one supreme head and king, having the dignity and royal estate of the imperial crown of the same, unto whom a body politic, compact of all sorts and degrees of people divided in terms and by names of spirituality and temporalty, be bounden and owe to bear next to God a natural and humble obedience . . .

And so it goes on, sentence upon sentence, trumpeting to the world that England has returned to her destiny as a great and independent nation, under one supreme monarch answerable to none but God. We notice, too, the appeal to history—false history as it happens—the secular history of Renaissance scholarship, breaking away from the monkish chronicles which record no such triumph for the worldly order, and a good deal which tells a different tale.

The Act of Supremacy of 1534 does not quite reach the heights of the previous measure. It more or less rounds off a revolution which has already been accomplished. But it yields nothing in the bold, confident grandiloquence of its style and content:

Albeit the King's Majesty justly and rightfully is and oweth to be the supreme head of the Church of England, and so is recognized by the clergy of this realm in their Convocations; yet nevertheless for corroboration and confirmation thereof, and for increase of virtue in Christ's religion within this realm of England, and to repress and extirp all errors, heresies and other enormities and abuses heretofore used in the same, be it enacted by authority of this present Parliament that the King our sovereign lord, his heirs and successors kings of this realm, shall be taken, accepted and reputed the only supreme head in earth of the Church of England called *Anglicana Ecclesia*, and shall have and enjoy annexed and united to the imperial crown of this realm as well the title and style thereof, as all honours, dignities, preeminences, jurisdictions, privileges, authorities, immunities, profits and commodities, to the said dignity of supreme head of the same Church belonging and appertaining.

However many times one reads these passages one cannot wholly lose the excitement of reading the work of some master of English prose or escape that sense of involvement in a revolution in the making. For in spite of all the evidence of the long roots of the Reformation stretching well back into the Middle Ages, there is nothing like this in the past which depicts the emergence of kingship in its full supremacy and with all its panoply of power over men's lives and thoughts. If ever England had a Renaissance kingship, it was surely now.

It was now, too, that Italian political literature gained a special relevance to the English scene when, for example, Thomas Cromwell set in motion the translation of *Defensor pacis*, a 14th-century treatise in elevation of the secular power, written by Marsiglio of Padua. Castiglione's *Courtier* and Machiavelli's *Prince* had to wait some decades for an English translation; but their work was sufficiently familiar already to educated Englishmen. At the same time the classical and biblical texts were being ransacked for evidence of the just and historic claims of a supreme kingship.

p 55
(33)
p 27
(49)

Secular voices were just as loud in their acclaim of monarchy. The Speaker of the House of Commons, Richard Rich, a follower of Thomas Cromwell, addressing Parliament in 1536, declared that Henry VIII was 'worthily and justly to be compared to Solomon on account of his wisdom and justice, to Samson on account of his strength and courage, to Absalom on account of his form and beauty.'

This new doctrine by no means went unchallenged. Thomas More was merely the greatest of those who set a boundary to the advancing claims of royal supremacy. Cardinal Reginald Pole, a kinsman of Henry VIII, found England impossible to live in under the new order, and denounced from Rome this intolerable usurpation of spiritual authority by the Crown. But whether these aggrandized powers were welcome or otherwise in the minds of the king's subjects, their very existence and the enlarged responsibilities of the state called for an enlarged government service, well-

p 253
(8)

adapted for these purposes. This meant both an extension of the range of education and a change in its character. And all this lay at the heart of the English Renaissance.

'Such as by their Learning shall do Good'

Long before, when in 1517 Bishop Fox was making his plans to found Corpus Christi College, Oxford, he had thought of a monastic foundation designed to raise standards among regular monks. But Bishop Oldham, his co-founder, emphatically thought otherwise:

> What, my lord, shall we build houses and provide livelihoods for a company of buzzing monks, whose end and fall we ourselves may live to see; no, no, it is more meet a great deal that we should have a care to provide for the increase of learning and for such as by their learning shall do good in church and commonwealth.

From now onwards it is possible to see, over and over again, this inner conflict of policy throughout the whole field of education. Put in its crudest form, the question could be posed as: should education primarily be directed towards the service of God or of the state? Of course many believed that it could in one sense do both, that is, breed worthy men serving the Christian commonwealth presided over by a God-fearing king. But once the question of curriculum, instructors, organization, finance had to be faced in detail, then the major problems of definition and aims pressed too hard on the educationists to allow the old order to survive intact. We no longer believe, as was once thought, that on the eve of the English Reformation there flourished under monastic inspiration and control a splendid, wide-ranging educational network which was shattered by the Reformation and the Dissolution of the monasteries. Many of the chantry schools, it is true, were outstandingly good but, as Mrs Joan Simon has recently shown, long before the Reformation there had been a growing demand for the new kind of school under secular patronage and to meet secular needs. The belief that Henry VIII and Edward VI, in their destruction of monastic schools and chantries, dealt a severe blow to education can only survive now as a pious legend. Instead, she writes: 'Reformation legislation, following on a long and gradual undermining of ecclesiastical jurisdiction, cleared the ground for much more widespread and rapid developments ... not least so far as the universities were concerned.' This change in emphasis was reflected in the large-scale diversion in the trend of charitable bequests from ecclesiastical to educational purposes, which, as Professor W. K. Jordan has established, is so impressive a feature of the second half of the 16th century. All this fits logically into the pattern of political thinking of Thomas Cromwell and his successors.

The executions of Thomas More and John Fisher are among the incidents in a book of Spanish-directed propaganda published abroad late in the century. Ignoring the Marian persecution of Protestants, it dwelt with heavy emphasis on the relatively few executions of Catholics under Henry and Elizabeth. (8)

By the middle of the 16th century the belief that education was for clerkly men under instruction from clerkly men, already dying before the Reformation, was a thing of the past. It is possible to see a tripartite system adapting itself to new needs. There were the old grammar schools, often refounded on the basis of ecclesiastical predecessors like Westminster School, the King's School, Canterbury, the King's School, Worcester. (Winchester and Eton were exempted from the act dissolving chantries.) But many grammar schools were new, arising from the initiative of town authorities, who often petitioned the Crown for the grant of monastic lands for the purpose or found the money from other sources. At Hull, Chelmsford and elsewhere new grammar schools came into existence, including one at Stratford, where Shakespeare may in due course have become a pupil. This process continued. By the end of the 16th century there were some three hundred and sixty grammar schools of which about two-thirds survive. For girls there was no provision for organized education, but private tutors were widely used for them in the families of the governing classes. Of the high level reached, Lady Jane Grey and Elizabeth I are each in their own way exemplars; while the Cooke daughters, children of Sir Anthony Cooke, became the most famous bluestockings in Tudor England. One of them, Mildred, became the mother of Sir Robert Cecil, Secretary of State under Elizabeth I, Lord Treasurer under James I and by then the most powerful man in England. His mother's learning is commended in the contemporary verse:

> *Coke is comely and thereto*
> *In book sets all her care.*
> *In learning with the Roman dames*
> *Of right she may compare –*

a passage worth quoting if only to indicate how bad Elizabethan verse could sometimes be. Another daughter, Anne, became the mother of Sir Francis Bacon. Thus, in the second generation, the Cooke family gave a Lord Chancellor as well as a Lord Treasurer to England.

The two universities at Oxford and Cambridge were attracting more and more the sons of aristocrats and gentry who would stay for a year or two learning the good and bad habits of their class and imbibing a little learning on the way. There were the Inns of Court in London, England's third university, where professional lawyers could be trained but where many more young men would attend simply as a finishing school and to learn just sufficient law to prevent them making fools of themselves when they sat as justices of the peace at quarter sessions. p 260 (21) p 259 (19)

But the important development inherent in these changes is the change in direction of the whole educational outlook. Reforming pressures were brought to bear on schools and universities alike. The new doctrines were to be taught, the Bible was to be read in English. In the universities mathematics, astronomy, cosmography, philosophy moved into positions of importance in the curricula. If theology remained—at least in theory—queen of the arts, she found her court dwindling before the gathering competition of the new sciences. But it was not simply that the students were being taught different things, they were being taught more often and more intensely. The *jeunesse dorée* which, even while at the university, was never far from the sight and sound of the hunt, was caught up none the less in the new educational pressures. If the universities were less crowded by poor men's sons seeking education and advancement in the Church, the gentlemen's sons who were moving in soon learned that scholarship was just as much a means of entry to state office as it had hitherto been in the Church. The most succinct expression of the revolution which was taking place is to be found in the words of the Protector Somerset, written to Bishop Ridley in 1549, about a plan to reform the teaching at Cambridge: p 264 (34) *f 10*

> We are sure you are not ignorant how necessary a study that study of civil law is to all treaties with foreign princes and strangers, and how few there be at this present to do the king's majesty's service therein.

To do the king's majesty's service. That was the task confronting the universities.

Ideals of Public Service

The intense discussion going on at this time as to the scope and purpose of education reflected both the intellectual and the social crisis of the age. To many scholars, the compromise of Christian humanism continued to be viable. Sir John Cheke, tutor to Edward VI, who was as good a Protestant as Thomas More was a Catholic, believed, as did More, that the new education need shed nothing of its earlier Christian idealism. Cheke at St John's College Cambridge, during a period that would later be described as its Golden Age, saw no conflict between a study of the scriptures and the secular philosophy of the ancient Greeks. 'Eloquence without godliness', wrote Thomas Becon, 'is as a ring in a swine's snout.' But the compromise was under heavy strain. Sir Thomas Elyot's *The Book named the Governor*, published in 1531, had little regard to theology as essential to a gentleman's education. Indeed intellectual training altogether should be set within limits. 'Continual study', he warned, 'without some manner of exercise shortly exhausteth the spirits vital.' In his view:

> . . . The most honourable exercise . . . and that beseemeth the estate of every noble person, is to ride surely and clean on a great horse and a rough, which undoubtedly not only importeth a majesty and dread to inferior persons, beholding him above the common course of other men, daunting a fierce and cruel beast, but also is not little succour, as well in pursuit of enemies and confounding them, as in escaping imminent danger, when wisdom thereto exhorteth.

There were other reasons for restricting the educational resources available to the community at large. If one of the reasons that More had preferred to publish his *Utopia* in Latin rather than in English was to prevent his book falling into the wrong hands, Henry VIII lived to regret the speed with which he had hastened to put the Bible in English in every parish church. Cromwell's Injunction of 1538 which had this purpose proclaimed throughout the land was followed, in the time of reaction after his fall, with the Statute of 1543 which stringently restricted Bible reading to a small section of the community.

This was the generation which had lived through the Peasants' Revolt in Germany of 1525 when the Bible and Protestant doctrine had appeared to set large parts of Germany ablaze. This was the time of the Anabaptists who menaced the whole established order with their biblical commonwealth in Münster, a revolutionary, egalitarian society of terrifying proportions. The arch-conservative sitting on the English throne held the door fast against the very Protestantism which had aided him in his struggle against the pope.

All this formed part of a larger debate. To men like Archbishop Cranmer a university education should be free to a man who was qualified to benefit from it. But this was not a view widely accepted or seriously applied. It was felt by some that it was better 'for the ploughman's son to go to the plough, and the artificer's children to apply the trade of his parent's vocation, and the gentleman's children are meet to have the knowledge of government and rule of the commonwealth'. Sir Thomas Smith, writing in 1565, saw education as indeed the distinguishing feature of a gentleman. Trying to define a gentleman, he acknowledges that it is impossible to do so with any precision, especially at a time when the class has been inflated by the climbing zeal of the new propertied men, aided for fees by the College of Heralds. So Smith falls back on certain general marks of identification. 'For whosoever studieth the laws of the realm', he confesses, 'who studieth in the universities, who professeth liberal sciences, and to be short, who can live idly and without manual labour, and will bear the port, charge and countenance of a gentleman, he shall be called master, for that is the title which men give to esquires and other gentlemen.'

f 7

The English Gentleman

p 258–259 (19)

The port, charge and countenance of a gentleman, meant education, wealth, ostentation, courtliness, public service. That at least was the theory. It is, however, this same Thomas Smith who tells us elsewhere in the same work of the conditions meted out to many of the sons of the gentry who had the ill-luck to become feudal

wards of the Crown. By some extraordinary anachronism, by then peculiar to England, heirs to lands held by a certain outdated (but still formally maintained) tenure known as knight-service-in chief became royal wards, if they were not yet of age at their father's death. These wardships were being bought and sold on the open market because they carried the right of marriage with them (that is, the right to impose a marriage upon the ward, or exact a heavy forfeit). Until the heir came of age his care and education were entirely in the hands of his guardian. And this, according to Smith, quoting contemporary opinion, was what happened: a gentleman could be 'bought and sold like an horse or an ox'. This, moreover, was why 'many gentlemen be so evil brought up touching virtue and learning, and but only in daintiness and pleasure; and why they be married very young and before they be wise, and many times do not greatly love their wives.' There was, said Smith, another reason put forward why these children received so little education. 'The buyer will not suffer his ward to take any great pains, either in study, or any other hardiness, lest he should be sick and die before he hath married his daughter, sister or cousin, for whose sake he bought him: and then all his money which he paid for him should be lost.'

This was no isolated allegation. Hugh Latimer earlier had condemned the whole wardship system on moral, social and educational grounds. Sir Nicholas Bacon, Smith's contemporary, denounced the whole business as 'a thing hitherto preposterously proceeding.' Sir Humphrey Gilbert, a decade later, painted a black picture of the education of wards, brought up 'in idleness and lascivious pastimes, estranged from all serviceable virtues to their prince and country, obscurely drowned in education for sparing charges'. And all this, he said, was deliberate. Guardians preferred to 'abase their [wards'] minds lest, being better qualified, they should disdain to stoop to the marriage of such purchasers' daughters.' We should not, of course, set too much store by these charges: they come often from social and educational reformers with specific purposes in mind; and we know from other evidence that their accounts of the treatment of wards are by no means universally true. We know of plenty of cases where guardians lavished every care upon their charges. Lord Burghley, Elizabeth I's Master of Wards, set up a private school for his wards in his own house where the standards of education reached the highest in the country. But there is no doubt that many guardians did abuse their rights, that these abuses reached scandalous proportions, that they aroused a great outcry in the House of Commons in the early 17th century, and that foreigners were astounded that such an extraordinary situation could survive so long. We should bear these conditions in mind when we think of the enormous educational advances of the time.

Robert Greene's 'Quip for an Upstart Courtier', or dialogue 'between velvet breeches and cloth breeches', is an allegorical dispute between Italianate and traditional England. Velvet breeches 'is sprung from the ancient Romans' but cloth breeches, of English manufacture, deplores the vices which have crept into 'this glorious Iland' with Italian fashions. (9)

Yet the broad outlines of change are clear enough and these may be briefly re-stated. In the second half of the 16th century more men were going to schools, to the universities and to Inns of Court. Secondly, the kind of education now offered was changing in character and purpose: it was training men in the secular arts in the service of the world. It was now that the conditions favourable to Renaissance influences flourished in England: a cultured court presided over by a prince, Elizabeth I, who saw herself in a special rôle as a patron of the arts; a nobility which, for all its masquerades and formal splendours, was in fact a nobility of service; and below it there was a new generation of administrators many of whom had been bred in the universities and Inns of Court precisely with a public career in mind.

p 264
(35)

It was now, in fact, more than thirty years after it was published in Italy, that Castiglione's *Courtier* was translated and published in England. It appeared in the year 1561 and its translator was Sir Thomas Hoby, husband of yet one more of the celebrated Cooke daughters. It was impossible wholly to anglicize the Italian model. The overwhelming majority of English aristocrats continued, at least until the end of James I's reign, to be firmly rooted in the country. The de-racinated 'court' nobleman, familiar enough in France, was virtually unknown until we come to the Scottish aristocrats of the early 17th century whom James brought south with him from Scotland, and the London merchants whom he elevated as the reign wore on. But the notion of a courtier had already come to mean the artificial man, with the false and forced political language, the double standards of ruthless ambition, the mailed fist in the velvet glove. Yet when Castiglione's courtier became a naturalized Englishman, he retained much of the Italian's patrician ways with the cultivated mind and social graces but mellowed and softened with the rustic traditions of provincial England. If Elizabeth I is the English version of the Renaissance prince, Sir Philip Sidney, soldier, poet, courtier, patron, is the native version of the Renaissance aristocrat.

f 9

p 264
(36)

The Flowering of the Language

There was also another and fundamental difference in the English response to the Renaissance as compared with that of Italy. Machiavelli it is true had seen the vision of Italian nationalism and unity, a nationalism which would be fulfilled by the skilful use of Renaissance political methods employed by a great prince in the service of the state. But the age of the Renaissance in Italy began and ended with national unity still centuries away. Machiavelli's scheme needed one great prince. In Italy, in fact, there were too many princes, none of them great. In England there was in the second half of the 16th century, one Prince who, whether great or not, somehow responded to—and herself inspired—a large measure of national feeling. In this the birth of a great national literature also played an important part.

Here, the contrast between the late 16th century and its first half is enormous. At the beginning of the century John Skelton had lamented:

f 13

> *Our natural tongue is rude*
> *And hard to be ennewed*
> *With polished terms lusty.*
> *Our language is so rusty,*
> *So cankered and so full*
> *Of frowards and so dull,*
> *That if I would apply*
> *To write ornately,*
> *I wot not where to find*
> *Terms to serve my mind.*

Of the earlier poets, he found the English of Gower 'old', with his matter vastly superior to the manner in which he expressed himself. Lydgate he thought diffuse and difficult to follow. Chaucer 'that famous clerk', was the great exception. His English was:

> *... Pleasant, easy and plain*
> *No word he wrote in vain.*

Hence, he complained, it was absurd for men of the 16th century to take his early English and try to bring it up to date:

Education in the early 16th century, from a manual on astronomy and calendar calculation published at Oxford in 1519. The syllabus is advertised as 'ad usum Oxoniensium'. (10)

> *And now men have amended*
> *His English, whereat they bark*
> *And mar all they work.*

This consciousness, that to the world of literature England had contributed only one great poet, survived right through the 16th century until the rise of Spenser. More than two generations after Skelton, and on the eve of the greatest age of English poetry, Sir Philip Sidney in his *Apologie for Poetrie* could write of Chaucer: 'Truly, I know not whether to marvel more, either that he in that misty time could see so clearly, or that we in this clear age walk so stumbling after him.'

But as long ago as 1530 Thomas More had rejected the notion that English was too coarse a language for literary expression. 'For as for that our tongue is called barbarous', he wrote, 'is but a fantasy; for so is, as every learned man knoweth, every strange language to other. And if they would call it barren of words, there is no doubt but it is plenteous enough to express our minds in anything whereof one man hath used to speak with another.' He was here defending the use of a Bible in English (if properly safeguarded against heresy); and it was indeed in sacred literature, the Bible, the Book of Common Prayer, Foxe's Book of Martyrs, the homilies and the printed sermons that, on the eve of Elizabeth's reign, English was already displaying its vigour, flexibility, colour, and resourcefulness as a medium of almost limitless promise.

It is, of course, true that much of the prose of this period could be heavy, sluggish, colourless and insensitive; and we should not forget that even in the golden decades of the eighties and nineties more bad than good poetry was written. But there can be little question that these later years were one of the greatest creative periods in the history of English literature. If Shakespeare had never lived, one would still be astounded at the succession of incomparable masterpieces pouring from the pens of Sidney, Spenser, Marlowe, Ralegh, Bacon, Donne, Jonson and others on

In Spenser's 'Shepherd's Calendar' the month of April is 'intended to the honour and praise of our most gratious Soveraigne' shown here among her ladies who are making music for her. Such flattery was part of a life dependent on patronage, as most literary men knew. (11)

'The Spanish Tragedy' by Thomas Kyd rivalled even Marlowe's 'Tamberlaine' in popularity in the late 1580s. It is a story of horror and murder, written in the vigorous blank verse which was just becoming the accepted medium of serious drama. Kyd evidently knew contemporary Spanish plays and introduced the 'revenge-tragedy' into England—a type which culminated in 'Hamlet'. (12)

into the 17th century. We are not here primarily concerned with a history of English literature but with the society which made possible the expression of such richness and diversity of talents. Part of the achievement is to be explained in the changing character of English patronage.

'To Feed on Hope'

English patronage during the Elizabethan period derived from three main sources: the royal court, the great provincial nobility, and the people of London. Of these, the central patronage of the Queen was the most complex and subtle in its operation and in retrospect has long been the most elusive to grasp. To Elizabeth and her contemporaries the court was an instrument for the expression of the personal will of the Queen, in politics no less than in culture. The grant of high office to a minister was handled in exactly the same way as the grant of a small reward to some literary man for writing a pamphlet. There was in all this a strong element of caprice but contemporaries also understood this, for they did not forget—as historians sometimes do—how essentially personal government was. Sir John Harington, Queen Elizabeth's godson, who is remembered as a court wit, as well as a pioneer of English sanitation, kept a fascinating notebook in which he entered brief observations about events at the royal court. In one such passage we read that he met the Lord Chancellor, Sir Christopher Hatton, coming away from the royal presence. Hatton, he says, 'came out from her presence with ill countenance and pulled me aside by the girdle and said in a secret way, "If you have any suit today

I pray you put it aside. The sun doth not shine."' Hatton, of course, was not commenting on the weather. The sun in politics as in contemporary literature was the Queen. The Queen was not in the mood.

Edmund Spenser understood the situation as clearly as did Hatton, the Lord Chancellor or Harington, the wit. Here for example is Spenser's dedication of his *Faerie Queene*, published *f 11* in 1590:

> To the most high, mighty, and magnificent Empress, renowned for piety, virtue, and all gracious government, Elizabeth, by the grace of God, Queen of England, France and Ireland, and of Virginia, Defender of the Faith, etc., her most humble servant, Edmund Spenser, doth in all humility dedicate, present and consecrate these, his labours, to live with the eternity of her fame.

And this is how he says the same thing in verse:

> *. . . O Goddess heavenly bright,*
> *Mirror of grace and Majesty divine*
> *Great lady of the greatest Isle, whose light*
> *Like Phoebus' lamp throughout the world doth shine,*
> *Shed thy fair beams into my feeble eyne,*
> *And raise my thoughts too humble and too vile,*
> *To think of that true glorious type of thine . . .*

For good measure, the printed version of the *Faerie Queene* is accompanied by dedicatory sonnets, to the Lord Chancellor, ten noblemen, three knights, two noble ladies and there is one sonnet finally to 'all the gracious and beautiful ladies in the Court', making seventeen sonnets in all.

Spenser in all this was conforming to an already established pattern, one which was to go on for centuries. It is therefore worth glancing for a moment at the ten noblemen and three knights (apart from the Lord Chancellor) who were the objects of these verses. They include Lord Burghley, Lord Treasurer; the Earl of Oxford, Lord Chamberlain; the Earl of Essex, one of the most influential members of the Privy Council and the Queen's favourite; Lord Charles Howard, Lord High Admiral; Sir Francis Walsingham, Secretary of State; and Sir Walter Ralegh. Amongst these and the others listed are the greatest patrons of the arts, of poetry and of the drama in England. But they were also the most powerful men in politics, the great channels through which flowed the royal bounty in Church, in state, in culture. Yet even so powerful a minister and favourite as Lord Chancellor Hatton might fail to persuade the Queen to grant a suit; but if he failed, then no one else would succeed. For these were the established means and no other existed. That is how politics work in conditions of personal government; and even in modern times, with western constitutional government, it remains true that patronage in practice is a highly personal thing, though never completely monolithic. In Elizabethan England it was.

Hence arose the bitterness with which unsuccessful suitors assailed the court, the attacks upon the corrupt exercise of monopoly power—attacks not against the Queen personally but against Burghley especially, regarded by contemporaries as the most influential adviser of the Queen, though he himself minimized his influence. The weakness inherent in any such system of personal government is that it breeds faction and that able men are thwarted from obtaining recognition and reward. It is Spenser again, this time in *Mother Hubbard's Tale*, who gives the most vivid picture of the relationship between suitor and patron:

> *Full little knowest thou, that hast not tried,*
> *What hell it is in suing long to bide;*
> *To lose good days, that might be better spent;*
> *To waste long nights in pensive discontent;*
> *To speed today, to be put back tomorrow;*
> *To feed on hope, to pine with fear and sorrow;*
> *To have thy prince's grace, yet want her peers';*
> *To have thy asking, yet wait many years;*
> *To fret thy soul with crosses and with cares;*
> *To eat thy heart through comfortless despairs;*
> *To fawn, to crouch, to wait, to ride, to run,*
> *To spend, to give, to want, to be undone.*

John Skelton was a royal tutor, and later in life a satirist of court life and an outspoken critic of Wolsey. In this woodcut from one of his works he is holding a posy—a pun on 'poesie'. (13)

Spenser belonged to the Essex faction, the faction which ultimately lost in the last grim struggle of the closing years of the reign. In 1601 Essex himself was crushed in a hopeless attempt to gain by force what he had failed to obtain by pleading, by pressure and by all the established processes of the Elizabethan Court; and Robert Cecil, son of Lord Burghley, emerged into an unchallengeable position at the centre of power.

Royal Progress

But there were also lesser courts scattered over the provinces where the landed aristocracy itself exercised a considerable cultural patronage in several branches of the arts. It took visible form in the building, or vastly extending, of castles and palaces. There was Lord Burghley's expenditure on the great house in Northamptonshire which bears his name; Leicester on his great castle at Kenilworth; the Sidneys on Penshurst Place; the Herberts on Wilton; Hatton on Holdenby and scores of others. If they gave work to architects, they also encouraged painters for their halls and galleries, goldsmiths and silversmiths for their plate, furniture designers, tapestry workers and, when they died, sculptors and monumental masons to erect massive tombs for their memory. One of the justifications for the magnificent scale of this building was to be able to receive the Queen in a manner worthy of Her Majesty when she came on progress in the shires; and, although this has a strong element of special pleading, it was none the less true. Every summer the Queen would go on a tour of some parts of southern England—she never got more than a hundred miles from the capital—and this was an occasion of both political and cultural significance.

All this was, of course, part of the great effort to identify the Queen with the nation at a time when communication, in every sense, was poor. It was a great display of monarchy: Queen, ministers, servants, hundreds strong moving slowly through the countryside staying a few days in the various great houses on the way. Often the full splendours of the masque and dance would be brought into play with its heavy symbolism of monarchy and nation. Here local talent would, for a brief spell, display itself before the Queen. On the most famous of these occasions, at Kenilworth in 1575, the Queen stayed for three weeks to a veritable festival of the arts; but there were numerous other times and places where her visit proved the opportunity for local poets for the first time—and no doubt the last—to appear before a national audience. In London at the Inns of Court and on Lord Mayor's Day, at the universities during her visitations, the same elaborate ceremonials brought forth an abundance of skills, some of it of a very high order. At Oxford and Cambridge, at St Paul's School, the plays were often the work of scholars. The Inns of Court put on the work of Shakespeare and Ben Jonson. Apart from this, some noblemen like the Earl of Leicester kept their own company of players. Other leading men in Church and state encouraged scholars to live as tutors and secretaries in their households. Thomas Whythorne, the composer, lived under the patronage of Matthew Parker, Archbishop of Canterbury; John Harte, the antiquary and spelling reformer, lived as a tutor to Burghley's wards, as did other distinguished scholars like Sylvius Frisius and Lawrence Nowell.

p 263 (32)

p 254 (11)

p 265 (42)

p 265 (37, 38)

But if we think of this complex cultural Renaissance as a response to native inspiration at court, in the country and in the capital, it continued to draw from Italy much of its impetus and form. For a spell in Italy, especially Venice and Padua, was considered an important phase in the education of a patron. To Sir Philip Sidney, as to so many of his contemporaries, such a visit, with its contact with Italian culture—it is possible but by no means certain that he met Tasso—proved a great formative period. His work *Arcadia* shows the influence of Sannazaro but also of the Greeks Heliodorus and Homer; and of much else too. 'It gathers up', wrote C. S. Lewis, 'what a whole generation wanted to say.' It is 'medieval, Protestant, pastoral, Stoical, Platonic'. A more striking, and more famous, example of the merging of the Renaissance outlook with English domestic culture is Spenser's *Faerie Queene*. It shows the marks of Vergil's *Aeneid*, of Aristotle but much more of Plato, it shows Christian predestinarianism; it reflects the contemporary Italian epic yet with it all it reaches back to English Chaucer and Malory and at the same time presents as its central figures an Arthur who is essentially Spenserian and Tudor, and a Gloriana who is Elizabeth.

p 68 (6, 7)

Shakespeare's London

If court and nobility were, then, of great importance as patrons, the capital itself was in its own way a major impulse in English Renaissance culture. To think of London in the late 16th century is to think of the Thames—and of Spenser's *Prothalamion*—and of Shakespeare. The fate of the capital, the nation, the river and the dramatist are intimately interwoven. For the capital (in effect the twin cities of London and Westminster) was now completely dominant in English industry, commerce, finance, law and government. For all this the great line of communication was the Thames with its estuary which gave London direct access by water—the cheapest means of communication—to the coastal region of all England and the Continent of Europe. 'All our creeks seek to one river', lamented Thomas Milles, the customs official at Sandwich, in 1604, 'all our rivers run to one port, all our ports join to one town, all our towns make but one city, and all our cities and suburbs to one vast unwieldy and disorderly Babel of buildings which the world calls London.' It was indeed a stranglehold and Milles was expressing a widespread provincial outcry against its supremacy. To others it had long been a source of national pride. An English propagandist of the mid-century thus spoke of the capital:

p 256– 257

> And as concerning the ancient and famous city of London . . . no city in France is to be compared unto it: first for the most pleasant situation; then consider the magnifique and decorate churches, the godly predications and services in them; the true and brief administration of justice; the strong Tower of London; the large and plenteous river; the beautiful palaces, places and buildings royal, as well all alongest the said river as in every street of the City and round about the same; the rich merchants and other people; the fair ladies, gentlewomen and their children; the godly bringing up of youth and activity of their children to learning; the prudent order amongst the occupations; their beautiful halls; the great number of gentlemen there always studying the laws of the realm; the high estate of the mayor and sheriffs, and the keeping of their sumptuous households; the bridge of London, with the fair mansions on it; the large and mighty suburbs; the pleasant walks without every port, for recreation of the inhabitants; and the exceeding number of strong archers and other mighty men which they may make to serve their king furnished for the wars.

Parliament, the Law Courts, the Inns of Court, the whole administration in Whitehall, the great companies in the City, the foreign merchants, all these brought to London a great and ever-growing concentration of population and therefore a mass of trades and men to serve them. By the end of the 16th century London and its suburbs had a population of some 200,000 and a strong, secular demand (and resources to pay) for its own secular culture. In 1577 *The Theatre* was opened in the suburb of Shoreditch. *The Curtain* came in the same year, *The Swan* in 1595 and in 1599 *The Globe*. The audience, the theatre and the playwright came

p 265 (39, 40, 41)

Holinshed's chronicles were used by Shakespeare as source material for some of his plays—this is the meeting of Macbeth with the three weird sisters. (14)

together; and, though Shakespeare belongs to a timeless world stage, and his plots are drawn from the world literature available to him, he remains also and characteristically the great expression of High Renaissance London. It is not a deterministic view of history to say that without London there could have been no Shakespeare, at least in the full richness that we know him. It is also true that without the Renaissance even Shakespeare would have lacked the wealth of cultural resources upon which his genius drew and which it transmuted into imperishable drama.

Shakespeare's predecessors as dramatists had extensively drawn on classical sources, more particularly Seneca, Plautus, Terence, as well as on the Italian *novella*, the short stories so fertile in comic and tragic plot. *Gorboduc*, a blank verse tragedy with a moral had been produced in 1562 (written by two parliamentarians, Thomas Norton and Thomas Sackville). John Lyly's comedies began to appear in the 1580s as did George Peele's and Robert Greene's, while Thomas Kyd broke new ground with his blank verse play *f 12* *The Spanish Tragedy*, composed on Senecan lines. But it was Christopher Marlowe who exploited the wide range of Senecan tragedy with his *Tamburlaine* and *Dr Faustus* and at the same time gave full and memorable expression to one of the central themes of Elizabethan thought, the nature of power, a theme to which Shakespeare himself returned over and over again. But to think of these men as forerunners and contemporaries of Shakespeare is grossly to underrate their best work. It was men like Norton, Sackville, Lyly, Kyd who delivered the English drama from the traditions of medieval morality and miracle plays. It was men like Kyd and Marlowe who, as it were, took the drama out of the royal and noble palaces, universities and Inns of Court to the people of London themselves. It was they who began the cultural—and social—revolution which Shakespeare carried forward to a matchless victory.

We can, in one sense, see Shakespeare as the culminating point of the English Renaissance in the whole range of culture. The extensive study of classical models dating back to the impact of humanism upon education earlier in the 16th century, the influence of Terence, Seneca, the classical poets, the modern Sannazaro and Petrarch; the abundant material of the ancient histories now available also in North's translation of Plutarch's *Lives;* the whole humanist dream of the perfectability of human reason; all these, and much else, gave form, thought and substance to the magisterial achievements of Shakespeare. But it was not just the fulfilment of a great humanist tradition. In Shakespeare as in many of his great contemporaries this was combined with the new pressures of his age: the Protestant crisis of the place of the individual soul and will in the universal order; the central problems of kingship and power to which Shakespeare constantly returned in the history plays, and in *Macbeth, Hamlet, Lear,* drawing his material in many cases not from the classics but from the great school of English *f 14* historians of which the chronicles of Holinshed, published in 1577, was the best example. Shakespeare's comedies likewise show his debt to the Elizabethan rediscovery of the classics but *A Midsummer Night's Dream* is as English as anything that our language has produced.

Conflict and Compromise

So Shakespeare like his contemporaries reflects the conflict within the humanist compromise, between the two faiths, the one in the ultimate fulfilment of man's greatness, the other in the frailty of man condemned by original sin. Thus he confronts the problem of the classical man in the Christian world in a famous passage in *Hamlet*:

> What a piece of work is man! How noble in reason, how infinite in faculties, in form and moving how express and admirable! In action how like an angel, in apprehension how like a god! The beauty of the world, the paragon of animals! And yet, to me, what is this quintessence of dust?

If this tension was felt right through English Renaissance culture—and indeed inspired some of its greatest masterpieces—the same conflict was implicit in the first responses in England to the new scientific thought. The problems raised by the work of Copernicus, which threatened the whole cosmological system of the Church, by the medical researches of Vesalius and his successors which undermined the hallowed concepts of the human body, the new work being done in mathematics, geography, all bred the grave inner doubts which John Donne in the early 17th century was to express so vividly. Science itself did not break the established moulds of English thought. But in the early 17th century it lived with increasing unease alongside the traditional doctrines of Church and society. Sir Walter Ralegh, scientist, colonist, politician, poet, historian—the Renaissance virtuoso—could not restrain his doubts and earned himself, unjustly, the name of atheist. Bacon, with still larger vision, under cool intellectual control, set out to establish a system of knowledge of universal compass. Harvey the scientific analyst of true independence, broke through to the fundamentals of human anatomy. These men each in their own way were outstanding products of the English Renaissance. But they each set limits to its survival in its original form. The classical as well as the Christian concepts were in danger.

p 261
(28)
p 206
(25)

A new tension was also emerging. Radical Protestantism, or Puritanism as it was coming to be known, looked to different authorities than a Renaissance culture or a princely state. To them the Bible was the unchallengeable source of authority about man, God, the state and the world order. And what they found in the Bible had little in common with the late Elizabethan England in which they lived. In Parliament, pamphlet and sermon they preached on behalf of a different society, pre-dating the Renaissance. Intransigently Puritan and soon to become severely sabbatarian as well, they were intolerant of much that they saw in the secular world around them. And their intransigence was met by severe censorship under episcopal control. Long afterwards, in the middle of the 17th century, the Puritans would try to establish a biblical commonwealth which was hostile to much in the English Renaissance. But their commonwealth collapsed and the continuing pressure of the late Renaissance outlook was resumed.

p 253
(5)

In the early 17th century we have a society which—even with the heavy under-current of doubt—manifested the vigour and confidence of a nation entering on the period of its greatness. The nationalism we find in Shakespeare, the imperialism we find in the achievements of Drake and the writings of Hakluyt, the enormous patriotic literature flowing from the press, much of it focussing on the Queen, establish the clear outlines of a nation-state governed by a Renaissance prince. Yet to see it in perspective we turn for a last view of her, not to the familiar passages of Shakespeare and the poets, but to the funeral eulogy pronounced upon her by Dr King at Whitehall:

> ...There are two excellent women, one that bare Christ and another that blessed Christ. To these may we join a third, that bare and blessed him both: She [Elizabeth] bare him in her heart as a womb, she conceived him in faith, she brought him forth in abundance of good works.

A Renaissance prince yet the mother of Christ! How much longer could this extraordinary compromise—and the compromise of a whole age—endure?

X THE NORTH TRANSFORMED

Art and Artists in Northern Europe

L. D. ETTLINGER

'What is painting?
To paint is to be able to portray upon a flat surface
anything that one chooses of all visible things,
howsoever they may be.'

DÜRER

The barrier of the Alps

held back more than men and nations. Ideas too, and forms of expression in art, crossed them only with effort, suffering subtle translations in the process. The Renaissance in Italy, doubtless because of the strong classical tradition which remained alive throughout the Middle Ages, has a unity and consistency which are easy to recognize. In the north it is always a mixture. In France, England, Germany and the Netherlands there was no 'natural' Renaissance style as there had been a Gothic style. Change was at first discontinuous and erratic, depending on the comings and goings of individual artists—which countries they visited, whom they met, who their patrons were, what works of art they saw, what works were exported. Every artist had to adapt the new ideas to his own native idiom, at first merely as interesting novelties, then with deeper understanding. In a sense, the story of the Renaissance in the north is the story of numberless personal Renaissances.

What are the signs that a painter has been influenced by Italy? Some are easy to see—the use of classical motifs in architecture and of classical poses in the figures (especially nudes, where the northern convention was markedly different), and the mastery of linear perspective, a Florentine discovery. Others are harder to isolate—qualities of scale, design and colour. The intimacy and rather naïve charm of Gothic 15th-century art tended to give way to more monumental forms, simpler settings and a more generalized treatment of men and women.

But it must not be forgotten that the process was a two-way one. From the very beginning Italy felt the impact of the north. Pisanello and Gentile da Fabriano belong to the International Gothic tradition; the Florentines were powerfully impressed by Hugo van der Goes; while the technique of oil painting, carried to such perfection in Venice, was an invention of Flanders.

Gossaert's *St Luke Painting the Virgin* (opposite) displays visibly the mingling strands of north and south. The subject itself is typically medieval (St Luke, by tradition an artist, was the patron saint of the painters' guild). The attitudes of the two figures, the slightly sentimental beauty of the Virgin, the playful baby, the meticulously painted drapery and such small details as St Luke's slipper lying on the floor are typically late medieval Flemish. The architectural setting, on the other hand, with its Ionic columns (not quite correct), its pedestals, consoles, mouldings, round arch, shell-niche and coffered vault, is Italian. And so one could go on: the fantasy chapel and fountain in the distance are Gothic; the calculated perspective, Italian; the saints in their traceried niches are medieval; the male nude and the cherub riding a bird, classical . . . The result is a true union of cultures, a successful assimilation of new ideas to a traditional theme. (1)

The **northern centre** of the new art during the late 14th century—the years following the innovations of Giotto and Duccio in Italy—was Prague. Its influence was felt as far away as England, where the portrait of *Richard II* (left) in Westminster Abbey owes much to the fact that the King's wife, Anne of Bohemia, came from that city, perhaps bringing artists with her. (2)

Sienese models appealed to the painters of Prague. *The Apostles taking leave of the Virgin* by Duccio (above) may be compared with *The Death of the Virgin* by an unknown Bohemian master (top right) and with the Master of Višši Brod's *Agony in the Garden* (right). (3, 4, 5)

Vigorous patronage and a new wave of interest in Italian art towards the turn of the 14th century led to bold changes in book-illumination. The *Brussels Hours*, commissioned in about 1400 by Jean duc de Berry, is the masterpiece of Jacquemart de Hesdin. On the dedication page (left) he showed the duke with St Andrew and St John the Baptist kneeling to the Virgin. The picture is clearly 'framed' by a decorative border; it is no longer simply part of a page. (6)

Fifty years later the development from illuminated book to self-contained picture is complete. Right: Etienne Chevalier from a book of hours by Jean Fouquet. The basic conception is still the same, but the details are now all of the Italian Renaissance. Heaven, however, where the Virgin sits enthroned (far right), remains Gothic—an interesting sidelight on the way in which the new style was still confined to earthly splendours. (7, 10)

'Greatest of all pre-Eyckian painters', Melchior Broederlam of Ypres, 'international' as he was, shows many influences from Italy. The fanciful little chapel in which the *Presentation* takes place (below) looks back to Sienese examples. (8)

Who painted the *Aix Annunciation* (above)—a Neapolitan influenced by Van Eyck, a Fleming impressed by Witz or by Sluter, a Frenchman from Provence? The question is perhaps unimportant, but the fact that it has been posed demonstrates the extreme cosmopolitan quality of European art during this period. (9)

The sparkling light of Lucas Moser's *Tiefenbronn Altarpiece* (right) puts it among the most original works of its time. Moser is known only by this one altarpiece, dated 1431. He was a German, but had clearly learnt the lessons of Flemish art. This detail is from a panel showing one of the legends of St Mary Magdalen. After Christ's Ascension, the tradition ran, Mary, Martha, Lazarus and some other disciples were expelled by the Jews and sailed on a raft to the shores of southern France. St Lazarus became the first bishop of Marseilles. (11)

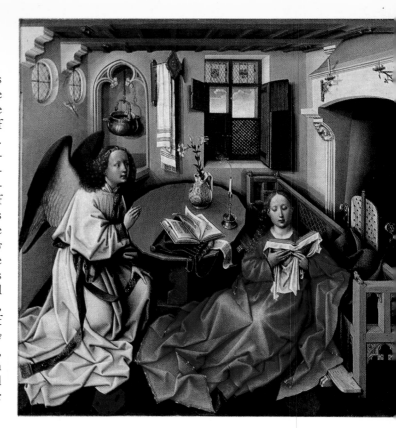

Three great painters made Flanders the artistic leader of northern Europe as absolutely as Florence was of the south—Jan van Eyck, the Master of Flémalle and Roger van der Weyden. What above all impressed their contemporaries was the meticulous naturalism of their detail. Instead of concentrating on the heroism and pathos of the human figure, the Flemish artists painted every object with the same loving attention. Left: *St Jerome in his Study*, probably by Jan van Eyck. The saint, the lion, the desk, books, papers and instruments seem, in the joyful clarity with which they are rendered, almost to attain the same degree of holiness. Right: part of the *Mérode Altarpiece* by the Master of Flémalle, with its homely Virgin, seated in an ordinary Flemish interior, painted without idealization or striving for dramatic effect. (12, 13)

Roger van der Weyden (Roger of the Meadow) was by far the most influential of the three leaders of Flemish painting. He also became aware of events outside Flanders. He travelled to Italy, carried out works for Italian patrons and had at least one Italian pupil. His *Entombment* (left) was painted in Italy. Wholly northern as it is in spirit and in many points of style (the lack of monumentality and weight in the figures, the careworn faces, the evident delight in drapery and landscape) it is in fact closely modelled on a picture from the school of Fra Angelico. In the north Roger had many followers, including Hans Memlinc and Dieric Bouts, a detail of whose *Entombment* is shown above. (14, 15)

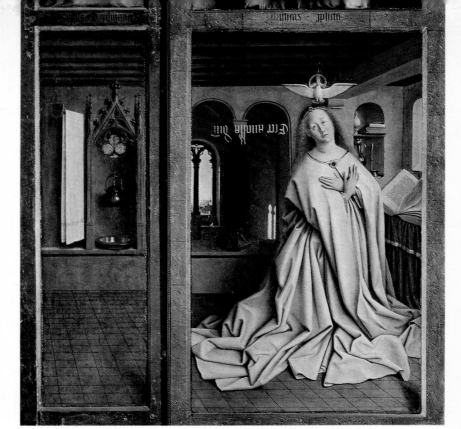

The immense altarpiece which Hubert and Jan van Eyck painted for the Cathedral of St Bavon at Ghent, with its twenty separate panels and hundreds of figures, would need a whole book to illustrate it adequately. This small tranquil scene, the *Annunciation* (above), appears on the back of the wings. Household articles stand on shelves and in cupboards; through the window, a tiny vignette of a Flemish town. (16)

Real tears seemed to flow from the eyes of Roger's men and women. He had inherited the expressionist legacy of the Northern Middle Ages and the Italians were astonished at the anguish and poignancy that could be conveyed in paint. In the *Descent from the Cross* at Madrid (below), the figures, isolated in a narrow recess, crowd to the very threshold of the picture-space —he has deliberately abjured the charm of a landscape background. (17)

A **revelation** of what had been achieved in the north came to the Florentines when Hugo van der Goes' *Portinari Altarpiece* was unveiled, about 1476, in the church of S. Egidio in Florence. It had been commissioned by the Medici agent in Bruges, Tommaso Portinari, and besides being in itself a work of considerable significance its effect was increased by being so prominently displayed. From a Florentine point of view it was not well designed: the space is not firmly articulated and the figures do not belong within it as solidly as, for instance, in a Botticelli or Ghirlandaio; they tend to break up into groups whose scale varies according to their importance. But the mastery of technique in the portrayal of faces, drapery, flowers, animals, stone, light and shade was something which the Florentines studied with fascinated attention. On the wings of the altarpiece are the members of the Portinari family and their patron saints—on the left (not shown) Tommaso and his sons; on the right his wife Maria and their daughter with St Margaret and St Mary Magdalen. In the background of the latter panel can be seen the three kings asking their way to Bethlehem. (20, 21)

A **literal 'quotation'** by one painter from the work of a contemporary is not common, but can be found in Ghirlandaio's *Nativity*, painted in Florence in 1485. Van der Goes' shepherds obviously impressed him deeply, and he copied them fairly closely, as well as the position of the Child lying on the bare ground. Note, however, that the columns behind are of a correct Composite Order and the manger is a Roman sarcophagus. (19)

287

Earth and Heaven meet in Jan van Eyck's revolutionary *Madonna of Chancellor Rolin*. Rolin, the shrewd and successful Chancellor of Burgundy, kneels before the Madonna, without requiring the intercession of any saint. The brocade of the chancellor's robe and the jewels on the Virgin's mantle and crown all show the minute realism for which Van Eyck was famous. Modern in technique (e. g. the perspective, and the confident handling of the middle-ground and distance), it is yet full of symbolism. The sculp- ture above the chancellor's head shows scenes from Genesis—the expulsion of Adam and Eve, the murder of Abel by Cain and the drunkenness of Noah—representing the entry of sin into the world. The Christ Child, Saviour from sin, carries the orb of the world in his hand. The rich palace (strongly Italianate in style) looks out on a landscape where earthly things seem suffused with a supernatural light, where reality is transcended and becomes a vision of Paradise. (18)

289

Patronage cut across frontiers. It was an age when private citizens, not just the Church and nobility, commissioned major works; when travellers commemorated their journeys in portraits from foreign artists, and artists themselves went abroad, taking their own style into new territory. Above left: Jean duc de Berry at table, from the Limbourg brothers' *Très Riches Heures*. The duke's court was for a time the leading centre of patronage in northern Europe. Right: the main panel from the Donne Altarpiece, commissioned by a Welsh knight, Sir John Donne, from the Bruges painter Hans Memlinc. Born in Germany, Memlinc worked in the manner of Roger van der Weyden, becoming one of the most successful artists of the later 15th century. (22, 23)

An Italian merchant: Giovanni Arnolfini was a merchant of Lucca, settled at Bruges. His wedding portrait (above), was painted by Jan van Eyck. (24)

An Italian prince: Francesco d'Este, a member of the ruling family of Ferrara, as Roger van der Weyden saw him—Italian features characterized with Flemish honesty. (25)

An English nobleman: Thomas Howard, Duke of Norfolk, painted by Holbein the Younger, of Basle. Holbein combines northern naturalism with the warmth of Italian colouring. (26)

A feeling for landscape developed in northern Europe independently of Italy. The *Boucicaut Hours* (above left) foreshadows Van Eyck, while Conrad Witz' *Miraculous Draught of Fishes* (centre) shows his impact. The Lake of Geneva becomes the setting of Christ's miracle. Above right: Cranach's *Rest on the Flight to Egypt*—the Holy Family in a German forest. (27, 28, 29)

Pentecost (below left) by Hans Multscher has none of the 'International Style' lyricism. The figures are robust, earthy, almost primitive but the colonnade must have been learnt from Italy. Holbein the Elder's *Flagellation* (below right), about seventy years later (1502), is still in the northern tradition, except for one detail—the classical pillar to which Christ is bound. (30, 31)

The climax of Gothic art

in Germany comes paradoxically in the midst of the intellectual ferment of the Renaissance. We find painters who have learned all they needed from Italy and then applied it, not to the expression of humanist values, but to the more complete realization of late medieval preoccupations.

The Raising of Lazarus (above) by Michael Pacher owes something to Mantegna. The foreshortening of the tomb is a typical piece of Renaissance virtuosity (the tomb itself is a classical tabernacle with a pointed lierne vault!). Yet the painting as a whole, and the elaborate altarpiece of which it is a part, belong firmly to the world of Gothic sensibility. (32)

The Crucifixion (above)—the central picture of Matthias Grünewald's *Isenheim Altar*—likewise springs from the background of German late Gothic art with its emphasis on suffering. The terrible tortured figure of Christ is wholly un-Renaissance—has indeed been called 'anti-Renaissance'. Grünewald, technically as accomplished as Dürer, turns his back on humanist optimism. (33)

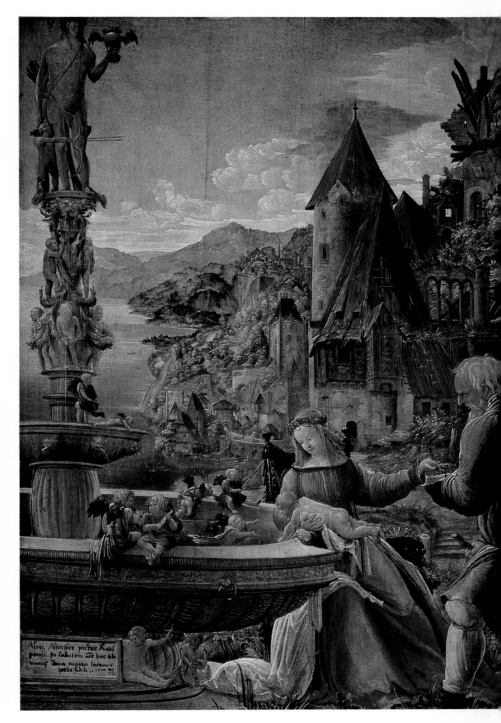

Christ in the Tomb (below): Holbein's merciless picture of physical death and the agony of dying. Deeply felt, and very much under the influence of Grünewald as it obviously is, this can also be regarded as a masterpiece of sheer technique, the body seen slightly foreshortened from below and portrayed with all the resources of Renaissance illusionism. (35)

The Rest on the Flight to Egypt (above) shows Albrecht Altdorfer living happily in two worlds—the rivers, mountains and high-roofed towns of the north, and a fantasy-land of the south where there could exist a fountain like the one on the left. Sculptured putti become one with angel-cherubs and even with the Christ Child himself. (34)

The susceptible art of architecture quickly learnt to assume the frills of the new style, but the ability to think a building through in consistent classical terms came much more slowly. Serlio's château of Ancy-le-Franc (below), though on French soil, was not an example which French architects could whole-heartedly imitate. (36)

Echoes from Italy are caught at Fontainebleau in 1528, where Gilles le Breton's Porte Dorée (above), with its pedimented windows, pilasters and big, formerly open, loggias, may be based on Laurana's palace at Urbino (p. 54, pl. 28). A more learned architect, Philibert de l'Orme, in about 1550, built the 'frontispiece' of Anet (right), the three orders correctly superimposed. (37, 38)

The rebuilding of the Louvre (above) was begun in 1546 under Pierre Lescot. The basic design is still traditionally French; its crisp classical details look as if copied from engravings, and indeed mostly were. (39)

Familiar features of Gothic architecture often seem incongruous in their new classical dress. Above: Antwerp Town Hall (1561–65), the old high-gable now transformed into a composition of columns, pediments and obelisks. Right: Holbein's design for a chimney-piece—Renaissance motifs crowded together without real insight into the style as a whole. (40, 41)

Painters who made the journey
to Italy in the early 16th century included Jan Gossaert, Jan van
Scorel, Maerten van Heemskerck, Hans Burgkmair, Holbein and
Dürer. With all of them the experience was crucial, but its effects
varied according to the capacity of each artist to assimilate what
he learnt. Burgkmair, who came from Augsburg, filled his *Virgin
and Child* (right) with Italian decorative details, but neither the
figures themselves nor their attitudes owe much to Renaissance
models. And the Roman ruins amid which they sit are covered
with the lush undergrowth of a northern landscape. (43)

Giorgione's vision of Venus (top), a magical evocation of warmth,
richness and sensuous beauty, did not survive translation at the
hands of painters from the north. Cranach's *Nymph of the Source*
self-consciously displays her body for admiration, the provo-
cative effect being emphasized by the necklace and transparent
drapery. (42, 44)

When Heemskerck reached Rome in 1532 the Italians had
already embarked on the experiment of Mannerism. In his
St Luke drawing the Virgin he caught the style adroitly, even
adding curious touches of his own. The background includes
specimens of antique sculpture (the artist's sketchbook doubtless
came in useful) and, as befits a physician, there are Greek medical
books on the shelves and the floor. (45)

The unhappy case of Jan Gossaert
shows that a visit to Italy was not
always an unmixed blessing. Below: a
detail from the fine *Adoration of the
Magi*, painted before he went, in his
own Flemish style. Bottom: *Neptune
and Amphitrite*, a pompous display of
classicism ill-understood. (46, 47)

Beneath a coffered vault and dome, the family of St Anne (above)
gather in tranquil communion. Quentyn Massys, who may have
gone south between 1514 and 1519, seems to have copied the
architecture from an Italian print. (48)

At the court of England Renaissance fashions came in at second
and third hand, and the most successful artists were themselves
foreigners. Hans Eworth, from Antwerp, adopted a stiff classical
manner in his *Queen Elizabeth confounding Juno, Minerva and Venus*.
The three goddesses realize that the Queen outshines them all. (49)

Dürer alone, the supreme genius of the northern Renaissance, can stand as an equal with the great southern masters, Bellini, Raphael and Michelangelo. He visited Italy twice, studying contemporary art and theory with deep understanding. In the *Virgin with the Siskin* (right) the Christ Child in particular shows strong influence from Italy (the siskin is the little bird on Christ's arm). The theme of the Madonna and Child was one to which Dürer returned many times, stressing the human motherhood of Mary (every religious picture in Germany at this time was significant in the great debate of the Reformation). Below: the *Adoration of the Magi*, painted in 1504 before his second journey. The unforced grouping of figures in an architectural framework is another achievement which owes much to Italian models. (50, 51)

'Ye rulers of the world', runs the ▶ inscription beneath the *Four Apostles* (right), 'beware in these troubled times not to take the words of men for the Divine Word. Heed the warning of these four, Peter, John, Mark and Paul.' The two panels are among Dürer's last works and are certainly his most monumental. They may have been intended as the wings of an altarpiece. On the left are St John and St Peter, on the right St Mark and St Paul. Dürer was personally involved in the upheavals of the Reformation and the picture makes its own statement on the tragic divisions of his age. (52, 53)

The same forces that were at work on German painting, producing simultaneously a last flowering of Gothic realism and a turning towards Italian models, also moulded the course of sculpture. (A parallel development in France is shown on p. 174-5). The great wooden altarpieces carved by Veit Stoss and Tilman Riemenschneider at the turn of the 15th century are among the most intense and dramatic works in all art. Riemenschneider's *Creglingen Altarpiece* (left) shows the Ascension of the Virgin; the composition, built up in billowing masses of drapery, is echoed in the soaring lines of the tracery above. Right: the *Death of the Virgin* by Veit Stoss, made for the Church of Our Lady at Cracow. (54, 55)

The sandstone crucifix (above) by Nicolaus Gerhaert which still stands in the Old Cemetery of Baden-Baden links the work of Claus Sluter with the later art of the north. Individual, observed suffering is raised to a universal level. (56)

Adam and Eve by Riemenschneider may be contrasted with the nudes shown on the opposite page. In keeping with the Gothic tradition, their humanity is expressed in emotional and spiritual terms rather than through a close study of anatomy. (57, 58)

The lure of Italy drew sculptors south in the early years of the 16th century. Peter Flötner of Augsburg went twice, and his *Apollo Fountain* at Nuremberg (left) shows clear Italian influence, though it may be based on an engraving rather than on an actual statue. Above are three small figures illustrating the same trend towards a more classical treatment of the nude. Left: *Judith*, by Conrad Meit. Centre: *Inkwell with the figure of Vanitas* (there is a skull at the girl's feet) by Peter Vischer the Younger. Right: *Christ Child Blessing*, a small bronze by an unknown sculptor, made about 1550 but reflecting Italian models of a century earlier. (59-62)

Sharp contours and rich decoration, combined with the heroic classical pose of the figure, give Hans Leinberger's *St George* (left) a hybrid quality of German and Italianate motifs. Neither artist nor patrons would renounce the medieval past.(63)

A dynasty of merchants, the Fuggers of Augsburg, displays the same pattern from the point of view of patronage. Their family chapel was the most Italianate ensemble north of the Alps. Its decoration (above) came from the Vischer workshop. (64)

Art and Artists in Northern Europe

L.D. ETTLINGER

A medieval theme treated by a Renaissance master: the woodcuts known as the Great Dance of Death (designed in the 1520s) rank with Holbein's greatest works in this medium. Here it is the monk who resists grinning Death. (1)

'EMULATE, noble man, the ancient nobility of Rome, which after taking over the empire of the Greeks, assimilated all their wisdom and eloquence, so much so that it is hard to decide whether it has equalled all the Greek discoveries and array of learning or surpassed them. In the same way you who have taken over the empire of the Italians should cast off repulsive barbarism and seek to acquire Roman culture.'

These sentiments as expressed here in the incisive words of Conrad Celtis (1459–1508), the German humanist who was an admirer and patron of Albrecht Dürer, may serve to bring into focus the problem of the northern Renaissance more sharply than any modern historical analysis could hope to do. For if in recent years some scholars have questioned the validity of the concept 'Renaissance' as far as the period from about 1300 to 1600 in Italy is concerned, others have been eager to deny the very existence of any related phenomenon in the countries of northern Europe. They have done so for not always creditable reasons, and unfortunately art historians in particular have been at fault in this respect.

In attempting to explain away the patent dependence of northern art on Italian precedent, the fateful heritage of a nationalistic Romanticism—above all the Hegelian philosophy of history which forms its core—has played havoc with historical objectivity.

The Northern Renaissance as we have seen, was a gradual process, lacking in decisive steps, the beginning of the new age overlapping the end of the old. Grünewald's *Meeting of St Erasmus and St Mauritius* may, however, fittingly stand at the end of the German Middle Ages. In spite of its up-to-date technique (the textures of brocade and armour, for instance, reflect Venetian preoccupations), it is essentially a medieval picture. The subject is a (purely imaginary) meeting between two early martyrs. Erasmus Bishop of Antioch was executed during the persecution of Diocletian by having his intestines pulled out on a windlass, which he is shown holding in his right hand. (Erasmus' bones had been collected at Halle, and a new abbey had been dedicated to him). St Mauritius was the leader of a Roman legion from Thebes in Egypt (and so is represented as a Moor or Negro), massacred about 300 AD for refusing to sacrifice to the Emperor. He is the patron saint of many places in Germany and Switzerland, including Magdeburg.

Historically too, this painting stands at the end of the Catholic north. It was commissioned about 1518 for the Collegiate Church of St Mauritius (St Moritz) and Mary Magdalen at Halle. Grünewald's patron was Albrecht von Brandenburg, Cardinal Archbishop of Mainz and Halle, who is portrayed in the likeness of St Erasmus. The Archbishop was at first not unsympathetic to the new ideas (a personal friend of Ulrich von Hutten, he had had a humanist education and earned a rebuke from Leo X for allowing books hostile to the Church to be published under his eye at Mainz); but as he grew older he hardened into a severe defender of Catholicism and a champion of the Jesuits. When the violence of the Reformation made Halle unsafe he had the painting moved to Aschaffenburg. (65)

Writers have insisted that the Germans, Flemish and French discovered the world and man by their own unaided efforts and terms such as 'a national concept of form', 'race', 'Germanic Genius' and even 'the destiny of nations' have been introduced into the debate only to obscure the fact that after the early 14th century all European art received its decisive impetus from Italy, even if artists in north and south travelled along rather different routes once the north had absorbed the first impact of the new realism which had arisen in Florence and Siena.

This must be obvious to even the most superficial observer. Jan van Eyck's *Annunciation* on the *Ghent altarpiece*, completed in 1432, has more in common with Duccio's rendering of the *Annunciation of the Death of the Virgin* on one of the narrative panels of his Siena *Maestà*, painted some 125 years earlier, than with any medieval rendering of a similar theme. Dürer's *Four Apostles* dated 1526, are the true contemporaries of Raphael's or Titian's monumental and solid figures, and they are separated by a whole world from the lithe and less substantial saints on a Gothic panel, as for example the *Wilton Diptych*, or for that matter from figures appearing on any late medieval painting produced anywhere in northern Europe.

p 285 (16)

p 299 (52, 53)

Celtis—though he spoke of Letters rather than of the Fine Arts—was aware that his countrymen were faced with a task far more challenging and complex than that which had faced the Italians. For he knew that to the latter, revival simply meant the taking up of the broken strands of a previous civilization, but he also knew from reading the writings of his Italian colleagues what Petrarch had meant when he introduced the term 'Dark Ages'. The barbarians descending across the Alps had extinguished the lights of classical culture, but the New Learning—and, as Petrarch's followers argued, also the new realism in the arts—was the beginning of a new and better age. Thus Celtis and the northern humanists who shared his convictions were really faced with a twofold problem. First in accepting the values of the Italian humanists they had to prove that they were no longer barbarians, but at the same time had to translate the classical heritage, received through its Italian transformation, into their own culture. Celtis' choice of words should be carefully noted: 'repulsive barbarism' and 'Roman culture' are set in antithesis. If these aspirations had not been shared by painters and sculptors they would hardly have travelled to Italy to complete their education, as was done by Dürer, Holbein, Gossaert, and many others.

'Windows on to the World'

However, more or less extended tours of study did not become the fashion until the late 15th century, but long before that time, at the very beginning of the Italian Renaissance, those masters whom Vasari was to call 'the first lights' of the new art had made an almost immediate impact north of the Alps. Echoes of Giotto's

The Emperor in the artist's studio—a detail from a woodcut by Hans Burgkmair of Augsburg to illustrate Maximilian I's unfinished romance of his own reign, 'Weisskunig'; Maximilian saw himself as the embodiment of both medieval chivalry and Renaissance patronage. (2)

frescoes in the Arena Chapel of c.1305 can be found in Austria within a generation. The French miniaturist Jean Pucelle during the 1320s was familiar with models which allowed him to introduce Italianate details; he had even grasped some of the new ideas of perspective—as yet not systematic and scientific—as well as the emotive vocabulary of Giotto's expressive gestures. English illuminators, particularly those of the East Anglian School, must also have been conversant with the latest achievements of Italian painting.

While truth of detail and even a rendering of human emotions had already been part of Gothic art all over Europe, it was only in the early 14th century that the carefully observed details were fused into a coherent and convincing narrative when they were presented in a manner which gave tangible reality to a picture. It was precisely this lively and dramatic way of story-telling which French, German and English artists learned from their Italian p 282 (3) models. It has often been claimed that Giotto and Duccio reintroduced picture space into an art which for centuries had been satisfied with flat pictographs, however animated these may have been. But such a bland statement is too modern and it oversimplifies the artistic development. Giotto and Duccio, as well as those who took up their inventions, were not so much concerned with the purely aesthetic problem of pictorial space as with a much more practical problem implied by the function of their images. They had to provide life-like representations of sacred and legendary art which would appeal immediately to the beholder, and in doing this the creation of pictorial space, giving verisimilitude, was only a means to an end. When Vasari claimed that Giotto stands at the beginning of this development towards greater realism he was perfectly right, and Giotto's quick appeal well beyond the frontiers of Tuscany and even Italy is based on this fact. But this does not imply that he had to be slavishly imitated, for his artistic language could be transformed and fitted into varying contexts or adapted to local traditions. It is interesting that Italy and the north, once they had got hold of the new pictorial devices, developed them independently so that a hundred years after Giotto's death both Italy and the north—or strictly speaking Flanders—had pictures which in Alberti's words were 'windows on to the world', though the world as seen by the painters of Florence and Ghent was hardly the same.

In our present state of knowledge (and considering the comparative scantiness of surviving examples) it is impossible to say with any degree of certainty by what means northern artists first became aware of Giotto's and Duccio's methods of pictorial representation. But one puzzling problem may be noted. Giotto had demonstrated his style in monumental frescoes and Duccio's no less revolutionary art had first appeared in a gigantic altarpiece in Siena Cathedral. Yet in France and England the new style p 282 (6, 7, makes its first appearance in *de luxe* illuminated manuscripts destined for wealthy and perhaps discriminating princes or ecclesiastics. Unfortunately we do not know whether in the north the new realism was still regarded as an acquired taste, appreciated only by the educated, or whether it had reached these countries through illuminated books which served as models and sources of inspiration for native artists.

The New Art at Prague

p 282 (2–5)

In one case, however, we are somewhat better informed about the adaptation and transformation of Italian Trecento art. In 1346 Charles IV, whose father John had been killed in the battle of Crécy, came to the throne of Bohemia and he was crowned Emperor in 1348. He knew Italy at first hand and set out at once to make his capital Prague into an intellectual and artistic centre, rebuilding the castle and cathedral, founding a university and calling scholars as well as artists from all over Europe to his court. Both Rienzo and Petrarch were among his visitors and the latter wrote: 'I must say that I have not seen anything less barbarous and nothing more civilized than the Emperor and his courtiers', handsome praise, even if we have to make allowances for some flattery.

Yet it cannot have been only flattery. Among the higher clergy and the imperial officials were well educated men who had studied in Italy and France. John of Neumarkt, Charles' Chancellor, was a widely travelled scholar and author, who admired not only Petrarch but also the latest achievements of Italian art, since for the illumination of his breviary he employed an artist (of unknown nationality) thoroughly familiar with the salient characteristics of Sienese painting. Still, it is true to say that most of the artists working for the Emperor and his circle were of German origin—called to Prague from as far afield as Strasbourg—but Italian manuscripts did reach Prague and we know of at least one Italian artist who was closely connected with the enterprises of Charles IV. Tommaso da Modena either came to Prague to help with the decoration of the chapel in the castle of Karlstein or he was commissioned to send pictures for it. His impact would have been felt either way.

Although native Czech artists are documented only at the end of the century in the reign of Charles' successor Wenceslas there must have been some earlier among the anonymous masters, and it has often been asked whether the art of Prague and its provincial derivations should be called Bohemian or German. In fact, the question is pointless. The patronage of Charles IV gave rise to a truly international court style of great sophistication, and in it many elements of different origin intermingled. Obviously French elements were strong, not only because of the influence of *quell'arte che alluminare è chiamata in Parisi* (the art which is called 'illuminating' in Paris), but also because the imperial family, the House of Luxembourg, had strong links with the west. Nevertheless, Italian pictorial inventions were of decisive importance.

p 282 (5) The Master of Višši Brod's *Passion* panels are full of Italian elements although they are not immediately obvious since there has been a regression to a more Gothic manner of representation. p 282 (4) On the other hand a picture like the *Death of the Virgin*, dating probably from the third quarter of the 14th century, is almost purely Sienese in character and must derive from a slightly earlier Italian model. There are not only the telling details, such as the coffered ceiling and slender pillars, there is also the intricate spatial arrangement suggested by the complex interior with its three bays. Yet the model has hardly been used with complete understanding. The scene seems crowded and the figures are placed rather in front of than inside the chamber. Pictorial space is suggested but not fully realized.

Like all styles dependent on the patronage of dynamic individuals, the Caroline court style was short-lived, extending into the time of Wenceslas, but losing its creative energy even before the Hussites destroyed many of its works early in the 15th century. Nevertheless it had served an important function in disseminating —even if often in a simplified or superficial manner—some of those pictorial ideas which had revolutionized Italian Trecento painting, for the influence of Prague extended deep into Germany, p 282 (2) to the Baltic, and even to England. The portrait of *Richard II* in Westminster Abbey is only one of the few remaining witnesses of this and we should perhaps remember that this monarch's first Queen had been Anne of Bohemia, in whose entourage artists from Prague could have come to London.

'Barbarous Gothic'

Vasari, writing in the mid-16th century and with the arts of Italy in mind, claimed that the break with the immediate past had first of all occurred in painting while sculpture and architecture abandoned the 'barbarous Gothic' manner only at a later date. As so often Vasari was right, and his criticism may be extended to

The sculptor, from Schopperus' 'Book of Trades' (1568). The verse accompanying this woodcut by Jost Amman reads: 'I carve effigies of former kings from Parian marble, or the events of my own time from wood', and refers to Praxiteles as the greatest of sculptors. (3)

the arts and architecture in northern Europe. In Italy churches in the local variant of Gothic continued to be built throughout the Trecento, and work on the big cathedrals of Milan and Bologna went on well into the 15th century, even if with occasional help from German masons. Sculpture, after the premature return to classical models used by Nicola Pisano, became Gothic once more in the hands of his son Giovanni. These facts must be remembered if we want to understand why only Italian Trecento *painting* was of particular fascination to the peoples of northern Europe. Far from feeling threatened by an allegedly alien mode of expression—as some modern historians would have it—artists and patrons alike eagerly grasped the new visual vocabulary and with it all the richer methods of rendering the visible world and a greatly enlarged range of human emotions. Yet in the early phase, which we are considering at present, Gothic tradition and Italian innovation were fused into a new style which has a strong character of its own. Even so it is hardly fortuitous that both Italian humanism and Italian art were patronized by men like Charles IV and John of Neumarkt.

It has already been mentioned that Parisian miniaturists were acquainted with contemporary Italian art by about 1330 and a decade later the Sienese master Simone Martini took up residence p 128 (24) in Avignon where the Papacy was in exile. Of the work he did there little survives and his impact on French 14th-century art cannot be assessed properly. In any case, in our context it is sufficient to look now at the turn from the 14th to the 15th century when vigorous patronage and a new wave of interest in Italian art brought yet another vogue for book illumination and painting whose style is usually, though not very happily, referred to as 'International Gothic'. Since however this style differs from that of the 13th century—the period of greatest efflorescence of Gothic—the alternative and less specific 'International Style' may be preferable.

Burgundy's Golden Age

The French kings of the period not surprisingly had political and military worries which fully occupied their minds, but Angevin princes, and above all Philip the Bold and Jean duc de Berry, employed some of the finest painters and sculptors of their day, making Dijon and Bourges into artistic capitals outshining even the splendour of Paris. Philip the Bold, who succeeded to the duchy of Burgundy in 1384 and died in 1404, not only held his hereditary lands, but also acquired through marriage a sizeable section of Flanders including Bruges, Ghent and Ypres—and much of Burgundian wealth depended upon the cloth trade. He richly endowed the Chartreuse de Champmol, situated just outside his capital Dijon.

Melchior Broederlam, who came from Ypres and has rightly been called 'the greatest of all pre-Eyckian painters', worked for the duke from 1387 onwards. In 1394 he was paid for the shutters of a carved altarpiece, depicting the *Annunciation* and *Visitation* on the one wing and the *Presentation* and *Flight into Egypt* on the p 283 (8) other. The delicately painted, elaborate and fanciful little chapel, serving as a setting for the *Presentation*, certainly owes its existence to Sienese models and so does the rocky landscape with the little castle surmounting a crag behind the Holy Family in the *Flight into Egypt*. All this, within the given conventions, is real enough; on the other hand, the gold background—a convention of an earlier manner—tells us that complete realism had as yet not been accepted in northern panel painting. There are still other features which give Broederlam's art originality and a character of its own. He obviously takes great delight in depicting his skeletal and graceful buildings, but they obey a scale of their own and are not related to the whole of the picture. Italian masters, on the other hand, 'built' more solidly, applied one unifying scale throughout, and made use of architectural features to give a firm structure to their compositions. But perhaps even more important is the rôle of light and luminous colouring, most obvious in the *Flight into Egypt*. Light not only delicately models the figures, it gives variety to the landscape, even picking out the leaves on the trees. The world which Broederlam depicts is less consistent than that of an Italian painter, but it is infinitely richer in detail, more colourful and more intimate.

Among the sculptors working in Champmol for Philip the Bold the outstanding genius was another Netherlander, Claus Sluter, who carved the figures for the portal of the Chartreuse and the *Well of Moses*, a well-head surrounded by six life-sized prophets and surmounted by a Calvary.

p 174
(23)

In arrangement the portal of the Chartreuse takes up the decorative scheme of medieval cathedral porches with its *trumeau* Madonna and lateral jamb figures. But the figures, and particularly those of the kneeling donors—Duke Philip and his wife Margaret of Flanders—are no longer parts of an architectural structure. These stone carvings are truly three-dimensional and they can be detached from the wall without losing their identity, because they have been conceived as organic figures following their own laws instead of those of the surrounding architecture. Sluter began working on them in 1391, and it should be noted that they antedate Donatello's *St George* at Orsanmichele by twenty-five years.

Donatello comes to mind again when we look at the powerful figure of *Moses* . Yet it is not only the expression and the intensity of gestures which convey a presence of dramatic reality; there is at the same time a new feeling for the artistic essentials of sculpture which imparts to the hard stone immense vitality. Today the *Well of Moses* is a torso (of the crowning Calvary only fragments survive) but when it was completed in all its polychrome and gilded splendour it must have looked spectacular. Such a colourful appearance might jar on our tastes, but it belongs to the International Style, and the preference for monochrome sculpture—in part at least due to a certain misunderstanding of the aesthetics of classical art—was to come later.

A Great Patron

p 290
(22)

The greatest patron and collector of the period (who must rank among the great art lovers of all times) was Jean duc de Berry, the youngest brother of Charles V. The personality of this prince has been admirably described by Professor Panofsky, who wrote: 'His main concern was to amass riches by all imaginable methods, possibly including being bribed by the enemy. For his overweening passion was to call into being or to acquire buildings, tapestries, sculptures, paintings, jewelry, models, carvings in crystal or ivory, enamels and, above all, illuminated manuscripts. Cautious, cultured and personably affable, he… died in 1416 at the age of seventy-six, leaving behind him an equally enormous amount of possessions and of debts.'

The duke's activities as a collector should be considered for a moment since they show certain interests which we associate normally with Italian *amateurs* of the Renaissance, and an incident from the Hundred Years' War may introduce his tastes.

In 1384 French and English representatives met at Lelinghem to discuss the possibility of an armistice. Their meeting place, a bare chapel, had been hung by the duke with tapestries depicting famous battles of antiquity. John of Gaunt, however, horrified by these images of violence, demanded their removal so that others showing the instruments of the Passion might be put up in their place. Both men obviously had the psychological effect of such decorations in mind, but they were thinking along different lines. John of Gaunt wished to instil piety and humility in the negotiators, but to Jean de Berry warlike valour was best exemplified by the deeds of classical heroes.

We cannot assume that these tapestries in style or even costume echoed ancient art. Like the illuminations in so many classical texts of the time they must have shown the ancients in a thoroughly contemporary disguise, the ladies in elegant Burgundian dresses and the gentlemen in heavy armour. Nevertheless the duc de Berry did possess a number of genuine classical silver vessels, coins and cameos, among them the famous *Gemma Augustea* (now in Vienna), as we hear from the 15th-century Italian artist and writer Antonio Filarete in an admiring reference to the duke's love for ancient art. In fact, Jean's passion for precious objects of this kind was such that clever dealers planted on him pseudo-classical gold medallions showing those Roman emperors from Augustus to Heraclius whose names are linked with the rise of Christianity. These medallions are the earliest Renaissance forgeries known to us. Yet in their day they were celebrated as exemplary specimens of classical refinement, and the *Constantine*

f 4

Medallion served as a model for one of the *Magi* in one of the duke's devotional books.

Still Jean de Berry's most lasting claim to fame rests on his patronage of living artists who were commissioned to illuminate his luxurious Books of Hours. Two examples only can be quoted here, the *Très Belles Heures de Jehan de France, duc de Berry*, known as the *Brussels Hours* since they are now one of the treasures of the Belgian Royal Library, and the *Très Riches Heures du duc de Berry*, in the Musée Condé at Chantilly. The former is documented as being by Jacquemart de Hesdin, who was in the duke's service from about 1384 until his death in 1411. He too came from Flanders and it is possible that he had visited Italy. The double-spread dedication picture of the *Brussels Hours*, which surely must be by the master's own hand, shows the duc de Berry with his patron saints St Andrew and St John the Baptist commending him to the Virgin Mary. The iconographic motive is common enough, but the handling is Jacquemart's alone. The perfect mixture of lyrical sweetness—best seen in the face of the Madonna—and firm plasticity, of linear rhythm and three dimensional modelling of figures set freely in space could only have been achieved by an artist whose style had been moulded equally by Gothic heritage and by lasting memories of Italian Trecento art. One revolutionary innovation is particularly striking: the miniature is emphatically framed and no longer forms part of a page. This novelty has so much surprised some modern critics that they suggested this miniature must have been an independent devotional picture which only later was stuck into the *Hours*. But this hypothesis seems to miss the critical situation in which Jacquemart de Hesdin was working. By 1400 realistic pictorial representation had become *de rigueur* and the demands for it superseded the old conventions which had forced illuminators to regard the book page as nothing but a place for flat decorations.

p 282 (6

p 290
(22)

The new manner is even more strikingly demonstrated in one of the most beautiful manuscripts of the period. It is again a Book of Hours, illuminated by an anonymous artist for Jean le Meingre *dit* Boucicaut, Marshal of France, and it is therefore known as the *Boucicaut Hours*. Since the owner was captured at Agincourt in 1415 and spent the next six years until his death as prisoner of the English, the *Hours* must date from the first or the beginning of the second decade of the 15th century. Moreover, the Master of the *Boucicaut Hours* certainly knew the works of Jacquemart de Hesdin, and he too treats each illustration as a little picture in its own right. When he depicts, for example, the *Visitation* he stages the meeting between Mary and Elizabeth in a tranquil rural scene, embedding the figures between hills and trees, silhouetting them against a lake in the middle-ground. The background is studded with minute yet exquisite details of peasant life. Most miraculous of all, however, is the sensitive treatment of light flooding over lake and hills, truly coming out of the sky. This feeling for atmosphere is an achievement which anticipates the art of Jan van Eyck.

p 291
(27)

Among this master's immediate predecessors were also the three brothers Paul, Herman and Jean Malouel—better known as the Limbourg brothers from their place of origin—who about 1411 entered the service of Jean duc de Berry. The meticulous realism of the Limbourg workshop is as remarkable as is the brothers' familiarity with the conventions of Italian painting. They were, in fact, the most knowledgeable and accomplished practitioners of a truly International Style, taking occasionally whole compositions from their Italian models. Outstanding among their works is again a Book of Hours which has become one of the most famous illuminated manuscripts of all times, the duc de Berry's *Très Riches Heures*. The *January* picture gives us not only a lively impression of the luxurious court life which the duke loved—it is a splendid banquet scene—but also contains all the elements which make up this glittering and elegant style. There is a wealth of detailed observation and with it the ability to deploy figures within convincing pictorial space. The men serving at table are really in front of it while Jean is sitting behind it, and the landscape with armed horsemen recedes further back still. The colours are brilliant and give to the surface of the miniature a shining jewel-like effect. Within a small compass the miniature has already all the elements of a full-scale panel painting.

p 290
(22)

This is hardly surprising. The new conquests of Italian Trecento painters—we should recall that Vasari saw them as the initial phase of a 'rebirth' of the arts—had at first been taken up by northern miniaturists only, but by the early 15th century these in their turn evolved a formal vocabulary fitted for the suggestion of pictorial space, for proper expression and gestures—in short, for the realistic rendering of a narrative. They had perfected a style which offered itself readily for tasks on a much grander scale.

Flanders takes the Lead

The painters who performed this miraculous transformation of the miniature were Jan van Eyck, the so-called Master of Flémalle and Roger van der Weyden, contemporaries of those Italian Quattrocento masters with whom Vasari opens the second phase of the Renaissance—Masaccio, Masolino and Uccello. Yet in spite of a common root in Trecento practice Italian and Flemish art by now looked different. Briefly—and what follows must be in the nature of things a drastic oversimplification—Italian painters and sculptors began to re-discover classical art, once the realism of the 14th century had prepared their eyes for its aesthetic values. This does not mean, however, that they indulged in sterile imitation or in an academic classicism. They rather allowed their joy in realism to be restrained by the principles of idealism inherent in classical art. Flemish artists on the other hand—by now the leaders in the north—retained to the end of the 15th century (and in some cases even longer) that enthusiasm for meticulous naturalistic detail which can be found already in the middle of the 13th century at the very height of Gothic. But the details whose effect up to this time had been merely cumulative became now part of an ordered universe held in its frame by the unifying power of picture space. Furthermore Italian artists, again following classical precedent, concerned themselves with human figures in a setting, putting all emphasis on the figures. But to Flemish artists the saint in his study was no more important than the quill in his hand or the street scene glimpsed through an open window behind him. The picture was a microcosm in which everything was described with the same accuracy and with undivided attention.

Italian reactions to this style are interesting and, in our present context, rather revealing. There is ample evidence for the popularity of Flemish art. Our most explicit witness is the Genoese humanist Bartolomeo Fazio who wrote just after the middle of the 15th century brief biographies of famous contemporaries, including four painters. Two were Italians—Gentile da Fabriano and Pisanello, and two northerners—Jan van Eyck and Roger van der Weyden. Of the former he has to say this: 'John of Gaul (*Johannes Gallicus*) is thought to be the foremost painter of our age, no less learned in literature than in geometry (i. e. perspective) and in all the skills which add to the embellishment of painting.' He goes on to mention several pictures he had seen in Italy, among them a *St Jerome* in the possession of Alfonso of Naples: 'Very life-like, in his study depicted with marvellous skill, since if you step back a little the room recedes and you see the whole books, but if you go nearer only the spines are visible.'

This picture does not survive but a similar one was in the Medici collection and it may be identical with a little panel now in Detroit. Its authorship has been disputed, but even if it was completed by Jan's pupil Petrus Christus it still has all those characteristics which Fazio so much admired. This admiration for Jan van Eyck must have been shared by Italian artists of the Quattrocento, for two Florentine frescoes were inspired by the Medici panel: Botticelli's *St Augustine* and Ghirlandaio's *St Jerome* in the church of Ognissanti.

The splendour and richness of Jan van Eyck's art, the variety of his invention and the brilliance of his technique are all evident in his most famous work, the *Ghent Altarpiece*, completed in 1432. This, however, raises so many problems of collaboration with his brother Hubert, of composition and of iconography that it cannot be discussed adequately in the space at our disposal. But the *Madonna of Chancellor Rolin*, painted probably a year or two later, contains everything which makes Jan van Eyck so great an artist. The motive—the donor venerating the Virgin—is an old one,

p 80–81
(8–10)

p 121 (1)

p 285
(16)

p 286
(18)

One of the earliest forgeries of an ancient Roman work of art is this French gold medallion of Constantine from the collection of Jean duc de Berry. It was made about 1400 and in spite of its Gothic appearance was accepted in its day as a fine classical specimen. The Limbourg Brothers copied it in the 'Très Riches Heures'. (4)

but the treatment which brings into our presence Rolin and the Madonna, both characterized with great feeling, is revolutionary. We are made to share the donor's vision of heaven, and the artist has bestowed on this heaven all his skill in order to give us a glimpse of unearthly majesty. The architecture is palatial, yet grander than that of any palace we know; the garden seen through the arcade is rich with many flowers and a shining river winds its way past a town into the far distance. The utmost realism has been employed to produce an enhanced image of reality. But this realism is not simply a display of skill, nor has it been employed for its own sake. The style communicates a religious concept.

The same may be said of a painting in the National Gallery, London, usually referred to as the *Double Portrait of Giovanni Arnolfini and his Wife*. But this picture does not depict some conjugal genre scene, nor is it a conversation piece. As Professor Panofsky has shown in a brilliant and learned analysis, it is a kind of painted marriage certificate in which almost every object has a symbolic meaning and every gesture legal significance. Of course, we are at liberty simply to admire Jan's unrivalled handling of every detail, his feeling for the warm light which fills the room, and his ability to convey an atmosphere of solemnity appropriate to the occasion. But we miss the deeper mystery of his genius if we divorce the technical achievement from the meaning of the picture. As Panofsky put it: 'In the London Arnolfini portrait, then, Jan van Eyck not only achieved a concord of form, space, light and colour which even he was never to surpass, but he also demonstrated how the principle of disguised symbolism could abolish the borderline between *portraiture* and *narrative*, between *profane* and *sacred* art.' It is worth noting that this work which is dated 1434 was commissioned by a merchant from Lucca, who had settled in Bruges. It is therefore yet another witness of the esteem in which Flemish painting was held by Italians. Giovanni Arnolfini represents a characteristic patron: the rich businessman of the Flemish trading centres. But reasons other than wealth also account for the rise of towns like Bruges, Ghent or Tournai as flourishing centres of patronage. The duc de Berry, who had drawn so many artists to his court had died in 1416 and a year earlier the French had suffered a decisive defeat at the hands of the English.

p 290
(24)

Changes in Patronage

Jan van Eyck had begun his career still as a court artist and although he lived in Bruges from 1430 until his death in 1441 he also remained in the service of Philip the Good, Duke of Burgundy. His rôle as a miniaturist has been much debated, but there can be little doubt that some of his earliest works were in this genre. His great contemporaries, the Master of Flémalle and Roger van der Weyden, were exclusively panel painters who received their commissions from private patrons or corporations. Roger was official Town Painter of Brussels for many years. These changes in the type of patron and in the kind of art ordered are closely related. The well-to-do bourgeois were not collectors vying with each other in the amassing of precious objects; they were businessmen who had their portraits painted or ordered altarpieces which served a liturgical function in chapels or churches and were meant also to raise the donors' stock in heaven.

p 284 (13) The Master of Flémalle, probably to be identified with Robert Campin of Tournai, must have been familiar with all the refinements of Italianizing illumination and his *Mérode Altarpiece* depicts the *Annunciation* in a domestic setting, an iconographic type in the last resort derived from Italian models. Two things are remarkable about this triptych. There is first of all the loving care with which the scene is described in its charming details, particularly striking in the genre-like character of the right wing showing St Joseph in his carpenter's shop. Next there is the serious if exaggerated attempt to give us convincing picture space. Recession is certainly over-emphasized—note, for example, the bench against which the Virgin is leaning—but we really see the donors kneeling just beyond the open door of the Virgin's room, and we look over St Joseph's shoulder through a window out on the market square filled with minute but lively figures. There are certain similarities suggesting that Jan van Eyck knew this panel when he painted the *Annunciation* of the *Ghent Altarpiece* and it is interesting to observe that his treatment is much more restrained than the Master of Flémalle's.

Still, Jan van Eyck's serenity is a personal quality and not the sign of a more mature style. Roger van der Weyden—a follower of the Master of Flémalle and probably his pupil—outlived Van Eyck by more than twenty years (he died in 1464): he was fully acquainted with Eyckian techniques and methods of representation, but he employed this artistic language in a far more emotional manner. The *Descent from the Cross*, painted probably about p 285 (17) the same time as the *Arnolfini* portrait or a little later, is a case in point. Bartolomeo Fazio describing a similar (lost) painting praised the faithful expression of grief and the truth of the painted tears, indistinguishable from real ones. The eulogy is in this case more than a cliché. The Italians were fascinated by Flemish realism, and in Jan van Eyck's works Fazio had admired a microscopic accuracy of representation. But in the paintings of Roger, truth to outward nature apart, he was struck by the psychological truth of expression. For the *Descent from the Cross* the painter has used a subtle device in order to stress the expressive quality of his figures: he has placed them in a shallow shrine so that they gesticulate before our eyes like dancers in front of a plain backdrop. It is hardly surprising that the dramatic composition and the expressive vocabulary of this picture were imitated over and over again by succeeding generations of artists.

Italy looks North

During the 14th and 15th centuries the north had benefited through the importation of a new art from the south. But by the time of Jan van Eyck and Roger van der Weyden painting in Flanders was no longer dependent. In fact, Italians were ready to buy Flemish paintings and to learn from them. Reference has already been made to works by Jan van Eyck and to their influence in Florence. Roger van der Weyden received Italian commissions and had at least one Italian pupil, whose works unfortunately are not known. Moreover, van der Weyden himself went to Italy and, again according to Fazio, visited Rome 'in the year of the Jubilee', that is in 1450.

p 284 (14) A painting of his was once in the Medici Villa at Careggi where Vasari saw it. It represents the *Entombment* and it so happens that the rather unusual iconography has its closest parallel in a picture

by a follower of Fra Angelico. Yet Roger borrowed only composition and iconography from his Florentine model. The poignant grief and the modes of expressing it are all his own. He did not try to don an Italian costume and his patrons certainly liked his Flemish ways. This can also be seen in portraits he painted from Italian sitters, such as *Francesco d'Este*, an offspring of the famous p 290 (25) house who lived in Flanders. Unlike his Italian contemporaries Roger did not smoothe the features of his sitter. It would be truer to say that he characterized them sharply in the same way in which he stressed the expressions in his narrative pictures.

The three painters just discussed did for the north what the first generation of Quattrocento painters had done for Italy; they created a new pictorial idiom which was to determine the course of painting not only in the Netherlands but all over northern Europe for almost a century. But of the three founding fathers Roger van der Weyden became by far the most influential, and this is hardly surprising. Jan van Eyck's manner was too remote or aloof (this is not meant in any pejorative sense), and his presentation was too perfect to allow much scope for followers. In this respect he may be compared with Piero della Francesca. Roger van der Weyden was hardly a more medieval artist than Jan —as has often been claimed—and more accessible to painters still steeped in the Gothic tradition. Technically he was as advanced as Jan van Eyck, but his emotional range was wider and in consequence his style was more pliable. This was apparent already when considering his use of an Italian model for the *Entombment* and it is obvious again if we look at one of his major works, the *Last Judgment*, commissioned shortly before 1451 by Nicolas Rolin for the hospital at Beaune.

Without eschewing the effects of the new pictorial devices —perspective, light playing over figures and landscape, vivid gestures and expressions—Roger with noteworthy single-mindedness concentrates all his efforts on the emotional content of his picture. He never loses sight of the religious (and more precisely liturgical) function of an altarpiece and we are made aware of it before we go on to appreciate his artistry. It would therefore be wrong to assume that Roger's impact, as compared with Jan van Eyck's, simply rested on style. To his age the function of a work of art was still of surpassing importance.

Flemish painters of the 15th century attained a high degree of skill in working the rich ore they had inherited, but with the notable exception of Hugo van der Goes none of them found a new method for extracting the precious metal. In fact, we may classify them in accordance with faithfulness to their models rather than on the basis of chronology or geography. For this reason it will suffice if we refer to only three painters.

Hans Memlinc was born in Germany but he must have come in his early youth to the Netherlands, where he became an orthodox disciple of Roger van der Weyden (probably as a member of his workshop) though he never grasped the essence of his master's style. Like many unimaginative but competent men he was highly successful, and when he died in 1494 in Bruges, where he had settled some thirty years earlier, he was among the richest men in a rich town. The *Donne Altarpiece*—commissioned by Sir John p 290 (23) Donne of Kidwelly—is a typical example of the Roger tradition at its most uninspired. The outer trappings are all there—the facial types, the draperies, the landscape seen through the openings of an arcade, the clear colours—but the gestures, always vital in Van der Weyden's pictures, have become stilted and empty, and intensity of emotion is lacking. Where Roger had used a simple composition for the strongest dramatic effect, Memlinc only manages a dull symmetrical grouping of figures.

Dieric Bouts, though no less indebted to Roger van der Weyden, showed more independence. We do not know where he was trained but his pictures suggest that he was familiar also with the Eyckian manner. The *Entombment* demonstrates Bouts' real grasp p 284 (15) of the pictorial idiom at his disposal. He turns the broken body of Christ towards the beholder for the sake of emphasis, as Roger van der Weyden had done on the Prado *Descent from the Cross*. All gestures and expressions are psychologically motivated and the arrangement of the figures in a shallow strip in front of a landscape back-drop strengthens the impact of the action. All these elements are clearly derived from Roger, but the monumentality of the figures and the almost hieratic stillness of the composition echo the methods of Jan van Eyck. Nevertheless the fusion of the various components is successful. By rendering certain Eyckian traits in an essentially Rogerian idiom Bouts became one of the most important mediators between Flemish and German painting.

The Inheritance Transformed

Only one Flemish artist of the second half of the 15th century can claim the attribute 'great': Hugo van der Goes. He was born in Ghent where he also spent the greater part of his working life until, late in the seventies, he entered a monastery. He died insane in 1482 and it was said at the time that a feeling of insufficiency before the *Ghent Altarpiece* had unhinged his mind. Yet the *Portinari Altar* is the work of a genius who had thoroughly transformed his inheritance. The *Nativity* (on the central panel) is enacted on a deep and wide stage with a disconcertingly empty centre. The Virgin, St Joseph, the adoring angels and shepherds are arranged to the left and right of the tiny Child lying isolated on the bare ground in the middle. The Child, however, is the principal source of light within the picture and our attention is drawn to this radiance. Other tensions and contradictions strike us when we consider the picture a little further. The distribution of light suggests a centrifugal scheme of composition; the placing of the figures, on the other hand, appears symmetrical round a central axis running down along the corner of the building in the background and through the gap between the two kneeling angels to the head of the Child. Still, between the two halves of the *Nativity* there is a subtle difference of startling effectiveness. The calm of St Joseph on the left has its counterpart in the agitation of the three shepherds on the right. The melancholy air of the serene Virgin kneeling in prayer is contrasted again with wild gesticulation of the shepherds whose forward rush has only just been arrested by the sight of the Christ Child. And there are still further contradictions. The spatial setting is consistent and indicates understanding of the problems of perspective. Yet van der Goes has varied the scale of the figures in accordance with their significance —a device also used on the wings in distinguishing between donors and their patron saints. We can hardly call this a regression to medieval practice since in this case scale has become an expressive device.

The altar was ordered about 1475 by Tommaso Portinari, the Medici agent in Bruges. As soon as it was completed it was shipped to Florence where it made a lasting impression on the painters, once it had been set up in Sant'Egidio. When Ghirlandaio painted in 1485 a *Nativity* for the Sassetti Chapel of Sta Trinita he 'quoted' Hugo van der Goes' shepherds. What was it that fascinated the Italians about this Flemish painting?

Thirty years earlier Bartolomeo Fazio had been charmed by the realism of Van Eyck; he admired his representations of a world in little. Ghirlandaio—at a moment when the systematic and scientific rendering of picture space no longer presented a problem to Italian painters—turned to Hugo van der Goes for the sake of a different kind of realism. Flemish masters, true to their Gothic inheritance, had perfected the realistic depiction of emotions through expressive human figures. This true-to-life intensity of expression, portrayed so beautifully by Hugo van der Goes, was something new to Italian artists of the late Quattrocento, and the return flow from north to south merging with the native Quattrocento stream contributed its share to that style we call the High Renaissance. Both Leonardo and Michelangelo were in the debt of the Flemings.

Across the Frontiers

Even so, in Italy the impact of Flemish art was less profound than in Germany and, though to a lesser degree, in France. Artistically speaking Germany after about 1430 became a province of Flanders, and much of the painting produced was 'provincial' also in the qualitive sense of the word. Moreover even the best artists —Hans Multscher, Lucas Moser, Conrad Witz, Martin Schongauer—looked to the north-west rather than towards Italy. French painters, on the other hand, true to their geographical position looked both to Flanders and to Italy. This vigorous internationalism of French mid 15th-century painting is apparent

in one of its finest and best known works: an altarpiece (now dismembered) of which the central panel with the *Annunciation* remains in the Eglise de la Madeleine in Aix-en-Provence.

p 283 (9)

The *Aix Annunciation* presents us with a puzzling mixture of ingredients. The iconography—the setting of the scene in a church rather than in a chamber—is French. The figures of the Virgin and the angel, however, can only have been painted by someone familiar with the *Annunciation* of the *Ghent Altarpiece*. But the plasticity of these figures, the broken folds of their bulging draperies, the oblique angle from which we see the church interior— these devices are constantly used by artists who had learned their trade in the circle of the Master of Flémalle or Roger van der Weyden. Lastly the complex perspective of the panel is constructed by mathematical rather than by empirical means, indicating knowledge of contemporary Italian art. Still, in the end the imaginative effort of a powerful artist fused everything, creating an original work of art in its own right.

We do not know who painted the *Aix Annunciation*, but it is hardly surprising that various candidates have been put forward; a Neapolitan influenced by Jan van Eyck (some of whose pictures could be seen in Naples, we remember), a Fleming conversant with the style of Conrad Witz, a Fleming deeply impressed by the sculpture of Claus Sluter, a Frenchman working in the south of France in the circle of René of Anjou. This kind of clever guesswork could be amusing if it did not betray an unhealthy and unhistorical pre-occupation with nationality or race. Stylistic characteristics can be acquired; they do not constitute a kind of physiognomy which allows us to determine the ethnic origins of an artist. As far as the 15th century is concerned we must accept the fact that styles and masters were mobile and frequently crossed the so-called frontiers.

In the case of the Master of the *Aix Annunciation* Italian links had to be inferred from his style, but we know that Jean Fouquet visited Rome and Florence between 1443 and 1447. He was in fact the first northern painter who encountered and absorbed the fruits of the Florentine Quattrocento Renaissance, and the style resulting from his journey has aptly been described as 'a new equilibrium between the two extremes of Italian and Flemish art'.

The dedication page of the most splendid manuscript attributed to Jean Fouquet, the *Hours of Etienne Chevalier*, shows the owner with his patron saint Stephen kneeling before the Madonna. Some fifty years earlier Jacquemart de Hesdin had used the same iconographic scheme in a manuscript he decorated for Jean duc de Berry. If we compare the two, we realise that the process of turning the illustration on the book page into a picture comparable to panel painting has now been completed. Fouquet's dedication picture can no longer be called a 'miniature'. The overt Italianism of his style is obvious. Pilasters, cornices, putti, garlands—all are pure classical motives. The oblique angle view—characteristic of earlier Flemish art—has been given up. Instead the scene is enacted on a box-stage conforming to the perspective rules laid down by Leone Battista Alberti. But there is still one amusing typically northern trait. Etienne Chevalier, kneeling in his palatial marble-clad room, is not actually in the presence of the Virgin: in his prayer he visualizes her in Heaven, and the painter has made his vision manifest for us. But the earthly and heavenly sphere are clearly distinguished. Heaven, like the churches of northern Europe, is built in the Gothic style, while the minister of Charles VII inhabits an earth adorned with the latest refinements of the new Renaissance architecture. No Italian would have used the two modes for these symbolic ends.

p 282–3 (7, 10)

The portrait of *Guillaume Jouvenel des Ursins* shows the same amalgamation of different elements. The pose of the sitter before a *prie-dieu* belongs to Flemish art—the donor of Roger's *Rolin Madonna* comes to mind—but the background overladen with strange (and not correctly used) gilded classical detail must be made up from memories of the trip to Italy.

It may not be chance that Fouquet is also the first French artist whose self-portrait has survived, a small circular enamel which may originally have been set in the frame of one of his paintings. But it is noteworthy that this enamel must be described as a portrait *all' antica*, for the composition used by Fouquet—head and shoulders seen from the front and framed by a roundel—is a

p 287–9 (20, 21)

p 287 (19)

painter's adaptation of a well-known type of Roman portrait sculpture, the *imago clipeata*.

Fouquet's sensitivity to all the implications of Italian Quattrocento art was perhaps exceptional among his French contemporaries. Most of them kept closer to the Flemish tradition even when they used a more methodical treatment of picture space, which they could only have learned from Italian sources. German artists of the period, as has already been said, surrendered completely to the lessons of Flemish painting. The painter and sculptor Hans Multscher—his workshop was in Ulm—followed the Master of Flémalle so closely that training or at least a sojourn in the Netherlands seems likely in his case. The *Pentecost* panel of his *Niederwurzach Altar*, dated 1437, is a rather robust example of the Flemish manner in a German guise. The lyricism of the 'Soft Style'—the German variant of the International Style—has gone. The figures have become dumpy and heavy. Multscher's Apostles have an air of earthiness—one is almost inclined to say primitivism—not found in his models which, after all, had sprung from the courtly art of Burgundy. Incidentally, the hexagonal colonnaded room in which the Apostles are assembled reproduces a Sienese Trecento model, which could hardly have reached Multscher directly but must have come to him through a Burgundian or Flemish intermediary.

p 291
(30)

'Cry out art, cry out and complain'

It is difficult to put a finger on the sources of another German painter, Lucas Moser. He is known to us through only one work, an altarpiece dated 1431 depicting the story of the Magdalen. This, the earliest surviving example of the Flemish manner on German soil, is astoundingly original, particularly in the handling of light. The journey of the saints on a raft silhouetted against the sun-drenched waves with their foamy crests is unique in European panel painting of the period. A comparable luminosity might be found only in the (somewhat earlier) miniatures of the Boucicaut Master or in others attributed to Jan van Eyck. The delightful group asleep outside the city-gate shows an acute gift for observation paired with the ability to render naturalistic details.

p 283
(11)

The frame of the *Tiefenbronn Altar* bears with the painter's signature a famous much debated inscription: 'Cry out art, cry out and complain, for nobody wants you now.' This agonized plea can hardly be a piece of implied art criticism—either a grumble that the new style still has too few devotees or a lament for the passing of the 'Soft Style'—it can only be the disgruntled voice of an artist who feels himself inadequately recompensed for his labours. It is well worth remembering that in Europe as a whole the 15th century was not a time of general affluence, but of continuing economic stagnation.

Reference has been made several times to the cosmopolitan attitude of 15th-century artists and patrons. Conrad Witz has been called 'the greatest Swiss painter before Holbein', but he was born in Germany, lived in Constance while the Council was in session (1414-18), settled in Basle during the early thirties when the town was filled with clergy from all over Europe for another Council, and finally worked in Geneva for a French patron. His highly original art shows traces of the study of both Jan van Eyck and the Master of Flémalle.

The Miraculous Draught of Fishes is part of an altarpiece which was commissioned in 1444 by the Bishop of Geneva. The landscape with the mountains on the further shore is an accurate portrayal of the view as we still see it from the Quai Montblanc. It is true that Jan van Eyck had painted 'real' prospects but the town and river behind the Chancellor Rolin cannot be identified for the scenery has been made up from many observations—all true by themselves—which have been assembled in order to convey an idea of the whole world. We would be mistaken if we regarded Witz' view of Lake Geneva simply as an example of topographical art introduced to please a local patron. Jan van Eyck had used a painstaking realism to disguise symbolism, and Conrad Witz had fully understood this essential quality of Eyckian art. The miracle, which took place on Lake Genesareth, is made real and immediate to the people of Geneva by being enacted before their own eyes. Witz, unlike so many of his contemporaries, was not content with learning the mechanics of Flemish painting.

p 291
(28)

He had penetrated the meaning of the new realism and expressed it in his own way.

It is perhaps not surprising that neither Moser nor Witz left a 'school' since their highly individual styles could not easily be learned or imitated. Moreover after the middle of the century Roger van der Weyden's influence became all-pervading. It was claimed by a 16th-century author that Martin Schongauer, the leading German master from about 1460 until his death in 1491, had actually been his pupil. This is not impossible, though there are difficulties over dates. In any case, the suggestion is telling, for Schongauer's art—he was an engraver in the first place and only one painting of his is known today—is permeated with the flavour of Roger's style. There is also one document, particularly precious to the historian, which witnesses his contact with one of Van der Weyden's main works. Schongauer drew the Christ of the Beaune *Last Judgment*, and the drawing came later into the possession of Dürer who proudly noted the author's name on it.

Humanism: Italy's Cultural Export

Schongauer was influential not only because of the high quality of his prints but even more because engravings are an ideal medium for the dissemination of a popular style. His standing was such that in 1493 Dürer, at the end of his training in Nuremberg, set out to meet him. He arrived in Colmar just too late, for Schongauer had died a few months previously, and Dürer turned to Basle, one of the centres of German humanism and publishing. The change of plan, though occasioned by the engraver's death, is of considerable historical significance. With Martin Schongauer, the last great representative of the Roger School had gone. The new generation, to which Dürer belonged, once again sought inspiration from humanism and from the general cultural movement of which humanism forms a part: the Italian Renaissance.

This does not mean that there was a sudden general change in the arts. Many masters and their customers remained satisfied with well-established habits, and some workshops went on well into the 16th century happily using a retarded style. The fact that advanced taste and fashion demanded something else from painting—and by now also from sculpture and architecture—must be seen as forming part of a wider cultural pattern. After the middle of the century people at the French and English courts and in the big commercial centres of south Germany took a growing interest in the 'New Learning', in literature, historiography, philosophy and art as they were practised in Italy.

Certainly these countries had political and ecomomic ties with the south. Students went to Bologna, Padua and other famous Italian universities. Ecclesiastics of all ranks went to Rome. But it is at least doubtful whether a taste for Renaissance art and architecture would ever have crossed the Alps if Italy's most important cultural export had not preceeded it: humanism. Italian scholars taught in Paris by the middle of the 15th century, in England they held secretarial positions with Henry VII, they visited the German centres of learning. A dean of Lincoln was inspired by his Italian friends to write rather dull Latin poetry and English publishers printed not only medieval romances but also Aristotle's *Ethics* in the Latin translation of Leonardo Bruni. Dürer and Holbein were contemporaries of Lefèvre d'Etaples, John Colet and Erasmus. All this, however, does not mean that some *Zeitgeist* touched all these men with his mysterious wand. The humanists, in reviving classical letters, concerned themselves with the rules of moral conduct they found enshrined in ancient literature. Leone Battista Alberti wrote not only about architecture, painting and sculpture but also a treatise *Della Famiglia*. These books are not the unrelated exercises of a dilettante; they share a common outlook. The exemplary character of classical art was seen not just in its aesthetic qualities, but—like that of literature—in its moral essence, or rather, with a truly Platonic spirit, in both.

The consequences of this outlook were profound. Vasari (a much better historian than detail-obsessed art historians are willing to admit) put the case for the early Renaissance clearly when he said that Masaccio had returned to nature, Brunelleschi to classical models, while Donatello held the balance between the imitators of nature and the followers of ancient art. He went on to argue that the perfection of the High Renaissance was only

Chambord, begun in 1519; the plan (from Ducerceau's 'Les plus excellents Bastiments de France', 1576) shows the medieval features of a square keep with ranges of lower buildings, all with corner towers and surrounded by a moat. The influence of the original Italian designer remains only in the Greek-cross division of the keep, each corner forming a suite of one large and two smaller rooms and a closet. (5)

reached when rule and order, learned from classical monuments, had been applied to all the arts. Rule and order, it should be noted, are moral as well as aesthetic qualities.

For obvious reasons this Italian pattern could not be repeated in the north. Moreover, there was a fundamental difference between the northern Renaissance of the 15th and that of the 16th century. The masters of the former had been content with the adoption of the pictorial means offered by Italian Trecento painting, and the process of absorption had been painless. But by the late 15th century, when a new wave of Italianism reached the north, Petrarch's seeds had yielded a rich harvest, and now the acceptance of the Renaissance meant more than the adaptation of Italian or antique forms. It implied the acceptance of a philosophy of life which had to be expressed in a classical language. In the different social and cultural context of the northern countries this was by no means easy and the resulting clash was often bound to be painful. Nor can we expect patrons and artists to comprehend at once the lessons learned from the south.

Architecture and the Roman Heritage

Of all the arts architecture proved to be the most conservative and at the same time, by a seeming paradox, also the one most susceptible to the frills of an extrinsic Renaissance. There were good reasons for resistance to any fundamental change. Architecture is conservative by nature because buildings have to satisfy needs deeply rooted in the social habits of people. Lay-out and appearance of buildings cannot be changed overnight for the sake of a new fashion. As far as Renaissance forms were concerned patrons and builders in France, England and Germany were also faced with a more specific problem. Brunelleschi, Alberti and their followers had wished to revive classical architecture which they considered their country's heritage. The situation in northern Europe was entirely different. Though some northern countries had once formed part of the Roman Empire, only southern France could boast substantial Roman remains, and without imposing ruins there was no feeling for any binding tradition. Moreover the Renaissance is a learned style, demanding from its practitioners acquaintance with both the monuments and the theory of antiquity. But Vitruvius' *Ten Books on Architecture* did not become available in French until 1547 and in German until a year later. As to Renaissance theory, Alberti's *De re aedificatoria* was first published in 1485 in an unillustrated edition which would hardly have helped an uninitiated student. A French edition appeared in 1553, but England had to wait for Leoni's translation of 1726. By the middle of the 16th century, however, a taste

for Renaissance architecture had been established and the Italian theoreticians of the day were eagerly studied on the other side of the Alps. Serlio's *Regole generali di architettura* of 1537 came out in a Dutch edition only two years later; a German translation followed in 1542, a French one in 1545. Vignola's *Regole delli cinque ordini* became by far the most popular of such treatises and was translated into many European languages. By the second half of the 16th century authors in northern Europe had become well enough acquainted with the new material and published their own treatises, as for example Ducerceau (*Livre d'Architecture*, 1555) Vredeman de Fries (*Architectura*, 1565), Wendel Dietterlin (*Architectura von Ausstheilung . . . der fünff Seulen*, 1593) and John Shute (*The First and chief groundes of architecture*, 1563).

Since systematic studies began late, Renaissance architecture when it first appeared in France, Germany and England, was little more than a novel form of decoration for basically Gothic structures. Moreover at first these embellishments could only be executed by imported craftsmen working for a class of patron who could afford costly extravaganzas.

'Extrinsic Renaissance' in France

France had closer political ties than her neighbours with Italy but the transalpine invasions of Charles VIII, Louis XII and François Ier produced as a direct result a reverse invasion of France by Italian taste. As early as 1475 Francesco Laurana had been employed by René of Anjou. Fra Giocondo and Giuliano da Sangallo were in France about the turn of the century. Leonardo accompanied François Ier back to France in 1517 and lived for two years until his death in 1519 near Amboise. Primaticcio and Rosso were the two leading masters working at Fontainebleau, and Serlio as well as Vignola paid visits during the early 40s of the 16th century.

The Château de Gaillon in Normandy, built for Cardinal Georges d'Amboise from 1501 onward, is one of the earliest and most characteristic examples of an extrinsic Renaissance. Italian craftsmen arrived on the scene only when the basic structure—a sturdy medieval castle—had gone up, and they were responsible among many other things for the decoration of the main entrance gate. The classical details, correct in themselves and rather fine, look strangely inappropriate between the two hefty corner turrets. In England we find the same thing happening at Hampton Court, begun by Cardinal Wolsey in 1514. Italian artists helped with the decoration and Giovanni da Maiano, a Florentine, made the terracotta roundels with the heads of Roman emperors surrounded by wreaths which adorn the gateway of this late Gothic English country-house.

The persistence of habits in architecture can best be seen at Chambord. Though the building was designed about 1519 for François Ier by an Italian from the school of Giuliano da Sangallo the plans were modified during execution by French masons and today we see an essentially medieval castle-keep, corner towers and all, decked out with rather bizarre classical details invading the tall gables, chimney pots and roof balustrades. The result is rather uncomfortable, a rich confection ideally suited for the garish spectacle of *Son et Lumière*, but hardly in keeping with the purer classical style expected in the age of Bramante. Henry VIII, not to be outdone by François Ier, may have wanted to build Nonesuch Palace, begun in 1538, in competition with Chambord. The building, completed only after the king's death, was destroyed in the 17th century, and is known to us only from drawings, on which it appears as an exotic and vulgar mixture of French, Italian and English elements.

f 5
p 176-7
(33, 34)

p 262
(30)

The Second Wave

A purer classicism became possible in France after about 1540 when architects with a thorough understanding of the Renaissance took over. Philibert de l'Orme as a young man had spent three years in Rome, moving in artistic and humanist circles. There he met Cardinal du Bellay through whom after his return he was introduced to the Dauphin (later Henri II) and Diane de Poitiers for whom between 1547 and 1552 he built the Château of Anet. Little of it survives today but the entrance (now in the courtyard of the Ecole des Beaux-Arts, Paris) shows a fundamental change from Gaillon or the Porte Dorée at Fontainebleau.

p 294
(38)

Philibert de l'Orme uses three classical orders, superimposed and in a proper context, with carefully blanced proportions. Yet the function of this entrance gate is in no way sacrificed to the demands of style. In 1568 Philibert published a treatise, *Le premier tome de l'architecture*, which is naturally modelled on Vitruvius and Alberti. But with the latter the French author shares a truly humanist concern with the moral problems facing the architect. Comfort, convenience and advantage of the inhabitants are more important than decoration, beauty and richness of houses, which should be built for the 'health and life of men'.

Pierre Lescot, de l'Orme's contemporary, may not have gone to Rome, but he was familiar with current architectural literature and with the monumental Roman remains of southern France. In 1546 he was commissioned with the rebuilding of the Louvre. In looking at Lescot's work we are struck by a curious paradox. The classical detail is correct and in itself of some considerable refinement. But there is rather too much of it—it is as if Lescot had wanted to employ everything he had ever learned—so that this magnificent façade looks like a rich display in front of a building, rather than an organic part of it.

It is interesting to compare Lescot's Louvre with a building erected by an Italian working in France, Sebastiano Serlio's château of Ancy-le-Franc begun also in 1546. If Lescot did his utmost to give the royal palace an Italian appearance, Serlio took care to assimilate himself. The high roof, the corner towers, though relieved by pilasters and cornices, the shallow relief of the sparse decorations—they all accord with native traditions. On the other hand architectural details, the niches between the windows and the open bays on the ground floor, are derived from Italian models. But all in all Ancy-le-Franc is an Italianate rather than an Italian building.

After Henry VIII had broken with Rome in 1534, cultural contacts between England and Italy became for a time tenuous and the main inspiration of Renaissance forms came through books or from France—that is at one remove. *The Gate of Virtue* at Caius College, Cambridge, put up during the sixties by the founder who in his youth had studied in Padua, derives from a design of Serlio's.

Serlio and French architecture also inspired to some extent the finest and most original example of Elizabethan architecture, Longleat House, built by its owner Sir John Thynne with the help of his master mason Robert Smythson. Thynne knew France well; moreover when he began Longleat he had already some building experience. Astonishing refinement of all architectural details, symmetry and restraint make Longleat House outstanding. 'It represents', as Sir John Summerson has said, 'as no other building does, the momentary "High Renaissance" of our architecture.' Nevertheless Thynne applied Renaissance principles to an essentially English house and he did not put up an Italian villa. Indeed the deeper understanding of Italian Renaissance architecture came to England only with Inigo Jones in the early 17th century.

The pattern was very much the same in the Netherlands and in Germany. An Italian architect from Bologna rebuilt Breda Castle in Holland during the 1530s. Antwerp Town Hall by Franz Floris, built between 1561 and 1565 combines elegant Italian motifs with many reminiscences of the northern tradition and the wing which the Elector Otto Heinrich added to Heidelberg Castle at about the same time is remarkable rather for picturesque agglomeration of Renaissance elements than for their rational application.

Much northern Renaissance architecture looks incongruosus and downright ugly because its style is inflated and pompous. Architects (or more often their exacting patrons) made the same mistake as Monsieur Jourdain in a comparable situation: they aimed beyond their station by using an idiom which they had not mastered. They covered all available surfaces with ornaments culled from prints and books without comprehending the principles of classical or Renaissance structure. Only where these decorations were employed on a smaller scale—on Holbein's design for a chimney piece, now in the British Museum, or on the carved screen of King's College Chapel, Cambridge can we appreciate the weird combination of fine craftsmanship and unbridled imagination. This love for elaborate decoration remains essentially Gothic in character.

p 191 (12)
p 295 (39)
p 294 (36)
f 6
p 263 (32)
p 295 (40)
p 205 (21)
p 295 (41)

Longleat—from the plan of the ground floor now at Hatfield. Whoever was responsible for the design, this building was unique in Elizabethan England for its classically-influenced symmetry. The traditional English courtyard house looked inwards for safety and convenience; Longleat was entirely extrovert with uniform, shallow bay-window units (derived probably from Somerset House) on all four sides. The Long Gallery on the first floor ran the length of the north side. (6)

The Transition in Sculpture

In fact, all over northern Europe a strong Gothic tradition survived well into the 16th century alongside the experiments with the new style. In the end sculptors found it easier to come to terms with the Renaissance, for they had to change less than the architects. Moreover two circumstances came to their aid: imported Italian masters set up examples which could be studied, and young northern sculptors went to Italy to learn about the Renaissance. They brought back prints, medals, plaquettes and small bronzes, which were carried north also by connoisseurs.

The transition from late Gothic to Renaissance sculpture is particularly striking in France. Michel Colombe's relief with *St George and the Dragon* dates from 1509 and was carved for the altar of the chapel at Gaillon. The picturesque and detailed landscape background, the variations in the scale of the figures, the dragon looking like a medieval beast, and the bold carving derive directly from the conventions of Gothic art. The marble frame, however, with its faultless grotesques seems curiously out of key with Colombe's style; it was supplied by a migrant Italian sculptor.

When François Ier commissioned in 1515 the tomb of Louis XII at St-Denis he employed two Italian artists who had settled in France, Antonio and Giovanni Giusti. The elaborate mausoleum with the kneeling figures on top, the *gisants* under an arcade surrounded by the Apostles, and the figures of Virtues at the four corners betray both in style and iconography a mixture of French Gothic and Italian Renaissance elements, though the latter come out more strongly. Torrigiani's almost contemporary tomb of Henry VII in Westminster Abbey is a parallel case in every respect. The monument is modelled on previous royal tombs in the Abbey, the figures of king and queen combine classical dignity with Gothic precision of line, but the angels at the corners of the sarcophagus are full-blooded Italian putti.

But the subsequent developments in France and England were different. The French kings had their favourite residence at Fontainebleau where Rosso Fiorentino, Primaticcio and Niccolò del' Abbate worked. The royal collection of Italian paintings was housed there, and in 1540 Primaticcio brought from Rome plaster casts of the most celebrated antiques—the Belvedere Apollo, the Laocoön, the Ariadne and others—which were cast in bronze and shown together with replicas of some 16th-century Italian sculptures. Benvenuto Cellini was a much admired if troublesome guest between 1540 and 1545 while he made, among a number of less spectacular things, the famous salt-cellar for François Ier (now in

f 3
p 174 (24)
p 174-5 (25)
p 251 (1)
p 173 (21)
p 172 (20)

Vienna). We know from Cellini's autobiography that French artists collaborated with their Italian colleagues and both Goujon and Pilon formed their style in such surroundings.

An elegant court style resulted from these contacts, and it is characteristic that until recently Goujon's name was attached to a piece of sculpture which shows the influence of Primaticcio and Cellini so clearly, that it has also been attributed to the latter: the *Diana of Anet*. Goujon's documented works from the late forties and fifties add to influence from Italian Mannerism yet another element, a real feeling for the use of clinging draperies which must have been learned from classical sculpture. Within the limited range of the decorative relief Goujon emerges as a sensitive and sophisticated artist.

Germain Pilon, on the other hand, was one of the greatest masters of the northern Renaissance, bringing insight and originality to his tasks. During the sixties he collaborated with Primaticcio on the tomb of Henry II and Catherine de' Medici at St-Denis. The monument follows the long established tradition of French royal tombs, but Pilon has gone a long way even from the Giusti tomb of Louis XII. The unmistakable Renaissance appearance is not simply due to the design, which in any case was Primaticcio's. It rather rests on the free handling of the figures. The four Virtues at the corners of the structure have classical poise and dignity, while the kneeling figures of king and queen are rendered with full understanding of their organic structure. Pilon avoided the Mannerist temptation to make the poses complex or striking, and the simplicity of posture is matched by the unaffected use of bronze.

Pilon's imaginative power is seen at its best in a marble which seems inspired by Michelangelo's *Risen Christ* in Sta Maria sopra Minerva, of which a cast was to be seen at Fontainebleau. The French sculptor's *Christ* belongs to a *Resurrection* which was destined for the (never completed) Valois mausoleum at St-Denis. Expressive gestures, emotional intensity and a real grasp of the principles of classical sculpture make this work intensely moving. It belongs to that rare moment during which an artist of genius transformed his native tradition in the light of knowledge gained from a different sphere.

By the side of France, English sculpture of the 16th century presents a sorry spectacle. Court patronage was lacking and with the dissolution of the monasteries and the Reformation the Church too ceased to be an effective patron. Hence (soon after Torrigiani's visit in the second decade of the century) it became unprofitable for foreign artists to come to England. Native sculptors continued to turn out funerary monuments, but they neither succeeded in keeping alive a Gothic tradition, nor did they manage more than a superficial application of Renaissance decoration. The tomb of the first Lord Marney, dating from about 1530, may stand here as a typical example.

The Last Flowering of Gothic

While German painters during the latter part of the 15th century rarely rose above dull mediocrity, sculptors hardly had their equals anywhere north of the Alps. Elaborate carved wooden altarpieces, sometimes further enriched by painted wings, were one of their notable contributions, and Veit Stoss made between 1477 and 1488 for St Mary's Church in Cracow the most monumental of them. With its predella and lofty finials it is some thirty feet high. The *Death of the Virgin* in the central shrine has rare dramatic power, and the drama is expressed not only through highly individual heads of the Apostles but also by billowing draperies which have a dynamic impetus of their own. Tilman Riemenschneider's *Creglingen Altar*, completed some twenty years later, is more lyrical in mood, but still testifies to the lasting appeal of this type of altar. In this case, however, there is a significant innovation: no paint or gilding is applied to the carved figures, and the intricate pattern of light and shade weaving over them enhances their sculptural quality. Nevertheless, Riemenschneider was not familiar with the ideals of the Italian Renaissance. The charming stone figures of *Adam and Eve* from the porch of a chapel show nothing of the interest in the organic structure of the human body which characterizes Italian sculpture since Donatello. They seem insubstantial and linear, and typi-

cally Gothic swaying movement uncontrolled by their own will.

Choir stalls were another task allowing German sculptors to exercise their skill and inventiveness. Those of Ulm Cathedral were completed by Jörg Syrlin in 1474. The bench ends are adorned with busts of sibyls and classical sages which are remarkable for their subtle psychological differentiation. The complex iconographic programme must have been devised by some local scholar, but Syrlin's formal idiom remains Gothic.

The same is true of Syrlin's great contemporary the Dutchman Nicolaus Gerhaert, whose art harks back to Claus Sluter. A sandstone *Crucifix* of his in the Old Cemetery at Baden-Baden is signed and dated 1467. The meticulous rendering of the tormented body of Christ is mitigated by restraint and dignity. The head is individual, yet the expression of suffering is raised to the level of the universal. Gerhaert's insistence on individuality is something new, and it is hardly surprising that the heads of a *Prophet and Sybil* at Strasbourg, have been taken for the portraits of some local nobleman and his mistress.

Gerhaert, Stoss, Riemenschneider and others exercised a powerful influence well into the 16th century. Hans Leinberger's magnificent *St George* of about 1525 shows, however, that the Gothic tradition did in the end clash with the Renaissance. The deliberately ornamental treatment of the draperies and the broken contour are in striking contrast to the well understood contraposto and the organic articulation of the figure of the saint.

Still, in Germany the Renaissance hardly left its mark on monumental sculpture. The lasting taste for Gothic apart, there were no princes who (like the kings of France) could afford to employ good Italian artists. The Emperor Maximilian dreamt of the ideals of medieval knighthood, and at the same time wanted to be a patron with a contemporary taste. Yet he had to content himself with a *Triumphal Arch* on paper—woodcuts made to Dürer's design—and his gigantic tomb was never completed. He wished his effigy to be surrounded by his Hapsburg ancestors with their patron saints, in all about a hundred bronze statues, of which only twenty-three were finished. Though they were designed by various masters, they have certain characteristics in common: while forcefully modelled, these figures retain a good deal of the Gothic love for flowing decorative lines and rich broken-up surfaces. Hans Leinberger's *Albrecht IV* and Peter Vischer the Elder's *King Arthur* are among the most distinguished.

Italianate Bronzes

Though patronage on a large scale was lacking, the much travelled and sophisticated merchants of the big international trading centres, notably those of Nuremberg and Augsberg, developed a taste for medals, plaquettes and small bronzes *all'antica* which had to be satisfied by native artists. The flourishing bronze foundry of the Vischers in Nuremberg became one of the centres for producing this new art. When Peter the Elder designed the *Shrine of St Sebald* his idiom was still Gothic, but his two sons were to add ornamental details picked up abroad. Hermann, the elder son, went to Rome in 1515 'for the sake of art', and Peter the Younger must have been familiar with north Italian bronze work. His *Inkwell with the figure of Vanitas* belongs to the precious world of humanist art in which iconographic subtleties were treasured as much as a classicizing style and exquisite workmanship.

We meet this Italianizing mode also in the art of Peter Flötner. After working for the Fuggers in Augsburg he went to Italy and settled in Nuremberg in 1522, visiting the south once more at the end of the decade. The *Apollo Fountain* of 1532 at Nuremberg has been attributed to him. The motive of Apollo shooting an arrow was probably derived from an Italian engraving and, in the last resort, it should be traced back to the *Belvedere Apollo*. Yet Flötner's Apollo is not a copy but the sensitive rendering of a typical Renaissance theme. The nude human figure is shown in a pose which guarantees the utmost formal restraint.

In Augsburg the Fuggers made their family chapel, which was begun in 1510 and consecrated in 1518, into one of the first and most resplendent examples of Renaissance decoration in Germany. Little of this remains today, but the altar group of the *Dead Christ supported by the Virgin and St John* is remarkable for its stately rhythm, equipoise and symmetry. Its authorship is uncertain, but

p 175 (26)
p 175 (27–30)
p 174 (22)
p 300 (55)
p 300 (54)
p 300 (57, 58)
p 300 (56)
p 301 (63)
p 204–5 (19)
p 301 (61)
p 301 (59)

p 301
(64)
whoever made it must have been familiar with north Italian sculpture. The bronze screen of the chapel came from the Vischer foundry and was completed only in 1540. The reliefs in the lunettes are among the most Italianate of the north.

The dichotomy running through German sculpture of the first half of the 16th century is most obvious in the work of Conrad Meit. Maximilian's daughter, Margaret of Austria, made him her court sculptor and during the late 1520s he was in charge of the decoration of her burial chapel at Brou. The tombs of Margaret and her husband Philibert follow Gothic, and more specifically Burgundian, tradition. But Meit was at his best in small boxwood statuettes, emulating bronze. His female figures such as *Eve* or *Judith* have a sensuous charm which shows how freely a northern artist could treat the nude.

p 301
(60)

The comparative scarcity of proper Renaissance sculpture in the north was also due to the absence of that all-pervading classical tradition which served Italian artists as a constant guide. Moreover the taste for the 'modern' idiom came without much warning so that sculptors going straight from Gothic to the High Renaissance had to miss the artistic development which between Giovanni Pisano and Verrocchio had transformed the nature of Italian sculpture. It is therefore excusable that some fell back on outmoded Quattrocento models, as for example the unknown Nuremberg master who about 1550 made the charming bronze of a *Christ Child Blessing* now in the Victoria and Albert Museum, London, while others found the step from Gothic to Mannerism easier, as we suspect when looking at Conrad Meit's *Judith*.

p 301
(62)

The Challenge to Painting

Painters too lacked almost everything which during the latter part of the 15th century had prepared the way for the 'classic art' of the early Cinquecento. While still working with the formulae of Flemish realism they were abruptly faced with an infinitely more complex and demanding style. A small number, who had sensibility and intelligence, survived the challenge, but for many it brought disaster since through lack of understanding they produced a hybrid—and often repellent—style.

English and French painting of the first half of the 16th century were poles apart. In France the School of Fontainebleau with its outstanding Italian masters created works of the highest quality and guaranteed the undisputed victory of Italian taste. Only in portraiture do we find for a time the continuance of northern traditions, as in the picture of *Louis XII* attributed to Jean Perréal or in the *Man with a Petrarch* perhaps by Jean Clouet, who may have been a Fleming. Jean's son François, however, made fashionable an Italian, and more specifically Florentine, type of portrait, exemplified by his *Charles IX*.

p 166 (2)

p 167 (7)

England, on the other hand, became familiar with Renaissance painting only through intermediaries who, with the exception of Holbein (who will be discussed in a different context) were inferior artists. Two characteristic examples will suffice. Guillim Scrots—court painter to Henry VIII—was a Netherlander who portrayed the English nobility in a flat and dull imitation of the grand Italian manner. Hans Eworth came to England from Antwerp where he had been born and trained; his *Queen Elizabeth confounding Juno, Minerva and Venus* of 1569 is a piece of flattery—the Queen of England assumes the rôle of Paris but keeps the apple for herself—painted with faint echoes of the School of Fontainebleau. In short, the aspect of Tudor and Elizabethan painting is as depressing as that of the sculpture of the same period, the miniatures of Nicholas Hilliard being perhaps the sole exception. In their own way these too reflect Italian art but again as transmitted by France where Hilliard stayed during the late seventies. His treatise *The Art of Liming* is deeply indebted to Italian sources from Alberti to Lommazzo.

p 297
(49)

p 261
(31)

p 321
(11)

While France enjoyed a colony of Italian painters on her own soil and England had to be content with feeble camp-followers of Flemish origin the artistic scene in the Netherlands and in Germany was far more varied. Certainly nothing could compare with the School of Fontainebleau and some of the painting was hardly better than in England. Yet apart from those who imitated superficial details and achieved no more than an extrinsic Renaissance there were a few great masters with a deeper understanding who joined innovation to tradition and thus created a style of their own. Besides there was much fine painting which falls into neither of these categories. In painting, as in sculpture, the late Gothic tradition was still vigorous, coming in fact to a triumphant climax during the second decade of the 16th century in Grünewald's *Isenheim Altar*. Moreover, some painters with a particular interest in the poetry of landscape founded a new genre which at the time was without parallel elsewhere.

p 292–
(33)

The Gothic tradition is particularly noticeable in the graphic arts in which the Germans had always been more original than in painting. Dürer's early woodcuts—the *Apocalypse* and the *Great Passion* for example—should be set in this context. Though he introduced technical refinements, the linear treatment of his prints, the interest in rich fold patterns, the carefully observed details and the preference for strong facial expression clearly indicate the traditional roots of his graphic style, and we should remember that as a young man he had greatly admired Martin Schongauer. But with Dürer this was a passing phase and he worked his way to a fuller comprehension of the Renaissance than any of his contemporaries.

f 7

The World of Matthias Grünewald

Matthias Grünewald (whose real name was Mathis Neithardt Gothardt), on the other hand, ignored or rejected the Renaissance, though there are occasional indications in his treatment and use of colour suggesting that he may have known something of Venetian art. Strangely enough, his principal work, the folding altar for the Anthonite Hospital in Isenheim (Alsace) was commissioned by the two Italian heads of this institution and for one of the panels Grünewald used an Italian popular print as a model. Nevertheless, the gruesome *Crucifixion* is wholly northern and medieval in concept. It is not a narrative representation of the scene on Golgotha but a symbolic rendering of its mystic meaning, and this is made clear through the gigantic figure of the Baptist as well as by inscriptions. The tormented body of Christ with its overpowering suggestion of agony has no parallels in Renaissance art and stems from a much older German line of ancestors. One of the wings shows the *Temptation of St Anthony* set in the tangle of some northern forest haunted by beasts which bring to mind Grünewald's equally 'medieval' contemporary Hieronymus Bosch. A later work, the *Meeting of St Erasmus and St Mauritius* is an allegorical portrait since St Erasmus bears the features of Grünewald's patron Cardinal Albrecht of Brandenburg. The rich glow of colour, the fascination with the difference in texture of the brocade of the Cardinal's chasuble and the martyred knight's armour may remind us of the preoccupations of Venetian painters of the same period. In every other respect however the picture belongs to a world which is fundamentally different from that of the Renaissance.

p 302
(65)

Grünewald was not a lonely and misunderstood 'reactionary'; in fact, many of his contemporaries must have found it easier to come to terms with his art than with that of Dürer. Even in Augsburg—a town which maintained close ties with Italy—Hans Holbein the Elder went on working in an essentially traditional manner. The *Flagellation* from an altarpiece of 1502 contains one archaeologically interesting detail: the column to which Christ has been tied. But the spidery figures with their angular movements and the almost caricatured heads belong to a late Gothic imagination. The *Martyrdom of St Sebastian*, painted over a decade later, makes one concession to the new taste: the painter now uses a strictly symmetrical composition. The *Christ in the Tomb* which his son and pupil Hans Holbein the Younger painted in 1521 still maintains a relentless realism lacking in all restraints. It is wrong to complain in this case about an alleged lack of 'spirituality'. The tragic power of this image springs from the strict application of a principle of late Gothic art: the beholder is shown the agony of Christ in all its physical horror. This brings the young Holbein near to Grünewald though his personal style is different.

p 291
(31)

p 293
(35)

Another painter who must be mentioned in this context is the Austrian Michael Pacher (who was also active as sculptor). Though he seems to have been familiar with Mantegna's methods of constructing pictorial space, his figure treatment and his love for expressive distortions remain essentially Gothic. The *Raising*

p 292
(32)
of Lazarus at St Wolfgang contains a few Italianizing details and the extreme foreshortening of the tomb with *Lazarus* is again reminiscent of Renaissance interests, but the figure of Christ has its nearest relatives in German wood-carvings.

The Beginning of Landscape

Besides the masters just briefly discussed there were many others of great ability working in a similar vein, but German artists of the early 16th century made their most notable contribution in landscape painting. The origins of the new genre are still not fully investigated but it can be said that Lucas Cranach and Albrecht Altdorfer were among the first and pre-eminent in this field. Cranach came to Vienna in his late twenties soon after 1500 and painted pictures with romantic landscape settings. Previously a high view-point had given to landscape the character of a backdrop, but Cranach—for example, in the *St Jerome in the Wilderness*—lowered the view-point so that the beholder feels himself drawn into the landscape. Moreover the scenery has a particular charm since it is familiar; his *Rest on the Flight to Egypt* shows the Holy Family in a German forest clearing, dominated by a giant fir tree overgrown with moss.

p 291
(29)

p 293
(34)
Albrecht Altdorfer a few years later painted the same subject, setting it in the Danube valley which he knew well. He added one piece of fancy, the splendid Renaissance fountain in which the little angels take a dip, but this blends well with the sunlit landscape. Altdorfer also made pure landscape drawings, as Leonardo had done, and unlike any Italian of his time he painted 'landscapes without figures' which must have been made for discerning connoisseurs since they are small in scale and painted with great skill on parchment.

The somewhat later landscapes of Pieter Bruegel—who is best known for his pictures of peasant life—are a greater puzzle. He visited France and Italy during the 1550s, but his paintings show no trace of Italian influence. When he painted the seasons, his concern was not with man's changing occupations, but with fields, hills, atmosphere and light, all of which he conveyed with unsurpassed imagination and skill.

But the majority of northern 16th-century painters tried to emulate the Italian Renaissance. Quentin Massys, while remaining faithful to the traditions of Flemish art, nevertheless introduced borrowed decorative motifs into his portraits and altarpieces. The *Kinship of the Holy Family* (1509) displays a characteristic example of fantastic architecture, most likely copied from an Italian print. There is also evidence that Massys knew about the art of Leonardo, but he changed his style less than did those who through visits to Italy were completely re-educated.

p 297
(48)

Jan Gossaert (called Mabuse after his birthplace) was in Rome in 1508–9 with a patron who wanted to have drawings after antiquities. Jan van Scorel stayed in Venice on a pilgrimage to the Holy Land, and during the short pontificate of the Dutchman Hadrian VI he was in charge of the Vatican collection of antiquities. Maerten van Heemskerck spent the early thirties in Rome filling his sketchbooks with drawings of classical remains. Of German painters Burgkmair and Holbein had personal knowledge of north Italian art, and Dürer went twice to Venice.

p 46–7
(4, 5)

For Mabuse's art the results of his Italian studies and of succumbing to the new taste were fatal. The fine *Adoration of the Magi* in London painted just before this journey, should be seen against the *Neptune and Amphitrite* of 1516, a picture as hollow and pompous as the Latin signature 'Johannes Malbodius', now adopted in place of the vernacular 'Hennin Gossart'. The sumptuous niche with the lumbering flesh-coloured figures looks like a parody of classical art, and the sentiment is a little too obvious. Fritz Saxl described Italian Renaissance painting as 'sensual and chaste at the same time', but here the chastity has been lost while sensuality has turned into sexuality.

p 297
46, 47)

'Endless Imitation'

The classical revival was misinterpreted in this particular way because northern artists were not sufficiently prepared for order, proportion and design—Vasari's decisive criteria of the High Renaissance. When Jan van Scorel painted a *Cleopatra* or Lucas Cranach a *Nymph of the Source* both used as their model Giorgione's

'And I took the little book out of the angel's hand and ate it up; and it was in my mouth sweet as honey: and as soon as I had eaten it, my belly was bitter.' This detail (actual size) from Dürer's woodcut of the Apocalypse (X, 10) shows his early interest in fold patterns and strong facial expression. (7)

Sleeping Venus but neither understood the Venetian master's magic, the paradox of allurement and restraint making up this masterpiece. Cleopatra and the Nymph are self-consciously naked; wide awake they display their bodies before the admiring gaze. Cranach moreover, as often in his mythological pictures, makes the nude vulgar and cheap by a transparent veil and a piece of jewellery.

p 296
(42, 44)

Religious painting too adopted Renaissance trappings for the sake of modernity. The Augsburg master Hans Burgkmair borrowed from Italy composition and decorative details for his *Virgin and Child* of 1509 but the attenuated proportions of the Madonna and the gaucheness of the child cannot have belonged to his models. A complicated architectural composition, derived from Lombard architecture, serves Holbein's *Man of Sorrows* as a setting, but it dwarfs the expressive figure of Christ. When Mabuse treated the popular subject of *St Luke drawing the Virgin*, artist and sitter meet in a vast marble hall in which Gothic and Bramantesque elements incongruously intermingle. But the most endearing example of this type of painting is Maerten van Heemskerck's picture of the same subject. The Evangelist works in a studio—reminiscent of the Vatican Belvedere—filled with statuary rather unbecoming for an artist of his saintliness: an Apollo, a Hermaphrodite, and even a Venus.

p 296
(43)

p 281 (1)

p 296
(45)

Netherlandish artists further were exposed to the impact of Raphael's tapestry cartoons which arrived in Brussels about 1516. Their influence was still strong a quarter of a century later when Jan van Scorel completed an altarpiece for the Abbey of Marchiennes near Douai, though he turned Raphael's measured rhetoric into hollow grandiloquence. Nevertheless works like this helped to maintain a 'Romanist' tradition, preparing the way for the fuller understanding of Italian art during the 17th century.

p 103
(61)

Clearly, the naturalization of the Renaissance required more than the picking up of classical forms or the depicting of classical subjects. Those who had to paint likenesses of humanists or merchants in Augsburg, Nuremberg or Basle found it comparatively easy to follow Italian models and Christoph Amberger's *Christoph Fugger*, dated 1541, and other pictures of this type can hold their own by the side of Venetian or Florentine portraiture. But on a deeper level only two artists seem to have grasped the principles of the Renaissance, and both grew up in towns which had close contacts with the south.

The Two Masters of the Northern Renaissance

Hans Holbein the Younger left his native Augsburg for Basle in 1515 at the age of eighteen. Drawings, illustrations and portraits prove his close contact with scholars and publishers of that town. In 1526 he arrived in England with an introduction from Erasmus to Thomas More. But in spite of links with the New Learning Holbein's attitude to the Renaissance differed from Dürer's. He was not interested in theory, and everything he drew or painted is a cold record, showing the incredible accuracy of his eye and hand. There is no documentary evidence for a visit to Italy, though we know that he went to France in 1523. Nevertheless his knowledge of Italian decorative details and a brilliant handling of colour make such a visit virtually certain. The serene symmetry of the *Solothurn Madonna* of 1522 could have been conceived only by an artist who had seen Italian compositions. Yet this *sacra conversazione* seems so natural and effortless that we can hardly speak of 'imitation'.

When Holbein settled for good in London in 1532, becoming eventually court painter to Henry VIII, religious painting was no longer in demand. There were opportunities for festival decorations in the Italian manner—among them the *Parnassus* for the king's wedding with Anne Boleyn—for the designing of jewellery, of goblets and so forth, and in every instance Holbein's designs accord with Renaissance fashions. But in the end he became almost exclusively a portrait painter, bringing to the northern tradition of veristic portrayal (which came easy to his talent) that nobler conception of the sitter which he had learned in Italy. Though he was unsparing in rendering the obese features p 254 (9) of *Henry VIII*, strict frontality and a simple composition give the king true majesty, an effect enhanced by the sumptuous colours. p 290 The noble poise of *Thomas Howard, Duke of Norfolk*, the brilliant (26) evocation of the Garter collar, and of the silk and ermine of the robe make such a portrait comparable with those of Titian.

Obviously, Holbein was not a reflective artist; moreover the Reformation restricted his activities and made it impossible for him to exercise his gifts in subjects peculiar to Renaissance painting. Even so, his intuitive grasp of Italian art is apparent. Dürer, on the other hand, though his background was similar, came to terms with the Renaissance by deeply pondering its principles. Born in 1471, he was a quarter of a century older than Holbein. He too was trained in a late Gothic workshop—that of Michael Wolgemuth in Nuremberg—and early in his life he came into contact with the world of humanism. His godfather was a publisher; at *f 1* the beginning of the nineties he worked for printers in Basle, p 214 (6) making woodcuts for Sebastian Brant's *Narrenschiff* and designing illustrations for a (never published) *Terence*. Twice he visited Venice, first in 1496, and again for some eighteen months in 1505–6.

All this is significant, but the decisive artistic experience had been an encounter with a minor Italian painter which Dürer himself has recorded. He tells us that as a young man he met Jacopo de Barbari who showed him drawings of ideally proportioned human figures constructed with the help of mathematics, without however revealing their 'secret'. Dürer tried to find out the secret by reading Vitruvius' chapter on human proportions, by copying Italian drawings and by tracing Mantegna engravings. He recognized, more clearly than did any other artist in the north, that the representation of the human figure was central to Renaissance art. Its morphology, proportion, motion and expressions—encountered perhaps already on the first Italian journey through knowledge of Leonardo's studies—remained his most absorbing interest throughout life.

Early in life another Renaissance problem took hold of his enquiring mind: the convincing pictorial rendering of a narrative. To this end he took up the quest for the mathematical construction of perspective. It is characteristic of Dürer that late in life he wrote treatises on human proportions and on perspective, while he never completed a more general book on the theory of art. In his art all pursuits went hand in hand. An engraving of 1504, *Adam and Eve*, summarizes his early search for the human figure of ideal beauty, and a painting of the same year, the *Adoration of* p 298 *the Magi* in the Uffizi demonstrates that he could place a harmoni- (51) ous group of figures within an intricate architectural setting. The choice of subjects was not fortuitous, for he meant to put the new pictorial means into the service of Christian art. Mythological subjects occur only among Dürer's early works, during the first flush of Renaissance enthusiasm.

As Dürer gained in experience he solved the problems of perspective, but the search for improved proportions and more beautiful human figures went on to the end, culminating two years before his death with the *Four Apostles*, figures in which he p 299 attained a poise and monumentality which ranks them with those (52, 53) of Giovanni Bellini, Raphael or Michelangelo. Yet the strongly characterized heads remind us of the northern veristic tradition.

Renaissance aesthetics influenced Dürer's ambition in yet another and significant way. By nature he was a draughtsman, and Erasmus appropriately called him an 'Apelles of black lines'. But in Italy Dürer saw something of the higher standing accorded to the painter and his work. He may have heard of Leonardo, and in 1505 he met Giovanni Bellini whom he greatly admired. Pictures like the *Feast of the Rosegarlands* or the *Virgin with the* p 298 *Siskin* are obviously indebted to the Venetian master's colour (50) and compositions. This emulation of fine Italian painting was a conscious act, for in a letter to his friend Pirckheimer Dürer boasted about his progress as a colourist. But after his return home circumstances forced him to spend much of his time and energy on woodcuts and engravings, though he had some important commissions for paintings. Characteristically, late in life in a kind of retrospect, he returned on his own accord to Venetian memories, planning in the manner of Bellini a large picture of the Virgin surrounded by saints and angels. It was never executed and is known only from sketches, but the *Four Apostles* may have been part of this undertaking.

There are of course many aspects of Dürer's art but we are concerned only with his response to the Italian Renaissance. This encounter caused a deepseated and painful conflict, always apparent in his praxis and theory. How could he find a true balance between the new aesthetic demands and, as he saw it, the overriding task of every artist to express the eternal verities of Christian beliefs?

His most famous engraving, the *Melencolia*, speaks most p 149 (movingly of his struggles. Its imagery, symbolic of the restless and brooding nature of a man born under Saturn, was a commonplace of contemporary belief. The artist's temperament in particular was thought to be 'Saturnine', eternally searching. Dürer (though he himself was not born under Saturn) had encountered a new art promising perfection. But the longer he sought the more elusive he found it. Still, *Melencolia*, huddling motionless in a bleak landscape, has a counterpart in another famous Dürer print, *St Jerome in his Study*, showing the church father ensconced in a warm sunlit room, busily absorbed in the unchanging truth of the Bible. Both engravings date from 1514. A few years later the Reformation was to shatter the foundations of Dürer's religion. During the twenties he worked out for himself a new certainty by increasingly turning to Luther, and at the same time he summed up his life's endeavours. The *Four Apostles* resolved both struggles.

As an artist Dürer stands alone among his contemporaries. But one of the great thinkers of the northern Renaissance can be compared with him, Erasmus of Rotterdam. A theologian and humanist who tried to find a synthesis between the New Learning and devout Christianity, he was faced with the same dilemma which confronted the Nuremberg master. But the political and religious developments of the 16th century made it impossible to build on the foundations Dürer and Erasmus had laid.

XI 'A WORLD ELSEWHERE'

Geographical horizons and mental horizons

JOHN HALE

'I believe that this is a very great continent,
which until today has been unknown'.

COLUMBUS

The expanding Universe

is a concept which would not have sounded strange to the men of the Renaissance, since their own Universe was expanding as rapidly and as disconcertingly as ours. The old Earth, a neat comprehensible pattern of Europe, Africa and Asia, with the Holy City of Jerusalem in the exact centre and the dark ocean all round, had gone for ever. In its place was another world—bigger, more alien, more frightening, a world to whose marvels there seemed no end.

The link between the revival of learning and the Age of Discovery is hard to define. Humanists in general were little interested in the stories brought back by the explorers, except as curiosities or moral examples. The explorers' own motives, and those of the organizations that financed them, were only partially concerned with the expansion of man's mental horizons. There was a time-lag before philosophy caught up with discovery. Ancient Rome seemed to those interested in ideas to have more to teach than modern Brazil.

Even so, the deluge of geographical information which descended upon Europe was bound to have a sweeping effect on subjects remote from geography—above all on the study of man, of society, ethics and 'natural' religion. Ideas which seemed self-evident were shattered; codes of conduct which seemed absolute were found to be relative after all. It was by no means as certain as it had been that civilization was in every respect superior to 'the state of nature'. By thinking about the New World, Europe had to think again about itself.

The detail reproduced here is from Pieter Brueghel's *Landscape with the Fall of Icarus*. It shows a two-masted ocean-going ship of about 1550, an accurate picture of the type of vessel in which the explorers sailed across unknown seas. Her prow points west. She belongs neither to the ordered cosmos of the Middle Ages, nor to the classical environment of the Renaissance. Brueghel's world is already the inheritance of the Age of Discovery— mysterious, remote, and infinite in possibility. (1)

A new type of man appeared on the scene to answer the needs of the new age—the explorer. He had to be more than a captain. He needed education, a knowledge of world geography to know the significance of what he discovered. He needed to be a leader, an organizer and a man with a sense of mission.

Christopher Columbus (right)—then in the service of Ferdinand and Isabella of Spain—discovered the Caribbean Islands while looking for the east coast of Asia. (When he set out he believed, in fact, that Japan was nearer to Spain than the West Indies turned out to be.) But his landfall at San Salvador, in the Bahamas, on October 12th, 1492 began the rush across the Atlantic by every maritime nation of Europe. (2)

Amerigo Vespucci of Florence (above) claimed to have reached North America slightly earlier than Cabot, but this is now doubted. His name was first given to the new continent in a book published in 1507, thus acquiring an immortality that it hardly merited. (3)

Vasco da Gama (left), the leader of the first Portuguese expedition to India, was descended from a noble family and combined the functions of admiral, general and diplomat. Sailing round the Cape of Good Hope (already rounded by Diaz in 1488), he dropped anchor at Calicut, in Madras, in May 1498. (5)

Martin Frobisher (below), a Yorkshireman, led expeditions to find the 'North West Passage' (the route into the Pacific via northern Canada) in 1576, 1577 and 1578—all ended in failure. He also brought back some 'black earth' in the belief that it was gold ore. (7)

John Cabot (above), of Italian origin, set out from Bristol in 1497 on behalf of some English merchants and Henry VII to find new lands across the Atlantic. He reached North America but believed, like Columbus, that he had found a way to China. (4)

Ferdinand Magellan (right) finally realized Columbus' dream of reaching Asia by sailing west. He passed Cape Horn and crossed the Pacific, only to be murdered by natives in the Philippines (1521). His deputy, Sebastian del Cano, returned to Spain, the first man to circumnavigate the earth, with one ship out of five and 18 men out of 237. (6)

Jacques Cartier, greatest of the early French explorers, joined the fruitless search for the North West Passage in 1534. Although he failed, like all the others, he did survey large areas of Canada for the first time and discovered the St Lawrence river. He brought back the first Red Indians to be seen in Europe, two Huron-Iroquois, who described a marvellous realm called Saguenay, 'rich in precious stones'. François Ier saw himself the happy ruler of another Peru and Cartier was despatched to find it. But by 1541 the dream was admitted to be hopeless and Cartier set about actively colonizing the new lands—the beginning of French Canada. This early drawing (right) shows the arrival of the first colonists against a map of the east coast and St Lawrence estuary. (8)

Hudson and Ralegh both met their deaths in the cause of exploration—Hudson (left) murdered by his crew while attempting to sail round the north of Canada (1611); Ralegh (above) executed after failing to find El Dorado in the jungles of Venezuela. (10, 11)

Sir Francis Drake (above)—admiral, explorer, national hero and pirate—was the first Englishman to sail round the world (1577–80), an enterprise prompted mainly by the hope of loot from the Spaniards. (9)

Pedro-Alvarez Cabral of Lisbon took possession of Brazil by accident. In March 1500, on his way to India, he was blown off course in mid-Atlantic and landed at Cape St Augustine. He claimed the country for Portugal and resumed his voyage. Right: part of Cabral's fleet, his own flagship seen centre left. (12)

The princes of Europe saw the world opening up before their eyes and were fearful of losing their share. Spain was the only country literally to discover a gold-mine: the treasure brought back from the New World made her, while it lasted, the richest and strongest state in Europe. Portugal was all-powerful in the east, and succeeded in snatching Brazil before the Spaniards. The great age of English, French and Dutch colonization did not come until the next century.

Henry the Navigator (above), a prince of the Portuguese royal house, was one of the most able and active patrons of scientific discovery in the mid-15th century. He lived most of his life at Sagres, in southern Portugal, where he supervised expeditions along the west coast of Africa and promoted the study of geography, astronomy, mathematics and mapmaking. (14)

The 'Virgin of the Navigators' (left) symbolizes one of the many motives behind the Age of Discovery – the desire to carry Christianity to the ends of the earth. It was painted by Alejo Fernández in about 1535 and forms the centre of an altarpiece. The Virgin, hovering over the waters, spreads her cloak protectingly over a fleet of ships. The identity of the men kneeling round her is a matter of dispute; the prominent figure on the left may be Columbus, the old man with the stick Bishop Fonseca y Sancho of Natienzo, and the others three pilots who were present at the Council of Burgos (Américo, Yánez Pinzón and the cartographer Juan de la Cosa). The bearded man on the other side may be Hernán Cortez, the conqueror of Mexico. In the background are some of the Indians, newly converted. (13)

Charles V (right), King of Spain, ruler of the Netherlands, Holy Roman Emperor, was the man who reaped most benefit from the exploitation of the New World. When he came to the throne in 1518, Spanish colonization was confined to the Caribbean Islands; when he died in 1558 the whole of Central and large parts of South America were firmly under Spanish control. He knew the Conquistadors personally, shrewdly trusting Cortez more than Alvorado or Pizarro, and did his best to safeguard the rights of the Indians. (15)

Elizabeth of England, victor over the Armada (seen in the background), proudly rests her hand on the globe – a gesture that typically exaggerates the facts. English trading ventures were, however, world-wide, and although Ralegh's colonization of Virginia proved in the end a failure, it contained the promise of things to come. (16)

How the earth grew and was transformed, almost from year to year, can best be realized by studying the development of maps in the hundred years between 1450 and 1550. The old medieval *mappamundi*, with its continents crowded together and the oceans reduced almost to nothing, was abandoned, and map-makers went back to the great geographer of late classical Alexandria, Ptolemy, first translated into Latin in 1409. For some time, however, there was an uneasy attempt to fit the new facts into the old pattern. In 1459 a huge decorative map of the world, over six feet in diameter and filled with information in words and pictures, was made by Fra Mauro of Venice. A detail showing the Mediterranean is reproduced below. South is at the top, so everything looks upside down. Although Fra Mauro's circular world is almost entirely filled with land, and although Jerusalem keeps its place very near the centre, it was in many ways a great step forward. Some information, as he acknowledges, is 'according to Ptolemy', but the discoveries of Marco Polo are incorporated, as well as those of later travellers to the east and to Abyssinia. (17)

The world we know had taken shape by the mid-16th century, and all that remained was to fill in the details. In the world map of Pierre Desceliers (1550) only a few areas are seriously wrong—Scandinavia, the north and east coasts of Asia, and, of course, Australia, not properly mapped until the 18th century. Other parts are astonishingly accurate, for instance South America and Indonesia. Desceliers made use of information from every available source—English, Spanish and Portuguese as well as French. But in spite of its modernity, the naïve little figures and monsters with which he decorates it recall the *mappamundi* of two centuries earlier; there are men with heads in their chests and men with huge ears; the King of Guinea has a white elephant; the Red Sea is literally red; and there are vignettes of scenes of exploration. Desceliers, who was the parish priest of Arques, near Calais (see the inscription in the bottom right-hand corner) probably made his map for the Dauphin, later Henri II. It was meant to be placed on a table to be read—hence the way the lettering changes direction. (18)

Fold out ▶

The limit of discovery along the West African coast is vividly shown in the world map of Henricus Martellus Germanus (above), made in 1489. Bartholomew Diaz had passed the Cape of Good Hope in 1487 but had been forced to turn back. Da Gama had not yet set out for India. The names on Martellus' map stop abruptly, and the shape of Asia is still largely guesswork. (19)

The first map of America (below) appeared on a chart of the world made by Juan de la Cosa, one of Columbus' companions, in 1500. (Here west is at the top.) The outline has been fairly judged from his own observations and those of Pinzón (for Brazil) and Cabot (for North America). Cosa was certain by then that Cuba and Hispaniola (Haiti) were islands. (20)

A Red Indian village, with its agriculture and tribal festivities, is portrayed with delicate sympathy by the English settler John White (left). White went out in 1585 with the second of Ralegh's expeditions to what is now North Carolina. The colony failed largely because the colonists were more interested in gold than in settlement, but White was able to make a unique record of Indian life before its fatal contact with Europe. Each part of the picture (which is one of many) has its written explanation. Notice the watchman in a little shelter in the cornfield, to frighten off birds. (21)

Jesuits in Japan receive a party of merchants (religion and trade—the two faces that Europe showed to the world), seen through the eyes of a Japanese artist. Japan was open to the Portuguese between 1543 and 1614, after which all Europeans were expelled. Here the Jesuit mission house is on the right. The ship has brought a delegation with presents for the local ruler—a horse, a chair, a dog and other goods. (24)

Salvation or slavery? was the great question that faced the imperialist powers. In Spain many churchmen and administrators sought to protect the peoples of the New World. Accounts of native life and customs were compiled by the friars. This illustration (right) shows a Franciscan presenting the Spanish viceroy, Antonio de Mendoza, with his *Ceremonies and Rites of the Muchuacán Province*. Behind him stand his Aztec converts. (22)

Spices from Asia had been the main spur to exploration and the opening up of trade-routes with the East. Marco Polo, as early as the 13th century, had stressed the riches of China and the Indies in this respect. A manuscript illumination (right) shows him visiting the pepper-growing district of Malabar, in southern India. 'Here', he wrote, 'there is pepper, ginger, cinnamon, cubebs, nutmeg and many other spices, and the finest cotton in the world.' (23)

Prester John, the ruler of a mighty Christian kingdom in the midst of Africa, was part of accepted belief in the later Middle Ages and Renaissance. Embassies were often sent to him and occasionally fabricated replies were received. He figures prominently in this map of 1558 (left). The African coast was by this time accurately known (as can be seen from the number of place-names) but the interior was still a complete mystery. (25)

Savage society fascinated the sophisticated taste of Europe. In 1550 the city of Rouen welcomed Henri II and his young queen Catherine de Médicis with a *Fête Brésilienne* on the banks of the Seine (right). The trees were painted to look tropical and were stocked with exotic birds and monkeys. The 'natives' were fifty genuine Brazilians, plus about 300 sailors who had been to Brazil and so were able to act the part—many of them naked, with their ears, lips and cheeks pierced for ornaments. They hunted, danced, shot with bows and arrows, split into two tribes, fought each other and burned each others' villages. Other details of primitive life are given in a work published eight years later (above and below) showing the same Grecian-looking natives making fire, smoking and fighting a battle. (26, 27, 28)

Explorers expected monsters and they found them. Stories of giants and dwarfs, extraordinary humans and fabulous beasts had been current for so long that it was almost impossible not to believe in them. Even conscientious scholars fell into the trap. Right: an illustration from Sebastian Münster's great description of the world, *Cosmographia universalis* published in 1544: headless men with faces in their chests (Ralegh *almost* saw them in South America), men with one huge foot, which they could use as sunshades, and dog-headed men. Far right: a 'monster like to a satyr' from Conrad Gesner's *Historia animalium*. This genuinely learned work, which went on being reprinted into the 17th century, contains serious descriptions of such animals as the sphinx, the gorgon, the lamia and the unicorn. (29, 30, 31)

Theory and practice combined to make the art of navigation. Beautifully illustrated books of travel, maps, charts, globes and instruments such as the astrolabe and compass were produced with a degree of craftmanship that went far beyond mere utility. It is interesting to realize, from this detail of a picture gallery in the early 17th century, that even at that date they were becoming valued as works of art in themselves. The astrolabe now reached its most perfect form. One of them lies on the table in front of the globe: it consists of two plates, the lower one representing the sky divided by lines of equal altitude and bearing, the upper one, which could be rotated, showing the relative position of certain fixed stars. When the two are correctly set the position of the observer can be easily calculated. Globes had been increasingly used since the beginning of the 16th century. One of the earliest, showing the world before the discovery of America, is that made by the Nuremberg geographer Martin Behaim in 1492 (see p. 207). They had the great advantage of not distorting the lines of longitude, as all two-dimensional projections do. (32)

Geographical horizons and mental horizons

JOHN HALE

The carrack—the type of oceangoing merchant ship in most general use by the 1490s—represented a revolution in rigging from the clumsy one-masted cog. The many small sails on the carrack made it easier to manoeuvre, to tack and sail into the wind. From an engraving of 1486. (1)

DURING the 15th and the first half of the 16th century two great movements coexisted: the Renaissance and the Age of Discovery —a period of intense cultural achievement and a period of fervent expansion. At no previous time had there been so much variety, experiment and achievement in the arts; before the exploits of the explorers all other phases of discovery—Greek, Roman, Mongol, Arab—pale into insignificance. In the lifetimes of Donatello and Leonardo Bruni, Portuguese mariners revealed the west coast of Africa as far as Cape Verde. During the careers of Leonardo da Vinci and Machiavelli, Africa was rounded and India and the East Indies reached by sea. Columbus' discoveries had led to the emergence of the coasts of Central and South America, Verrazano had sailed into New York harbour, and after Magellan's death in the Philippines one of his captains brought home the first ship to have circumnavigated the globe. By the death of Michelangelo, Cartier had reached Montreal, trade had been established with Japan and English seamen had discovered Novaya Zemlya and entered the Kara Sea. Two peaks of achievement, one of the imagination the other of action. What had they in common? How far did Erasmus write, Raphael paint, Bartholemew Diaz venture past the Cape of Storms in obedience to a common impulse, derived from a shared experience—a way of thinking, an approach to living that historians have agreed to call the European Renaissance?

Again, Michelet's characterization of the Renaissance as the discovery of the world and of man (which Burckhardt took as the heading for the most brilliant chapter in *The Civilization of the Renaissance*) is an invitation to try to discover the relationship between the two contemporary forms of exploration: that of the inner world of the mind and the senses, and that of the coral beaches and the ice-locked shores of the material world. What was there about the purposeful urge to discover new lands that derived from the intellectual ferment of the Renaissance, and what effect had the broadening of geographical horizons on the mental horizons of the stay-at-homes who heard and read about them? Europe had never been so deluged with new information—more than 150,000 square miles of America alone had been explored between 1492 and 1540—and to see how it was absorbed is an important check on our understanding of that abstraction, Renaissance Man.

Certainly, what made the exploration of the world possible, improvements in ship design and in the efficiency of guns, had nothing to do with the intellectual Renaissance. It was not until the 15th century that a fruitful interbreeding of Mediterranean and Atlantic types produced vessels that could go anywhere and get back. The explorer needed a ship whose sails could be worked by a small crew (shortage of food and water was the main hazard of long voyages), which could be sailed reasonably close to the wind and which, as to rudder and hull design, could be held to a course with the minimum of deflection from the direction aimed at. Such vessels were arrived at as a consequence not of the theoretical, antiquarian-inspired planning that influenced changes in galley design in mid-16th-century Venice, but of the practical tinkering with hull shape and sail plan that had gone on throughout the Middle Ages. Such hardy, nimble ships, armed with better guns than could be found outside Europe, meant that governments could not only send out expeditions of discovery but protect the trade routes that resulted from them.

f 1
319 (1)

If the means of exploration rose naturally from the Middle Ages (artillery was in use before the birth of Petrarch and Giotto) so did the motives behind it. Governments were primarily interested in gold and silver to supplement the dwindling sources at home for the manufacture of coin, and in spices, necessary then as previously to make food palatable rather than more delicious. A third motive, universally stated and at least widely believed in, was the extension of Christianity. Here too the Age of Discovery saw the redirection of an earlier motive which had linked conquest and gain with missionary enthusiasm, an extension of the mood which had sent crusaders to the Holy Land and the Teutonic Knights towards Russia. Nor was the rivalry between Spain and Portugal in the East Indies in the early 16th century different in kind from the competition for Levantine markets between the trading powers of the medieval Mediterranean.

p 329
(23)
p 322
(13)

Of these four motives, the one that may appear to pass least naturally into the Renaissance centuries is the Christian. But the Muslim advance into south-east Europe and the presence of Moors in the Iberian peninsula until their expulsion by arms in 1492 had kept the crusading ideal as an active force, and monarchs who would not have financed expeditions without the hope of cash reward, nevertheless sought, in words written of Vasco da Gama, for Christians *and* spices. To preach to natives, to bring some home to receive religious instruction—the motive was sincere, even if it may be looked on as analogous to the expenditure on charity in the *Conto di Messer Domeneddio* of the Renaissance merchant's account book: a salve to his conscience. Columbus was aware that the Spanish monarchs wanted gold and spices from his newly discovered islands, but he could nevertheless write of 'what I conceive to be the principal wish of our most serene King, namely, the conversion of these people to the holy faith of Christ'. There was a feeling that the discoveries themselves were part of a divine plan. Manuel I of Portugal

333

explained to the ruler of Calicut that Europeans had always wished to reach the Malabar coast by sea, but 'as long as God did not wish it to take place, all the men of the past times were unable to accomplish it'. And he was warned that now God has allowed Christians to break into the Indian Ocean 'it would be a wrong and injury to God to wish to resist his manifest and known will'. And while the missionary impulse was strongest among the Catholic powers, Hakluyt urged Englishmen to turn their attention to America not only to enlarge the Queen's dominions, but to enlarge 'the glory of God by planting of religion among those infidels'.

From the governmental point of view, the most 'Renaissance' aspect of discovery lies in the co-operation between the crown, geographical 'experts', and highly educated merchants whose acquisitive instincts were accompanied by a strong and well-informed sense of curiosity. We glimpse such a combination at Sagres, the headquarters of Henry the Navigator's attempts to tap the gold of the Saharan caravans at its source by exploring the West African coast. It recurs in the groups that launched expeditions from the Thames to find a north-east or north-west passage to Cathay.

'To See Interesting Sights'

As for the seamen themselves, their adventurousness and self-reliance repeated the qualities that had given Sicily to the Normans and built up medieval trade-routes by sea as long and hazardous as that between Venice and Southampton. From the point of view of danger and discomfort, the voyages of discovery were of the same order as the long hauls far into the Atlantic that English and Portuguese fishermen had taken as a matter of course and which they extended, without any thought of exploration or adding to the sum of geographical knowledge, when news came

The traveller marking his route on a globe, from Varthema's account of his travels. In 1505 he claimed to have reached the Spice Islands during a voyage round Egypt, Arabia, Persia and India. The information he gathered was later used by the Portuguese in their trading operations. (2)

of the great shoals off Spitzbergen and the Newfoundland Banks. Scurvy was a new hazard, the result of longer voyages without fresh meat or vegetables, but endurance and fatalism were bred deep into seamen: no voyage of discovery was thought to be so 'different' from a normal trading or fishing trip that crews could not be found. There were mutinies—Magellan, Drake and others lost ships *en route* from this cause, though Henry Hudson was the only explorer to suffer personally—based on the fear, particularly among the married men, of never returning home, but while some expeditions were cut short by a discrepancy between the confidence of a captain and his crew, none failed to reach at least its initial objective.

There is one further continuity to note before we turn to the explorers, the leaders of voyages of discovery, themselves. Wanderlust, the desire to see new lands, is not the product of particular historical circumstances: it is a constant of human nature. In the Middle Ages, before the existence of the Americas was suspected, and before the possibility that Europeans could stay alive in equatorial Africa was taken seriously, it was the Far East that beckoned. Among the travellers who set off for China some, like Giovanni de Plano Carpini, were sent on diplomatic missions, but many others, like the Polos, went on a free-lance basis, looking, it is true, for trade, but looking for it in the most adventurous way. Travel to India and beyond was blocked in the mid-14th century by the collapse of the Tartar Empire in China and the growing power of the Christian-hating Ottoman Turks, but the opening of new routes by sea provided a fresh outlet for this perennial wanderlust. Men like the Venetian Alvise da Cadamosto, who joined in the Portuguese exploration of West Africa 'to see interesting sights' in 1455 and 1456, and Antonio Pigafetta, another Italian, who joined Magellan's expedition 'to experiment', he said, 'and go and see with my eyes a part of those things', were part of a tradition which owed little to anything we associate specifically with the Renaissance. The same is true of overland travellers like Ludovico Varthema, who reached Mecca and *f 2* Aden in 1503 before crossing to India and penetrating as far as Vijayanagar, or the European merchants whom Vasco da Gama and his successors found on the Malabar Coast.

It is only when we leave the common seaman and the free- *p 320–* lance traveller and turn to Columbus and his peers that we feel in *321* the presence of a new type of man. Our opinion must, alas, be *(2–12)* blurred. The free-lance was much readier with his pen; the richest veins in the literature of travel are the records of men who had no responsibility to others, no sense of mission save that of diverting and proving something to themselves. We know Magellan through Pigafetta; Da Gama through an anonymous companion; Cabral, the discoverer of Brazil, through an unknown member of his fleet. The journals of Columbus are a rare case, both because they survived and because they reflect his character with a clarity unusual before the journals of Captain Cook. Generally we are shown the actions of the explorers, not their thoughts.

Moreover, part of the seeming novelty of the explorers' rôle is due to the fact that they were pursuing a new occupation. The Norse discovery of Greenland and Labrador around 1,000 A.D. was in the nature of a *Völkerwanderung*, a search for living space rather than a carefully planned reconnaissance. Exploration, on the other hand, involves as great a determination to get back as to set out. Its purpose is to extend knowledge which may or may not be exploited through trade or settlement. No European nation in the Renaissance was so overpopulated that emigration was a necessity. The explorer needed more than the qualities of an Eric the Red or the captain of a merchant vessel on an ordinary trading voyage, however long. He had to have qualities of leadership and seamanship—even though he might lean heavily on his pilots in matters of pure navigation—but he also had to be able to imagine his task within the context of an emerging knowledge of the world as a whole. He was part of a programme which was both practical and intellectual. He had to keep in mind the hypotheses of medieval geography and deliberately, critically test them.

Marco Polo and other medieval travellers of whom we have knowledge were as curious about what they saw as were their Renaissance successors, and they were hardly more credulous.

On his second voyage in 1577, Frobisher captured and brought back a family of Eskimos, who excited much amazement in the brief time they survived in England. The queen allowed them to hunt any birds—even swans—on the Thames, and the man was often seen shooting ducks from his skin-covered boat as he had done in Greenland. (3)

But their curiosity was more indiscriminate, and taking their world picture for granted, they neither criticized it nor felt the need to relate their experiences to it. Physically determined, they were intellectually irresponsible. Polo's travels were digested into a series of stories and fascinating scraps of information from a far land which he (and his editor Rustichello) knew Europeans would want to hear about. The Renaissance explorer was not only opening up new territory and new routes, he was consciously adjusting his inheritance of guesses about what the world looked like in the light of what he found. And whereas medieval travellers sometimes point up a moral for their readers from their observation of other peoples, it is always within the context of the norms of European conduct. When Polo emphasized the modesty and decorum of Cathayan girls he was merely expressing the preference of a Venetian paterfamilias. When Cabral's companion Covilhan contrasted the true modesty of a naked Brazilian girl with the false modesty of the overdressed women of fashion at home he was setting one culture against another.

Conflicting Values

The nakedness of the races found during the exploration of Africa and the Americas of course emphasized the difference between their culture and manners and those of Europeans. But this sense of contrast, which deepened throughout the 16th century and did much to break down the narcissism of European thought about morals and political organization, was directly related, as we shall see, to the intellectual Renaissance of the 14th and 15th centuries. It was the outcome of an increasing ability to think historically and to imagine life lived in terms of a different culture; the product of the imaginative rehabilitation of ancient Rome as a self-contained civilization.

And whereas Polo set out to tell an entertaining story, and was not concerned to emerge as a personality himself or to follow and extend the trail he had blazed, the characteristic personal and pedagogic notes of the Renaissance are heard in Cadamosto's remark that he wrote of his explorations 'in order that those that shall come after me may be able to understand what my thoughts were in the midst of varied things in strange new places', and in Richard Chancellor's statement that he was describing his search for a north-east passage in 1553 so that he 'may encourage others to the like travel'. This awareness of self, and of being part of an evolving process, again connects the discoveries with the intellectual temper of the Renaissance.

There is one further point at which the discoverers may be related to a Renaissance trait: the appetite for fame. Generally speaking, the material rewards of exploration were not great. Fortunes could be made by settlers and colonial administrators, but the explorer's rôle was to prepare the way for exploitation, not to indulge in it. Columbus was the only explorer who could envisage enjoying the fruits of his discovery as an administrator, and he died disappointed and only moderately well-to-do. Drake returned from his voyage round the world with the *Golden Hind's* flanks stuffed with gold and silver and spices, but his instructions were unusual in that they had positively ordered him to pillage Spanish shipping off the coasts of Chile and Peru. And while every voyage of discovery was potentially a trading voyage, contact with a profitable market was necessarily in the nature of an experiment; any goods shipped were, in any case, the property of an expedition's sponsors, not of its leader. While explorers might hope for wealth, therefore, they could not confidently expect it, nor is there an indication that any explorer before Quiros (who badgered the King of Spain into financing an expedition to found a Christian commonwealth in the South Pacific in 1605) was predominantly motivated by missionary zeal. Fame, therefore, the desire to be known for great deeds, was a strong component in an explorer's motivation, especially as with the publication of voyage-collections the explorer's name entered a heroic literature so widely read as to be the successor to the romances of chivalry. Discovery and Renaissance interpenetrate in the words written of Frobisher's attempt to find a north-west passage: 'He determined and resolved with himself to make full proof thereof and to accomplish or bring true certificate of the truth or else never return again, knowing this to be the only thing of the world that was left yet undone whereby a notable mind might be made famous and fortunate.'

We must not make too much of this point, however, in an attempt to distinguish between the timeless and the specifically 'Renaissance' elements in the first phase of global discovery. We know too little about the personal motives of the explorers—just as we know too little about the motives of medieval men of action.

Maps of an Expanding World

We are on firmer ground when we turn to geographical theory. Theory was the fuel of action in the Renaissance as it had not been in the Middle Ages. Not that the Middle Ages had been without theories: systems of politics and adventurous re-systematizations of theology and philosophy. Not that during the Renaissance the business of governing, worshipping, making a living went forward in terms other than of habit and day-by-day practice. But men had come to feel in some respects more detached from the wheel of circumstance. The revival of antiquity, the disinterment of theories which appeared to have influenced actions in the past—this produced new concepts, some of which were taken as models for action. Men really did try to live according to the 'all-round' thesis propounded by Cicero and Quintilian and re-tailored by the practice of Vittorino da Feltre and the persuasion of Castiglione. Architects and artists were actually affected by theoretical treatises based on assumptions about what had produced great art in antiquity. Politicians, who cannot afford to be less than pragmatic, ignored Renaissance political theory even when it mirrored their behaviour as closely as did Machiavelli, but soldiers, who have longer pauses between crises, did have time to adopt some of the organizational hints of the theorists who had rediscovered Vegetius.

In some ways the rediscovery of ancient theory checked the progress of medieval rule-of-thumb methods. It is true of medicine, it is probably true of physics, it is true of literature, where the vitality of the vernacular was nearly throttled when the powerful ghost of Ciceronianism got at its throat. But the basic energy of the age, its political and economic momentum, the tolerance it extended to the eccentricity of the individual broke through its admiration for the norm and the ideal.

If Renaissance Europe had not acquired new ships and an urgent need of precious metals it is possible that the re-acquired classical geographical orthodoxy of Ptolemy would simply have overtaken the medieval orthodoxy and double-checked the conviction that there was nothing new to be found and, even were novelty suspected, no way of looking for it. For medieval man the world consisted of three continents, Europe, Asia and Africa. His maps showed the earth's surface crammed with them, land crowding out the oceans: no Atlantic, no Pacific, the Indian Ocean conventionally shown as an inland sea squeezed up from the south by the vast mass of Terra Incognita. Maps of the world were not so much aids to travel, or to the imagining of the actual relationship of one land mass to another, but visual commemorations of divine purpose, commonly with Jerusalem at the centre and the rest of creation grouped about it.

f 5 During the 15th century, Ptolemaic maps, reflecting the actual shape of the world as it was known to 2nd-century Greeks, exerted a strong influence on the Jerusalem-centred diagrams. How far this shift was due to an increasing appetite for accurate visual representations of the earth's surface is not clear. Medieval maps were more for reflection or delight than for use. They were symbols of God's power, repositories of legends and marvels, the visual equivalents of Genesis. Even when the influence of ancient geography gained ground the maps that reflected it were tributes to the newly discovered classical authorities rather than things to use. By putting Europe in the top left hand corner and providing a far larger Asia than had the *mappamundi*, the Ptolemy maps made it possible to record journeys to the Far East like those of Marco Polo and of Niccolò Conti, whose early 15th-century travels in India and as far as Java were written down by the humanist Poggio Bracciolini. But such maps still remained symbols of knowledge rather than aids to travel or to imagining the actual shape of the continents. The land traveller relied on asking his way from town to town. He did not need more than a symbolic itinerary telling him what to ask for. It was the seaman, who had no one to ask, who needed accurate maps, and he got them in the portolan charts which, from the early 14th century at least, showed parts of the Mediterranean coast. By the mid 15th-century portolans showed the coasts of Europe and West Africa in detailed 'real' terms, but humanist cartographers still preferred the world picture of the ancients. Even when exploration was in full swing, map-makers, with some exceptions, were slow to make the symbol correspond to the truth; the cult of Ptolemy influenced maps more than the contemporaneous expansion of actual knowledge. This was not the result of wilful obscurantism. Until a map was generally seen as an aid to imagining what the world really looked like, the cartographer was naturally concerned to refine his symbols according to the best—and this meant the classical—authority. Eventually the deluge of geographical information brought back by the explorers was to drown the 'unreal' tradition and to encourage the notion that all maps should record the actual shape of the world. The gift of 'Discovery' to 'Renaissance' is clear. How far did humanist geography influence exploration?

The long-term aim of gold-and-spice-hungry nations was contact with the sources of peppers, cloves and other medicinal and flavouring spices of 'the Indies', a term which included India, China, Japan and South-East Asia. These reached the Mediterranean via Muslim maritime and overland routes but were expensive and the supply was well below the demand. It was also universally believed that Cathay was filled with gold which did not reach Europe at all. So Cathay was the goal, and it showed up far more clearly on Ptolemaic than on Jerusalem-centred maps. Serious study of Ptolemy dates from the beginning of the 15th century and his influence was partly encouraging and partly negative. His Africa extended well south of the Equator and he believed that the Indian Ocean was an inland sea; as far as an eastwards sea route to Cathay was concerned he made it appear more unlikely than ever. On the other hand his theory that life was possible in the southern hemisphere suggested that the medieval assumption that no-one could survive the scorching heat of the Equator was wrong. All men—this was the medieval theological contribution—were descended from the sons of Noah, the Flood's survivors. If there were men in the southern hemisphere they must at some time have crossed the Equator, and so then could 15th-century seamen.

Ptolemy by himself was a warning against rather than an argument for an attempt to reach Cathay by circumnavigating Africa—there was nothing to circumnavigate: Africa blended

into the continent of Terra Australis which filled almost the whole of the southern hemisphere and linked Africa to India. Nor did he suggest that the 'Ocean Sea'—the deep waters outside normal fishing and coastal voyages which were believed to be different from them in kind—provided a medium in which men could survive. To the Middle Ages the Ocean Sea was rather like the upper atmosphere before the invention of oxygen masks and pressurized aircraft, a fatal zone delineating the physical limits of existence. But Ptolemy was not the only classical geographer to be discussed in humanist circles. Strabo, a predecessor of Ptolemy, was also the subject of much commentary, and particular attention was paid to Strabo's notion that the Ocean Sea washed the southern shores of Asia and that there was at least one large island ('Taprobane') lying off the Asian coast to the south. Still more crucial was his treating the globe—both classical and medieval geographers believed that the earth was round—as habitable in all its parts and likely to contain unknown lands. While not committing himself as to the navigability of the Ocean Sea, he strongly suggested that it was not different in kind from off-shore waters. 'The inhabited world', he wrote, 'forms a complete circle, itself meeting itself; so that if the immensity of the Atlantic Sea did not prevent, we could sail from Iberia to India along one and the same parallel over the remainder of the circle.'

We know little about the theoretical discussions that went on at Henry the Navigator's court at Sagres. But certainly, at the time when Henry was sending out his first African expeditions, the implications of classical geography were being discussed in a centre as noted for humanist as for mercantile initiative: Florence. From 1428, when Henry's brother Prince Pedro paid a map-collecting visit to Florence, to 1474, the date of the important letter Toscanelli sent to Columbus, there was contact between the practical exploits of the Portuguese and the theory of the Italians.

The Portuguese exploration of West Africa did not entail a great imaginative leap into the dark, as did Columbus' first expedition westwards across the Atlantic. It groped, handhold by handhold, down the coast. But as successive voyages showed that men could come and go as safely through these waters—even beyond the Equator which was crossed in 1473 without anyone turning black—as in the seas of Europe, the idea that the Ocean

Columbus landing on an island in the Indies in 1492, with the king of Spain figuratively supervising the undertaking. This woodcut is from a Florentine edition of 1493, proof of the speed with which Columbus' original letter was copied and distributed through Spain and Italy. (4)

p 324–
327
(17–20)

p 122 (5)

p 322
(14)

Although the Ptolemaic maps may not themselves have been designed by Ptolemy, they were revered as part of the classical text and widely copied. This version of the world-map, made in 1503 for Reisch's encyclopaedic work 'Margarita Philosophica', retains many features which had in fact been disproved. The east-north-east wind, known as Vulturnus or Caecias, is shown wearing spectacles, possibly a pun on the Latin for blind (caecus). (5)

Sea itself might be navigable became firmer and Strabo's idea of an 'open' Indian Ocean became increasingly attractive. In 1445 Diniz Diaz saw the coast beyond Dakar tending to the east: was this the tip of Africa? The interaction of theory and practice was shown on the Venetian Fra Mauro's world map, commissioned by the Portuguese crown and completed in 1459. The basic shape is that of Ptolemy, but unusual emphasis is placed on the detailing (mostly erroneous) of the Indies, and Strabo, not Ptolemy has been followed for the Indian Ocean.

p 324 (17)

Prince Henry's own motives, as given by the chronicler Gomez Eannes de Azurara, did not include the aim of reaching Cathay. They were to trade and to convert and to look for black Christians who would aid the Portuguese against the Moors of Morocco. But throughout this great operation, which culminated in Bartholomew Diaz' rounding the Cape in 1487, an overall plan can be sensed: longer and longer leaps down the coast leading to an increasing confidence that Cathay could be reached. The cost of the longer expeditions was considerable, it was only justifiable in terms of a firmly imagined goal, Cathay, and that goal could not have been imagined without a changed attitude to space, an attitude in which space was seen conceptually, as a whole within which tests could be made, and experiments carried out. It was an attitude reflected in the work of painters and architects and nourished by the Renaissance passion for geometry.

'It is Possible'

The 'Renaissance' did not produce the ships, the men or the motive for exploration, but it did provide the excuse for raising the large sums of money involved, an excuse based on a new view of the world as *open* to discovery and a map picture that incorporated information which was believed, however uncritically, to be true, a picture which represented a blend of classical authority and travellers' reports.

Without such a frame of mind—('it is possible'), and such a frame of reference—the prestigious modified Ptolemaic world map, the Age of Discovery would have been postponed. All the great voyages were based on a theory of what could be achieved by them. The trust in theory was prepared for by the coastal nature of West African exploration and the gold, ivory and slaves that provided an insurance against the theory of a route to Cathay proving wrong. But even when Diaz' voyage strongly suggested it was right, Columbus found it hard to persuade the rulers of Spain to invest in a voyage that looked far more tempting on the map (he was a trained cartographer himself); he shrank the circumference of the globe even more drastically than classical geographers had done, and by selecting his authorities carefully he had produced an Asia which was even longer than Ptolemy's and Marco Polo's and stretched as far towards Europe as the latitude of the Virgin Islands. Once Columbus had sailed, however, and once the enormous surprise of the Americas had been digested and roughly plotted on world maps, monarchs became readier to follow the suggestions of cosmographers. Magellan's suggestions, doubtless made with the advice of his geographer friend Ruy Faleiro, that a route might be found to Cathay round the new continent's southern shore was attractive because Diaz and Da Gama had shown that Africa did not run straight into Terra Australis: the same might well be true of America. The voyages in search of north-eastern and north-western passages to Cathay of which there were so many, mostly English, in the second half of the 16th century, were based on theoretical notions about the navigability of the Ocean Sea north of Asia and America; theories so stubbornly believed in that they led to failure after failure and to scores of deaths by exposure and scurvy in ice-locked ships. Until Cook's second voyage the history of the South Pacific consists of voyages in search of Terra Australis, the stubbornest geographical myth of all until it was whittled down to Antarctica.

f 4

p 320 (6)

The process of exploration was the first demonstration of the scientific method: hypothesis, experiment, new hypothesis. It was demonstrated for all interested men to see, in the largest and most dramatic way. The hypothesis that there was open water between Europe and Asia to the west was disproved not by an abstract calculation, in the way that the reinstatement of the classical world picture 'disproved' the medieval one by substituting a more fashionable and intellectually respectable hypothesis, but concretely, by revealing an enormous new territory full of exotic peoples and providing a new way of life for thousands of soldiers and settlers. And the process was continuous. Verrazano's survey of the east coast of North America in 1523 led to a new hypothesis, that over the promontory (which he took to be a continuous bar) separating Chesapeake Bay from the Atlantic was an extension of the Pacific which drove a wedge through the continent and almost divided North America into two halves. The hypothesis was entered on the maps until further experimental voyages disproved it. And in the same way, the island groups of the Far East only came to take their true shape on maps gradually from pieces of isolated information discussed by sea captains and shipwrecked sailors in Malacca, and patiently re-phrased into successive hypotheses by the cartographers of Lisbon. Scientific method, which we rightly take as a hallmark of the thinking of modern man, could not be applied rigorously in a pure scientific field, in astronomy or physics or chemistry, until the appearance of the pendulum clock, the telescope and the microscope. Though Renaissance attitudes to finance and politics became increasingly hard-headed, the thinking behind them could only be pseudo-scientific, as their effects were incapable of proof. Theory could only be verified in the field of discovery, through the co-operation between the hypothesizers at home and the observers in their ships. The first scientific laboratory was the world itself.

It is only, then, when we look at the exploration movement as a whole that we see a necessary partnership between Discovery and Renaissance, Renaissance providing the programme, as it were, for a machine that had evolved from the character, skills and needs of the Middle Ages. This partnership, however, was fumbling and confused. While the process was as we have described it, it was achieved by observers who could not see what was in front of their eyes, and hypothesizers who represented a minute fraction of the intelligent public. In trying to estimate the impact of the discoveries we must remember that the first explorers carried with them a host of medieval presuppositions which prevented their making a properly objective report on what they saw, and that the information they brought back was of interest only to a small section of the community, and of that section it was only of direct concern to a few rulers, merchants and cosmographers. Others added the new knowledge to their old categories of thought without it affecting their outlook on the world. For most men the new reality and the old legends co-existed harmoniously, just as the Jerusalem map had co-existed with a need to take long journeys. An awareness of the hypothesis-observation-new hypothesis process was present in the few who were making a living out of it, but it was not until the end of the 16th century that it began to change the way in which more than a very few men thought.

The explorers were the reverse of open minded; they expected to find certain things and it was difficult for them to see past these expectations. Just as a space traveller without a scientific training might come back from Mars reporting the bug-eyed monsters his reading of science fiction had conditioned him to expect there, the explorers saw certain aspects of the truth through a haze of presuppositions derived from their reading of medieval travel literature.

Monsters and Legends

These presuppositions fell into three main categories: monsters and marvels, biblical legends and Golden Age legends. All appealed very strongly to the 15th-century imagination. Monsters both mythical and 'real' had played a prominent part in ancient thought, from the quasi-divine centaurs and sirens to the dog-headed or single-footed men who were live to live on the fringes of the Greek world, especially in India. The vitality of such conceptions, and the large class of 'mixed' creatures, like the mantikhora, which had the face of a man, the tail of a scorpion and a lion's body, was, for some psychological reason, very

f 7, 8

p 331
(31)

'*When the fruit is ripe, it opens to disclose a real animal like a lamb*' —this strange plant is described in all seriousness in Mandeville's '*Travels*', a 14th-century compilation containing real and fabulous information on the east. The illustration is from a printed Spanish edition of 1521. (6)

great: they passed readily into early medieval folklore, and were accepted and explained by educated men, by Augustine, for instance. Monsters figured largely in medieval art and literature. Conceived as dwelling mostly in India they played an especially large part in romances set there, like the *Romance of Alexander*. They figured largely, of course, in the immensely popular *Travels* by Mandeville. Interest grew still stronger in the Renaissance; monstrous births, human and animal, were studied as portents, linked to the motion of the stars and foretelling the deaths of princes and the fortunes of war.

f 6

Explorers and travellers, then, expected to find monsters in Africa and Asia and also in America, since, until Balboa discovered the Pacific in 1513, America was looked on as the eastern extension of Asia and shared that continent's freight of marvels. No voyager actually saw them, but the monsters, widely known through startling late medieval woodcuts, had an extraordinary hold over the imagination, weakening objectivity by surrounding what was real with a ghostly retinue of non-facts. They were constantly felt to be round the corner. Haunted by one such woodcut, Pigafetta, sailing home through the East Indies after Magellan's death, quoted his pilot to the effect that 'in this neighbourhood was an island named Aruchete, the inhabitants of which, men and women, are not more than one cubit high, and they have ears as large and long as themselves so that when they lie down one serves them for a mattress, and with the other they cover themselves. They are shorn and naked, their voices are shrill, and they run very swiftly. They dwell underground, live on fish and a certain substance which grows between the bark and the wood of a tree which is white and round like coriander comfits, and which is named ambulon.' The circumstantiality of this description is pure Mandeville, but Pigafetta, alert and cultivated as his narrative shows him to have been, accepts what ought to be on the same plane of reality as what was. 'We would have gone there willingly', he added, 'but the shoals and the currents did not allow of it.' In the same vein Ralegh, speaking of the headless men whom he did not see in Guiana but knew to exist 'because every child in the provinces of Orromaia and Canuri affirms the same', pointed out that 'such a notion was written of by Mandeville, whose reports were holden for fables many years and yet, since the East Indies were discovered, we find his relations true of such things as theretofore were held incredible.'

p 330–331
(29, 30)

Belief in composite monsters had a double effect on the voyager who tried to describe a new type of real animal. It encouraged description in similar terms, and it made the animal sound like a monster. Here, for instance, is Pigafetta again, this time on the guanaco of South America (a type of llama). 'This beast has its head and ears of the size of a mule, and the neck and head of the fashion of a camel, the legs of a deer, and the tail like that of a horse.' The medieval trait of describing something in terms of something else rather than objectively fostered this unscientific approach, and so did the habit of seeing new things in terms of pious wonder and the acceptance of classical authority. As late as 1554 an English description of the head of an African elephant notes correctly that the tusks grow from the upper jaw downward 'wherein the painters and arras workers are deceived', but the writer then goes on to say that he 'beheld it not only with my bodily eyes but much more with the eyes of my spirit, considering by the work the cunning and wisdom of the workmaster, without which consideration the sight of such strange and wonderful things may rather seem curiosities than profitable contemplations. Pliny and Solinus write that they use no adultery.'

The temptation to see new creatures in terms of monster and marvel was all the stronger because readers at home were seldom satisfied with factual descriptions of the newly found lands. They looked to travel literature to confirm, rather than to extend, the detail of their mental horizon. All the main intellectual currents of the day—neo-biblicism, secular history, classical learning—led reflective men back, not outwards. An age of intellectual ferment, as the Renaissance undoubtedly was, is not necessarily open minded; the effort to make a synthesis of classical wisdom, Christian revelation and national identity was too great for the discoveries to impinge in more demanding forms than those of corroboration and recreation.

Readers were reluctant to give up the marvels and fables to which they had become used. Editions of Mandeville and Pliny (another of the main sources of geographical and anthropological myths) were published in the early 16th century at the same time as the letters of Columbus and Vespucci, and part of the success of the first important account of discoveries in the New World, *The Decades* of Peter Martyr (completed in 1530) was due to his retaining many legends among his facts. Rabelais, satirizing the geographical writers both of antiquity and of his own day in *Gargantua and Pantagruel*, pictured them as hiding behind a tapestry and writing their works at the dictation of Hearsay, a hunchback who possessed seven tongues, but who was blind and unable to move.

Quest for the Earthly Paradise

Another feature in the newly-discovered lands that readers most longed to hear about was the existence of an Earthly Paradise or some precious spot where men still lived as they had in the Golden Age, happy, naked, free, without poverty, disease or melancholy, without the responsibilities of property or the need of goverments. In the late 15th century there was a widespread pessimism, a nostalgia for a time when men were not distracted by plagues and wars. The taste for a pastoral life was increasing, and one motive for interest in Eden and in the Arcadian theme in Greek literature was the desire to escape imaginatively from the harsh present.

The Middle Ages placed Paradise in Asia—'And the Lord God planted a garden eastward in Eden'—and from the 12th century Paradise was associated not only with tranquillity and innocence but wealth, for the empire of Prester John was associated with it. Prester John was supposed to be a Christian ruler, of fabulous riches, who had somehow preserved the faith amid the infidel people around him. He was seen as a potential ally against the enemies of Christendom. A succession of embassies was sent to make contact with him in the 13th and 14th centuries; he was reported in India, Ceylon and China, but never found. By the late 15th century his court was commonly held to be somewhere in unexplored Africa, with Ethiopia as its most likely setting. Prince Henry's captains hoped to get news of him, and at intervals throughout the exploration of the coast, natives who had been captured, converted and taught Portuguese, were returned with instructions to find him and urge him to make contact with Portugal.

Such legends, and the stories of lost civilizations like Atlantis, added a fabulous geography which blurred an understanding of the real peoples found by the explorers just as the fabulous bestiary complicated their account of real animals. Columbus was as convinced that the Orinoco flowed from the Terrestrial Para-

p 329
(25)

Animals from imagination and observation: (above) the hydra from Gesner's 'Historia animalium', published 1551–87, and (below) a selection of the animals which Breydenbach claimed to have seen on his journey to the Holy Land in 1483–4. Even in the 16th century, natural history was still largely a matter of guesswork and hearsay, and in the 17th-century editions of Gesner the existence of the unicorn is still debated. (7, 8)

dise as he had been that Cuba was Japan and as he remained convinced that Central America was the Malay Peninsula. And the discovery of the real and immensely rich empires of the Aztecs and Incas gave added strength to mythical ones like Cibola, in search of whose seven cities of gold De Soto explored the southern United States, or the empire of El Dorado, the Golden Man, whose will-of-the-wisp flickered temptingly before the imagination of the Conquistadors who hunted for him in the hinterlands of Colombia, Venezuela and Guiana. Explorers were tempted to colour their facts to fit in with their hopes. Columbus assumed from a few nose-ornaments worn by the primitive Tainos that the gold mines of Cathay were nearby; Ralegh's remark of

Guiana that 'every stone that we stopped to pick up promised either gold or silver by his complexion' reflected his conviction that the land of the 'men whose heads do grow beneath their shoulders' was on the confines of El Dorado's empire.

More important than these dreams, which did, after all, lure men into exploration and led to an extension of knowledge, was the damper put on 'scientific' anthropology by myths of the Golden Age and pre-Fall man. Intensifying Covilhan's first description of the Tupi of Brazil (1500) King Manuel told Ferdinand and Isabella that his expedition had 'found the people nude as in the first innocence, gentle and peaceable'. Of the same natives Vespucci wrote: 'They have no laws, no religion, live according to nature . . . they have all things in common, they have no frontiers or kings, obey no-one, each is his own master . . . they live to extreme age in a country of marvellous beauty.' And Ralegh wrote in the same terms of the entirely different natives of Virginia: 'We found the people most gentle, loving and faithful, void of all guile and treason, and such as live after the manner of the Golden Age'. If this was not true it was felt that it ought to be, and such accounts were received with gratification.

If the voyagers themselves were inclined to underplay the less ideal aspects of Indian life, the men who popularized their adventures for the general public at home added another layer of exaggeration, so that the reader saw the New World twice distorted, saw reality at two removes. And although from report after report evidence piled up that could have given the lie to the idyllic nature of life among the natives of America, the legend was
f 9 stubbornly believed. In his essay *Of the Cannibals* Montaigne wrote: 'What in those nations we see by experience, doth not only exceed all the pictures wherewith licentious Poesie hath proudly embellished the Golden Age, and all her quaint inventions to paint a happy condition of man, but also the conception and desire of Philosophy.' When he goes on to say that 'the very words that import lying, falsehood, treason, dissimulations, covetousness, envy, detraction, and pardon were never heard of amongst them', it is clear that he is not concerned to imagine the natives as they really were, but to use them collectively as a stick with which to beat his fellow Europeans—who did use words that imported lying, treason and the rest. The Indians were seen not as individuals but as symbols.

It was not only writers with a taste for moralizing who saw the Americas with the mind's eye rather than with the real eye. 'Golden Age' descriptions continued throughout the century in the work of geographers. Artists portrayed Indians as heroic classical nude figures as though they were competing in the Olympic
p 330 Games instead of scuttling through the swamps of the Amazon.
(26, 27) And it was not as if stay-at-homes had no chance to see what

Indians actually looked like. Columbus had brought some back on his first two voyages. Other explorers followed his example and *f 3* returned with natives as curiosities or as proofs of their having reached the Americas. In France seven Indians had been exhibited in 1507 at Rouen, together with their canoes, while in 1550, when Henry II visited that city, he was welcomed with a grandiose *p 330–* spectacle in the Indian taste. Outside the walls a meadow and its *331 (28)* trees were made to look as much like a Brazilian forest as possible, and in it was a model village, with huts and fires. It was populated by three hundred 'Indians', some completely naked. Fifty were genuine imported natives, the rest sailors who were supposed to have been to Brazil and could be expected to give authentic performances. They were carrying on the ordinary life of an Indian village: cooking, carrying loads, cutting down trees, reclining in hammocks, smoking tobacco. Evidence as to real conditions in the Americas was in fact at hand, through actual specimens, *p 328* through books, through the accounts of eye-witnesses, but it was *(21)* not willingly absorbed.

Salvation or Slavery?

Possibly the main intellectual interest in the New World for the stay-at-home was not in any case scientific, but religious; the first question asked was not 'What are they like?' but 'Can they be saved?' Had the Indians been evangelized? The Gospel was supposed to have gone through the whole world, but the Indians showed no sign of having received it. Had they heard the word of God—from St Thomas, for instance—but relapsed? Or were they pagans? Were they indeed capable of becoming Christians? Had they reasoning powers? Were they like animals who had no souls? If they were not responsible human beings, were they natural slaves?

This last question was of prime importance, for on the answer to it depended the sort of treatment the Indians might expect from their Spanish taskmasters. And the 'animal, therefore natural slave' view was put with some force. In a speech before the Council of the Indies in 1525 the Dominican Tomas Ortiz said that the Indians had no justice, no respect for law or truth. They were incapable of learning. Their personal habits were loathsome; 'they eat fleas, spiders, and worms raw, whenever they find them. They exercise none of the humane arts or industries. When taught the mysteries of our religion, they say that these things may suit Castilians, but not them, and they do not wish to change their customs . . . the older they get the worse they become.' This malign tradition had roots deep in popular superstition: black was the devil's colour; it was a strikingly original paradox that made Shakespeare's Othello into a heroic shamer of Christians.

Yet on the other hand, African slaves had throughout the later Middle Ages been customary inmates in well-to-do homes in southern Europe and had been liked and treated no better or worse than white menials: they had on occasion become specially privileged pets. And if the natives of tropical Africa and the Americas had not had the Gospel preached to them, no more had Homer or Vergil or Ovid—yet the humanists preached the inherent goodness, the natural religious impulse of man in order to be able to accept the teaching of illustrious pagans. And yet, again, Aristotle had taught the inevitable distinction between free men and slaves, and this view, too, found a congenial hearing in the Renaissance, in Castiglione's *Courtier*, for instance.

The range of opinion applicable to natives was, then, large: from the liberal view that Indians should be peaceably converted *p 328* and could be guided into living like Europeans, to the contemp- *(22)* tuous and brutal 'spiders and worms' view. There were even attempts made by Spain to put the liberal view into practice. In the West Indies experimental villages were set up in the 1520s and 1530s where natives were coached in the life of Spanish farmers and left alone to see if they could match the industry of the originals. All these experiments failed; the Indians would not work the hours, wear the clothes or follow the diet of Europeans. The way was open for the pessimists to point out that they were incapable of living virtuous and free lives, and must be, by nature, slaves. And as at this time there was a growing clamour for cheap labour to work in mines or sugar estates, in a climate which sapped the energy of white men, the pessimists were confirmed

Columbus in the description of his first voyage mentioned that the inhabitants of Dominica ate human flesh, and although cannibalism was not frequently found by the explorers the very fact of its existence fired the horrified imagination of European artists. From an engraving of 1558. (9)

by economic need. The slave trade took on a new and long-enduring lease of life, and conversion by force was accepted as a common necessity. 'If gentle polishing will not serve', as Richard Hakluyt wrote of the natives of North America, 'then we shall not want hammerers and rough masons enow, I mean our old soldiers trained up in the Netherlands, to square and prepare them to our preachers' hands.'

It will be seen that this is in striking contrast to the Golden Age view, but both led to the Indians being thought of not as individuals but as a category. By one school they were idealized, by the other they were despised. The Age of Individualism was not greatly concerned to distinguish one Indian from another. Man had acquired a confident self-consciousness: but this was western, humanistically educated man. Indeed, the 16th-century concept of man and his place in the universe tempted him to shrink from a close consideration of 'savages'; they lacked the definite place in an ordered hierarchy that was demanded by the Renaissance World Picture. By 16th-century Englishmen, for instance, the Indians were on the whole assumed to be wild, ignorant and animal-like. It is in this guise that they appear in Spenser. It was this view that produced that strange denizen of a newly discovered island, Caliban. It was this frame of mind which resisted the detailed information contained in growing volume in the reports of explorers and travellers. These men were becoming objective, more anthropologically minded. But as with modern journalism, the opinions of the man-on-the-spot had to be edited down to meet the presuppositions of his readers at home.

The Slow Response

It is useful to recall just how slowly reader interest in the New World grew. In France, the *Mémoires* of Commines, which go up to 1498, contain no mention of America. Nor do those of Fleuranges, which run up to 1522, nor do those of Du Bellay, which go up to 1536. As late as 1604, in the vast biographical dictionary of Antoine du Verdier, out of 2,600 folio pages, Columbus is allotted five *lines*. And works specially devoted to geography reflect the same indifference. Signot's *La Division du Monde*, which went through many editions between 1539 and 1555, made no mention of America. The *Cosmographie* of Belleforest (1575) gave more space to Semiramis than to Cortes and Pizarro, and Thévet's *Cosmographie*, published in the same year, placed the Straits of Magellan, Mexico and Brazil all on the same side of the Equator—and Thévet was the king's official geographer. The demand for accuracy remained slight until the second half of the century, though France had become a major exploring power from Verrazano's expedition of 1523, when much of the east coast of North America, including New York harbour, was surveyed. Indifference was possible even in Spain. In all the voluminous writing of the humanist Lucio Marineo Siculo, who was teaching at Salamanca when Columbus was discussing geographical theory with his colleagues, and who was one of Ferdinand's official historians, there is only one reference to Columbus. It calls him Pedro, not Cristoforo, and smugly records the discovery of a Roman coin in Central America: 'This took the glory from our soldiers who were boasting of their navigation, since the coin is proof that the Romans had sailed to the Indies long before.' For most humanists, indeed, the rediscovery of the ancient world was more absorbing than the discovery of the new.

Nor did creative writing—poetry, the drama—show any signs of being seriously affected by the discoveries throughout the 16th century. Some authors referred to America, and the voyages were reflected in a stray image here and there, but there is no sign that the mental horizon of any writer was widened or that the quality of his imagination was affected. In France, the poets of the *Pléiade* were still more interested in the classical world. Their references to antiquity were warm and immediate, to the Americas dispassionate or moralizing. Shakespeare showed little interest in the discoveries, apart from some gibes in *The Tempest* at those who thought that the white man brought benefits to the native. 'You taught me language', retorts Caliban to Prospero's claim that he gave him reason, 'and my profit is, I know how to curse: the red plague rid you for learning me your language.' It would be folly to suggest that the discovery of the New World had any ascer-

Columbus and his crew trading with the inhabitants of Hispaniola (Haiti), one of the islands discovered on his first voyage in 1492. Columbus commented on the willingness of the natives to barter their gold for worthless scraps—'a sailor received for a strap, gold to the weight of 2½ large coins'. From an edition of Columbus' letter, printed in Basle 1493. (10)

tainable effect upon Shakespeare's genius, or the manner in which it was expressed.

These reactions, so negative from a scientific point of view, only represent two strands in Renaissance thought: the popular wish to retain the 'escape' element involved in reading about marvels and monsters, and the moral element in humanism which believed that education should concentrate on the authoritative expression of human wisdom rather than on the study of nature. Montaigne expressed this humanist view that the sciences were irrelevant to the best development of the character: 'Being beaten with ambition, with avarice, with rashness, and with superstition, and having such other enemies unto life within lives—wherefore shall I study and take care about the mobility and variation of the world?' Cosmology, which of all humanist studies was the most suited to absorb the hypothesis-observation-new hypothesis method, was reluctant to be as scientific as the evidence of the discoverers would have allowed it to be. There was a well-developed Two Cultures crisis in the Renaissance.

Prosaic Fact

The other strand is the contribution of less sophisticated men whose first-hand experience was not doctored to meet popular or learned taste. Beneath the literature of exploration we must always sense the spread of accurate information in the form of a captain's oral report or in the correspondence between merchants and their sea-going factors. Accurate observation, precise description: just as in politics we look for these qualities not in formal treatises or the wording of alliances or in proclamations but in the dashed-off, frequently pithy and racy correspondence of working diplo-

f 10

mats, so the workaday reactions to new lands must be looked for below the level at which the cultivated reading public received them. The scientific temperament, as we see it expressed in Galileo's statement that science is concerned with 'the sensible world and not one on paper' was shaped not only by 'texts and authorities' but by conversations with foundrymen, dyers and glass manufactures and with clockmakers and artillerymen. Beneath the books we have been looking at, then, we must imagine the new information spreading in real terms uncontaminated by learned or moralizing associations, and flowing not only from pioneering voyages where the temptation to glamorize and distort was at its height, but from the more prosaic and routine ventures which followed them.

Humanist geography did, however, have its practical side. Its intellectual justification was stated by the German Vadian. 'As long as the human mind lives in the body it obeys that law of knowledge which decrees that the intellect can only grasp that which is conducted to it by the senses, and that all our thinking and imagining is analogy. This law of knowledge requires first and foremost the study of geography so that we may begin our quest for knowledge by understanding the earth, the scene of human habitation.' This theory chimed with actual need: governments wanted maps which showed the administrative divisions of their countries, soldiers maps from which they could plan campaigns—'I have been asked,' wrote Conrad Turst of Zürich in the early 1490s, 'to describe the regions of our Confederation and their environs so that you may realize . . . how useful such a description is to all those princes who are about to take the field with their armies'; growing national pride also fostered the production of regional maps. This led to political frontiers being defined as accurately as possible, and the atlas began to make its contribution to the way in which a man imagined his own country and its neighbours and rivals—a factor of some importance in international relations; frontier mentality has dominated political thinking ever since, but it was literally unthinkable until maps produced the frontier image.

In this way, just as an extension of the use of clocks and watches by making the hour and the minute as prominent as the day and the season influenced men's sense of time, so the realistic, standardized detail of maps influenced their sense of space. In time a man's consciousness could still switch from urgency to indulgence, in space from reality to symbols, but another step had been taken in the organization of thought in the direction of observable, checkable reality.

World maps, which were older than regional maps, continued to set the tone for all map making, and influenced as they were by the discoveries, passed on their increasingly uniform conventions—north at the top, latitude scales—to them; the inclusion of world maps in atlases helped the countries of Europe to be seen in a global context. This influence was particularly important because humanist geography tended to be strongly regional; the visual equivalent of national history. The illustrated world descriptions, like that of Münster, became increasingly more marvel-struck the further their authors turned from their native country. It was not only the Italians who were parochial during the Renaissance; Germans, French, Spanish and English topographers were intent on celebrating their own locality first, their country as a whole second, Europe third, with the world well in the rear. Against this localism, however, were set two modifying forces; the discoveries, and a belief that foreign travel was an important part of the education of a man of means. Less strong in England, where after the Reformation travel was seen as spiritually dangerous, the need for foreign languages in diplomacy, the cult of the alert, widely informed and talented man led to travel being seen as desirable on general grounds, and not merely for the purposes of trade or pilgrimage or formal enrolment in a foreign university. Montaigne, turning from a discussion of books in his essay on Education, said: 'to conclude, I would have this worlds-frame to be my Schollers choise-booke: so many strange humours, sundry sects, verying judgements, diverse opinions, different lawes, and fantasticall customes teach us to judge rightly of ours, and instruct our judgement to acknowledge his imperfections and natural weakness, which is no easy an apprentisship.'

Comparison and Contrast

Though Montaigne did not counsel travel to countries outside Europe, he was prepared to use information from the margin of the 'worlds-frame', as we have seen, to contrast his decadent fellow-Europeans with the noble savages of America. 'Compare and contrast': this familiar formula, with its invitation to mental agility, is of considerable importance to our theme. Characteristic of medieval reasoning was the tendency to think of an object by connecting it to a category of similar objects, to see what writers had said about such an object or why God had created it. Rumination pursued widening circles of significance—from the literal meaning to the allegorical, to the moral, to the mystical—enclosing the fact or theme in a synthesizing, hierarchical view of existence. Because of this habit of mind, few of the meteorites of information from the discoveries entered the closed mental atmosphere of Europe without being burned out of shape. Modern reasoning patterns involve contrast as well as association: this is different from that: what do I learn from the comparison? The first strengthening of contrast-thinking came from the humanists' bringing into focus the civilization of pre-Christian antiquity, and from the existence on Europe's eastern frontier of a threatening and radically different political organization, that of the Turks. The newly-discovered societies, however, accelerated the process by confronting Europeans with a wide range of governments, religions and social habits that were different from their own. More's *Utopia* contained the first literary portrait of a Renaissance explorer, Raphael Hythlodaeus, 'discoverer' of Utopia. As a result of his travels, More noted, 'just as he called attention to many ill-advised customs among these new nations, so he rehearsed not a few points from which our own cities, nations, races and kingdoms may take examples for the correction of their errors.'

Before the sophisticated races of the East or the more primitive ones of the West could present thought-provoking contrasts to Europeans, they had to be seen not as merely picturesque but as the product of a specific environment. It was necessary to see deeper than the immediately striking detail—nakedness in Africa and in the New World, the sex customs which Europeans found so intriguing in the East—and to pass from the first impulse to see the native as a potential slave or Europeanized Christian to a more anthropological approach. Such an approach made remarkable strides during the 16th century from its occasional beginnings, as when Vasco da Gama's captain-major persuaded his chief to let him spend a night with the natives of the Cape of Good Hope in order to see how they lived and what they ate. Knowledge flowed from the explorers themselves—Columbus' account of the Tainos is a valuable portrait of this soon-to-vanish people—from the experience of slavers looking for the hardiest and most intelligent of African tribes and from settlers and colonial administrators. But it was above all the missionary orders who were forced into the most sympathetic contact with non-Europeans. For conversion to be more than skin deep they had to learn the languages and sympathize with the religious beliefs of the peoples they wished to Christianize.

The New Objectivity

It was religion, more than trade, more even than the needs of secular administration, that forced Europeans to understand how other peoples lived and thought. It was from works like the Jesuit newsletters, circulated in Europe from mission stations running p 328–329 (24) from Japan to Paraguay, that some of the background to the explorers' accounts was filled in, and that the mental horizons of Europeans were helped to catch up with the expanded geographical horizons of their world. It was a landmark in this mental expansion when an English venturer in search of a north-east passage to Cathay was asked 'to bring thence some old printed book, to see whether they have had print there before it was devised in Europe.' It was a sign of what progress Europeans had made in seeing their civilization as one among others that a generation later Carletti could write of the Chinese, *à propos* the invention of gunpowder and printing: 'It is possible to believe beyond any doubt that all these things came from them. And I agree to the statement that not only these, but every invention for good or for evil, of beauty or ugliness, must have come from that region, or at least it can be affirmed that they have in themselves the knowledge of everything, not having had it from us or from the Greeks or other nations who taught it to us, but from native creators in that huge and very ancient country.'

The long-term effect on Christianity in Europe of the contact with other religions was of great importance, though difficult to define with precision. It led to a more relaxed view of dogma, a concentration on the promise rather than on the law of Christianity. It was realized that all men, however remote or primitive, had a religious sense that led them to worship something outside themselves and their immediate environment. This led to tolerance, in extreme cases to the vague pantheism which was so widespread in the 18th century; the belief that God dwells in everything and every man, and has not declared Himself exclusively to any one nation or sect. As it came to be seen that the world was hugely populous, the idea of a personal God who scans the actions of each individual became harder to accept. He moved further from the day-to-day affairs of every man. He became more a source of distant inspiration than of watchful judgment. Morality itself became less a clean-cut issue of right or wrong when it was seen that non-Christian moralities could produce upright and responsible conduct.

In fact, as an anthropological point of view developed, God became less anthropomorphic. And in a similar way, as societies were examined which gave or seemed to give little weight to law, or property, or kings, an ideal of the Noble Savage took form and came to underlie the work of 18th-century political writers like Rousseau who saw Europeans as born in the chains of a needlessly elaborate and unfair social structure.

The Renaissance is often described in terms of subjectivity, of men like Petrarch who were fascinated by their own thoughts and feelings, whose self-consciousness came to give a new status to the concept of the individual. But consciousness of self simply intensified the medieval habit of seeing life concentrically: the stronger the sense of individuality, the stronger the macrocosmic-microcosmic thought structure which saw man as the world writ

small or the universe as man writ large. The liberating element in Renaissance thought—to use a Whiggish phrase—was not subjectivity (what progress is involved in changing a small prison for a larger one?) but objectivity, empiricism, pragmatism; these are the attitudes that lead from the Middle Ages to modern times. The much-lauded self-consciousness of the Renaissance, secular self-scrutiny replacing mere conscience-searching, was in itself no more than a glamorizing of an essentially medieval state of mind. Objectivity was the liberator, the widener of mental horizons, and it was fed less by Machiavellian political realism, which placed the individual in yet another microcosm-macrocosm structure, or by naturalism in art, which by adding a dimension to the medieval world view made men feel all the more at home in it, than by forcing the imagination outwards, by feeding it with challenging information about different ways of life.

This information could only be challenging when it was exact, and exact descriptive prose grew as much from travel books as from the diplomatic and technical literature of Europe. Here is a late 16th-century description of a Japanese sandal: 'Their shoes are made entirely of a single straw sole of strands twined together, or perhaps of leather, with a thong fastened to the ends of both sides of the sole which comes up over the foot. And there is also another strand that is joined to the first one mentioned but is fastened to the end of the sole a little inside, so that it may pass through the opening between the two large fingers of the foot. And thus that shoe or sole is held firmly on the foot. And when they want to remove it, they have only to raise their heel a little and shake the foot, which quickly slides out.'

This homely description by the Florentine traveller Carletti typifies the new objectivity; laconic, precise, uncommitted. It is information, pure and simple, ideal nourishment for the scientific temperament. The Age of Discovery was no more than a facet of the cultural and intellectual Renaissance and, as we have seen, a partly independent one, but the voyagers' information, once it was precisely recorded and firmly related to unfamiliar ways of life, significantly affected Renaissance intellectual life in its rôle as the transition between medieval and modern ways of thought.

Exploration in the Renaissance. In 1493 the pope divided the New World between the Spanish and Portuguese to avoid future dissension. The dividing lines, originally favourable to Spain, were altered in 1494 after the Portuguese objected. (11)

CHRONOLOGICAL CHART

| 1400 | 1410 | 1420 | 1430 | 1440 | 1450 | 1460 | 1470 | 1480 | 1490 | 1500 | 1510 | 1520 | 1530 | 1540 | 1550 | 1560 | 1570 | 1580 | 1590 | 1600 |

ITALY

1370–1460 GUARINO DA VERONA: educationalist, humanist
1377–1446 BRUNELLESCHI: first Ren. architect
1378–1446 VITTORINO DA FELTRE: educationalist, humanist
1378–1455 LORENZO GHIBERTI: sculptor—*Baptistery Doors, Florence*
c.1386–1466 DONATELLO: sculptor—*Magdalen, Gattamelata, David*
1401–?28 MASACCIO: painter—*Brancacci Chapel frescoes*
1404–72 ALBERTI: humanist, architect, writer—*De re aedificatoria 1450–72*
1407–57 LORENZO VALLA: humanist scholar—*Elegantiae 1444*
1410/20–92 PIERO DELLA FRANCESCA: painter, mathematician—*Arezzo frescoes 1452–66*
c.1430–1516 GIOVANNI BELLINI: Venetian painter—*sacre conversazioni in S. Giobbe*
1432–68 reign of SIGISMONDO MALATESTA, Rimini
1433–99 MARSILIO FICINO: Florentine neo-Platonist, philosopher
1434–92 MEDICI ascendancy in Florence: COSIMO, PIERO, LORENZO IL MAGNIFICO
1441–71 reigns of LEONELLO and BORSO D'ESTE, Ferrara
1442–94 reigns of ALFONSO V and FERDINAND I, Naples
1444–82 reign of FEDERIGO DA MONTEFELTRO, Urbino
1444–1514 DONATO BRAMANTE: architect—*Tempietto; plans for St Peter's*
1444–1519 reigns of LODOVICO and FRANCESCO GONZAGA, Mantua
c.1445–1510 BOTTICELLI: painter—*Birth of Venus; Primavera*
1447–55 pontificate of NICHOLAS V
1450–1515 ALDUS MANUTIUS: major scholar-printer, Venice
1452–1519 LEONARDO DA VINCI: painter, scientist, inventor—*Last Supper 1491/98*
1454–94 POLITIAN: humanist, poet, Greek and Latin scholar
1456–1530 JACOPO SANNAZARO: Neapolitan poet—*Arcadia 1504*
1458–64 pontificate of PIUS II (Aeneas Sylvius Piccolomini)
1463–94 PICO DELLA MIRANDOLA: neo-Platonist, mystic
1465 SWEYNHEIM and PANNARTZ started printing in Italy
1469–1527 NICCOLÒ MACHIAVELLI: political theorist, historian, statesman—*Prince 1513*
1470–1547 PIETRO BEMBO: Venetian humanist, historian, champion of vernacular
1474–1533 ARIOSTO: Ferrarese poet—*Orlando Furioso 1516*
1475–1564 MICHELANGELO: sculptor, painter, poet, architect—*Sistine Chapel 1508–12*
1478–1529 CASTIGLIONE: writer, courtier, diplomat—*Courtier 1528*
1479–1500 reign of LODOVICO SFORZA, Milan
1483–1520 RAPHAEL: painter, architect—*Vatican Stanze 1508+*
1487/90–1576 TITIAN: Venetian painter—*Assumption 1516*
1491–98 influence of SAVONAROLA in Florence
1503–13 pontificate of JULIUS II
1518–80 PALLADIO: architect, designer in Venice and Vicenza—*4 Books of Architecture*
1527 Sack of Rome
1544–95 TASSO: Ferrarese poet—*Gerusalemme liberata 1575*
1545–63 Council of Trent: beginning of Counter-Reformation

FRANCE

1433–1501 ROBERT GAGUIN: humanist, statesman, educational reformer
1450–1536 LEFÈVRE D'ÉTAPLES: humanist, Hellenist, religious reformer
1456–59 GREGORIO TIFERNATE taught Greek and rhetoric in Paris
1468–1535 JODOCUS BADIUS ASCENSIANUS: scholar-printer
1468–1540 GUILLAUME BUDÉ: major humanist, philologist—*De asse 1515*
1470 first printing press established in Paris
c.1490–1538 GERMAIN DE BRIE: Greek scholar, vernacular poet
1492–1549 MARGUERITE DE NAVARRE: writer; poet and patron—*Heptameron 1558*
1494–1553 FRANÇOIS RABELAIS: writer, satirist—*Pantagruel 1532*
?1496–1544 CLÉMENT MAROT: poet—*Adolescence Clémentine 1532*
1500/15–70 PHILIBERT DE L'ORME: architect, architectural writer—*Château Anet 1552*
c.1501–c.1564 MAURICE SCÈVE: poet—*Délie 1544*
1503–59 ROBERT ESTIENNE: scholar-printer
1505–75 MICHEL DE L'HÔPITAL: humanist, Chancellor of France
1508–85 JEAN DORAT: court poet, Latinist
c.1510–c.1563 JEAN GOUJON: sculptor—*Fontaine des Innocents 1547–9*
1519 designs for Chambord, work continued until at least 1550
1522–60 GUILLAUME DU BELLAY: poet, member of Pléiade, court poet—*Déffense 1549*
1524–85 PIERRE DE RONSARD: member of Pléiade, court poet—*Odes 1550/2*
1530 establishment of Royal readerships, later Collège de France
1530,32 arrival in Fr. of Rosso and Primaticcio—start of Sch. of Fontainebleau
1533–92 MICHEL DE MONTAIGNE: writer—*Essais 1580*
1540–45 BENVENUTO CELLINI in France—*salt cellar 1540/3*
1550s years of most important activity of Pléiade

NORTHERN EUROPE

Scale: 1400 · 1410 · 1420 · 1430 · 1440 · 1450 · 1460 · 1470 · 1480 · 1490 · 1500 · 1510 · 1520 · 1530 · 1540 · 1550 · 1560 · 1570 · 1580 · 1590 · 1600

- Jan van Eyck: artist—*Ghent Altarpiece finished 1432*
- c.1400–64 Roger van der Weyden: artist—*Deposition 1435*
- 1401–64 Nicholas of Cues: theologian, humanist, mathematician
- c.1440–82 Hugo van der Goes: artist—*Portinari Altarpiece 1475*
- 1440–50 Gutenberg's printing press established
- Rudolf Agricola: humanist, educationalist
- mid 15th C—mid 16th C: Family of Vischers: Nuremberg sculptors and bronze-workers
- 1442–85 Johann Reuchlin: Hebrew scholar—*De arte cabbalistica 1517*
- 1455–1522 Conrad Celtis: humanist, polymath, poet
- 1459–1508 Johann Froben: scholar-printer—printed Erasmus' Gk. New Testament 1516
- 1460–1527 Erasmus: *Praise of Folly 1509, Greek New Testament 1516*
- 1469–1536 Willibald Pirckheimer: wealthy Nuremberg scholar and patron
- 1470–1530 Albrecht Dürer: artist—*Apocalypse woodcuts 1498*
- 1471–1528 Lucas Cranach the Elder: artist, court painter to Electors of Saxony
- 1472–1553 Matthias Grünewald: artist—*Isenheim Altarpiece, finished c.1515*
- c.1475–1528 Martin Luther—ninety five Theses, Wittenberg 1517
- 1483–1546 Ulrich Zwingli: Swiss Reformer, humanist
- 1484–1531 Ulrich von Hutten: Reformer, adventurer, humanist
- 1488–1523 Philip Melanchthon: Reformer, humanist—Augsburg Confession 1530
- 1497–1560 Jean Calvin: French Calvinist, first head of Geneva University
- 1509–64 Théodore de Bèze: French Reformer, emigrated to Geneva—*Institutes 1536*
- 1514–64 Andreas Vesalius: anatomist
- 1519–1605 Confession of Augsburg, 1555 'Peace of Augsburg: cuius regio, eius religio'
- 1530 Otheinrichsbau built—Italianate decoration

SPAIN

Scale: 1400 · 1410 · 1420 · 1430 · 1440 · 1450 · 1460 · 1470 · 1480 · 1490 · 1500 · 1510 · 1520 · 1530 · 1540 · 1550 · 1560 · 1570 · 1580 · 1590 · 1600

- 1427/8 *Aeneid* translated into Spanish—first complete translation into modern language
- 1442–1522 Antonio de Nebrija: humanist, grammarian—*Spanish grammar 1492*
- 1456–1517 Cardinal Jiménez de Cisneros: church reformer, educationalist
- 1474–1566 Bartolomé de las Casas: writer, preacher, anti-slavery in America
- 1478 establishment of Inquisition
- 1479 foundn. College of Sta Cruz, Valladolid – one of first Renaissance buildings in Spain 1486–93
- 1482 publication of *Carcel de Amor*—fashion for spiritualized love
- ?1490–1541/1532 Juan and Alfonso de Valdés: religious and literary critics
- c.1490–1561 Alonso Berruguete: sculptor, pioneer of Spanish mannerism
- 1491–1556 St Ignatius of Loyola: founded Society of Jesus
- 1492–1540 Luis Vives: greatest Spanish humanist, philosopher, educationalist
- 1495–1563 Diego de Siloé: architect, sculptor—*Granada Cathedral 1528+*
- 1498 foundn. University of Alcalá: immediate prestige and influence
- 1501–36 Garcilaso de la Vega: poet—imitated Italian style
- 1502–17 Complutensian Polyglot Bible
- 1508 publication of *Amadis de Gaula*—initiated great vogue of novel of chevalry
- 1527 Conference of Valladolid to judge orthodoxy of Erasmus' works
- 1527–91 Luis de León: poet, religious writer—*La Perfecta Casada 1583*
- 1527+ Palace of Charles V, Alhambra—pure Italian classicism
- 1529–88 Juan Huarte de San Juan: educationalist, medical writer
- 1530–97 Juan de Herrera: architect of Escorial (1563–84)—restrained classicism
- 1534–97 Fernando de Herrera: humanist poet—*Algunas obras 1582*
- 1534 design for Jaen Cathedral, masterpiece of Spanish Renaissance style
- d.1540 Arias Barbosa: Greek scholar—*Greek grammar 1538*
- 1541–1614 El Greco: painter—*The Burial of Count Orgaz 1586*
- 1559 *Diana*—pastoral/neo-Platonist novel

ENGLAND

Scale: 1400 · 1410 · 1420 · 1430 · 1440 · 1450 · 1460 · 1470 · 1480 · 1490 · 1500 · 1510 · 1520 · 1530 · 1540 · 1550 · 1560 · 1570 · 1580 · 1590 · 1600

- 1427–70 John Tiptoft, Earl of Worcester: humanist, visited Italy
- ?1446–1519 William Grocyn: humanist, scholar and teacher of Greek
- c.1460–1524 Thomas Linacre: humanist, physician, royal tutor, Greek scholar
- ?1467–1519 John Colet: humanist, founder of St Paul's School
- c.1475–1530 Thomas Wolsey: cardinal, statesman, patron of New Learning
- 1476 establishment of Caxton's printing press
- 1478–1535 Sir Thomas More: lawyer, statesman, satirist—*Utopia 1516*
- ?1485–1540 Thomas Cromwell: politician, administrator—Dissolution of Monasteries
- 1489–1556 Thomas Cranmer: Archbishop of Canterbury—*Book of Common Prayer 1549*
- ?1490–1546 Sir Thomas Elyot: scholar, educationalist—*Book of the Governor 1531*
- c.1506–52 John Leland: topographer, antiquary—*Laboryouse journey 1549*
- 1526, 1532–43 Hans Holbein in England—*Portraits of Henry VIII*
- 1533, 1534 Act in Restraint of Appeals; Act of Supremacy
- 1536+ Dissolution of the Monasteries
- ?1536–1614 Robert Smythson: architect—*Wollaton Hall 1580*
- 1538+ Nonesuch Palace built: quasi-Renaissance extravaganza
- 1547–52 Somerset House built: influenced Eng. Ren. architecture
- c.1547–1619 Nicholas Hilliard: miniaturist—*Arte of Limning*
- 1552–99 Edmund Spenser: poet—*Faerie Queene 1590*
- 1552–1618 Sir Walter Ralegh: poet, explorer
- 1554–86 Sir Philip Sidney: poet, courtier, soldier
- 1557, 95, 99 first four theatres opened
- 1561–1626 Sir Francis Bacon: *Essays 1597*
- 1564–93 Christopher Marlowe
- 1564–1616 William Shakespeare

Select Bibliography

General

New Cambridge Modern History, vols. I and II (Cambridge, 1957–8)

ALLEN, J. W. A History of Political Thought in the XVIth Century (London, 1928; reprinted 1957. Paper edn. 1960)

FEBVRE, L. and MARTIN, H-J. L'apparition du livre (Paris, 1958)

FERGUSON, W. K. Renaissance in Historical Thought (Boston, 1948)

GARIN, E. L'umanesimo italiano (Bari, 1952)

HAY, D. The Italian Renaissance in its Historical Background (Cambridge 1961)

HEXTER, J. H. Reappraisals in History (London, 1961)

JACOB, E. F. ed. Italian Renaissance Studies: a tribute to the late Cecilia M. Ady (London, 1960):
includes contributions by MARKS, L. F. 'The Financial Oligarchy in Florence under Lorenzo'
GOMBRICH, E. H. 'The Early Medici as Patrons of Art'
RUBINSTEIN, N. 'Politics and Constitution in Florence at the end of the fifteenth century'

KRISTELLER, P. O. Renaissance Thought (New York, 1961)

SANDYS, J. E. A History of Classical Scholarship from the sixth century B. C. to the end of the Middle Ages (Cambridge, 1921)

TIEGHEM, P. VAN La littérature latine de la Renaissance. Etude d'histoire littéraire européenne (Paris, 1944, reprinted 1966)

WOODWARD, W. H. Studies in Education during the Age of the Renaissance 1400–1600 (Cambridge, 1905)
Vittorino da Feltre and Other Humanist Educators (Cambridge, 1897)

I Cradle of the Renaissance

ADY, C. M. Lorenzo de'Medici and Renaissance Italy (London 1955)

BARON, H. The Crisis of the Early Italian Renaissance: Civic humanism and republican liberty in an age of classicism and tyranny (2nd edn. Princeton, 1966)

BROWN, A. M. 'The humanist portrait of Cosimo de'Medici, Pater Patriae', Journal of the Warburg and Courtauld Institutes, XXIV (1961)

BRUCKNER, G. A. Florentine Politics and Society, 1343–1378 (Princeton, 1962)

GILBERT, F. Machiavelli and Guicciardini: Politics and History in sixteenth-century Florence (Princeton, 1965)
'Florentine political assumptions in the period of Savonarola and Soderini', Journal of the Warburg and Courtauld Institutes, XX (1957)

GUTKIND, C. S. Cosimo de'Medici, Pater Patriae, 1389–1464 (Oxford, 1938)

JONES, P. 'Florentine families and Florentine diaries in the 14th century', Papers of the British School at Rome, XXIV (1956)

MARTINES, L. The Social World of the Florentine Humanists, 1390–1460 (Princeton and London, 1963)

RUBINSTEIN, N. The Government of Florence under the Medici 1434–1494 (Oxford, 1966)

WACKERNAGEL, M. Der Lebensraum des Künstlers in der florentinischen Renaissance (Leipzig, 1938)

II Widening Circles

General

ROSSI, V. Il Quattrocento (Milan, 1938)
TOFFANIN, G. Il Cinquecento (Milan, 1945)
VALERI, A. L'Italia nell'età dei principati, dal 1343 al 1516 (Milan, 1949)

Rome

PASCHINI, P. Roma nel Rinascimento (Bologna, 1940)
PECCHIAI, P. Roma nel Cinquecento (Bologna, 1948)

Naples

CROCE, B. Storia del regno di Napoli (Bari, 1925)
GOTHEIN, E. Il rinascimento nell'Italia meridionale (Florence, 1915: translated from the original German, Breslau, 1886)

Milan

MALAGUZZI-VALERI, F. La corte di Lodovico il Moro 4 vols. (Milan, 1913–23)
Storia di Milano, Fondazione Treccani, vols. V–VII (Milan, 1955–56)

Venice

CESSI, R. Storia della Reppublica di Venezia (Milan, 1944)
La civiltà veneziana nel Quattrocento (Florence, 1957)

Mantua

CARTWRIGHT, J. Isabella d'Este, Marchioness of Mantua, 1474–1539 (London, 1903)
LUZIO, A. and RENIER, R. Mantova e Urbino (Turin, 1893)

Ferrara

BERTONI, G. L' 'Orlando Furioso' e la rinascenza a Ferrara (Modena, 1919)
GARDNER, E. G. Dukes and Poets in Ferrara (London, 1904)

Urbino

CARTWRIGHT, J. Baldassare Castiglione (London, 1908)
DENNISTOUN, J. Memoirs of the Dukes of Urbino (2nd edn. London, 1909)

Rimini

RICCI, C. Il Tempio Malatestiano (Milan–Rome, [1924])

III A New Vision

BLUNT, A. Artistic Theory in Italy 1450–1600 (Oxford, 1940; paper edn. 1962)

MURRAY, P. and L. The Art of the Renaissance (London, 1963)

MURRAY, L. The High Renaissance (London, 1967)
Late Renaissance and Mannerism (London, 1967)

MURRAY, P. The Architecture of the Italian Renaissance (London, 1963)

POPE-HENNESSY, J. An Introduction to Italian Sculpture 5 vols. (London, 1955–63)

SEYMOUR, C. Sculpture in Italy 1400–1500: Pelican History of Art (London, 1966)

VASARI, (ed. BULL, G.) Lives: Penguin Classics (London, 1965)

WÖLFFLIN, H. Renaissance und Barock
English trans. by Kathrin Simon Renaissance and Baroque (London, 1964)
Die klassische Kunst (Munich, 1899)
English trans. by Peter and Linda Murray Classic Art (London, 1952)

IV The New Learning

BILLANOVICH, G. I primi umanisti e la tradizione dei classici latini (Freiburg, 1953)

GAETA, F. Lorenzo Valla—Filologia e storia nell'umanesimo italiano (Naples, 1955)

NOLHAC, A. M. P. G. DE. Pétraque et l'humanisme (2nd edn. Paris, 1907)
Poliziano e il suo tempo—Atti del IV congresso internazionale di studi sul Rinascimento (Florence, 1957)

SABBADINI, R. Il metodo degli umanisti (Florence, 1922)
Le scoperte dei codici latini e greci ne' secoli XIV e XV 2 vols. (Florence, 1905–14)

ULLMAN, B. L. The humanism o Coluccio Salutati (Padua, 1963)

WEISS, R. The Dawn of Humanism in Italy (London, 1947)
Humanism in England during the Fifteenth Century (2nd edn. Oxford, 1957)

V Reason, Unreason and Faith

ANGELERI, C. Il problema religioso del Rinascimento: (Florence, 1952)

CANTIMORI, D. Eretici italiani del Cinquecento (Florence, 1939: revised German edn., trans. W. Kaegi, Basle, 1949)
Prospettive di storia ereticale italiana del Cinquecento (Bari, 1960)
Studi di storia (Turin, 1959. Reprinted 1965)

DICKENS, A. G. Reformation and Society in Sixteenth-Century Europe (London, 1966)

ELTON, G. R. Reformation Europe, 1517–1559 (London and Glasgow, 1963)

WILLIAMS, G. H. The Radical Reformation (Philadelphia, 1962)

VI France in Transition

BUSSON, H. Le rationalisme dans la littérature française de la Renaissance (1533–1601) (2nd edn. Paris, 1957)

DOUCET, R. Les institutions de la France au XVIe siècle (Paris, 1948)

IMBART DE LA TOUR, P. Les origines de la Réforme 4 vols. (Paris, 1905–35)

MORÇAY, R. La Renaissance (2nd edn. Paris, 1957)

NOLHAC, A. M. P. G. DE. Ronsard et l'humanisme (Paris, 1921)

REESE, G. *Music in the Renaissance* (London, 1954)

RENAUDET, A. *Préréforme et humanisme à Paris pendant les premières guerres d'Italie 1494–1517* (2nd edn. Paris, 1957)

RICE, E. F. *The Renaissance Idea of Wisdom* (Cambridge, Mass., 1958)

TILLEY, A. A. *The Dawn of the French Renaissance* (Cambridge, 1918)

VII 'The Egg that Luther Hatched'

ALLEN, P. S. *The Age of Erasmus* (Oxford, 1914) *Erasmus. Lectures and Wayfaring Sketches* (Oxford, 1934)

HUIZINGA, J. *Erasmus of Rotterdam* (London, 1952)

HYMA, A. *The Christian Renaissance. A history of the 'Devotio Moderna'* (New York and London, 1925) *The Youth of Erasmus* (Michigan, 1930)

PHILLIPS, M. M. *Erasmus and the Northern Renaissance* (London, 1949)

RENAUDET, A. *Etudes érasmiennes, 1521–1529* (Paris, 1939)

RUPPRICH, H. *Humanismus und Renaissance in den deutschen Städten und an den Universitäten* (Leipzig, 1935)

SMITH, P. *Erasmus* (New York, 1923; paper edn. London and New York, 1962)

SPITZ, L. W. *Conrad Celtis, the German Arch-Humanist* (Cambridge, Mass., 1957) *The Religious Renaissance of the German Humanists* (Cambridge, Mass., 1963)

THORNDIKE, L. *Science and Thought in the Fifteenth Century* (New York, 1929)

VIII An Age of Gold

BATAILLON, M. *Erasme et l'Espagne: Recherches sur l'histoire spirituelle du XVIe siècle* (Paris, 1937)

BELL, A. F. G. 'Notes on the Spanish Renaissance', in *Revue Hispanique*, LXXX (1930). Translated into Spanish as *El Renacimiento español* (Saragossa, 1944)

CAMON AZNAR, J. *La arquitectura plateresca* (Madrid, 1945)

DIAZ-PLAJA, G. ed. *Historia general de las literaturas hispánicas*, Vol II (Barcelona, 1951)

ELLIOTT, J. H. *Imperial Spain 1469–1716* (London, 1963)

GOMEZ-MORENO, M. *La Escultura del Renacimiento en España* (Florence and Barcelona, 1931)

GREEN, O. H. *Spain and the Western Tradition: the Castilian mind in Literature from 'El Cid' to Calderón* 4 vols (Madison, Wisconsin, 1963–66)

HANKE, L. *The Spanish Struggle for Justice in the Conquest of America* (Philadelphia, 1949) *Aristotle and the American Indians: a Study in Race Prejudice in the Modern World* (London, 1959)

HARVEY, J. H. *The Cathedrals of Spain* (London, 1957)

LASSAIGNE, J. *Spanish Painting* Vol I: *from the Catalan Frescoes to El Greco* (New York, 1952)

POST, C. R. *A History of Spanish Painting*, vols IX–XII (Cambridge, Mass., 1947–1958)

SOLANA, M. *Historia de la filosofía española: época del Renacimiento* (Madrid, 1941)

SOLDEVILA, F. *Historia de España*, vols II, III, and IV (2nd edn. Barcelona, 1962–63)

IX Tradition and Change

BENNETT, H. S. *English Books and Readers 1475–1557: being a study in the history of the book trade from Caxton to the incorporation of the Stationers' Company* (Cambridge, 1952) *English Books and Readers 1558–1603: being a study in the history of the book trade in the reign of Elizabeth I* (Cambridge, 1965)

CASPARI, F. *Humanism and the Social Order in Tudor England* (Chicago, 1954)

LEWIS, C. S. *English Literature in the Sixteenth Century* (Oxford, 1954: reprinted 1959)

NUGENT, E. M. ed. *The Thought and Culture of the English Renaissance* (Cambridge, 1956)

SIMON, J. *Education and Society in Tudor England* (Cambridge, 1966)

STONE, L. *The Crisis of the Aristocracy, 1558–1641* (Oxford, 1965)

WRIGHT, L. B. *Middle-class Culture in Elizabethan England* (University of North Carolina, 1935; reissued Ithaca, N. Y., 1958)

WRIGHT, L. B. and LA MAR, V. A. *Life and Letters in Tudor and Stuart England* (Ithaca, N.Y., 1962)

X The North Transformed

BLUNT, A. *Art and Architecture in France 1400–1500* Pelican History of Art. (London, 1953)

MONTAGU, J. *Bronzes* (London, 1963)

MÜLLER, T. *Sculpture in the Netherlands, Germany, France and Spain 1400–1500* (London, 1966)

PANOFSKY, E. *Albrecht Dürer* (4th edn. Princeton, 1955) *Early Netherlandish Painting* (Cambridge, Mass., 1953)

PEVSNER, N. and MEIER, M. *Grünewald* (London, 1958)

RING, G. *A Century of French Painting 1400–1500* (London, 1949)

SAXL, F. and WITTKOWER, R. *British Art and the Mediterranean* (London, 1948)

STRONG, R. *Holbein and Henry VIII* (London, 1967)

WATERHOUSE, E. *Painting in Britain 1530–1790* Pelican History of Art (London, 1953)

WHINNEY, M. *Sculpture in Britain 1530–1830* Pelican History of Art (London, 1964)

XI 'A World Elsewhere'

ATKINSON, G. *Les nouveaux horizons de la Renaissance française* (Paris, 1935)

BREBNER, J. B. *The Explorers of North America 1492–1806* (2nd edn. London, 1964)

CHINARD, G. *L'exotisme américain dans la littérature française* (Paris, 1935)

HAKLUYT, R. *Voyages* (Everyman, 7 vols. London)

HOFFMAN, B. G. *Cabot to Cartier* (Toronto, 1961)

MORISON, S. E. *Admiral of the Ocean Sea: a life of Columbus* (Boston and Oxford, 1942)

PARKER, J. ed. *Merchants and Scholars: Essays in the History of Exploration and Trade* (Minneapolis, 1965)

PARRY, J. H. *The Age of Reconnaissance* (London, 1963)

PENROSE, B. *Travel and Discovery in the Renaissance* (New York, 1962)

PRESTAGE, E. *The Portuguese Pioneers* (2nd edn. London, 1966)

List and Sources of Illustrations

The page on which an illustration appears is shown by the first set of numerals, its plate or figure number by the second.
Sources of photographs are given in italics

I Cradle of the Renaissance

11 Printer's device of Lucantonio Giunta, from Ovid's *Metamorphoseos vulgare*, lily of Florence with the initials of Lucantonio; Venice, 1497

13 1. *Marzocco*, copy of the original by Donatello of 1418–20 now in the Bargello, Florence; c.1440. Piazza della Signoria, Florence. Photo *Scala*

14–15 2. Florence: view of the Cathedral (Sta Maria del Fiore) from the east; c. 1300–1467; dome begun by Filippo Brunelleschi 1420, finished after his death in 1446 by Michelozzo and others. Photo *Mansell-Alinari*
3. Woodcut, *Chain view of Florence*; Italian School, 1486. *Kupferstichkabinett, Staatliche Museen zu Berlin*
4. Florence: view of the Baptistery of S. Giovanni from an upper storey of the Campanile. Photo *Martin Hürlimann*
5. Florence: view of Sta Maria Novella from the south; 1246–1330, upper façade, columns and pilaster strips by Alberti, c. 1456–70. Photo *Martin Hürlimann*
6. Florence: view of Orsanmichele from the west; 1336–50 (statue of St Matthew by Ghiberti, 1419–22). Photo *Martin Hürlimann*
7. Florence: view of the Palazzo Strozzi; probably designed by Giuliano da Sangallo, built by Benedetto da Maiano, 1489–1507; later cornice by Cronaca, 1533–36. Photo *Mansell-Alinari*
8. Florence: view from the south-east. Photo *Mansell-Alinari*

16–17 9. Cassone showing the festival of St John the Baptist; Florentine, late 14th C. Museo Nazionale del Bargello, Florence. Photo *Scala*
10. Detail from the *Confirmation of the Franciscan Rule*, fresco by Domenico Ghirlandaio, showing the Loggia dei Lanzi; 1485. Sassetti Chapel, Sta Trinita, Florence. Photo *Scala*
11. Detail from *St Francis resuscitating a child*, fresco by Domenico Ghirlandaio, showing two girls of the Sassetti family; 1485. Sassetti Chapel, Sta Trinita, Florence. Photo *Scala*
12. Detail from the *Raising of Tabitha*, fresco by Masolino, showing two fashionable young men; c.1425. Brancacci Chapel, Sta Maria del Carmine, Florence. Photo *Scala*
13. Detail from *St Francis resuscitating a child*, fresco by Domenico Ghirlandaio, showing members of leading Florentine families; 1485. Photo *Scala*

18–19 14. Portrait of Coluccio Salutati from a MS initial; Italian, second half of 14th C. Plut.53.18, fol.1r. Biblioteca Medicea-Laurenziana, Florence. Photo *Dr G.B. Pineider*
15. Detail from the *Execution of Savonarola*, showing the Palazzo Vecchio; artist unknown, c.1500. Museo S. Marco, Florence. Photo *Mansell-Alinari*
16. Detail from a page of the scrutiny in the *Lion d'oro* district; 1440. Archivio di Stato, Florence. Photo *N. Rubinstein*
17. Detail of monument to Leonardo Bruni, Chancellor of Florence, by Bernardo Rossellino; 1440s. Sta Croce, Florence. Photo *Mansell-Alinari*
18. Bust of Brutus by Michelangelo; c.1542, unfinished. Museo Nazionale del Bargello, Florence. Photo *Mansell-Anderson*
19. *The Signory discusses the war against Pisa*, by Giorgio Vasari; 1567–71. Palazzo Vecchio, Florence. Photo *Soprintendenza alle Gallerie, Florence*

20 20. Detail from the *Procession of the Magi*, fresco by Benozzo Gozzoli, showing Cosimo and Piero de'Medici; c.1459. Palazzo Medici-Riccardi, Florence. Photo *Scala*

21 21. Reverse of medal commemorating the Pazzi conspiracy, by Bertoldo di Giovanni, showing the assassination of Giuliano de'Medici; 1478. British Museum, London. Photo *John Webb*
22. Detail of the *Confirmation of the Franciscan Rule*, fresco by Domenico Ghirlandaio, showing Lorenzo de'Medici and three members of the Sassetti family; 1485. Sassetti Chapel, Sta Trinita, Florence. Photo *Scala*
23. *Palazzo Pitti*, lunette by Giusto Utens; 1599. Museo Mediceo, Florence. Photo *Scala*
24. *Il Trebbio*, lunette of the Medici villa by Giusto Utens; 1599. Museo Mediceo, Florence. Photo *Scala*

22–23 25. Detail from side-panel of the *St Matthew Altarpiece*; begun 1367 by Orcagna (Andrea di Cione), completed 1368 by Jacopo di Cione. Uffizi, Florence. Photo *Mansell-Brogi*
26. Drawing from Filippo Calandri's *Trattato di Aritmetica*, woolmerchant; 1492. MS 2669. Biblioteca Riccardiana, Florence. Photo *Dr G. B. Pineider*
27. Façade of Medici Bank in Milan, drawing by Filarete; mid-15th C. From M. Lazzaroni and A. Muñoz, *Filarete, scultore e architetto del secolo XV*, 1908
28. Poggio a Caiano: façade of the Medici villa, by Giuliano da Sangallo; conversion begun 1480, loggia pediment and Della Robbian frieze under Pope Leo X, curving stairs 17th-C. addition. Photo *Mansell-Alinari*
29–30. Obverse and reverse of gold florin; Florentine, 15th C. British Museum, London. Photo *John Webb*
31. Florence: view of inner courtyard of the Palazzo Medici-Riccardi by Michelozzo, 1444–c.1460. Photo *Mansell-Alinari*
32. Florence: exterior of the Palazzo Medici-Riccardi from the south-east; by Michelozzo, 1444–c.1460. Arches closed and windows inserted after designs by Michelangelo in 1517. Photo *Mansell-Alinari*

24 33. Agate cup inscribed LAUR MED; probably Byzantine, 9th or 10th C., silver-gilt mount 15th C. Museo degli Argenti, Palazzo Pitti, Florence. Photo *Scala*
34. Ewer of oriental sardonyx; late antique (probably 3rd or 4th C. AD), silver-gilt mount 15th C. Pyx composed of two amethyst cups; perhaps antique, base and mount 14th C. Venetian. Both inscribed LAUR MED. Museo degli Argenti, Palazzo Pitti, Florence. Photo *Electa*
35. Florence: interior of the Biblioteca Medicea-Laurenziana; built from designs by Michelangelo 1523–59. Photo *Scala*
36. Detail from the *Birth of Venus* by Botticelli; c. 1485. Uffizi, Florence. Photo *Scala*

26 37. Drawing of John Argyropoulos by one of his pupils from a copy of Aristotle's *Organon*; Italian, mid-15th C. MS Barocci 87, fol.33v. *Curators of the Bodleian Library, Oxford*
38. Detail from the tomb of Carlo Marsuppini, Chancellor of Florence, by Desiderio da Settignano; 1450s. Sta Croce, Florence. Photo *Mansell-Alinari*
39. Reverse of medal of Alberti by Matteo de'Pasti, winged eye; 1446–50. British Museum, London. Photo *John Webb*
40. Medal of Alberti, by Matteo de'Pasti; 1446–50. *Trustees of the British Museum, London*
41, 42. Obverse and reverse of medal of Marsilio Ficino, attributed to Niccolò Fiorentino; before 1500. British Museum, London. Photo *John Webb*
43, 44. Obverse and reverse of medal of Politian, attributed to Niccolò Fiorentino; before 1500. *Kunsthistorisches Museum, Vienna*.
45. Medal of Pico della Mirandola by Niccolò Fiorentino; c. 1495. *Trustees of the British Museum, London*
46. Reverse of medal of Pico della Mirandola by Niccolò Fiorentino; c.1495. British Museum, London. Photo *John Webb*

27 47. Woodcut from Luigi Pulci's *Driadeo d'amore*; Florence, c.1498
48. Detail of bust of a young man attributed to Donatello, medallion with charioteer and two horses; mid-15th C. Museo Nazionale del Bargello, Florence. Photo *Mansell-Alinari*
49. Bust of Machiavelli, polychromed terracotta; artist unknown, perhaps a pastiche in the manner of the 16th C. Palazzo Vecchio, Florence. Photo *Mansell*
50. Detail from *Zacharias in the Temple*, fresco by Domenico Ghirlandaio, four humanists; 1485–90. Sta Maria Novella, Florence. Photo *Mansell-Alinari*

28 51, 52. Obverse and reverse of bronze medal of Girolamo Savonarola, reverse showing the allegory of the Divine Punishment; School of Della Robbia, 1497. British Museum, London. Photo *John Webb*
53. *Siege of Florence* by Giorgio Vasari; mid-16th C. Palazzo Vecchio, Florence. Photo *Scala*

29 1. Woodcut from Girolamo Savonarola's *Della Semplicita della vita christiana*; Florence, 1496

30 2. Woodcut from Jacobus de Cessolis' *Libro di Giuocho di Scacchi*, a wool-merchant; Florence, 1493
3. Titlepage woodcut from Giorgio Chiarini's *Libro che tracta di Mercantantie e usanze de paesi*, bankers; Florence, 1490

31 4. Titlepage woodcut from Piero Crescentio's *De Agricultura*, villa; Venice, 1495

33 5. Engraving of *Mercury*, showing a Florentine street scene, from a copy of an earlier set of the *Planets*; Florence, c.1465

35 6. Woodcut from Niccolò degli Agostini's *Li Successi Bellici*, the siege of Padua; Venice, 1521

36 7. Woodcut from Masuccio da Salerno's *Novellino*, the author presenting his book to his patron; Venice, 1492

37 8. Woodcut from Le Chevalier Paris' *Innamoramento de Paris e Viena*, jousting; Venice, 1522

38 9. Titlepage woodcut from Cristoforo Landino's *Formulaio di Lettere e di orationi volgari con la proposta e riposta*, a lecture; Florence, 1492

39 10. Woodcut from Luigi Pulci's *Morgante Maggiore*, concert scene; Florence (Pacini), 1500

40 11. Titlepage woodcut from Lorenzo de' Medici and Politian's *Canzone a ballo* (probably taken from a lost earlier edition), group of singing girls; Florence, 1568

II Widening Circles

43 Printer's device of Aldus Manutius, dolphin and anchor with the motto *Festina lente*, from Xenophon's *Hellenica*; Venice, 1503

45 1. *Entry of Pius II into the Lateran*, fresco by Pinturicchio; begun 1502. Piccolomini Library, Siena Cathedral. Photo *Scala, reproduced by permission of the Opera della Metropolitana di Siena*

46–47 2. *Platina appointed Vatican Librarian by Sixtus IV*, by Melozzo da Forlì; 1477. Vatican Galleries. Photo *Archivio Fotografico Gallerie e Musei Vaticani*
3. Portrait of Pope Alexander VI Borgia from the *Resurrection*,

348